THE PRICE DISCRIMINATION LAW

The Price Discrimination Law

A Review of Experience

BY CORWIN D. EDWARDS

THE BROOKINGS INSTITUTION, *Washington, D.C.*

Library of Congress Catalogue Card Number 59-15197

Printed in the United States of America
The George Banta Company, Inc.
Menasha, Wisconsin

THE BROOKINGS INSTITUTION is an independent organization engaged in research and education in the social sciences. Its principal purposes are to aid in the development of sound public policies and to provide advanced training for students in the social sciences.

The Institution was founded December 8, 1927, as a consolidation of three antecedent organizations: the Institute for Government Research, 1916; the Institute of Economics, 1922; and the Robert Brookings Graduate School of Economics and Government, 1924.

The general administration of the Institution is the responsibility of a self-perpetuating Board of Trustees. In addition to this general responsibility the By-Laws provide that, "It is the function of the Trustees to make possible the conduct of scientific research and publication, under the most favorable conditions, and to safeguard the independence of the research staff in the pursuit of their studies and in the publication of the results of such studies. It is not a part of their function to determine, control, or influence the conduct of particular investigations or the conclusions reached." The immediate direction of the policies, program, and staff of the Institution is vested in the President, who is assisted by an advisory council, chosen from the professional staff of the Institution.

In publishing a study the Institution presents it as a competent treatment of a subject worthy of public consideration. The interpretations and conclusions in such publications are those of the author or authors and do not necessarily reflect the views of other members of the Brookings staff or of the administrative officers of the Institution.

Foreword

IN 1936 THE ROBINSON-PATMAN ACT was enacted by the Congress to protect trade and commerce against unlawful price discrimination and trade practices. A voluminous literature has developed on the legal and economic issues arising out of the enforcement of this legislation. But no comprehensive review of the experience under the act or its economic effects has heretofore been made.

An appraisal of this experience after twenty years seemed desirable, especially in view of the widespread implications of the law. Hence, Brookings welcomed the opportunity to sponsor such an investigation under the direction of Professor Corwin D. Edwards, of the University of Chicago. Professor Edwards, as a former long-time staff member of the Federal Trade Commission and as a student of regulatory practices, was uniquely qualified to make this appraisal with insight into both the economic and the legal intricacies of enforcement.

He presents in this volume a detailed review of experience, under the Robinson-Patman Act, stressing particularly the litigation of economic issues and the modifications in business practices that followed.

Brookings is deeply indebted to Professor Edwards for this contribution to public understanding; it is also indebted to the interviewing staff of economists that worked with him, and to the members of the Advisory Committee, who offered helpful criticism and suggestions to the author.

The views expressed are those of the author, as they are in all Brookings studies, and are not to be taken as necessarily reflecting the views of the staff, officers, or trustees of the Institution.

I wish to acknowledge with gratitude the financial support of the Institution by the Ford Foundation, which has made this study possible.

ROBERT D. CALKINS
President

October 1959

Author's Preface

THIS STUDY OF EXPERIENCE under the Robinson-Patman Act differs substantially from that which was initially planned. The original intention was to give minimum attention to litigation before the Federal Trade Commission and the courts; to take the facts found in decisions and opinions as a starting point; to ascertain from interested parties—sellers, favored and disfavored customers, and competitors of these—what happened after orders under the Robinson-Patman Act were issued; and to endeavor, from case studies of subsequent events, to formulate generalizations about the impact of the statute on business practice.

This plan guided the conduct of field work for the study. To obtain the names of interested parties, it was necessary to examine the findings of the Federal Trade Commission and the underlying public records in cases in which the Commission had issued orders to cease violations of the Robinson-Patman Act. This was done for 239 of the 244 cases decided prior to January 1, 1955.[1] Unfortunately, however, the public records of most of the cases supplied no such information. Only 41 of the decisions had been preceded by a formal trial. Twenty-five more cases were based on stipulations of fact, most of which were brief and lacking in details. In the remaining 178 cases, decision had been based on blanket admissions, consent, or default, so that the complaint of the Commission, and findings that paraphrased it, furnished the only information about the facts. Since the complaints were often general, these cases seldom furnished the names of any interested persons except the respondents.

In view of these difficulties, the initial plan was to conduct field interviews for each case in which official public records disclosed the name of at least one interested person other than the respondent. Fewer than one hundred cases met this criterion. Since the list of the cases that did

---

[1] Since no complete list of orders in cases under the Robinson-Patman Act was available, one was compiled from published decisions. It contained 239 cases. After field work had been completed, a further check found 5 additional cases, involving violation of the brokerage provision.

so was top-heavy with violations of the brokerage provision, many of which appeared to raise similar issues and to meet only the minimum requirement regarding possible sources of information, about 15 brokerage cases were arbitrarily deleted from the list. Field work was undertaken on the remaining 84 cases. In the complete list of cases that resulted in orders, which is given in Appendix A, these are designated by an "x" in the column headed "Included in Sample."

For each case in the sample thus selected, a list was prepared showing the names, addresses, and affiliations of interested persons, so far as such information was available. For a few cases so many names were obtained that interviews were sought with only a selected group, chosen to include persons from the concerns granting the discrimination, beneficiaries of it, and competitors of both, with, so far as possible, coverage of different areas and enterprises of different sizes. In most instances, however, the available names were so few that an effort was made to interview every person named. A particular effort was made to interview the respondent in each case.

Interviews were based on questionnaires differentiated according to the type of practice involved in the case and the relation of the person interviewed thereto. There were 18 such questionnaires, as follows:

Brokerage
    For Sellers
    For Buyers
    For Intermediaries
    For Buying Groups
    For Members of Buying Groups
    For Market Information Services
    For Clients of Market Information Services

Porportionality
    In Payments
      For Sellers
      For Buyers
    In Services
      For Sellers
      For Buyers

Discriminations
    Volume or Quantity—For Sellers
    Unsystematic—For Sellers
    Volume or Quantity or Unsystematic—For Buyers

Functional
    For Sellers
    For Buyers

Territorial
    For Sellers
    For Buyers

In spite of the effort to develop questionnaires relevant to varying situations, it was obvious from the beginning that planned questions could serve only as general guides to the interviewer because of (1) the many qualitative differences in the circumstances of different cases; (2) probable variations in the character and completeness of business records; (3) probability that persons interviewed would differ substantially in their willingness to supply detailed information. Accordingly, the questionnaires were intended to be subject to modification as the circumstances of each interview might suggest.

Field interviews were conducted in 1956 by a staff of seven persons, and during the early part of 1957 by two additional persons. Each interviewer was asked to familiarize himself with the Commission's findings in the cases covered by his interviews. In addition, he was supplied with (1) excerpts and summaries of relevant materials from the docket records of cases that were tried, of which some were prepared by John Baney and others by the author; (2) copies of the reports of related interviews as these became available. A report of each interview was submitted in writing.

The interviewing staff was as follows: John J. Baney, former member of the staff of the Federal Trade Commission; Joseph D. Coppock, professor, Earlham College; Joel B. Dirlam, professor, University of Connecticut; Walter Gerhardt, graduate student, Tulane University; Earl A. Graham, former member of the staff of the Federal Trade Commission; Theodore J. Kreps, professor, Graduate School of Business, Stanford University; Bernard Shull, graduate student, University of Wisconsin; Irwin M. Stelzer, economist, Boni, Watkins, Jason, & Co. (on leave); John T. Wheeler, professor, School of Business Administration, University of California.

After a considerable number of interviews had accumulated, the original plan for the study was substantially modified. Three considerations led to the decision to do this: first, that considerable analysis of the facts of the situations preceding the Commission's orders was proving to be indispensable to an understanding of subsequent situations disclosed by the interviews; second that the interviews, though valuable sources of information, were not supplying enough detailed, reliable, and comparable information for use in the way originally planned; and third, that analysis of the public records of the Commission and the interviews jointly would produce a result with greater meaning than analysis of the interviews alone.

The first consideration rested on the fact that the circumstances to which the orders of the Commission had been addressed were more various than had been anticipated. The cases did not fit neatly into a few categories of business practice. Instead, the range of significant variation in the facts was so great that an understanding of it, and of its bearing on the impact of the Commission's orders, required a substantial analysis of the cases themselves.

The second consideration meant, in effect, that the interviews were disappointing. It had been anticipated that many persons, particularly those subject to the orders of the Commission, would be reluctant to talk candidly. Though such situations were encountered, particularly in interviews with small enterprises, they were fewer and less important than had been anticipated. On the other hand, deficiencies in the information available were substantially greater than had been anticipated: (1) Many small enterprises had gone out of business or had changed ownership; and the new owners were unfamiliar with the relevant facts, while the old owners were dead or unavailable. (2) In large enterprises, persons familiar with the particular case and its aftermath were often no longer employed, and their whereabouts were often not known. (3) Relevant business records had often been destroyed. (4) In a considerable number of large concerns, and in some small ones, the proceeding had been concerned with aspects of the business regarded as unimportant and with sums of money regarded as trivial, so that those who handled it had no clear memory of it; and the relevant records were buried in inactive files where they could not be located without time and effort greater than the persons interviewed were willing to give. (5) Persons interviewed were often so busy that the interviews were too short to cover all relevant aspects of the subject. (6) In particular instances, information supplied was inconsistent with documentary evidence or with conflicting statements by others; and without inquisitorial rights the interviewers could not resolve the contradictions. (7) Even the most detailed and apparently reliable interviews involved so many variations in the kind of information supplied that comparable data as to price movements and similar quantitative matters could not be compiled from them. Because of these limitations, an analysis resting on the interviews alone would have been, at best, a collection of significant fragments.

The interviews, however, often supplemented and illuminated the public record of a case, and the public record often supplied valuable interpretative background for the interviews. The best parts of the interviews consisted in descriptions of market structures and trade practices and in evaluations of changes in them and of related changes in the business environment. These were usually matters about which the findings of the Commission and the underlying public records were least revealing, since they were often tangential to the questions of legality with which the Commission was concerned. In functional discount cases, for example, the Commission's attention had centered on the question whether the recipients of different discounts had been competitors, and the information provided by the cases as to the nature and rationale of the particular functional discount structures had sometimes been scant. By filling such gaps, the interviews provided a basis for a better understanding of the cases and of the changes in practice that were necessitated by the orders of the Commission.

Accordingly, the plan of the study was revised to include an analysis of the litigation under the Robinson-Patman Act as well as of the changes in business practice that followed this litigation.

Under the final plan, the book is based on six bodies of material. First are the findings, orders, appellate decisions, and underlying public records of the 84 cases included in the original sample. Second are the field interviews with persons participating in or affected by these cases. These two groups of data are the primary sources on which the analysis rests. Third are the findings and orders of the remaining 160 cases in which the Commission found violation of the act in decisions rendered before January 1, 1955. Since the poverty of the findings was the reason for omitting these cases from the original sample, few of them have contributed significantly to the analysis except in statistical totals. Fourth are the findings and orders in the 67 cases in which violation was found in decisions rendered between January 1, 1955 and December 31, 1957, and in the appellate decisions rendered during that three-year period. During the period 19 cases were tried, some of them of unusual importance; and the analysis set forth in this book has been substantially modified by them. Because of their recency, however, it has not been possible to conduct field interviews in these cases or even to examine the public records underlying the findings of fact. In one or two instances in which decisions were issued in 1958 or later on matters discussed in the book, last minute changes in text or footnotes have taken account of these decisions. However, the decisions in cases since December 31, 1957 have not been systematically studied. Fifth are the complaints and orders in cases dismissed by the Commission prior to December 31, 1957. These have been examined only for the purpose of checking conclusions regarding the policies of the Commission and interpretations of the law by ascertaining whether or not dismissals have been consistent with these conclusions. Sixth are the major court decisions in private litigation under the statute, so far as the author has been able to find them. They have been used only to supplement the analysis of judicial interpretations of the law where points developed in private litigation modify or extend those developed in the Commission's cases.

No effort has been made in this book, however, to analyze the scope and effect of the private lawsuits. Information about such proceedings is not readily available. When litigation terminated in a settlement out of court, there is typically no public record of the settlement. When a judgment was entered by consent of the parties, the court has a record of the settlement, though there is no summary of the facts other than the usually contradictory allegations of the plaintiff's formal complaint and the defendant's formal answer. In cases that were settled after trial before a jury, the jury's estimate of the facts was summarized in a verdict for one of the parties, without findings of fact or conclusions of law. Only in contested cases in which jury trial was waived are there findings of fact and conclusions of law. The decisions, whether reached by consent or by contested verdicts, are not centrally compiled; and many of them cast so little light on the facts and the law that their compilation would be useful only for statistical purposes.

The readily available records pertaining to these cases consist mostly of judicial decisions on procedural motions, findings in cases in which a contested case was tried by a judge without a jury, and opinions rendered by judges of the appellate courts. (There have also been a few opinions from state courts in cases in which a claim based on the Robinson-Patman Act was advanced in litigation under state law.) The appellate court opinions and the more important decisions of the lower courts are printed, and annual lists of them are compiled and published by Commerce Clearing House. Many of the decisions of the lower courts, however, were rendered in disposing of procedural questions that did not raise substantive issues. They had to do with such matters as whether it was proper to sue several defendants jointly, whether complaints were clear and complete, how far the parties to the litigation might demand access to each other's documentary records, and whether there were controverted issues of fact that required trial and precluded the court from deciding the case by a summary judgment. Even the decisions that concerned substantive matters frequently decided questions that, though administratively important, were remote from the central problems of public policy toward price discrimination. For example, they determined whether particular dealings were in interstate commerce, whether the plaintiff was actually a customer or a competitor of the defendant, whether the plaintiff had proved that a discrimination affected not only business in general but also his particular business, and what was the proper measure of the amount of pecuniary damage done by an injurious discrimination. In a number of cases, the issue raised was whether an enterprise could escape a contractual obligation because the contract violated the law—to which the answer was yes; or whether it could escape paying for goods it had bought because it had paid a discriminatory price—to which the answer was no. In a number of cases the principal basis for suit was not discrimination, but a complaint that prices had been set unreasonably low in violation of Section 3 of the Robinson-Patman Act. Lower courts differed on whether the provision for triple damage suits covers Section 3. In January 1958, this question was settled in the negative by the Supreme Court.[2]

In a few of the cases, decisions focused on important substantive issues. Most of those cases were appealed, so that opinions of the appellate courts are also available.

Because of these limitations, no independent attempt has been made in this book to determine the frequency of private suits, the success of the victims of discrimination in protecting themselves thus, or the effectiveness of the deterrent to violation of the law which such suits have provided. Estimates have been used, however, from Lee Loevinger's article, "Enforcement of the Robinson-Patman Act by Private Parties."[3]

So far as decisions and opinions in private suits are readily available and appear to be significant, they have been read in order to cull from

---

[2] See *Nashville Milk Co.* v. *Carnation Co.* 355 U.S. 373 and *Safeway Stores* v. *Vance*, 355 U.S. 389.

[3] Commerce Clearing House, *1957 Antitrust Law Symposium*, pp. 145-63.

them the ones that throw light on the substantive issues here discussed. Since most cases that involve novel questions are appealed, it is believed that this procedure has been adequate to cover the proceedings in which private litigation has extended or modified the judicial interpretation of the law. Each important private case has been discussed in connection with the topic to which it is relevant.

The author desires to express his gratitude to those who have helped him obtain access to relevant information, interpret it, and correct weaknesses in the plan and execution of the book. Particularly, he is grateful to Cyrus Austin, Richard B. Heflebower, A. D. H. Kaplan, Mark S. Massel, and George W. Stocking, who, as members of the advisory committee for the study, gave their time generously to review the research plan and criticize the manuscript; to Joseph E. Sheehy and Earl W. Kintner of the Federal Trade Commission, who helped him obtain access to official documents and to understand their meaning; to the late Robert B. Dawkins, of the Federal Trade Commission, whose interpretations of various difficult points of law and policy were very helpful; to J. M. Clark, who read critically the chapters on territorial discrimination; to the interviewing staff, on whose resourceful insight much of the interpretation rests; to Mary O'Donnell, who, when the author was ill, added co-ordination of the field work to her secretarial duties. If the book has merits, it is partly due to the assistance these persons so generously gave; its defects are attributable soley to the author.

CORWIN D. EDWARDS

Table of Contents

1 / The Problem and the Plan of This Book

THE IDEA OF DISCRIMINATION has a shadowy origin in the social and legal preconceptions of democratic society. In a democratic community equality of status is taken for granted. Such equality implies equal position before the law, equal political rights and duties, and equal economic opportunities. It requires equal treatment of all members of the community by persons exercising political or judicial authority. So far as private persons have the power to affect substantially the rights and opportunities of their fellows, it implies that they, too, have a duty to treat their fellows equally.

This democratic ideal is modified by the knowledge that many kinds of inequality are practically necessary. Children and adults, men and women, the sane and the insane, the law-abiding and the criminal, citizens and foreigners are in various respects treated differently. Equality of treatment is taken to mean equal treatment for persons similarly situated. Where there are substantial differences of condition, inequality is thought to be appropriate; but the differences in treatment are expected to be appropriately related to the underlying differences in condition. To discriminate is to apply unequal treatment to persons similarly situated or to apply, to persons dissimilarly situated, unequal treatment that is inappropriate to the dissimilarity.

Alongside these vague but compelling preconceptions, we have inherited from the thinking of economists ideas about discrimination that are more precise but less comprehensive. To the classical economist, the tendencies of a free market economy were both inevitable and admirable. Through the bargaining of buyers and sellers, prices came to be appropriately related to costs, and costs came to be appropriately related to underlying scarcities of resources and skills. For prices to vary with costs was not only natural but also proper.[1] Any other price relationship

[1] Marginal rather than average costs were used in applying this standard. However, the nature of the cost concept is not important to the distinction between legal and economic concepts of discrimination.

1

expressed inefficiency and injustice and could prevail only because of interference with the free play of markets. To the economist of this tradition, discrimination consisted of a distortion of the relation between the prices and costs of a seller, so that either costs or prices varied without corresponding variation in the other.

These two ideas of discrimination—which, for convenience, will be called respectively the political and the economic idea—differ from each other. According to the political idea, discrimination is found only in unequal treatment. Though difference of condition is an excuse for inequality, even where different conditions prevail, equality should be approached as closely as possible. Undue equality is never subject to criticism. According to the economic idea, on the contrary, discrimination exists whenever prices and costs do not vary concomitantly. Price difference without cost difference is discrimination; so is cost difference without price difference. By the cost standard, prices may be either unduly different or unduly similar, and in either case they are discriminatory. Thus the economic idea of nondiscriminatory prices requires appropriate degrees of unequal treatment.

As applied to the marketing of goods, the economic idea is broader than the political idea. In political thinking only the buyers or the sellers of a particular commodity are similarly situated. Indeed, only those among them who are in competition with each other are clearly included within a similar group. Consequently, the political demand for equality applies only within a commodity market and usually only to groups of persons in that market who are competitors. The economist, however, is concerned with the allocation of resources and purchases among different uses of a commodity and among different commodities in different markets. His test of discrimination is logically applicable not only to differences in a seller's prices in selling the same commodity in competition with different sellers or in transactions with competing buyers but also to a seller's price differences in selling a commodity to buyers who do not compete with one another or in selling different commodities in different markets.

When applied to a specific situation these differences are striking. If a particular commodity is bought and sold at a uniform price by all who compete in its purchase and sale, it can raise, according to the political idea, no problem of discrimination. According to the economic idea, however, this very uniformity of price may be evidence of discrimination if it prevails in spite of substantial differences in cost. Moreover, if the sellers are also engaged in selling other commodities, they may be discriminating in price by selling this commodity too dearly or too cheaply relative to the others, in the light of the costs applicable to each. An economist may inquire whether a steel company discriminates between competing buyers of steel strip, whether it discriminates between buyers who purchase strip for different noncompeting uses, and whether it discriminates between buyers of strip and buyers of its other rolled products.[2]

The political idea of discrimination has long had some application to business affairs. Its beginnings can be found in medieval conceptions of the just price. Its modern American employment is to be found not only in its use under the antitrust laws, which is the subject of this book, but also in other politico-economic legislation. For example, we seek to avoid discrimination in railway rates, both by limiting the power of the railroads to make extortionate charges and by limiting (through such rules as the carload quantity limit) their power to make price concessions that reflect economies. Underlying such rules is the belief that any departure from a uniform schedule of rates is suspect.

The economic idea of discrimination has had relatively little impact on public affairs. One part of it has been borrowed as an addition to the political idea: the belief that a difference in cost will usually constitute such a difference in circumstances as to justify a discrimination that would otherwise be objectionable. However, public policy has not accepted the full logic of the economist's position; though a cost difference

---

[2] Not all economists accept the full implications of the view here expressed. Some, for example, would not apply the term discrimination to a seller's prices for products that are quite dissimilar even though the price differences bore no relation to cost differences (Compare, for example, Joe S. Bain, *Price Theory* (1952), pp. 400-01 with George J. Stigler, *The Theory of Price* (1952), pp. 214-15.) To the present writer it appears that the economic concept of discrimination was a consistent and intelligible part of the classical theory of equilibrium, where its logic was that set forth above; but that use of the concept of discrimination in theories of monopolistic competition has been diverse and obscure. For the careful working out of a view similar to that expressed here see Eli W. Clemens, "Price Discrimination and the Multiple-Product Firm," *Review of Economic Studies,* Vol. 19, 1951-52, p. 1, reprinted with alterations in Richard B. Heflebower and George W. Stocking, eds., *Readings in Industrial Organization and Public Policy* (1958), p. 262. It is noteworthy that in the regulation of railroads undue preference in rates may be found to exist between competing commodities. See D. Philip Locklin, *Economics of Transportation,* 3d ed. (1947), pp. 525-32.

may permit a price difference, it is not thought to require it. There has been no effort in the antitrust laws to condemn prices because they are unduly similar.[3] Except in regulating transportation, there has been little effort to condemn as discriminatory the different prices at which a seller offers different commodities for sale or to insist that if discrimination is to be avoided, prices must vary with costs.[4]

The dominance of the political idea over the economic is peculiarly evident in the place of the concept of discrimination in the antitrust laws. Since these laws are broadly designed to preserve competition, they are concerned especially with activities that impair competition. The Sherman Act of 1890 forbade restrictive agreements and monopolization without mentioning discriminatory practices. In some of the cases under that statute, attention was given to price discrimination and to discriminatory refusal to sell goods, but only because such practices might be used to

[3] The Interstate Commerce Commission, however, has repeatedly applied such a concept in regulating transportation rates. See *Commercial Association* v. *Galveston & San Antonio Ry. Co.*, 128 I.C.C. 349 (1927), 160 I.C.C. 345 (1929); *Inland Empire Shippers League* v. *Director General*, 59 I.C.C. 321 (1920); *Kansas Grain Association* v. *Chicago, Rock Island & Pacific Ry. Co.*, 139 I.C.C. 641, 670 (1928); *Dutton Lumber Co.* v. *New York, New Haven & Hartford R. R. Co.*, 151 I.C.C. 391 (1929). In a separate opinion in the latter case Commissioner Eastman said (p. 415): "Other things being equal, it is as unduly preferential to give one shipper twice as much transportation for the same charge as it is to give him the same amount at half the price."

In the United Kingdom a similar concept has been offered to the courts in a proceeding under the electricity acts, *British Oxygen Ltd.* v. *Scottish Electricity Board*. The electricity bought by British Oxygen from the Board was cheaper to produce than the electricity which the Board sold to others. British Oxygen bought at a discount which was less than the Board's saving in cost. It sued the Board under a provision of the electricity laws that forbids undue discrimination. The case went to the House of Lords on a point of law: the Board's contention that, as a matter of law, the customer paying the lower price could not claim discrimination. Refusing to adjudicate the matter finally at this stage of the proceedings, the House of Lords referred it back to a court for trial. It is not yet decided.

[4] In certain antitrust cases high prices and profits on items in a line of goods have been regarded as evidence that the seller had a monopolistic position in selling that line. See, for example, the contentions of the government on the sale of electric light bulbs by General Electric and Westinghouse. In distribution there has been repeated condemnation of so-called loss-leaders, on the theory that large distributors who sell certain items in their line at little or no profit do so with predatory purpose and effect. Interpretations such as these have always been hotly challenged. In the aggregate, they have constituted arguments designed to support particular conclusions or courses of action, but not coherent programs designed to bring the prices of different commodities into an orderly relation to one another.

destroy competitors. When the Clayton Act was passed in 1914, its provisions about price discrimination were concerned solely with the impact of discrimination on competition, and therefore conceived discrimination as something that should be uncovered in the relations among competitors. As will appear subsequently, the selective focus of the law was blurred by the Robinson Patman Act of 1936, but the blurring consisted in modifying a political tradition rather than substituting an economic analysis.

Discrimination in the Clayton Act

A law against price discrimination was first introduced into the American antitrust laws by the Clayton Act of 1914. It was intended, like other parts of the Clayton Act, to prevent monopoly in its incipiency by striking at practices by which powerful enterprises might attain or consolidate control of their markets. Experience under the Sherman Act had indicated that price discrimination was one of these practices. In particular instances powerful enterprises had weakened or destroyed smaller competitors by selective price reductions focused on segments of the market that were peculiarly important to these small rivals. With such practices in mind, the Congress included in the 1914 law a provision intended to curb discriminations by powerful sellers where anticompetitive effects on their competitors were reasonably probable.[5]

The purpose of the 1914 law was set forth clearly in a report by the House Committee on the Judiciary.[6] The committee said:

[5] This provision read as follows: "Sec. 2. That it shall be unlawful for any person engaged in commerce, in the course of such commerce, either directly or indirectly to discriminate in price between different purchasers of commodities, which commodities are sold for use, consumption, or resale within the United States or any territory thereof or the District of Columbia or any insular possession or other place under the jurisdiction of the United States, where the effect of such discrimination may be to substantially lessen competition or tend to create a monopoly in any line of commerce: *Provided,* That nothing herein contained shall prevent discrimination in price between purchasers of commodities on account of differences in the grade, quality, or quantity of the commodity sold, or that makes only due allowance for difference in the cost of selling or transportation, or discrimination in price in the same or different communities made in good faith to meet competition: *And provided further,* that nothing herein contained shall prevent persons engaged in selling goods, wares, or merchandise in commerce from selecting their own customers in bona fide transactions and not in restraint of trade." 38 Stat. 730.

[6] *Antitrust Legislation,* H. Rept. 627, 63 Cong. 2 sess., p. 1960.

Section 2 of the bill . . . is expressly designed with the view of correcting and forbidding a common and widespread unfair trade practice whereby certain great corporations and also certain smaller concerns which seek to secure a monopoly in trade and commerce by aping the methods of the great corporations, have heretofore endeavored to destroy competition and render unprofitable the business of competitors by selling their goods, wares, and merchandise at a less price in the particular communities where their rivals are engaged in business than at other places throughout the country.

In the 22 years between the enactment of the Clayton Act and the enactment of the Robinson-Patman Act, the Federal Trade Commission issued 43 complaints under the price discrimination provisions of the Clayton Act, but dismissed 31 of them. It issued 12 cease and desist orders, of which 4 were subsequently appealed and reversed by the courts.[7] Thus before the Robinson-Patman Act only 8 valid cease and desist orders were issued in price discrimination cases, and the courts reversed the Commission in every case that reached them.[8]

The thinness of the record of enforcement was apparently due to three major difficulties in the application of the statute. First, the courts were initially reluctant to apply the law to discriminations that tended to reduce competition not between the discriminating seller and his competitors but in the resale market served by the seller's favored customers. In the first of the commission's cases to be reversed, that against the Mennen Company, an appellate court held in 1923[9] that the law did not

[7] The cases which were not reversed had to do with the *Fleischmann Co.,* 1 FTC 119; *Cudahy Packing Co.,* 1 FTC 199; *Wayne Oil Tank and Pump Co.,* 1 FTC 259; *Galena Signal Oil Co.,* 2 FTC 446; *South Bend Bait Co.,* 4 FTC 355; *The Salt Producers Association,* 5 FTC 67; *U. S. Steel Corp.,* 8 FTC 1; and *Pittsburgh Coal Co. of Wisconsin,* 8 FTC 480. It is noteworthy that of these orders only that against U.S. Steel was appealed, and in this instance there was no appeal until after the passage of the Robinson-Patman Act.

The cases in which the Commission's order was reversed involved the *Mennen Co.,* 4 FTC 258, 288 F. 774; the *National Biscuit Co.,* 7 FTC 208, 299 F. 733; *The Loose-Wiles Biscuit Co.,* 7 FTC 218, 299 F. 733; and the *Goodyear Tire and Rubber Co.,* 22 FTC 232, 92 F. 2d 677, 304 U.S. 257, 101 F. 2d 620.

[8] Violation of the price discrimination provisions of the Clayton Act had also been enjoined in four proceedings by the Department of Justice; but in each of these violation of the Sherman Act was principally at issue. The cases were *U.S.* v. *A. Schrader's Son, Inc.,* decree July 14, 1923; *U.S.* v. *Flower Producers Cooperative Association,* consent decree Aug. 15, 1926; *U.S.* v. *Gillette Safety Razor Co.,* consent decree Aug. 4, 1927; *U.S.* v. *Amsterdamsche Chininefabriek,* consent decrees Sept. 20, 1928 and March 2, 1929.

[9] *Mennen Co.* v. *FTC,* 288 F. 774.

apply to this kind of damage to competition. However, five years later the Supreme Court reversed this interpretation in a private suit by declaring that the offense against the policy of preserving competition "by a discrimination in prices exacted by the seller from purchasers of similar goods is no less clear when it produces the evil in respect of the line of commerce in which they are engaged than when it produces the evil in respect of the line of commerce in which the seller is engaged."[10] Subsequent to this decision the statute applied to all discriminations that had the prohibited anticompetitive effect, no matter where that effect became apparent.

The other two difficulties were more enduring. First, the law provided that nothing therein should prevent discrimination "on account of differences in the . . . quantity of the commodity sold." Though the Federal Trade Commission argued that this language exempted only such discriminations as were reasonably related to the difference in the cost of providing different quantities, the courts interpreted the provision to mean that quantity discounts were exempt regardless of their amount or their effect. Thus an important class of discriminatory price concessions was exempted from the law. Second, the law provided that nothing therein should prevent "discrimination in price in the same or different communities made in good faith to meet competition." Through this provision retaliatory discrimination was sanctioned; the application of the statute was limited to those sellers that initiated, as distinguished from those that subsequently adopted, a discrimination; and harmful effects on competition among buyers were made unreachable if the discriminating seller could show that he had met competition in good faith.

The concern of the Federal Trade Commission over these limitations in the law of price discrimination came to a head during its investigation of chain stores in the early 1930's. The Commission concluded that "Many of the low buying prices of the chains had little if any relation to differences in quantity or cost of selling." Moreover, the Commission feared "that even discriminations justifiable on account of quantity or cost of selling might nevertheless in the long run lead to monopoly."[11] In a final report on the chain store investigation submitted to the Senate in 1934, the Commission recommended that the law of price discrimination be revised so that it would broadly prohibit unfair and unjust discrimination, leaving to the courts the application of this standard where

[10] *George Van Camp & Sons Co.* v. *American Can Co. et al.,* 278 U.S. 245.
[11] Federal Trade Commission, *Annual Report,* 1935, p. 33.

there were differences in quantity and cost and where a competitor's prices were met in good faith.[12] In its annual report for 1935, the Commission reverted to the problem but made a somewhat different recommendation. It now said that if the exemption on account of differences in quantity were so interpreted that any difference in quantity justified any amount of discrimination, the law could give no substantial protection, and that therefore the statute should be amended "to clearly define the discrimination in price intended to be forbidden." It suggested, too, that supplementary legislation be enacted "to require all manufacturers of merchandise, other than perishables, selling in interstate commerce to report promptly to the Federal Trade Commission whenever they make special discounts and allowances which were not openly and generally made and published to the trade."[13]

By the early 1930's, when the chain store report was completed, the time was ripe for a change in the price discrimination law. On the one hand, the old law had proved to be of limited usefulness. On the other, the problem of price discrimination had evolved with the development of the economy. Local price cutting to obtain a monopoly, such as Congress had had in mind in 1914, had ceased to be a major political problem.[14] New problems had come to the fore because of great changes that were taking place in the channels of distribution. The traditional sale of goods from manufacturer to wholesaler to retailer was being challenged or superseded by new methods. Manufacturers established retail outlets. Wholesaling and retailing functions were joined by vertical integration. Chain store selling grew rapidly; mail-order distribution became more

[12] *Ibid.*, p. 33.

[13] *Ibid.*, pp. 15-16.

[14] Indeed, in the orders issued by the commission prior to the Robinson-Patman Act, there were only two that were applicable to territorial price discrimination. One, against U. S. Steel, involved the use of a basing point pricing formula in a conspiratorial setting. The other, against the Pittsburgh Coal Co. of Wisconsin, involved price differences between the Twin Cities and Duluth. Even these cases did not present the traditional pattern of predatory local price cutting. The problem in the Pittsburgh Coal case was competition among distributors. In the U. S. Steel case, though monopolistic effects on competition among sellers were alleged and found, the center of attention was injury to Middle Western customers who competed with others more favorably located.

Of the ten other cases in which orders were issued, six were concerned with discriminations among classes of customers, one with special prices to a mail order house, one with volume discounts, and two with more complicated forms of nonterritorial discrimination. In five of these cases, the commission found a probability of damage to competition among customers, and in three of them it found no other kind of damage.

prominent; voluntary organizations of retail stores undertook wholesaling functions. Specialized distributors appeared who performed only a part of the functions traditionally associated with their level of distribution. In the general scrambling of relationships, established groups felt their interests threatened, newcomers maneuvered for advantage, and traditional norms of business methods, markups, and business ethics were no longer reliable.[15]

The unrest and clamor for protection that inevitably accompany rapid institutional change were given strength and focus by the fact that much of this change was undertaken by powerful distributors who, in undertaking it, rapidly became more powerful. The corporate chains became the symbols of the new methods of distribution. The sales of chain groceries almost quadrupled between 1919 and 1927. In the same period, the sales of chain variety stores, drugstores, and candy stores more than doubled, and those of chain cigar stores and shoe stores grew about 50 per cent. The sales of wearing apparel chains quintupled. Mail-order sales increased by nearly one third.[16] The great mail-order houses began to supplement their catalog selling by the establishment of chains of retail stores. The various forms of mass distribution gave rise to alarm among small distributors in the trades affected, to organized agitation by trade associations composed of such distributors, and to assorted proposals for legislative curbs on the growth of the corporate chains. State legislatures were asked to apply progressive taxes based on the number of stores under a common ownership, and many of them did so. Price cutting by chain stores was attacked by proposals for state laws to curb sales below "cost" or to permit resale price maintenance on branded goods. The chain stores were accused of monopolization; and although even the largest of them had percentages of their markets so small as to make the accusation implausible, they resembled monopolies in the fact that their scale of operations had outrun that of their small competitors and in the fact that their size had given them not only certain functional advantages but also bargaining power and power of maneuver that were not available to small enterprises.

[15] For an account of changes in distributive methods, see R. M. Clewett, ed., *Marketing Channels for Manufactured Products* (1954), especially articles by Fred M. Jones, "The Development of Marketing Channels in the United States to 1920" and Nathaniel H. Engle, "The Development of Marketing Channels in the United States since 1920."

[16] See U.S. Bureau of the Census, *Statistical Abstract of the United States 1928*, p. 325.

With the advent of depression, special discounts to powerful buyers increased in number, and chain stores, selling necessities at low prices, suffered less than other distributors. Thus the chain store problem that became important in the 1920's resulted in political action that culminated in the 1930's.

The Federal Trade Commission's belief that the law of price discrimination was weak and needed amendment would not in itself have evoked the political support needed to make amendment possible. The recommendation that the law be amended was given political impact partly by the growing concern over the power of chain distributors, particularly in the food industry, and partly by the readiness to adopt new economic policies that was generated during the depression of the 1930's.

In 1926 the Senate directed the Federal Trade Commission to make a comprehensive investigation of chain stores.[17] This investigation produced a series of 33 reports culminating in a final report in December 1934.[18] The Commission found in the chains many advantages "flowing from the integration of production and of wholesale and retail distribution, from the savings involved in avoiding credit and delivery service, and from the ability of chains to realize the benefits of large-scale advertising," all of which, in the opinion of the Commission, were plainly lawful and could not be eliminated without "radical interference with the rights of private ownership and initiative, virtual abandonment of the competitive principle, and destruction of the public advantage represented by lower prices and lower cost of living." However, the Commission also found that the chains enjoyed buying advantages derived from price discrimination by suppliers, which accounted for "a most substantial part of the chains' ability to undersell independents,"[19] and that the chains engaged in local price discrimination in reselling. It thought that the selling practices of the chains were intrastate and hence unreach-

[17] S. Res. 224, 70 Cong. 1 sess. (1926).

[18] Federal Trade Commission, *Annual Report*, 1935, pp. 32-40.

[19] This conclusion has been challenged, on the basis of a reanalysis of the Commission's figures, by Joseph Cornwall Palamountain, Jr., *The Politics of Distribution* (1955), pp. 63-72. Mr. Palamountain asserts that about one fifth of the difference in retail prices between chains and independents was attributable to the advantages of the chains in buying prices. See also Richard B. Heflebower, "Mass Distribution; A Phase of Bilateral Oligopoly or of Competition?" Papers and Proceedings of the Sixty-ninth Annual Meeting of the American Economic Association, *American Economic Review*, Vol. 47 (May 1957).

able by federal authority, but that the discriminatory buying advantages should be subjected to federal attack. Seeing difficulties in the use of existing law because of the exemption of discriminations based on quantity and discriminations made in good faith to meet competition, it recommended amendment of the statute to facilitate an attack on the chains.[20]

The economic and political environment of the day was suited to new legislative ventures. Concern over a severe depression had resulted in 1933 in unprecedented legislative experiments. In the years before the Commission's final report on chain stores, the National Industrial Recovery Act had given legal effect to "codes of fair competition" expressing the aspirations of nearly every substantial and well-organized interest in manufacture and distribution. The codes were both radical and diverse in their departure from accepted standards for federal legislation; and the scope of the code-making process was so extensive that it necessarily entailed a flow of decisions about complicated questions of public policy with minimal time for consideration of the issues involved. Included in the codes for the food industries were many provisions concerned with price discrimination and related matters. Most common were provisions against secret rebates, requirements to prevent advertising allowances from becoming concealed price reductions, and prohibitions of free deals and brokerage payments to buyers. Some codes also limited quantity discounts and sought to prevent retailers from receiving wholesale discounts.[21]

Though the Supreme Court invalidated the National Recovery Act a few months after the Commission's recommendations about chain stores became available, and though the end of the code-making process was widely greeted as a relief from a proliferation of ill-considered experiments, much of the attitude that had been expressed in the National Recovery Administration continued to be influential in economic politics. Legislative proposals that would previously have seemed drastic were regarded as conservative. Procedures in considering legislative recommendations that would previously have seemed superficial and summary were regarded as adequate. There survived from the NRA period and from the continuing economic depression a sense of urgency and a

[20] Federal Trade Commission, *Annual Report*, 1935, pp. 32-33.

[21] NRA Division of Review, *Work Materials No. 35, The Content of NIRA Administration Legislation*, Part C: Trade Practice Provisions in the Codes by Daniel S. Gerig, Jr. and Beatrice Strasburger (February 1936), pp. 7-25.

willingness to experiment. There was also a belief that major evils called
for action, and that discriminatory pricing was among these evils.[22]

Discrimination in the Robinson-Patman Act

When legislation resulted from the forces discussed above, it took the
form of an amendment of the existing price discrimination law and hence
was fitted into the general framework of the antitrust laws. This fact
obscured the difference between what had previously been done and
what was now attempted. The political impulse underlying the law was
an impulse to control changes in the channels of distribution, to curb the
power of the stronger distributors, and to enhance the opportunities of
the weaker ones. It was akin to that which underlay the NRA codes in
the distributive trades, the chain store tax laws, and the state laws permitting resale price maintenance and forbidding sale below cost. It expressed, not a concern to preserve free markets, but rather a concern to
assure the survival of small business. Legislation shaped to these ends
could be fitted into the antitrust matrix because, in the laws against
monopoly, there was also concern to limit concentrations of power and
to secure as much survival of competitors as was necessary to maintain
competition. Since discrimination might lead to monopoly and monopoly
was inconsistent with adequate opportunity for the weak, the law of discrimination had an appropriate place in an antimonopoly statute. It
could be stretched beyond the limits of what was strictly necessary to the
antimonopoly purpose, and thus could be used to curb powerful distributors at points where these concerns were not endangering competition and to strengthen the opportunities of small enterprises more fully
than was necessary to the preservation of competition. This could be
done more easily by giving old words new meanings than by frankly
building a new superstructure of meaning on an old foundation. Indeed,
a stretching of old concepts is the way in which the law most commonly
evolves in democratic societies.[23]

[22] It is surprising but apparently true that the programs contained in NRA
codes were not directly related to the program subsequently incorporated in the
Robinson-Patman Act. The provisions of the codes concerned with distribution
were not reviewed during the hearings on the price discrimination bill.

[23] The author does not intend to imply condemnation of the Robinson-Patman
Act by this analysis. One of the major problems of public policy in this field is
whether or not it is desirable to curb the power derived from bigness even when
it is not monopoly power. If the answer is yes, one can argue that it would be

In stretching the political concept of discrimination beyond that contained in the original Clayton Act, the writers of the Robinson-Patman Act did not, however, adopt the economic concept of discrimination. The new law was no more concerned than the old with relationships among the prices of different commodities. It was no more concerned than the old with broad effects on the allocation of resources among the various lines of activity in an economic society. Like the old, it was concerned with the bearing of discrimination on the relations among groups of competitors. Like the old, it conceived discrimination as price difference, and embodied no concern lest prices be unduly similar when costs differed. It accepted from the economic theory of discrimination the same general idea that had already been included in the previous law, namely that a price difference can be justified by a cost difference. It endeavored to make this idea more precise than the previous law had done.

The broad plan of the Robinson-Patman Act was to cope with price discrimination that had significant effects on business opportunities, whether or not these effects changed the vigor of market competition or increased the probability of monopoly. Attention was to be given to the opportunities of both sellers and buyers, but with primary concern for the latter. Since the broadened scope of the statute necessarily entailed a more pervasive intervention in price making, care was to be taken to leave adequate scope for the encouragement of efficiency in distribution by safeguarding all price differences that were based on cost differences. The new ambitious controls over pricing practices were to be applied in the same way as the old ones: that is, by cease and desist orders issued against offenders after appropriate legal proceedings, by judicial injunctions obtained by the government, and by private suits for damage or for injunctive relief instituted by persons damaged or threatened with damage.

Many questions about the scope and impact of the new law were inherent in its pervasive character. First was a series of questions on the scope of the concept of discrimination itself. It could no longer be sought merely in the tactics by which a would-be monopolist sought to consolidate his position. Were all price differences to be regarded as discrimin-

---

well to superimpose on the monopoly concept, either by interpretation or by new legislation, something appropriate to cope with the power that inheres in great size. To characterize the Robinson-Patman Act as an effort of this general kind is to express neither approval nor disapproval but merely to seek to define the place of the statute in the evolution of public policy.

atory? If not, how were discriminatory differences to be recognized? Was the attack on discrimination to be confined to an attack on differences in price? If not, what other discriminations were to be subject to the law— differences in the quality of goods, differences in the service provided to the buyer, selective assistance to him in reselling, differences in willingness to make goods available to him? To ignore such differences was difficult, for differences in quality and in terms of sale, and refusals to sell could be means of discriminating supplementary to or alternative to price discrimination itself. Yet the law could scarcely undertake to require uniformity in the characteristics of articles sold and in the conditions under which they were sold. The difficulty appeared most clearly in the dual status of refusal to sell. On the one hand, no discrimination could be clearer than a willingness to make goods available to some customers while denying them to others. On the other hand, the right to choose one's own customers and one's own sources of supply lay close to the heart of a free market.

A second central question was the way in which a harmful discrimination was to be recognized. It would have been possible to provide by statute that any price difference among competing customers was to be regarded as harmful. The Congress did not attempt to go so far. The practical meaning of the law would necessarily depend on the standards that were developed to distinguish between harmful and harmless differences. On the buying side of the market, this distinction would go far to determine how much flexibility could remain in a seller's price structure. On the selling side of the market, the standards used in identifying harm were even more important; for in making a sale a seller necessarily inflicts some harm on his competitors, and if this harm was to be regarded as the target of the statute, price difference would be ruled out as a competitive weapon. Thus the concept of harm would directly determine the scope of sellers' competition.

In another respect, perplexing questions were necessarily involved: how far a seller might be free to meet the prices of his competitors by introducing differences into his own price structure. Adjustment of prices to meet competition could be regarded as the essence of competitive give and take, or as a device by which powerful sellers isolated the limited markets of less powerful competitors in order to cope with these concerns one by one. The old law had permitted discrimination in price without limit when it was made in good faith to meet competition. What limitations, if any, were to apply in the new law?

Various difficult questions lurked behind the effort to safeguard efficiency of distribution by authorizing cost-justified price differences. To what extent are there elements of efficiency that do not at once translate themselves into savings in the seller's cost? To what extent will use of the cost standard permit experiment with promising new methods without legal penalties if the experiment proves a failure? Can cost information be provided readily enough to enable concerns to take advantage of the leeway afforded by the statute?

Alongside these conceptual problems inherent in the basic plan of the law were important questions of the impact of such a statute on the economy. To what extent would buying and selling become a game too hazardous to be played without the constant surveillance of lawyers? Would the effort to protect small business be generally successful or would its principal effect be to induce large concerns to evade the statute by vertical integration and similar methods of consolidating their power? Would price differences be replaced by more general price changes without diminution in the flexibility of prices, or would concerns that could no longer make selective price adjustments refrain from making any price changes? Would competition be enhanced because small concerns had a better chance, or would it be reduced because sellers had less incentive to compete by price reductions? Would market bargaining be more vigorous because there were more concerns engaged in it, or would it entail so much danger of unlawful discrimination that it would be avoided? Would goods be cheaper or more expensive for the ultimate consumer?

Questions such as these are the focus of this book. In many instances, unfortunately, the limitations of the data make it possible to provide only a tentative or a fragmentary answer.

The book is confined solely to a study of the problems of discriminations that have arisen and the remedies that have been applied under the Robinson-Patman Act. Although cases under the Sherman Act and the Federal Trade Commission Act have been concerned from time to time with discriminatory aspects of business agreements, monopolies and unfair practices, and orders under these statutes have sometimes sought to curb discrimination, no effort is made herein to summarize or analyze such activities. Proceedings under other statutes are discussed only to the extent necessary to an understanding of cases under the Robinson-Patman Act to which they have some relationship.

The first section of the book sets forth in some detail the concepts of the law and the general characteristics of its administration. A chapter on legislative history seeks to determine what Congress was trying to do. A chapter on the statute analyzes the legislation that emerged. A chapter on administration classifies the cases and sets forth the peculiarities that were introduced by the administrative processes of the Federal Trade Commission.

The main body of the book analyzes the operative meaning that the legal concepts have acquired in cases decided by the Federal Trade Commission and in a few of the major private cases. It also contains a study of the effects of the decisions in 83 cases, so far as these could be ascertained by interviews with persons affected thereby.

In this part of the book it has seemed desirable to simplify the discussion by considering the various parts of the Robinson-Patman Act out of sequence. The act contains four sets of prohibitions. One, contained in Sections 2(a) and 2(f), forbids sellers to engage in price discrimination and buyers to receive unlawful price concessions. Another, contained in Section 2(c), forbids buyers and sellers alike to participate in the payment of brokerage by a party on one side of a transaction to a party on the other side of the transaction or to his agent. A third, contained in Sections 2(d) and 2(e), forbids sellers from making payments for selling services and from providing selling services unless the payments and services are available to all competing customers on proportionally equal terms. A fourth, contained in Section 3, is enforceable by criminal penalties and is not under the jurisdiction of the Federal Trade Commission. It has been little used and receives only passing attention herein.

It has seemed wise to discuss the sections concerned with brokerage and with proportionality in services and payments for services before discussing those concerned with discrimination in price. The brokerage section is the easiest to understand because the test of illegality is simple and applies equally to buyer and seller. It is also the one that has been most frequently used. The proportionality sections, though more difficult and until recently less important, are also relatively simple, since they depend on a single test of whether the service or payment is available to all in proper proportions. By contrast with these, the sections concerned with price discrimination involve the major conceptual difficulties of the act—the meaning of injury to competition, the nature of the cost defense, the extent and meaning of the right to meet competition in good faith, and the relative responsibility of the Commission and the respondent to supply proof pertinent to these various subjects. Moreover, though the brokerage section and the proportionality sections have been applied in various settings, their application has been less diverse than that of the price discrimination sections. The problems that arise in a price discrimination case involving quantity discounts are so different from those that arise in a case involving functional discounts or territorial discrimination that separate analyses are required for these different subjects.

Accordingly, the first two chapters that discuss the applications of the law deal with the brokerage section. One is concerned with the effort to prevent powerful corporate and voluntary chains and co-operatives from obtaining brokerage; the other with the application of the law of brokerage to various types of relatively small enterprises. The next chapter deals with the sections on proportionality, treating together the closely related parts of the law that have to do with provision of and payment for services.

With these sections out of the way, a series of chapters deal with the provisions against price discrimination. Most of the cases that have arisen under this part of the law are concerned with discrimination by sellers. Most of them fall into three classes: First, those in which the seller grants quantity or volume discounts, that is, discounts dependent on the amount of goods a buyer takes in a single transaction or over a period of time; second, those in which price concessions to buyers depend on the buyer's distributive function, that is, the place he occupies in the channels of distribution; and third, those in which prices vary according to the location of the buyer. Separate analyses are made of these three types of discrimination. In the case of territorial discrimination the analysis has been complicated by the fact that the policies of the Federal Trade Commission in this field produced a major political controversy, as a result of which the focus of the application of the law was substantially changed. Accordingly, the matter is dealt with in three chapters, of which the first discusses the Commission's proceedings against formula price discrimination before the controversy, the second the controversy itself, and the third the cases concerned with unsystematic local discrimination, most of which have arisen since the controversy.

Some cases fit into none of the categories already mentioned, and some of them are important for their contribution to the development of the law's major concepts. They are discussed in a chapter on miscellaneous types of discrimination.

Since the cases concerned with the receipt of unlawful discriminations have come to involve problems different from those that arise in cases against sellers, they are discussed separately in a chapter that follows those concerned with discrimination by sellers.

The analysis of the various categories of discrimination is followed by three chapters that endeavor to summarize the significance that has been acquired by the three main concepts of the statute. They are concerned respectively with the nature of injury to competition, meeting competition as a defense to a price discrimination charge, and cost justification.

The substantive portion of the book is followed by two chapters devoted to an appraisal of American price discrimination policy. The first attempts to appraise the Robinson-Patman Act itself. The second sets forth tentative suggestions for a modification of the statute and of the policy that underlies it.

Three warnings are necessary in view of the nature of the material.

First, it has been difficult to fit some of the cases into the classification by types of discrimination, which has furnished the main skeleton of the book. Although the classification appears to be required by the major differences that exist among relatively clear examples of each type, it is not convenient for every case. In some cases, two or more types of discrimination were present, so that it has been necessary either to discuss a case fully by going beyond the subject of the chapter in which the case appears or else to divide the discussion and place parts of it in the various relevant chapters. Each procedure has been used, and neither has been wholly satisfactory. In some instances, the facts were complex and ambiguous, so that the proper classification of the case was not clear. In other instances, the Federal Trade Commission's description of the discrimination was so meager as to make it quite possible that the case has been misclassified. Accordingly, though the classification of the major cases is believed to be meaningful, little reliance should be placed on the exactness of the classification of the less conspicuous cases. In the table of cases in the appendix, the classifications should be used with reserve. In the text, the total numbers of cases in the various classes should be regarded as no more than approximations.

Second, the analysis of injuries to competition found by the Commission in the various cases should also be treated with reserve. Since most of the cases were not contested, and since the legal consequences of one type of injury were the same as those of another, the Commission was not always careful in making distinctions among the various kinds of injury. In a few instances, the lack of care is apparent from internal inconsistencies in the Commission's findings. In many instances, it has been necessary to interpret ambiguous language in the findings in assigning the case to one or more of the classes of injury recognized by the statute. In many of the more recent cases that were settled by consent orders, the Commission made no substantive findings, and nothing is available on injury except the allegations of the complainants. In view of the fact that a prosecutor often claims more than he can prove, these cannot be taken as definitive, even though they are accredited by the consent of the respondent to an order. The Commission's thinking about injury to competition appears clearly in some of the cases. Defects in the thinking appear in the ambiguity of many of the findings and in the inconsistency of the findings that have been made in similar cases. Statistical summaries of the treatment of injury should be regarded as no more than approximately correct, and conclusions should be drawn from them only so far as these do not depend on exactness in the figures.

Third, the reader should bear in mind that in most instances the account of the aftermath of one of the Commission's orders has all the weaknesses of information obtained by interview. Sometimes relatively few people could be found who had direct knowledge of the facts. Usually these people were talking about matters that lay several years in the past; and often they had not regarded these matters as of major importance, even at the time. Reliable business records were sometimes no longer available and sometimes not consulted because the person interviewed could not give enough time to do so. Interviews were often shorter than was desirable. Persons interviewed were not always candid. Where the law or the order of the Commission was currently being violated or where practices were of a type the legality of which is questionable, frank declaration that this was so was not to be expected. When contradictions appeared in the information obtained from different sources, no process of subpoena or cross-examination was available to ascertain the truth.

On the whole, the persons interviewed were co-operative and well-informed. What they said supplies a broad account of the effect of the act that is believed to be reliable. If this had not been so, the interviews would not have been used. But the reliability of the general picture does not guarantee that each detail in the picture is accurate. Thus there have been many problems of judgment in determining what should be said about the aftermath of particular cases. Statements that were clearly un-reliable have been discarded. Where there were differences of opinion or conflicting allegations of fact on some matter that is discussed, these have been noted. Where a story comes from only one or two sources, this fact has been made plain. Nevertheless, it remains possible that particular situations have been incorrectly understood. It is believed that the in-formation derived from the interviews is useful for the purpose for which it was collected—that of understanding the types of effect that have been produced by cases under the Robinson-Patman Act. It is believed that it is far from satisfactory and may be misleading as a basis for an under-standing of the current practices of a particular enterprise or the current situation in a particular industry. It is believed that it is valueless for one purpose—ascertaining the degree of compliance with the law or with the orders of the Commission.

2 / Legislative History of the Robinson-Patman Act

AS THE PREVIOUS CHAPTER has indicated, the setting of the early 1930's was an appropriate one for revision of the price discrimination law. Concern over the growth of chain stores, unrest arising from the depression, dissatisfaction with the existing law of price discrimination, and the experimental bent of the New Deal combined to make legislation politically possible.

The chain store report of the Federal Trade Commission became a catalyst for legislative action. Its effect was supplemented by a hearing conducted in 1935 by a committee of the House of Representatives, ostensibly to investigate the American Retail Federation.[1] Much of this hearing was concerned with the practices of chain stores in the food industry, particularly the Great Atlantic & Pacific Tea Company. When the consideration of bills to amend the price discrimination law began, digests of the Commission's report and of the hearings of the committee were submitted to the House Committee on the Judiciary by the proponents of the bill.

Early in 1935 several bills were introduced proposing amendment of the law. One, by Representative Mapes, based on the recommendation of the Commission in the chain-store report, proposed to amend Section 2 of the Clayton Act to make it unlawful "either directly or indirectly to discriminate unfairly or unjustly in price between different purchasers of commodities." Another, introduced in the Senate on May 13 by Senator Robinson and in the House on June 11 by Congressman Patman, contained a more ambitious proposal.[2] Mr. Mapes apparently made

[1] *Investigation of the Lobbying Activities of the American Retail Federation,* Hearings before the House Special Committee to Investigate American Retail Federation, 74 Cong. 1 sess. (1935). The resolution to investigate and a portion of the committee's conclusions appear in *Congressional Record,* Vol. 80, Pt. 7, 74 Cong. 2 sess., p. 8105.

[2] Both bills, H.R. 8442 and H.R. 4995, are reprinted in *To Amend the Clayton Act,* Hearing before the House Committee on the Judiciary, 74 Cong. 1 sess.,

no sustained effort to obtain consideration for his bill, and in practice the Robinson-Patman bill and successors thereto became the focus for congressional attention. The Robinson-Patman bill was drafted by H. B. Teegarden, attorney for the United States Wholesale Grocers' Association, and Congressman Patman relied heavily on Mr. Teegarden during committee consideration of the bill.

As introduced, the bill contained a flat prohibition of discrimination in prices or terms of sale on commodities of like grade and quality, with no test of the effect on competition such as was contained in the existing law. There were, however, two exemptions, one to authorize price differentials that made only due allowance for differences in cost, and the other to authorize differentials depending solely on whether the purchase was for resale to wholesalers, to retailers, to consumers, or for use in further manufacture. In addition to prohibiting discrimination generally, the bill struck directly at brokerage payments and advertising allowances. It prohibited the payment and receipt of brokerage commissions when the recipient was not acting for and controlled by the person who made the payment. It forbade payments to customers for sales services rendered by them, unless either these payments were offered on proportionally equal terms to all competing customers or the customer's interest was in no way publicly associated with the furnishing of the service and the payment did not exceed the fair value of the service rendered. A final provision of the bill set forth a formula for measuring the damage done by unlawful discrimination, to be used by injured parties in private damage suits.

Testifying on behalf of the proposal, Mr. Teegarden described it as directed at unreasonable quantity discounts, dummy brokerage allowances, and pseudo-advertising allowances, because in the experience of the food trades, these were the three principal ways in which price concessions were granted to buying organizations.[3]

Hearings on the Patman and Mapes bills were held by the House Judiciary Committee in July 1935, covering a period of five days. Of the 23 witnesses other than members of Congress who testified, 18 represented various portions of the food industry. Farmers were represented only by a spokesman for a farm organization in the Lehigh Valley and

---

p. 2. Mr. Mapes also incorporated his proposal in a more comprehensive bill, H.R. 5062, which included also proposals for amendment of Secs. 7 and 11 of the Clayton Act and Sec. 5 of the Federal Trade Commission Act. *Ibid.*, pp. 2-3.

[3] *Ibid.*, p. 16.

by a Pennsylvania vegetable grower, both of whom opposed the bill. Manufacturers were represented by spokesmen for the Associated Grocery Manufacturers and the Association of Ice Cream Manufacturers. The former expressed sympathy with the purpose to amend the price discrimination law but opposed specific features of the bill. The latter opposed the bill as written, and suggested changes in it. A spokesman for the National Food Brokers Association supported the bill vigorously. Representatives of three wholesale grocery associations testified, two of them supporting the bill and one opposing it as unconstitutional and offering a substitute. The National Association of Retail Grocers endorsed the bill. The National Voluntary Groups Institute, represented by a vice president of Independent Grocers Alliance, opposed it. Two associations of chain stores and officials of three chain-store companies were also in opposition. Thus organizations in the food industry divided, as might have been expected, with the principal support for the amendment coming from wholesale and retail associations and the principal opposition coming from the chains. Food manufacturers desired to limit the scope of the legislation, and the major farm organizations were apparently uninterested.

Of the five witnesses not representing the food industries, two were concerned with retail distribution. The National Association of Retail Druggists supported the bill; Sears Roebuck opposed it. The other three witnesses represented, respectively, the National Coal Association, the American Mining Congress, and the Manufacturing Chemists Association. They all expressed the view that the bill was concerned with chain-store problems not found in their industries, and that its enactment as a statute of general application would be seriously disruptive of their ways of doing business.

The opposition encountered from other sources than the food industry apparently generated some hesitancy within the committee. No further formal steps were taken for about six months. On January 22, 1936, Representative Utterback introduced an amended version of the Patman Bill, H.R. 10486. A subcommittee of the Judiciary Committee was established under his chairmanship, and in February this subcommittee held hearings for four days on the Patman bill, the Utterback bill, and the Mapes bill.[4] Eighteen witnesses appeared, other than members of Congress. Of these, eight came from organizations represented in the

[4] *To Amend the Clayton Act,* Hearing before the House Committee on the Judiciary, 74 Cong. 2 sess.

previous hearings and expressed substantially the same points of view as before. In addition, the food industries were represented by another association of wholesale grocers and by Cooperative Food Distributors, both supporting the bill. From outside the food industries, there were six new witnesses, all of whom opposed the bill. Three represented manufacturers of rubber goods, wood-working power tools, and scissors. Two represented the National Retail Dry Goods Association and the Mail Order Association of America. One represented the Institute of Distribution, speaking for mass distributors in various industries.

Thus, with the sole exception of the National Association of Retail Druggists, all business interests outside the food industries opposed the bill in both hearings.[5] Within the food industries, the second hearing did nothing to change the division of forces that appeared in the first.[6] No hearings on the bill were held by the Senate, on the ground that hearings in the House had adequately covered the field.

The program set forth in the Utterback bill was significantly different from that in the original Patman bill. It forbade discriminations only when they reduced competition; modified the provision about payment for sales service so that it no longer permitted selective advertising allowances; added a companion provision covering the furnishing of sales help to distributors; sought to define the use of basing-point price formulas as discriminatory; and included an exemption for perishable commodities.

The bill reported by the House Committee on the Judiciary on March 31 combined portions of the Utterback and Patman bills, but included

[5] Group conflicts affecting congressional consideration of the bill are analyzed in Joseph Cornwall Palamountain, Jr., *The Politics of Distribution* (1955), pp. 188-234. See also Newell W. Ellison, "The Robinson-Patman Act, Its Political and Commercial Background," Trade Association Executives, *Proceedings on the Robinson-Patman Anti-Discrimination Act* (1936), pp. 4-19.

[6] During subsequent debate in the House, Congressman Celler, an opponent of the bill, named the following national organizations as opposing it: National Retail Dry Goods Association, National Retail Lumber Dealers Association, National Retail Hardware Association, Mail Order Association of America, Institute of Distribution, National Cooperative Council, National Cooperative Milk Producers Federation, National Voluntary Groups Institute, American Farm Bureau Federation, the dairymen's leagues, Evaporated Milk Association, National Manufacturers Association, Manufacturing Chemists Association, Associated Grocery Manufacturers, National Coal Association, National Publishers Association, National American Wholesale Grocers Association, General Federation of Women's Clubs, American Home Economics Association. See *Congressional Record*, Vol. 80, Pt. 7, pp. 8107-08.

important provisions that had been contained in neither.[7] It made discriminations unlawful not only when they reduced competition in the market but also when they reduced competition with the beneficiaries of a discriminatory price. It authorized the Federal Trade Commission to set quantity limits designed to reduce the permissible justification of price differences by cost differences. To the exemption for functional discounts, it added a provision concerned with the treatment of distributors who performed dual functions. It modified the brokerage provision by extending it to cover allowances in lieu of brokerage and by incorporating in it an exception covering payments made for services rendered. It added new provisions authorizing the payment of co-operative dividends, dealing with the respondent's burden of proof, and authorizing the introduction of evidence that a competitor's price had been met in good faith. At the suggestion of the committee, the House changed this version of the bill before it was passed on May 28, by deleting the provisions concerned with functional discounts and basing-point systems.[8]

[7] *Prohibition of Price Discriminations,* H. Rept. 2287, 74 Cong. 2 sess. Hereinafter cited as H. Rept. 2287.

[8] These changes appear to have been primarily due to opposition by farm organizations to the version of the bill that had been reported by the Judiciary Committee. On May 18 a joint letter from the American Farm Bureau Federation, the National Grange, the National Cooperative Council, the National Cooperative Milk Producers Federation, the Farmers National Grain Corporation, and the Northwest Farmers Union Legislative Committee said that the bill would "greatly restrict and hamper the operations of producer-owned and producer-controlled cooperative associations" by depriving them of wholesale discounts and by placing a "strait jacket" on their "legitimate merchandising and advertising operations." On May 25 this opinion was set forth in greater detail in another joint letter from all of the groups except the National Cooperative Council. Objections were expressed: (1) to the elimination of the multiple basing-point system; (2) to the functional discount provision, "under which farmer-owned and farmer-controlled cooperative associations would be deprived of their wholesalers' and jobbers' discounts"; (3) to a possible interpretation of the price discrimination provision by which a seller could not charge different prices in different markets—an interpretation which, it was said, "would destroy the business operations of many of our great farmers' cooperative associations"; (4) to the possibility that the advertising provisions might require farm co-operatives to cease placing their limited advertising budgets strategically and instead advertise only on a national basis; (5) to limitations in the provision for meeting competition, by which a competitor's price might not be undercut and the discriminating seller must carry the burden of proof as to the price he was meeting. The letter asked that the first two objections be met by deleting the offending provisions; that the next two be met by clarification of meaning; and that the last be met by amending the bill to authorize meeting competition in good faith without specifying a price limitation.

In the Senate the successive versions of the bill displayed wide variations both from one another and from the House versions. The original Robinson bill, S. 3154, was identical with the Patman bill. The bill reported by the Senate Committee on the Judiciary[9] had been modified to include provisions regarding the effect on competition like those proposed by the House committee and, as in the version of the House committee, to authorize the Federal Trade Commission to fix quantity limits, though with more explicit requirements regarding the findings on which such action must be based. However, the bill of the Senate committee contained nothing on dual function distributors, co-operative dividends, the burden of proof, or meeting competition in good faith. Its brokerage provision omitted the amendment on payment for services rendered that had been introduced by the House committee; and its provision on a showing of cost differences was designed to prevent the inclusion of differences in payment to brokers among the relevant costs.

On the day the bill was reported by the Senate committee, Senators Borah and Van Nuys introduced two bills, S. 3670 and S. 3835, apparently modeled on the Canadian Price Discrimination Act of the previous year,[10] that would have applied criminal penalties to certain types of price discrimination. On February 25 these bills were consolidated as S. 4171. Though hearings were held on them on March 24 and 25, the testimony was concerned primarily with the Robinson and Patman bills.[11] Much of it came from manufacturers and mass distributors who opposed these bills.

The letters were printed in the *Congressional Record,* Vol. 80, Pt. 7, pp. 8116-18, and became the focus of debate. The provision about basing points had been criticized by various members of Congress, and the functional discount provision was not thought by the sponsors of the bill to be necessary to its purpose. These two provisions were deleted, therefore, at the suggestion of the Judiciary Committee. In debate, sponsors of the bill denied that it could have the meanings that were the basis for the next two objections. No concession was made, however, in the provision as to meeting competition. See *ibid.,* pp. 8106, 8113-40; Pt. 8, 8223-38.

[9] *To Amend Antitrust Act Relative to Wholesale Prices, etc.,* S. Rept. 1502, 74 Cong. 2 sess. Hereinafter cited as S. Rept. 1502.

[10] Canadian Statutes 25 and 36, George V, C56, Sec. 9, 1935.

[11] *Price Discrimination,* Hearings before the Senate Committee on the Judiciary, 74 Cong. 2 sess. Twenty-one witnesses were heard. Various organizations of distributors that had been represented at previous hearings presented statements again. So did Associated Grocery Manufacturers. One important farm organization appeared, the National Cooperative Council. Among the new witnesses were small manufacturers of textiles, hosiery, buttons, shipping bags, and metal boxes,

Before passing the bill reported by the Judiciary Committee, the Senate, apparently influenced by the opposition expressed in the hearings on the Borah-Van Nuys bill, virtually re-wrote the bill by amendment during debate.[12] It added a provision prohibiting buyers from receiving unlawful discriminations; appended criminal provisions taken from the Borah-Van Nuys bill; completely exempted discriminations made in good faith to meet competition; and incorporated various exemptions pertaining to broad classes of goods such as imports, crude minerals and metals, and commodities sold for use in further manufacture or in the production of new products.

Although the Senate bill was passed on April 30 and transmitted to the House, the House ignored it and passed its own version of the amended Patman bill on May 28. When the Senate received this bill, it struck out all but the enacting clause, substituted the text of its own bill, and with this change passed H.R. 8442 on June 1. Thus two versions of H.R. 8442, passed by the two houses, contained all the differences between that bill as passed by the House of Representatives and S. 3154 as passed by the Senate.

The bill went to conference before a consensus had developed on its scope and content and before differences of opinion had come to focus on a few well-understood alternatives. In the House of Representatives the versions of Mr. Patman, Mr. Utterback, and the Judiciary Committee differed significantly from one another and from that finally adopted by the House. In the Senate the versions of Senator Robinson, Senators Borah and Van Nuys and the Judiciary Committee differed sharply from one another, and the version passed by the Senate included important matters that were considered for the first time during debate. Whereas committee reports usually crystallize issues, so that subsequent action consists in choosing among alternatives that have been clearly formulated or devising compromises on a few controverted points, committee action

---

a spokesman for "various" tire and rubber manufacturers, and a representative of Associated Coffee Industries.

[12] The texts of the original Patman bill, the bill reported by the House Judiciary Committee, the bill reported by the Senate Judiciary Committee, the bill that passed the House, the bill that passed the Senate, and the final Act appear as appendices in Franz Otto Willenbucher, "The Robinson-Patman Anti-Price Discrimination Act," dissertation for the degree of Doctor of Jurisprudence, Georgetown University Law School, Washington, D.C., 1937 (mimeo.). The texts of the House bill before and after amendment by the Judiciary Committee appear in *Congressional Record*, Vol. 80, Pt. 7, pp. 8138-40.

in each house presented, in this instance, only one of a series of ideas on the scope and focus of the bill. Because of the differences between the versions passed by the two houses, the task of the conference committee resembled that ordinarily performed by the judiciary committees. This was recognized at the time. In debate in the Senate, Senator Robinson accepted one amendment with the statement, "There is one feature of the amendment about which I am in doubt; and little opportunity is afforded to study the proposition, as I had not seen the amendment before it was brought forward here. I see no objection to its incorporation in the bill so that the conferees may consider it along with the McNary and Austin amendments which have heretofore been agreed to." In the same debate Senator McNary said, "I think it might be well, since it will probably be necessary to write the bill in conference, that all worth-while suggestions that may be offered should be incorporated in the bill so that the conferees may sit down and finally perfect a bill."[13] Similarly, Senator Robinson assented to an amendment by which the substance of the Borah-Van Nuys bill was added to his, on the ground that "if the conferees finally prefer the plan of that bill to either the House bill or the Senate bill . . . they will have the opportunity of doing so."[14]

The conference report was adopted by the House on June 15 and by the Senate on June 18, 1936. The bill was approved by the President on June 19.

As a result of the haphazard way in which the bill was developed, there are unusual difficulties in ascertaining the intent of Congress from a study of the legislative history. In regard to some matters, no explanation was offered for the version finally adopted by the Congress. As to others, conflicting expressions of opinion were reconciled in ways susceptible to varying interpretations. Nevertheless, a partial light is cast on congressional thinking by the reports of the judiciary committees of the two houses, the conference report to the House,[15] the statements of the sponsors of the bill during debate, and expressions of opinion from the floor.

[13] Quoted in Federal Trade Commission, *Robinson-Patman Act, Congressional Expressions and Formal Decisions* (February 1942), pp. 37 and 34.

[14] *Congressional Record,* Vol. 80, Pt. 6, p. 6277.

[15] The conference report to the Senate consisted of the text of the bill as amended in conference, with no explanatory comment. The entire debate on it occupies less than one page of the *Congressional Record.* See *ibid.,* Pt. 9, pp. 9902-04.

Objectives of the Legislation

The broad objectives of the legislation were set forth in similar terms in the reports of the Judiciary Committees of the Senate and the House. The purpose was not merely to strengthen the precautionary element in the antitrust laws but to afford equality of opportunity to commercial buyers. In the language of the House report,

> The purpose of this legislation is to restore so far as possible, equality of opportunity in business by strengthening antitrust laws and by protecting trade and commerce against unfair trade practices and unlawful price discrimination, and also against restraint and monopoly for the better protection of consumers, workers, and independent producers, manufacturers, merchants, and other businessmen.

Though the committee expressed the opinion that "the evidence is overwhelming that price discrimination practices exist to such an extent that the survival of independent merchants, manufacturers, and other businessmen is seriously imperiled," its attention was not focused solely on the dangers to competition thereby implied. It announced the guiding ideal as:

> . . . the preservation of equality of opportunity so far as possible to all who are usefully employed in the service of distribution and production, taking into consideration their ability and equipment to serve the producing and consuming public with efficiency and the protection of the public from a threat of monopoly or oppression in the production and manufacture of the things it needs and the distribution of the same fairly and honestly without employment of unfair trade practices and unlawful price discrimination.

It said that the general object was "to suppress more effectually discriminations between customers of the same seller not supported by sound economic differences in their business positions or in the cost of serving them." It decried discriminations "in excess of sound economic differences between the customers concerned," on the ground that they involve losses that must be recouped from the business of other customers. Thus, although the committee thought competition was endangered and intended to reduce that danger, it pursued a broader aim. It explained the new language in regard to injury to competition included in the bill by saying: "The existing law has in practice been too restrictive in requiring a showing of general injury to competitive conditions in the line of commerce concerned, whereas the more immediately important concern is in injury to the competitor victimized by the discrimination. Only through such injury in fact can the larger, general injury result."[16]

Similarly, the Senate Judiciary Committee set forth as its guiding ideal "the preservation of equal opportunity to all usefully employed in the service of distribution comportably with their ability and equipment to serve the producing and consuming public with real efficiency, and the preservation to that public of its freedom from threat of monopoly or oppression in obtaining its needs and disposing of its products." The committee thought that "discriminations in excess of sound economic differences involve generally an element of loss, whether only of the necessary minimum of profits or of actual costs, that must be recouped from the business of customers not granted them." It explained the new language regarding injury to competition in words identical with those in the report of the House committee.[17]

The Meaning of Discrimination

The concept of price discrimination incorporated in the bill was not explicitly discussed in the reports of the committees of the two houses or in the conference reports. However, in debate on the conference report, Congressman Utterback, chairman of the House managers, explained the meaning of the concept as follows:

> In its meaning as simple English, a discrimination is more than a mere difference. Underlying the meaning of the word is the idea that some relationship exists between the parties to the discrimination which entitles them to equal treatment, whereby the difference granted to one casts some burden or disadvantage upon the other. If the two are competing in the resale of the goods concerned, that relationship exists. Where, also, the price to one is so low as to involve a sacrifice of some part of the seller's necessary costs and profit as applied to that business, it leaves that deficit inevitably to be made up in higher prices to his other customers; and there, too, a relationship may exist upon which to base the charge of discrimination. But where no such relationship exists, where the goods are sold in different markets and the conditions affect-

[16] H. Rept. 2287, pp. 3-8.
[17] S. Rept. 1502, p. 3.

ing those markets set different price levels for them, the sale to different customers at those different prices would not constitute a discrimination within the meaning of this bill.[18]

As originally introduced in each house, the bill was designed to cover discrimination both in prices and in terms of sale. In the Senate, this scope was retained throughout. In the House, however, the Committee on the Judiciary eliminated the bill's application to terms of sale. The conferees accepted the House version. The conference report to the House explained that the managers were of the opinion "that the bill should be inapplicable to terms of sale except as they amount in effect to indirect discriminations in price within the meaning of the remainder of sub-section (a)."[19]

Like Grade and Quality

The original Robinson-Patman bill pertained to discriminations on commodities of "like grade and quality." The language remained unchanged in both houses and was included in the bill that became law. From the hearings before the House Judiciary Committee,[20] it is evident that the wording was carefully chosen to prevent price concessions to large distributors who sold commodities under their own private brands. Supporters of the bill testified that it would let a manufacturer sell merchandise for private branding, but only if he sold at his usual price for branded goods or made his price concessions on unbranded merchandise available to all buyers. The committee did not accept suggestions from other sources that provision be made for price reductions on private brands.

The Test of the Effect on Competition

As originally introduced in both houses, the bill flatly prohibited discrimination in price on commodities of like grade and quality without reference to the effect of the discrimination. The substitute bill introduced in the House of Representatives by Congressman Utterback for-

[18] *Congressional Record*, Vol. 80, Pt. 9, p. 9416.
[19] *Ibid.*, p. 9414.
[20] *To Amend the Clayton Act*, Hearing, 74 Cong. 2 sess., pp. 355, 421, 469. See also *Congressional Record*, Vol. 80, Pt. 8, pp. 8234-35.

bade discrimination only where it might lessen competition among either sellers or buyers or their competitors or might restrain trade or tend to create a monopoly. Thus it was designed to invoke a test of the effect on competition similar to the test incorporated in the existing price discrimination law and in Section 3 of the Clayton Act. The judiciary committees of both houses retained the test of effect on competition but enlarged it. They provided that discrimination should be unlawful where its effect "may be substantially to lessen competition or tend to create a monopoly in any line of commerce, or to injure, destroy, or prevent competition with any person who either grants or receives the benefit of such discrimination or with customers of either of them."[21] With the exception of a slight verbal change, to be discussed below, this provision remained unaltered during further consideration of the bill.

The comments of the judiciary committees of both houses as to the meaning of the new language about competition have been quoted above in discussing the purpose of the law. A further explanation was given by Congressman Utterback during debate on the conference report. He said that existing law required "a showing of effect upon competitive conditions generally in the line of commerce and market territory concerned, as distinguished from the effect of the discrimination upon immediate competition with the grantor or grantee." He described the impact of the new language as follows:

> The difference may be illustrated where a nonresident concern opens a new branch beside a local concern, and with the use of discriminatory prices destroys and replaces the local concern as the competitor in the local field. Competition in the local field generally has not been lessened, since one competitor has been replaced by another; but competition with the grantor of the discrimination has been destroyed. The present bill is, therefore, less rigorous in its provisions as to the effect required to be shown in order to bring a given discrimination within its prohibitions.[22]

In debating the new language about competition that had been inserted in the Senate bill by the Judiciary Committee, the Senate added the word "knowingly," so that the language forbade discrimination where the effect might be to injure, destroy, or prevent competition with any person

---

[21] S. Rept. 1502, p. 8. In the version of the House Committee, the language of the Utterback bill as to effect upon competition was also retained. It was eliminated by the conference committee.

[22] *Congressional Record*, Vol. 80, Pt. 9, p. 9417.

"who either grants or knowingly receives the benefit of such discrimination," or with the customers of either. This amendment was adopted by the conference committee. The conference report to the House said that the purpose of the change was "to exempt from the meaning of the surrounding clause those who incidentally receive discriminatory prices in the routine course of business without special solicitation, negotiation, or other arrangement for them on the part of the buyer or seller and who are therefore not justly chargeable with knowledge that they are receiving the benefit of such discrimination."[23] This explanation is as obscure as the phrase it proports to explain.[24]

Cost Justification

In both houses the original Robinson-Patman bills contained a proviso "that nothing herein contained shall prevent . . . differentials which make only due allowance for differences in the cost of manufacture, sale, or delivery resulting from the differing methods of quantities in which such commodities are to such purchasers sold or delivered."[25] The Utterback bill contained a similar exemption for differences in price to purchasers of different quantities "not in excess of the differences in cost of selling the commodity in question, together with the cost of any service rendered by any such person in connection therewith." The provisions of the original Robinson-Patman bills were retained by the judiciary committees of the two houses with minor changes. The House committee amended the language of the proviso to make it clear that though differentials that were cost justified were not prevented, they were also not required. The Senate committee retained the original provision with a modification designed to prevent savings in brokerage from being included among the costs used to justify a price difference. The two houses accepted the versions of their respective committees. The conferees returned to the version contained in the original bill.

[23] *Ibid.*, p. 9414.

[24] The provision in which the word "knowingly" appears makes price discrimination by sellers unlawful but does not impose any liability on buyers. Thus the exemption supplied for discriminations that give advantage to persons who do not knowingly receive the benefit is not an exemption for the ignorant buyer but for the seller, who may not be ignorant. If read literally, this means that the buyer's ignorance becomes an excuse for the seller's discrimination. In practice no such interpretation has been proposed.

[25] *To Amend the Clayton Act*, Hearing, 74 Cong. 1 sess., p. 1.

The provision on cost was regarded as of great importance in making the bill consistent with the requirements of economic efficiency. The House Judiciary Committee emphasized the authorization for price differences based on cost differences and explained that this provision "leaves trade and industry free from any restriction or impediment to the adoption and use of more economic processes of manufacture, methods of sale, and modes of delivery." Relying on this provision, it said that the bill contained nothing to discourage efficiency or reward inefficiency.

> Any physical economies that are to be found in mass buying and distribution . . . whether those economies are from more orderly processes of manufacture, or from the elimination of unnecessary salesmen, unnecessary travel expense, unnecessary warehousing, unnecessary truck or other forms of delivery, or other such causes—none of them are in the remotest degree disturbed by this bill.[26]

Similarly, the Senate committee said that the bill "leaves trade and industry free from any restriction or impediment to the adoption and use of more economic processes and to the translation of appropriate shares of any savings so effected up and down the stream of distribution to the original producer and to the ultimate consumer."[27] A similar explanation was given by Congressman Utterback in debate on the floor of the House:

> It is through this clause that the bill assures to the mass distributor, as to everyone else, full protection in the use and rewards of efficient methods in production and distribution in return for depriving him of the right to crush his efficient smaller competitors with the power and resources of mere size. There is no limit to the phases of production, sale, and distribution in which such improvements may be devised and the economies of superior efficiency achieved, nor from which those economies, when demonstrated, may be expressed in price differentials in favor of the particular customers whose distinctive methods of purchase and delivery make them possible.[28]

The language of the cost proviso had been carefully chosen. The Senate Committee on the Judiciary explained that the phrase *due allowance:*

[26] H. Rept. 2287, pp. 9, 17.
[27] S. Rept. 1502, p. 5.
[28] *Congressional Record,* Vol. 80, Pt. 9, p. 9417.

. . . marks the zone within which differentials may be granted. The bill neither requires nor compels the granting of discriminations or differentials of any sort. It leaves any who wish to do so entirely free to sell to all at the same price regardless of differences in cost, or to grant any differentials not in excess of such differences. It does not require the differential, if granted, to be the arithmetical equivalent of the difference. It is sufficient that it does not exceed it.[29]

The committee explained that, in referring to cost differences "resulting from the differing methods or quantities in which such quantities are to such purchasers sold or delivered," the bill limited the acceptable differences in cost:

. . . to those marginal differences demonstrable as between the particular customers concerned in the discrimination. It is designed, among other things, to preclude the grant of a discrimination to a particular customer equal to the whole saving in cost resulting to the seller's entire volume of business as augmented by that customer's patronage; to preclude also differentials based on allocated or imputed, as distinguished from actual, differences in cost, representing particular facilities or departments which the favored customer may not have immediately utilized, but with which the seller cannot dispense in the general conduct of his business. It is designed, in short, to leave the test of a permissible differential upon the question: If the more favored customer were sold in the same quantities and by the same methods of sale and delivery as the customer not so favored, how much more per unit would it actually cost the seller to do so, his other business remaining the same?[30]

The House committee gave a similar explanation. Congressman Utterback further elaborated the point during debate in the House. He said:

As between purchasers in equal quantities, for example, where one takes multiple store-door delivery, and the other single warehouse delivery, with consequent savings in trucking or other delivery costs to the seller, that saving may be expressed in a price differential. Or where one places a single order calling for periodic deliveries over an extended period of time, whereas the other places smaller successive orders requiring more frequent and therefore more costly salesman solicitation, such a difference in cost may be expressed in a price differential. Or where one customer, devoid of storage facilities requires spot deliveries during the rush of the season, for which the manufac-

[29] S. Rept. 1502, p. 5.
[30] Ibid., pp. 5-6.

turer must produce in advance and store himself in order to make the fullest utilization of his plant capacity; while another customer orders for delivery in off seasons, handling the storage himself and saving the manufacturer that cost, such a saving may be expressed in a price differential. Or where one customer orders from hand to mouth during the rush of the season, compelling the employment of more expensive overtime labor in order to fill his orders; while another orders far in advance, permitting the manufacturer to use cheaper off-season labor, with the elimination of overtime, or perhaps to buy his raw materials at cheaper off-season prices, such savings as between the two customers may likewise be expressed in price differentials. So also where a manufacturer or merchant sells to some customer through traveling-salesman solicitation, to others across the counter, and to others by mail order from catalog, price differentials may be made to reflect the differing costs of such varying methods of sale. These examples are illustrative of the way in which the bill permits the translation of differences in cost into price differentials as between the customers concerned, no matter where those differences arise. But the bill does not permit price differentials merely because the quantities purchased are different, or merely because the methods of selling or delivery are different, or merely because the seasons of the year in which they enable production are different. There must be a difference in cost shown as between the customers involved in the discrimination, and that difference must be one "resulting from the differing methods or quantities in which such commodities are to such purchasers sold or delivered". . . . Where the methods of delivery are the same, but the distance is different, price differences in such cases may, of course, be made to reflect those differences.[31]

Quantity Limits

In spite of Congressman Utterback's statement that there was no limit to the economies that could be expressed in price differentials, the bill did authorize the setting of such a limit. The House Judiciary Committee added a proviso authorizing the Federal Trade Commission to issue orders to establish quantity limits on particular commodities and stipulating that the cost exemptions should then not be construed to permit differentials based on differences in quantities greater than those so established. The Senate committee added a similar provision, but included a requirement that in fixing such quantity limits the Federal Trade Commission must find "that available purchasers in greater quantities are so

[31] *Congressional Record,* Vol. 80, Pt. 9, p. 9417.

few as to render differentials on account thereof unjustly discriminatory or promotive of monopoly in any line of commerce."[32] The versions of the two committees were accepted by the respective houses. The Senate version was accepted by the conferees and included in the final bill. The House committee explained the provision by saying:

> This proviso rests upon the principle that where even an admitted economy is of a character that is possible only to a very few units of overshadowing size in a particular trade or industry, it may become in their hands an instrument that lessens competition and that tends to create a monopoly; and that in forbidding its use and foregoing its benefits the public is merely insuring its freedom from monopoly control.[33]

The committee pointed to the analogy of the requirement that concessions in freight rates not be granted for quantities greater than a carload. Similarly, the Senate committee said:

> . . . that where even an admitted economy is of a character that is possible only to a very few units of overshadowing size in a particular trade or industry, it may become in their hands nonetheless the food upon which monopoly feeds, a proboscis through which it saps the life blood of its competitors; and that in forbidding its use and foregoing its benefits the public is but paying a willing price for its freedom from monopoly control.[34]

This committee, too, pointed out the analogy to the rules concerning freight rates. Senator Logan told the Senate, "What we had in mind . . . was that there might be one concern or two concerns with such purchasing power that they could buy in such tremendous quantities that they would be buying without competition."[35]

Meeting a Competitor's Price

Neither in the original version of the bill nor in the Utterback substitute was there any authorization to meet competition in good faith. The Senate Judiciary Committee reported that one of the two principal weaknesses of existing law was that:

[32] S. Rept. 1502, p. 6.
[33] H. Rept. 2287, p. 10.
[34] S. Rept. 1502, p. 6.
[35] *Congressional Record,* Vol. 80, Pt. 6, p. 6428.

... It permits discriminations to meet competition, and thus tends to substitute the remedies of retaliation for those of law, with destructive consequences to the central object of the bill. Liberty to meet competition which can be met only by price cuts at the expense of customers elsewhere, is in its unmasked effect the liberty to destroy competition by selling locally below cost, a weapon progressively the more destructive in the hands of the more powerful, and most deadly to the competitor of limited resources, whatever his merit and efficiency.[36]

The House Judiciary Committee, however, inserted in the bill a proviso "that nothing herein contained shall prevent a seller rebutting the prima-facie case thus made by showing that his lower price to any purchaser or purchasers was made in good faith to meet an equally low price of a competitor."[37] The committee apparently regarded this provision as an authorization to meet competition in stated circumstances. It said:

> This proviso represents a contraction of an exemption now contained in Section 2 of the Clayton Act which permits discriminations without limit where made in good faith to meet competition. It should be noted that while the seller is permitted to meet local competition, it does not permit him to cut local prices until his competitor has first offered lower prices, and then he can go no further than to meet those prices. If he goes further, he must do so likewise with all his other customers, or make himself liable to all of the penalties of the act, including treble damages. In other words, the proviso permits the seller to meet the price actually previously offered by a local competitor. It permits him to go no further.[38]

In debate in the Senate a similar provision was added to the Senate bill. It was broader, however, in that it permitted a showing that a competitor's offer had been met in good faith not only for prices but also for the furnishing of services or facilities. By further amendment during debate, the Senate bill provided also "that nothing herein contained shall prevent discrimination in price in the same or different communities made in good faith to meet competition." Still another amendment made in debate in the Senate, applicable only to crude mineral products or metals in the form in which they are loaded for shipment, exempted discrimination in the price of such products "in the same or different communities made in good faith to meet competition."[39]

[36] S. Rept. 1502, p. 4.
[37] H. Rept. 2287, p. 2.
[38] *Ibid.*, p. 16.
[39] *Congressional Record,* Vol. 80, Pt. 6, p. 6349.

The conference committee reverted to the version of the House Judiciary Committee. The conference report explained that the authorization to meet competition in good faith "is found in existing law and, in the opinion of the conferees, is one of the obstacles to enforcement of the present Clayton Act." Although the House language was retained, the interpretation of that language was no longer that formerly given to it by the House Judiciary Committee. The conference report to the House said that the provision was "intended to operate only as a rule of evidence in a proceeding before the Federal Trade Commission."[40] Senator Van Nuys explained to the Senate that the provision set forth a rule of evidence rather than substantive law.[41] In the House, Congressman Utterback explained the provision as follows:

It is to be noted, however, that this does not set up the meeting of competition as an absolute bar to a charge of discrimination under the bill. It merely permits it to be shown in evidence. This provision is entirely procedural. It does not determine substantive rights, liabilities, and duties. . . . It leaves it a question of fact to be determined in each case, whether the competition to be met was such as to justify the discrimination given, as one lying within the limitations laid down by the bill, and whether the way in which the competition was met lies within the latitude allowed by those limitations. This procedural provision cannot be construed as a carte blanche exemption to violate the bill so long as a competitor can be shown to have violated it first, nor so long as that competition cannot be met without the use of oppressive discriminations in violation of the obvious intent of the bill. To illustrate: The House committee hearings showed a discrimination of 15 cents a box granted by Colgate-Palmolive-Peet Co. on sales of soap to the A.&P. chain. Upon a complaint and hearing before the Federal Trade Commission, this proviso would permit the Colgate Co. to show in rebuttal evidence, if such were the fact, an equally low price made by a local soap manufacturer in Des Moines, Iowa, to A. & P.'s retail outlets in that city; but this would not exonerate it from a discrimination granted to A. & P. everywhere, if otherwise in violation of the bill. But the committee hearings show a similar discount of 15 cents a case granted by Procter and Gamble to the same chain. If this proviso were construed to permit the showing of a competing offer as an absolute bar to liability for discrimination, then it would nullify the act entirely at the very inception of its enforcement, for in nearly every case mass buyers receive similar discriminations from competing sellers of the same product. One violation of law cannot be permitted to justify another. As in any case of

[40] *Ibid.*, Pt. 9, p. 9414.
[41] *Ibid.*, p. 9903.

self-defense, while the attack against which the defense is claimed may be shown in evidence, its competency as a bar depends also upon whether it was a legal or illegal attack. A discrimination in violation of this bill is in practical effect a commercial bribe to lure the business of the favorite customer away from the competitor, and if one bribe were permitted to justify another the bill would be futile to achieve its plainly intended purpose.[42]

Right to Select Customers

Various provisions were included in the original bill or inserted subsequently to make sure that particular practices were not to be regarded as unlawfully discriminatory. One of these, contained in the original bill and retained without alteration, was "that nothing herein contained shall prevent persons engaged in selling goods, wares, or merchandise in commerce from selecting their own customers in bona fide transactions and not in restraint of trade." This provision was similar to one contained in existing law. In opening the debate on the conference report, Congressman Utterback explained to the House of Representatives that the provision:

> . . . permits, however, the selection of customers and not the selection of what shall be sold to them. It is intended to protect the buyer against customers who are troublesome in their methods or insecure in their credit. It does not permit the buyer, once he has accepted a customer, to refuse discriminatorily to sell to him particular distinctions of quality, grade, or brand which the seller has set aside for exclusive sale at more favorable prices to selected customers in evasion of the purposes of this bill.[43]

Price Change Through Time

The original bill contained no reference to price changes through time. The Utterback version provided that it was not to be unlawful to make quantity differences in price or terms of sale when in good faith necessitated by actual or imminent depreciation in the utility of perishable commodities or of commodities that had become obsolescent. The House

[42] *Ibid.*, p. 9418.
[43] *Ibid.*, pp. 9413, 9418. It is obvious that in using the word buyer, Mr. Utterback intended to use the word seller.

Judiciary Committee adopted this provision in broadened form: "that nothing herein contained shall prevent price changes from time to time where in response to changing conditions affecting the market for or the marketability of the goods concerned, such as but not limited to actual imminent deterioration of perishable goods, obsolescence of seasonal goods, distress sales under court process, or sales in good faith in discontinuance of business in the goods concerned."[44] The same provision was added to the Senate bill in debate on the floor, and was retained by the conference committee. The House Judiciary Committee explained that "while it is not believed that the principal prohibitions of Section 2(a) apply in any case to such price changes, nor has such construction ever been suggested or contended for under present Section 2, this specific exemption is included as an added precaution to safeguard the ready disposition of goods characterized by fluid market conditions."[45]

Co-operatives

The original bill contained no reference to co-operatives. The House Judiciary Committee inserted a provision that: "Nothing in this section shall prevent a co-operative association from returning to its members, or a co-operative wholesale association from returning to its constituent retailer members, the whole or any part of the net earnings resulting from its trading operations, in proportion to their purchases or sales from, to, or through such association."[46] A similar provision was added to the Senate bill during debate. The House committee explained that while the bill contained no provision either express or implied prohibiting the distribution of patronage dividends, the section was added as a precautionary reservation "in a spirit of encouragement to the co-operative movement."[47]

The conferees retained the provision with certain changes in wording. The conference report to the House explained that:

. . . The words "or a co-operative wholesale association from returning to its constituent retail members", which appeared following the word "consumers" in the Senate amendment, have been eliminated. As

[44] *Ibid.*, p. 9413.
[45] H. Rept. 2287, p. 11.
[46] *Ibid.*, p. 2.
[47] *Ibid.*, p. 17.

so modified, this section serves to safeguard producer and consumer co-operatives against any charge or violation of the act based on their distribution of earnings or surplus among their members on a patronage basis. While the bill contains elsewhere no provisions express or implied to the contrary, this section is included as a precautionary reservation to protect and encourage the co-operative movement. Whether functioning as buyers or sellers, co-operatives also share under the bill the guaranties of equal treatment and equal opportunity which it seeks to accord to trade and commerce generally.[48]

In the ensuing debate, Congressman Utterback explained to the House that the provision:

> . . . leaves the members of co-operatives free to seek through co-operative endeavor the economies and savings of mass operations, and assures to them, as compared with their larger corporate competitors, any real economies and savings to which those mass operations entitle them and which they often now do not receive. There is nothing in the last section of the bill that distinguishes co-operatives, either favorably or unfavorably, from other agencies in the streams of production and trade, so far as concerns their dealings with others.[49]

Several provisions defining the scope of forbidden discrimination were considered during the legislative process but eventually were eliminated from the bill.

Functional Discounts

Both the original bill and the Utterback version contained a provision intended to establish the legality of functional discounts. The Robinson-Patman bill provided that nothing therein should prevent price differentials between purchasers "depending solely upon whether they purchase for resale to wholesalers, to retailers, or to consumers, or for use in further manufacture."[50] Similarly the Utterback bill authorized independently established differences in price or in terms of sale "founded solely and in good faith upon classification of customers as wholesalers or jobbers, remanufacturers, or processors, retailers or consumers."[51]

[48] *Congressional Record,* Vol. 80, Pt. 9, p. 9415.
[49] *Ibid.,* p. 9419.
[50] *To Amend the Clayton Act,* Hearing, 74 Cong. 1 sess., p. 1.
[51] *Ibid.,* 74 Cong. 2 sess., p. 271.

The Senate committee retained the original version of the Robinson bill. It explained that the existing law permitted such differentials but that:

> . . . since added restrictions are here imposed in these respects [as to quantity differentials and differentials not affecting general competition], a separate clause safeguarding differentials between different classes of purchasers becomes necessary. Such differentials, so long as equal treatment is required within the class, do not give rise to the competitive evils at which the bill is aimed; while to suppress them would produce an unwarranted disturbance of existing habits of trade.[52]

The House committee likewise retained the original provision, but elaborated it by the statement that, for the purpose of classifying customers, the character of the selling of the purchaser and not of his buying should determine his classification, and that purchasers who performed both wholesale and retail functions should be classified as retailers on purchases for sale to consumers and as wholesalers on purchases for sale "to retail dealers only, not owned or controlled, directly or indirectly, by the purchaser."[53] Like the Senate committee, the House committee saw no evil in differentials between functional classes of purchases and did not wish to disturb existing habits of trade. It gave a further explanation as follows:

> It should be noted that there is nothing in this exemption to prevent consumers when buying co-operatively or otherwise in quantities characteristic of retailers or retailers when buying in quantities characteristic of wholesalers from being accorded the same prices as those dealers respectively so long as their prices are respectively justified within their own class on the basis of differences in cost. . . . Wholesalers frequently find it necessary to supplement existing stock by additional purchases in smaller quantities and the above exemption . . . permits wholesalers to be accorded wholesale prices on these smaller purchases as incident to his business without the seller having to accord them at the same time on the whole body of purchases in similar quantities on sales direct to retailers. This protects the usefulness of the wholesaler in serving retailers dependent upon him for their source of supply. . . . Whether retailers acting co-operatively in their purchasing activities will be classified as wholesalers or retailers will depend naturally upon whether their co-operative organization functions as a separate entity taking title and reselling it to its retailer members, or merely as repre-

---

[52] S. Rept. 1502, p. 5.
[53] Committee Amendment to H.R. 8442, H. Rept. 2287, p. 19.

senting them severally in their dealings direct with the selling source of supply. . . .[54]

The House provision was completely eliminated during debate. The Senate provision was modified during debate[55] and eliminated in conference. No explanation was given by the conferees.[56]

Basing Point Systems

The Utterback bill contained a provision, not found in the original Patman bill, defining the word "price" to mean "the amount received by the vendor for each commodity unit, after deducting actual freight or cost of other transportation, if any, allowed or defrayed by the vendor."[57] This provision was retained in the bill reported by the House Judiciary Committee. The report explained that the purpose was "to put an end to price discrimination through the medium of the basing-point or delivered-price system of selling commodities. It will require the use of the f.o.b. method of sale."[58] In support of this provision, the report said that the use of basing-point systems had resulted in identical delivered prices at any given destination, in charges for freight at railroad rates when delivery was made by waterway or highway, in excessive cross-hauling for which the public paid the bill, and in imposing sacrifices on certain local customers as compared with distant customers. After reciting experience with basing-point pricing methods in the cement and steel industries, the report concluded that in the latter industry there was practically no competition and that price discrimination had resulted in both industries in building up practical monopolies. The provision defining price was deleted from the bill during debate in the House of Representatives and was not subsequently considered.[59]

[54] *Ibid.*, p. 9.
[55] As the bill passed the Senate, it provided "that nothing herein contained shall prevent differentials in prices as between purchasers depending solely upon whether they purchase as factors, or wholesalers, or retailers, or consumers or for use in further manufacture." *Congressional Record*, Vol. 80, Pt. 6, p. 6427.
[56] The deletion of the provision was apparently due almost entirely to opposition by farm organizations which feared that farm co-operatives as well as corporate chains would suffer loss of functional discounts. See above, p. 25n.
[57] *To Amend the Clayton Act,* Hearing, 74 Cong. 2 sess., p. 271.
[58] H. Rept. 2287, p. 14.
[59] The deletion was proposed on behalf of the House Judiciary Committee, apparently in part because the provision was opposed by farm organizations (see above,

Miscellaneous Proposals for Exemption

In debate on the floor of the Senate, various provisions were inserted in the Senate bill for the purpose of exempting particular classes of business. One of these amendments would have applied the provision forbidding sellers to discriminate only to goods manufactured or produced in the United States and would thus have exempted imports. A second would have authorized discrimination in price based on differences in quantity where commodities were sold "for use in further manufacture and in the production of a new product to be sold to the public."[60] A third would have provided that in the case of crude mineral products or metals in the form in which they are loaded for shipment nothing should prevent differences in price or terms of sale "based upon differences in the grade, quality, or quantity of such products, or that make only due allowance for differences in the cost of selling or transportation, or discrimination in the price of such products in the same or different communities made in good faith to meet competition."[61] These amendments were deleted by the conference committee, but were not specifically discussed in the conference reports. In the Senate, Senator Van Nuys explained that the second of these amendments was omitted because "the conference committee saw no reason why that type of commodity should be exempted to the exclusion of other types."[62]

Liability of Buyers

As originally introduced, the bill made price discrimination by sellers unlawful but did not apply to the receipt of discrimination by buyers. The Utterback bill and the bills as reported by both judiciary committees were similarly limited. During debate in the Senate, a provision was inserted making it unlawful for any buyer engaged in commerce, in the

---

footnote 8, p. 25) and in part because certain members of the Rules Committee were opposed to it. Statements in the debate implied that insistence on the provision might have made it difficult to get the bill scheduled for consideration. Opinion expressed in debate was various—that the provision was objectionable and, conversely, that the purpose was desirable but extraneous to that of the bill. See *Congressional Record*, Vol. 80, Pt. 5, pp. 5715, 5716; Pt. 7, pp. 8106, 8113, 8117, 8118, 8138-40; Vol. 8, pp. 8223, 8229.

[60] *Ibid.*, Pt. 9, p. 9903.
[61] *Ibid.*, Pt. 6, p. 6349.
[62] *Ibid.*, Pt. 9, p. 9903.

course of commerce, "knowingly to induce or receive a discrimination in price or terms of sale, which is prohibited by this section." Thus, although the central problem of the bill was the power of large buyers, the application of the law to buyers was an afterthought.[63] The Senate provision was retained by the conference committee.[64] Congressman Utterback explained it to the House as follows:

> This affords a valuable support to the manufacturer in his efforts to abide by the intent and purpose of the bill. It makes it easier for him to resist the demand for sacrificial price cuts coming from mass-buyer customers, since it enables him to charge them with knowledge of the illegality of the discount, and equal liability for it, by informing them that it is in excess of any differential which his difference in cost would justify as compared with his other customers.[65]

Measure of Damage

The original Robinson-Patman bill contained a provision establishing a formula for measuring the damage done by price discrimination. It was retained in the Senate committee's version of the bill. However, it did not appear in the Utterback bill in the House, or in the version reported by the House Judiciary Committee. The provision was eliminated in conference.

Brokerage

The original bill contained a provision forbidding the payment or receipt of brokerage where the payment was made to an intermediary representing the person on the other side of the transaction. The Senate committee enlarged the scope of this prohibition by making it apply not only to commissions, brokerage, and other compensation, as in the original bill, but also to any allowance or discount in lieu thereof.[66]

---

[63] The provision originated in a bill (S. 4024, 74 Cong. 2 sess.) introduced by Senator Copeland. This bill had been written by Charles Wesley Dunn, an attorney who has often represented the National Grocery Manufacturers Association. The substance of the bill was proposed by Senator Copeland as an amendment during the Senate debate. See Charles Wesley Dunn, *Sections 2(d) and (e) of the Clayton Act, as Amended by the Robinson-Patman Act,* undated, p. 9.

[64] The phrase "terms of sale" was deleted from this provision, as from Sec. 2(a).

[65] *Congressional Record*, Vol. 80, Pt. 9, p. 9419.

[66] See S. Rept. 1502.

The committee also expanded the prohibition to cover the other party to the transaction as well as his intermediary or agent. Both enlargements were retained in the bill that passed the Senate. The House Judiciary Committee added the same enlargements, but proposed a qualification by which the payments were prohibited "except for services rendered in connection with the sale or purchase of goods, wares, or merchandise."[67] These changes were all retained in the bill that passed the House and in the one reported by the conference committee.

Both judiciary committees explained the brokerage provision as an attempt to cope with the discriminatory practices of large buyers. The House committee said:

> . . . When free of the coercive influence of mass buying power, discounts in lieu of brokerage are not usually accorded to buyers who deal with the seller direct since such sales must bear instead their appropriate share of the seller's own selling cost. Among the prevalent modes of discrimination at which this bill is directed is the practice of certain large buyers to demand the allowance of brokerage direct to them upon their purchases, or its payment to an employee, agent, or corporate subsidiary whom they set up in the guise of a broker, and through whom they demand that sales to them be made. But the positions of buyer and seller are by nature adverse, and it is a contradiction in terms incompatible with his natural function for an intermediary to claim to be rendering services for the seller when he is acting in fact for or under the control of the buyer, and no seller can be expected to pay such an intermediary so controlled for such services unless compelled to do so by coercive influences in compromise of his natural interest.[68]

In addition, the committee said that the relation of the broker to his client is a fiduciary one, that to collect from a client for services rendered in the interest of a party adverse to him is a violation of that relationship,

[67] In the hearings in 1936 that preceded the legislation (*To Amend the Clayton Act*, 74 Cong. 2 sess., pp. 311, 334, 337-38), spokesmen for Cooperative Food Distributors and the National Voluntary Groups Institute asked that the principle of payment for services be recognized in the brokerage provision. Apparently they expected the reference to services to prevent the payments that their groups received from being declared unlawful. To the organized food brokers, the exception constituted "a perfectly damnable four words." (See Association of Independent Food Dealers of America, *The Case for Freeing Independent Merchants from Restraints Against Their Competitive Opportunity to Earn Brokerage*, pp. 17-18.) The attitude of the National Food Brokers Association was set forth in a pamphlet issued by it in 1935 entitled *Unfairness in the Food Industry*.

[68] H. Rept. 2287, p. 15.

and that "to protect those who deal in the streams of commerce against breaches of faith in its relations of trust, is to foster confidence in its processes and promote its wholesomeness and volume."[69] Similarly, the Senate committee said that the bill was directed at the practice of large buyers and that to permit the payment "where in fact, if a 'broker', so labelled, enters the picture at all, it is one whom the buyer points out to the seller, rather than one who brings the buyer to the seller, is but to permit the corruption of this function to the purposes of competitive discrimination."[70] The Senate committee, too, spoke of the desirability of preserving the purity of the fiduciary relationship.

Neither committee referred in its report to the enlargement of the brokerage provision to cover allowances and discounts in lieu of brokerage. Apparently this language was regarded as a means of preventing evasion, and neither committee realized that it might have the effect of creating conflicts of principle between the price discrimination section and the brokerage section where both were applicable to a particular discount.

The exception authorizing payments for services rendered was explained by the House committee in language, also adopted in the conference report to the House, that deprived this exception of significance. The committee said:

> Section (b) permits the payment of compensation by a seller to his broker or agent for services actually rendered in his behalf; likewise by a buyer to his broker or agent for services in connection with the purchase of goods actually rendered in his behalf; but it prohibits the direct or indirect payment of brokerage except for such services rendered. It prohibits its allowance by the buyer direct to the seller, or by the seller direct to the buyer; and it prohibits its payment by either to an agent or intermediary acting in fact for or in behalf, or subject to the direct or indirect control, of the other.[71]

After the conference report Congressman Utterback reinforced this interpretation by saying to the House that where sales are made "from buyer to seller" in the nature of the case "no brokerage services are rendered by either," and no brokerage payment "can be made by either party to the other."[72]

[69] Ibid.
[70] S. Rept. 1502, p. 7.
[71] Congressional Record, Vol. 80, Pt. 9, p. 9414.
[72] Ibid., p. 9418.

Proportionality of Payments

The original Robinson-Patman bill contained a provision concerned with payments to customers for selling services. It forbade those payments unless either they were offered on proportionately equal terms to all other competing customers or the business of the customer receiving the payment was in no way publicly associated with the services for which payment was made, and the payment did not exceed the fair value of those services. H. B. Teegarden, author of the bill, explained the purpose of this provision in the hearing in the House. He said that where payments were made on proportionately equal terms no other restriction was placed upon the seller. He continued:

> Now, if he wants to pick out particular customers, which he may legitimately want to do sometimes—he may have an advertising appropriation limited in size, not large enough to spread among all his customers, yet which he wants to spread among selected communities over the country for the purchase of newspaper advertising, billboard posters, or any other form of local advertising—what are his alternatives? He must either hire someone locally to do that, or pay a salaried representative and send him into the community from without.
>
> Certainly there it is to the interest of the local community, local welfare, to employ local personnel for local services. The only thing is to guard that against being used as a medium to promote, or to shoulder onto the manufacturer the advertising costs of that customer's own business, where the competitor has to pay his own.
>
> So subsection (2) . . . affords that protection. It permits the selection at will of customers for these local services provided in the rendition of the service it is kept separate from any public association or reference to the business of the customer, keeps him purely on the basis of a salaried representative.[73]

The Utterback version of the bill likewise forbade payments for sales services unless they were available on proportionately equal terms to all other customers but did not authorize the alternative procedure of maintaining the anonymity of the distributor rendering the services. The Utterback version of the provision was adopted by the House Judiciary Committee and retained in the bill which passed the House. The original version, which permitted the alternative of anonymity, was retained by the Senate Judiciary Committee and included in the bill that passed the

---

[73] *To Amend the Clayton Act,* Hearing, 74 Cong. 1 sess., p. 218.

Senate. The conference committee adopted the House version without explaining the grounds for its action.

The Senate Committee explained the provision as follows:

Still another favored medium for the granting of oppressive discriminations is found in the practice of large buyer customers to demand, and of their sellers to grant, special allowances in purported payment of advertising and other sales promotional services, which the customer agrees to render with reference to the seller's products, or sometimes with reference to his business generally. Such an allowance becomes unjust when the service is not rendered as agreed and paid for, or when, if rendered, the payment is grossly in excess of its value, or when in any case the customer is deriving from it equal benefit to his own business and is thus enabled to shift to his vendor substantial portions of his own advertising cost, while his smaller competitor, unable to command such allowances, cannot do so. Section 2(c) of the bill addresses this evil by prohibiting the granting of such allowances unless made available to all other customers of the seller concerned on proportionately equal terms, or unless in the rendition of such services the customer's own business is kept out of the picture. The first of these conditions is designed to rob this practice generally of its discriminatory character, and the second to leave open a legitimate field for the use of customer services as mere employees or agents in local advertising, in lieu of salaried representatives sent in from without, or of other local personnel strangers to the seller's acquaintance. The frequency with which limited advertising appropriations admit of their expenditure only in selected communities makes it important both to the seller and to the local community to preserve this freedom so long as it is properly protected against discriminatory use. The phrase "proportionally equal terms" . . . is designed to prevent the limitation of such allowances to single customers on the ground that they alone can furnish the services or facilities in the quantity specified. Where a competitor can furnish them in less quantity, but of the same relative value, he seems entitled, and this clause is designed to accord him, the right to a similar allowance commensurate with those facilities. To illustrate: Where, as was revealed in the hearings earlier referred to in this report, a manufacturer grants to a particular chain distributor an advertising allowance of a stated amount per month per store in which the former's goods are sold, a competing customer with a smaller number of stores, but equally able to furnish the same service per store, and under conditions of the same value to the seller, would be entitled to a similar allowance on that basis.[74]

[74] S. Rept. 1502, pp. 7-8.

The House Judiciary Committee used the same language except that it omitted the portion of the statement, not relevant to its version of the provision, concerned with the use of distributors as anonymous agents. Neither committee discussed the possible case in which a competitor who was unable to furnish services of the same quantity was also unable to furnish services of the same relative value.[75] After the conference committee's report, Congressman Utterback said to the House:

> The existing evil at which this part of the bill is aimed is, of course, the grant of discriminations under the guise of payments for advertising and promotional services which, whether or not the services are actually rendered as agreed, results in an advantage to the customer so favored as compared with others who have to bear the cost of such services themselves. The prohibitions of the bill, however, are made intentionally broader than this one sphere in order to prevent evasion in resort to others by which the same purpose might be accomplished.[76]

Proportionality of Services

The original Robinson-Patman bill contained no provision concerned with the furnishing of services by the seller to his distributor. The Utter-

---

[75] However, in debate in the House on May 27th, Representative Bloom raised this type of question. He said, "If you have a window at Fourteenth and F Streets, and the manufacturer wants to make a contract with that store at 14th and F Streets, where thousands of people pass by every day, are you going to pay the same price for one down at Fourth and B Streets where only 50 people pass in the course of a day? . . . There are no two windows alike, no two counters alike. One side of the street is different from the other side. . . . How can you do it on proportionately equal terms when there are no two places alike? Suppose one store is 25 feet and the other store is only 10 feet; what are you going to do with the ten-foot fellow? Give him half a sign?"
Mr. McLaughlin: "You can give him a smaller sign. . . . They have all different kinds of signs now. What do you do today?"
Mr. Bloom: "We do not do that. We would go broke if we did."
However, on behalf of the Judiciary Committee, Mr. McLaughlin said: "The committee, in considering the measure, gave a great deal of time to a discussion of the very things suggested by the gentleman from New York. It is the opinion of the committee that the bill in the form in which it is presented to the House fully protects all purchasers in the matter of advertising discounts, but it is also the opinion of the committee, after due deliberation, that if the bill were amended in the manner suggested by the gentleman from New York, it would be destructive of the purposes intended by the bill itself." *Congressional Record*, Vol. 80, Pt. 8, pp. 8236-37.
[76] *Ibid.*, Pt. 9, p. 9418.

back bill, however, provided that to furnish such services should be unlawful unless they were available to all purchasers on proportionately equal terms. This provision was retained in the version reported by the House Judiciary Committee. No similar provision was included in the Senate bill. The conferees accepted the House provision.

The report of the House Judiciary Committee contained no separate analysis of the provision about services. Instead, having set forth the objections to discriminatory payment for advertising services, the report said:

> Sections (c) and (d) of the bill address this evil by prohibiting the granting of such allowances, either in the form of services or facilities themselves furnished by the seller to the buyer, or in the form of payment for such services or facilities when undertaken by the buyer, except when accorded or made available to all competing customers on proportionally equal terms.[77]

After the conference report, Congressman Utterback said to the House that the phrase *proportionally equal terms,* as used with reference to services,

> . . . has reference to the several purchasers' equipment and ability to satisfy the terms upon which the offer is made, or the services or facilities furnished to any other purchaser. There are many ways in which advertising, sales, and other services and facilities may be either furnished or paid for by the seller upon terms that will at once satisfy the requirements of the bill concerning equitable treatment of all customers and at the same time satisfy the legitimate business needs of the seller and the purchaser.[78]

Criminal Provisions

No criminal provisions were included in the original Robinson-Patman bill nor in the Utterback version of a substitute. Such provisions appeared for the first time in bills that were introduced by Senators Borah and Van Nuys on the day the Robinson bill was reported to the Senate,[79] and were subsequently consolidated into a single bill. During debate in

---

[77] H. Rept. 2287, p. 16.
[78] *Congressional Record,* Vol. 80, Pt. 9, p. 9419.
[79] S. 3670 and S. 3835, later consolidated as S. 4171.

the Senate on the Judiciary Committee's version of the Robinson bill, provisions from the Borah-Van Nuys bill were added thereto. They applied criminal penalties to buyers and sellers who participated in a transaction in which any discount, rebate, allowance, or advertising service charge was granted in excess of that available to competitors on goods of like grade, quality, and quantity. They provided similar criminal penalties for territorial price discrimination undertaken for the purpose of destroying competition or eliminating a competitor and for sale at unreasonably low prices undertaken for such a purpose. The conference committee retained these provisions. The conference report to the House said that they were not inconsistent with the amendment of the Clayton Act. The criminal section, the report said, "authorizes nothing which that amendment prohibits, and takes nothing from it. On the contrary, where only civil remedies and liabilities attach to violations of the amendment provided in Section 1, Section 3 sets up special prohibitions as to the particular offenses therein described and attaches to them also the criminal penalties therein provided."[80]

[80] *Congressional Record,* Vol. 80, Pt. 9, pp. 9414-15.

3 / *Content of the New Statute*

THE AMENDMENT OF THE PRICE discrimination section of the Clayton Act that emerged from the legislative process includes five separate prohibitions based on four prohibitory principles. It will be convenient to discuss these in a sequence different from that of the statute, in order to dispose of the simpler parts of the law before discussing those that are more complex.

Brokerage

Section 2(c) made it unlawful for a person on one side of a transaction to pay brokerage or any allowance or discount in lieu thereof, except for services rendered, to a person on the other side of the transaction or to the agent of such a person.[1] Such payments were unlawful without reference to the purposes for which they were made or to their effect on competition or on the persons directly involved. The statutory meaning of the proviso authorizing payments for services rendered could be explored in litigation, but, apart from this proviso, there was no exemption or limitation on the complete outlawry of the specified kind of payment. Since allowances and discounts in lieu of brokerage were forbidden, as well as brokerage commissions themselves, it was to be anticipated that the prohibition would extend to an uncertain degree over price reductions that were associated with, or were historical sequels to, payment of the prohibited commissions. It is noteworthy that the prohibition applied

[1] Sec. 2(c) provides: "That it shall be unlawful for any person engaged in commerce, in the course of such commerce, to pay or grant, or to receive or accept, anything of value as a commission, brokerage, or other compensation, or any allowance or discount in lieu thereof, except for services rendered in connection with the sale or purchase of goods, wares, or merchandise, either to the other party to such transaction or to an agent, representative, or other intermediary therein where such intermediary is acting in fact for or in behalf, or is subject to the direct or indirect control, of any party to such transaction other than the person by whom such compensation is so granted or paid." 49 Stat. 1527.

uniformly to buyer, seller, and intermediary agent, and to both the payment and the receipt of the payment. The questions determinative of illegality were relatively simple: whether brokerage or something in lieu of it had been paid; whether the parties concerned were on opposite sides of the sales transaction; and, if these two questions were answered affirmatively, whether the payment was exempt under the proviso about services rendered.

Payment for Sales Services

Section 2(d) applied to payments by a seller to his customer for sales services rendered by the customer.[2] Such payments were forbidden unless they were available on proportionally equal terms to all other customers competing in the distribution of the product. The law was silent as to the measure by which proportional equality was to be determined. Granted, however, that the standard of proportionality was violated, the payment was to be unlawful without regard to the purposes for which it was made or to its effect on competition or on the persons immediately involved. The prohibition of disproportionate payment applied to the seller only. The receipt of the prohibited payment was not made unlawful.

Provision of Sales Services

Section 2(e), like Section 2(d), rested on the principle of proportionality.[3] It forbade sellers to discriminate against one purchaser for resale

[2] Sec. 2(d) provides: "That it shall be unlawful for any person engaged in commerce to pay or contract for the payment of anything of value to or for the benefit of a customer of such person in the course of such commerce as compensation or in consideration for any services or facilities furnished by or through such customer in connection with the processing, handling, sale, or offering for sale of any products or commodities manufactured, sold, or offered for sale by such person, unless such payment or consideration is available on proportionally equal terms to all other customers competing in the distribution of such products or commodities." 49 Stat. 1527.

[3] Sec. 2(e) provides: "That it shall be unlawful for any person to discriminate in favor of one purchaser against another purchaser or purchasers of a commodity bought for resale, with or without processing, by contracting to furnish or furnishing, or by contributing to the furnishing of, any services or facilities connected with the processing, handling, sale, or offering for sale of such commodity so purchased upon terms not accorded to all purchasers on proportionally equal terms." 49 Stat. 1527.

in favor of another by furnishing sales services or facilities "upon terms not accorded to all purchasers on proportionally equal terms." Apparently Sections 2(d) and 2(e) were intended to incorporate parallel standards of proportionality applicable respectively to payments for selling services and the furnishing of such services. In both sections the measure of proportionality was omitted. In both sections liability was placed on the seller only. In both sections disproportionality was unlawful regardless of its purpose or effect. In minor particulars, however, differences in wording in the two sections presented possibilities of divergence in meaning. Section 2(d) applied to persons engaged in commerce, whereas Section 2(e) did not contain a reference to commerce. Section 2(d) spoke of customers, Section 2(e) of purchasers of commodities bought for resale. Section 2(d) required proportionality among customers competing in the distribution of the products, whereas Section 2(e) required proportionality among purchasers for resale.[4] Moreover, Section 2(b), which is concerned with procedure, provided explicitly that proof of discrimination in services or facilities furnished should have the effect of shifting to the respondent the burden of disproving the prima facie case thus made, and that in rebuttal the seller might show that he acted in good faith to meet services or facilities furnished by a competitor.[5] There was no parallel provision about payment for sales services. In spite of such discrepancies, it was clear that these two sections sought broadly to enforce on sellers a standard of proportional payments or proportional services, wherever either payments or services were provided for competing customers as a part of sales effort.

Price Discrimination by Sellers

The heart of the statute was Section 2(a), which dealt broadly with discrimination in price.[6] The application of this section was limited to

[4] Although the requirement is not explicitly limited to competing purchasers, it has been consistently construed to imply this limitation.

[5] See below, footnote 8, p. 58, and footnote 10, p. 59.

[6] Sec. 2(a) provides, in part: "That it shall be unlawful for any person engaged in commerce, in the course of such commerce, either directly or indirectly, to discriminate in price between different purchasers of commodities of like grade and quality, where either or any of the purchases involved in such discrimination are in commerce, where such commodities are sold for use, consumption, or resale within the United States or any Territory thereof or the District of Columbia or

sellers alone, though Section 2(f), which will be discussed below, applied a corollary prohibition to recipients of price discrimination. The section forbade discrimination in price between different purchasers of commodities of like grade and quality where there was a reasonable probability of effects injurious to competition. The relevant effects were placed in two categories. The first consisted in substantial lessening of competition or tendency to create a monopoly, that is, in effects on market competition analogous to those that were invoked in the previous law of price discrimination and in the part of the Clayton Act concerned with exclusive dealing and tying arrangements. The second type of harm was conceived as injury to or destruction or prevention of competition "with any person who either grants or knowingly receives the benefits" of the discrimination or "with customers of either of them." This concept of harmful effect had no statutory precedent and obviously was intended to enlarge considerably the application of the law of price discrimination.

Three points are noteworthy with reference to the new language. First, in regarding the prevention of competition as unlawful, the statute broke new ground. The previous law had been concerned solely with reductions of existing competition. It was possible now to apply the law where, but for a discrimination in price, additional competition might reasonably have been expected. Second, the concepts of injury, prevention, and destruction were made to cover not only competition in the market generally but competition with particular persons benefited by the discrimination. Impairment of the competition of the disfavored class or group of customers that competed with the beneficiary of the discrimination was sufficient to constitute the statutory injury, even when the competition of this class or group had been fully replaced by competition from others, so that competition in the market had not been reduced. Similarly, discrimination that drove a competing seller out of business might be found injurious to competition even if the seller was replaced by another and market competition remained as vigorous as before.

---

any insular possession or other place under the jurisdiction of the United States, and where the effect of such discrimination may be substantially to lessen competition or tend to create a monopoly in any line of commerce, or to injure, destroy, or prevent competition with any person who either grants or knowingly receives the benefit of such discrimination, or with customers of either of them: *Provided,* That nothing herein contained shall prevent differentials which make only due allowance for differences in the cost of manufacture, sale, or delivery resulting from the differing methods or quantities in which such commodities are to such purchasers sold or delivered: . . ." 49 Stat. 1526.

Third, injury, prevention, and destruction of competition were to be stopped, not only among the customers of the discriminating seller but among the customers of these customers as well, so that indirect effects in resale markets were brought within the purview of the statute.[7]

When any of the injurious consequences specified in the statute was a reasonably probable result of a price discrimination, the illegality of that discrimination did not automatically follow. Instead, the discrimination was made unlawful only if various grounds for exemption were inapplicable to it. The most important of these are exemption through cost justification and exemption because the discrimination was made in good faith to meet the price offered by a competitor.

As to cost, the statute provided explicitly that nothing should prevent differentials that make only due allowance for differences in the cost of manufacture, sale, or delivery "resulting from the differing methods or quantities in which such commodities are to such purchasers sold or delivered." The language of this proviso had been carefully chosen to make sure that the cost differences used to justify price differences should consist of items of expense directly attributable to particular transactions and should not include any allocations of overhead reflecting calculations of advantage by the discriminating seller. Section 2(b), which is concerned with procedure, provided that the burden of showing cost justification shall be on the recipient.[8] Thus, the effect of the statute

[7] The language by which these results were accomplished is, in various respects, inept. The prohibition of injuries to competition with the customers of the grantor of discrimination achieves nothing more than was already accomplished by the language pertaining to competition with the beneficiaries of discrimination. Moreover, in cases in which competition with a beneficiary of discrimination is injured, it is far from clear why the application of the statute is made to depend on whether the beneficiary was aware of his benefit, particularly since the prohibition is applicable to the seller's discrimination and not to the buyer's receipt of it. These peculiarities of the statutory language make the boundaries of the law fuzzy, but do not deprive it of the significance stated above.

[8] The relevant language is as follows: "Upon proof being made, at any hearing on a complaint under this section, that there has been discrimination in price or services or facilities furnished, the burden of rebutting the prima facie case thus made by showing justification shall be upon the person charged with a violation of this section, and unless justification shall be affirmatively shown, the Commission is authorized to issue an order terminating the discrimination: . . ." (49 Stat. 1526.) This language appears to impose upon the respondent rather than the Commission the burden of introducing evidence as to the effects of discrimination upon competition; and in the Moss case a court so decided (see below, pp. 480-81). However, the courts have generally assumed that the Commission carries the burden of showing that the discrimination may be harmful to competition. The Commission has consistently held that it carries that burden.

was to enable the Federal Trade Commission to rest its case after showing injurious discrimination, and to place on the respondent the burden of deciding whether a cost justification should be attempted and of proving any such justification affirmatively.

The law also provided, however, that the extent of justification through a cost defense might be reduced by the Commission in stated circumstances. The Commission was authorized, after investigation and hearing, to find that for particular commodities purchasers buying large quantities were so few that price differentials based on these quantities would be "unjustly discriminatory or promotive of monopoly"; and, on the basis of this finding, to fix quantity limits for the commodities in question.[9] The effect of the establishment of a quantity limit would be to prevent differentials in price based on differences in quantity exceeding the limit. Even if a price reduction on a larger quantity were fully justified by cost differences, the cost justification would be precluded by the Commission's having previously, in a separate proceeding, fixed quantity limits for the particular commodity.

The second major ground for exemption had to do with the seller's meeting of competition in good faith. Section 2(a), which contained the substantive provisions governing price discrimination by sellers, made no reference to meeting competition, differing in this respect from the previous law of price discrimination. However, in assigning to the recipient the burden of rebutting the Commission's prima facie case, the procedural Section 2(b) carried a proviso that nothing should prevent a seller from showing that his lower price (or the furnishing of services or facilities) was made in good faith to meet an equally low price of a competitor (or the services or facilities furnished by a competitor).[10] Though the statute thus explicitly authorized the showing that competi-

[9] The relevant language is as follows: "*Provided, however,* That the Federal Trade Commission may, after due investigation and hearing of all interested parties, fix and establish quantity limits, and revise the same as it finds necessary, as to particular commodities or classes of commodities, where it finds that available purchasers in greater quantities are so few as to render differentials on account thereof unjustly discriminatory or promotive of monopoly in any line of commerce; and the foregoing shall then not be construed to permit differentials based on differences in quantities greater than those so fixed and established: . . ." 49 Stat. 1526.

[10] The relevant language is as follows: "*Provided, however,* That nothing herein contained shall prevent a seller rebutting the prima-facie case thus made by showing that his lower price or the furnishing of services or facilities to any purchaser or purchasers was made in good faith to meet an equally low price of a competitor, or the services or facilities furnished by a competitor." 49 Stat. 1526.

tion had been met, it was not explicit on the result of such a showing. The ambiguity of the language and the fact that the reference to meeting competition appeared in a procedural section rather than a substantive one provided grounds for subsequent controversy over the significance of meeting competition as a defense against a charge of price discrimination.

Receipt of the Benefit of Discrimination

Section 2(f) was a corollary to Section 2(a).[11] It provided that to induce or receive a prohibited discrimination in price should be unlawful. Apparently the congressional purpose was to provide equivalent weapons against the seller and the favored buyer who took part in a discriminatory transaction. However, since the buyer's liability under the statute was made to depend on the seller's having granted a prohibited discrimination, the provision against buyers was subsidiary to the provision against sellers. In a proceeding against a buyer, the statute required proof that the act of the seller was unlawful. The provision afforded no basis for a charge against a buyer based merely on the buyer's conduct. Moreover, the prohibition applied only to knowing inducement or receipt of the prohibited discrimination, and the statute was ambiguous in regard to the character of the knowledge that was a necessary element of the offense. It did not state clearly whether the guilty knowledge of the buyer consisted merely in his knowledge that he had received a price concession or must also include knowledge that in granting it the seller had acted unlawfully. Furthermore, the statute did not clearly state to what extent the burdens of proof established for sellers under Section 2(b) of the act were also applicable to buyers in proceedings under Section 2(f).[12]

[11] Sec. 2(f) provides: "That it shall be unlawful for any person engaged in commerce, in the course of such commerce, knowingly to induce or receive a discrimination in price which is prohibited by this section." 49 Stat. 1527.

[12] Sec. 2(b) explicitly imposed on the person charged with a violation the burden of rebutting the Commission's prima-facie case by showing justification. As to cost defenses, however, the information that was available to a seller from his own business records was not necessarily available to his customer who might be involved in a 2(f) proceeding. Moreover, the provision of Sec. 2(b) concerned with the good-faith defense specifically spelled out the seller's right to show that his lower price was made in good faith to meet a competitor's equally low price. No mention was made of a buyer's right to present such information. It is reasonable to suppose that the provisions of Sec. 2(b) were written with sellers in mind and without careful consideration of their effect in a proceeding under Sec. 2(f).

Criminal Offenses

Appended to the various provisions that have been summarized above was an additional section of the statute establishing new criminal offenses punishable by fine and imprisonment. However, these offenses did not consist of any of the violations already described, but rather of three new ones.[13] One was to sell goods at unreasonably low prices for the purpose of destroying competition or eliminating a competitor. Presumably the prohibition of such conduct with such a purpose added little, if anything, to the provision against attempts to monopolize already contained in Section 2 of the Sherman Act. A second criminal offense was to sell goods in any part of the United States at prices lower than elsewhere in the United States for the purpose of destroying competition or eliminating a competitor. Since the offense involved a prohibited purpose, this prohibition, too, covered ground similar to that of Section 2 of the Sherman Act. The third criminal offense was to take part in a transaction knowing that it discriminated against competitors of the buyer by giving the buyer a discount, rebate, allowance, or advertising service charge greater than that available to his competitors on goods of like grade, quality, and quantity. If one assumes that the terms "discount," "rebate," and "allowance" cover all forms of price concession and that an advertising service charge is the equivalent of a payment for sales services, it is obvious that this provision pertained to activities similar to those covered by Sections 2(a), 2(f), and 2(d), previously discussed. However, the standards of illegality differed from those of these sections. Grants for advertising service were to be appraised, not by the special standard of proportional equality, but by the same standard as was used for discounts generally. Difference in the price concessions available to com-

[13] The relevant language is as follows: "Sec. 3. It shall be unlawful for any person engaged in commerce, in the course of such commerce, to be a party to, or assist in, any transaction of sale, or contract to sell, which discriminates to his knowledge against competitors of the purchaser, in that, any discount, rebate, allowance, or advertising service charge is granted to the purchaser over and above any discount, rebate, allowance, or advertising service charge available at the time of such transaction to said competitors in respect of a sale of goods of like grade, quality, and quantity; to sell, or contract to sell, goods in any part of the United States at prices lower than those exacted by said person elsewhere in the United States for the purpose of destroying competition, or eliminating a competitor in such part of the United States; or, to sell, or contract to sell, goods at unreasonably low prices for the purpose of destroying competition or eliminating a competitor.

"Any person violating any of the provisions of this section shall, upon conviction thereof, be fined not more than $5,000 or imprisoned not more than one year, or both." 49 Stat. 1528.

peting buyers was sufficient to establish the illegality of the larger concession, without proof of damage to competition thereby and without opportunity to justify the concession by showing either difference in cost or good faith in meeting a competitor's prices. However, the price differences that were to be compared pertained only to like quantities; and thus the prohibition became inapplicable to price concessions that depended on the size of the purchase. Because of the lack of comparability between the criminal offenses set forth here and the offenses set forth elsewhere in the law, it should have been obvious that a vigorous effort to enforce all portions of the statute simultaneously could scarcely be practicable—that it would result in the capricious application of criminal penalties to particular discriminations that were not more serious in their consequences than others that were immune from such penalties.

Weaknesses in the New Law

Certain basic weaknesses were apparent on the face of this statute. One consisted of the various ambiguities that have been summarized above. These foreshadowed unnecessary controversy over the meaning of the law and unnecessary delay in providing legal guidance for business conduct. A second closely related difficulty lay in the unco-ordinated application of different principles of illegality to different ranges of business conduct. Concessions by sellers might take the form of services or allowances subject to the principle of proportional equality set forth in Sections 2(d) and 2(e), of discounts in lieu of brokerage, prohibited under Section 2(c) unless granted for services rendered, or of price concessions, to be evaluated under the standards of competitive injury, cost justification, and good faith in meeting competition set forth in Sections 2(a) and 2(b). Receipt of benefits by buyers was categorically prohibited (if not for services rendered) if it involved transmission of brokerage commissions or of allowances in lieu thereof; was prohibited under Section 2(f) if the receipt was knowing and involved illegal price discrimination by sellers; and was not prohibited at all if the benefits took the form of advertising allowances or sales services. Criminal liability was incurred by buyer and seller in accord with none of the foregoing standards, but rather when there was knowing participation in a transaction in which a favored buyer received a discount, rebate, allowance, or advertising service charge greater than that available to his competitors on similar goods bought in like quantity. These conflicting standards not only impaired the intelligibility of the law and the likelihood that there would be voluntary compliance with it, but also invited changes in the form of business transactions by persons who saw an advantage in subjecting themselves to one of the legal principles rather than another. Particulaily, the statute provided an incentive for powerful buyers to obtain concessions in the form of advertising allowances and sales services, for which the seller alone was liable, rather than in the form of price reductions or brokerage payments, for which the buyer might be liable along with the seller.

A third weakness in the statute consisted in its general focus on the conduct of sellers rather than the power or conduct of buyers. The avowed purpose of the Congress was to use the law of price discrimination to curb the buying power of chain stores and other large buyers. However, the means to be employed consisted primarily in forbidding sellers, the presumed victims of that buying power, from granting the concessions that were exacted from them. Only in the brokerage section and in the part of the criminal provisions that did not depend on a predatory purpose did the statute establish equal liability for buyers and sellers. As to advertising allowances and sales aids, the seller alone was liable. In regard to price discriminations generally, the liability of the seller and the character of his applicable defenses were worked out in detail in Sections 2(a) and 2(b), whereas the corollary liability of the buyer was summarily set forth in Section 2(f) in language that made the buyer's violation depend on a showing of violation by the seller and possibly on a further showing that the buyer knew the seller's action was illegal. Thus, whereas a proceeding against a seller under Section 2(a) could be based solely on his own conduct, viewed in the setting in which it took place, a proceeding against a buyer under Section 2(f) necessarily covered not only his conduct but the conduct of the seller as well. If the statute was an effort to protect competition from the pressure of powerful buyers on weak sellers, it was anomalous to provide that protection primarily by action against the weak sellers who succumbed to the pressure. Such a process bears some resemblance to an effort to stamp out mugging by making it an offense to permit oneself to be mugged.

Because of this peculiarity in the new law of price discrimination, the approach of the law to the problems of power with which it sought to deal was oblique rather than direct. In this respect the statute differed from the antitrust laws generally. The prohibitions of the Sherman Act are designed to curb the activities by which single enterprises or groups of enterprises attempt to enhance their own power or to use power already acquired. In so far as the Federal Trade Commission Act is applied to collusion and to monopolistic practices, this statute has a similar focus. The provisions of the Clayton Act that pertain to tying arrangements or acquisitions of stock or assets are also designed primarily to curb conduct that, if unchecked, would reduce competition with the persons whose activities are to be curbed. The previous version of the law of price discrimination was also focused primarily on discriminations undertaken with the purpose or effect of enhancing the power of the discriminating enterprise or exploiting that power more successfully. By contrast, the effort of the Robinson-Patman Act to curb the power of great buyers consisted, in large part, of an attempt to alter the conduct of those who deal with powerful buyers and thereby to reduce the power of those buyers indirectly. An alteration of trade practices and price relationships was expected to produce an environment less favorable to the big buyer, and this alteration was to be brought about primarily by curbing the conduct of the enterprises which constituted that environment rather than by curbing the conduct of the big buyer himself.

Because of this contrast of technique, there was a difference of spirit between the Robinson-Patman Act and the antitrust laws generally. Whereas the other antitrust laws provide occasion for a series of attacks on manifestations of business power, many of the proceedings under the Robinson-Patman Act would necessarily be directed at weak enterprises rather than powerful ones. Whereas the orders in antitrust cases are generally designed to diminish the power of the powerful enterprises and groups subject to those orders, the orders in Robinson-Patman cases would be designed to bring about alterations of trade practices or price relationships. There was a resemblance between the techniques of the Robinson-Patman Act and the techniques used in other legislation concerned with trade practices. In spite of the contrast between the purpose of the Robinson-Patman Act to preserve competition and the purpose of N.R.A. codes to assure acceptable prices and business practices, the act resembled some of the codes. This resemblance consisted in the fact that both bodies of regulation were designed to accomplish their purposes by curbs on prices and marketing methods imposed on persons whose conduct was thought to be harmful for reasons other than the possession or pursuit of excessive power by those persons.

. The fact that the Robinson-Patman Act was designed to control trade practices and price relationships created in the statute a peculiar possibility of ambivalent results. In those parts of the antitrust laws that provide for direct attack on business power, the consistency between the purpose of the law and the focus of the various proceedings brought under it is usually apparent. Although there is ample room for dispute about the wisdom of particular ventures in law enforcement, there is seldom reason to believe that a particular proceeding points in a direction irrelevant or opposite to the policy of the law. In any regulation of trade practices, however, various purposes can be served by the curbs imposed, and there may often be legitimate dispute over whether or not a proceeding serves some particular one of these purposes. In this respect the Robinson-Patman Act resembled trade-practice legislation more than it did the remainder of the antitrust laws. Controls such as those applied to brokerage had a bearing on the status of the broker in the distributive process as well as on the problems of buying power associated with the receipt of brokerage commissions by big buyers. Curbs on price concessions by sellers had a bearing on the interests of selling groups in price stability and in the elimination of so-called chiseling as well as on the advantages that powerful buyers might obtain from price concessions. In altering the environment that surrounded the big buyer, proceedings under the Robinson-Patman Act would necessarily alter the environment that surrounded other buyers and sellers as well, and thus produce effects diverse in character. Unlike proceedings under other parts of the antitrust laws, these proceedings were exposed to frequent challenge as to whether, on balance, they tended to enhance or to reduce competition. In using the techniques of control over trade practices and price relationships, the statute lacked the clarity of focus characteristic of the parts of the antitrust laws that involve direct attack on manifestations of business power.

4 / The Commission's Enforcement of the Statute

BETWEEN THE EFFECTIVE DATE of the Robinson-Patman Act in 1936 and December 31, 1957, the Federal Trade Commission decided 430 cases in which it had alleged a violation of the price-discrimination law.[1] (These included one case in which complaint had been issued under the old law before the effective date of the new one.) In 311 of these cases—about 72 per cent—a cease and desist order was issued against one or more practices forbidden by the statute.[2]

These 311 orders did not, of course, constitute the full impact of the law on American business. The Department of Justice had concurrent jurisdiction to enforce the amended provisions of the Clayton Act and also exclusive jurisdiction to enforce the criminal provisions that the Robinson-Patman Act added to the law. Private persons had rights to bring suit for violation of the Clayton Act amendments.[3] The concepts of the Robinson-Patman Act may have influenced the enforcement of other statutes such as the Sherman Act.[4] Moreover, as in all law en-

---

[1] This figure includes all cases in which orders as to price discrimination were issued and all in which the entire complaint was dismissed. It does not include cases in which a charge under the Robinson-Patman Act, included in the complaint, was dismissed while an order was issued as to other types of violation. Short of examining every complaint issued by the Commission, not all cases of the latter type can be identified. Moreover, such dismissals are of uncertain significance—for in some instances the allegation under the Robinson-Patman Act was dropped as a part of an agreed settlement that resulted in an order under the Federal Trade Commission Act broad enough to stop the alleged discrimination.

[2] For a list of the cases in which orders were issued, see App. A, Table 1. For a list of those dismissed without orders, see App. A, Table 3.

[3] Private litigation also took place for a time for alleged violation of the criminal provisions of Section 3 of the new statute. In January 1958, however, the Supreme Court held that this part of the law is not subject to triple damage suits. See *Nashville Milk Co.* v. *Carnation Co.*, 355 U.S. 373, and *Safeway Stores* v. *Vance*, 355 U.S. 389.

[4] Orders against conspiracy under the Sherman Act and the Federal Trade Commission Act have included prohibitions of price discrimination, and proceedings

forcement, there has undoubtedly been a considerable amount of voluntary compliance with the principles that appear to have been expressed in the law or to have emerged from the litigated cases.

To trace the effect of the Robinson-Patman Act on the enforcement of related legislation such as the Sherman Act would be a formidable task, requiring both an appraisal of previous policies in enforcing such laws and a consideration of other influences toward change in these policies. It has not been attempted here. The activities of the Department of Justice in enforcing the Robinson-Patman Act have been few and episodic. They are summarized in Appendix B, but are not discussed elsewhere. Though there has been a considerable amount of private litigation, and probably a still larger amount of private settlement of damage claims that might have resulted in litigation, not much of this private action has contributed to the development of the policy aspects of the law.[5] The formal suits have been too few and difficult to provide effective private remedies for those who experienced discrimination; and there is no way of knowing the degree of success attained by injured private persons in obtaining informal settlement of their claims without suit. Important private cases are discussed herein where relevant, but no attempt is made to cover the private litigation systematically.[6]

---

under the Federal Trade Commission Act have been directed against such practices as payment of discriminatory sales commissions on tires and receipt of disproportionate advertising allowances. Such proceedings are considered in this book only where they throw light on the application of the Robinson-Patman Act.

[5] See, for example, footnote 27, p. 600.

[6] In an article on "Enforcement of the Robinson-Patman Act by Private Parties" (CCH 1957 *Anti-Trust Law Symposium*, pp. 145-63), Lee Loevinger estimates that to the end of 1956 about 75 private proceedings under the statute had been reported. In 28 of these, the reports covered judicial rulings and did not show the final disposition of the case. In 41, final judgment had been rendered for the defendant—in 13 without appeal and in 28 after appeal. In only 6 cases had there been final judgment for the plaintiff. One of these (*United Cigar-Whelan Stores Corp.* v. *H. Weinreich Co.*, 107 F. Supp. 89) resulted in a summary judgment that a contract was unenforceable. Five resulted in monetary awards, totaling about $484,000. Each of the 5 damage cases was appealed: in 1 the decision of the court of appeals was accepted by the defendant; in 2 the Supreme Court denied certiorari; in 1 there were 2 decisions by the circuit court followed by dismissal of certiorari; and in 1 the case went twice to the Supreme Court.

The successful damage suits were: (1) *Elizabeth Arden Sales Corp.* v. *Gus Blass Co.*, 150 F. 2d 988, certiorari denied, judgment $3,030 plus attorney's fees; (2) *American Cooperative Serum Association* v. *Anchor Serum Co.*, 153 F. 2d 907, certiorari denied, judgment $15,850; (3) *Moore* v. *Mead's Fine Bread Co.*, 184 F. 2d 338, 340 U.S. 944, 348 U.S. 115, judgment $68,400; (4) *Fitch* v. *Kentucky-*

The proceedings of the Commission have been dominant in determining the scope and direction of legal activity and in formulating the issues of law and public policy.[7] They constitute the center of attention in this book.

Voluntary compliance with the law has undoubtedly been important, but its extent and character cannot be satisfactorily measured. In the first few months after the Robinson-Patman Act became effective, the Federal Trade Commission encouraged informal conferences between its staff and business enterprises that wished to adjust their pricing practices voluntarily to make them consistent with the new statute. Many conferences were held, and presumably the pricing practices of a considerable number of enterprises were modified by this means without formal legal process. After formal enforcement began, there probably were further changes in the conduct of the business community. But it is reasonable to suppose that voluntary modifications of business conduct have been primarily responses to the public policies of enforcement, and that their extent and character have depended on the vigor and clarity of those policies. Thus the Commission's 311 cease and desist orders may be regarded not only as the larger part of formal law enforcement but also as the principal determinants of the patterns of private litigation and voluntary compliance.

Distribution of Emphasis Among Types of Violation

A striking feature of the application of the Robinson-Patman Act by the Commission has been the disproportionate emphasis placed on the various parts of the statute. This is evident in the tables on pages 69 and 70. Forty-seven per cent of the cease and desist orders—145 out of

---

Tennessee Light & Power Co., 136 F. 2d 12, affirming *Kentucky-Tennessee Light & Power Co.* v. *Nashville Coal Co.*, 37 F. Supp. 728, judgment $176,364; (5) *Bruce's Juices* v. *American Can Co.*, 87 F. Supp. 985, 187 F. 2d 919, 190 F. 2d 73, certiorari dismissed, judgment $220,000.

[7] Loevinger concludes in his article (*op. cit.*, pp. 161-63) that the interpretation and application of the law "tends to be much more restrained and conservative" in private suits than in proceedings by the government, and that the treble damage provision has been applied "most conservatively, both as to the situations in which liability has been imposed and as to the amount of damages awarded." He thinks private enforcement is effective "only where the violation is relatively gross or obvious," but that the sanction it affords "is probably more effective than the bare statistics as to the number of plaintiffs' judgments would indicate."

311—were issued in cases involving solely the payment or receipt of unlawful brokerage. Three more orders were concerned with unlawful brokerage as well as other violations of the law. Price discrimination by sellers in violation of Section 2(a) was the sole offense covered by 101 orders, slightly more than 32 per cent. The other kinds of unlawful action received relatively little attention.[8] Twenty-seven orders were concerned solely with disproportionate advertising allowances and similar disproportionate payments in violation of Section 2(d); five orders solely with disproportionate furnishing of sales services in violation of Section 2(e); and seven orders solely with unlawful discrimination by a buyer in violation of Section 2(f).

Number of Violations of Each Part of the Act Found in Successive Groups of Robinson-Patman Cases, 1936-57[a]

Section of Act Violated	Group I Dockets 2986–4227	Group II Dockets 4229–4915	Group III Dockets 4920–5502	Group IV Dockets 5516–6103	Group V Dockets 6104–6752	All Cases
2(a) only (discrimination)..	30	8	11	36	16	101
2(c) only (brokerage)......	17	40	43	16	20	145
2(d) only (disproportionate payments).............	1	1	2	5	18	27
2(e) only (disproportionate services)..............	2	0	0	1	2	5
2(f) only (receipt of discrimination)..........	2	1	3	1	0	7
More than one section.....	10	3	3	3	7	26
Total cases in group.......	62	62	62	62	63	311

[a] The groups consist of 62 cases each (except the final group, which is 63), arranged in sequence by docket numbers, which were assigned serially as complaints were issued. Thus the successive groups show changes in emphasis through time. The alternative method of establishing groups by time periods was rejected because the total number of price discrimination orders varied greatly from year to year: direct comparison of numbers of cases in particular categories would be misleading, and comparison of percentages would, in some periods, attribute too much importance to a small number of proceedings. The time period covered by each group of dockets is as follows, as shown by the dates of the first and last complaints therein: Group I, 11/21/36–8/7/40; Group II, 8/8/40–2/13/43; Group III, 2/23/43–6/20/47; Group IV, 11/20/47–6/17/53; Group V, 6/17/53–3/27/57.

[8] Neither the importance attributed to a part of the statute nor the effort devoted to it can be more than roughly measured by the number of cases arising under it. Cases differ greatly both in relative importance and in the relative amount of effort they require. A part of the difference is due to the differing requirements of dif-

There were also 26 orders that covered violation of more than one section of the statute. This multiple-violation group included 17 violations of Section 2(a), 3 of Section 2(c), 20 of Section 2(d), 10 of Section 2(e), and 5 of Section 2(f).

Types of Violation Found in Cases of Multiple Violation of the Robinson-Patman Act, 1936-57

Sections of Act Violated	Group I	Group II	Group III	Group IV	Group V	All Cases
2(a) and 2(c)............	1	0	0	0	0	1
2(a) and 2(d)...........	5	2	2	0	1	10
2(a) and 2(e)...........	1	0	0	1	0	2
2(a) and 2(f)............	2	0	0	0	0	2
2(c) and 2(d)...........	0	0	1	0	0	1
2(c) and 2(f)............	0	0	0	1	0	1
2(d) and 2(e)...........	0	0	0	1	6	7
2(a), 2(d) and 2(f).......	1	0	0	0	0	1
2(a), 2(d), 2(e) and 2(f)...	0	1	0	0	0	1
Total cases of multiple violation in group..........	10	3	3	3	7	26

When the simple and multiple violations are grouped together, the orders are distributed as follows:

	Number	Per Cent of Total Violations	Per Cent of Total Orders[9]
Price discrimination by sellers................	118	34.7	37.9
Payment or receipt of brokerage..............	148	43.5	47.6
Disproportionate payment for sales service......	47	13.8	15.1
Disproportionate furnishing of sales service....	15	4.4	4.8
Receipt of unlawful discriminations by buyers..	12	3.5	3.8

That orders involving unlawful brokerage have been almost as numerous as all other orders combined suggests a substantial distortion of focus in the administration of the law. There is no reason to believe that

ferent sections of the statute; but even more of it is due to the varying complexity of particular problems and to the variation in effort between contested and uncontested proceedings. The routine cases under the brokerage provision probably have required less effort than the routine price discrimination cases. To this extent, the comparison by number of cases probably overemphasizes Sec. 2(c).

[9] Because of multiple violations, the percentages in this column, when added, exceed 100.

during the more than twenty years since the passage of the Robinson-Patman Act, the payment of brokerage commissions by sellers to buyers has constituted the principal threat to competition evident among discriminatory practices. Public concern about such brokerage payments arose, prior to the enactment of the statute, almost wholly with reference to the buying practices of a small number of corporate chains in the food industry. Outside this limited field, concern over anomalies in brokerage payments was frequently expressed by food brokers and their trade associations; but the problems raised do not seem to have had wider application or greater significance than those presented by numerous other industries, each concerned with anomalies in its own trade practices. Since the brokerage provision incorporated in the statute made the specified payments unlawful without reference to their effect on competition or their justification by cost differences, proceedings concerned with such payments were unlikely to uncover evidence of damage to competition sufficient to justify great emphasis on this part of the law.

The preponderance of brokerage proceedings appears to be due primarily to the simplicity with which such cases can be investigated and tried. After an initial burst of litigation concerned almost wholly with efforts by buyers and their agents to take advantage of the provision in the statute regarding services rendered, the law, as interpreted by the courts, became enforceable by simple proceedings. Violation consisted merely in the payment of brokerage or an equivalent to a party on the other side of a transaction or to his representative. In proving that a payment was made, that it constituted brokerage, and that the payer and recipient came from opposite sides of a transaction of sale, the Commission could establish a conclusive case. There was no need to consider competitive injury, cost justification, good faith in meeting competitors' practices, or even the significance of services rendered. Investigation could be short and inexpensive, evidence could be brief and conclusive, and once the simple facts were established, no valid defense was available. The Commission had an incentive to institute brokerage cases, partly because they could provide an impressive statistical total, and partly because, when an apparent violation came to its attention, the facts were so readily ascertainable and a proceeding based on them was so simple that there was no need to consider policy questions or litigating strategy. Moreover, the principal organization of brokers in the food field was actively interested in vigorous enforcement of the brokerage provision and probably was zealous in bringing violations of this part of the act to the attention of the Commission.[10]

A second striking feature of the distribution of emphasis is the fewness of the cases in which the Commission has proceeded against buyers of goods for inducing or receiving illegal discriminations. Twelve orders out of 311 were issued against such buyers, less than 4 per cent of the total. Although the amended statute was intended primarily to cope with the problem of the powerful buyer, its use for direct attack on buyers has been negligible. Presumably, the neglect of this part of the law is to be attributed to the fact that the statute is so drawn as to emphasize law violations by sellers and to create unusual difficulties in proceedings against buyers based on any other charge than receipt of unlawful brokerage. As appears below in Chapter XV, the first proceeding against a buyer which was sharply contested resulted in judicial interpretation of the law that emphasized these difficulties. Since this proceeding, further enforcement of Section 2(f) appears to have come to a practical standstill. It is an anomaly that, in a statute largely concerned with the power of buyers to induce discriminations that injure their weaker competitors, such activities by buyers have been seldom attacked directly.

As was to have been expected, orders under Section 2(a), concerned with price discrimination by sellers, have been more numerous than orders under Sections 2(d) and 2(e), concerned with disproportionate payment for or provision of sales services. Section 2(a) incorporates the basic prohibition of price discrimination by sellers. Its language is broad enough to be applied to a wide variety of discriminations—special price concessions, quantity and volume discounts, functional discounts, and territorial price discriminations.[11] Enforcement of this part of the

[10] The attorney for the National Food Brokers Association is quoted as having reported to the association in January 1939, "The Federal Trade Commission, upon the presentation to the Commission by your officers and counsel of the fact and law situation as we saw it, started the work. . . . Every assistance was given to make sure that the brokers' interpretation of the Act was understood. . . . We have to the best of our ability kept in contact with the attorneys of the Federal Trade Commission to be of any assistance we could, leaving no stone unturned to the end that those lawyers would know what our interpretation of Section 2(c) is. . . ." See Association of Independent Food Dealers of America, *The Case for Freeing Independent Merchants From Restraints Against their Competitive Opportunity to Earn Brokerage,* pp. 17-18.

[11] As used in this book, the term *quantity discount* means a price reduction based on the amount bought in a single transaction; the term *volume discount* means a price reduction based on the total amount bought during a period of time; the term *functional discount* means a price concession based on character-

law applies the basic prohibition of discriminatory pricing to most of the methods by which a seller can discriminate. By contrast, Sections 2(d) and (e) are concerned with a relatively narrow subject, the provision of sales service by a supplier to his distributor or by a distributor to his supplier. That only 15 orders have been issued under Section 2(e) is not surprising. That Section 2(d) has produced as many as 47 orders appears to be due primarily to two circumstances—first, that special problems are created by policies of selective advertising (see Chapter VII below), and second, that business enterprises have increasingly used advertising allowances as convenient substitutes for risky types of price discrimination.

It is noteworthy that the distribution of emphasis among cases of different types has changed substantially during the period of 21½ years covered by the tables on pages 69 and 70. In those tables the cases that resulted in corrective orders are divided into 4 groups of 62 and 1 of 63, arranged in the sequence in which they were instituted by the Commission. Hence these groups indicate roughly the changes in the Commission's distribution of emphasis among different types of proceedings. In Group I, cases concerned solely with price discrimination by sellers in violation of Section 2(a) were nearly half of the total, and every case of multiple violation included such discrimination; so that price discrimination was at issue in nearly 65 per cent of all proceedings. By similarly combining the violations shown in the tables on pages 69 and 70, percentages can be computed for other types of violation. Payment or receipt of unlawful brokerage was found in 29 per cent. Less than 15 per cent of the cases involved the proportionality provisions or unlawful receipt of discrimination, and in most of these the offense was combined with violation of Section 2(a).

In Groups II and III, the emphasis changed sharply. Price discrimination was found, alone or in combination with other violations, in 18 per cent and 21 per cent of the cases, respectively. Violation of the brokerage provision rose to 79 per cent in the former period and was still 71 per cent in the latter. Cases concerned wholly or partly with other parts of the statute continued to be a small part of the whole—8 per cent and 13 per cent, successively.

---

istics of the buyer, such as his place in the channels of distribution, his structure, or the types of service he performs; the term *territorial discrimination* means a price difference based on the location of the sale or of the buyer's place of business.

In Groups IV and V, cases concerned with brokerage lost importance, though they still constituted about 27 per cent in the former and about 32 per cent in the latter. Cases involving price discrimination rose to 60 per cent in the former group and receded to 27 per cent in the latter. More important in the last group than either brokerage or price discrimination was disproportionate payment for sales services, which, alone or with other violations, appeared in over 40 per cent of the cases.

The major movements shown by these figures are: (a) a rise of brokerage cases from about 30 per cent to nearly 80 per cent, followed by a decline to the original level; (b) great fluctuation in the relative importance of price discrimination cases, which, however, never attained again the importance they had in the initial group; (c) a recent sharp increase in the importance of the cases concerned with advertising allowances and similar payments for service, which have become more numerous than any other type of case.[12]

It is noteworthy that the provision of the law authorizing the Commission to fix quantity limits has been invoked only once, and then unsuccessfully.

Distribution of Emphasis Among Industries

Although the Robinson-Patman Act is so written as to apply to the entire range of interstate commerce in commodities, the orders issued by the Commission under it have been heavily concentrated on the food industries. Of the 148 orders concerned with brokerage, 129, or 87 per cent, pertain to these industries. Of the 19 remaining, 13 have to do with apparel—5 with furs and fur garments, 5 with women's garments generally, 2 with millinery, and 1 with men's clothing. The other 6 brokerage orders are concerned, respectively, with containers, crystal phosphate, plumbing products, drugs, tires, batteries and accessories, and hardware and general merchandise.

The orders that prohibit violations of other sections of the act have a wider distribution among industries. Fifty-seven of a total of 166 have

---

[12] In the cases decided during the first six months of 1958, violations of Sec. 2(d) continued to be important, violation of the brokerage provision rose to almost equal importance, and price discrimination fell in importance. Of 25 cases, 10 were concerned with disproportionate payment only, 8 with brokerage only, and 5 with price discrimination only. Two cases involved multiple violations, 1 of Secs. 2(a) and 2(f), the other of Secs. 2(a), 2(d) and 2(e).

to do with food products, and 109 with other products.[13] In the latter group, 8 are concerned with clothing and related items; 20 with medical, dental, and optical supplies, drugs, and cosmetics; 18 with automotive parts, gasoline, and tires; 11 with various rubber products; 9 with building materials and equipment; 7 with industrial materials and equipment; 12 with books and school supplies; 10 with personal equipment—watches, jewelry, baby walkers, cigars, and shoe polish; 4 with animal feeds; 4 with commercial inoculants; and 6 with miscellaneous items—golf balls, snow fence, greeting cards, mattresses, savings systems, and mops and waxes. Most of the orders apply to the sale of finished goods ready for consumption. Presumably this fact reflects a persistent tendency to give closer scrutiny to the dealings of manufacturers with distributors than to transactions among manufacturers. It is noteworthy, too, that even of the orders concerned with other matters than brokerage more than one third pertain to the food industries. When these and the brokerage orders are combined, the food industries account for about 60 per cent of the total.

The concentration on food products is consistent with the history of the Robinson-Patman Act. Problems arising in the food industry, particularly with reference to corporate chains therein, were at the center of congressional attention when the act was considered. The first draft of the statute was prepared by an attorney for a trade association in the food industry. The concepts of the act—for example, those pertaining to brokerage—are fitted to the institutions of the food industry. It is probable that the bias toward proceedings in this industry reflects the relative weight of complaints received by the Commission and the relative ease with which the language of the statute can be applied to the institutions of this part of the market.

It is also probable, however, that the distribution of emphasis among industries reflects a haphazard application of the statute, not guided by any general plan of attack based on the relative importance of different problems. Within the food industries no less than 9 of the 57 orders concerned with other matters than brokerage have to do with corn products, primarily corn syrup used in making candies, and 9 more orders apply directly to candy manufacture and distribution. Another 5 of the orders have to do with yeast and 2 with salt, relatively unimportant food products, as measured by total value of production. Portions of

[13] This total includes three cases in which violation of the brokerage provision was accompanied by other violations.

the food industry substantially more important in their magnitude have received much less attention. Only 1 order not concerned with brokerage applies to meat, 1 to fish, 2 to frosted foods, and 3 to fruits and vegetables and their juices.

A similar imbalance is evident in the other industrial groups. Among the 12 orders concerned with rubber products, 5 are applicable to heels and soles, and 4 to rubber stamps, as compared with 2 for tires and 1 for rubber and canvas footwear. Among the 14 orders pertaining to automotive supplies other than tires and tubes and gasoline, 3 are concerned with spark plugs.

Cases have tended to cluster in particular industries without regard to the importance of those industries and without any clear evidence that there is a similar clustering of the problems of price discrimination. It appears probable that most cases arise from complaints, that information developed in one case points to the existence of related problems, and that when one competitor is subject to an order, there are pressures and considerations of equity that make it seem desirable to impose on his rivals a comparable standard of conduct. When proceedings develop in this way, the progression from case to case is both convenient and logical, but the entire body of proceedings is likely to present a distorted reflection of the business scene.

Attention to Disorderly Industries

Outside the food field, the Commission has spent a substantial part of its effort on industries that have a relatively chaotic or disorderly price structure. Where there is no well-recognized market price, the transactions of buyers and sellers involve large amounts of higgling and often result in a series of special prices applicable to particular sales. In such circumstances, prices to competing customers will be the same only by accident. Whereas in a more orderly market structure, particular discounts or concessions may constitute relatively enduring anomalies and may have relatively enduring effects, the discounts and concessions of such a disorderly price structure constitute a welter of ephemeral discriminations, the benefits of which may be enjoyed now by one customer and now by another, with a considerable cancellation of benefits in successive transactions. As in an oriental bazaar, the widespread resort to such higgling practices expresses a particular form of competition, rather than an interference with competition. Though less dangerous to competition and to competitors than systematic discrimination, it is more conspicuous. It often gives rise to complaint; its existence can be readily demonstrated; and the immediate injury to the disfavored customer at a particular moment is as apparent as in more orderly discriminations. Hence it is not surprising that, in so far as legal proceedings are not guided by a well-considered plan, they may include a considerable number addressed to such disorderly markets.

This appears to have been the case in proceedings of the Commission in such fields as rubber stamps and automotive supplies. Rubber stamps are made by small producers and sold in small transactions. The evidence in the cases underlying the Commission's four orders in this field indicates that the violations by these producers consisted in selling their goods on a haphazard basis for whatever they could get from each customer. This appears to have been the practice of every producer. From the point of view of buyers, the purchase of stamps was an expenditure for one small item of miscellaneous office supplies, the effect of which was lost in the total transactions of the concern.

In the case of automotive parts, manufacture and distribution for the replacement market show similar disorder. Many manufacturers of specialties, operating on a small scale, offer their products to parts distributors in haggling transactions in which the bargaining power of the parties changes with the rapidly changing public acceptance enjoyed by particular parts and accessories. The bargaining relationships are affected by the fact that some parts are produced by large makers and that powerful chains are to be found among distributors, but special price concessions appear to be at least as numerous in the catch-as-catch-can relationships of small parts makers and distributors as among the larger factors in the industry. The Commission's eight orders in the field have been concerned largely with the activities of small manufacturers and with discriminations that the disfavored customers said were not important.

The examples cited have common elements in the fact that competition is vigorous on both sides of the market and that much of the discrimination apparent in the industry reflects competitive maneuvering for position in which no sustained advantage for a favored group is clearly discernible. A program of legal proceedings designed to give priority to attack on discriminations from which monopolistic results are likely to flow would presumably have given a low level of priority to cases in such fields. The fact that these cases are prominent among the Commission's proceedings is attributable to the fact that discriminations become more apparent as the price structure becomes less orderly and hence are likely to receive disproportionate attention in a legal program not carefully planned to take account of the degree to which competition is jeopardized.

Infrequency of Contested Proceedings

A major characteristic of the litigation underlying the Commission's 311 orders has been the fact that most of the orders were issued without a full legal contest. The typical pattern has been one in which the respondent acquiesced in the proceeding without offering a vigorous defense.

Method of Disposing of Cases Resulting in Orders Under the Robinson-Patman Act, 1936-57

Method of Disposition	Group I	Group II	Group III	Group IV	Group V	All Cases
Full Trial...............	15	5	6	12	7	45
Partial Trial............	6	3	2	3	2	16
Stipulation of Facts.......	13	3	6[a]	4[a]	0	26[a]
Admission Answer........	27	52	47[a]	24	3	153[a]
Consent Order..........	1	0	1	18[a]	51	71[a]
Default by Respondent ...	0	0	0	2	0	2
Total Cases in Group.....	62	63	61	62	63	311

[a] In one case some respondents stipulated the facts, while others filed admission answers; so that the case is recorded twice. In another case, a stipulation of facts accompanied a consent order and there has been similar double recording. Therefore the listings in the columns for Groups III and IV and for All Cases, when added, exceed the number of cases in the line covering Total Cases in Group.

In 249[14] cases the Commission found it unnecessary to present evidence and argument because the respondents admitted the material allegations of the complaint, stipulated the relevant facts and waived argument, consented to the entry of an order, or in some equivalent way chose to forego their defense. In 2 additional cases the respondents filed no answer

[14] This is the total of lines 3, 4, and 5 of the accompanying table, minus the two duplicate entries.

and did not present themselves to contest the proceeding. Only 61 of the orders were preceded by trials; and in 16 of these trials the proceedings were curtailed by respondents' decisions not to present evidence for the defense or to forego the filing of briefs, the presentation of oral argument, or both. In only 45 instances—less than 15 per cent of the total number of cases resulting in orders—was a cease and desist order issued after a full trial of the case. Trials were more frequent in the initial group of 62 cases than subsequently; but even in this group there were full trials in less than one fourth of the cases. (It should be noted, however, that in a few of the cases in which legal proceedings were curtailed, the curtailment did not reflect even partial acquiescence in the decision. Thus, in the Automatic Canteen case, the respondent took the position, eventually supported by the Supreme Court, that the Commission had not presented evidence on all the matters necessary to prove violation and therefore chose to offer no evidence on behalf of the defense. The case was hotly contested on legal points, both before the Commission and on appeal, and with eventual success for the respondent.)

There were various reasons for enterprises accused of violating the act to avoid a full legal contest. By avoiding a trial they could minimize adverse publicity among their disfavored customers. By a suitably guarded consent settlement or admission answer they could prevent the Commission from building a trial record that might be used against them in subsequent triple damage suits. In some instances, too, respondents who had granted discriminatory concessions under pressure or in compliance with trade custom may have welcomed orders to cease these concessions. The willingness of some large respondents to accept orders was probably due to the fact that they regarded discriminations on minor parts of their business as too unimportant to warrant an expensive contest. The willingness of some small respondents was probably strengthened by trepidation at the costs and uncertainties of a trial of strength against the government. Some respondents, particularly in brokerage cases, may have thought their violation of the law was so clear that a defense was hopeless. Comment from attorneys indicates that until recently some clients were unconcerned about orders because they thought there was little chance of a check on their compliance. For reasons such as these, enterprises, large and small, have often accepted orders without full challenge of the Commission's conclusions regarding complex issues of fact or of its interpretations of unadjudicated and sometimes obviously ambiguous provisions of law.

Victories for the Government in Appellate Courts

The tendency of respondents to accept the views of the Commission was undoubtedly strengthened, as time passed, by the almost unvarying support given to the Commission by the courts in cases that were appealed. In the 10 brokerage cases that received judicial review, the Commission's orders were uniformly sustained. In the 23 cases that were appealed after orders concerned with price discrimination by sellers or with disproportionality in provision of sales services, the Commission was sustained fully in 15 cases, sustained with modifications of its order in 4 cases,[15] and reversed in 4 cases.[16] Moreover, in 1 of the 4 cases lost by the Commission, that against Minneapolis-Honeywell, the Supreme Court refused to hear the case on procedural grounds amid indications that, had it rendered an opinion, it might have reversed the lower court. In this body of cases the only significant interpretations of law regarding which the Commission's views were overturned by the courts had to do with the right of a seller to meet a competitor's prices in good faith and the relevance of a cost defense in a proceeding for violation of Section 2(e).

However, in the sole case having to do with the interpretation of Section 2(f) that reached the courts on appeal, the Commission's decision was reversed. The court decided, contrary to the view of the Commission, that burdens of proof that rest on respondent sellers who are accused of discrimination in price rest on the Commission in proceedings against respondent buyers accused of receiving such discriminations.

It is noteworthy that the Commission suffered no significant reversal

---

[15] *Morton Salt* v. *FTC,* 334 U.S. 37; *Standard Brands* v. *FTC,* 189 F. 2d 510; Maryland Baking Co., Fourth Circuit, Decision April 8, 1957; *C. E. Niehoff & Co.* v. *FTC,* 241 F. 2d 37. In the first three cases the modifications were minor. In the fourth the court accepted Niehoff's plea that an order while Niehoff's competitors were not similarly restrained would jeopardize Niehoff's existence. Accordingly, in sustaining the order, the Court modified it so that it was to become effective when the court so directed. However, the Supreme Court set aside this part of the ruling of the lower court. See below, pp. 88-89.

[16] *Minneapolis-Honeywell* v. *FTC,* 191 F. 2d 786, 344 U.S. 206; *Standard Oil Co. of Indiana* v. *FTC,* 340 U.S. 231, and 78 S. Ct. 369; *Atalanta Trading Corp.* v. *FTC,* 258 F. 2d 365; *Simplicity Patterns* v. *FTC,* CCH, *Trade Cases 1958,* par. 69047. In the first three cases, the matter at issue was finally decided. In the last, the court held that, contrary to the Commission's view, a cost defense was relevant to a violation of Sec. 2(e), and remanded the case to the Commission to consider respondent's evidence as to cost justification. The decision is being appealed.

on appeal until 1951, 15 years after the passage of the act, and that the significant issues pertaining to the defense of meeting competition under Section 2(a), the burden of proof under Section 2(f), and the relevance of a cost defense under Section 2(e) were not adjudicated until 1951, 1953, and 1958, respectively.

Lag in Clarification of the Law

Because of the fewness of the litigated cases, important questions on the meaning of the Robinson-Patman Act have been less than fully explored. Though the courts have determined that meeting competition in good faith is a complete defense for a seller in a price-discrimination case, the nature of the conduct that constitutes good faith has been adjudicated in only two cases,[17] those against Staley and Standard of Indiana, and many problems as to the interpretation of good faith still remain to be considered. Although the Automatic Canteen case established the responsibility of the Commission for proving the unlawfulness of the discriminatory price received by a buyer, there have been no later decisions to determine the boundaries of the Commission's responsibility in this respect or the feasibility of the suggestions made by the Supreme Court in the Canteen case in regard to the way in which the Commission might undertake the task. The ruling that a cost defense may be offered in a proceeding under Section 2(e) is recent, and presumably will not be conclusive until the question is decided by the Supreme Court. Some important problems of interpretation have never been raised before the Federal Trade Commission. For example, no respondent in a proceeding under Section 2(d) has yet defended his advertising allowances to his customers on the theory that they constituted, not discounts on sales, but purchases of advertising;[18] that in such a context a duty to buy advertising on proportionally equal terms can reasonably mean only a duty to make payments proportional to the value of the advertising; and that any other interpretation of the statute would constitute an imposition of arbitrary requirements to buy worthless services, unrelated to the purposes of a price discrimination law.

[17] The defense has been rejected in several other cases in which attention centered on other problems, so that the decision cast little or no light on the legal meaning of good faith.

[18] Such a defense was offered in a case that was dismissed for lack of evidence and was successful in a lower court in a private suit decided in 1957. See below, pp. 160-64.

Similarly, matters that have loomed large in controversy about the Robinson-Patman Act have often been argued on the basis of few actual cases. We are often told, for example, that, although discriminatory prices can be legally justified by a showing that they merely reflect differences in cost, such a showing is practically impossible either because the standards of the law are too tight or because the Commission's application of these standards is too rigid. Yet the claim of cost justification has been brought to the Commission in few cases, and when this issue has arisen, the Commission has not always decided it unfavorably. Until December 31, 1957, there were only 32 orders in litigated cases under Section 2(a) in which a cost defense might have been offered.[19] In 13 of these, such a defense was actually offered, but was incomplete or was rejected as unsatisfactory.[20] A cost defense was also offered in 1 case that was decided on the basis of an agreed stipulation of facts. In 4 cases before December 31, 1957, in which a complaint under Section 2(a) was dismissed by the Commission, cost justification was stated to be one of the grounds for dismissal.[21] Many cost problems that might arise in price discrimination cases have never come before the Commission for decision.

Since industries differ greatly in types of competitive relationship, distributive channels, price structures, terms of sale, techniques of computing costs, and many other aspects of trade practice, a decision appropriate to the circumstances of one industry is not necessarily applicable to the dissimilar relationships of a different industry. Because of the fewness of decisions on controverted issues, there is a constant temptation

[19] Until the circuit court decision in the Simplicity Patterns case in May 1958, it was generally assumed that cost justification was not relevant to violations of Secs. 2(c), 2(d) and 2(e).

[20] Among the 13 were 2 in which a cost defense was accepted in regard to some of the discriminations. In 1 it was offered for only part of the discriminatory prices and was accepted by the Commission as to the prices for which it was offered; in the other, it was accepted in regard to some of the discriminations and rejected as to others. The first was Docket 4920, *Minneapolis-Honeywell Regulator Co.,* the second Docket 4972, *U.S. Rubber Co.*

[21] These cases were Docket 2937, *Bird & Son,* closed July 17, 1937; Docket 4636, *Bissell Carpet Sweeper,* closed March 6, 1945; Docket 5677, *B. F. Goodrich,* closed Jan. 31, 1954; and Docket 5728, *Sylvania Electric Products,* closed Oct. 1, 1954. In a fifth case, in which an order was issued against other violations of law, a portion of the complaint alleging violation of Sec. 2(a) was dismissed because the discrimination was cost-justified; see Docket 5701, *Horlicks Corp.,* order Sept. 19, 1950. Another case, Docket 6721, *Hamburg Brothers, Inc.,* was dismissed for this reason on April 30, 1958.

to apply these decisions not only to like situations but also to situations that are substantially different and have not yet been explored in litigation. In such circumstances misinterpretations of the law are probable, and gaps in awareness of the meaning of the law are inevitable. Thus the general acquiescence in the Commission's enforcement of the Robinson-Patman Act has had the dual result of expediting the enforcement procedures and delaying the development of a well-understood and fully worked-out body of law.

The infrequency with which the Commission's complaints have resulted in contests has also reduced the pressure on the Commission for clarity, accuracy, and substantive adequacy in its findings and orders. At first, when uncontested cases were usually settled on the basis of an admission answer or a stipulation of facts, the Commission formulated findings of fact and conclusions of law in each case, even though these were sometimes unrevealing. Subsequently, when uncontested cases were usually settled by a newly developed procedure for consent orders, the Commission formulated, in addition to its formal order, only findings as to the portion of the facts that established its jurisdiction in the case. In such a proceeding, the nature of the violation can be ascertained only from the Commission's complaint; and the authority of this document is reduced (a) by the well-known tendency of prosecutors to allege more than they can prove in order to leave themselves leeway for new developments during the progress of the case; and (b) by the fact that the respondents have not admitted the truth of the allegations. Under the first two procedures, the consent of the respondents has meant that findings of fact and conclusions of law have not been challenged; under all three procedures, it has meant that the scope of orders had been unilaterally determined by the Commission.[22] The judicial process is based on the presumption that substantial justice will emerge from the clash of opposing contentions. Where that clash has been sporadic, as in proceedings under the Robinson-Patman Act, it is not surprising that the findings and orders have been sometimes vague, sometimes perfunctory, and sometimes unusually broad in scope. The Commission has been forced to substitute for the pressures of litigation a control exercised through its own administrative processes of surveillance and review. The decisions justify doubt that these processes have been adequate to the task that has been imposed on them.

[22] In most instances, however, there has been informal negotiation about the nature of the order before the formal settlement of the case.

The case against Adolph Gottscho, for example,[23] was decided on the basis of an answer in which the material allegations of the Commission's complaint that there had been violation of Section 2(a) in selling rubber stamps were admitted by the respondents. The record of the case, therefore, consists of the complaint, the admission answer, and the findings of the Commission. The entire findings on the nature of the discrimination and its effect were as follows:

> Par. 5. In the course and conduct of their aforesaid business, respondents, since June 19, 1936, have been, and are now, discriminating in price between different purchasers of their products of like grade and quality by selling such products to some purchasers at higher prices than the prices at which they sell similar products of like grade and quality to other of such purchasers. Such products are sold and distributed for use within the various States of the United States.
>
> Par. 6. The effect of respondents' discrimination in price has been, and may be, substantially to lessen, injure, destroy, and prevent competition between respondents and their competitors in the sale and distribution of rubber stamps and other products in commerce as aforesaid, and has been, and may be, to tend to create a monopoly in respondents in said line of commerce.[24]

The process by which such findings are produced is intelligible. Where an admission answer is accepted, the Commission has no legal basis for findings that extend beyond what was admitted and no factual basis for failing to find what was admitted. Where a complaint was drawn in general terms, an admission was likely to be equally general. Within wide limits, respondents had no incentive to be precise in their admissions of fact, particularly as to the damage caused by a discrimination; for the Commission's power to issue an order was not increased or decreased by a difference in the injury found.[25]

In thus closely paraphrasing the language of the statute without providing supporting details, the Commission not only has frequently failed to provide information about the economic content of its proceedings, but also has sometimes reached conclusions so sweeping that they raise

[23] Docket 5517, *Adolph Gottscho, Inc.* The complaint, findings and order in this and all other cases under the Robinson-Patman Act appear in the bound volumes of *Federal Trade Commission Decisions.* Volume and page references appear with each case in the listings in Appendix A. Table 1 lists cases in which cease and desist orders were issued; Table 3 lists cases that were dismissed.

[24] 46 FTC 104-05.

[25] See below, Chap. 8, p. 217; Chap. 16, p. 521.

a question in the reader's mind whether they were well-considered. The Gottscho case and other related cases illustrate this point also. Having supplied no information about Gottscho's size and no information about the size and power of competing sellers, the Commission found, nevertheless, that Gottscho's discrimination not only lessened competition but also tended to give Gottscho a monopoly. In a case against another manufacturer of rubber stamps, also based on an admission answer, the Commission found that this manufacturer's discrimination also tended to produce monopoly.[26] In two other rubber stamp cases, which were tried, the discriminations were similar and the manufacturers were small.[27] In the Moss case a tendency toward monopoly was found, while in the case of the Krengel Manufacturing Company the finding was limited to a reduction of competition. No information was supplied by the Commission showing how it was possible for each of three competing manufacturers to benefit from a tendency to monopoly by discriminating in price. Neither was information supplied as to why a similar discrimination by a fourth competitor had a more limited effect.

Obscurity in the language and excess in the conclusions of the Commission in cases that are settled by admission answer or by consent does not usually trouble the private bar; attorneys assume that uncontested cases do not set precedents, and that in taking a case to trial they can build a trial record that will preclude extravagant findings or assure reversal on appeal. Where cases that have an element of novelty are typically litigated, it is doubtless true that an occasional uncontested case has no significant effect on the development of the law. It may also be true that the prevalence of uncontested cases with findings dubious in scope and clarity has not affected decisions by the courts in the relatively few cases that have been appealed under the Robinson-Patman Act. But the concepts used by the Commission in applying the law have been visibly affected. The effect has been greatest where obscurity and excess do not have specific legal consequences. Since corrective orders may be applied as readily to a discrimination that jeopardizes competition with particular competitors as to one that does so in the market generally, no legal right is affected by the distinction between the two effects. There has been no incentive for respondents to seek to limit the sweep of the Commission's findings of injury. These findings have been made with so

[26] Docket 5048, *Unity Stamp Co.* The findings in this case set forth the various prices at which Unity sold stamps, but contain no other relevant detail.
[27] Docket 4405, *Samuel H. Moss;* Docket 5516, *Krengel Manufacturing Co.*

little precision that in practice much of the difference between the new and old concepts of injury has disappeared; indeed, in some instances the reader cannot tell what kind of injury is being found. As will appear in later chapters, such confusion can cause difficulties when proposals for further development of policy toward price discrimination are being considered. Moreover, there is a continuing possibility that where cases are not contested, the Commission's lack of precision may extend to matters in which substantive rights are involved, so that the rules applied by the Commission and obeyed by business men who try to stay out of trouble may reach further and include more than the law applied by the courts.

Obscurity and vagueness have crept into some of the Commission's orders as well as into its findings. To draft a satisfactory order is a formidable task: if the order narrowly forbids what the respondent has been doing, minor changes in his conduct may enable him to comply with it without ceasing his offense. If it broadly forbids all acts and practices in which the offense might be concealed, it is likely to prevent harmless and even useful activities; moreover, it is likely to be worded in such a way that its scope is uncertain. To draw an order that neither falls short nor goes too far requires a penetrating analysis of the discrimination and of the setting in which it appeared. Without a trial, there is increased danger that such an analysis will be wanting. The infrequency of contests has encouraged the Commission to make perfunctory orders. Among the worst examples are some that merely paraphrase the language of the statute; some that merely forbid the exact discrimination found; and some that forbid not only price differences that have been found to be potentially harmful but also price differences that appear to be harmless or even desirable. Some of these will be discussed in later chapters.

Scope of Compliance Activity

A striking feature of the Commission's enforcement of the Robinson-Patman Act has been the infrequency of efforts to ascertain the extent of compliance with the Commission's orders and the effectiveness of those orders in accomplishing their intended results. When the law was passed, the Commission maintained no systematic procedures for the review of its orders and assigned no employees to that review. A compliance section was established within the Commission for the first time in 1947, and for some time thereafter its work was limited by the fact that it consisted of only four employees.[28] In every cease and desist order a provision was included requiring the respondent to report within sixty days the steps he had taken to comply with the order; and when such reports were, on their face, unsatisfactory, they sometimes led to immediate discussion of the matter with the respondent. However, in the usual case, relatively vague reports of compliance were accepted, and no subsequent check was made. After the organization of the compliance section, a selective study of compliance was undertaken in particular cases. The scope and frequency of such studies has increased as the growth of the section has made such an increase possible. In August 1954, a systematic survey of compliance with the Commission's orders was begun, covering not only the price discrimination cases but all of the Commission's proceedings. By July 1, 1958, orders in more than 3,000 cases had been examined. Supplementary reports of compliance had been requested in nearly 1,200 cases, and further investigations and negotiations had been undertaken where they appeared to be necessary. More than 1,000 orders were still not surveyed. Work had been completed on all orders issued under the Robinson-Patman Act before 1947.

This burst of activity, however, is recent. During the first 18 years of the Robinson-Patman Act, compliance with orders was reviewed only where charges of noncompliance came to the Commission in the form of complaints. Until the end of 1954 there had been only eight cases in which the Commission had charged and found that a respondent had violated an order under the act.[29] In six of these cases the proceedings resulted in a judicial order enforcing that of the Commission.[30] In a seventh, after the court had affirmed the Commission's order, the respondent was fined $500 in a subsequent proceeding for contempt of court.[31] In an eighth, although the Commission found violation, the

[28] In April 1958, the division had 21 employees, of whom 6 were temporarily assigned to other work.

[29] When little was done to investigate compliance, instances in which noncompliance was found usually resulted in formal proceedings. Present policy is to negotiate informally for modification of the practices of those subject to the order and to accept a modified compliance report without publicity where the negotiations produce a result satisfactory to the Commission.

[30] They were Docket 2986, *Standard Brands;* Docket 4142, *American Crayon Co.;* Docket 4143, *Binney & Smith;* Docket 4240, *David M. Weiss;* Docket 4257, *Jack Herzog;* Docket 5279, *Carl Rubenstein.*

[31] *FTC.* v. *Biddle,* 33 FTC 1796.

offending organization had changed ownership shortly before the Commission's report, and therefore no action was taken.[32] The infrequency of the Commission's review of compliance with its orders during the early years of the Robinson-Patman Act may have contributed to the willingness of respondents to accept those orders without contest.

Under the Robinson-Patman Act, as under all statutes, enforcement proceedings against particular respondents have gone forward singly rather than in co-ordinated groups. This has meant that orders were issued against particular enterprises while some of their competitors were not subjected to similar orders and perhaps not even to similar legal proceedings. Since the purpose of an order is to require compliance with the law, such disparities are, in theory, unimportant; for an enterprise has an obligation to obey a statute whether or not it has been specifically directed to do so. In practice, however, the specific requirements imposed by some orders on respondents are designed to circumscribe action in a way that is not clearly required by law in the case of other enterprises not subject to orders. Moreover, disobedience to a Commission order may result in a judicial order and subsequently in punishment for contempt, whereas no such consequences attach to the failure of one enterprise to follow the apparent implications of a decision in a case against another enterprise.

Accordingly, the selective nature of the Commission's proceedings has created business problems. Because the Robinson-Patman Act has a pervasive importance for daily transactions, these problems have been more acute under this statute than they apparently are under most other parts of the antitrust laws. In the rubber stamp industry, for example, only four out of more than seventy manufacturers in New York City have been subjected to proceedings and orders under the statute, although it is alleged that the pricing practices involved in the cases against these four were similar to those of other enterprises. In the seed inoculant industry, orders cover four out of fourteen producers. Similar situations prevail elsewhere. In one recent case,[33] the respondent vainly requested the Commission to defer applying an order on the ground that competitors were not similarly restricted. On appeal, the Seventh Circuit was impressed by the respondent's argument that it "would be forced out of business if the traditional pricing practices which it now follows were

[32] Docket 4915, *Dentists' Supply Corp.*
[33] Docket 5768, *C. E. Niehoff & Co.*

denied to it while its competitors are free to continue such practices."
Though affirming the Commission's order, the court rejected its argument that the effective date of the order could not be deferred. It characterized this argument as a statement that "we may witness and participate in but not interfere with the economic death of Niehoff, while the
Commission machinery continues to operate toward cease and desist
orders against Niehoff's competitors."[34] It stayed the order to take effect
at such time in the future as the court might direct, indicating that this
time would "depend upon the future course of the Commission's proceedings against Niehoff's competitors." A similar plea was made vainly
on appeal by another respondent who had not raised the question of
delay before the Commission.[35] In February 1958, the Supreme Court
disposed of both cases by ruling that when the Commission had not been
asked to delay its order, an appellate court could not consider doing so,
and when the Commission had refused a request for delay, its action
could not be overturned "in the absence of a patent abuse of discretion."
The court held that the propriety of deferment depended "on a variety
of factors peculiarly within the expert understanding of the Commission."[36]

It seems obvious that law enforcement cannot be effective if correc-
tion of the conduct of one lawbreaker must wait on effective action
against all others in the same competitive field. It seems equally obvious
that those chosen for initial proceedings will inevitably be handicapped
so long as their competitors continue to engage in conduct they can no
longer emulate. Something can be done to prevent law enforcement itself
from becoming a source of haphazard discrimination by co-ordinating
the investigation and disposition of related cases in the same industry.
It is evident that the Commission has sometimes tried to do this. In the
corn products industry, for example, complaints against eight producers
on similar charges were instituted in the same year—1939. Of the eight
cases in which orders have been issued in regard to price discrimination
on automobile parts, six were initiated in two groups of three cases each.
Four cases concerned with seed inoculants were initiated at the same time
and decided by orders issued on the same day. As to spark plugs, one
case was initiated much earlier than the other two; but although two of

[34] 241 F. 2d 37, 41.
[35] Docket 5723, *Moog Industries, Inc.*
[36] *Moog Industries* v. *FTC* and *FTC* v. *C. E. Niehoff & Co.*, Supreme Court
Reports, lawyers ed. (Feb. 17, 1958), pp. 370, 373.

the cases were tried, the orders in all three cases were issued simultaneously.

Sometimes, however, there was no such effort at co-ordination. An example is rubber stamps, regarding which four parallel complaints against small manufacturers located in the same city were issued at dates ranging from December 6, 1940 to November 21, 1947, and four orders were issued at dates ranging from May 1, 1943 to July 15, 1949. Another example is school supplies. Complaints against American Crayon Company and Binney & Smith were issued at the same time on May 24, 1940, and orders against both were issued on December 31, 1940; but in a similar case against American Art Clay Company the complaint was issued on September 17, 1943, and the order, based on an admission answer, on May 12, 1944. Still another example is the series of cases concerned with receipt of brokerage by voluntary chains and co-operatives in the food industry; complaint was issued against United Buyers on August 31, 1937, Modern Marketing Service on May 6, 1939, and Independent Grocers Alliance on April 18, 1946; orders were issued respectively on November 13, 1941, September 8, 1943, and March 7, 1952. Discriminatory effects were inherent in unco-ordinated proceedings such as these.

Efforts to co-ordinate cases are likely to be ineffective where, as in food brokerage, proceedings are numerous, so that simultaneous investigation and trial is not possible, and where respondents differ in their willingness and ability to contest the cases. Although all the corn products cases were started in the same year, the Commission's orders ranged from January 29, 1940 to June 10, 1942, because of the varying degrees of opposition encountered; and in the two cases that were appealed, the decisions of the Supreme Court were not issued until April 23, 1945. Similarly, the varying pace of the trials in the automobile parts cases resulted in orders in the first six cases that ranged from March 17, 1953 to December 27, 1957.

The discriminatory effects of staggered orders can be reduced in such situations by taking care that the first complaints shall be brought against powerful offenders whose offenses are among the most flagrant; that complaints against other offenders are brought, if possible, before the first cases are tried or during their trial; and that the cases against the more powerful concerns are decided before orders are issued against their less powerful competitors. In the yeast industry, the Commission's order against Standard Brands preceded those against National Grain Yeast and Federal Yeast. In the proceedings concerned with industrial trucks, a complaint against Yale and Towne in September 1954, was followed by five other complaints in April and May 1955, before the Yale and Towne case went to trial; no trial took place in the later cases prior to the decision to dismiss the Yale and Towne case in June 1956; and thereafter, in September 1956, the other cases were dismissed for similar reasons. If techniques such as these were consistently used, the problem of discriminatory enforcement would be held to a minimum.

5 / Brokerage to Corporate Chains and Buying Groups

THE SECTION of the Robinson-Patman Act that has to do with the payment of brokerage is the only one the meaning of which has been adequately tested by litigation. Eight of the orders of the Federal Trade Commission under this section were appealed to the courts. In the resulting decisions, judicial interpretation of this part of the law became clear.

One question raised had to do with the relation of the brokerage provision to the rest of the Robinson-Patman Act. In early cases it was urged that the prohibition of brokerage payments appears as one of a set of provisions designed to prevent price discrimination which is injurious to competition and that, therefore, the prohibition applies only when such discrimination can be found and when the respondent cannot establish the defenses available to him in a price discrimination case. In the proceeding against the Great Atlantic & Pacific Tea Company,[1] the FTC and the court gave some support to this view, for the Commission specifically found that the payment of discounts in lieu of brokerage to A. & P. tended to injure competition. In 1939 the Third Circuit affirmed this finding. Nevertheless, in reviewing the case, the judges of the Third Circuit held that the act "expresses an absolute prohibition of the payment of brokerage or compensation in lieu thereof to the buyer upon the buyer's own purchases." The court also held that the Commission was right in rejecting the claim of A. & P. that the allowance it received merely reflected the seller's saving of brokerage expense. To accept a cost defense in a brokerage case, said the court, would be to frustrate the congressional intent.[2]

Similarly, in the Biddle case in 1938 the Second Circuit rejected the

---

[1] Docket 3031, *The Great Atlantic & Pacific Tea Co.* References to decisions by the Federal Trade Commission and the courts appear opposite each case in the list of cases in App. A.

[2] 106 F. 2d 667, 673-74.

argument that the brokerage section should be construed in the light of the price-discrimination section.[3] In the Oliver case, decided in 1939, the Fourth Circuit said that the practices specified in Section 2(c) of the Robinson-Patman Act, as well as in Sections 2(d) and 2(e), were "forbidden because of their tendency to lessen competition and create monopoly, without regard to their effect in a particular case."[4] The court saw no reason to read into these sections the limitations contained in the parts of the act that dealt broadly with price discrimination. In the Webb-Crawford case, decided in 1940, the Fifth Circuit held that the effect on competition need not be considered in adjudicating an alleged violation of the brokerage provision. "The Congress considered the effect on commerce of the things named in subsection (c), and absolutely prohibited them. The Trade Commission is not to enter on any inquiry about their evil effect, nor whether a proceeding would be in the public interest. Its duty is to enforce the prohibition."[5] In the Southgate case, decided in 1945, the Fourth Circuit took a similar position. Southgate had argued that its receipt of brokerage on goods that it bought involved no discrimination, since the wholesalers to whom it sold these goods paid what they would have paid if they had bought from a manufacturer through Southgate as a broker. Said the court, "The answer is that price discrimination . . . is not necessary to a violation of Section 2(c), quoted above, which specifically forbids the payment of brokerage by the seller to the buyer or the buyer's agent."[6]

Regarded as a self-contained prohibition, the brokerage provision presented a major problem of interpretation in its language in regard to services rendered. To pay or receive brokerage was unlawful.

> . . . except for services rendered in connection with the sale or purchase of goods, wares, or merchandise, either to the other party to such transaction or to an agent, representative, or other intermediary therein, where such intermediary is acting in fact for or in behalf, or is subject to the direct or indirect control, of any party to such transaction other than the person by whom such compensation is so granted or paid.[7]

Respondents in the early brokerage cases interpreted this language to mean that if a buyer or a buyer's agent rendered services to the seller, a

[3] *Biddle Purchasing Co.*, 96 F. 2d 687.
[4] *Oliver Brothers, Inc.*, 102 F. 2d 763, 767.
[5] *The Webb-Crawford Co.*, 109 F. 2d 268, 269.
[6] *Southgate Brokerage Co., Inc.*, 150 F. 2d 607, 609.
[7] 49 Stat. 1527.

payment of brokerage for these services was to be exempt. Accordingly, they sought to prove that the payments they paid or received were compensation for services.

This contention was first offered to a court in the Biddle case in 1938. Biddle sold a market-information service to buyers, placed buyers' orders with sellers, collected brokerage from the sellers, and credited this brokerage to its buyer customers as an offset to the charges for the information service. It argued that it rendered service to both sellers and buyers and therefore had a right to collect compensation from both. The court rejected the argument on the ground that Biddle transmitted to the buyer what was received from the seller, took its own compensation entirely from the buyer, and so could not be regarded as a seller's agent or as the recipient of the seller's brokerage payments.

In the A. & P. case, likewise decided in 1938, A. & P. offered voluminous evidence designed to show that its field buyers furnished services to sellers, including market information, advice on improvement of quality and advice on size of containers, information on the routing of shipments, and attempts to move surplus merchandise and thereby relieve gluts in the market. Rejecting this evidence, the court said,

> The agent cannot serve two masters, simultaneously rendering services in an arm's-length transaction to both. . . . The record clearly requires the conclusion that the field buying agents of the petitioner were the agents of the petitioner and that such services as were rendered by them to sellers were purely incidental to such representative capacity. For such incidental services the petitioner may not be compensated.[8]

In the Oliver case, decided in 1939, the Fourth Circuit took a similar view. Oliver conducted a market-information service similar to Biddle's. As in the Biddle case, the court held that the payments made to Oliver were not for services rendered because they were eventually received by the buyers, not retained by Oliver. It added that the benefit to the sellers was incidental to the service rendered by Oliver to the buyers and was not the result of a service undertaken for the benefit of the sellers. But, even if Oliver had rendered service to the sellers, said the court, this would not have changed matters, for to regard Oliver as the seller's broker would also be to regard Oliver's payments of brokerage to the buyer as payments on behalf of his principal. "We may assume that under the section

[8] 106 F. 2d 667, 674-75.

it is permissible for a broker to render services to both buyer and seller and to receive from both compensation for the services rendered; but this is a very different thing from the buyer himself receiving the compensation."[9]

The implication in the Biddle and Oliver cases that the buyer's agent might be capable of rendering sales services to a seller for which he might legally be compensated was substantially weakened in the following year by decisions in the Webb-Crawford and Quality Bakers cases. Webb-Crawford was a wholesale grocery company. The dominant personalities in it were engaged as partners in a brokerage undertaking with Webb-Crawford as a principal customer. They contended that in sales to Webb-Crawford they performed for sellers the same brokerage functions as in sales to other customers and that their brokerage income was retained by the partners, not transmitted to Webb-Crawford. In sustaining the Commission's order in 1940, the Fifth Circuit accepted the reality of the brokerage services rendered by the partnership.

> . . . Nor do we see that the brokers failed to render selling service to the sellers. . . . What in our opinion is fatally important is that one of the brokers, E. L. Wier, as vice-president of the Webb-Crawford Company, does all its buying. He acts as the representative of the buyer; and, as one of the brokers, receives one-fourth of the commission paid by the seller. Ed D. Wier, who sells the purchased goods for the Webb-Crawford Company, and must have a voice in determining what shall be bought, gets a fourth of the commission; and Carter W. Daniel, who checks the bills and pays them, gets the remainder of the commission. Without reflecting on the faithfulness or honesty of anyone here concerned, it is evident that the tendency and general results are precisely the same as if the Webb-Crawford Company, the buyer, had gotten the commissions. And the law equally condemns both things. . . . Sellers who sell to the Webb-Crawford Company cannot pay brokers' commissions to these men, who, in fact, act for and represent the buyer in making the purchases. The interposition of C. R. Daniel as manager for the brokers does not change the fact that the commissions are paid to his principals who are the officers and representatives of the buyer.[10]

In thus holding that representatives of the buyer cannot receive brokerage payments even when they render true brokerage services to the seller, the court was troubled by the words, "except for services ren-

[9] 102 F. 2d 763, 770.
[10] 268 F. 2d 268, 270.

dered," that appeared in the statute. It disposed of them by changing the punctuation found in the law. It asked whether these words "qualify the whole subsection, so that any person having any relations whatsoever to the opposite party to a commercial sale can take a commission, provided he renders service." It answered,

> Such a construction would largely destroy the statute, and nullify its plain intent. The words can, by transferring a comma, be attached to those immediately preceding: "or any allowance or discount in lieu thereof, except for services rendered." The statute would then prohibit "a commission, brokerage, or other compensation, or any allowance or discount in lieu thereof except for services rendered, in connection with the sale or purchase, etc." The punctuation as published is confusing. We think the true meaning is better indicated by taking the comma out after "thereof," and inserting it after "rendered." Commas are not to be suffered to defeat the legislative meaning.[11]

In the same year the First Circuit took a similar line in the Quality Bakers case. Quality was a co-operative association of bakery companies which collected brokerage from sellers on purchases made through it by its members. The court said:

> Undoubtedly the sellers received valuable benefits and advantages from the business given them by the Service Company other than the ordinary profits on the sales. For instance, they were saved the expense incident to obtaining the business and dealing separately with numerous customers taking a large amount of merchandise. In that way and to that extent the Service Company rendered services and had contractual relationship with the sellers. For those benefits the sellers were willing to pay and did pay. . . . The petitioners contend that by the language in paragraph (c) above quoted, reading "except for services rendered in connection with the sale or purchase of goods," the Congress recognizes that a buyer, or his agent, may perform services for the seller in connection with the transaction for which the seller may pay and the buyer or his agent receive compensation by way of a brokerage fee or commission on the sale. We do not take such a view of the paragraph. The construction contended for makes much of its language meaningless; it does violence to the purpose of the Act and has been explicit rejected in other circuits. It is plain enough that the paragraph, taken as a whole, is framed to prohibit the payment of brokerage in any guise by one party to the other, or the other's agent, at the same time expressly recognizing and saving the right of either party to pay

[11] *Ibid.*

his own agent for services rendered in connection with the sale or purchase. . . . Even if the Service Company here renders services to the sellers under agreement to do so, as claimed by petitioners, it cannot lawfully collect brokerage fees from the sellers since it is acting as agent for the purchasers.[12]

By 1945, when the Southgate case was decided on appeal by the Fourth Circuit, the view that control by the buyer made the question of service to the seller irrelevant had become firmly established. In this case, the FTC had excluded evidence offered by Southgate as to the services that it rendered to sellers in transactions in which Southgate took title to some of the sellers' merchandise while acting as the sellers' broker in other transactions. The court held that the evidence was properly excluded, saying: "It is perfectly clear that this provision forbids the payment of brokerage on a sale or purchase of goods to the other party to the transaction."[13] The court added that it was not impressed by Southgate's argument as to services, since the services rendered were services to itself. In the same year the Seventh Circuit sustained on appeal the Commission's finding that a brokerage establishment, Modern Marketing Service, though owned by certain individuals, was in fact controlled by Red and White, an association of wholesalers. On this ground the court found unlawful the receipt of brokerage by Modern Marketing on sales made to the members of Red and White. The court said:

We assume, in fact, we think the proof shows, that such services were genuine and of benefit to such sellers. . . . We are of the view that where such relationship exists it is immaterial whether the services rendered the seller were genuine or fictitious and whether they were incidental or otherwise. Even good faith on the part of both the broker and the seller cannot be utilized to escape the condemnation of the provision.[14]

The same court reiterated this view in 1953 in the case of Independent Grocers Alliance, holding that "intermediaries acting in behalf or under the control of buyers may not receive brokerage payments upon the purchases of such buyers."[15]
In the Southgate case the problem regarding the bearing of brokerage service on the legality of brokerage payments was complicated by South-

[12] *Quality Bakers of America,* 114 F. 2d 393, 398-99.
[13] 150 F. 2d 607, 609.
[14] *Modern Marketing Service, Inc.,* 149 F. 2d 970, 978.
[15] *Independent Grocers Alliance Distributing Co.,* 203 F. 2d 941, 945.

gate's effort to relate the brokerage provision to Section 2(d) of the Robinson-Patman Act. This section makes it unlawful to pay anything of value to a customer "for any services or facilities furnished by or through such customer in connection with the . . . sale or offering for sale of any products" of the person making the payment "unless such payment or consideration is available on proportionally equal terms to all other customers competing in the distribution of such products."[16] Southgate argued that this section recognizes the reality of service by a buyer to a seller and the legitimacy of a seller's payment for such service; and that, in the light of this section, payments of brokerage by a seller to a buyer must be appraised under Section 2(c) as to whether or not services are actually rendered and under Section 2(d) as to whether or not those services are proportionately available to all competing customers. In rejecting this argument, the court treated Section 2(d) as forbidding discrimination on services such as advertising actually rendered by buyers and denied the reality of the services about which Southgate was arguing, "For sellers to pay purchasers for purchasing, warehousing, or reselling the goods purchased is to pay them for doing their own work and is a mere gratuity."[17]

In the Quality Bakers case, Quality argued that its transmission of brokerage to its members was exempt from the provisions of the brokerage section of the act, because Section 4 of the same act "specifically permits a co-operative organization, such as this, to return to its members the whole or any part of the net earnings or surplus resulting from its operations in proportion to their purchases from, to, or through the association."[18] The court found that the exemption thus accorded to co-operatives does not authorize them to receive brokerage under the circumstances specified in the brokerage provision.[19]

Thus the First, Second, Third, Fourth, Fifth, and Seventh Circuits have all agreed in rejecting the claim that a brokerage payment to a buyer or his agent is justified by services rendered to the seller. The claim was made and rejected in cases involving the field agents of a large buyer, purchases for his own account by a broker, sales by a broker to a customer controlled by the same individuals as those in the brokerage house,

---

[16] 49 Stat. 1527.

[17] 150 F. 2d 607, 611.

[18] U.S. Circuit Court of Appeals for the First Circuit, October Term, 1939, *Record* (Proceedings before the FTC), p. 44.

[19] 114 F. 2d 393, 400.

payments to a market-information service on purchases made by its customers (with the payments credited to the customers), payments to a co-operative association on purchases by its members, and payments to a brokerage concern controlled by a trade association on purchases by members of that association. Although the earlier cases show some diversity in the grounds on which the brokerage arrangements were held to be unlawful, the later ones consistently applied one simple test—whether or not the recipient of the payment was on the side of the transaction giving rise to the payment or was controlled by someone on the other side thereof.

The breadth of application given to the brokerage provision by the interpretations that have been summarized above was further enlarged by the willingness of the Commission and the courts to disregard corporate forms and base decisions on underlying identities of interest. In the Webb-Crawford case, the facts were that three individuals owned 95 per cent of the stock of the Webb-Crawford Company and were the company's principal officers. As partners, these same persons operated a brokerage enterprise, the management of which was entrusted to the brother of one of them, who was himself a small stockholder in the Webb-Crawford Company. The partners in the brokerage enterprise retained its profits, though from time to time they individually extended loans to Webb-Crawford. The FTC found that the partnership was controlled by Webb-Crawford and that the loans constituted transmission of brokerage to Webb-Crawford. The court overruled the Commission on both points. It held that the partners could and did control the corporation and that Webb-Crawford did not get any of the brokerage fees. Nevertheless, because of the dual functions and dual interests of the controlling individuals, it found that the results were "precisely the same as if the Webb-Crawford Company, the buyer, had gotten the commissions," and that the partners in fact acted for and represented the buyer in making purchases.[20]

With this judicial precedent, the FTC has consistently disregarded the corporate fiction when there is an underlying identity of interest between purchaser and intermediary. Thus, in the Mississippi Sales case,[21] it issued an order against a brokerage company and a jobber, because the former received brokerage commissions on sales to the latter and because the two corporations were almost wholly owned by the same individual.

[20] 109 F. 2d 269, 270.
[21] Docket 3511, *Mississippi Sales Co., Inc.*

Similarly, in the case against Thomas Page Mill,[22] it ordered a seller to cease paying brokerage to a brokerage enterprise on sales to a wholesale grocery company on the ground that two of the three partners in the brokerage concern owned most of the stock in the wholesale company and the third was an executive of the wholesale company. The Commission's findings included the addition that there was no evidence that the seller knew of the connection between the broker and the wholesaler.

The brokerage provision, as thus interpreted, is a complete bar to any payment of brokerage by a party on one side of a transaction to a party on the other side.[23] Moreover, the provision explicitly covers not only the brokers' commissions but also "any allowance or discount in lieu thereof." Through this language, price concessions and payments that might otherwise be subject to the general law of price discrimination contained in Section 2(a), or to the law applicable to advertising allowances and other similar payments contained in Section 2(d), are, instead, subject to the brokerage provision if these concessions or payments are found to be in lieu of brokerage. The inevitable result of the language is to apply different rules to price concessions and payments that are identical in amount and in economic effect.[24]

If, for example, a seller grants a buyer a quantity discount of 5 per cent on purchases in excess of 1,000 units, the legality of this discount will ordinarily be determined under the provisions of Sections 2(a), (b), and (f) of the act. The seller's grant of the discount will be unlawful provided (1) the discount is discriminatory, (2) its effects may be injurious to competition, (3) the seller fails to show that the grant is justified by a difference in his cost, and (4) there is no proof that the concession was made in good faith to meet the equally low price of a competitor.[25] The buyer's receipt of the discount will be unlawful if the concession is one that the seller could not lawfully grant and if the buyer knowingly induced or received it. If, however, the discount was given "in lieu of

[22] Docket 4286, *The Thomas Page Mill Co., Inc.*

[23] *Cf. Report of the Attorney General's National Committee to Study the Antitrust Laws* (March 31, 1955), pp. 188-89.

[24] The Attorney General's Committee thought that "the present disparity in the statutory consequences which attach to economically equivalent business practices . . . facilitates manipulation and fosters confusion. . . . Such legal incongruities, we believe, frustrate equally the Commission's legitimate enforcement objectives and businessmen's good faith attempts to comply." *Ibid.*, pp. 191-92.

[25] There are other provisos on which a case less frequently turns; for example, that the goods sold to buyers who are differently treated be of like grade and quality.

brokerage," it is automatically unlawful without regard to any of the conditions that have been listed.[26] There is no relevance in a showing that it works no competitive injury,[27] that it is cost-justified,[28] or that it was made in good faith to meet a competitor's equally low price. Buyer and seller alike have violated the statute if the discount has been substituted for a brokerage payment.

Similarly, if a seller makes an advertising allowance to a customer, the legality of that allowance will ordinarily be determined by the provisions of Section 2(d), and the allowance will be unlawful if it is not available on proportionally equal terms to other customers. If, however, the allowance is made in lieu of brokerage, no inquiry need be made as to whether similar allowances are available to other customers on proportionally equal terms.[29] Instead, the allowance will be found

[26] A price concession to a direct buyer, made by a seller who sells to others through brokers, is suspect. For example, in a proceeding settled by consent (Docket 6366, *Union Malleable Manufacturing Co.*), the Commission's complaint alleged that the seller gave Sears Roebuck a discount not available to customers who bought through brokers and that the lower price reflected "all or a portion" of the brokerage. However, in Docket 6386, *Maine Fish Co.*, the Commission dismissed a complaint of this type on the ground that the price differences were not "arithmetically commensurate with the pattern of brokerage." (Opinion of the Commission, p. 3.) In Docket 5989, *Fruitvale Canning Co.*, the Commission proceeded against a seller who had made concessions to large direct buyers while selling to others through brokers; but the concessions exceeded the amount of the brokerage, and the proceeding was brought under Sec. 2(a) instead of 2(c).

[27] In Docket 6230, *Rocky Mountain Wholesale Co.*, the total brokerage payment involved in the case was $34.76. The hearing examiner rejected the argument that no order was appropriate as to so small a matter, holding, "It is the character of the act charged and admitted which the law denounces, not the extent thereof, be it small or great."

[28] One attorney with whom the writer has talked believes that, although cost differences do not make lawful a discount granted in lieu of brokerage, evidence that such differences exist is relevant to a decision whether or not the discount is to be regarded as in lieu of brokerage. He thinks that for this reason data about cost may be offered in a proceeding in which the Commission challenges a discount under the brokerage provision, and may, if adequate, acquit the respondent of the charge. If his opinion is correct, the practical effect is the same as if the cost defense were explicitly allowed, except that the costs offered in justification could not include the savings from avoiding payment of a broker's fee. However, the point has not been tested before the Commission or in the courts.

[29] The formal distinction between an allowance in lieu of brokerage and an advertising allowance is that the former applies to the buyer's purchase from the seller, the latter to the buyer's resale of what he has purchased. In practice, however, a lump-sum payment to a buyer may sometimes be interpreted as either the one or the other type of payment or both. (See the discussion of the Carpel case, pp. 179-80). Moreover, an advertising allowance may be interpreted as a trans-

to be unlawful as soon as its substitution for a brokerage payment has been demonstrated.

The case against the Great Atlantic & Pacific Tea Company illustrates both the reason for the congressional effort to cope with allowances that replace brokerage and the awkwardness of the legal standard that has emerged from this effort.

Before the effective date of the Robinson-Patman Act, June 19, 1936, A. & P. had regularly asked for and obtained brokerage commissions on the ground that its field buying agents eliminated the need for the use of brokers by its suppliers. The amount paid to A. & P. was usually the same that the seller paid to his ordinary brokers. After the effective date of the act, A. & P. instructed its field buying agents to cease receiving brokerage and instead (1) to buy for net prices reduced below the seller's price to other customers or the general market price by amounts equivalent to the former brokerage payments, or (2) to buy under quantity-discount agreements providing for discounts equal to the brokerage formerly paid, or (3) to have the brokerage placed in escrow until their legality under the act could be determined. Each of these methods of purchasing was actually used by A. & P.'s field buyers thereafter. The Commission found that, "with extremely few exceptions, in no wise affecting the facts in this matter," A. & P. was the only customer to whom suppliers sold in these ways, and that under the quantity-discount agreements A. & P. received brokerage whether or not the quantity-buying provisions of the contracts were fulfilled. It is obvious that the congressional intent to stop the payment of brokerage commissions to large chains like A. & P. would have been thwarted if the prohibition of the statute had turned on the question whether the payments made were described as brokers' commissions or were given some other name.

It is also obvious, that the concessions received by A. & P. in the form of net prices or quantity discounts were condemned in accord with standards wholly different from those that would have been applied if these concessions had not been preceded by concessions described as brokerage. Although the court and the Commission agreed in finding that the concessions received by A. & P. injured competition, this finding was not essential to the case, since a payment in lieu of brokerage by a seller to a buyer was held to be absolutely prohibited. Moreover, the

mission of brokerage because the concern paying the allowance has received brokerage. See the discussion of the Modern Marketing and United Buyers cases, pp. 103, 120-21.

Commission had found that the concessions made to A. & P. consisted of the savings on brokerage services, and the court held that if the cost defense was to be read into the brokerage provision, "then it is obvious that the petitioner is entitled to the relief it seeks from this court. . . . In other words, if the allowances and discounts in the case at bar be deemed to be permissible by reason of the cost-differential provisos of paragraph (a), it is clear that the petitioner is entitled to have the cease and desist order of the Commission set aside."[30] Thus the effect of the case was to forbid A. & P. to receive price concessions that were justified by a saving in cost because that saving happened to be a brokerage commission.

In the Modern Marketing case, the court sustained the Commission's findings that the brokerage fees collected by Modern Marketing were distributed to and accepted by the trade association, Red and White, and its member wholesalers. Most of what was distributed took the form of advertising allowances for point of sale advertising of the Red and White brands, which the trade association had licensed to Modern Marketing for a $30,000 annual payment. In this case, the condemnation of Modern Marketing depended on the finding that it was controlled by Red and White, but the condemnation of Red and White and the member wholesalers depended on the finding that they received brokerage. As recipients of advertising allowances, they would not have been subject to the prohibitions of Section 2(d) of the act, which applies only to payment by the seller and not to receipt by the customer. They were in violation in the Modern Marketing case because the allowances were held to be payments in lieu of brokerage. Similarly, as the donor of an advertising allowance, Modern Marketing itself would have been in violation under Section 2(d) only if it had failed to make the allowance available on proportionally equal terms. It was in violation in the actual case because it was transmitting an allowance in lieu of brokerage, regardless of the terms on which the allowance was available to the various customers involved.[31]

Frequency of Brokerage Cases

The interpretations of the brokerage provision that have been discussed above have simplified the task of the FTC in coping with bro-

[30] 106 F. 2d 667, 676.
[31] 149 F. 2d 970.

kerage problems. The Commission's task in proving a violation is merely to show that a payment of brokerage was made and that the parties between whom it passed were on opposite sides of the sales transaction. Even when the problem involves allowances in lieu of brokerage, the burden of proof is thought to be increased only by a need to show that the challenged allowance has superseded, or has otherwise been regarded as the equivalent of, a brokerage payment. When such relatively simple facts can be demonstrated, the respondent has no basis for a successful defense.

Brokerage cases are, therefore, economical of time and effort as compared with other cases. Violations can be established with certainty. Few respondents have found it worthwhile to present a defense. Even the cursory investigation required to establish the limited facts needed to prove violation is likely to produce evidence of other violations; for a single broker usually deals with several sellers and buyers, a single seller usually sells through several brokers, and a single buyer usually purchases from several sources. The simplicity of the cases and their interlaced character have encouraged the Commission to pursue them actively; and the vigilance of organized food brokers has brought many cases to the Commission's attention and made it difficult to disregard the complaints.[32]

Of the 311 cease and desist orders issued between June 19, 1936 and December 31, 1957 by the Commission, 148 were concerned with violations of the brokerage provision, and in all but three of these cases the brokerage provision alone was involved.

Since the prohibitions regarding brokerage apply equally to the seller, the intermediary agent, and the buyer, all parties to an illegal payment of brokerage are equally in violation. Buyer and seller violate the law jointly in every case. If an intermediary participates in the transaction, he, too, is a violator. In practice, however, the Commission's brokerage cases have seldom been brought against all who participated in an illegal transaction. Sometimes the proceeding has involved only the seller who made the payment, sometimes only the buyer who received it, and in a few instances only the intermediary who received it or passed it on. Fifty-two of the 148 orders concerned with unlawful brokerage cover

[32] See, for example, criticism of the Commission for delay in the IGA case by Watson Rogers, President of the National Food Brokers Association, in testimony in *Functional Operation of the Federal Trade Commission,* Hearings before the House Select Committee on Small Business, 81 Cong. 2 sess., p. 24.

only those making the payment. Sixty-four cover only the recipients—buyers, buyers' agents, or both. In only 32 instances does the order apply to both the receipt and the payment.[33] The Commission's selection of respondents appears to have been based on administrative convenience. Where diverse payments were made to a single recipient, as in the A. & P. case, proceedings were brought against the buyer rather than the numerous sellers. Where payments from various sellers converged on an intermediary before being transmitted to various buyers, proceedings were brought against the intermediary, with a few of the buyers and sellers sometimes included, as in the cases against Quality Bakers and Biddle. In instances in which there was no evident convergence, the focus of the case appears to have developed accidentally from the way in which the facts were obtained. Thus, in the case against Thomas Page Mill, the Commission's findings and the underlying stipulation of facts indicate clearly that the intermediary which received brokerage was controlled by the buyer, but that there was no evidence that the seller had knowledge of this fact. Nevertheless, the case was brought against the seller and the order covers him alone.

Types of Brokerage Cases

Since the brokerage provision forbids a particular practice without regard to its effect on competition or to the size and power of those participating therein, it has necessarily been applied to a wide range of situations, some of which are unrelated to the issues that gave rise to the Robinson-Patman Act. The diversity of the relationships that have been held to be illegal appears in the following classification:[34]

1. Brokerage, or allowance in lieu thereof, given direct to the buyer
   a. Paid or allowed by the seller
      (1) As a price concession to a large buyer
      (2) As an allowance to a buying broker
      (3) To anyone buying direct

[33] In 23 of the cases sellers and buyers who dealt with one another directly or through an intermediary are jointly covered by the order, the intermediary being also covered where appropriate. In the nine remaining cases the respondents are subject to orders in both their buying and selling activities.

[34] For this classification the writer is indebted to Cyrus Austin of the New York bar, member of the advisory committee for this study.

   b. Broker's fee split by a seller's broker
      (1) In particular instances, to get business
      (2) As a general practice, to anyone buying direct, by field
          brokers who generally use sub-brokers
2. Brokerage, or the equivalent, allowed to an intermediary
   a. Owned or controlled by the buyer, or by the buyer's officials or
      stockholders
      (1) A true broker, but selling substantial amounts to a buyer
          who is the source of ownership or control
      (2) A false front, set up by a single buyer or a small group to
          collect brokerage
          (a) By deceiving the seller
          (b) By concealing the relationship from enforcers of the law
      (3) Representing a large group and functioning openly
          (a) As a cooperative
          (b) As a group-buying organization
              (aa) Serving as a buying intermediary and passing
                   brokerage to buyers in price reductions, money,
                   or services
              (bb) Performing no buying service, but getting fees for
                   promotion (either a flat fee or based on sales to
                   members)
              (cc) Owning trademarks that are affixed to the goods
                   sold by members
   b. Independent concern acting as a buyer's agent
      (1) A brokerage enterprise
          (a) Passing brokerage, or part of it, to the buyer
          (b) Retaining brokerage, but getting it from the seller rather
              than the buyer
      (2) A market-information service which buys for its customers,
          passing brokerage to them

For purposes of the ensuing discussion, a less elaborate classification
will be used. We shall consider successively (1) brokerage concessions
to the large buyer (equivalent to 1.a.(1) of the previous classification);
(2) brokerage payments to trade associations and co-operatives (equivalent to 2.a.(3) of the previous classification); (3) brokerage payments to
market-information services (equivalent to 2.b.(2) of the previous classification); (4) brokerage payments to brokers on sales to a buyer affiliated
with the broker (equivalent to 2.a.(1) and (2) of the previous classification); (5) brokerage payments to so-called buying brokers (equivalent to
1.a.(2) of the previous classification); (6) brokerage payments to so-

called resident buyers (equivalent to 2.b.(1)(b) of the previous classification). This abbreviated classification is designed to throw light on the differing economic situations in which the brokerage provision has been applied, rather than on the formal differences in the relationship of the parties to one another, which are the bases of the more elaborate classification. It omits cases in which the seller's broker makes sporadic price concessions to get business (equivalent to 1.b.(1) of the previous classification); cases in which the seller or the seller's broker allows brokerage generally to anyone buying direct (equivalent to 1.a.(3) and 1.b.(2) of the previous classification); and cases in which an independent broker, acting as the buyer's agent, collects brokerage from the seller and passes it on to the buyer (equivalent to 2.b.(1)(a) of the previous classification). These cases appear to be relatively rare, and none of them is included in the group of brokerage cases that has been specifically studied during this inquiry. The issues raised by the sporadic price concessions made by sellers' brokers have to do with price discriminations similar to those involved in price concessions to large buyers, except that the power of the buyer is probably less evident. The issues raised by the case of the independent broker who acts as buyers' agent and transmits brokerage to the buyer are similar to those raised by the market-information service that does the same thing. Only the type of case in which the seller or his broker follows a general practice of granting brokerage to all who buy direct presents a situation appreciably different from those that have been specifically studied. It is noteworthy that in this instance the seller (or his broker) has adopted a pricing system under which he obtains a uniform realization from all his sales by giving the benefit of the brokerage commission wherever he does not have to pay it. It is ironical that the law treats as discrimination this avoidance of variation in net receipts from different buyers. However, the practice is rare and the issue raised by it is, therefore, relatively unimportant.

Allowances to Powerful Buyers

Of the 26 brokerage cases that have been specifically studied, 3 have had to do with the type of allowance to powerful buyers that was stated by the Congress to be the basis for the inclusion of the brokerage provision in the act. Two of these may be treated as a single case, since they had to do respectively with the Great Atlantic & Pacific Tea Company and its wholly owned subsidiary, Atlantic Commission Company.[35] Another case, against Atlas Supply Company, involved brokerage allowances received by a joint buying organization established by five large petroleum companies.[36] In no other brokerage case in which the Commission has issued an order has one of the large national chains or one of the largest corporate buyers been the focus of attention.[37]

The A. & P. case was a successful use of the brokerage provision against price concessions masquerading as brokerage.[38] The Commission's order prohibited purchase at net prices reflecting the deduction of brokerage in whole or in part; accepting quantity discounts representing brokerage in whole or in part; accepting prices, allowances, or discounts representing brokerage savings effected by sellers; and accepting allowances or discounts in any form in lieu of brokerage.

After the Commission's order had been sustained by the circuit court and the Supreme Court had denied certiorari, A. & P. held meetings of its buyers to make sure that they understood the order and issued instructions regarding observance thereof. It gave wide circulation within the company to its report to the Commission setting forth the way in which it was complying with the order. It required its buyers to file written acknowledgment that they understood and would follow a letter of instructions which was also circulated. Subsequently, in a manual on the Robinson-Patman Act for use by its buyers and officers, it explained the program of compliance and illustrated the application thereof to specific situations. It sent a letter to all suppliers asking for their assurance that they would not "offer or give any discount or allowance in lieu of brokerage or any price discount, allowance, payment, or other conces-

---

[35] Docket 3344, *Atlantic Commission Co.*

[36] Docket 5794, *Atlas Supply Co.*

[37] Since most of the cases against small sellers and small brokers were settled summarily with minimal findings, it is often impossible to determine whether or not they involved any substantial payment of brokerage to powerful buyers. The respondents in the uncontested cases were mostly individuals and small corporations, with occasionally a larger concern such as Booth Fisheries, Clover Farms, or Columbia River Packing. All of the cases that were tried prior to Dec. 31, 1957, are discussed in this chapter except Docket 6255, *Florida Citrus Exchange*, and Docket 6484, *Henry Broch & Co.* The first of these had to do with brokerage paid to pool-car buyers; the second, with brokerage to a canner of moderate size (J. M. Smucker Co.).

[38] Presumably, however, the concessions would have been lawful under the standards of Sec. 2(f) of the Robinson-Patman Act. See below, Chap. 15.

sion which reflects in whole or in part any brokerage or brokerage savings or which otherwise violates the Robinson-Patman Act."[39]

However, A. & P. did not immediately cease its efforts to obtain buying advantages. A part of the manual for its buyers and officers set forth ways of obtaining low prices without violating the law. Among these were (a) buying the entire output of a seller's plant or all of his output of a particular commodity or grade of commodity; (b) having the seller make for A. & P. goods of substantially different grade or quality from those he sells to others; (c) buying for private branding at a price below that of the manufacturer's brand; (d) buying from sellers who use salesmen instead of brokers.[40] In subsequent litigation under the Sherman Act, which ended in conviction in a criminal case and a consent decree in a civil case, one of the contentions of the government was that A. & P. gave preference to suppliers who used no brokers; and in the consent decree a provision was included prohibiting A. & P. from requiring its suppliers not to use brokers.[41] However, A. & P. has consistently denied that it had any such policy.

In 1946 A. & P. adopted a program by which its legal department would review all offers of "advertising and promotional allowances, quantity discounts, cost-savings allowances, and similar arrangements." This review was designed to replace the Robinson-Patman manual that had been previously used. The company continued through 1946 to include on its purchase order forms a statement by which the supplier assured A. & P. that he was not making any allowance in lieu of brokerage. In a compliance statement filed July 15, 1956, A. & P. assured the Commission: "The Company does not solicit any allowances or discounts by suppliers and does not accept any offerings made by suppliers when there is evidence that they are not freely made to other customers. The company has discontinued the use of its own contract forms for advertising and promotional allowances, quantity discounts, cost-savings allowances and the like."

In September 1946, A. & P. was convicted of violation of the Sherman Act in a case in which much of the evidence concerned its buying prac-

---

[39] Compliance Report by A. & P., June 6, 1940.

[40] See American Institute of Food Distribution, *Robinson-Patman Guide Book* (1940), pp. 29, 33, 35, 59-60. See also Carl H. Fulda, *Food Distribution in the United States: The Struggle Between Independents and Chains,* Association of American Law Schools (1951) (mimeo.), pp. 91-92.

[41] CCH, *Trade Cases 1954,* par. 67658.

tices.[42] In February 1949, this conviction was sustained on appeal.[43] In 1954 a consent order was entered in a companion civil case.[44]

The combined effect of these cases and the proceeding by the Federal Trade Commision appears to have been a substantial change in the buying practices of the company. In interviews for the present study with various concerns that supply food to A. & P., there was agreement that the company now takes care to avoid receipt of special allowances. A representative comment by a supplier is that A. & P. is "very anxious that our prices and terms to them are the same as to any other buyer of like quality, quantity, market, and time."

In ceasing to press for special concessions, A. & P. has continued to rely chiefly on direct buying through field agents. Without allowances in lieu of brokerage, this appears to be more expensive than purchase through brokers; but it permits a closer check on the quality of what is bought. However, purchases are made through brokers to a minor degree. Some suppliers say that they sell to A. & P. entirely through brokers, others that they do so in large part. Some say that A. & P. now buys in small quantities, operates on a budget system, and expects immediate delivery. One supplier indicates that this practice on the part of A. & P. and other chains has made it necessary for him to carry inventories in public warehouses. Another attributes to this buying practice his decision to establish a large number of his own warehouses throughout the country.

The suppliers also indicate that, since the case, A. & P. and other chains have increased their emphasis on integrated manufacturing operations and on the sale of private-label merchandise. A. & P., however, has informed the writer that whereas its own products furnished 15.5 per cent of its total sales in 1940, the percentage in 1958 had fallen to approximately 11. It also states that although it does not keep records

[42] 67 F. Supp. 626. The facts of the case are admirably summarized in Fulda, *Food Distribution in the United States*, pp. 124-73. In deciding the case, Judge Lindley expressed doubt that the Robinson-Patman Act was necessary: "I have thought that the Sherman Act, properly interpreted and administered, would have remedied all the ills meant to be cured."

[43] 173 F. 2d 79.

[44] CCH, *Trade Cases 1954*, par. 67658. The decree in this case required dissolution of Atlantic Commission Co., forbade A. & P. to act as buying agent for others while it engaged in retailing, forbade acceptance of volume discounts based on purchases by more than one unit of the company, required parity of the prices of products made by A. & P. between sales to outsiders and transfers to controlled retail operations, and imposed various other restrictions.

of purchases under private label, it does not believe that there has been any substantial change in these.

One supplier complains that he cannot meet the prices quoted on private label business without making a general price reduction. The predominant opinion among suppliers, however, is that, even with a greater proportion of private-label goods, pressure from A. & P. has decreased, and sellers' margins have improved.

The other case in which the brokerage provision has been used against the power of a large buyer involved certain major oil companies. The Standard Oil companies of New Jersey, Ohio, Kentucky, Indiana, and California are successors to the Standard Oil Company that was dissolved as an unlawful monopoly in 1911. In 1929 these companies jointly organized Atlas Supply Company as a buying agent in the purchase of tires, batteries, and other automobile parts and accessories for resale through the filling stations that carried gasoline. Since the Commission's case against Atlas was primarily directed at price concessions received in violation of Section 2(f), the case is discussed more fully below in the chapter on receipt of unlawful concessions.[45] In addition to obtaining low prices, however, Atlas sometimes succeeded in establishing itself as a supplier's agent and obtained commissions on sales to the oil companies that controlled it. The complaint in the case says that Atlas purported to be the agent of General Electric and Westinghouse in distributing electric lamps, and received commissions from these concerns. Accordingly, the complaint included a charge that Atlas had violated the brokerage provision.

The case was disposed of by answers in which respondents admitted the allegations of fact, waived hearings, and consented to the Commission's order. The order included a requirement that the buyers cease to receive brokerage. Subsequently, Atlas not only complied with this requirement, but discontinued its buying activities altogether. Instead, each oil company made its own purchases directly from the suppliers.

Although the A. & P. and Atlas cases furnish a slender basis on which to appraise the effect of the brokerage provision on the buying advantage of powerful buyers, both cases point to the successful use of this part of the statute in such situations. Elimination of brokerage commissions to the buyer has apparently taken away one of the forms of price concession enjoyed by the powerful before 1936. Elimination of allowances re-

---

[45] See below, pp. 495-98.

ceived in lieu of brokerage has apparently exposed powerful buyers who formerly received brokerage payments to great risks in receiving a price advantage even when, but for its connection with brokerage, it might be lawful.

From interviews with manufacturers and distributors generally, it appears probable, however, that this obstacle to the direct receipt of price concessions has encouraged the large buyer to obtain low prices in ways that do not violate the brokerage provision and perhaps do not violate the price-discrimination law. Four types of activity have been emphasized by those who believe that powerful buyers still enjoy important buying advantages. The first is purchase from suppliers who make no sales through brokers and hence can make price concessions without fear that they may be considered to be in lieu of brokerage. The second course of action is a resort to advertising allowances in place of brokerage commissions and other forms of concession. Since disproportionate advertising allowances may also be violations of the Robinson-Patman Act, this matter will be further considered in discussing Section 2(d) of the act. The third course of action is purchase of the entire output of one or more small producers or purchase from small producers who sell only to other large and powerful buyers.[46] Though the seller is forbidden to discriminate in price, nothing in the law prevents him from quoting a low price that is not discriminatory. When a single buyer takes the entire supply, or a few large buyers divide it at a uniform price, no question of discrimination arises even if the purchase price is lower than that paid by other buyers in dealing with other sellers. The fourth course of action is the vertical integration of the powerful buyer, by which he produces what he formerly bought and thus substitutes for a market price in an arm's-length transaction a mere administrative transfer of values between the parts of a single corporate entity.

[46] An official of A. & P. predicted that resort to suppliers who did not use brokers would establish two price levels differing by more than the amount of the brokerage, since "the direct sellers are going to save and be able to pass on to their customers a great deal more than mere brokerage. In addition to the brokerage differential, exclusively direct sellers will have for their customers only large concerns who buy in quantity lots, pay promptly, and immediately put the merchandise into consumption." See A. & P. Transcript, Vol. 28, p. 5850, quoted in Fulda, *Food Distribution in the United States*, p. 94. In 1940, however, the National Food Brokers Association estimated that, of the 3,500 fruit and vegetable canners, fewer than 50 had shifted to some form of direct selling. See *Business Week* (Aug. 10, 1940).

Although by buying from sellers who avoid all sales through brokers, the powerful buyer can avoid problems under the brokerage provision of the statute, he and his suppliers are still subject to the other provisions, which strike directly at price discrimination. So far as this course of action is followed, the prohibition of allowances in lieu of brokerage is evaded, but the prohibition of discriminations injurious to competition is not. In the process, however, suppliers who sell to powerful buyers may be induced, for legal reasons, to avoid using brokers in transactions where such use would be economical.

It is clear that in so far as powerful buyers may have succeeded in obtaining advantages through exclusive purchase or vertical integration, they may have consolidated their buying advantage along lines not subject to the Robinson-Patman Act. But it is also clear that, though both courses of action are open to a big buyer, neither is free from difficulties. Small sellers are usually reluctant to become wholly dependent on one purchaser. Even if such sources can be found, the large buyer who relies on them must take chances on the quality and uniformity of the product he receives, must incur problems in assembling his purchases from small sources, and must face risks on the stability of his suppliers, all of which could be avoided if he could obtain an equivalent price from a few large producers. Similarly, the big buyer who undertakes vertical integration must find additional capital for this form of expansion, must acquire the know-how requisite to success as a producer, and must carry the continuing costs of a producer's overhead at times when markets are bad enough that some supplies may be available below cost.

Neither the effectiveness of the statute in preventing discriminatory concessions to powerful buyers nor the importance of these alternative ways of buying at low prices has been sharply tested. The scarcities and allocations of the Second World War and of the Korean Crisis and the boom markets that have prevailed generally since the close of the war have reduced the need for sellers to grant low prices either on a discriminatory basis or otherwise. In most lines of business, price competition at retail has not been keen. As compared with the 1930's, low prices have been less effective in transferring business, and there has been a tendency for powerful buyers, who, in reselling, formerly relied on price appeal, to emphasize other forms of sales appeal instead. Until buyers' markets intensify competition on a price basis, the conclusion that the brokerage provision has significantly altered the concessions available to big buyers can be only tentative, and the importance of exclusive purchase and vertical integration as substitute ways to low buying prices cannot be appraised.

Brokerage to Voluntary Groups and Co-operatives

In another group of cases, more numerous but perhaps not more important, the brokerage provision has been applied to the activities of voluntary chains and co-operatives. Of this type are the cases against Modern Marketing Service, United Buyers Corporation,[47] Quality Bakers, Independent Grocers Alliance, and National Modes.[48] Closely related to these is the case against Carpel Frosted Foods,[49] in which Carpel was found to have violated the advertising and brokerage provisions of the act as a seller and District Grocery Stores, a voluntary chain, was found to have received brokerage unlawfully as a buyer.[50] In another related case involving San Pedro Fish Exchange,[51] exaction of brokerage from sellers was a part of an agreement by trade associations to fix prices and allocate business.

In some instances, the payment of brokerage to a buyers' group appears to the seller to be only a form of price concession to the powerful, though the power of the buyers may be derived from joint action rather than from individual strength. In the case of San Pedro Fish Exchange, for example, shippers of fish to Los Angeles and San Pedro were asked to quote prices and pay brokerage to a single broker appointed by the wholesalers' associations of the two cities, under a promise that, if they did so, they would obtain a fair share of the business, and with an implication that refusal would result in a boycott. Though the pressure exerted on sellers by the joint action of buyers is less obvious in other cases, it is clear that wherever the business of the members of the buying group could be effectively guided by the central office, sellers had much to gain or lose through the group's good will.

[47] Docket 3221, *United Buyers Corp.*
[48] Docket 5338, *National Modes, Inc.*
[49] Docket 5482, *Carpel Frosted Foods, Inc.*
[50] As a case concerned with advertising allowances, the Carpel case is significant. Its brokerage portion contributes nothing to the pattern visible in the other cases; indeed, the Commission found a brokerage payment in what the parties apparently regarded as an advertising arrangement. Accordingly, the case is not analyzed in this chapter. It is discussed below, pp. 179-80.
[51] Docket 3739, *San Pedro Fish Exchange.*

The Red and White group (the buying organization involved in the case against Modern Marketing Service) apparently covered 43 jobbers who sold to about 5,000 retail stores, and about $7,000,000 of business was done in goods bearing the group's private brand. Between 1936 and 1941 the United Buyers group represented from 40 to 51 wholesalers; in 1937 it bought through the central organization merchandise worth $49,000,000. In the year ending June 30, 1936, Quality Bakers, representing about 70 wholesale bakers, bought more than $5,500,000 worth of goods. National Modes bought on behalf of 72 member stores in various cities,[52] and had buying arrangements in 1937 with about 60 nonmembers. Independent Grocers Alliance had nearly 5,000 affiliated retail grocers on January 1, 1937, and, with brokerage rates varying from 2 per cent to 8 per cent, had total brokerage income of more than $600,000 in 1937.[53] Access to business on this scale was regarded by many suppliers as worth paying for.

Sale through a buying group or a buyers' co-operative was also, for certain small suppliers, a ready-made solution for a difficult marketing problem. Labels such as those of Red and White and I.G.A. were given a national meaning through the advertising programs of the groups and through the wide distribution of the products on the shelves of the participating stores. Whereas distribution of a small seller's product through brokers would have required him to establish a series of agents in various places and would have made it necessary for each agent to attempt to sell his little-known brand against the competition of well-known national brands, sale through large buying groups or through large chains, voluntary or corporate, required only contact with one or two central buying offices and made it possible for the product to move through the many participating stores under a well-known private brand that these stores were anxious to push. Moreover, in selling through a co-operative or a voluntary group or corporate chain, a small producer avoided credit problems, which were likely to be annoying if he attempted to sell through brokers to widely scattered small distributors. Thus the production of goods for private-label sale became a significant field of operation for small producers, and the presence of a substantial and growing number of co-operatives and voluntary groups alongside the corporate chains increased the opportunity to place private-label goods

[52] Of these, 28 did an annual ready-to-wear business of more than $250,000 each, the others less than that.

[53] The figures in this paragraph are taken from the Commission's findings of fact.

and diminished the dependence of each private-label producer on any particular distributive organization, whether co-operative, voluntary, or corporate. The pressure of the co-operatives and voluntary groups on the private-label producers appears to have been less than that of the corporate chains, because the former could not readily undertake self-supply through vertical integration.

Two classes of intermediaries were involved in the FTC cases concerned with brokerage payments to groups. The first was the cooperative, in which the organization was controlled by, and operated solely for the benefit of, participating business enterprises. United Buyers Corporation, for example, was, until the Commission's order of November 1941, an organization controlled by its member stockholders, each of whom had no more than five shares. The other type of group was one wholly or partly controlled by persons who endeavored to make a profit from rendering service to the members. A clear example is I.G.A. The capital stock of I.G.A. was owned by Market Specialty Company, organized to own it, and at the outset the stock of this holding company was wholly owned by four persons who had conceived the idea of I.G.A. In 1933 affiliated wholesalers organized another holding company, the Grocers Company, which bought half of the stock in the first holding company for $500,000. The other half continued to be owned by the family that had initiated the undertaking. In 1942, when the secretary of the Grocers Company resigned in a dispute over the future character of the organization, he asserted that I.G.A. was operated primarily for the purpose of paying dividends and managers' salaries.

Most of the intermediaries involved in the group brokerage cases were like I.G.A. in that they expressed compromises between ownership by participants and individual profit. The Red and White Corporation, the principal group involved in the Modern Marketing case, was formed around a brand originally owned by a single wholesale grocer, and developed into a corporate intermediary in which there was considerable inequality of ownership. In 1938 the original wholesale grocery company and two members of the family that controlled it owned 105 of the 555 shares in Red and White, while 31 other stockholders divided the remainder.[54] National Modes was organized under a plan that provided that a single individual could own 50 shares out of a total of 200; and, in fact, only 74 shares were issued to the retailers who were to own

[54] Docket 3783, Commission Exhibits 35A, 35B.

the remainder of the stock. The individual owner became the president, treasurer, chief executive officer, secretary, and major stockholder of the holding company that he organized to control the operation. Quality Bakers was owned in November 1937 by 57 bakeries, of which the largest owner, with 5 plants, held 60 shares and no other more than 15 or less than 7½.

In several of the group brokerage cases, the strength of the group rested in part on control of brands or trademarks. Red and White Corporation originated in the successful use of the Red and White brand by a wholesale grocer, followed by the licensing of other wholesalers to use the same brand in their respective trade areas. In due course the brand was transferred to a corporation formed to own it, license it, and buy goods to be sold under it. National Modes was organized with the central purpose of allocating exclusive rights to use brands that would be nationally advertised, selecting manufacturers to produce the branded goods, and placing orders with those manufacturers on behalf of the participants. Similarly, I.G.A. was concerned largely with the placement of orders for merchandise bearing the I.G.A. label and with the distribution of this merchandise through affiliated wholesalers and retailers.

The brokerage that such intermediaries received from sellers served two purposes. If all or part of it was retained in the intermediary organization, it met operating expenses and permitted the organization to perform a service for affiliated concerns without charging them the full equivalent cost. If all or part of the brokerage was transmitted to buyers, the payment consolidated the buyers' loyalty to the organization and encouraged them to buy through it and to emphasize the sale of the products thus bought.

The concerns affiliated with such buying groups were manufacturing consumers, as in the case of Quality Bakers; wholesalers, as in the case of San Pedro Fish Exchange; wholesalers with affiliated retailers, as in the case of United Buyers, Red and White, and I.G.A.; or retailers, as in the case of National Modes and D.G.S. Among them were some relatively large enterprises, such as Best's, the Hecht Co., and Broadway-Hale (which made purchases through National Modes), and S. M. Flickinger (which was the founder of Red and White). However, many of the participants were relatively small. To them the joint ownership or franchise control of a private brand appeared to be a way of competing effectively against manufacturers' national brands and against the private brands of corporate chains. Moreover, joint purchasing through the

buying group afforded an opportunity to offset the buying advantage of
the corporate chains and to obtain merchandising assistance such as a
corporate chain could render to its outlets but an individual store could
not provide for itself.

The buying advantage that the participants found in the voluntary
group apparently had four aspects: First, receipt of brokerage commissions in so far as these were passed on by the intermediary or were used
by the intermediary to provide services without charge;[55] second, receipt
of quantity and volume discounts in so far as these became available for
purchases pooled through the buying group but would not have been
available for the separate purchases of the members; third, participation
in whatever price advantage accrued to the purchase of merchandise for
sale under the private label, as compared with the purchase of similar
merchandise under sellers' brands; and fourth, enjoyment of whatever
special discounts or low net prices might be extended by producers
anxious to obtain the business of the group. One of the possibilities for a
special price concession was that a national-brand manufacturer, anxious
to minimize the voluntary group's emphasis on its private label, might
offer price concessions on the national brands similar to those he gave
to corporate chains under the shadow of their private brands.

The services that became available to the participants through the
voluntary group were varied. Through Quality Bakers, baking companies
received engineering and sanitary services and help in quality control
and accounting—types of service that had no pertinence to the merchandising activities of concerns associated with other voluntary groups.
In the other groups the central organization provided help in store layout, field men to assist reorganization, advisory and supervisory service,
aid in quality control (for example, meat grading and the establishing of
quality standards for private-label merchandise), and similar managerial
assistance. They collected advertising allowances and distributed them
to participants, provided signs, layouts, and mats for advertising campaigns, devised and promoted private labels, issued bulletins, issued market reports, provided information about the availability of specific commodities, supplied store equipment, and maintained systems of insurance.
Not all of these services were supplied by every voluntary group, but

[55] Quality Bakers, for example, credited its members with half the brokerage
on their orders. In 1936 the credits more than covered the dues of 36 members
out of 69, and the total credits exceeded the total dues.

some form of service having to do with store layout, quality control, advertising, and market information was to be found in each.

There was no uniformity in the pace at which the voluntary groups adjusted their operations to take account of the brokerage provisions of the Robinson-Patman Act. When the act was passed, United Buyers, which had previously defined itself as a co-operative, began calling its members customers, but made no other change in its method of doing business. I.G.A., which had been transmitting 80 per cent of its brokerage receipts to the affiliated enterprises that bought the goods, discontinued this practice and, instead, paid out the same proportion of its brokerage receipts in the form of advertising allowances offered to participants in ratios proportional to the brokerage earned on their purchases. Red and White ceased to collect brokerage. Instead, it licensed its brands for $30,000 a year to Modern Marketing Service, a brokerage organization that had been independently established by certain former officers of Red and White. The announced purpose of this change was to place the collection of brokerage in an independent agency that would be a seller's agent. One immediate effect was a reduction in the advertising allowances received by members of Red and White.[56] Until April 1937 Quality Bakers made no change in its way of doing business other than to designate as service fees what it had previously called brokerage commissions. Thereafter it ceased collecting brokerage, bought in quantity to supply the pooled orders of its participating bakers and charged the participants a buying fee. Since the complaint of the Commission was issued in August of the same year, it is probable that the change was made because of the Commission's investigation.

The orders against receipt of brokerage by buying groups were issued in series over more than a decade. The first was that against Quality Bakers in 1939. This was followed by an order against San Pedro Fish Exchange in 1940; but since the fish case turned primarily on a price-fixing plan, it contributes little to an understanding of the brokerage provision. In 1941 an order was issued against United Buyers, in 1943 against Modern Marketing Service, in 1950 against National Modes, in 1951 against Carpel Frosted Foods and D.G.S., and in 1952 against

[56] Whereas most of the brokerage income of Red and White went to members in advertising allowances ($254,000 out of $328,000 in fiscal 1935 and $340,000 out of $340,000 in fiscal 1936), advertising allowances by Modern Marketing were less than half of the brokerage received—$136,000 out of $321,000 in fiscal 1937, and $111,000 out of $300,000 in fiscal 1938.

I.G.A. The orders against Quality Bakers, Modern Marketing Service, and I.G.A. were appealed and sustained.

After its unsuccessful appeal, Quality Bakers, which had been operated for profit, sold its assets to a successor that was a pure co-operative. The successor company purchases goods in wholesale quantities and resells them to members, but instructs the supplier to ship directly to the member. It obtains quantity discounts from some suppliers, but other suppliers refuse to give discounts on purchases thus handled.[57] The purchasing operations are regarded as less important than the engineering, sanitation, quality control, and accounting services that are rendered to members (for which the members pay dues and fees), and the promotion of a brand owned by the cooperative. The members now buy a larger part of their requirements direct than before the case. Nevertheless, their savings on purchases may cover as much as nine tenths of their payments to the association. The case did not prevent the continued payment of patronage dividends, since brokerage income was never a large part of the total receipts. Such dividends are now derived from quantity discounts. Membership has increased.[58] Net sales by all members in 1956 exceeded by $100,000 the sales reported by Continental Baking. Interviews with members indicate a general opinion that the services rendered by the organization are better now than before the case. One member thinks that the cost of goods bought through Quality has gone up slightly, that dues have increased, and that the size of patronage dividends has fallen, but apparently attributes this change less to the case than to higher costs and to an increase in the amount of service rendered.

The United Buyers and Modern Marketing cases will be considered together, since each turned on the treatment of private labels. After the Commission's order against United Buyers in 1941, United filed a compliance report saying that all stock in the central organization had been transferred to the former president, vice president, and secretary-treasurer of the organization, and that these owners would operate the concern as a seller's agent and would license its labels to wholesale and retail dealers on an exclusive basis within their respective territories. The

[57] One producer informed us he cannot sell to Quality because it demands 5 per cent.

[58] According to one estimate, membership has doubled since the order and now includes about 150 wholesale brokers. According to another, membership has grown about 15 per cent.

report announced an intention to pay advertising and promotional allowances to these licensees. The Commission initially received the report without demur.

Meanwhile, the Modern Marketing case was decided in 1943 and the Commission's order was affirmed on appeal in 1945. The Red and White brands had been licensed to a privately owned brokerage concern known as Modern Marketing Service at the time of the passage of the Robinson-Patman Act, and this concern had sought to establish itself as a seller's agent competent to collect brokerage and to issue licenses for use of the labels by wholesalers and retailers affiliated with Red and White. The Commission and the court concurred that Modern Marketing Service was not a manufacturers' agent but actually the agent of Red and White Corporation and its stockholders, and that in paying an annual license fee and substantial advertising allowances to Red and White and the concerns affiliated with it,[59] Modern Marketing Service was actually transmitting brokerage to buyers in violation of the law. As a result of the Commission's order, Modern Marketing Service went out of existence. Control of the Red and White brand reverted to Red and White, which was no longer receiving brokerage.

The close resemblance between the arrangement that had been struck down in the Modern Marketing case and that which had been set up after the order in the United Buyers case led the Commission to reopen the latter case in November 1945. An additional compliance report was ordered, followed in March 1946 by a proceeding to modify the order against United Buyers. This proceeding turned on the advertising and promotional allowances that United Buyers (now rechristened U.B.C. Distributors) was extending to wholesalers and retailers for the promotion of goods bearing U.B.C. labels. In June 1947, the order (which had applied to brokerage payments) was modified to prevent U.B.C. from transmitting brokerage in the form of services as well. The revision also enlarged the scope of language in the order which pertained to control of the intermediary by the buyer. Thereupon, U.B.C. eliminated its advertising and promotional allowances, but said that it would continue to reimburse buyers for the actual cost of advertising and promotion. A compliance report to this effect was held in abeyance by the Commission pending decisions in the cases against Cooter[60] and I.G.A. In the Cooter

---

[59] The advertising allowances were discontinued in May 1939, to conserve resources for defense of the case before the Commission.

[60] Docket 5460, *The Cooter Co. et al.* The case was decided Dec. 13, 1951.

order the Commission specifically forbade the rendering of service to the buyer by a broker who owns the trademarks that are applied to the goods bought. Apparently U.B.C. modified its program still further in the light of this decision. A re-examination of the matter by the Commission in 1955 indicated that U.B.C. then collected advertising allowances from sellers but did not pass these on to buyers and that it published bulletins in which commodities bearing U.B.C. labels were advertised, but without mention of the name of any buyer. Upon this showing, the Commission dropped its investigation. The view apparently held by the Commission is that a broker may collect brokerage for the sale of goods that bear his trademark and may undertake institutional advertising of that trademark but may not transmit the brokerage to a buyer either in the form of an advertising or promotional allowance or in the form of advertising or other service on the buyer's behalf.[61]

In the cases of both U.B.C. and Red and White, the effect of the Commission's action was a substantial impairment of the strength of the voluntary group. U.B.C. has substantially fewer wholesale customers. When payments to buyers were discontinued, some buyers dropped their participation. The volume of business decreased from the time of the order until 1954. It is believed that U.B.C. could sell more if it could pay brokerage to buyers; but those expressing the opinion comfort themselves with the thought that, if payment of brokerage were permissible, the corporate chains would enjoy a similar advantage. U.B.C. continues to emphasize the importance of U.B.C. labels as guarantees of quality.

Interviews with several concerns formerly affiliated with U.B.C. suggest that the loss of payments from it was one reason for severing their connection but not the only one. Three of them say that the services were not particularly valuable apart from the buying advantage. Four stress the loss of buying advantages as reasons for dropping their connection. One refers to a growing consumer preference for national brands, and another to a belief that U.B.C.'s service was too narrowly confined to buying and did not include adequate assistance in marketing goods. Among the concerns interviewed that are still affiliated, one

[61] If this is a correct statement of the law, it illustrates the anomaly in the statute. A supplier who does not use brokers may advertise goods for the benefit of his customer provided he makes the service available to other customers on proportionally equal terms. But a broker who does the same thing, or a supplier who does so through a broker as intermediary, has violated the provision against making an allowance in lieu of brokerage.

expresses the view that the service is improved, another that it is the same as before, and a third that less service is rendered than before. One who thinks the service has not changed would not rejoin the former type of buying group if he could.

One former participant refers bitterly to the substitution of a privately owned brokerage concern for the co-operative in 1941. He asserts that this change resulted in sale of U.B.C. assets to the new concern for much less than their true value.

The effect of the Modern Marketing case on Red and White must be considered in two stages—from 1936 to 1945 during the period of voluntary adjustment, and after 1945 under the impact of the Commission's order. During the first period there was some decline in the amount of business done, as indicated by the total amounts received in brokerage commissions and expended in advertising allowances. In 1935 Red and White had a total income of $444,000, of which $340,000 consisted of brokerage, all of which was paid out to jobbers as an advertising allowance on Red and White brands. For the fiscal year beginning December 1, 1936, the total income of Modern Marketing Service was nearly as great—$433,000, of which $321,000 was brokerage. In the two ensuing fiscal years, total income fell first to $427,000 and then to $322,000, brokerage in the first of the two years being $300,000 and in the second $302,000. But, whereas Red and White had paid all of its brokerage to affiliated jobbers, Modern Marketing paid in advertising allowances only $136,000 in the fiscal year beginning December 1, 1936 and only $101,000 in the following fiscal year. Meanwhile, however, Red and White retailer affiliation was apparently rising from 5,000 retail stores to 8,500.

After the Commission's order was affirmed in 1945, Modern Marketing Service ceased to exist. Personnel engaged in brokerage activities was taken over by a new concern, Bushey and Wright, organized by certain former stockholders of Modern Marketing. The new enterprise differed from Modern Marketing in at least two respects: First, it was not, like Modern Marketing, the beneficiary of agreements between Red and White and concerns affiliated with Red and White as to the channeling of purchases by the latter; second, it did not, like Modern Marketing, control Red and White brands under the terms of a license renewable annually. Apparently its status as an independent broker has been accepted by the Commission. It has succeeded in establishing itself in many instances as representative of sellers formerly served by Modern Marketing. Apparently it sells most of what is packed with the Red and White label (though the labels are available for merchandise bought direct).

In 1955, apparently as a result of compliance negotiations with the Commission, the Red and White brand was sold to Bushey and Wright. The price is said to have been nominal, apparently because, since it would necessarily be paid from or constitute a capitalization of brokerage income, a substantial price might have been interpreted as a transfer of brokerage to buyers.

Red and White has declined in numbers and influence. The number of affiliated retail stores has fallen from 8,500 to between 4,000 and 5,000. Loss of brokerage has meant reduction of income. Though services such as assistance in store layout, advertising, and merchandising are provided and 250 field men are employed, participants must pay for them directly by service fees of from $1,000 to $3,000 per year. Affiliated concerns also incur new costs for advertising the Red and White brands. Discontinuance of the advertising allowance has removed the incentive to push the brand. Hence the importance of the Red and White brand in the business of the affiliated companies is apparently declining.

The concerns affiliated with Red and White that were interviewed were giving less emphasis to Red and White products. One wholesaler, for example, reported that in 1935 such products accounted for 25 per cent of his total sales as compared with 9 per cent today. Another, 30 per cent of whose sales in 1933 carried the Red and White label, sold only 15 per cent under that label in 1950. He attributes the decline to the case, and offers as an example Red and White salad dressing, which had been made by Kraft but could not be promoted during the period of readjustment and therefore lost its market and was dropped by Kraft. He says that Red and White brands are losing out to national brands because they cannot be promoted similarly. According to one estimate Red and White products have declined about 50 per cent in position relative to the national brands. Another wholesaler says that as a result of the case he had to let several salesmen go and had less incentive to deal with the sellers who supplied Red and White products. He now regards the Red and White business as his least important source of revenue and speaks of Red and White stores as grade B and C stores that are being replaced by supermarkets. A third concern dropped Red and

White during the war in favor of local sources less affected by war priorities and now sees no sense in pushing Red and White products instead of products bearing his own private label. A fourth has dropped the organization, thinking that it has nothing to offer and that there is no advantage in pushing Red and White labels instead of his own. A fifth thinks the court case had little effect: For a time after the Commission's order he emphasized Red and White products; subsequently he abandoned the wholesale grocery business for more attractive lines of investment.

Among those involved in the Red and White case, as was true in the United Buyers case, there is an undercurrent of criticism directed at the individuals who took over the brokerage business. One affiliate of Red and White said the case put money in the pockets of the owners of Modern Marketing Service and later of Bushey and Wright. One of the suppliers also commented that a few individuals who operate the brokerage business are making all the money.

Most of the sellers who were interviewed about this case regard it as unimportant, partly because a minute fraction of their total volume was involved and partly because they continued to make the same sales through Bushey and Wright or other brokers or direct to jobbers. One thought direct sale to small buyers had increased his overhead. One noted a substantial decline in the proportion of his private-label business. One said that he had lost his best business and had to scratch around for new customers. One said that at the time of the complaint he supplied four Red and White wholesalers with about $2,000,000 of goods annually and now supplies two with about $300,000. One thought the case helped him: "Why give away 2½ per cent?"

When the Commission's order was issued against National Modes, the holding company offered to buy all shares in National Modes at their book value and to merge the two companies, with the effect that the merged company would have title to the trademarks under the new name of Carolyn Fashions. Carolyn was to become a jobber, buying trademarked goods on its own credit and selling them to one selected store in each city without contractual agreement to do so. This plan went into effect. Thus the assets of National Modes, including its important trademarks, were acquired by the holding company at a cost of about $7,400, and the retailers who had participated in building up the trademark received their original cash investment without any capital gain.

The principal owner of the holding company and of its successor,

Carolyn Fashions, now does business not only through this company but also as a partner in a large buying agency, which operates from the old National Modes office. This agency is reputed to purchase about $500,000,000 worth of goods per year. Its income is said to be derived exclusively from fees paid by buyers.[62]

Carolyn now advertises its brands, issues bulletins to retailers, and licenses selected stores to sell the brands in designated territory. Apparently, however, Carolyn does not operate as a jobber for stores selling the Carolyn brands; instead the stores buy these brands direct from the manufacturers whose names are given in the bulletins. One customer indicates that he sells about the same volume of the branded goods as before. Another buys less because he regards the label as having become less popular. In his opinion, the shortage of supplies during the war crippled the National Modes plan, and at the time of the Commission's complaint it was already dead on its feet.

I.G.A. had been experiencing a decline before the Commission's order in 1952. This fact is evident in the changes in its gross income, brokerage receipts, and payments for advertising allowances, as shown in the accompanying table.

I.G.A. Gross Income, Brokerage Receipts, and Advertising Allowances, 1937-46

(In thousands of dollars)

Year	Gross Income	Brokerage Receipts	Advertising Allowances Paid
1937	1114[a]	608	438
1938	1046	541	368
1939	1072	539	375
1940	1039	495	303
1941	1013	485	308
1942	884	448	282
1943	849	431	278
1944	830	401	253
1945	808	396	229
1946[b]	825	390	163

[a] A misprint in the Commission's findings makes this figure 1141. *Cf.* 48 FTC 926 and the figures in the table, *ibid.,* 925.

[b] For eleven months only.

[62] An interview was sought with this partner but was refused.

It appears probable that the decline of I.G.A. reflected in the foregoing figures should be attributed at least partly to the decisions of the Commission and the courts against such similar organizations as United Buyers and Red and White. In 1942 the secretary-treasurer of the Grocers Company (the holding company that had been formed by affiliated wholesalers) resigned because the management refused to accept his view that a drastic reorganization of I.G.A. was necessitated by the decision in the United Buyers case. Moreover, the case against I.G.A. itself began with a substantial investigation prior to a complaint in 1946, and was then pending before the Commission until 1952. Though the long contest enabled I.G.A. to continue to collect brokerage for a considerable period of time, it presumably discouraged many of the affiliated enterprises. Apprehensions as to the law may have had a significant effect, but other influences were probably important. Wartime scarcities, food rationing, and postwar price increases provided a setting in which participants might well have thought I.G.A.'s services and private brands less important, and suppliers might well have been reluctant to pay brokerage to a buying group.[63]

Apart from brokerage activities, the structure of I.G.A. was not affected by the Commission's order. Stock in the organization continues to be divided equally between Market Specialty Company and The Grocers Company. The former continues to be owned by the original group, and the latter continues to be owned by wholesale grocers affiliated with I.G.A. I.G.A. now centers its activities on advertising and merchandising service. It issues weekly price lists for available goods; operates a "store engineering" department; furnishes field men to help improve the efficiency of operations; furnishes advertising signs, mats, and posters; owns and licenses the use of I.G.A. labels; grades meat; and is developing a program for quality control of perishables. It also operates an insurance service. Its income is derived from retailers' dues, payments for use of its field men, payments for the use of its labels, payments by retailers for advertising materials, payments for advertising in its magazine, and receipts for insurance.

I.G.A.'s loss of its brokerage activities was followed by an increase, rather than a further decline, in the number of affiliated concerns, and in volume of business. It now has about 80 affiliated wholesalers (as com-

[63] For a discussion of the I.G.A. case see John Parkany, "Federal Trade Commission Enforcement of the Robinson-Patman Act, 1946-52" (doctoral dissertation, Columbia University, 1956), pp. 228-36.

pared with 58 in 1946), through whom it deals with nearly 6,000 retailers. No wholesalers were lost at the time of the decree. The number of affiliated retail stores has increased by about 20 per cent since 1950. The dollar volume of affiliated stores has approximately doubled. In spite of the loss of brokerage revenue, the personnel at headquarters has not been reduced, and the services rendered by the organization have been expanded.

One manufacturer, who formerly paid brokerage to I.G.A., stopped making sales through it and other buying groups when the legality of such brokerage payments was challenged, and thereafter lost his private-label business. However, since this business was an unimportant part of his volume, he found that he could sell wholesalers individually with no significant change in total sales. His average realization on the goods he sold was increased, largely because a sellers' market was developing. Another manufacturer found that as a result of the case he lost his business with I.G.A. east of the Rockies, though he continues to sell to I.G.A. on the West Coast.

One of I.G.A.'s wholesalers expresses satisfaction with I.G.A.'s service both before and after the Commission's order and says that he now obtains a larger part of his business from affiliated I.G.A. stores than he did several years ago. A wholesaler who severed his connection with I.G.A. before the Commission's case was instituted says that he did so partly because I.G.A. was retaining an increasing part of its brokerage receipts and partly because it was difficult to sell the I.G.A. private labels against the competition of the national brands.

As a result of the Commission's order, the persons who had previously handled I.G.A.'s brokerage operations formed Food Brokers, Inc., as a separate company. Food Brokers, Inc. is owned by six employee stockholders, each of whom has agreed to offer his stock to the group before selling it elsewhere. It was able to establish relationships with all I.G.A. suppliers. Its gross income and the number of its suppliers and customers have increased since 1953. Though there is no obstacle to prevent the purchase of I.G.A. items through other brokers, Food Brokers makes most of the sales of commodities bearing the I.G.A. brands. Its separation from I.G.A. has facilitated its establishment of brokerage connections with additional manufacturers.

There are marked similarities in the impact of the Commission's orders on the various voluntary chains and co-operatives that have been involved in violations of the brokerage provision. When the group could no longer collect brokerage for establishing the contacts between suppliers and its members, this function was taken over in four instances by a private brokerage concern established by former employees of the group. In three of the four instances, valuable trademarks or brands that had been developed in the group were transferred to the new private organization. Windfall profits apparently accrued to strategically placed individuals.

The effect of the cases on the size and vigor of the groups concerned was not uniform. In one instance, the group disintegrated and only a private enterprise was left. In two instances, there can be no question that the Commission's proceeding contributed substantially to a decline in the number of enterprises participating, in income, and in the sales of its private brands. In one instance in which brokerage had been relatively unimportant, the group's methods of doing business were altered without visible effect on its well-being. In one instance, there was a marked decline in the group's strength in the years preceding the order of the Commission, apparently due in part to controversy over the appropriate course of action, followed by a revival of strength after the order, when the group reconciled itself to the performance of service without collecting brokerage.

In general, the changes brought about by the orders involved a decline in the relative importance of the private brands that were involved, an increase in the amount of direct buying done by participants, even when the group continued to act as a purchasing agent, and a decrease in the amount of money expended on the systematic promotion of the group's trademarks, brands, and labels.

There was no uniformity in the steps taken to make the exploitation of private brands consistent with the law regarding brokerage. In the case of I.G.A., the organization continued to own the brands and license their use while divorcing itself from the purchase and sale of goods. In the case of Quality Bakers, the group continued to own and promote a brand while acting as a buying cooperative. In the case of United Buyers and Modern Marketing, the brand was transferred to a privately owned organization that collected the brokerage, and the program of advertising and promotion was curtailed to avoid passing on brokerage in the form of advertising allowances. In the case of National Modes, the brand was transferred to an owner that did not represent sellers.

When the groups were deprived of their brokerage income and of their opportunity to refund brokerage to buyers, they found it necessary to rely wholly on other types of appeal. Ownership of trademarks was found by some to be impracticable and by others to be of declining importance. The result was an increased emphasis on the quality and variety of other services. These services were improved and enlarged in most instances, in spite of the loss of brokerage income.

On balance, the brokerage cases appear to have reduced the size and effectiveness of voluntary groups, with the amount of the damage depending on the previous division of emphasis between group buying and other activities. As a result of the cases, the importance of group buying has been substantially diminished, with a consequent increase in the relative and absolute importance of other services rendered by the groups. The weakening of the groups was less severe than has often been asserted. But it may, nevertheless, have been of major importance in halting, and even reversing, the growth of organizations that had great capacity for further growth.

6 / Brokerage: Other Applications of the Law

SINCE SECTION 2(c) of the statute forbids the payment of brokerage from one party in a transaction to the other, regardless of the setting in which the payment takes place or the economic effect it produces, the law governs not only the conduct of big buyers, powerful buying groups, and those who sell them, but also the business relationships of all other concerns, large and small. Most of the proceedings under Section 2(c) have been unlike those discussed in the previous chapter. They have resulted in orders that had little or nothing to do with the problems of advantage for the powerful on which the statute was intended to focus. The function of this chapter is to summarize these aspects of the Commission's use of the law.

Market Information Services

The brokerage provision has been applied to market information services in two cases, one involving Biddle Purchasing Company and the other Oliver Brothers, Inc. Although Biddle operated primarily in the food field, and Oliver primarily in the hardware field, the two companies were so similar in their methods of doing business and the cases were so similar in the issues they raised that the Biddle case was regarded as an adequate test of the problems presented by both. The Oliver case was disposed of by stipulation that the findings of the Commission concerning Biddle would apply to Oliver also; and when Oliver appealed the order of the Commission, the record presented to the court which decided the appeal, was that of the trial of the Biddle case. Accordingly, the discussion here will consider Oliver separately only when dealing with developments after the order. Otherwise, it will treat the Biddle case as representative of both.

In 1937 Biddle Purchasing Company sold a market-information

service to nearly 2,450 clients for a fee ranging from $25 to $50 per month. Biddle stood ready to buy for these clients any merchandise described and priced in the market-information service. When it made such a purchase, it collected brokerage from the seller and credited the amount as an offset to the fee due from the purchaser. For about 14 per cent of the clients, the brokerage credits equaled or exceeded the fee. For the others, the credits reduced the size of the fee in varying percentages but left something due from the buyer to Biddle. Biddle made purchases from more than 5,000 manufacturers. Its buying transactions provided the information included in its market-information service. The buying privileges that were extended to the purchasers of the service provided the basis for the buying transactions.

Biddle contended, and the Commission did not deny, that most of the buyers and sellers who were brought together by Biddle were relatively small enterprises without wide contacts in the market. To support this contention, Biddle submitted evidence to show that many of those who bought its information service were located in small cities. Their distribution was as follows:

Population of City	Number of Buyers
Under 25,000	522
25,000 to 35,000	156
35,000 to 50,000	156
50,000 to 75,000	174
75,000 to 100,000	136
Over 100,000	1,301

The Biddle case was the first in which the Commission issued an order about brokerage payments. Accordingly, it was regarded as a test case on the meaning of the brokerage provision. Biddle relied primarily on testimony by sellers and buyers that Biddle rendered a service to both. Various sellers testified that Biddle not only provided them with the same services they obtained from other brokers but also did so more effectively than most brokers. The Commission did not find it necessary to evaluate this evidence. It based its order on the findings that Biddle acted as the buyers' agent and collected brokerage for transmission to the buyers and that the buyers gave the sellers no service in making the purchase. The court sustained this position on appeal, though one judge dissented in part, in the belief that Biddle rendered brokerage service to sellers and, to comply with the law, needed only to keep the fees that it collected.

Soon after the order of the Commission was sustained on appeal in

1938, the Commission began to investigate complaints that Biddle was not complying with the order. In 1940 it instituted a proceeding asking that Biddle be punished for contempt. After the court had sustained Biddle's contention that the Commission must be required to particularize the nature of the violation, the matter was referred back to the Commission as a special master to take evidence as to whether or not there had been a violation. In the early stages of the contempt hearings, Biddle made charges that the Commission's attorney was engaged in improper collaboration with the National Association of Food Brokers. Midway in the hearings, however, the attorney who represented Biddle was changed, the charges against the Commission attorney were dropped, and Biddle waived any further challenge of the Commission's allegation that the order was being violated. Thereupon, in June 1941, the Second Circuit found Biddle in contempt and fined it $500.

As a result of this proceeding, the nature of the violation can be ascertained only from the claims made by the Commission. The Commission's bill of particulars in the compliance case described particular transactions in which Biddle received brokerage and credited it to customers and other transactions in which Biddle received a discount in lieu of brokerage and made this discount available in whole or in part to the customer by a resale at or slightly above the purchase price.

After the contempt proceeding, Biddle continued to sell its market information successfully. It now has about 5,500 customers who pay a monthly service fee for a combined information and buying service. Although forbidden to receive and transmit brokerage, it has maintained its offer to buy for its customers. In representing the buyer, it purchases at prices that reflect the usual discounts. According to some of its suppliers, it is aggressive in hunting for low prices, and places its orders mostly with concerns that sell unbranded goods or are quoting promotional prices.

Five sellers who dealt with Biddle were interviewed. Two of them said that the percentage of their business that was placed with Biddle had not changed. Three said that this percentage had declined. For one the decline had varied from item to item, with a range of from 2 to 40 per cent; but the change was attributed to competitive price reduction apparently unrelated to the case. For the second the decline had been slight in percentage and nonexistent in absolute volume. The third did not particularize.

Of the three customers who were interviewed, one thought that the case had slightly reduced his income. The others had noticed no effect. One of these said that, because of the rise in freight rates, the growth in regional manufacturing, the increase in national advertising, and the possibility of buying through co-operatives, the Biddle type of service was less valuable than it used to be.

Like Biddle, Oliver vainly appealed the Commission's order. Like Biddle, it continues to buy, when requested to do so, on behalf of the customers who pay a flat fee for its information service. Of the five customers of Oliver who were interviewed, one is a wholesaler who ceased to deal with Oliver because, in quoting the retail trade, Oliver was competing with him. Another has switched from Oliver to Biddle. The other three continue to use the Oliver service and to make purchases through Oliver. There is general agreement among these customers that this kind of buying service is useful chiefly in obtaining goods that are not usually included in the buyer's line. One customer also uses Oliver to buy goods that cannot be bought directly from the manufacturer because the manufacturer has assigned the territory to an exclusive distributor.

Biddle and Oliver have apparently adjusted their business successfully to the Commission's order. Information is not available as to the effect on the scope of Oliver's business. Biddle, however, has more than doubled its clientele since 1937, and the volume of business it places for its subscribers has grown substantially. Sale of market information for a monthly fee has been found practicable even without brokerage credits as an offset to the sale price. The transition was made easier by the fact that other ways by which buyers had obtained brokerage were also being blocked by the Commission.

The effect of the cases on the profits of Biddle and Oliver is not known. Since brokerage was credited to the buyers, there was obviously no direct effect. It is possible, however, that if brokerage credits could still be offered, the information service could be sold at higher prices than are actually charged. An appraisal of this possibility is not feasible with the information at hand.

Since both Biddle and Oliver continue to buy on behalf of their clients when requested to do so, there is no reason to believe that the orders have significantly reduced the selling opportunities of concerns that formerly sold through Biddle and Oliver. These sellers can have lost business only in cases in which they (1) depended substantially on the market-information service for contact with buyers, (2) have lost that contact because buyers, without the incentive of brokerage credits, make less use of the information service in their purchasing, and (3) have been unable to find new channels to reach these buyers. Though such a combination of circumstances is possible, there is no reason to believe that it is common.

The effect of the cases on buyers has apparently been to make their market information more expensive in that none of the cost of it is covered by brokerage. The services of Biddle and Oliver are still available as purchasing agents where the buyer wishes to use them.

Thus the harmful effects that were predicted by Biddle and Oliver when the cases were instituted have not materialized. On the other hand, it is difficult to see that any public interest has been served by the Commission's orders. For at least 86 per cent of Biddle's customers the total credits received for brokerage before the case amounted to less than the fee, which usually ranged from $300 to $600 per year, and since credits could not be enhanced by using more than one information service, these small sums cannot be regarded as part of a larger cumulative total of discriminatory advantage. That various small concerns in the food industry and elsewhere bought market information at a discount appears to be unrelated to the public issues that underlie the law of price discrimination.

Neither is it apparent that the orders have served any appreciable private purpose. When the cases were pending, they were hailed at a convention of food brokers as a victory for legitimate brokers. Presumably, this attitude was based on the belief that the goods moving through Biddle and Oliver would come to move through ordinary brokerage channels. The continued willingness of the two concerns to buy for their clients has destroyed the basis for this belief; and interviews with sellers suggest that, with minor exceptions, goods move through the market-information services in about the same volume as before. Thus the orders have accomplished nothing significant, even for the brokers whom they seemed most likely to benefit.

Affiliated Brokers

The simplest use of the brokerage provision has been to stop the receipt of brokerage by dummy brokers that were controlled by a single buyer and used for the sake of obtaining an indirect discount in the form of a broker's commission. Where such a broker concealed from the seller his relationship to his principal, his activities were quasi-fraudulent.[1] Where the nature of the broker was known to the seller, the grant of a brokerage allowance was merely a decorous way of giving a price concession. However, since the payment of brokerage was inherently unlawful, the statute could be invoked to stop it, whether the size of the payment and the power and competitive relationships of the buyer were such as to jeopardize competition.

Three of the cases studied involved relationships in which the brokerage house was essentially a masquerade for a single buyer.

In the case against Thomas Page Mill, the offense consisted in the payment of $1,578 brokerage on sales of flour through Minetree Brokerage Company to Poplar Bluff Wholesale Grocery Company, of Poplar Bluff, Missouri. Minetree Brokerage consisted of three individuals, of whom two owned 88 per cent of the stock in Poplar Bluff Wholesale Grocery and the third was an executive thereof. There was no evidence that the seller, Thomas Page Mill, knew of the connection between the brokerage establishment and the wholesale grocery company. After the Commission's order in 1941, the seller ceased doing business both with the broker and with the wholesaler.

Similarly, the Reeves-Parvin case involved the receipt of brokerage by Tri-State Brokerage Company on purchases made by Reeves-Parvin, a wholesale grocer, when the two companies were corporate affiliates.[2] The same individual was president and major stockholder of both companies, and the two concerns occupied the same office and had employees in common. Tri-State did a legitimate brokerage business with other companies at one time; in 1933 only 38 per cent of its income was derived from sales to Reeves-Parvin. However, its sales to others declined rapidly, and this proportion rose in successive years to 65, 86, and 94 per cent. The Commission's order was designed to stop the payment and receipt of brokerage in connection with the transactions between Reeves-Parvin and Tri-State. Thereafter, Reeves-Parvin continued to buy from the same sellers through the same distributive channels, but Tri-State

[1] In private litigation, Sec. 2(c) has sometimes been invoked against wrongs that have little logical relation to it: bribery of a buyers' employee (*Fitch* v. *Kentucky-Tennessee Light and Power Co.*, 136 F. 2d 12) and coercive exaction of secret rebates (*Avon Publishing Co.* v. *American News Co.*, 122 F. Supp. 660). It has been invoked successfully as a justification for canceling contracts. See, for example, *Baysoy* v. *Jessop Steel Co.*, 90 F. Supp. 303, and *Jarrett* v. *Pittsburgh Plate Glass Co.*, 131 F. 2d 674.

[2] Docket 3129, *Reeves-Parvin & Co.*

ceased to collect brokerage on purchases that Reeves-Parvin made through it.

A similar case against Webb-Crawford Company involved the relationship of this wholesale grocer, the largest in Northeast Georgia, to Daniel Brokerage Company. Daniel Brokerage was originally organized under the name of G. A. Christian Brokerage Company by three individuals who were stockholders in Webb-Crawford. In 1936 one of them, G. A. Christian, retired, selling his interest and his stock in Webb-Crawford, and the brokerage concern was renamed Daniel Brokerage. Thereafter, the largest stockholder in Webb-Crawford owned 50 per cent of Daniel, the second and third stockholders in Webb-Crawford 25 per cent each. Together these three men owned 706 shares in Webb-Crawford out of a total of 744. Another stockholder in Webb-Crawford, who owned 32 of the remaining 38 shares, became Daniel's manager.

When the Federal Trade Commission's case was brought, 75 to 85 per cent of Daniel's brokerage income was derived from sales to Webb-Crawford, which constituted about 10 per cent of Webb-Crawford's total purchases. The cost of carrying on the brokerage business was slight. Indeed, in 16 months in 1936-37 Daniel distributed $16,000 in profits out of total brokerage receipts of $23,000.

The extent to which the sellers who paid brokerage were aware of the connection between the two concerns is a matter of dispute. Some sellers disclaimed knowledge, and the record contains evidence of inquiries by some of them in response to which Daniel gave assurance "that none of the proceeds of this firm has ever at any time been diverted to the firm of The Webb-Crawford Co., it will never benefit so far as the proceeds of the new firm are concerned, they are two distinct and individual firms."[3] However, there was an identity of persons in the management of the two firms, and Daniel's brokerage office was located in the building occupied by Webb-Crawford. It is probable that the corporate fiction did not prevent most suppliers from knowing the relationship between the two companies.

The relation between Daniel and Webb-Crawford impaired the opportunity of the principal competing broker, North Georgia Brokerage Co., to sell to Webb-Crawford. Since the two owners of North Georgia Brokerage were father and son, and one of them was a brother of the

[3] It is noteworthy that Daniel wrote to H. B. Teegarden of U.S. Wholesale Grocers Association in an effort to get a "ruling" that it might lawfully receive brokerage.

second and third largest stockholders in Webb-Crawford, whatever discrimination existed was between one relative and another.

Though no findings as to injury were necessary under the law, the Commission found that the arrangement diverted business from sellers who did not pay brokerage to Daniel, prevented competing brokers from selling to Webb-Crawford, and enabled Webb-Crawford to injure its competitors by making sales below prevailing market prices.

After the case, the manager of Daniel Brokerage, who owned 32 shares of Webb-Crawford stock, purchased the brokerage company and changed its name to Athens Brokerage. Webb-Crawford now purchased from both Athens Brokerage and North Georgia Brokerage. Five or six years after the order, North Georgia Brokerage acquired Athens Brokerage, and the two concerns were merged. Subsequently, the father and son who owned the merged brokerage company sold the business to two persons unrelated, so far as the record shows, to the stockholders of Webb-Crawford. Thus the practical identity between the wholesale grocery company and the brokerage house was replaced successively by a connection through a minor stockholder, a connection through blood-brothers, and disappearance of all connection.

The effect of the case on the channeling of Webb-Crawford's purchase is a matter of dispute. Competitors have suggested that in the two sales of the brokerage house the value of the relationship to Webb-Crawford must have been capitalized and included in the sale price, and that thus the owners of Webb-Crawford succeeded in obtaining the present worth of future payments of brokerage to a preferred broker. According to various estimates Webb-Crawford purchases constitute from 25 to 75 per cent of the present volume of business of North Georgia Brokerage. It is clear that Athens Brokerage and subsequently North Georgia Brokerage continued to make substantial sales to Webb-Crawford. Since North Georgia Brokerage was a local concern representing suppliers whose products Webb-Crawford was accustomed to buy, substantial sales to Webb-Crawford were, perhaps, to be expected.

At the time of the acquisition of Athens by North Georgia, Athens had from 25 to 30 accounts and North Georgia about 50. After the acquisition, North Georgia had between 60 and 70 accounts. In some instances it had not taken over the Athens accounts because it had conflicting arrangements with a competitor. Prior to the acquisition, the brokerage income of Athens was between $14,000 and $16,000 a year, and that of North Georgia about $30,000. Eight years later, when North

Georgia was sold to new owners, its brokerage income was about $48,000. These figures suggest that, although Daniel Brokerage was originally little more than a dummy broker, the acquisition of new accounts and the merger eventually converted its successor into a legitimate broker.

Information about the competitive effect of the change in relationship between Webb-Crawford and Daniel is scanty and conflicting. Several competitors of Webb-Crawford were confident that the arrangement did not hurt them and praised Webb-Crawford as a company not given to price cutting.[4] Two competitors thought the arrangement had hurt them by making it possible for Webb-Crawford to cut prices from time to time. Most of the brokers who were interviewed said that they had not been hurt, apparently because they were exclusive representatives of particular brands. One thought that the arrangement had reduced his sales to Webb-Crawford and that these had never recovered to the previous level.

Apart from dummy brokers, there have also been cases in which a concern doing a legitimate brokerage business included among its customers an affiliated wholesaler and collected brokerage upon the sales made to this customer. In such situations the brokerage provision has been invoked against the collection of brokerage on sales to the affiliate.

Mississippi Sales Company, of Meridian, Mississippi, was a brokerage concern that in 1937 received about $73,000 in brokerage commissions. Between 13 and 14 per cent of its brokerage income was derived from sales to a jobber, a chain of retail groceries, and a wholesale grocery, with each of which it was connected by interlocking ownership. The president of Mississippi Sales owned 98 per cent of its stock, 98 per cent of the stock of the jobber, Jobbers Produce Company, nearly 33 per cent of the stock in the grocery chain, Penney Stores, and over 47 per cent of the shares in the wholesale grocery, Buckley Young.[5] While the Commission's case was in progress, he sold his shares in Penney and Buckley Young, and subsequently the Commission dismissed the case against these two companies on the ground that Mississippi Sales had not acted as their agent. Because of the identity of ownership, the Commission issued an order designed to prevent sellers from granting brok-

[4] Since Webb-Crawford's sales were about $2,000,000 per year and the profits of Daniel Brokerage about $1,000 per month, the opportunity to cut prices by diverting brokerage profits was necessarily narrow.

[5] Except for three shares, one other stockholder held the rest of the Penney stock, and he and one other family held the rest of the stock in Buckley Young.

erage to Mississippi Sales on purchases made by Jobbers Produce and to prevent Mississippi Sales from receiving or transmitting brokerage on such purchases. After the order, Jobbers Produce Company was dissolved. Its assets were acquired by a new enterprise in which the majority stockholder of Mississippi Sales had no interest. Mississippi Sales made sales to the new company in amounts substantially equal to its previous sales to Jobbers Produce but charged no brokerage on these sales. There is no indication that the case had any other effect on the relation of Mississippi Sales to suppliers or customers.

The effect of the Commission's cases involving these relatively simple problems was to bring about relatively simple changes in business relationships. In some instances the ties of ownership and control between broker and buyer were dissolved, and thereafter the broker collected brokerage on all his sales, including those to the previous affiliate.[6] In other instances, the affiliation was maintained, but the broker ceased to collect brokerage commissions on sales made to the affiliated buyer. Sellers sometimes ceased to deal with broker, buyer, or both, and reported this fact as showing their compliance with the order of the Commission.

Buying Brokers

Several of the Commission's cases have been directed at the payment and receipt of brokerage on purchases made for their own account by concerns doing a brokerage business. Although such purchases bore a superficial resemblance to the collection of brokerage by a buyer through a dummy broker,[7] some of them expressed a substantially different motive, took place in a different economic setting, and therefore deserve separate discussion.

[6] But Mississippi Sales played safe by collecting no brokerage on sales to Jobbers Produce even after the ties of ownership were broken.

[7] Such a case was directed against G. B. Shelton (Docket 4585, *G. B. Shelton Brokerage Co.*), which did business partly as a wholesale grocer and partly as a broker of sugar and crystal phosphate. When it bought crystal phosphate for its own account, American Agricultural Chemical allowed from 50 to 75 cents per 100 pounds in lieu of brokerage. Admission answers were followed by an order against both buyer and seller in March 1946.

According to the compliance reports, American Agricultural Chemical ceased to deal with Shelton in February 1944, while the case was pending. In compliance with the order, Shelton ceased to collect brokerage or receive allowances in place of it on purchases that it made for its own account.

The characteristic pattern presented by these cases is one in which a concern doing business as a broker represented distant sellers in transactions many of which were for less than carload lots. In some instances, l.c.l. sales were necessary because the buyers were too small to make carload purchases. This was true, for example, of many wholesale buyers of fish in the southern states and in New York City. In other instances, the demand was too limited to permit even a substantial buyer to move the commodity in carload quantities. This was true, for example, of such commodities as cauliflower and early watermelons in markets such as Memphis. If buyers had been required to pay the transportation rates for less than carload lots, they would have been at a substantial cost disadvantage as compared with corporate chains. Consequently, brokers who sold in such circumstances attempted to arrange for shipment in pool cars in order to give their small customers the benefit of carload rates.

However, there were difficulties in selling on a pool-car basis. Those who placed the first orders were likely to be reluctant to wait while the rest of the carload was sold. Consequently, it became common practice before the Robinson-Patman Act for brokers who had sold a substantial part of a pool car to order shipment of the whole car, relying on their ability to sell the remainder while the car was in transit. If any part of the car remained unsold at the time of arrival, the broker took delivery in his own name and subsequently resold. As to such deliveries, his legal status was that of a wholesale buyer, not a broker.

Even when the entire pool car was sold, brokers, their principals, and their customers often found it convenient for the car to be shipped to the broker as buyer. If goods in the car were invoiced to several different buyers, the death or bankruptcy of any one of them, or his refusal to take delivery because of alleged spoilage or for any other reason, might tie up the entire shipment and cause inconvenience to the other buyers. Moreover, if the seller looked to each buyer separately for payment, he found it necessary to explore the credit standing of a considerable number of distant small wholesalers and to take the trouble of making out invoices and keeping accounts for each of them separately. He preferred to ship to his broker, in whose credit he had confidence, and to handle the entire car with a single invoice and a single accounting entry. In such transactions, the broker was formally the buyer, even though the change in his actual relationship to the seller and to the wholesalers might be merely formal.

From this kind of nominal purchase, it was easy for brokers to move toward a less nominal status as wholesalers. Having substituted their credit for that of their customers and made arrangements to warehouse goods that they had not succeeded in selling at the time the shipment arrived, they thought themselves entitled to compensation for these expenses and risks. In some instances they charged sellers the actual cost of such expenses as warehousing. In other instances, having taken title to the goods at a price that differed from the going market price by no more than the brokerage fee, they took advantage of a subsequent rise in price to make a profit in addition to their brokerage. From such windfall gains, it was a short step to the making of speculative purchases when they thought the price was about to rise. Moreover, some of them found that, by controlling goods in local storage, they could increase their sales by promising an attractive quick delivery; and to this end they began to keep warehouse stocks regularly, even though they continued to think of themselves as brokers.

During the war, brokers of some products had an additional incentive to buy goods because of wartime shortages. When goods were in short supply, distant buyers who could be reached only through brokers were likely to be neglected; and the broker, anxious to maintain his business and preserve his clientele, sometimes found that he could buy goods from suppliers who would not sell through him as agent.

This fluid relationship between seller, buyer, and intermediary contained nothing that was inherently unfair to any one of them or to competitors of any one of them. Still less did it contain anything that was likely to impair competition. However, when appraised under the standards of the brokerage provision of the Robinson-Patman Act, it was unlawful, since it did not maintain a sharp distinction between broker and buyer and did not limit the collection of brokerage strictly to the transactions in which the broker had refrained from acquiring a buyer's status.

Relationships of this kind were the basis of the Commission's cases against Columbia River Packers Association, Custom House Packing, Ketchikan Packing Company, Southgate Brokerage Company, and Jake Felt.[8]

Columbia River Packers was a canner of West Coast fish that dis-

[8] Docket 5033, *Columbia River Packers Association, Inc.;* Docket 5404, *Custom House Packing Corp.;* Docket 5164, *Ketchikan Packing Co.;* Docket 3765, *Fruit and Produce Exchange et al.*

tributed its product through from 40 to 45 brokers. Ten of these were named in the Commission's complaint and five in its findings. Columbia River Packers invoiced shipments to these brokers against cash payment on arrival. The broker took title, paid for the shipment, and subsequently collected from those to whom he had sold. The principal broker for Columbia River Packers was W. H. Stanley of New York City, to whom Columbia River Packers sent more than 40 per cent of its output. About 85 per cent of Stanley's business consisted of Columbia River Packers products. Stanley paid for the goods before they arrived, reimbursed Columbia River Packers for insurance on them en route, maintained warehouse stocks in New York to fill small orders, and on occasion borrowed from banks against warehouse receipts. On December 31, 1940, Stanley's books showed an inventory of merchandise valued at nearly $365,000.[9]

Southgate also represented Columbia River Packers as a broker. It made purchases for its own account, warehoused portions of them, and insured its inventory without billing Columbia River Packers for its insurance and warehousing. During the year ending April 27, 1940, it bought $21,000 worth of canned salmon from Columbia River Packers. Although it sold at prices authorized by Columbia River Packers, it followed changes in the market price without specific authorization.

In the Columbia River Packers case the Commission proceeded against the seller for paying brokerage to buying brokers, rather than against the various buying brokers who received the payments.

The case against Ketchikan Packing Company involved similar facts. Ketchikan is a canner of Alaska red salmon. At the time of the case it sold from $200,000 to $300,000 per year, a considerable part invoiced to William H. Stanley of New York. Stanley's status as a buyer was the same as in the Columbia River case. The Commission's case was brought against both Ketchikan as a seller and Stanley as a buyer.

A third case was brought against Southgate Brokerage because of its receipt of brokerage on goods it bought for its own account. These included, of course, the fish that it received from Columbia River Packers. The Commission found that 60 per cent of Southgate's business consisted of purchases for its own account and that in many instances it received on such purchases either brokerage or discounts in lieu thereof. The amount thus received in the last half of 1941 was nearly $26,000.

[9] Docket 5033, Exhibit 215A.

As a result of these cases, Columbia River Packers adopted the practice of maintaining consignment stocks in various principal markets. It has found this practice expensive. In 1955 it had a finished-goods inventory valued at nearly $4,000,000 (on a f.i.f.o. basis) out of total assets of less than $10,500,000. It finds that even large buyers now follow a formula of maintaining minimum stocks with maximum turnover; they compute the re-orders of their branch stores on business machines; and they place limited orders when inventories fall below the minimum level.

Instead of invoicing shipments to brokers, Columbia River Packers now retains title until the goods are sold to customers. It has not experienced difficulties in selling under the new system.

Like Columbia River Packers, a considerable number of large sellers have found it necessary to establish consignment stocks in various parts of the country. They have been induced to do so partly by the Commission's proceedings against buying brokers and partly by the increased emphasis the chains and other large buyers place on the quick deliveries that enable them to carry small inventories. The availability of warehouse stocks has encouraged nearby distributors to pick up supplies directly at the warehouse, instead of dealing through brokers. Banks have come to serve as sellers' collection agents.[10] The consigned stocks of one shipper are estimated to have ranged from 50 to 70 carloads, with an investment in prepaid freight of about $100,000.[11] Small producers have not been able to maintain widely distributed warehouse stocks because of the expense that this would involve. Thus the elimination of the buying broker has handicapped them in comparison with their larger competitors.

After the case, Ketchikan ceased to sell directly in eastern markets. Instead it sold its entire output exclusively through a single broker in Seattle.

Brokers like Southgate are encountering difficulties, some of which are attributable to the Commission's cases. In the buyers' markets of the 1930's, surpluses were sold cheaply in the South through brokers of the Southgate type. During the war and subsequently, shortages appeared

[10] According to one commission merchant, the carrier gets his money through a bank, which presents the invoice to each buyer and wires collection to the canner. A bill of lading attached to a sight draft is sent to the bank. This involves "no demurrage, no merchandise delivery, no orders for payment."

[11] See California Lima Bean Growers Association, *36th Annual Report*, 1952, p. 6.

that reduced the willingness of sellers to use such channels, and rising incomes in the South diverted southern consumers to other products that had not been sold through brokers. For example, beef and pork replaced sardines in many Southern diets. Corporate chains, voluntaries, and supermarkets provided outlets for substantial quantities and were preferred by sellers as easier ways to achieve volume sales. Thus the small outlets, the wholesalers who served them, and the brokers who served these wholesalers are being squeezed out. The inability of the broker to preserve his small customers by flexibly combining purchase with the performance of brokerage functions is hastening the process. Moreover, large sellers, who, like Columbia River Packers, are maintaining warehouse stocks and sending invoices to each customer, are encouraged to make more use of their own sales organizations and to rely more heavily on customers who buy in substantial volume.

The Custom House Packing case presented a similar pattern. Custom House Packing, a packer of seafood, sold exclusively through an affiliated company, Wilbur Ellis,[12] a broker specializing in fish meal. Wilbur Ellis resold through sub-brokers with whom it split its brokerage commission. It passed on a part of the commission when these sub-brokers bought for their own account as well as when they acted as brokers. Though the incentives for purchase by sub-brokers were in part the same as in the cases involving Columbia River Packers and Ketchikan, the principal inducement for a sub-broker to buy appeared during the war, when fish products were scarce and the purchase of them was easier than the discovery of sellers who were willing to consign the merchandise.

The Commission's case was begun in November 1945, and the order was issued in September 1946. As a result of the case, Wilbur Ellis ceased to make an allowance of part of its brokerage on purchases made by sub-brokers. According to the compliance reports, this practice was discontinued even before the Commission's complaint. Custom House Packing was dissolved at the time of the Commission's order, but apparently for reasons unconnected with the order. Wilbur Ellis continues to do business as a fish broker. Interviews with sub-brokers indicate that the percentage of their business that consists of purchases for their own account has declined, but that the change is primarily due to the fact that supplies are no longer so hard to get and to the availability of consignment stocks that are now carried by the canners of fish products rather

---

[12] Stockholders in Wilbur Ellis and their families controlled Custom House Packing.

than to an unwillingness to buy without receiving a brokerage allowance. One such broker says, however, that since brokerage fees are now lower than before and during the war, the margin they provide is so small that it would no longer be feasible for a broker to carry the risks and costs of taking title, warehousing, and insuring, even if such an arrangement were lawful. This same broker has ceased to represent Wilbur Ellis because he does not think Wilbur Ellis carries adequate stocks of consigned merchandise. Partly because of the case, this broker has only a residual interest in the canned-fish business.

In certain borderline situations, there may be an overlap between the patterns of the buying broker and the dummy broker. This was apparent in the case of Jake Felt. Felt operated in Memphis, Tennessee, as a food broker under the name Fruit and Produce Exchange. He was also president and manager of M. E. Carter and Company, which carried on a wholesale food business in the same city. He owned 84 per cent of Carter's stock. Most of his brokerage business consisted of sales to Carter. About 75 per cent of Carter's purchases were made through Fruit and Produce Exchange. The suppliers who were involved in the case asserted that they were unaware of the connection between the broker and the wholesaler. Thus, although Felt retained the brokerage commissions in his brokerage business without passing them on to Carter, the pattern of Felt's business had the characteristics of dummy brokerage.

However, the arrangement also displayed the pattern of the buying broker. When Carter wished to buy in less than carload quantities, Fruit and Produce Exchange placed carload orders in its own name and sold the remainder of the car to other buyers as rapidly as it could, sometimes completing the transaction before the car arrived and sometimes afterward. By this means, Carter and others found it easier to distribute celery, cauliflower, early watermelon, and similar products for which the demand was not great enough to justify the purchase of a carload by a single wholesaler.

After the Commission's order, some suppliers ceased doing business both with Carter and with Fruit and Produce Exchange. Others continued to sell to Carter but used other brokers. A few apparently continued to sell through Fruit and Produce Exchange, and two paid brokerage on sales to buyers other than Carter. This business, however, was slight. Three or four years after Felt's death in 1950, Fruit and Produce Exchange gave up its brokerage license. Carter now buys about 50 per cent of its volume direct from sellers, about 45 per cent through sellers' brokers not related to it, and about 5 per cent through purchasing agents.

Resident Buyers

Except for the case of National Modes, the brokerage cases thus far discussed have all pertained to the food industry. This fact fairly reflects the scope of the Commission's enforcement of the brokerage provision; for of the 148 orders involving brokerage, 129 were concerned with food. Thirteen of the remaining 19 orders had to do with apparel—furs and fur garments, women's clothing, millinery, and men's clothing.

The clothing industries have constituted a special problem because certain long-established trade practices in the sale of clothing are inconsistent with the brokerage provision of the Robinson-Patman Act, which was drafted after consideration of the problems of the food trades and without regard to the problems of the garment industries. In the women's apparel and fur industries, production has long been concentrated primarily in a few metropolitan centers and most producers have been small. Style change and imitation of successful designs have been rapid. Distributors not located in the garment centers have found it imperative to keep in close touch with the changes, particularly as their customers have been made increasingly aware of the latest fashions through the nationwide circulation of periodicals, moving pictures, television programs, and the like. Contact between the outlying distributor and the producers at the urban center has long been maintained via so-called resident buyers who purport to act as agents of the distributors in selecting and buying merchandise. In some cases the resident buyer is compensated by a fee from the distributor; and in some cases he is a salaried employee of the distributor. Frequently, however, such buyers receive their compensation in the form of commissions paid by sellers on the purchases of the buying agent. The practice does not involve subterfuge or concealment, but is generally understood and accepted by sellers, distributors, and resident buyers alike.

As an agent of the buyer the resident buyer who derives his income in commissions from the seller is, however, clearly in violation of the Robinson-Patman Act; and the seller who pays the commission also violates the act. This pattern has resulted in five cease and desist orders addressed to furs and fur garments, five addressed to women's clothing, two addressed to millinery, and one addressed to men's clothing. Two of the orders involving fur garments were subsequently reviewed by the courts. One, against Jack Herzog & Co.,[13] had to do with Herzog's operation as a resident buyer on behalf of 80 fur garment retailers and department stores who bought, in the aggregate, from $600,000 to $800,000 worth of such garments yearly. The other had to do with David M. Weiss, who acted as resident buyer for about 60 retailers of fur garments.[14] The Commission's orders against both resident buyers were based on answers in which the respondents admitted all the material allegations of fact set forth in the Commission's complaint. When the Herzog case reached the Second Circuit through the Commission's request for enforcement of its order, Herzog contended that he was an independent broker, neither compensated nor controlled by buyers; but the court held that the admission answer conclusively established the existence of an agency relationship between Herzog and the buyers and that the arrangement therefore violated the statute. Since Weiss had agreed with the Commission that the decision as to the Commission's request for enforcement of the order against him should be governed by the decision of the court in the Herzog case, the ruling in regard to Herzog disposed of the Weiss case as well. In both cases the court appointed the Commission as special master to determine whether the order was being violated. Subsequently, both respondents entered into stipulations admitting that they had violated the orders against them. Thereupon the Second Circuit granted a decree of enforcement in each case.

Two brokerage cases involving the garment trades were covered by the present study. The first was concerned with the receipt of brokerage by Jasper W. Efird on purchases for a chain of retail department stores and an affiliated jobber in Virginia and the Carolinas.[15] Efird was an officer and director in the various companies, which were controlled and almost wholly owned by his brothers and himself. He operated a buying office on their behalf in New York City. From 26 of the companies he received salaries aggregating $9,840 per year, and from his stock he received dividends varying between $3,101 and $6,815 per year. On his purchases for the stores, which constituted about 10 per cent of their total requirements, he received brokerage payments from sellers that, on a yearly basis from 1936 to 1939, fluctuated between $5,436 and $4,280. From these various revenues he paid the expenses of the New

[13] Docket 4257, *Jack Herzog & Co.*
[14] Docket 4240, *David M. Weiss.*
[15] Docket 3955, *Jasper W. Efird.*

York office, which amounted to from $5,000 to $7,000 per year. His brothers were not aware that he received brokerage commissions but took no action to change the arrangement when the Commission's investigation gave them knowledge of it. The Commission issued an order directing Efird to cease receiving brokerage on his purchases for the stores and directing the stores not to receive brokerage or allowances in lieu thereof on such purchases. The inclusion of the stores in the order was apparently based on two findings: First, that in some instances in which Efird beat down a buying price so far that no commission was paid him, the price concession constituted an allowance in lieu of brokerage that was received by the stores; and second, that in so far as Efird paid his buying expenses from the commissions he deposited to his own account, the stores were receiving the benefit of the commissions in the form of service by him.

Efird has been dead for more than eight years. The buying office is still maintained in New York but does not accept brokerage. Interviews with various dress manufacturers in the New York market indicate that the payment of brokerage by sellers to buyers who purchase women's dresses is common there, though probably less common now than during the depression. As a result of the Commission's cases, some effort is made to conceal the payments.

The other case studied had to do with Harry Bitterman,[16] who bought about $200,000 worth of fur garments per year on behalf of retailers and obtained brokerage from sellers. Bitterman and the seller respondents filed admission answers that resulted in an order against them in 1942. Bitterman is now dead. Operations such as his are apparently criticized in the fur industry not on the ground that the brokerage relationship is perverted, but on the ground that they involve price cutting and chiseling. According to one critic, clients of such firms are mostly bad credit risks; the agent diverts their business to inferior fur houses; he represents to them that the goods they buy are shipped on approval and can be returned; and the result of his activity is price cutting. The effect of the case is said to have been the stoppage of overt brokerage payments to resident buyers in the fur trade and the substitution of the same payments under other names, such as service fees.

It is common knowledge that, although the Commission's brokerage proceedings in the garment industry may have resulted in some changes of form, they have done little to stop the payment of commissions to resident buyers by sellers who are not subject to specific cease and desist

[16] Docket 4229, *Harry M. Bitterman, Inc.*

orders. The Commission probably could find a basis for proceedings analogous to those against Weiss, Herzog, and Bitterman against several hundred concerns in New York City alone.

However, there is no reason to believe that any public or private harm is done by the continuance of the unlawful practices. A distributor who wishes to maintain contact with an urban garment center has access to buying agents of whom some will look to him for their buying fee and others will rely on sellers' commissions for their fees. If his volume of business is large enough, he also has the option of maintaining his own buying office. Each of these methods of doing business must justify itself in competition with the others. Similarly, sellers have ready access to buying offices where they need not pay commissions on sales and to resident buyers who expect commissions. There is no reason to believe that commissions are exacted from them except where they receive equivalent advantage. Since competition is keen in the garment trades, it is reasonable to expect that, whether the buying office is supported by sellers' commissions or buyers' fees, prices and margins will be so adjusted that neither seller nor buyer finds any consistent advantage in the one way of doing business as compared with the other. To impose on the industry a requirement that its contractual arrangements shall conform to preconceived ideas as to the appropriate functions of brokers would be to force the abandonment of harmless or useful relationships on doctrinaire grounds.

So long as the brokerage provision applies in theory to all business, the Federal Trade Commission must necessarily be embarrassed in failing to enforce it consistently in the garment industries. Moreover, the few concerns that are subject to orders against the payment or receipt of brokerage commissions in these industries are handicapped so long as their competitors continue to engage in such transactions and are not curbed by similar orders. Nevertheless, the Commission has been wise to refrain from devoting a large part of its time and man power to proceedings such as these, that can have no economic significance.

Summary

Viewed as a whole, the brokerage cases appear to include many that did not express the central purposes of the Robinson-Patman Act and that had effects partly inconsistent with those purposes.[17] Of those that

[17] In the opinion of the Attorney General's Committee, the brokerage provision gives a "virtual legal monopoly" to one type of middleman and thus "clogs com-

have been studied, two have terminated concessions to large buyers that it was the obvious purpose of the statute to curb; and one of these cases appears to have induced the abandonment of similar concessions to other large buyers. Several other cases have forced voluntary chains and co-operatives to look for their income to other sources than sales commissions and to rely for their usefulness on service functions or co-operative buying rather than on an ambiguous agency relationship to buyers and sellers. This group of cases has done something to weaken the voluntary organizations in their struggle against the corporate chains. Two cases have prevented buyers from continuing to obtain market information at a discount, apparently with no other significant effect. In reducing the fluidity of the activities of buying brokers, several cases have substantially impaired the competitive strength of small wholesalers who are dependent on l.c.l. purchases and of the brokers who serve them, and probably have also weakened smaller producers in their competition with large producers. Some chiseling for price concessions, a part of it quasi-fraudulent, has been prevented by the cases brought against dummy brokers. In the few applications of the brokerage provisions outside the food industries, an ineffective attack has been made on well-established trade practices, with little result except to handicap a few respondents whose activities have been specially curbed and to provide incentives to use subterfuges to conceal relationships that had been candidly avowed.

A by-product of the cases appears to have been to encourage certain inefficiencies in the distribution of food. Corporate chains that had formerly taken brokerage payments have moved in the direction of purchase in smaller quantities and insistence on more service, since they are not free to obtain price concessions even where cost-justified. Sellers have found it necessary to maintain expensive consignment stocks, partly to meet the new demands of the corporate chains and voluntaries for quick delivery, and partly to fill the gap left by the elimination of the buying broker. Neither of these changes can be attributed entirely to the brokerage cases, but each appears to have been accentuated thereby.

The effect of the brokerage cases on the relative well-being of cor-

petition in the channels of distribution, and exacts tribute from the consumer for the benefit of a special business class." However, the Committee's recommendation was merely an amendment of the law "to restore the original vigor of the exception 'for services rendered' in Section 2(c)." See *Report of the Attorney General's National Committee to Study the Antitrust Laws* (March 31, 1955), pp. 191-93.

porate chains and small independent distributors is uncertain, with considerable probability, however, that on balance the independents have been hurt rather than helped. The gains for the independents have been narrowly limited. Except where the seller previously paid them brokerage, corporate chains can obtain price concessions in the form of quantity or volume discounts, discounts for purchase at the supplier's place of business, and the like, to the full extent that such discounts can be justified under the general law of price discrimination,[18] and they can obtain advertising allowances to the full extent that suppliers can be induced to grant them, since the recipient incurs no liability under the Robinson-Patman Act.

They can buy from concerns that do not use brokers without being troubled by Section 2(c). A. & P. continues to be restrained by an order against allowances in lieu of brokerage, and a few other national chains may be vulnerable to analogous proceedings (though less so with the passage of time); but a growing number of local and regional chains of supermarkets can buy direct from the supplier where it pays to do so, can get such advantages as the rest of the statute allows, and need not fear to be tripped up by a heritage of loose practices in taking brokerage before 1936, when these enterprises did not yet exist. Though such concerns may move more cautiously in direct buying than they otherwise would, they are limited by the brokerage provision in matters of form rather than substance.

Independents, on the other hand, are enduringly prevented from getting some of the advantages of direct buying through pool cars in which brokers perform both brokerage and wholesaling functions. Associations of independents that do not actually become wholesalers can provide collective strength only if they can grow without receiving brokerage payments from sellers and can advertise their collective trade-marks without receiving from sellers advertising allowances that might be interpreted as the equivalent of brokerage. The difficulties that the brokerage provision presents to independents appear to be more enduring, more general, and less readily avoided than those that it presents to the corporate chains.

---

[18] It is noteworthy that proceedings against Safeway Stores and Kroger for receiving unlawful discriminations were dismissed by the Commission after it lost a similar case against Automatic Canteen Co. See below, pp. 510-11.

7 / *Proportionality in Payments and Services*

SECTIONS 2(d) and 2(e) of the Robinson-Patman Act are based on a special principle and have to do with closely related subjects. The first makes it unlawful for a seller to make payments to a customer for sales services unless the payments are proportionately available to all competing customers. The second makes it unlawful for the seller to render sales services to persons who buy for resale unless these services are proportionately available to all buyers.[1] The characteristic practice forbidden by the first is the payment of an advertising or promotional allowance to selected customers. The most common practice forbidden

---

[1] The language of the two sections is not parallel and in consequence there are various uncertainties about the comparative scope of the two prohibitions. Thus, the prohibition as to payments applies to persons engaged in commerce, whereas the prohibition as to the provision of services makes no reference to commerce; the prohibition as to payments concerns payments to "customers," whereas the prohibition as to the provision of service has to do with service to "purchasers"; the prohibition as to payments has to do with payments that are not "available" on proportionally equal terms, whereas the prohibition as to the provision of services has to do with services that are not "accorded"; the prohibition as to payments directly forbids payments that lack the required proportionality, whereas the prohibition as to the provision of services forbids "discrimination" in the disproportionate services; the prohibition as to payments has to do with payments in connection with any of the commodities offered by the seller, whereas the prohibition as to provision of services has to do with services connected with the particular commodity bought by the particular customer; the prohibition as to payments requires proportionality to all other customers "competing in the distribution of such products," whereas the prohibition as to provision of services requires proportionality "to all purchasers." What importance should be attributed to these differences in wording is uncertain, for the Commission has issued only fifteen orders under Sec. 2(e), and only three of these and two involving Sec. 2(d) have been reviewed by the courts. The tendency has been to minimize the importance of the variation in statutory language. Thus, in the Arden case, the Second Circuit assumed that the omission of the reference to commerce in Sec. 2(e) was inadvertent. In the same case the court held that the Commission's order properly extended to indirect as well as direct purchasers, and emphasized the competitive relationship among the purchasers.

by the second is the furnishing of demonstrators to aid selected customers in displaying and selling goods.

The practices covered by the two provisions are closely related. Payments to a customer for promotional services and provision of promotional services in a customer's establishment are both methods by which a seller intervenes in the resale of commodities he has furnished. The exact form of the intervention is largely a matter of convenience, and within wide limits one form can be replaced by the other. A seller may pay his customer to mention the seller's brand in the customer's advertising or may himself place advertisements for the brand, in which the customer's name is mentioned; he may pay demonstrators to work in the customer's establishment, or, alternatively, he may pay the customer to employ clerks who will demonstrate the goods; he may pay the customer to arrange merchandise so that the brand is conspicuously displayed, or he may supply a delivery service that includes the arrangement of the customer's merchandise. Whatever form the promotional co-operation takes, the incentives for the seller to offer it and for the customer to accept it are likely to be the same, and discriminations in the amount of it available to different customers are likely to have similar consequences. A parallel treatment of payment for service and the provision of service is an appropriate recognition of these relationships.

Relation to Other Parts of the Law

Difficult conceptual problems appear, however, when these two provisions are compared with other parts of the Robinson-Patman Act. The co-operation between buyer and seller, which is regulated here under the test of proportionality, is an issue also in the brokerage provision that has been discussed in the previous chapter and in those applications of the provision concerned with injurious price discrimination that have to do with functional discounts, to be discussed in a subsequent chapter. But in these other parts of the statute, different rules are applied. Co-operation between the buyer and the seller may be subject to three legal principles, depending on whether the form and history of the relationship present a problem of price discrimination, of disproportionate service, or of payment of brokerage to a buyer.

As interpreted by the courts, the brokerage provision of the statute rests on the view that neither the buyer nor the buyer's agent can render to a seller, in connection with the buyer's purchase of goods, a service substantial enough to justify the payment of a fee or commission. Section 2(d), however, explicitly recognizes that the buyer may render service to the seller in connection with the buyer's processing, handling, sale, or offer for sale of the seller's products, and treats the payment for this service as legitimate provided it is proportionately available to all. Furthermore, Section 2(e) recognizes that the seller may render service to the buyer in connection with the latter's processing, handling, sale, or offer for sale of the goods bought from the seller; it treats this service as legitimate if it is proportionately available. The brokerage provision envisages buyers and sellers as persons who deal with one another at arm's-length. Sections 2(d) and 2(e) envisage them as persons jointly interested in promoting the flow of the commodity through the channels of distribution to the ultimate consumer. Under the former concept, any payment across the transaction is regarded as unlawful. Under the latter concept, such a payment is regarded as lawful if it is made for services in resale and is generally available. Though in theory the former concept applies to the first sale of goods and the latter concept to their resale, in practice there may be payments that are applicable to both types of transactions simultaneously.[2]

A similar difference in concept separates the provisions regarding proportionality from the provisions as to price discrimination (Section 2 [a]) as they apply to functional discounts. If the promotional service of a distributor is recognized by the seller through specific payments for promotional activity, the lawfulness of these payments will depend on whether or not they are proportionally available according to the standards of Section 2(d). If, however, the seller recognizes by a functional discount the general promotional usefulness of a distributor, without specifying explicitly or without policing the services for which the discount is granted, the lawfulness of the discount is to be judged, not by its proportional availability, but by a consideration of the injurious effects that it may entail and of the applicability of the defenses available to sellers whose discounts may have these effects.[3]

Thus, in practice, different legal rules are applied to closely related matters. The form given to a business relationship, rather than its substance, determines the nature of the rule to be applied.[4] If a payment

---

[2] See for example, the Carpel Frosted Foods case, discussed below, pp. 179-80.

[3] See the discussion of the Binney & Smith case below, pp. 186-87; 188-90.

[4] Cf. Cyrus Austin, "Brokerage v. Service Payments: Another Look at Section 2(c)," in *Trade Regulation Series No. 3, Symposiu* (1956), pp. 57-64. See also footnote 29, pp. 101-02 above.

or a discount is described as brokerage or is the successor to a payment that was thus described, it is subject to the sweeping prohibitions of the brokerage provision. If a payment similar in amount is made in a lump sum rather than as a percentage of the invoice cost of goods and is conditioned on the performance of certain promotional services, it is likely to be tested by its proportional availability in accord with Section 2(d). If, without previous history of payments called brokerage, substantially the same amount is allowed to the same buyer, as well as to a number of others, because these buyers are said to have similar functional characteristics, the legitimacy of the allowance will be determined by a third standard—the effect on competition. There is considerable opportunity for buyers and sellers to change the form of their business relationship in order to subject it to one rule of law rather than another.

The Concept of Proportionality

In adopting the standard of proportionality in Sections 2(d) and 2(e), the Congress chose one out of several possible ideas of equal treatment, apparently without considering the claims of the others.

First, it defined equality in proportional rather than absolute terms. It provided that payments for sales services be made, not in equal amounts, but in proportional amounts. Presumably absolute equality was discarded as impossible; but if the law is assumed to mean what it says, it prohibits absolute equality. Its effect is to forbid a seller whose customers buy different amounts from paying all of them a uniform flat sum for advertising service.[5]

Apart from absolute equality, however, there are at least three reasonable standards of proportional equality. Customers might be said to be equally treated by either of two standards: (a) if the services and payments for service that they receive are proportional to the purchases they make from the seller; or, (b) if these services and payments are proportional to their value, that is, to the effect in promoting the seller's business that they can achieve.[6] Sellers might be said to be equally treated by a

[5] Charles Wesley Dunn, "Sections 2(d) and (e)," in CCH, *Robinson-Patman Act Symposium* (1946), p. 71, says that a manufacturer can proportionalize his payments either by making the same payment for a similar service by each dealer or by measuring the payment by a reasonable standard of relative value. He does not explain how he derived the first alternative from the language of the statute.

[6] The failure of Congress to distinguish clearly between these concepts is illustrated by an explanation given by Congressman Utterback, who was in charge of

third standard:[7] if the services provided by a customer to different sellers are proportional to the payments made to the customer by those different sellers. But these three different standards of equal treatment are inconsistent with one another. If a seller makes advertising allowances to his customers in proportion to their purchases from him, these allowances are unlikely to reflect accurately the relative value to the seller of the advertising services that he receives. If he makes payments proportional to the value of these services, they are unlikely to be proportional to the purchases of the customers. If several different sellers grant, to a given customer, advertising allowances each of which is proportional to the allowances made to other customers by the particular seller, it is almost inevitable that the payments received by any one customer from different sellers will be out of proportion to the relative services he renders to these sellers. If a buyer establishes a uniform scale of charges for advertising service rendered to his suppliers, the proportionality thus set up among the payments he receives is unlikely to be consistent with maintenance of proportionality between one seller's payment to him and that same seller's payment to other customers.[8] The three kinds of proportionality can seldom be simultaneously maintained.

---

the bill: "But proportional to what? Proportional naturally to those customers' purchases and to their ability and equipment to render or furnish the services or facilities to be paid for." (See *Congressional Record*, 74 Cong. 2 sess., Vol. 80, Pt. 9, p. 9416.) Thus two standards of proportionality were lumped together in one sentence.

[7] The failure of Congress to consider this standard was, of course, a natural consequence of the fact that, unlike Sec. 2(a), Secs. 2(d) and 2(e) were concerned with the effects among customers, to the exclusion of any concern with effects among competing sellers.

[8] District Grocery Stores has a printed scale of prices for such services as special mailings to its members, insertions in its catalogs, and displays of merchandise in its warehouse sales room. Its adoption and use of such a price list were apparently influenced by the case against *Holzbeierlein* (Docket 5020), which was based on his advertising arrangements with D.G.S., and the case against *Carpel Frosted Foods* (Docket 5482), in which D.G.S. was a respondent. If adhered to, this list maintains proportionality between the services rendered by D.G.S. in promoting a seller's goods to its members and the payments received by D.G.S. for such promotion. Any one seller who pays for the selling services at the prices listed can maintain proportionality in his own payments only by adjusting his advertising allowances to all his other customers so that they are consistent with what he pays D.G.S. If several voluntary chains were to adopt similar price lists, there would be only a remote mathematical possibility that a seller dealing with all of them could conform to the price list of each and still maintain proportionality between his own payments and sales to the various chains.

Assuming that a standard of proportionality is to be used, the choice between proportionality in the services provided by a buyer and proportionality in the payments made by a seller is a thorny one. Congress envisaged the probability that if sellers could make disproportional allowances, powerful buyers would get the large ones. It is equally clear that if a buyer is not held to standards of proportionality, he may provide for powerful sellers, without charge, advertising services for which he requires less powerful sellers to make payment. In the curtailed hearings that preceded the enactment of the present law, the relative importance of the various possibilities was not explored. Attention was focused on the fear that big buyers would get concessions; and here, as in most other parts of the law, an attempt was made to avoid this result through control of the seller's conduct. Fear that the big buyer would treat different sellers differently was not expressed.

The choice between payment in proportion to purchases and payment in proportion to the benefit received by the manufacturer from the buyer's advertising services is likewise a difficult one. An advertising allowance may be conceived as a concealed discount. If so, its primary effect is to alter the net price at which goods are bought, and in a price-discrimination statute this effect should either be sterilized through some such requirement as a proportional relation between the amount of the allowance and the amount sold, or be fully exposed to the law that regulates other forms of discrimination.[9] However, an advertising allowance may also be conceived as a price paid for a legitimate advertising service. In this view, the purchase of advertising is similar to a purchase of transportation or of raw materials. Some purchasers may be unable to provide the kind of advertising service desired; others may be able to provide only service of inferior quality. The seller may want only a limited amount of advertising service or only a particular kind. The general policy of the law in a free private-enterprise system is to leave buyers free to choose their sources of supply, to buy as much as they want from these sources in such proportions as they wish, and to pay the market value of what they buy. The application of these principles to purchases

[9] A private suit, *American Cooperative Serum Association* v. *Anchor Serum Co.* (153 F. 2d 907, certiorari denied) was concerned with an advertising allowance to the Illinois Farm Bureau Serum Association for which practically no advertising was performed. The difference between the allowance and the recipient's expenditure for advertising was regarded by the Court of Appeals of the Seventh Circuit in 1946 as a discriminatory secret rebate subject to the provisions of Sec. 2(a).

of advertising would suggest that it is inappropriate to require a buyer of advertising service to buy it from all his customers if he buys it from any and to buy it from them in stated proportions to which proportionate values are arbitrarily assigned. One might, with similar logic, require a steel manufacturer to buy railway transportation service from every railroad in proportion, not to his need for service from each, but to the amount of his steel products purchased by each.

Moreover, a payment for useless service, or a payment substantially in excess of the value of the service rendered, is, in effect, a concealed price concession; hence any standard of proportionality other than that of the value of advertising may readily be thought to foster discrimination. Overpayment closely resembles payment for service not actually rendered, which has long been condemned.[10]

One might reasonably expect that these rival conceptual views of proportionality in advertising allowances would have been sharply presented to the Commission and the courts; for although the law requires proportionally equal terms, it does not specify how proportionality is to be assured. In fact, proportionality to purchases has been taken for granted.[11] Until 1957 no decision in a case against an advertising allowance was dependent on the question whether payments proportional to the value of the advertising were sufficient to satisfy the law.[12]

[10] In dismissing the soap cases, the Commission included in its opinion the statement, "Certainly payments for services or facilities not furnished are not authorized. The same would be true of payments grossly in excess of the cost or value of the services rendered." See Docket 5585, *Lever Brothers,* 50 FTC 511; Docket 5586, *Procter & Gamble Distributing Co. et al.,* 50 FTC 513; Docket 5587, *Colgate-Palmolive-Peet Co.,* 50 FTC 525.

[11] The Attorney General's National Committee to Study the Antitrust Laws lists three ways of conforming to the law: (a) paying a dollar allowance per unit of service rendered by the buyer up to a uniform maximum percentage of his dollar volume of purchases; (b) paying a dollar amount per unit of goods bought, provided the buyer performs a specified minimum of service; (c) furnishing services to buyers worth a uniform percentage of their purchases. See *Report of the Attorney General's National Committee to Study the Antitrust Laws* (March 31, 1955), p. 189.

[12] In Docket 3915, *Larus and Brother Co.* was charged with violating Sec. 2(d) in 1938 by paying United Cigar Stores $1,000 for window space in New York City. Its answer said, "Respondent makes no advertising allowance to any of its customers as payment or consideration in connection with the sale of its products. Respondent purchases advertising space and advertising as a commodity in itself, based solely on its calculated advertising value, whether from individuals who may be customers of Respondent, or otherwise. After a test of many years' actual experience, Respondent learned that its purchase of advertising from United Cigar-

In July 1957, however, the legality of the purchase of advertising on the basis of its value to the concern buying it was adjudicated in a private suit in a district court in Illinois.[13] Twenty retail grocers and two wholesale grocers had sued General Foods, Hunt Foods, Morton Salt, and A. & P., charging that advertising placed by the first three in *Woman's Day,* a magazine published by A. & P., violated Sections 2(a), 2(d), 2(e), and 2(f) of the Robinson-Patman Act. The theory of the complaint was that the advertising was disproportionate because similar advertising was not made available to all other customers; that in paying for it the suppliers furnished A. & P. a disproportionate service, namely, a subsidy of a large part of the cost of the magazine; that the payments constituted injurious discrimination in price; and that A. & P. violated the law by inducing and receiving these injurious discriminations. Presumably the charge as to injurious discrimination was included in the case in an effort to cover A. & P. as well as the suppliers, since the receipt of dis-

---

Whelan Drug Store Corporation of New York City was the purchase of a commodity of real value to Respondent at a fair and reasonable price, and during all of the period covered by this proceeding such purchase has been solely on the basis of its calculated advertising value, and has no relation either in percentage or amount to any products sold by Respondent and purchased by said Drug Stores Corporation. Respondent will purchase advertising of this type only on the basis of whole windows, properly located, the concern selling same agreeing to prepare at its expense the displays with frequent changes, and furnish merchandise for display, the location of the advertising, the time and duration thereof to be approved by Respondent. In the very nature of things, the purchase of such advertising . . . could not be apportioned in any way amongst customers. Respondent would gladly purchase additional advertising of this same type from customers or noncustomers in position to furnish the same quantity and quality at the same price. . . ." Answer by Respondent, pp. 16-17.

The case against Larus was dismissed for lack of evidence to support the complaint. (See 44 FTC 1182.) Similar cases against other manufacturers were similarly terminated. Thus the issue raised by Larus was not pressed to a decision. Since the Larus answer, in effect, admitted the special arrangement with United Cigar Stores, one must presume that the lack of evidence cited as ground for dismissal pertained, not to the making of the payments, but to a relation between them and sales of the product to the customer.

After the order against A. & P. in the case involving allowances in lieu of brokerage, A. & P.'s instructions to its buyers included a statement that payments for advertising should be proportional to the ability of each customer to render the desired services and to the advertising value of the services to the seller. (See American Institute of Food Distribution, *Robinson-Patman Guide Book,* 1940, pp. 91-92.) The Commission has instituted no case against A. & P. because of such a practice.

[13] *State Wholesale Grocers* v. *Great Atlantic & Pacific Tea Co.,* 154 F. Supp. 471.

proportionate advertising allowances or services was not in itself a violation of the statute. The court treated this subordinate part of the complaint as worth consideration only if a violation of Section 2(d) or 2(e) were proved.

The charge under Section 2(e) was dismissed without difficulty. The court saw nothing in the payments for advertising that established a relation of subsidy different from the relationship between any advertiser and the publication in which he advertises. The advertisers did not furnish *Woman's Day* to A. & P.; A. & P. furnished it to the advertisers. "It is the high quality of *Woman's Day,* reflected by its editorial content, that sells the magazine to the public—these sales, in turn, attract the advertising revenue of such manufacturers as the defendant suppliers. It seems manifestly clear that a magazine the public will not buy cannot earn advertising revenue."[14]

The heart of the case was the charge under Section 2(d). The court found that the purchases of advertising in *Woman's Day* were based on the advertising value of the publication and were unrelated to the sales of merchandise to the suppliers by A. & P.:

> . . . These defendants chose to advertise in *Woman's Day* after having weighed the same criteria that they considered before advertising in any medium and, more specifically, in any magazine . . . there is no evidence of any ulterior motive . . . nor does it appear that the defendant suppliers had intended to favor A. & P. (New Jersey) over any of its other customers . . . it has been stipulated that the extent to which A. & P. promotes or merchandises the products of its suppliers is and has been in no way affected by the fact that such suppliers do or do not advertise in *Woman's Day* or by the extent of such advertising, if there is any.

The evidence "clearly . . . reveals that the defendant suppliers receive full value for their payments for their advertisments in *Woman's Day.*"[15]

In these circumstances, the court saw in the advertising neither favoritism to A. & P. nor harm to competing food distributors. The defendant suppliers had advertised in other magazines distributed through stores, one of which had been sold for a time by some of the plaintiffs. "A. & P. does not shift substantial portions of its own advertising costs to the defendant suppliers," and the evidence "conclusively shows that the de-

[14] *Ibid.,* p. 475.
[15] *Ibid.,* pp. 477, 478.

fendant suppliers' product advertising in *Woman's Day* aids in the sale of the advertised products by all grocers who carry the product advertised."[16]

Moreover, "plaintiffs do not publish or sell a store distributed magazine and, thus, they are unable and unequipped to render or furnish the services for which payment would be made and for which the defendant suppliers in this case pay *Woman's Day*. Being so unable to furnish these services, plaintiffs have no standing to complain about the defendant suppliers' advertising in *Woman's Day* even if it were assumed that these payments violated the Act."[17]

In deciding the case the court formulated standards which it thought could be generally applied. It held that "It was the intent of Congress that advertising payments are not unlawful . . . where advertising services are rendered as agreed and paid for and where the recipient derives only an incidental benefit therefrom. . . . It was not intended by Congress that Sections 2(d) and 2(e) should be applied so as to hamper legitimate advertising."[18]

Accordingly,

> . . . If a service can be said to benefit only the supplier or if the service benefits only the customer, there is no difficulty. . . . However, where it is conceivable that a service might benefit both the supplier and the customer, then, and only then, it becomes necessary to determine whom the services were *primarily* designed to benefit. If the services were primarily designed to benefit the supplier, the Act has not been violated; if the services were primarily designed to benefit the customer, then the Act has been violated unless proportionally equal treatment has been given that customer's competitor. If it is made to appear that equal benefits accrued to both the supplier and his customer from the service, then also the Act has been violated; and in determining whether the customer receives equal benefit, it must be made to appear that the customer has been able to shift to his supplier "substantial portions of *his own advertising costs.*"[19]

In July 1958, with one dissent, the circuit court reversed the decision on violation of Section 2(d).[20] Though it found that advertisers were

[16] *Ibid.*, pp. 482, 480.
[17] *Ibid.*, p. 483.
[18] *Ibid.*, p. 506.
[19] *Ibid.*, p. 479.
[20] CCH, *Trade Cases 1958,* par. 69089.

urged by their advertising agencies to place advertisements in the magazine "solely upon evaluation by such agencies of *Woman's Day* as an effective advertising medium" and that the price of the advertising was comparable to that charged by other magazines with comparable circulations, it did not regard these circumstances as controlling. It held that Section 2(d) made disproportionate payment for advertising unlawful regardless of the advertiser's motive. It rejected the argument that the independent stores, lacking a store magazine, would not have been able to furnish similar advertising even if payment had been offered. In this part of its opinion, it applied to proportionality of payment the principle that had been adopted in the Arden case[21] to govern proportionality in the provision of services. Citing the Arden case, it declared: "An offer to make a service available to one, the economic status of whose business renders him unable to accept the offer, is tantamount to no offer to him."

However, like the district court, the circuit court could find in payments for advertising no provision of a service and hence no violation of Section 2(e). It affirmed the dismissal of this part of the case.

Having decided that Section 2(d) had been violated, the court remanded the proceeding to the district court to determine whether or not the plaintiff had suffered damage from the violation. However, since the sections concerned with proportionality are applicable only against sellers, the charges against A. & P. were dismissed. The case now focused on the advertisers—General Foods, Hunt Foods, and Morton Salt.

Presumably the differing views of the district and appellate courts will be eventually carried to the Supreme Court. If the interpretation of the circuit court is affirmed, a supplier will be unable to buy advertising from a customer, even though he acts in good faith, unless he offers to advertise proportionately through all his customers. If the interpretation of the district court is affirmed, the prohibition of Section 2(d) will be inapplicable to advertising programs that sellers undertake in good faith except in the difficult cases in which these programs provide substantial benefits both for sellers and for participating distributors. However, since many types of advertising, such as store displays and newspaper advertising by distributors, are likely to provide joint benefits, a significant conflict will remain between the interest of the advertiser in buying only

[21] See below, pp. 168-69; 196-98.

the service he wants and the interest of the distributor in preventing rivals from obtaining preferential advantages through advertising allowances.

The Test of Illegality

In resting Sections 2(d) and 2(e) on the concept of proportionality, the Congress gave them an automatic character similar to that of the brokerage provision. Here, as in the case of brokerage, there is no need to show that the challenged arrangement has had or is capable of having an adverse effect on competition.[22] As in the case of brokerage, the respondent under Section 2(d) cannot excuse his special allowance by showing that it is justified by considerations of economy or efficiency. Neither can he excuse it by showing that it was made in good faith to meet an identical allowance already made by someone else.[23] A finding by the Commission that the allowance was not proportionately available to the seller's competing customers is sufficient to establish a violation of law.

Under Section 2(e), though no injury to competition need be shown, the statute explicitly provides that a respondent may rebut the Commission's case by showing that he provided services or facilities to meet those provided by a competitor. In May 1958, a circuit court held, in a case under this section, that a respondent also has the right to show that the disproportionality of his services is justified by differences in cost.[24]

[22] Dicta in certain private suits indicate that injury may be relevant. See *National Nut Co.* v. *Kelling Nut Co.,* 61 F. Supp. 76, 83, and *Chicago Sugar Co.* v. *American Sugar Refining Co.,* 176 F. 2d 1. The Commission, however, does not so interpret the law; and its orders have generally been unchallenged and have been enforced by the courts in several cases.

[23] The Commission's decision in Docket 5482, *Carpel Frosted Foods,* appeared to cast some doubt on this interpretation; but in Docket 6212, *Henry Rosenfeld, Inc., et al.,* the Commission specifically decided on June 21, 1956, that the defense of meeting competition is not relevant to a proceeding under Sec. 2(d). This position had been foreshadowed by the Third Circuit in a decision in the A. & P. case. See *Great Atlantic & Pacific Tea Co.* v. *FTC,* 106 F. 2d 667.

[24] *Simplicity Patterns Co.* v. *FTC,* 258 F. 2d 673. The Circuit Court for the District of Columbia decided that the reference to provision of services in Sec. 2(b) of the act has the effect, not only of authorizing the respondent to show that he met competition, as it explicitly does, but also of making available to him whatever justification may be relevant, including cost justification. In the autumn of 1958, petition for certiorari was filed. The Commission had consistently assumed that cost defenses were not relevant to Secs. 2(d) and 2(e). Since there is no reference in Sec. 2(b) to payment for services, as distinguished from the provision of services, it is

The latter interpretation, which was contested by the Commission, is being carried to the Supreme Court.

Sections 2(d) and 2(e) differ from the brokerage provision by applying only to the seller. Whereas he who receives illegal brokerage violates the law as fully as he who pays it, the Robinson-Patman Act does not forbid a customer to receive a disproportionate service or a disproportionate advertising allowance.[25]

---

unlikely that cost defenses will be acceptable under Sec. 2(d) even if the court's decision as to Sec. 2(e) is affirmed by the Supreme Court.

[25] Because of advertising allowances given to two regional chains, the Commission issued complaints against 11 sellers (Dockets 6460-70, inclusive). Seven of the cases eventually resulted in consent orders, one in an order based on a stipulation of facts, and two in orders after trial. The order in one of the cases tried (Docket 6464, *Atalanta Trading Corp.*) was subsequently set aside on appeal. See below, pp. 166-67.

However, the initiative in arranging the advertising allowances apparently came from the recipients, Food Fair Stores and Giant Food Shopping Center. Two cases (Dockets 6458 and 6459) were brought against them, not under the Robinson-Patman Act, but under Sec. 5 of the Federal Trade Commission Act. According to a statement by the trial examiner in denying a motion to dismiss the Food Fair case, the case turned on the question whether or not it is an unfair method of competition under the Federal Trade Commission Act to induce a violation of the Robinson-Patman Act. However, the attorney who represented the Commission's complaint assured the writer that he was not relying on this theory, but on substantive proof that would show that the activities of the respondent had damaged competition. Choice between these two theories was crucial to the significance of the decision. To hold that a consummated impairment of competition violates the Federal Trade Commission Act is not new, whatever may be the circumstances from which the result arises. To hold that the Federal Trade Commission Act is violated by anyone who contributes to a violation of the Robinson-Patman Act would be to apply the former statute not only where competition has been (or probably will be) damaged but also where there has been a lack of proportionality in payments for services, regardless of the effect on competition.

Extraneous circumstances prevented a decision of the issue in the Food Fair case. On Sept. 27, 1957, the Commission decided that, because of Food Fair's ownership of a meat packing plant, jurisdiction over Food Fair had been given to the Secretary of Agriculture by the Packers and Stockyards Act. Accordingly, the Food Fair case was dismissed. After a motion to dismiss the Giant case had been rejected by the Commission, Giant bought one hundred shares of Armour common stock and then renewed its motion. On April 16, 1958, the motion was reluctantly granted by the hearing examiner, whose ruling was appealed to the Commission. At the end of September the Commission had not yet acted on the appeal.

Meanwhile, largely as a result of the decision in the Food Fair case, the Congress had amended the Packers and Stockyards Act to give the Federal Trade Commission jurisdiction over retail sales of meat products. See Public Law 85-909, approved Sept. 2, 1958.

Judicial Interpretation

Except in the *Woman's Day* case discussed above, judicial review has contributed little to an understanding of the sections that incorporate the concept of proportionality. The *Woman's Day* decision is recent, and until its principles are finally tested on appeal, one cannot be certain of their authority. Only one order by the Commission under Section 2(d) has been appealed.[26] Two cases involving such orders have been brought before the courts in proceedings in which the Commission charged that its order had been violated. In one of these, the respondent consented to an order of enforcement, and no controverted issue was before the court. Although the other case involving Section 2(d) shuttled back and forth between the circuit court and the Supreme Court, the matter at issue was whether or not a judicial order was appropriate with reference to parts of the Commission's order that had not been violated, and no light was thrown on the substantive questions raised by the statute.[27] In a private suit in 1945,[28] the Eighth Circuit confirmed an award of damages to a department store in Little Rock, Arkansas, because Elizabeth Arden had paid a competitor in Little Rock the full salary of a clerk to demonstrate Arden cosmetics, yet paid the complaining department store only half the salary of a similar clerk. The difference in payment had been arbitrarily determined and was not proportional to Arden's sales to the two stores. In another private suit a district court said in 1956[29] that Section 2(d) might be violated if a manufacturer gave an advertising allowance to a retailer but not to a wholesaler whose customers competed with the retailer.

A decision by the second circuit in July 1958 in the case of Atalanta Trading Corporation provided further interpretation of Section 2(d). In the area around Washington, D.C., Atalanta had given Giant Food Shopping Center an allowance of $500 to promote pork shoulder pic-

[26] Docket 6464, *Atalanta Trading Corp.*

[27] See below, p. 188.

[28] *Elizabeth Arden Sales Corp.* v. *Gus Blass Co.,* 150 F. 2d 988. The complaint was brought under both Secs. 2(d) and 2(e). Arden contested the constitutionality of the latter section because no reference was made to interstate commerce therein. The court of appeals held that since Sec. 2(d) contained such a reference, the omission of it from the parallel Sec. 2(e) was inadvertent and would be disregarded; but that in any event Arden's payment violated Sec. 2(d). The Supreme Court denied certiorari.

[29] *Krug* v. *International Telephone and Telegraph Corp.,* 142 F. Supp. 230.

nics for the Fourth of July 1954, an allowance of $2,000 to promote specially packaged gift-wrapped canned hams for the Christmas holidays in 1954, and an allowance of $1,000 to promote precooked Canadian bacon in May 1955. To others in the Washington area, Atalanta had made no sales of bacon, only a single $600 sale of pork shoulder picnics five months after its allowance to Giant, and only a single $250 sale of canned hams eight months before its allowance to Giant. The Commission had analyzed the allowances on the theory that all could be considered together as allowances on pork products. Rejecting this classification, the court cited with approval a previous decision by the Commission that the law imposes "no requirements that a seller give advertising allowances on all his products if he elects to accord them on one or more articles." It thought that the time intervals precluded a finding that the concessions to Giant on hams and pork shoulder picnics had been withheld from others.

The Commission apparently assumed without discussion that if a supplier wishes to grant promotional allowances in a given territory, he must elect to do so upon the first sale made. Under the Commission's rationale any prior sale without an allowance would make a subsequent sale with an allowance unlawful. By the same token any allowance given on the first sale could never be adjusted to meet competition. . . . Assuming the validity of dispensing with proof of actual competitive injury, to hold that Section 2(d) has been violated in the face of a record revealing that the promotional allowances could not possibly have had any discriminatory effects would establish an inflexible rule at odds with the basic concept of free competition.[30]

Something was done to define the scope of the services that must be proportionalized under Section 2(e) in a decision by the Fifth Circuit in a private suit in 1956.[31] The complaint was that U. S. Steel Corporation had favored a wholly owned subsidiary by honoring assignments of wages covering goods purchased from the subsidiary while it gave no similar service to the plaintiff. In dismissing the complaint, the court said that Section 2(e) applies to merchandising services rendered on specific commodities, not to extensions of credit.

Three of the Commission's orders under Section 2(e) were appealed

---

[30] *Atalanta Trading Corp.* v. *FTC*, 258 F. 2d 365, 369, 371-72. The decision was not appealed. The Commission's case was Docket 6464.

[31] *Skinner* v. *U. S. Steel Corp.*, 233 F. 2d 762.

to the courts. In one of the cases, involving Corn Products Refining Company,[32] violation of Section 2(e) was accompanied by several kinds of price discrimination in violation of Section 2(a) and by requirements contracts that violated Section 3 of the Clayton Act. Both in the Commission's findings and order and in the decisions on appeal, attention centered on other matters than Section 2(e). In the relevant part of one case, the Commission found that in paying for advertising that mentioned the Curtiss Candy Company, Corn Products Refining Company had given Curtiss a service that had not been made available to other customers. The Corn Products defense rested on the contentions that the advertising payments had been made to advertising media, not to Curtiss; that their purpose had been to promote the sale of dextrose; that dextrose was bought by Curtiss as a raw material for candy manufacture, not as a product for resale; and that Curtiss had received no service not available to its competitors. The Seventh Circuit saw no difficulty in accepting the Commission's inference that the arrangement between Corn Products and Curtiss by which both companies would advertise dextrose was made to build up the sales of dextrose to Curtiss and others and resulted in large expenditures by Corn Products for the benefit of Curtiss to the detriment of other competing purchasers. The Supreme Court, too, found no difficulty in regarding the advertising as a service related to the purchase of dextrose by Curtiss and to Curtiss' sale of the candy containing dextrose. At both appellate levels, the decision turned primarily on two questions: First, whether Section 2(e) was applicable to a commodity the separate identity of which was lost in processing; and second, whether it applied to an advertising arrangement that was not made directly with the buyer of the commodity. Both questions were answered in the affirmative.[33]

In another case that was appealed, the Commission found that Elizabeth Arden had violated Section 2(e) by supplying demonstrators to some customers and not to others.[34] It rejected Arden's argument that demonstrator service is of a kind that cannot be proportionalized, on the ground that Arden was free to avoid any service that could be supplied only on terms violating the statute. It considered, and rejected as incon-

---

[32] Docket 3633, *Corn Products Refining Co.*

[33] See below, pp. 194-95.

[34] The case bore a close relation to the private case of *Elizabeth Arden Sales Corp.* v. *Gus Blass Co.,* which has been discussed above.

sistent with the evidence, Arden's contention that demonstrators had been supplied only to meet competition. In reviewing the case, the Second Circuit held that the Commission does not need to prove that competition has been adversely affected by a violation of Section 2(e). The Court also held specifically that the order had been properly made to apply to indirect as well as to direct customers. The Court mentioned the Commission's view that any service that is offered must be proportionately available to all and the finding that Arden's services had not been offered in good faith to meet services furnished by competitors. The interpretations of the law involved in these two points were not explicitly affirmed, but since they were necessary to the Commission's decision, which the Court sustained, they may be regarded as having received the Court's approval. However, the validity of the Arden case as a precedent has been clouded by the Commission itself, for in subsequently approving trade practice conference rules for the cosmetic industry, the Commission abandoned the principle of its Arden decision that any service offered to any one must be proportionately available to all. Instead, it adopted the view that the services offered to different customers may be of different kinds, if, in the aggregate, the group of services available to various customers satisfies the test of proportionality.

The third appeal was in the case against Simplicity Patterns, decided by the Circuit Court on May 29, 1958. The Court held that, in refusing to receive the respondent's cost defense, the Commission had misinterpreted the statute, and remanded the case to the Commission to hear the evidence as to cost.[35]

If the court's interpretation of the law is affirmed by the Supreme Court, cost defenses will be permissible under Section 2(e), and the difference between the rules of law applicable to the two sections concerned with proportionality will be significantly increased.

*The Frequency of the Cases
and the Scope of this Study*

Until December 31, 1957, the law as to disproportionate provision of service resulted in orders by the Commission in only 15 cases, of which only 5 turned solely on this section of the statute. Eight of the remaining

[35] See above, footnote 24, p. 164.

10 cases involved also disproportionate payments, 3 involved injurious price discrimination, 1 involved receipt of injurious discrimination, 2 involved unlawful tying arrangements, and 2 involved predatory attacks on competitors. Three of the 15 cases were appealed. In the Arden case, which had to do with disproportionate service only, the Commission was sustained by the circuit court and certiorari was denied. In the Corn Products case, where disproportionate service was accompanied by price discrimination and tying arrangements, the Commission was sustained both by the circuit court and by the Supreme Court. The Simplicity Patterns case was remanded to the Commission for consideration of a cost defense that the Commission had refused to receive, and on September 30, 1958, had not yet been finally decided.

In the same period, the Commission issued orders against disproportionate advertising allowances in 47 cases. In 27 of these no other unlawful practice was involved. In 12 others the disproportionate allowance was accompanied by injurious price discrimination,[36] in 8 others by disproportionate service, in 1 by illegal brokerage, in 2 by receipt of illegally discriminatory price concessions, in 1 by unlawful tying arrangements, in 1 by price-fixing, and in 2 by predatory attacks on competitors. No case was appealed. In 2 cases, however, the order was judicially enforced after the respondents had violated it.

Since the Commission assigns docket numbers to cases in the sequence in which complaints are issued, these numbers can be used as a rough guide to changes in the Commission's distribution of emphasis among different types of legal proceedings. If the orders under the Robinson-Patman Act are arranged in five equal groups[37] according to sequence of docket numbers, the 62 cases in the first group include 7 proceedings concerned with Section 2(d) and 3 concerned with Section 2(e). Only 3 of the 10 cases had to do with proportionality alone; the rest also involved other types of violation. The second group includes only 4 cases having to do with proportionality. All of them involved violations of Section 2(d), 1 involved Section 2(e) also, and only 1 did not include other types of

---

[36] This includes one case in which the Commission found also disproportionate services, illegal receipt of discriminatory prices, and tying arrangements; and one in which it found illegal receipt of discrimination and price-fixing.

[37] The fifth group has 63 cases, the others 62.

violation. In the third group, there are no violations of Section 2(e) and only 5 of Section 2(d), 3 of the latter involving other violations as well. In the fourth group, proportionality is slightly more important. There are 8 cases, 5 concerned with Section 2(d), 2 with Section 2(e), and 1 with both sections. Only 2 involved any other violation of law. In the final group, proportionality suddenly attains major importance. Section 2(d) was violated in 25 cases, 6 of which included violations of Section 2(e) also; and Section 2(e), standing alone, was also violated twice. In only 1 case was there any other type of violation. The 27 cases concerned with disproportionality were over 43 per cent of all the cases in the group. Of all the cases concerned with proportionality under the Robinson-Patman Act, exactly half fall in the last group. Presumably the increased activity reflects an increasing tendency for businessmen to substitute advertising arrangements for brokerage payments and price concessions and an increase in the importance of advertising as supermarkets and self-service by consumers have increased.

In the present study, attention has been given to 5 of the 8 cases involving Section 2(e) that were decided before December 31, 1955, and to 11 of the 25 cases involving Section 2(d) that were decided before the same date.[38] Among the 2(e) cases studied are 3 in which only this part of the law was violated; 1 in which the violation included Section 2(a) and Section 3 of the Clayton Act; and 1 in which the violation included Sections 2(a), 2(d), 2(f), and Section 3 of the Clayton Act. Among the 11 cases that were concerned with Section 2(d), 2 had to do with that section only; and 9 with it in combination with various other violations of law: 6 with Section 2(a); 1 with Sections 2(a), 2(f), and Section 5 of the Federal Trade Commission Act; 1 with Sections 2(a), 2(e), 2(f), and Section 3 of the Clayton Act; and 1 with Section 2(c).

The Growing Importance of
Advertising Allowances

There was a general agreement among those who were interviewed

[38] One of the cases, against *Curtiss Candy Co.* (Docket 4556), involved both types of violation. Thirty-two separate cases involving proportionality resulted in orders before Dec. 31, 1955. Of these, 15 have been studied.

that advertising allowances have become more prevalent since the effective date of the Robinson-Patman Act and that in many instances they have taken the place of other types of arrangement, particularly the payment of brokerage fees to buyers. There appear to be at least three reasons for this development: (1) the efforts to exploit brands without violation of the brokerage provisions; (2) the legal advantage of advertising allowances; (3) their suitability to institutional changes in the food industries.

In several of the brokerage cases that involved voluntary or cooperative groups, brokerage arrangements had been entangled with the exploitation of trademarks, which had won recognition and become valuable properties. Efforts to preserve the value of these trademarks after the brokerage arrangements were set aside took the form of advertising allowances designed to induce distributors to push goods carrying the marks. Where the ownership of the mark and the nature of the advertising were so arranged that the advertising allowance could not be interpreted as a payment by a seller to a buyer in lieu of brokerage, these programs succeeded in preserving at least a part of the prestige and value of the marks.

The use of advertising allowances also had legal advantages, particularly from the point of view of buyers. When the seller paid the buyer unlawful brokerage, buyer and seller were equally guilty. When the seller granted the buyer an unlawful discount, the buyer who knowingly induced or received the discount was himself violating the law. When the seller paid an unlawful advertising allowance, he violated the law in giving it, but the buyer did not do so in receiving it. Thus, where advertising allowances were substituted for other forms of concession to buyers, the legal liability of the buyer was reduced. Moreover, until recently the hazards of the seller were reduced by the fact that the Commission paid relatively little attention to this type of practice. Prior to 1951 only 14 orders had been issued against violations of Section 2(d) in more than 14 years, and only 4 of these were concerned with such violations alone. Before 1956 there were only three years in which more than 2 orders under Section 2(d) were issued.

In some cases it was possible for the seller, too, to escape illegality by resort to an advertising allowance. Where the purpose of an unlawful brokerage payment had been to induce a representative of the buyer (for example, a voluntary chain) to engage in promotional work on the seller's behalf, the same promotional services might be rendered and lawfully paid for through an advertising allowance provided care was taken in the legal form of the arrangement. It was necessary to tie the payment specifically to the service to be rendered and to divorce it from any relationship to the flow of goods between buyer and seller, yet at the same time to make the payment proportionally available to the seller's various customers. This was difficult but not impossible.[39]

In a variety of other circumstances, sellers could also accomplish their purposes through advertising allowances that were not disproportionate and hence not unlawful. A few examples will serve to indicate the diversity of such situations. A seller, wishing to introduce a new product by selective advertising, might place it first in only a few outlets, all receiving proportional advertising allowances, and subsequently place it in many outlets after the advertising allowance had been withdrawn.[40] At selected points where the seller wished to undertake special advertising programs, he might distribute his goods on consignment rather than by sale, thus converting the special advertising of his consignment agents into expenditures by an agent on behalf of a principal rather than expenditures for which an allowance was paid to a customer. Again, a seller might make some kinds of allowance generally available with reasonable certainty that they would be seldom accepted.[41]

Apart from such ingenious devices as these, each of which could be used only in special types of situations, there developed evasions of the law based on concealment rather than immunity. In some cases, for example, advertising allowances were paid personally by salesmen rather than by the companies they represented and were included under other names in the salesmen's expense accounts.

Third, advertising allowances have become more prevalent because they are appropriate to institutional changes and market strategies in the food industries. The increased emphasis on packaged and processed foods has enhanced the importance of brand names. The development of supermarkets and voluntary chains, as well as corporate chains, has

[39] *Cf.* Austin, "Brokerage *v.* Service Payments: Another Look at Section 2(c)," *op. cit.*

[40] See Ralph E. Axley, "Current Problems of Merchandising in the Face of the Proportionally Equal Terms Requirement," in *Trade Regulation Series No. 3, Symposia* (1956), pp. 147 ff.

[41] See below, p. 182.

established a pervasive rivalry between national brands and private brands. The growth of self-service by consumers has fostered a struggle of brand against brand. Efforts by the owners of the brands to win the co-operative support of those to whom they sell are to be expected.

National-brand manufacturers have resorted to advertising allowances, not only in their competition against one another but also in attempting to reduce the interest of distributors in private brands. They have preferred to make advertising allowances rather than payments of brokerage to buyers because the former made possible more control over the buyer's behavior. Powerful distributors, aware that under the price discrimination law they do not enjoy unlimited immunity in seeking discounts or brokerage commissions, have found it safe to press for maximum advertising allowances. As this pressure has become institutionalized, the buyers for chains and supermarkets have sometimes found that their employers placed more pressure on them to obtain maximum advertising allowances than to obtain minimum net prices; and, in response to this pressure, they have emphasized the importance of the advertising allowance in their buying. This development has probably gone further than would be justified by a rational evaluation of the advantages of advertising allowances.

Information is not available to show the pace at which the resort to advertising allowances has developed. It is probable, however, that the Commission has been slow in recognizing the importance of this type of practice. In any case, it is noteworthy that the Commission's emphasis on proceedings concerned with disproportionate advertising has been increasing.

Varieties of Advertising Allowances

The advertising allowances that have been involved in the Commission's cases have been paid for a wide variety of promotional activities. Among their purposes have been to induce distributors to mention the seller's goods in newspaper and other periodical advertising, in handbills, in direct mailings, in other forms of printed matter, and over the radio; to encourage such advertising at particular times such as the beginning of a season, a period of slack sales, or the time of a special promotion; to obtain special display and an advantageous position for brands of merchandise in the distributor's establishment; to induce the distributor to affix his private brand to the seller's product and thus give the seller the benefit of the promotional effort spent on that brand; to encourage constant promotional effort by the distributor in such forms as salesmen's calls, propaganda at business conventions, and the carrying of an adequate and representative inventory of the seller's goods; and to induce manufacturers of unrelated goods to encourage the handling of the seller's products by distributors whom they control. In its narrowest form, the allowance has been paid for specifically defined and limited acts such as the placement of a particular advertisement with a particular content. In its broadest form, the allowance has been paid for pervasive co-operation with the seller scarcely different from that which is often compensated by a functional discount.

Several kinds of disproportionality have been found by the Commission in the advertising allowances against which it has proceeded. In the most common type of case the seller granted an allowance to selected recipients without being willing to grant it to others. Usually the selection was direct and candid, but in a few cases it was accomplished indirectly through the choice of types of advertising or advertising media or standards of eligibility that would automatically prevent many customers from obtaining the allowance. Disproportionality sometimes took the form, not of refusal to grant allowances, but of disproportionate variation in the amount of advertising service bought from different customers or in the compensation offered for the service.

Neither the difference in the type of advertising service bought nor the difference in the nature of the disproportion established appears to have been significant in differentiating the kinds of business situations to which the advertising allowance provision has been applied and the kinds of economic results that have followed the Commission's orders. The important differences are traceable to the purposes rather than the forms of the advertising programs.

Advertising Allowances as Indirect Price Discrimination

Advertising allowances fall into two classes. One includes those that are intended primarily to give the buyer a price concession; the other, those that are intended primarily to enlist the buyer's co-operation in a promotional program. When an allowance for advertising is merely a price reduction, it can be treated as such and subjected to an order under the parts of the statute applicable to discriminations in price. Indeed, in two cases this has been done, and the recipients of the allowance, who would not have been liable under Section 2(d), have been subjected to orders under Section 2(f).[42] But where the seller purports to require advertising service, and to some extent receives it, the advertising aspect of the arrangement may make a price discrimination fuzzy. In such instances, the seller is liable under Section 2(d), if his allowances are disproportionate.

One case—that against C. F. Sauer—involved advertising allowances in which the price discrimination aspect was at least as conspicuous as the promotional aspect. Sauer granted advertising allowances to customers some of whom did not spend them on advertising. It selected these customers and determined the amounts of the allowances capriciously. Certain customers, it appears, became beneficiaries of the allowances partly because they were large and powerful and partly because of the personal friendship of Sauer's active manager, who is now dead. The allowance played a subordinate part in a broader program of capricious price discrimination by Sauer.[43] The Commission's order and Sauer's death have made a considerable change in the operations of the Sauer Company. All of Sauer's customers who were interviewed agree that Sauer no longer engages in unsystematic discrimination, either in the form of advertising allowances or otherwise. Advertising allowances are still paid, but at a uniform percentage of volume, on proof of actual expenditure for advertising. Price differentials have been generally eliminated. There are discounts for small quantities, such as 8 or 12 gallons. Information is conflicting as to whether or not the price structure includes volume discounts in addition to advertising allowances that are proportional to volume.[44]

Advertising Allowances as Payments
for Access to Controlled Markets

In three other cases studied, the advertising allowance challenged by the Commission was granted to concerns or associations that controlled

[42] See below, pp. 487-88.
[43] See below, pp. 473-74.
[44] See below, p. 474.

access to important segments of the market, under conditions suggesting that, if an allowance had not been granted, the seller might have suffered a disadvantage in his sales. These cases differ from the Sauer case in that the allowance was paid for some kind of advertising service that was actually performed. Nevertheless, the control of the market exercised by the recipient of the allowance was the most striking feature in each case.

In the case against Golf Ball Manufacturers Association, the allowance was paid by manufacturers of golf balls for the right to affix to their balls a trade-mark, P.G.A., owned by the Professional Golfers Association. The payment was made to the Association in the form of a royalty for use of the mark and was distributed by the Association to its members in proportion to their sales of balls bearing the mark. Balls with this mark were sold only through the shops operated by the members of the Association. The allowance was accompanied by the unlawful grant and receipt of discriminatory prices and by a price-fixing conspiracy.[45] Most of the manufacturers who paid the allowance had well-advertised trade marks of their own, and balls bearing these marks were also sold through the shops of the professional golfers. The inducement for the manufacturers to co-operate in the promotion of a private brand that competed with their own brands was obviously the fact that the professional golfers as a group could place a considerable amount of promotional effort behind their private brand and thus obtain for it a volume so large that no manufacturer wished to be excluded from this private-brand market. Moreover, there was a possibility that professional golfers might seek to divert trade from the advertised brand of a manufacturer who did not co-operate to the advertised brands of others who co-operated. That the allowance rested more on the power of the Association to influence a segment of the market than on the desire of the manufacturers to buy advertising service is apparent in the fact that some of the leading manufacturers welcomed the Commission's order as a way of reducing their promotional expenses and strengthening their own brands. Leading manufacturers have continued to sell their own brands through professional golfers as well as other channels and to supply balls with the P.G.A. trade-mark for sale by professional golfers, but without payment of advertising allowances. One of them apparently lost some sales in making the readjustment: in the year before the Commission's order, his sales of balls bearing the P.G.A. label were about

---

[45] See below, pp. 297, 332, and footnote 21, p. 300.

24 per cent of his total sales; in the first full year after the order, they were only 6 per cent, and his total volume was 7 per cent lower. While this book was being written, the Professional Golfers Association was endeavoring to find a lawful way by which it could obtain an income for the use of its brand.

Similarly, the case against United States Rubber involved payments that had been made partly to obtain access to private-brand markets. This case was concerned partly with discriminatory prices granted to certain mass distributors and commercial accounts.[46] However, it also covered commissions paid by United States Rubber to certain great oil company customers on sales that United States Rubber made directly to jobbers and filling stations whose primary business was the sale of the petroleum products of these oil companies. The commissions, frequently referred to in the trade as overrides, compensated the oil companies for using their influence to induce these distributors to buy United States tires. In thus paying a commission to bystanders through whom the goods did not flow, United States Rubber was recognizing the effectiveness of the influence exercised by the major oil companies over the concerns that distribute their products. The relevant part of the Commission's order directed United States Rubber to cease paying commissions to oil-company customers for services rendered in connection with the sale of tires unless these commissions were proportionally available to all other customers. Presumably, the reason the order was confined to payments made to customers was the belief that payments to concerns that were not customers did not violate Section 2(d). In compliance with the order, United States Rubber has ceased to pay commissions on its direct sales of tires to petroleum distributors where the oil company that has influence with these distributors is also a customer of United States Rubber. However, the payments are still made on similar direct sales where the recipient oil company is not itself a customer of United States Rubber. Thus, the effect of the case has been to establish a distinction between two classes of direct sale by United States Rubber, although there is no significant economic difference between the two classes. Where an influential oil company buys United States Rubber products, it receives no commission upon direct purchase of United States Rubber products by the distributors of its petroleum products. Where the oil company

[46] See below, pp. 257, 463, 471-72.

does not buy United States Rubber products, it receives a commission on similar purchases. In the latter class of cases, United States Rubber still pays an oil company for its influence in the market.[47]

The use of an advertising allowance to purchase admission to a market was also an aspect of the Carpel Frosted Food case. Carpel, a wholesaler of frozen foods, agreed in 1944 to pay a commission to District Grocery Stores, an organization of 275 groceries in and around Washington, D.C. In return, D.G.S. was to advertise one Carpel item each week at Carpel's expense, to warehouse Carpel products, and to refrain from advertising or sponsoring the frozen food of a competitor. After the arrangement had been discussed with the Federal Trade Commission, it was replaced by one that eliminated the provision for the exclusion of competitors. Under the new plan, Carpel was to pay D.G.S. $5,000 a year, and D.G.S. was to use the money in promoting Carpel products. Subsequently, members of D.G.S. purchased about 10 to 12 per cent of Carpel's total volume. The Commission found that Carpel and D.G.S. had both violated the brokerage provision of the act and that Carpel had violated the advertising-allowance provision in making advertising payments to D.G.S. that were not proportionally available to others. In distinguishing between these two kinds of violation, the majority of the Commission held that the portion of Carpel's payments to D.G.S. that was used to promote the sale of Carpel products to D.G.S. stores constituted brokerage payments, while the portion of the payments that was expended by D.G.S. to promote the sale of the products by the stores to the ultimate consumer constituted advertising allowances.

It is obvious, however, that in making the lump-sum payments, Carpel had no such legal distinction in mind. It was concerned to find an outlet through D.G.S. stores and found it necessary to enlist the co-operation of D.G.S. because the D.G.S. by-laws required the members to carry

[47] It is possible that proceedings under the Federal Trade Commission Act may result in broader effects on overrides. On Jan. 11, 1956, the Commission issued three parallel complaints against *Goodrich and the Texas Company* (Docket 6485), *Goodyear and Atlantic Refining* (Docket 6486), and *Firestone and Shell* (Docket 6487). In each complaint, the charge was that, since the oil company had effective control over the ostensibly independent distributors of its gasoline, its arrangement as to overrides closed the market to competing tire producers, deprived distributors of freedom of choice, limited the access of consumers to competing goods, damaged competition, and thus violated the Federal Trade Commission Act. On Sept. 1, 1958, the cases had not yet been decided.

all merchandise advertised by D.G.S. and to display it when called on to do so.[48] However, the arrangement involved more than the mere payment to a powerful intermediary. In 1944 frosted foods were relatively new, and few grocery stores had facilities for keeping and displaying them or experience in selling them. Promotional work by D.G.S., both with the member stores and with the general public, was appropriate in creating and enlarging a market for a new product. For this reason, the advertising allowance in the Carpel case was only partly an effort by Carpel to buy its way into a market through a monthly payment.

As a result of the order, the promotional arrangement between D.G.S. and Carpel was canceled, and D.G.S. ceased to distribute the Carpel frozen-food line under private label. With the discontinuance of this label, Carpel's volume was reduced. However, D.G.S. now buys various nationally branded frozen foods through Carpel as distributor and receives advertising allowances from the manufacturer for promoting them.

Advertising Allowances as
Payments for Advertising

Where the advertising allowance was intended primarily as a purchase of advertising, the impact of the Commission's cases differed widely with the differences in the nature and purpose of the particular advertising program. In some instances, the seller's purpose was to enhance the prestige of his goods in a way that, if successful, would increase his sales not only through outlets receiving the allowance but through others as well. In some instances the allowance was intended to facilitate an experiment with a particular method of sales promotion. In some instances its purpose was to achieve the maximum effect with a limited advertising budget by placing advertising where it would reach the most customers or the most desirable customers. In some instances the purpose was to win the good will of distributors by helping them undertake special merchandise promotions related to their own distributive strategy. Sometimes the purpose was to enlist a broad collaboration by the distributor equivalent to that expected in return for a functional discount.

The effort to build prestige for the product and thereby to enlarge its

[48] The by-laws also required the members to buy merchandise from those with whom D.G.S. made a purchase contract; but D.G.S. explained this requirement as having been used only prior to 1927, when D.G.S. had no warehouse.

market is illustrated by the case involving Kay Windsor. Success for a dress manufacturer depends on placing dresses in a considerable number of satisfactory outlets early in the season, so that an adequate volume of orders can be attained rapidly and so that there will be adequate time for the merchandise to be sold before mark-down sales begin. This objective of the manufacturer is inconsistent with the desire of many stores that sell dresses to delay their orders until they can be sure what styles can be successfully sold. A manufacturer can sell more easily to small stores at or before the beginning of the season if he can show these stores that others, particularly large department stores and stores with prestige, are featuring his dresses in their advertising. Manufacturers compete for advertising by the influential stores. They offer advertising allowances selectively to chosen customers who have not asked for allowances. They increase the offers when influential buyers bargain for concessions. They have no incentive to make similar allowances generally. Their purpose does not require advertising of their dresses by everyone. Indeed, such advertising might make their dresses seem too common to be desirable. Moreover, advertising by the ordinary small store would not help them make sales to others, since, in general, one small store does not imitate another.

The impression is widespread in the dress industry that advertisments by large stores that have prestige facilitate the sale of the same dresses by small competing stores. The small stores themselves often share this belief. To the extent that it is true, the question arises whether selective advertising allowances are always injurious to the competitors of those receiving them. But whether there is injury to competing stores, it is obvious that the seller's promotional purpose can be accomplished better by selective advertising than by general advertising.

Windsor's advertising allowances, so far as the case disclosed them, reflected these incentives and were similar to those of other dress manufacturers. Normally, Windsor's allowance was available to customers who bought an initial order of at least 600 cotton dresses during off-season periods for sales promotions in January or immediately after Easter. Actually, Windsor did not observe these limitations, but sought to interest certain department stores and a buying syndicate by making such allowances as seemed necessary in each instance, and did not inform other customers that an allowance was available. In New York City, Franklin Simon received an allowance of $3,500 between January and

June 1949, while R. H. Macy was not offered any allowance. In Newark, Kresge-Newark received $150 on 300 dresses bought through a buying syndicate, which was permitted to allocate the allowance it received among its members.

The Commission found that Windsor had violated Section 2(d) by offering advertising allowances that were not generally available. After the case, Windsor discontinued its program of selective allowances. One customer, a small department store, says that this change reduced its willingness to buy Windsor dresses. In place of special allowances, Windsor made a general offer to pay half of the cost of newspaper advertising up to a maximum of 4 per cent of the customer's net annual purchases. In practice, this plan has caused trouble. Some customers have deducted from their payments to Windsor the entire cost of their advertising of Windsor dresses; others have deducted 4 per cent of each invoice, whether or not they did any advertising. Such misunderstandings have led to disputes and ill will and to suits by Windsor for sums as small as $4.75—presumably undertaken lest failure to try to collect be interpreted as violation of the Commission's order.

Many small customers have made no effort to obtain Windsor's advertising allowances. A small buyer cannot claim a small promotional allowance because he does not find it practicable to advertise by brand name a dress of which he may have bought only six copies.[49] If he places newspaper advertisements, they are so small that there is no room for mention of the manufacturer's name.

The interviews with Windsor's customers indicate that other dress manufacturers still make selective advertising allowances similar to those condemned in the Windsor case. These customers did not appear to resent Windsor's allowances. Indeed, one of them said specifically that the advertising of a dress by a large department store competitor generates volume for other stores as well and that he, therefore, orders the dress he sees featured in the advertising of the department store. Several of these customers criticize advertising allowances, not on the ground that they are discriminatory, but on the ground that it is foolish for a store to allow its advertising program to be governed by the manufac-

[49] In dismissing a case against *Lever Brothers Co.* (Docket 5585) in 1953, the Commission recognized as relevant a contention that small buyers could not take advantage of a nominally available advertising allowance, but held that in the particular case the practical availability of the allowance had been shown. See 50 FTC 509-10.

turer's needs rather than its own. They think that there is danger in tying the store's prestige to that of a particular manufacturer's label, and that there is danger that the quest for allowances will lead to overbuying. One department store asserts that, by setting up an obstacle to selective promotional advertising, the Robinson-Patman Act has increased the pressure of time on the manufacturer of ready-to-wear clothing, and has thus made it easier for department stores to buy garments from distressed manufacturers for sale under distributors' private labels.

In the Curtiss Candy case, the advertising practice condemned by the Commission consisted in a catch-as-catch-can use by Curtiss of a wide variety of advertising and promotional expedients, each adopted in particular places in co-operation with particular distributors. It is not clear from the record to what extent these various practices were regarded as experiments with advertising techniques that might later be more widely applied and to what extent they may have been intended from the outset as special promotions. It is clear, however, that each was adapted to particular circumstances. Among the forms of advertising used were (a) payment of a monthly fee to a chain store for posters displayed in automatic machines; (b) grant of a discount for prominently displaying certain designated candy bars; (c) grant of a discount for the placement of only Curtiss Candy products on display racks; (d) grant of a discount to a chain for carrying five Curtiss Candy bars in every store, with good display; (e) grant of a discount to a chain for placing a Curtiss display figure prominently on each soda fountain; (f) payment of a monthly lump sum for the inclusion of a Curtiss advertisement on soda-fountain and lunch-room checks and for advertising, display, and promotion of Curtiss products in specified ways; (g) payment of a part of the lump-sum cost of a radio-advertising program; (h) payment of a monthly lump sum for participation in radio, newspaper, circular, and other advertising, and for concentrated efforts by salesmen; (i) payment of a monthly lump sum for poster advertising. These various forms of advertising payment were accompanied by the discriminatory provision of sales services, including the furnishing of free samples, the payment of demonstrators, and the rental of billboards.

The portions of the Curtiss case that had to do with payments for advertising and provision of sales services were incidental to various kinds of price discrimination and tying arrangements. Considered as a whole, the case turned on price discrimination rather than on promotional practices.[50] Nevertheless, the record of the case supports the opinion that the advertising promotions were primarily intended, not as additional forms of price concession, but as an assortment of devices to bring Curtiss products to the attention of the public. Some of these devices could be effective as advertising only because of their novelty. Others were capable of being generally used, but the Curtiss advertising program as a whole would have had to be less varied in order to take a form that could be made available to all customers.

The available information about the effect of the Commission's order on the Curtiss advertising program is not specific. The company still engages in co-operative advertising, but various competitors and customers think that it is "less aggressive" or "has reformed." This change is attributed to changes in executive personnel and less financial stress because of shortages of candy during the war, as well as to the order. One customer says that as a result of the discontinuance of special deals his purchases from Curtiss have fallen from about $50,000 per year to between $10,000 and $15,000. However, total sales by Curtiss did not decline. Apparently Curtiss now makes some advertising allowances available to all customers and seeks to establish proportionality among others by offering alternative allowances for alternative services. Performance of the services by those who receive payment for them is checked by tear-sheets of advertisements and by certification of other activities.

In the International Salt case, the unlawful advertising allowances on table salt constituted a minor part of International's advertising program. International provided a generally available advertising allowance of 10 cents per case of Sterling brand salt under a system of agreements with retailers for store display and sales service; and this program was found to be lawful. However, the Commission found that International had also accepted various offers by individual customers to provide advertising services under arrangements that differed in each offer. International's willingness to make such agreements had not been made generally known. In determining whether or not to accept these offers, International had followed no specific standards, but had made decisions in each instance after considering such matters as the type of store display offered, the shelf position offered, the type and quantity of the advertising to be provided, the quality, location, and cleanliness of the

[50] See below, pp. 291, 296, 314, 341, 493, and footnote 20, p. 299.

store, and the character of store personnel. The Commission found that the varying and selective advertising payments provided in these agreements violated Section 2(d).

Apparently the effect of the decision was the discontinuance of the varying arrangements with individual stores, without change in the general advertising program. No further information about the matter is available.

The effort to maximize the return from a limited advertising budget is evident in the activities of respondents in two of the cases studied—those against John B. Stetson and Holzbeierlein. The Stetson case involved price discrimination as well as disproportionate advertising.[51] The advertising aspect of the case was illustrated in the Commission's findings by advertising payments to three customers in New York and Chicago. One of these customers received a payment of $6,600 a year for window displays of Stetson hats on Fifth Avenue at 45th and 33rd Streets for 32 weeks of the year, and on 45th Street at Fifth Avenue for 22 weeks of the year. The second customer operated a chain of 26 retail hat stores in New York City. The third operated clothing stores in Chicago, St. Paul, and Minneapolis. Each received between $12,000 and $15,000 per year for advertising and display.

As a result of the case, Stetson discontinued these special advertising allowances. Apparently, its action contributed to a decision by one customer to cease carrying Stetson hats.

Holzbeierlein was a small baker in the District of Columbia, with a sales volume of somewhat more than a million dollars a year at its maximum. He thought he could compete with large bakers only by advertising. Finding advertising expensive, he based his advertising program upon advertising allowances to District Grocery Stores, United Food Stores, Nation-Wide Service Groceries, and others. For several years he paid District Grocery Stores $250 a month. In return, his product was mentioned in D.G.S. advertising, and D.G.S. supplied it to the customers who did not specify brands. In the Commission's case, which was aimed at the arrangement between Holzbeierlein and D.G.S., Holzbeierlein was found to have violated Section 2(d). As a result of the case, Holzbeierlein found it necessary to terminate his program of selective advertising allowances. The decision came in 1944. In 1953 Holzbeierlein's business was liquidated.

[51] See below, p. 257.

Before this case, D.G.S. made its arrangements for co-operative advertising on an *ad hoc* basis. Subsequently, it developed and published a schedule of rates to be charged for various types of service, such as mention in catalogs, mention in mailings, and provision of merchandise displays in its warehouses. It now applies these rates uniformly in its contracts with suppliers. As has been noted above,[52] maintenance of this type of proportionality by D.G.S. may create embarrassments for sellers who are trying to maintain proportionality in their payments to the various distributors to whom they sell.

The type of problem presented by Stetson and Holzbeierlein was thought to be important by various concerns that were not themselves involved in the Commission's proportionality cases. The officials of one buying group that was involved in a brokerage case expressed the opinion that the most restrictive feature of the Robinson-Patman Act is its effect on small producers who wish to engage in selective co-operative advertising.

Advertising Allowances as the Equivalent of Functional Discounts

In two cases that have been studied, concerned with school supplies, the Commission proceeded against the use of advertising allowances to set up a special functional class of distributors. These cases, against American Crayon Company and Binney & Smith Company, were similar in their facts and in the issues they raised. In each case the respondent was found guilty of unlawful discrimination in price as well as granting disproportionate advertising allowances.[53] The violation of the advertising-allowance provision consisted in setting up two classes of promotional distributors who received extra discounts of 10 per cent and 5 per cent, respectively, for carrying warehouse stocks and furnishing various promotional services. The purpose of the discounts was apparently to elicit exceptional service from those distributors who were believed to be best equipped to make sales to major school systems and other important customers. Apparently the sellers desired to rely primarily on a few such distributive organizations but were unwilling to cut

---

[52] See footnote 8, p. 157.
[53] See below, pp. 295-96, 340-41.

themselves off from some parts of the market by refusing to sell to other distributors of school supplies.[54]

Both of the school-supply cases resulted in 1940 in orders based on stipulations of facts by the respondents. Thereafter, American Crayon adopted written standards to determine the eligibility of a customer for the status of educational promotional distributor and announced that concerns enjoying this status would uniformly receive a promotional allowance of 10 per cent. The policy was announced in American Crayon's price lists for 1941 and 1942, but not thereafter. Salesmen were instructed to recommend for the preferred status all who could qualify. The requirements for the promotional allowance were that the distributor carry a representative stock, employ salesmen who regularly solicited large educational institutions, issue a catalog that included items produced by American Crayon, demonstrate merchandise with samples and displays to ultimate consumer groups and educational conventions, make regular quotations to educational institutions and also special quotations on American Crayon's request, report to American Crayon on competitive conditions, and maintain an adequate stock of samples and sales literature.

In 1951 the Commission began to investigate American Crayon's compliance with the order; in 1953, it reported that the company had violated the order in regard to both price discrimination and advertising.[55] The violation as to advertising was regarded as the more important. It consisted in failing to keep customers notified of the availability of the special discount for promotional service and in denying this discount to some customers who met the requirements for it, specifically to Gateway Paper and Supply Company, of Beloit, Wisconsin. American Crayon contended that Gateway was not active in displaying American Crayon's goods at educational meetings; did not report competitive conditions; did not list an adequate number of American Crayon products in its catalog; and employed only two salesmen to cover 1,500 schools

---

[54] It is noteworthy that these sellers were legally free to refuse to sell to all suppliers except those to whom they granted special discounts, even though the effect of the refusal would have been a harsher discrimination than was involved in the denial of an advertising allowance. Selective distribution by choice of distributors entails, however, an incomplete coverage of the market. In seeking to avoid this, Binney & Smith and American Crayon substituted preferential distribution by refusing to give uniform recognition to distributors' promotional services. But the gentler device was unlawful, though the harsher one was not.

[55] As to the former, see below, pp. 340-41.

in five states. It argued also that Gateway's catalog quoted prices lower than those of the educational promotional distributors with whom Gateway competed. During the compliance proceeding, American Crayon offered to re-examine the question of Gateway's eligibility, but Gateway refused the offer. In the investigation it appeared that American Crayon made sales to 94 educational promotional distributors (out of 3,500 jobber customers), as compared to 52 in 1942. In 1950 such distributors bought approximately half of the school supplies sold by American Crayon.

The Commission came to the conclusion that, whether or not Gateway was eligible for the special discount, American Crayon had violated the order by failing to inform Gateway of its deficiencies and to make the allowance available to others who sold to educational institutions.[56] In 1954 the Commission requested the Sixth Circuit to affirm and enforce the order. In April 1955 the Court determined that the order had been violated and granted enforcement of the portions involved in the violation. After considerable controversy the order of enforcement was extended in March 1957 to cover the whole of the order by the Commission.[57]

In 1951 the Commission also ordered an investigation of compliance with the order against Binney & Smith. In the investigation it appeared that Binney & Smith was extending a special promotional discount of 10 per cent to those distributors who agreed to carry a representative stock; to give Binney & Smith products prominent display in their catalog; to push the sale of Binney & Smith products, carrying only enough of other brands to fill insistent orders; and to submit bids on Binney & Smith products where bids were invited on commodities made by Binney &

---

[56] 49 FTC. 1799. The summary of the findings has been supplemented from the underlying record.

[57] In its order in April 1955, the Sixth Circuit set aside the first three paragraphs of the Commission's order, apparently on the ground that they had not been violated. In December of the same year the Supreme Court reversed this action. Thereupon, in February 1956, the Circuit Court reversed its entire decision, thus setting aside its own order enforcing the portion of the Commission's order that had been violated; it said that it was required to do so by the Supreme Court. In October 1956, this action was also reversed by the Supreme Court, and the Court below was ordered to affirm and enforce the part of the order that had been violated and to consider the Commission's petition for affirmance and enforcement of the rest. Thereafter, in February 1957, the Circuit Court affirmed and enforced the entire order. See 223 F. 2d 264; 350 U.S. 907.

Smith.[58] At the time of the investigation, such special discounts were being given to 38 school distributors, out of between 5,000 and 6,000 jobber customers. In 1945 Binney & Smith had also begun to grant a special discount of the same amount to certain school-discount customers who sold chiefly for its competitors but frequently obtained orders from schools for Binney & Smith brands. At the time of the investigation, there were 43 in this group. They were required to carry a representative stock; to give Binney & Smith prominent display in their catalog; and to bid on Binney & Smith brands where bids were invited and merchandise made by it was specified. The first of these two groups received the special discount not only on goods sold to schools but also on goods sold to retailers or through their own stores. The second group received it only on the merchandise resold to schools.[59]

In the investigation it appeared that Binney & Smith had not notified its customers that the extra 10 per cent was available and had established no definite standard for the selection of the distributors who were eligible for it. At least one received it while clearly failing to meet the stated requirements, and some to whom it was denied apparently met the requirements better than some to whom it was granted.

In 1954 the Commission asked the Second Circuit to enforce its order. A decree affirming and enforcing the order was entered with the consent of Binney & Smith.[60]

As a result of the compliance proceedings in the two cases, the special promotional discounts appear to have become available to concerns that could not previously obtain them. Gateway, which had been the principal complainant in both cases, had obtained the discount from another supplier, and refused to deal with either Binney & Smith or American Crayon. Apparently there still are controversies as to eligibility for the discounts. Nevertheless, various customers say that they are no longer at a disadvantage in bidding on orders from schools and that they now

[58] Report of the FTC on its investigation of alleged violation of its order to cease and desist, April 9, 1953, filed in FTC Docket 4143-1.

[59] The promotional discount was regarded by the Commission as subject to the requirements of Sec. 2(d), but the equal discount to school discount customers was regarded as subject to the requirements of Sec. 2(a), apparently because the Commission did not think the requirements as to services were made and applied in good faith. See below, p. 340.

[60] *Statutes and Court Decisions Pertaining to the Federal Trade Commission*, Vol. V, 1949-55 (1957), p. 676.

have the confidence to buy more at one time and to carry larger inventories.

Standards Invoked in Appraising Advertising Allowances

In dismissing the soap cases[61] the Commission expounded with unusual detail the considerations it regards as relevant to an appraisal of advertising allowances. Charges that the manufacturers had violated Sections 2(a) and 2(d) were dismissed by the trial examiner. His decision as to Section 2(d) was appealed; and the Commission affirmed it in an opinion covering all three cases.

The Commission said:

> Every customer knew, or could have easily learned, what payments were being offered and what he must do to get any of them. There was no singling out of favorite customers and making private and different deals with them as appeared in the matter of *John B. Stetson Company,* 41 FTC 244. There was no making of special allowances for promotional services to certain customers which were not made known (or even denied) to other customers, "who were able and willing to furnish the same services and facilities" as in *American Art Clay,* 38 FTC 463, *American Crayon Company,* 32 FTC 306, *Lifesavers Corp.,* 34 FTC 472, and other cases. . . .
>
> Counsel supporting the complaints . . . points out groups of customers who he claims could not make practical use of the newspaper program. These groups are:
>
> "(1) *Those Who Do Not Do Consumer Advertising Within the Meaning of That Term in the Contract.* . . . On this point, we adopt the finding of the trial examiner, which is as follows: '. . . There is no evidence . . . that an isolated advertisement placed by a customer would not be considered as regular consumer advertising or that the respondent has ever refused to grant an advertising allowance because the advertisement appeared as an isolated advertisement in a newspaper.'
>
> "(2) *Those Who Because of their Smaller Purchases of Respondents' Products Do Not Receive Enough in Payment to Pay for Newspaper Advertising Even Though Restricted to Respondents' Products.* . . . On this feature of the case we adopt the finding of the trial exam-

---

[61] Docket 5585, *Lever Brothers Co.;* Docket 5586, *The Procter and Gamble Distributing Co. et al.;* Docket 5587, *Colgate-Palmolive-Peet Co.*

iner, which is as follows: '. . . There is no evidence in this record to support a finding that even the highest rate of payment . . . is not reasonably available to all of respondent's customers. The customer can avail himself of this rate . . . on such products which he cares to advertise . . . with only one insertion of the advertisement. The respondent places no restrictions on the newspapers which he may use except that it cover the area where his store or stores are located thus enabling the use of neighborhood papers or weekly or monthly papers at a greatly reduced rate. The respondent has accepted as low as 2 or 3 lines of advertising as compliance with the contract. . . . No witness has appeared in this proceeding who testified that he wished to participate in the advertising allowance but could not do so because of the expense. Furthermore, any customer, who for any reason does not wish to advertise, can avail himself of promotional allowances at the rates provided by using handbills, radio or television or by conducting feature sales with display only.' "

. . . We will assume that among these many customers will be found some who do not find newspaper advertising practical. There is no proof, however, that either handbills or store displays are not reasonably practical for all.

There is no evidence in these cases that the promotional plans were tailored to fit the needs of favored customers as was condemned in *Elizabeth Arden, Inc.* v. *Federal Trade Commission,* 156 F. 2d 132. . . . Nor does the law require that a comprehensive plan must be so tailored that every feature of it will be usable or suitable for every customer. In many cases that would be an impossibility. . . .

Section 2(d) permits payments for services or facilities actually furnished. Certainly, payments for services or facilities not furnished are not authorized. The same would be true of payments grossly in excess of the cost or value of the services rendered. . . . There is no evidence from which it can be found that payments to any customers are in excess of their cost or value.

An additional question arises because of the fact that respondents' payments covered different types of services for which a differing scale of payment was fixed—a certain amount per case for newspaper advertising, a lesser amount for handbills, and still less for store displays. The argument is made that, to meet the requirement of proportionality, payment per case should be the same for each type of service rendered. . . . The proof generally is to the effect that advertising by newspaper is more expensive and more effective than advertising by either handbill or store display. . . .

The law does not prohibit a seller from paying for services of different types. In some cases it might be his duty to do so in order to meet the test of availability. Nor does the law require a seller to pay at the same rate, per unit of product sold, for types of services which are of unequal cost or value. The practical result of such a rule would be to restrict the payments to some type of service that every single customer could furnish. It would adopt uniformity as its goal rather than proportionality. Payments must be made in good faith for services or facilities actually rendered and there should be a fair and reasonable relation between the amount of the payment and the type of service rendered. . . . No standard could be laid down which would insure exact proportionality with the mathematical accuracy of a slide rule. . . . Nevertheless, the intent of Congress . . . is clear. Prior to the enactment of the Robinson-Patman Act, payments for services and facilities rendered (particularly in the advertising field) were often used for the purpose of discriminating among customers. It was that evil that Section 2(d) was intended to eliminate. Consequently, every plan providing payment for promotional services and facilities should be carefully scrutinized to see that it does conform to the express Congressional intent. It must be honest in its purpose and fair and reasonable in its application.[62]

The Effect of Advertising Allowances

From the various cases it is evident that where advertising allowances were intended in good faith to buy advertising service, their effect was not uniform. Some distributors chose their sources of supply in an effort to maximize the allowances they received, but others disregarded the availability of allowances in deciding where to buy. Certain large distributors received offers of allowances from so many sellers that, without losing the allowances, they could exercise a wide range of choice in buying. Without distorting their buying, advertising, and selling practices, they were able to obtain payments that defrayed a large part of their advertising expenditures. It was common but not universal for distributors to undertake more promotion on the goods to which allowances were attached; and in so far as the allowances induced special promotional efforts, they presumably affected the volume of sale and purchase by the distributor. In some cases the recipient of the allowance used it to increase his margin rather than to enhance his promotional expenditures; but in other cases the allowance was spent on promotion without any direct effect on distributors' margins. The level of the distributors' resale prices was seldom if ever affected by the size of the allowance.

[62] 50 FTC 507-12.

Effect of Proceedings Against
Advertising Allowances

The effect of the proceedings against disproportionate advertising allowances is difficult to ascertain. In 9 of the 11 cases that have been studied, the Commission's order covered other types of violation of the Robinson-Patman Act as well as violation of the advertising-allowance provision, and it is often impossible to determine separately the effect of the part of the order that had to do with advertising.

There was general agreement among those interviewed that advertising allowances are no longer used to increase distributors' margins but are uniformly spent in additional sales promotion. Since the allowances did not affect the level of resale prices before the cases, there is no reason to believe that the changes in advertising practice brought about by the cases had such an effect. So far as the interviews contained information on this matter, they confirmed the impression that resale prices were not affected. In several instances—the distribution of golf balls, tires, spices and extracts, and Stetson hats—the allowances were reduced or eliminated rather than made generally available at their previous levels. The effect was some increase in the net price received by the producer and some decrease in the distributors' margin. In the case of school supplies, however, the special allowance that had been available to some became available to a larger number, and the new recipients enjoyed a wider margin than before. Holzbeierlein's volume of sales was apparently reduced by the curtailment of his advertising program. In the cases of Stetson and Kay Windsor, at least one customer was alienated by the change in advertising practice; but apparently Stetson's total volume was not affected, and an apparently well-informed customer of Kay Windsor's expresses the belief that there was no significant effect upon Windsor's volume.

Provision of
Sales Services

In one case involving disproportionate provision of services by the seller—Corn Products Refining Company—only formal differences appear from the advertising allowance cases already discussed. The other cases concerned with the provision of sales services and facilities fall into four groups. One has to do with the provision of sales persons, usually known as demonstrators, to assist in reselling the merchandise of the manufacturer.[63] In the later cases in this group, this practice was accompanied by the provision of various displays and allowances, which apparently were offered, in the hope of reducing disproportionality, to distributors that did not receive demonstrators.[64] The second group has to do with the provision of goods in containers of special sizes or types, not available to all customers.[65] The third group has to do with the provision of display cabinets and racks, prizes for contests, and various other materials for advertising.[66] The fourth group has to do with the availability of the privilege of returning unsold goods.[67] Some companies engaged in more than one of these practices.

Provision of Advertising as a Sales Service

Eager to develop a market for dextrose as a raw material in candy manufacture, Corn Products Refining Company agreed with Curtiss Candy Company that Curtiss would use dextrose in its candy and feature it in its advertising, and that Corn Products would expend substantial sums in advertising Curtiss candies. The advertising by Corn Products was not placed through Curtiss, and the payments for it were made to the media rather than to Curtiss. Moreover, the size of the program was not conditioned either on the amount of dextrose bought by Curtiss or on the amount of advertising of dextrose by Curtiss. Consequently, the Commission interpreted the arrangement as the provision of a special service for Curtiss rather than as an advertising allowance.

It is obvious that Curtiss received a differential advantage from the fact that in four years—1936 to 1939—Corn Products spent $750,000

[63] Docket 3133, *Elizabeth Arden, Inc.;* Docket 6216, *Wooster Rubber Co.;* Docket 6264, *Knomark Manufacturing Co., Inc.;* Docket 6552, *O'Cedar Corp.*

[64] Docket 6441, *Helena Rubinstein, Inc.;* Docket 6442, *Yardley of London, Inc.;* Docket 6443, *Elmo, Inc.;* Docket 6519, *Revlon Products Corp.* probably belongs in this group, but the complaint refers vaguely to services and allowances, and since there was a consent order, there were no specific findings.

[65] Docket 3736, *Luxor, Ltd.;* Docket 6018, *General Foods Corp.*

[66] Docket 4556, *Curtiss Candy Co.;* Docket 5982, *American Greetings Corp.;* Docket 6221, *Simplicity Patterns;* Docket 6264, *Knomark Manufacturing Co., Inc.*

[67] Docket 5773, *Appleton-Century-Crofts, Inc.;* Docket 5982, *American Greetings Corp.*

in advertising Curtiss candy. It is equally obvious that, from the point of view of Corn Products, a major purpose of the advertising was to develop a new market. The record indicates that this purpose was accomplished, for the Commission found not only that the sales of dextrose by Corn Products to Curtiss rose during the four years from 1,347,000 pounds to 7,091,000, but also that Corn Products sold substantial quantities of dextrose to other candy manufacturers during this period. In essence, therefore, the case involved selective promotion similar to that of Kay Windsor or John B. Stetson. However, the advertising practice appeared in a setting of other violations of the Robinson-Patman Act as well as of Section 3 of the Clayton Act. The Commission's finding that the advertising arrangement for dextrose was unlawful was appealed by Corn Products along with the rest of the Commission's decision and was included in the orders in which the Circuit Court and the Supreme Court affirmed and enforced the order of the Commission.

The immediate result of the case was that Corn Products Refining ceased its program of advertising Curtiss candy as rich in dextrose. Information is not available as to whether Curtiss and other candy makers subsequently changed the proportions of dextrose used in their candies. One candy maker, on hearing of the dextrose arrangement, ceased to buy corn syrup from Corn Products and resumed doing so only when wartime shortages made alternative supplies less readily available.

Provision of Demonstrators as a Sales Service

The most important and widespread practice that is covered by Section 2(e) is the furnishing of demonstrators by manufacturers. In the cosmetic industry, particularly, it was common before the Robinson-Patman Act for the producers of the leading brands to furnish clerks to work behind the counters of large department stores in demonstrating and selling the products of the manufacturer. Some demonstrators were permanently stationed in particular stores; some moved from store to store, spending a limited time in each. In some cases the demonstrator was employed by the store, and all or a portion of her salary was paid to the store by the manufacturer. By the very nature of the practice, demonstrators could be made available only to stores with cosmetic departments large enough to make possible a mass display of the products of a single manufacturer and the use of all or most of the time of a sales girl in selling the products of that manufacturer. Indeed, shortly after the passage of the Robinson-Patman Act, one commentator suggested that, as applied to demonstrators, the proportionality provision must mean that, if a department store was to receive the services of a salesgirl for a month, a drugstore should receive the services of a midget for five minutes.

The demonstrator practice was challenged by the Commission in a case against Elizabeth Arden. Arden sold to about 3,000 retailers, including about 725 department stores, about 25 women's specialty shops, and about 2,250 drugstores. Arden spent about $250,000 a year in supplying more than 200 full or part-time demonstrators to 265 stores which, in the aggregate, bought less than 40 per cent of Arden's sales.[68] To be eligible for a demonstrator, a store was required to carry a representative stock of Arden products, to give them an adequate counter display, to display them in windows, to advertise them once or twice a month, to mention them in fashion shows, and to buy from Arden more than $5,000 per year; but the interpretation of some of these requirements differed from store to store. The salaries paid by Arden to demonstrators in various stores ranged from 1½ to 7½ per cent of the store's purchases from Arden. Where demonstrators were furnished, the sales of Arden products to consumers were increased and sometimes as much as tripled. Some department stores received no demonstrator service—for example, John Wanamaker in Philadelphia, which bought more Arden products in 1938 than six other Philadelphia department stores that received demonstrator service.[69] Drugstores and similar small outlets received no demonstrator service.

The Commission's order against Arden was sustained by the Second Circuit in 1946. Since Arden was unwilling to be interviewed for the present study, the effects of the order on Arden's practices and on the use of demonstrators generally can be ascertained only from interviews with others. One of Arden's customers said that it received from Arden the same demonstrator service as before. (This is possible under the order if compliance therewith by Arden consisted in offering proportional service to all customers who did not formerly receive it.)

Among Arden's competitors, one gives all customers a uniform per-

---

[68] In addition, Arden paid commissions to cover part of the salary of sales clerks in about 82 stores.

[69] Exhibit No. 5 shows that Wanamaker purchases were over $24,000, while none of the six who received demonstrators bought more than $15,000 and one bought less than $7,500.

centage allowance for demonstration. Another, with outlets in about 12,000 stores, pays all or part of the cost of "cosmeticians" in 10,500 stores. In 300 stores such clerks serve the manufacturer exclusively, and in the rest, on a part-time basis. This manufacturer prefers to reimburse the stores for its share of the salaries of these persons, since this procedure makes it easier to keep the payments proportional to sales. In the case of 35 to 40 leading stores, however, the manufacturer pays the clerk directly and thus incurs some risk that the allowance may be disproportional if the sales volume varies from what was expected. The conception of proportionality that is used has to do with the size of the store's display as well as with the amount of its purchases. The scale of allowances is 18 per cent where there are two girls using 12 continuous feet of exclusive space for the manufacturer's product, 15 per cent where there is one girl using 8 continuous feet, and 10 per cent where 8 continuous feet are used but only half of a girl's time is available. Similar adjustments are made for other combinations of time and space, and alternatives to demonstrators are offered, seven different plans being used in an effort to achieve rough proportionality. All plans have been made known to all customers. In general, the cost of providing the service is said to be higher per dollar of sales on the smaller amounts of service.

The maintenance of proportionality in demonstrator services involves substantial difficulties in addition to those that arise in service to small accounts. The larger the number of customers, the harder it is to be sure that they are treated proportionally. A manufacturer with four hundred customers has an easier problem than one with many thousands. Since each manufacturer must keep his services proportional, there is competitive difficulty wherever the same store buys from two or more concerns that provide demonstrator service, for only by accident will the amounts of service offered to the store be the same. The larger the number of his customers, the harder the manufacturer finds it to make competitive adjustments in a particular store without creating troublesome disproportions. There is considerable incentive to avoid the difficulties of providing proportional services to small accounts by ceasing to sell direct to such accounts. This incentive is enhanced by the belief among manufacturers that the services offered to the small stores are not worth their cost but merely increase the cost of distribution. But because of the difficulties attendant on the maintenance of proportionality in co-operative advertising with distributors, manufacturers are encouraged to place more emphasis on their own advertising; and they can benefit from such advertising only if the distributor has the goods in stock. Hence they hesitate to confine their direct sales to the larger and more profitable stores.

The Arden case no longer has authority as a legal guide for business practice. The decision was followed by widespread criticism in the cosmetic industry by manufacturers and large and small distributors alike. Manufacturers thought it impossible to proportionalize demonstrator service and undesirable to abandon the use of demonstrators; large distributors wished to retain the demonstrator service they were receiving; and most small distributors had no desire to receive the minute amounts of demonstrator service that would have been theirs under the standard of proportionality. This discontent was expressed in requests that the Federal Trade Commission approve trade practice rules for the cosmetic industry which would abandon the theory, expressed in the Arden decision, that each type of distributive service rendered by the seller must be separately proportionalized.[70] After much debate, the Commission acceded to this request. In 1951 it promulgated trade practice rules for the cosmetic industry that included a provision "clarifying" the application of the law as to proportionality. It said that when a customer was offered a service that was not suitable to the business of other customers, the requirement of the law could be met if the seller offered these others "an alternate type of promotional service, facility or allowance which is of equivalent measurable cost, is usable by the customer, and is suitable to his facilities and business. . . ." It provided, however, that all customers must be informed of the kind, amount, and terms of the offer, and that if the offer was conditioned on reciprocal performance by the customer "there be an equality of ratio among all customers as to the measurable cost of that which is supplied by the industry member and the reciprocal service, facility or payment required of any customer."[71]

[70] The Commission's decision in the case said, "the statute affords the seller a free election in the first instance as to what services or facilities, if any, he will provide to purchasers of his products; but having elected to furnish a particular service or facility to a particular purchaser or purchasers, he thereby assumes the obligation of according similar services to all competing purchasers to the extent required by the statute. The furnishing of a service or facility which cannot be proportionalized for the benefit of competing purchasers or, in the alternative, the failure or refusal to proportionalize the terms upon which services or facilities are granted . . . constitutes a failure to accord such services or facilities upon proportionally equal terms." The Commission's order included a paragraph specifically prohibiting failure to proportionalize demonstrator services. 39 FTC 302.

[71] FTC *Trade Practice Rules for the Cosmetic and Toilet Preparations Industry,* Promulgated Nov. 29, 1951, pp. 4-5.

In approving the rules, the majority of the Commission issued a statement defending its action:

> To insist on a narrow and impracticable interpretation of this law that services furnished must be "identical" would be to open wide the road to absurdity. . . . We must be practical. A window display may well be a more efficient "demonstrator" than is a girl employed in a department store, and the distributor should be at least as competent to appraise the value to his business of those services as is this Commission.

It said that the Arden case did not compel the proportionalization of identical services.

> Arden was offering its favored purchasers something and its unfavored purchasers nothing. The Commission stopped that by an order appropriate to the facts of that case and the court approved that action. Further than that, the decision did not go. The Commission has never officially construed the Arden or Gus Blass decisions as going further. Such construction was only that unofficially placed upon those decisions by a portion of its legal staff. . . . By the promulgation of these rules, it is placing its official interpretation that those decisions do not require limiting proportionalization to identical services or facilities but do permit the proportionalization of alternate services upon proportionately equal terms.[72]

Two commissioners opposed the rules. One of them, Commissioner Ayres, issued a dissenting statement. After quoting the parts of the Arden decisions that appeared to say that each service must be proportionalized, he said that if the interpretation was to be changed, the proper procedure was to ask the court to modify the previous interpretation, to apply the new interpretation in pending cases, and only thereafter incorporate it in trade practice rules. However, he objected to the new interpretation on three grounds: (1) that to apply it would require "unbelievably complex standards of cost comparison," requiring "multiple analyses of the comparative costs of the seller in furnishing the service, facility or payment to many buyers, and of the ratio among all customers as to the cost of what they receive and of what they give in return"; (2) that the discretion granted to the seller to select the alternatives to be offered would "permit arbitrary and unjust discriminations among com-

[72] *Ibid.,* pp. 12-14.

peting customers"; and (3) that the effect of the rule would be continuance of the use of demonstrators by a few of the larger manufacturers to pre-empt the most desirable retail outlets and exclude the smaller manufacturers from effective distribution through them.[73]

After issuing the rules, the Commission dismissed six pending cases against cosmetic manufacturers in which the charges were similar to those of the Arden case.[74] The reasons for dismissal were that voluntary acceptance of the new rules by the respondents could be expected to result in abandonment of the practices charged.[75] Four subsequent orders concerned with demonstrators and alternative services have been issued against cosmetic manufacturers. One of these involved a respondent in one of the dismissed cases; the other three involved concerns not previously charged with violation.

Provision of Small Packages as a Sales Service

The Luxor case had to do with the sale of Luxor cosmetics in ten-cent packages. Early in the 1930's Luxor decided to distribute its products in ten-cent sizes as well as in the larger packages in which they had been previously sold. A preliminary survey indicated that retail druggists were unwilling to sell the junior sizes. Thereupon, Luxor experimented for more than a year with the sale of these sizes through druggists in Cincinnati and Louisville. It found that in the stores handling both sizes the

---

[73] *Ibid.*, pp. 14-21.

[74] The cases were Docket 2973, *Richard Hudnut, Inc.;* Docket 2974, *Elmo, Inc.;* Docket 3017, *Charles of the Ritz, Inc.;* Docket 3039, *Primrose House, Inc.;* Docket 4435, *Coty, Inc.;* Docket 4436, *Bourjois, Inc.* All six cases were dismissed Jan. 9, 1953. On March 7, 1956, an order was issued against *Elmo* (Docket 6443) for disproportionality in the provision of demonstrators and substitute services.

[75] On March 1, 1956, in a conference sponsored by the Federal Bar Association and the Bureau of National Affairs, Commissioner William C. Kern referred to these dismissals as follows: "Respondents, represented as they were by competent counsel, apparently persuaded the Commission that they would abide by the rules and that the public interest did not require pressing the formal proceedings to final conclusion. As a result of a check on compliance with trade practice rules the Commission has been given reason to believe that many of these respondents are in open and flagrant violation of the rules and are continuing the very practices which were the basis of the original complaints. As a result the Commission has recently instituted a group of new proceedings, which are now pending. It is impossible for me to defend the handling of these cases as an example of effective enforcement of the Robinson-Patman Act." See *Congressional Record,* Vol. 102, Pt. 4, 84 Cong. 2 sess., p. 5391.

sales of the larger size decreased so much that there was a reduction in the store's total dollar volume. A later investigation by Luxor in Chicago confirmed its opinion that the junior sizes could not be effectively distributed through druggists. In 1932 Luxor adopted a policy of selling the junior sizes only through limited-price variety stores, most of its customers in this field being chains. The Commission found that 38 per cent of Luxor's dollar volume came from sales of the junior sizes. In testifying during the case, Luxor said that it was receiving only about 12 requests per year from druggists and department stores for the ten-cent size. But various druggists testified that their customers were demanding the ten-cent items and sometimes left the store without buying after finding that these items could not be obtained. The Commission found that in failing to make the small packages generally available, Luxor was giving service to some of its customers that was not proportionally available to all. It ordered Luxor to use no package of a size and style that was not made generally available.

Though Luxor was a subsidiary of Armour and one of the 12 largest cosmetic companies, it no longer exists. It was bought from Armour in 1948 by Lever Brothers and immediately dissolved. A druggist whose complaints were apparently significant in bringing Luxor's practices to the Commission's attention said that after the case he was able to buy the junior sizes but found that they were unprofitable because they decreased his sale of the larger sizes. He therefore tried to avoid selling them, refrained from displaying them prominently, and soon stopped carrying them. Another customer also expressed the view that the small sizes were unprofitable and that the demand for them was chiefly due to the depression. Distributors of cosmetics apparently agree that since the war there has been no need for a distributor to carry junior-size packages.

The principle of the Luxor case was applied again by the Commission in 1956 in a case against General Foods.[76] The case involved charges that General Foods had violated Sections 2(a), 2(d) and 2(e); violation of Sections 2(a) and 2(e) was found, while the charge under Section 2(d) was dismissed for lack of evidence. The facts relevant to Section 2(e) were that General Foods sold various products in two kinds of containers, one an "institution-pack" suited for use by hospitals, hotels, and similar consumers, the other a "grocery-pack," suited for use by households; and that the institution pack was not made available to all intermediaries who

[76] Docket 6018, *General Foods Corp.*, decided Feb. 15, 1956.

desired it. Some wholesale grocers obtained, and some did not obtain, cereals, baking powder and dessert preparations in this pack. Maxwell House coffee in the institution pack was not available to ordinary wholesalers, but was furnished to contract wagon distributors who resold to institutions. A complicating detail was the fact that the coffee sold under the Maxwell House brand for institutional use was a special blend containing, in addition to the five types of coffee beans ordinarily used, a sixth type added to insure a longer period of freshness in the coffee after brewing. In spite of this difference, the two blends were found to be of like grade and quality because they bore the same brand, which was different from other brands of coffee offered by General Foods, and because they were sold "for the same use, sometimes competitively." The Commission found that Section 2(e) had been violated, and ordered General Foods not to furnish any buyer any grocery product packaged in containers of a certain size and style unless the opportunity to buy the product in like containers was accorded proportionally to all competing buyers.

Provision of Assorted Services as a Sales Service

Among the violations of the Robinson-Patman Act involved in the Curtiss Candy case, one consisted in a violation of Section 2(e) by supplying free samples and demonstrators in the new stores of particular customers and by paying the rental cost of billboards on which a customer's advertising was to be placed. Services of this type were intermingled with more numerous advertising allowances and with various forms of price discrimination, as well as with certain exclusive-dealing arrangements. The Commission ordered the practices stopped. It is impossible, however, to disentangle the effect of this part of the order from that of other and more important aspects of the proceeding.

Acceptance of Returned Goods as a Sales Service

Another order under Section 2(e) was directed against the acceptance of unsold books from distributors by Appleton-Century-Crofts. The Commission found that Appleton followed a general practice of permitting book dealers to return unsold copies of educational books and that this privilege was denied to dealers a substantial part of whose business consisted in wholesaling second-hand books or selling second-hand books through multiple outlets. Treating the return privilege as a service not proportionally available to all, the Commission ordered Appleton to terminate the disproportionality.

One of the country's large second-hand book dealers says that it has been denied the return privilege only by Appleton but that it now enjoys the privilege because of the case. An interview with Appleton was requested but refused.

Runway Allowances as a Sales Service

A remarkable application of Section 2(e) was attempted in a private suit, *Russellville Canning Co.* v. *American Can Co.*[77] Russellville sued American Can for discriminatory volume discounts and freight allowances[78] and for provision of a disproportionate service to one customer. The service consisted of a runway connecting American's can-manufacturing plant at Austin, Indiana, with a canning establishment owned by Morgan, the plant's largest customer. Cans delivered across the runway were sold at a discount of 45 cents per 1,000. No similar runway was provided for other customers; indeed, no similar runway could be provided except for a customer with a contiguous plant. Cans were delivered across the runway at a discount, not only when they were made at Austin, but also when they were shipped to Austin from American's other plants.[79]

The lower court found that selective provision of runway service was a violation of Section 2(e) and that the impossibility of making similar service available to others was no defense.

> The defendant may in good faith construct its factories in certain localities and thereby incidentally create a locational advantage to those customers situated nearby. In such a case, defendant may sell f.o.b. the factory, provided it is the normal source of supply, and the nearer customers will receive their cans at a smaller delivered price than those less favorably situated. This, however, is not discriminatory for the difference is justified in delivery costs. When, however, additional

[77] *Russellville Canning Co.* v. *American Can Co.*, 87 F. Supp. 484 and 191 F. 2d 38.

[78] See below, pp. 244-46, 445-46.

[79] This fact was emphasized in another private suit, *Bruce's Juices* v. *American Can Co.*, in which the runway allowance was also challenged, but as a discrimination. See 87 F. Supp. 985 and 187 F. 2d 919.

facilities, the runway here, are furnished, so that those near the factory
receive their cans at a price lower than that normally incident to locational advantage, a discrimination does exist, and the seller, defendant
here, must either furnish proportionally equal facilities to all customers
purchasing that commodity, discontinue the furnishing of such facilities, or, in this case, discontinue the granting of a discount based upon
the existence of the facilities.[80]

American Can offered a cost defense based on a comparison of delivery
cost from the Austin plant with delivery cost from its plant at Terre
Haute. The court rejected it, not because cost defenses were inapplicable
to violations of Section 2(e) but because it covered only one year, because
conditions at the two plants were dissimilar, and because the costs at each
plant were averaged, without segregation of the costs of runway delivery
and with ut segregation of costs for the kinds of cans sold to Morgan.

On appeal the Eighth Circuit ruled that the runway allowance was not
a violation of Section 2(e) but possibly a discrimination under Section
2(a); that Russellville had proved no injury to its business, since the two
companies canned different kinds of vegetables, and there was no evidence of diversion of business from Russellville to Morgan; and that the
cost defense should have been accepted as evidence, since the only
way of showing the economies at one plant was to compare costs there
with costs at another.[81] The matter was remanded for a new trial; but the
case was settled privately by a payment to Russellville, and the trial was
not held.

The Significance of the Cases
Involving Proportionality

Among the practices against which the Commission has taken action
in its enforcement of Sections 2(d) and 2(e), a few were little more than
methods of discriminating in price under the pressure of powerful buyers.
In the cases involving these practices, the proportionality sections have
been applied with the same purposes and effects as the general law of
price discrimination.

[80] 87 F. Supp. 484, 489.

[81] In the Bruce's Juices case, the Fifth Circuit rejected the cost defense for the
runway allowance because the allowance was granted not only on cans made at
Austin but also on cans made at other factories and shipped to Austin to be delivered through the runway. In this case the court found the discrimination unlawful and awarded damages to Bruce's Juices.

However, in most of the cases, the enforcement of the proportionality sections has prevented the use of practices that had other aspects than the granting of price concessions to large buyers. The promotional efforts of producers have been curtailed through the requirement that, where promotion is undertaken jointly with distributors, it shall be carried on only in programs broad enough and varied enough to enlist all distributors in appropriate proportions. This requirement necessarily impairs the opportunity for the producer to limit his promotional budget by centering his campaign on certain strategic points, to focus his promotion on the prestige of particular distributors, and to experiment locally with new types of promotion. It also constitutes an obstacle to acceptance by the producer of requests that he co-operate with distributors in particular promotions that these distributors are undertaking. The law forbids a producer like Luxor to differentiate channels of distribution by package sizes (or by other devices that will be interpreted as the provision of services) even if, as in the Luxor case, the differentiation appears to conform to the market realities and to the desires of most distributors, large and small. Had the Arden case not been superseded by the extra-legal device of a trade practice conference, the application of the law to the use of demonstrators might have meant the enforced abandonment of this practice. With the modifications that the trade practice conference has introduced, the actual effect appears to have been a costly provision of demonstrators or of substitutes for demonstrator service in small outlets in order to avoid discontinuing the use of demonstrators in large outlets.

These interventions in the details of promotional practice cannot be lumped together as irrelevant to the price discrimination problems that underlie the Robinson-Patman Act. Forms of discrimination as significant as others condemned by the statute appear to be involved in some of these cases. Programs to take advantage of the prestige of particular distributors or to limit advertising campaigns to key spots may mean in practice that advertising allowances and special services are offered to large and powerful distributors and not to their small rivals, and the cumulative effect of such offers by various producers may be to give these large distributors substantial aggregate advantages. In some instances, a large part of a distributor's advertising program is financed by advertising allowances. One distributor with an advertising budget of about $400,000 per year finds that allowances cover 25 per cent of it. Another obtains from such allowances 20 per cent of the costs of his newspaper advertising, which is more than $40,000 per year, as well as a smaller percentage of the cost of other advertising. A third, with an advertising budget of half a million, obtains 10 per cent of it from allowances. One regional voluntary food chain apparently covers about half of its advertising costs through allowances, since the sums that it collects from its members for advertising are sufficient to meet only the other half of the costs. In the case of school supplies, the interviews indicate that the allowances that were received by favored distributors were large enough to prevent other distributors from bidding successfully on school contracts and to reduce the size of the inventories these other distributors were willing to carry and the purchases they were willing to make.

It is impossible to know how extensive and important the discriminatory effects may have been in the situations in which the Commission took action under the proportionality provisions. Proof of injury to competition was not required by the statute, and the Commission made no effort to supply it. The observer is forced to rely for his appraisal on the broad circumstances of the case and on comments by interested parties in interviews held years after the case. Opinions formed in this way are obviously inconclusive. For what it is worth, however, the information at hand suggests that in some cases, such as that of Luxor, there was nothing that would have justified a finding of injury to competition had a test of this kind been applied. In other cases, the application of the test of injury probably would have resulted in findings and orders different in scope from those actually issued.

The cases are persuasive that the price discrimination appearing in disproportionate advertising allowances and disproportionate services raise problems similar to and no more dangerous than those that appear directly in price differentials. Practices free from injurious impact appear to be common enough to raise questions about the wisdom of a rule of law that outlaws these practices regardless of their effect. The main part of the Robinson-Patman Act forbids price discriminations where certain types of effect are likely to be produced and where certain types of justification are not found. A standard of this kind, rather than a prohibition of anything that is not proportional, appears to be appropriate to the matters that have come before the Commission in the proportionality cases.[82] The legal standard that is applied to discriminatory pricing di-

[82] *Cf. Report of the Attorney General's Committee,* pp. 191-93. The Committee expressed disapproval of "the present disparity in the statutory consequences which attach to economically equivalent business practices." It favored "reconciliation" of the proportionality sections with Sec. 2(a). However, unlike the present writer, it saw no basic difficulty in the standard of proportionality. It thought that these

rects the Commission to explore the effect of price differentials and to curb the freedom of the price maker only where it finds specific reason to do so. Sales effort, like pricing, involves a complex body of practices, the results of which are complicated and sometimes obscure. In reshaping it in order to make it nondiscriminatory, an exploratory technique is more appropriate than the application of a fixed standard of proportional equality.

---

sections were "beginning to be administered in a workable way," and recommended that the Commission issue a policy statement sanctioning (1) percentage allowances of buyers' purchases conditioned on services of equivalent value; (2) allowances at set rates for given services up to a limit set by a uniform percentage; (3) services by the seller, of types best suiting each customer class, approximating a uniform percentage. Thinking interpretation could harmonize this part of the law with broad antitrust objectives, the Committee recommended no legislative modification of it.

8 / *Quantity and Volume Discounts*

THERE WAS INITIALLY a widespread belief that the Robinson-Patman Act would be used chiefly against discounts granted on large purchases; for the act was intended primarily to limit the buying advantages of large business enterprises, which characteristically can buy large amounts. The history of the act has partially justified this expectation. Proceedings against quantity discounts—that is, discounts based on the amount bought in a single transaction—have been relatively few. Proceedings against volume discounts—that is, discounts based on cumulative purchases during a stated period—have been the most numerous of those concerned with violation of Section 2(a).

From the passage of the Robinson-Patman Act until December 31, 1957, the Commission issued orders in 49 cases against unlawful discounts based on the quantity bought in a single transaction or the volume bought over a period of time. Most of these cases had to do with volume rather than quantity. In 37 instances the proceeding involved volume discounts only; in 3, both volume and quantity discounts, but with emphasis on the former; and in 9 quantity discounts only. However, in 5 of the 9 instances in which quantity discounts were not accompanied by volume discounts, other types of violation of law were also found—conspiracy to fix prices and unlawful discrimination among territorial markets in 1, unfair practices in 1, functional price discrimination in 2, and unlawful advertising allowances in 1. In only 4 of the quantity-discount cases was this type of discount the sole point of attention; and even in these 4, attention was centered, not on the size of the quantity discount, but on the fact that a preferential discount schedule was available to some customers. By contrast, 25 of the volume-discount cases involved no other form of a law violation, except certain irregular or selective discriminations arising from failure to observe the discount scale in all transactions.[1] In enforcing the law, the Commission has given substantial

---

[1] In two of the three cases in which the Commission condemned both volume and quantity discounts, no other violation was found. In the third, there were also unlawful advertising allowances.

attention to volume discounts and relatively little attention to quantity discounts.

The reasons for the difference in emphasis are not wholly clear; but among them three are probably important. First, soon after the Robinson-Patman Act became law, there was a substantial amount of change in the scale of quantity discounts in an effort to comply with the new statute. During the year after the passage of the Robinson-Patman Act, the Federal Trade Commission afforded opportunities for business enterprises to discuss their price structures informally with members of the Commission's staff.[2] Attention was given primarily to quantity discounts, which were then thought to occupy a central place among the practices affected by the law. The conferences indicated that quantity discounts usually began only at relatively high quantities and thereafter increased in amount at an accelerating rate, whereas the economies that were said to underlie these discounts were conspicuous at the lower end of the quantity scale and insignificant at the upper end.[3] As a result of these conferences, many enterprises voluntarily reduced the size of their discounts on large quantities or eliminated such discounts altogether. There is no way of knowing the frequency of such voluntary change, but it appears improbable that the alterations in discount structures went so far as to eliminate substantially all quantity-discount problems.

Second, cost justifications are more readily available for schedules of quantity discounts than for schedules of volume discounts. As between large and small shipments there may be differences in packaging, methods of handling and transportation charges, which, so far as they result in differences in cost, may justify quantity discounts. It is harder to show, for customers who buy comparable quantities, specific differences in cost based on the mere fact that some of the buyers purchase these quantities

[2] The author, employed by the Commission during part of this period, was one of the group to whom such discussions were assigned.

[3] In most instances, the cost justification for a quantity discount rested chiefly on the fact that a transaction involved certain lump-sum costs independent of the amount bought. If the aggregate of these lump-sum costs was $1, their cost per unit was $1 in the sale of 1 unit, but only 50 cents when 2 units were bought instead of 1 and 25 cents when 4 units were bought instead of 2. If the transaction covered 100 units, the lump-sum cost per unit was only 1 cent. Little saving could be achieved by a further spread of the allocation of the lump sum. Yet there was typically no quantity discount to encourage the purchase of 2 units rather than 1 or 4 units rather than 2. The first quantity discount might be granted only for purchases of 100 units or even more, and there might then be successively greater discounts for purchases of quantities such as 500, 1,000 and 10,000 units.

more often and thus buy larger total amounts in a stated period of time. Where a cost justification is available, it is usually offered during the Commission's investigation and prior to a formal complaint; so that the greater availability of such justifications for quantity discounts tends to reduce the relative number of cases in which the Commission challenges this type of practice.

Third, the incentives to make price concessions to powerful buyers are more likely to evoke volume discounts than quantity discounts. So far as the buyer's power is derived from his bigness, it is closely related to his volume of business and, hence, to the volume of his purchases. It has no similar obvious relation to his choice between frequent purchase in small amounts and less frequent purchase in larger amounts. Incentives to make frequent small purchases may exist for large buyers as well as for small ones, because of a desire not to speculate on changes in the value of inventories, desire to avoid problems of spoilage and similar merchandising considerations, and desire to minimize warehousing. In many lines of business, the opportunity to buy in relatively large quantities may be widespread, so that a quantity discount cannot readily reflect the unusual power of the largest buyers.

Patterns in Quantity-Discount Cases

Quantity discounts have been challenged by the Federal Trade Commission in 5 cases concerned with books, 2 cases concerned with salt, 1 concerned with rubber and canvas footwear, 1 concerned with lead products, 1 concerned with canned fruits and vegetables, 1 concerned with automobile parts, and 1 concerned with magnesium dockboards. In the salt cases and the dockboard case, there were both volume and quantity discounts, and attention was given primarily to the former. In the lead case, primarily directed against conspiracy to fix prices, attention was centered on a zone-pricing formula; but for one of several products —lead oxides—the conspiracy included the maintenance of discriminatory quantity discounts. It is doubtful that the Commission would have proceeded against the quantity discounts found in any of these three cases if they had not been entangled with other violations of law. In the automobile parts case and the footwear case, quantity discounts shared attention with functional discounts; in the fruit and vegetable case, with advertising allowances. In the five book cases there were related proceed-

ings under the Federal Trade Commission Act;[4] and as to quantity discounts the Commission's principal objection was not to the relative size
of the discounts for different quantities but to the fact that different discount schedules were used in dealing with different customers or a
single discount schedule was used for some customers but not for
others.[5]

Selective proceedings against quantity discounts are, of course, consistent with the standards of the law. Quantity discounts are unlawful, like
other discounts, only when they have the capacity to produce specified
effects on competition and when the seller does not show that they are
cost-justified or granted to meet the equally low price of a competitor.
The different treatment of the quantity discounts in various cases was due
to the fact that in certain instances the Commission found the requisites
of illegality, whereas in others it did not.

The observer, however, cannot readily distinguish the unlawful quantity-discount structures from the lawful ones. The Commission found
unlawful a discount of 10 cents per case given by Morton for the purchase of carload quantities of Blue-Label salt; a discount of from 4 to 5
per cent given by International Salt on purchases of 100 cases or more
of table salt; and differentials of 40 cents and 90 cents per 100 pounds,
respectively, between carload prices of lead oxides and 1.c.1. quantities
greater than and less than 5 tons. On the other hand, in the paint case,

[4] In spite of the fact that quantity discounts have been often challenged in
association with other practices, the Commission's record clearly refutes the view
that cases directed at other law violations will be automatically enlarged to cover
the quantity discounts associated with these violations. For example, in the cases
against Sherwin-Williams and Bausch & Lomb, the findings discuss quantity discounts which the Commission did not find unlawful.

[5] In two of the cases, Docket 5962, *Random House, Inc.* and Docket 5963,
Simon and Schuster, Inc., some customers were denied quantity discounts, while
others received them. In the other three cases, Docket 5898, *Harper and Brothers*,
Docket 5960, *Houghton Mifflin Co.*, and Docket 5961, *Little, Brown & Co., Inc.*,
different quantity-discount schedules were employed for different groups of customers. The Commission's findings do not disclose the basis for the difference in
treatment. The orders were so broad as to prohibit differences in prices charged to
competing buyers whether due to the use of different discount schedules in selling
to different customers or to purchase of different amounts by customers whose
purchases were subject to the same schedule.

Since the cases were settled by consent, an adequate statement of the facts is
not available in these cases. If one can assume that conditions were parallel to
those of the Doubleday case, Docket 5897 (see below, footnote 42, pp. 317-18), the
difference in treatment may have arisen from the fact that three concerns were
treated as jobbers.

the Commission noted discounts as high as 14 per cent on carloads and truckloads and discounts as high as 10 per cent on purchases of 84 gallons or more of paint, yet did not condemn these discounts.[6] Since most of the quantity discounts that were found to be lawful were treated as subordinate or co-ordinate elements in complicated price structures, and since the Commission seldom explains its reasons for dismissing portions of a complaint if it sustains other portions, one can obtain from the records of the various quantity-discount cases only scattered and incomplete explanations for the decisions that particular discounts were lawful while others were not.

Problems in the Volume-Discount Cases

The volume discounts involved in the cases raised the same issues that were important in the quantity-discount cases, along with others peculiar to volume discounts. Accordingly, most of the ensuing discussion will have to do with them.

Volume discounts provided for price concessions to buyers who bought stated amounts within stated time periods. They were condemned by the Commission on two grounds: First, the discount schedules were themselves unlawful. Second, in practice they were not uniformly applied: Volume discounts were granted to some buyers but not to others who bought as much; or discounts were granted to some buyers who had not purchased from the seller the amounts to which the discounts applied.

The second objection arose in about two fifths of the volume-discount cases. In certain instances, notably the sale of bakers yeast by Standard Brands and the sale of frit by the Ferro Enamel Corporation, the discount was based not on the buyer's total purchases from the seller but on his total purchases from all sources. In the absence of such concessions, volume-discount structures encourage buyers to buy their full requirements from a single source in order to reach the highest attainable discount bracket. Hence, the granting of such a concession may be a mark of competition for business among two or more sellers who use volume discounts, and the effect of the concession may be to mitigate the exclu-

---

[6] In the optical case, too, the Commission referred to variations in prices on lenses, frames, and mountings, involving quantities ranging from two pairs of a kind or five pairs assorted to 50 pairs assorted, but was so little impressed by these price differences that their amount is not set forth in the findings. Presumably, it thought the quantities small enough to be easily purchased.

sive-dealing features of volume-discount arrangements without making available to buyers levels of discounts greater than they could otherwise achieve by concentrated buying. Small sellers are likely to use this form of concession in an effort to obtain a portion of the business of large buyers who might otherwise place all of it with large sellers. However, the more attractive features of the practice were not visible in the two cases in which the Commission considered it. Standard Brands, the largest seller of yeast, apparently gave credit for portions of the buyer's volume bought from other sources in order to avoid the complete loss of customers who might be induced to purchase some yeast from smaller producers. In certain instances, the Commission found, discounts granted on this basis had been made in good faith to meet competition; but since there were other instances in which Standard was not meeting a competitor's prior offer, the Commission condemned the practice. Ferro Enamel was engaged with other producers of frit in a price-fixing conspiracy, and the use of purchases from all sources as a basis for volume discounts in this conspiracy was apparently a device for making prices to each buyer uniform from all sellers, even though the buyer might have bought different amounts from different sellers. In these settings, the Commission concluded that the sellers' grant of discounts on purchases made partly from other sellers was indefensible, and condemned the practice without hesitation.

Various volume-discount schedules had the common characteristic that sellers based discounts on the total amounts they sold to all parts of a large buying organization, even though the purchases were made separately by different buying units within the organization. American Optical Company, Kreisler, and John B. Stetson granted volume discounts to corporate chains on total sales, whether these sales were made to central offices, regional warehouses, or local stores. Some sellers— for example, Simmons and Kreisler—also permitted the pooling of the purchases of buyers who belonged to voluntary chains or co-operative buying groups. In some instances the privilege was granted to certain selected groups rather than to all; Master Lock, for example, granted it to only one chain. In some instances, the pooling privilege was available only for orders that were assembled in a central office and transmitted to the seller in combined form; in other instances, for orders transmitted directly to the seller by the different units of the buying organization. Rarely, buyers were allowed discounts on purchases pooled for discount purposes by informal agreement, even though these buyers had no other enduring ties of organization. In one instance, that of Minneapolis-Honeywell, oil-burner manufacturers were credited not only with their own volume of purchases of Honeywell's controls but also with the value of controls bought from Honeywell by their customers. The Commission treated all such pooling as a perversion of volume-discount programs, whether the pooling privilege was available generally or only to selected customers.[7]

Problems arose, not only in regard to pooling, but also as to discounts for volumes larger than those actually bought. In certain instances, notably the sale of mattresses by Simmons, the sale of industrial chucks by Jacobs, and the sale of dentists' supplies, the volume discount was granted in the form of a rebate after the period came to an end, based on the total amount that had actually been sold. Thus the discount granted was necessarily consistent with the discount schedule. In some instances, however, the volume discount was currently applied to the price of each purchase made by the buyer. Thus it reflected a computed volume that might not be identical with the volume bought in the period of time that included the transaction. Minneapolis-Honeywell, for example, granted volume discounts on automatic controls for volumes computed in any one of three ways: by the amount bought in the last previous year, by the average of two or more prior years, or by the estimated amount to be used in the current year. If the target volume was not attained, no additional charge was made; but if it was exceeded, the customer received an appropriate refund.[8] Except where the volume was determined prior to the application of the discount, it was inevitable that discrepancies between imputed and actual volume should result in the payment of volume discounts greater or smaller than those earned under the discount schedule. Unless offsetting payments were subsequently made, these deviations were treated by the Commission as discriminatory concessions to individual buyers. The difficulty of avoiding them constituted one of the hazards of the use of volume discounts.

The volume discounts condemned by the Commission differed greatly in complexity. In the simplest schedule, a single discount was available

[7] Sherwin-Williams permitted pooling as a method of earning quantity discounts. The discount schedule was not condemned, but the Commission's order applicable to it sought to stop the pooling practice.

[8] Apparently this practice was particularly prevalent in 1938, the year studied by the Commission, because the market declined unexpectedly so that customers fell below expected volumes under conditions that made it peculiarly difficult to ask them for more money.

to buyers who bought more than a stated amount during a stated period of time. In complex schedules, there were as many as eleven volume brackets, to each of which a different discount was applicable. Where there were few brackets, each bracket was necessarily wide, and the size of the discount separating one bracket from another was likely to be substantial. In such cases, the Commission raised questions as to the propriety of lumping together all of the buyers in a bracket, in disregard of the wide variation in the amounts they bought, and of differentiating the treatment of buyers who bought in similar volume when the boundary of a discount class fell between them. The fewer and broader the discount classes, the more vulnerable they were to close scrutiny of their scope and boundaries. In the discount schedules with numerous brackets, the difference in price between any two successive classes of buyers was usually smaller, and the buyers in any one class were usually more homogeneous in methods of buying and in amounts bought. Thus challenge of the propriety of the classification was less inviting. However, the validity of any discount was open to question as compared with any other. If there were eleven volume classes, the most favorable discount could be challenged by comparison with the discount received by each of the ten other classes, and challenges could also be based on similar comparisons among any of the other pairs of classes. The more elaborate the discount structure, the more varied were the ways in which problems of injury to competition might arise, and the more complicated were the allocations of costs that would be appropriate to a cost defense. Moreover, in the elaborate discount structures the segregation of the largest and smallest buyers in narrowly defined classes eligible for specified discounts, and separated by a considerable number of intermediate classes and discounts, tended to emphasize the magnitude of the concessions to the big buyer.

Findings of Injury to Competition:
the Primary Line

Volume or quantity discounts, like any other price discriminations by a seller, are unlawful only if there is a reasonable probability that their effect on competition will be injurious. Three types of damage to competition are recognized by the statute: (a) a tendency to monopoly; (b) a substantial lessening of competition; (c) injury, destruction, or prevention of competition with those who take part in the preferential transactions.[9] Any of the three types of damage may appear on the sellers' side of the market, that is, in the primary line of commerce; or on the buyers' side, that is, in the secondary line of commerce.[10] Thus there are six possibilities, which may appear together or separately. Some one of these must be probable if a discrimination is to be found unlawful.

Tendency to monopoly is a concept older than the Robinson-Patman Act. It can be thought of as a lessening of market competition so severe that monopoly is a probable result unless the process is checked. Substantial lessening of competition is also an older concept. It can be thought of as a reduction of competition in the market, not great enough nor cumulative enough to imply the probability of monopoly, but sufficient to reduce significantly the degree of competitive protection enjoyed by the consumer or the supplier or both. For convenience, it will often be referred to in subsequent discussion as the broad type of injury, or as injury to competition in the market sense. The third concept of damage —injury, destruction, or prevention of competition with participants in the preferential transaction—was brought into the law by the Robinson-Patman Act. It has to do with impairment of the opportunities of groups that suffer from the discrimination, not necessarily accompanied by a reduction of the vigor of market competition generally. For convenience, it will often be referred to hereafter as the narrow type of injury, as group injury, or as injury to competitors.

In the primary line, the meaning of impairment of the opportunities of the seller's competitors, as distinguished from a substantial lessening of competition, on the one hand, and as distinguished from the process of competition itself, on the other, is obscure; and the meaning attributed to the concept under the law must be left to develop in later pages. In the secondary line, the meaning of the narrow concept of injury is clearer: apart from any effect on market competition, the capacity to compete of a class of disfavored buyers may be impaired, and that of a class of favored buyers may be improved. If a discrimination has this effect, it is unlawful, unless justified, whether or not the substitution of one type of competitor for another changes the vigor of market competition in the resale market in which the buyers sell. The broad type of injury is damaging to the ultimate consumer (and perhaps, but not necessarily, to intermediate buyers who serve him). The narrow type of injury is

[9] See above, pp. 32, 57-58.
[10] The terms primary line and secondary line are habitually used in the Commission and by attorneys who try cases before it.

damaging to a class of intermediate buyers (and perhaps, but not necessarily, to the ultimate consumer).

Although potential damage to competition in one or more of these six senses is the essential element that makes price discrimination unlawful, the Commission's findings as to damage have often been perfunctory or vague. In many instances the probability of damage has been found in the language of the statute, with little or no explanation of the process by which the Commission decided that damage was likely in the particular case. The Commission's complaints have often alleged every kind of damage recognized by the statute, presumably to provide a basis for every possible development in the case; and in uncontested cases these sweeping claims of damage have frequently been reiterated in the Commission's findings whether or not the scope and character of the discrimination appeared to justify all of them. In some instances, the finding as to damage has been made in language that does not say clearly which of the various statutory types of damage is meant; and in a few instances, the findings have included more than one passage pertaining to damage, with differences in the scope of the damage set forth in the different passages. These peculiarities in the findings have not been seriously challenged; for the law is not more severe in censure of one kind of damage than another, and the Commission's power to issue corrective orders would be neither larger nor smaller if the scope of a finding of damage were changed. In the later consent settlements, moreover, orders have been issued without substantive findings, so that the Commission's complaints supply the only information about the nature and extent of the damage.

Since any of the six kinds of injury to competition is sufficient to make a discrimination unlawful and to permit the Commission to use its full remedial powers, there has been no incentive for the Commission to prove every kind of injury that may exist. The injury that is easiest to prove is sufficient for every legal purpose; and this is usually the narrow type of injury rather than the broad one. It was to be expected that narrow injury in one or both lines of commerce would be found more often than injury to competition in the market or a tendency toward monopoly. One should remember, however, that the Commission's failure to find one of the broader kinds of injury when an attempt to do so was unnecessary does not indicate whether or not such an injury was present. One can only guess whether the Commission could have found more if it had felt the need to undertake the task.

Nevertheless, an appraisal of the impact of the price discrimination law must be concerned with the effects on competition produced by discrimination and with the impact of the law in altering those effects. So far as the findings of the Commission permit, damage of different kinds must be distinguished in this appraisal.

In volume discounts, the Commission has found the probability of damage to competition in both the primary and secondary lines of commerce. The probability of damage in the primary line was found in 28 of the 40 volume-discount cases.

In two of these, the effect on competition in the primary line of commerce was of a type familiar in proceedings under the Sherman Act. One case concerned Jacobs Manufacturing Company,[11] the largest manufacturer of industrial chucks, which sold about 95 per cent of all industrial chucks used in connection with portable machine tools. Jacobs' volume discount plan, the Commission thought, induced buyers to concentrate their purchases with Jacobs, and thus made it difficult for competitors, actual or prospective, to compete with Jacobs. The Commission saw in the discrimination all three types of injury in the primary line—probable injury to competitors' opportunities, probable injury to market competition, and a tendency to create a monopoly for Jacobs.

Another case involved a price-fixing conspiracy by makers of frit which included discriminatory volume discounts running up to 20 per cent for purchases of more than $40,000.[12] In this case, too, the Commission found all three types of injury in the primary line.[13]

But in finding injury to competition among sellers, the Commission has not confined itself to situations such as that of industrial chucks, in which one manufacturer overshadows the market, nor to situations in

[11] Docket 6061, *Jacobs Manufacturing Co.*

[12] Docket 5155, *Ferro Enamel Corp. et al.* The case was decided on the basis of an admission answer.

In a quantity-discount case, too, discounts by producers of lead products were minor parts of a price-fixing conspiracy that involved use of discriminatory zone-pricing formulas. (See Docket 5253, *National Lead Co. et al.*) Here, too, the Commission found all three types of injury.

[13] The finding as to monopoly is ambiguous in that it might be interpreted as covering the secondary line also. The Commission found that the discrimination "tends to create a monopoly in said commerce in the various localities or trade areas in the United States in which said respondents and their customers are engaged in the sale and distribution of said product." (42 FTC 52.) In view of the fact that the broad type of injury in the secondary line was not found, the passage quoted is interpreted here as applicable to monopoly in the primary line only.

which the discrimination was a part of a conspiracy among sellers to reduce competition. It has seen such injury in volume discounts in 26 other cases, many of which were directed against manufacturers it would be difficult to regard as having achieved or aspired to monopoly.[14] In all of these cases the Commission found (or alleged in a case settled by a consent order)[15] that the discrimination had the capacity to lessen competition among sellers;[16] and in 20 of the 26 it also found (or alleged) a tendency for the discriminating seller to attain a monopoly.[17] Of the 26 cases 22 were decided summarily after the respondents had waived trial. In 11, there were consent orders without findings; and in most of the others the findings as to injury in the primary line are brief and general and throw little light on the Commission's reasoning.[18] In 16 of the cases the Commission's complaints and findings supply no information, other than a description of the discounts and a statement that seller was

[14] For example, Docket 5971, *Kentucky Chemical Industries, Inc.;* Docket 5969, *Benrus Watch Co.;* Docket 5696, *Central Soya Co.;* Docket 5446, *Jacques Kreisler Manufacturing Co.;* Docket 3840, *Simmons Co.;* Docket 5912, *Ubiko Milling Co.;* Docket 5973, *Early and Daniel Co.;* Docket 4571, *Life Savers Corp.;* Docket 5828, *Holtite Manufacturing Co.*

[15] Eleven of these cases were settled by a consent procedure in which the Commission made no substantive findings. In such instances, the breadth of the Commission's view of injury can be ascertained only from the allegations of the complaint. This is not wholly satisfactory, for there is a tendency to allege in complaints not only what the government can actually prove but also what its staff thinks might conceivably be proved as the facts of the case become more fully known. Nevertheless, since no other information as to injury is available, the allegations of such complaints have been included in these summaries.

[16] In 18 of these cases (of which 10 were settled by consent orders without findings), as well as in the frit and chuck cases, the finding (or allegation) of damage to competition in the market was coupled with one of injury to competition between the discriminating seller and his competitors; that is, injury in the primary line was alleged or found in both the broad and the narrow sense. In no case was the difference between the two explained; indeed, in some cases the language of the finding was such that it is difficult to decide whether the Commission meant to find the broad injury, the narrow injury, or both.

[17] Eleven of these were cases settled by consent, in which the complaint alleged a tendency to monopoly and the order was issued without substantive findings.

[18] The situation in the quantity-discount cases is similar. Injury to competition in the primary line was found (or alleged in cases settled by consent orders) in 8 of the 9 quantity-discount cases in which no unlawful volume discounts were found. Only 2 of these cases were tried; in 1 of these the findings of injury to competition cover territorial discrimination as well as quantity discounts, with the former more important in the case; and in the other the findings cover functional discrimination as well as quantity discounts. In the other 6 cases there were no findings or the findings as to injury in the primary line were not explained.

in competition with others, to show how it was determined that volume discounts were damaging to competition in the primary line. In one case the only further information given is that the price differences were substantial.[19] In another the conclusion is badly based on the probability that the discriminations will divert trade from competitors.[20] In two others the Commission explained that many retailers had ceased, wholly or partly, to buy from the seller's competitors.[21] In a fifth the nature of the diversion is briefly explained as the result of a tendency of buyers to concentrate their purchases in order to take advantage of higher rates of discount.[22] This point is elaborated in another case by the statement that competing sellers can obtain part of the purchases of a buyer only at lower prices, since the effect of buying from them is to reduce the buyer's discount on the part he still buys from the discriminator.[23] Though by piecing these brief statements together one can obtain a general idea of the nature of the injury the Commission believes volume discounts produce in the primary line, none of the cases contains any statement as to the number, size, and power of the seller's competitors nor as to the amount of trade that may be diverted. There is no explanation of the fact that a tendency toward monopoly was found (or alleged) in most of them, but not in all; nor of the fact that in some cases volume discounts were not found to produce damage to competition in the primary line.

Among the cases selected for the present study, there are only two in which particulars were given on the nature of injury in the primary line, those against Bausch & Lomb and Minneapolis-Honeywell.[24] In the Bausch & Lomb case, injury to Bausch & Lomb's competitors was found to be a consequence of injury to independent wholesalers. The Commission found that the wholesale branches of Bausch & Lomb were selling to large dealers at the same prices as to independent wholesalers and that therefore these wholesalers were unable to sell to a sub-

[19] Docket 6044, *Goodyear Tire and Rubber Co., Inc.*
[20] Docket 6370, *Magnesium Co. of America, Inc.* This statement appears in the Commission's complaint. The case was settled by consent, without findings, but with an agreement that the complaint would furnish the basis for interpreting the Commission's order.
[21] Docket 6152, *Aeration Processes, Inc. et al.;* Docket 4571, *Life Savers Corp.*
[22] Docket 5969, *Benrus Watch Co., Inc.*
[23] Docket 3840, *Simmons Co.*
[24] Docket 3233, *Bausch & Lomb Optical Co., et al.* and Docket 4920, *Minneapolis-Honeywell Regulator Co.* In the former the facts and the findings were similar to those of a companion case against *American Optical Co.*, Docket 3232, which has not been specially studied.

stantial part of the market except at a loss. Since independent wholesalers must be used by small independent manufacturers, who cannot
grant comparable volume discounts on their limited lines of product, an
exclusionary effect was discerned at the manufacturing level. Moreover,
the volume discounts tended to induce large dealers to concentrate their
purchases with Bausch & Lomb and thus to refrain from buying the
goods of independent manufacturers unless the latter quoted prices
lower than Bausch & Lomb by amounts sufficient to offset the loss of
discounts. All three kinds of injury in the primary line were found. In a
companion case against American Optical Company the same types of
injury were found for the same reasons. Thus discrimination by each of
two large competing companies was found to tend to create a monopoly
for each.

In the case against Minneapolis-Honeywell, the Commission's decision
was appealed, and the finding of injury in the primary line was subjected
to close scrutiny. Honeywell produced about 60 per cent of the automatic
temperature controls for oil burners. The Commission found that Honeywell's volume discounts had the capacity and tendency to induce the
purchase of Honeywell's temperature controls and had diverted trade to
Honeywell from its competitors, with a probability of damage to competition in the primary line of commerce.[25] In reviewing the case, the
Seventh Circuit found in the record "undisputed facts" showing:

(a) that the prices charged for controls by M-H's competitors were
generally lower than those of M-H and that there is no evidence of
any undercutting of its competitors' prices by M-H; (b) that throughout
the complaint period there existed the keenest kind of price competition among control manufacturers; (c) that the total business of M-H's
competitors increased, and the three new concerns which entered the
industry after 1932 have enjoyed a steady growth in sales volume; (d)
that M-H's share of the available control business was reduced from
73 per cent in 1937-1938 to only 60 per cent in 1941; (e) that in 1941
M-H lost to its competitors 53 per cent of the control business of 31

[25] Doubtless the Commission was encouraged to make this finding by the fact
that the charge of price discrimination was one count in a complaint other parts
of which were directed at agreements designed to require purchasers to buy various kinds of controls in combination and to buy from Honeywell unpatented
stoker switches for use in furnace-control systems subject to a Honeywell patent.
The Commission found that these other arrangements violated the Federal Trade
Commission Act and Section 3 of the Clayton Act. Though the findings make the
line of thinking clear, they are not wholly clear as to whether the Commission
found the broad type of injury, the narrow type, or both.

customers who previously had standardized on M-H's controls; and (f) that in that same year, 126 of M-H's other oil burner manufacturer-customers also purchased competitive controls.[26]

On these grounds the court concluded that

> M-H was entitled to meet the competition built up in its field, and even if it did succeed in retaining or diverting some business that might otherwise have gone to some of its competitors, where those competitors were able to enter its field and build thriving businesses in spite of M-H's commanding position and alleged wrongful practices, we think it cannot be said that the effect of those practices was substantially to injure competition.[27]

The Commission appealed the decision, but since its petition for review was filed too late, the Supreme Court rejected the appeal on procedural grounds.

In dismissing a complaint against Yale and Towne Manufacturing Company in 1956, the Commission discussed the question of injury in the primary line in terms reminiscent of the decision of the circuit court in the Minneapolis-Honeywell case. As to the standard to be used in ascertaining injury, Commissioner Anderson's opinion said:

> In contending that the initial decision is based on an erroneous construction of the Act, the appellant [the attorney supporting the complaint on behalf of the Commission] argues that a showing that a seller's discriminations are sufficient to divert business from his competitors suffices to establish a prima facie case of law violation and that, even assuming that the evidence fails to show actual diversion of business to respondent, such circumstance does not render the record deficient.

Admitting that the statute requires only a reasonable probability of the injurious effect, he said that this fact "does not support the proposition, however, that conclusive inferences may be drawn from isolated evidentiary facets of the case without consideration of those which may be drawn from the entire record. If the particular circumstances attending the discriminations refute conclusions that the proscribed adverse effects may result, the statutory requirements of proof of injury have not been

[26] *Minneapolis-Honeywell Regulator Co.* v. *FTC,* 191 F. 2d 786.
[27] 191 F. 2d 786, 790.

met."[28] In the particular case, the opinion found no probability of injury because the performance, specifications, and adaptability of the product, rather than price, were the controlling factors in inducing sales and because competitors who gave no discounts had succeeded in selling to customers who bought in large volume and who had previously bought from the respondent. It quoted with approval a passage from the hearing examiner's initial decision saying:

> This record affirmatively shows that in this industry in the years in question there has been ease of entry, opportunity for survival, growth, and profit, excellent consumer choice of alternative products, efficiency in production and an active race for improvement of product, redesigning and the introduction of new types with supplier preference by purchasers fluidly responsive thereto, technological advances, and a fluidity and flexibility of market and of competition therein. The evidence is unanimous that competition in this industry in respondent's line of commerce is active, keen, healthy and increasing.[29]

Findings of Injury to Competition:
the Secondary Line

The Commission has found volume discounts illegal primarily because of their effect on the secondary line, that is, on competition among buyers. This finding (or allegation) stands alone in 13 cases and appears in every case but 3. All three degrees of damage have been found (or alleged in cases settled by consent without findings) —the narrow type 35 times, the broad type 24 times, and a tendency to monopoly 14 times.[30] Trials took place in only 11 of the 37 volume discount cases in which the Commission found injury in the secondary line, and in most of the others in which there were findings as to injury, these were brief and unrevealing. In the secondary line, the Commission tended to emphasize the narrow kind of injury, presumably because that is the most readily shown.

In 11 cases involving injury in the secondary line, it found (or alleged

[28] Docket 6232, *The Yale and Towne Manufacturing Co.,* Opinion of the Commission, pp. 4, 7.
[29] *Ibid.,* p. 3.
[30] Because of ambiguities in the findings, the distinction between the narrow and broad types of injury is not always clear, and the figures as to these should be regarded as only approximate. Note also that in 11 cases that were settled by consent, allegations of injury rather than findings of injury are included in the totals.

in a case settled by consent) only the narrow type of injury in this line, and in 3 of these cases there was no finding of injury in the primary line of commerce. These limited allegations and findings do not necessarily mean that no other type of injury among buyers could have been discovered; for having proved all that was necessary as a basis for an order, the Commission had no need to push its case further.

More frequently, both the broad and narrow types of injury were found (or alleged) together in the secondary line, without indication of the ground for the conclusion that injury to a class of intermediate distributors was also damage to market competition.[31] Similarly, in the 14 instances in which the Commission found a tendency to create a monopoly among buyers, this finding stood unexplained.[32]

In 13 of the volume-discount cases, no explanation is given in the complaints and findings as to the scope of the injury found in the secondary line. In another, the full explanation is the bald statement that a difference in price gives a substantial competitive advantage.[33] In 3 cases, information is given as to the aggregate amount of the discounts given in a year; and in 2 of them there is also information as to the number or proportion of customers receiving discounts; but the significance of the data is not analyzed in any of the 3.[34] In the other cases, with different

[31] The situation as to injury in the secondary line in the quantity-discount cases is similar. In 8 of the 9 cases in which quantity discounts but not volume discounts were condemned, the Commission found (or alleged in a case settled without findings) both the broad and the narrow types of injury; and in 6 of the cases it found (or alleged) a tendency to monopoly as well. In 1 case, the narrow type of injury stood alone. Only 2 of the cases were tried. The reasons for the Commission's view of injury were not stated in 7 of the 8 cases.

[32] In a revealing decision in the Edelmann case (Docket 5770), Hearing Examiner Frank Hier said: "As for 'tendency to create a monopoly,' the doctrinaire approach regards this as an inevitable *sequitur* of any substantial lessening of competition. However, in the setting of this case, the Hearing Examiner construes this phrase to mean that the probable result of the discriminatory pricing practice found will be such a concentration of economic power in the price-favored as will enable them to affect substantially the market in which they sell, if not to dominate and dictate the commercial acts of the unfavored. The record here fails to establish this. The challenged pricing practices have been followed for a substantial number of years, but there is no substantial evidence of such concentration in the price-favored at the secondary level." (51 FTC 993-94.) The decision in this case, as in most others by this hearing examiner, distinguishes clearly among concepts of injury and analyzes the evidence as to each.

[33] Docket 5969, *Benrus Watch Co.*

[34] Docket 5971, *Kentucky Chemical Industries, Inc.;* Docket 5972, *Ubiko Milling Co.;* Docket 5973, *Early & Daniel Co.*

degrees of clarity and different amounts of supporting detail, the Commission alleged or found injury in the secondary line because the difference in the buying price between favored and disfavored customers must result either in a difference in resale price that tended to divert trade to the favored group or in a difference in operating margins that gave the favored buyers more money than the disfavored ones to expend on service, sales effort, more varied stocks of goods, and other aids in expanding sales. No effort was made to estimate the magnitude of these effects.[35]

In one case, the evidence offered to controvert the conclusion that the price differences were injurious included a showing that various small jobbers had been able to grow in spite of their low discounts and thus to qualify for larger discounts;[36] and that the total number of jobbers was growing. The hearing examiner thought this evidence inadequate because "the Clayton Act is concerned primarily, if not exclusively, with commanding equality of price among competitors at the time of purchase, rather than with the myriad factors of a reselling operation which may . . . offset disadvantage on the one hand or advantage on the other." The Commission's opinion disposed of the same evidence by the brief statement that it did not mean that Nichoff's discounts "were attainable by all of its jobbers."[37]

In the earlier cases there was a tendency to emphasize the substantiality of the sums of money involved, and the size of the buyers who received advantages. In the Standard Brands case,[38] for example, the Commission found that the discriminations favored the most powerful buyers, and in the Brill case it found that the result was an inevitable tendency toward centralization and elimination of the smaller buyers. In the later cases, however, small amounts of discrimination among small buyers were regarded as similarly injurious. In the Standard Motor Products case, decided in 1957, the Commission recognized that "The customers involved are, for the most part, small, although some maintain more than one place of business," but held that "a more advantageous price to one customer gives him increased margin of profit, permits additional

[35] The analysis is most fully set forth in certain recent cases: Docket 5721, *Standard Motor Products, Inc.;* Docket 5722, *Whitaker Cable Corp.;* Docket 5723, *Moog Industries;* Docket 5768, *C. E. Niehoff and Co.;* Docket 5770, *E. Edelmann & Co.;* and Docket 5913; *P. and D. Manufacturing Co.*

[36] Docket 5768, *C. E. Niehoff and Co.*

[37] 51 FTC 1121-22, 1145.

[38] Docket 2986, *Standard Brands, Inc.*

services to customers, more vigorous selling and other opportunities for the extension of his business at the expense of his less favored competitors."[39] Similarly, in the Edelmann case the Commission's opinion said that the principle of protecting merchants against competitive injury from discrimination was "in nowise affected by the fact that respondent is not one of our country's largest producers of automotive parts or that the recipients of its discounts do not appear to be concerns of great size and resources engaged in distributing the products on a national basis."[40]

But in most of the cases in which this general view of injury was expressed, the analysis was not sufficient to explain why in particular instances the Commission found only injury to a disfavored class of customers, while in others it found a lessening of market competition and even a tendency toward monopoly. In general, the nature of the damage to the disfavored was made clear, while the damage to market competition and thus to the consumer was left obscure.

In the Standard Brands case, for example, the Commission found that volume discounts on bakers yeast enabled large bakeries and chains to make large and substantial savings that could be employed in their keen competition with smaller bakeries; and that these savings might be used for periodic reductions in price or increase in service and for sales effort and sales appeal. The Commission concluded in general terms that the effect of the discrimination was "substantially to lessen competition or tend to create a monopoly in the sale and distribution of bread . . . and to injure, destroy, or prevent competition with customers receiving the benefit of such discrimination. . . ."[41] The findings made no effort, however, to show explicitly that the injury to small bakeries was of such magnitude or appeared in such a setting as to justify the conclusion that competition in the market sense would be also injured.

The Morton Salt case and the Minneapolis-Honeywell case were appealed, and in each the Commission's concept of injury in the secondary line was reviewed by the courts. The decisions afford a contrast between two conceptions of injury to competition in the secondary line—one held

[39] Docket 5721, *Standard Motor Products, Inc.*, Opinion of the Commission, pp. 4-5.

[40] Docket 5770, *E. Edelmann & Co.*, 51 FTC 1004. The opinion noted that Edelmann's volume of business was .07 per cent of the total business in automotive replacement parts and equipment, and that its aggregate volume in 1949 was $1,600,000.

[41] 29 FTC 123.

by the Federal Trade Commission and the Supreme Court, the other by the appellate court for the Seventh Circuit. In the Morton case, the Commission found injury from the fact that the wholesalers competing with the beneficiaries of Morton's discrimination "must either sell at competitive prices and in so doing reduce their possible profits by the amount of the discriminations against them, or attempt to sell at higher prices than those which the favored customers of respondent charge for the same product, with the result of inability to secure business and a reduction in the volume of their sales."[42] Relevant to this injury was the fact that "a difference of five cents per case may result in the loss of a sale to a customer, not only of the salt involved but of other commodities as well, the order for which might be placed with the salt purchase."[43]

In reviewing the finding, the Seventh Circuit held that it was supported by slender evidence and dubious reasoning.

By two hypothetical questions propounded to witnesses, many of whom were not shown to possess any qualifications for the opinion given, the Commission attempted to established a probable result from the continuance of the price-discount system of petitioner from which the possibility of injury to competition might be inferred. These opinions are at variance insofar as injury defined by the Act is concerned with the actual facts admitted by many of the witnesses whose opinions were sought, and as otherwise established. One question was, "If you were selling Morton's Blue Package salt at $1.65 per case while at the same time a competitor seller was selling it for $1.63 per case, would your business be affected?" The similar question was, "If you were paying $1.50 per case for Morton's Blue Package salt while a competitor was paying $1.40, would your business be affected?" Fifty-one of the Commission's witnesses were thus interrogated over petitioner's objection. Thirty-two thought their business might be affected. None specified in what manner, to what extent, or what bearing such injury might have upon their competitive position or business profit. Twenty-nine (some of the thirty-two included) observed that while the competitor

---

[42] 40 FTC 397. This method of analysis is in sharp contrast with that used by the Commission in an early case against Kraft-Phenix Cheese Company. The Commission found that Kraft's prices differed substantially, but that competition was not injured because resale prices were not related to the price differences; trade was not in fact diverted by the resale price differences; the net disadvantage of the disfavored customers was too small to make a significant change in their total profits; and reasonable changes in methods of buying would have enabled the disfavored customers to obtain the lower prices. Docket 2935, *Kraft-Phenix Cheese Company*, 25 FTC 537.

[43] 40 FTC 396.

enjoying the discount might have an opportunity to make more profit, there would be no effect on competition, if, as the record demonstrates to be the fact, the discount was not used to reduce the sale price of the product. This had not occurred in the past.

Any businessman would readily admit that to some degree the price paid by a competitor for a product sold by him affects his business, but that is far from establishing that such price differential would force either of them to resell at a substantially reduced profit or to refrain from reselling. . . . This does not inferentially establish that the competitive position of either of them is being or may be injured, or that competition in the wholesale or retail business in the same line of commerce in general is being or may be injured or that the price differentials in question actually affect or may affect the competitive resale fluctuations in the trade.

The record in this case shows that wholesalers and retailers attempt only to stay in general line with competitors' prices; they distinguish between the effect of regular and special sale prices, and between the prices of cash-and-carry houses or stores and those of regular service houses or stores; competition between other salt manufacturers or between salt wholesalers and retailers has not been injured, and monopoly has not been promoted by the quantity price structure for the salt products manufactured, sold and delivered by petitioner, and there is no evidence that such will be the probable effect from a continuance thereof.

Contrary to the inferences drawn by the respondent Commission upon this foundation, the evidence shows substantial increases in sales to all nondiscount customers in all trade areas for the entire period covered by the Commission's evidence. The inference, if any could be drawn, was that the quantity discount system of petitioner tended to increase, not injure, competition. The least that can be said for this evidence is that it completely rebuts the opinion evidence elicited upon the hypothetical questions and renders same a wholly insufficient foundation for the inference of injury, or probability of injury to competition.[44]

One judge, dissenting from this opinion, said:

If I, a small buyer of salt, have to pay more for my salt than a larger buyer does because he is a large buyer, it seems clear to me that I have been discriminated against as to price. . . . It does not have to be shown and therefore found by the Commission that such discrimination actually lessened competition, etc. It is sufficient if it is found that there is a reasonable possibility that the discriminatory acts "may"

[44] *Morton Salt Co.* v. *FTC,* 162 F. 2d 949, 956.

have such an effect. . . .This called for the expert judgment of the Commission. . . . The fact of the discrimination itself, it seems to me, would have supported an inference that the effect may be to lessen competition . . . but there was abundant evidence in the record to support the finding. . . .[45]

The Supreme Court agreed with the minority opinion in the Circuit Court. On the ground that, in fact, only a few customers could buy enough to qualify for Morton's volume discounts, it brushed aside Morton's argument that the discounts had been available to all customers. It found adequate evidence of injury.

> The Commission found what would appear to be obvious, that the competitive opportunities of certain merchants were injured when they had to pay respondents substantially more for their goods than their competitors had to pay. . . . That respondents' quantity discounts did result in price differentials between competing purchasers sufficient to influence their resale price of salt was shown by evidence. This showing in itself is adequate to support the Commission's appropriate findings. . . .[46]

The Court further developed its conception of injury in rejecting the argument that injury to competition was precluded by the fact that salt is a small item in the budgets of most wholesale and retail business.

> There are many articles in a grocery store that, considered separately, are comparatively small parts of a merchant's stock. Congress intended to protect a merchant from competitive injury attributable to discriminatory prices on any or all goods sold in interstate commerce, whether the particular goods constituted a major or minor portion of his stock. Since a grocery store consists of many comparatively small articles, there is no possible way effectively to protect a grocer from discriminatory prices except by applying the prohibitions of the act to each individual article in the store.

The comments of the court regarding the Commission's evidence further emphasized its view that injury to competition is inherent in any substantial difference in the prices made by competitors.

[45] *Ibid.*, pp. 956-60.
[46] *FTC* v. *Morton Salt Co.,* 334 U.S. 37. The term "quantity discounts" was used by the Court to cover what are here called volume discounts.

. . . The Commission need only prove that a seller had charged one purchaser a higher price for like goods than he had charged one or more of the purchaser's competitors. . . . The Commission here went much further in receiving evidence than the statute requires. It heard testimony from many witnesses in various parts of the country to show that they had suffered actual financial losses on account of respondent's discriminatory prices. Experts were offered to prove the tendency of injury from such prices. The evidence covers about two thousand pages, largely devoted to this single issue—injury to competition. It would greatly handicap effective enforcement of the Act to require testimony to show that which we believe to be self-evident, namely that there is a "reasonable possibility" that competition may be adversely affected by a practice under which manufacturers and producers sell their goods to some customers substantially cheaper than they sell like goods to the competitors of these customers. This showing in itself is sufficient to justify our conclusion that the Commission's findings of injury to competition were adequately supported by evidence.[47]

The difference in opinion between the Commission and the Seventh Circuit appeared again in the Minneapolis-Honeywell case. The Commission's finding as to injury in the secondary line of commerce rested on the point that disfavored manufacturers of oil burners found their sales and profits affected by higher prices for the most important component of their products. Undeterred by the overturn of its opinion in the Morton Salt case, the Seventh Circuit refused to regard the existence of substantial price differences as inherently injurious and, instead, examined the substantiality of the evidence supporting the conclusion.[48] It summarized the relevant information as follows:

The absence of causal connection between the price of controls and the price of the finished products generally is demonstrated by the stipulation entered into prior to the hearing:
"Some manufacturers paying higher prices for respondent's automatic temperature controls were able to, and often did, sell their oil burners complete with controls at prices below those which other similar manufacturers paying lower prices for respondent's * * * controls sold their oil burners.

[47] 334 U.S. 37, 49-50.
[48] *Minneapolis-Honeywell Regulator Co.* v. *FTC*, 191 F. 2d 786.
The Court took notice of the fact that in holding the discrimination injurious the Commission had overruled the report of its trial examiner, with one commissioner dissenting.

"Some manufacturers paying lower prices for respondent's * * * controls were able to, and often did, sell their oil burners complete with controls at prices below those which other similar manufacturers paying higher prices for respondent's * * * controls sold their oil burners."

Even though some manufacturers did testify that "the question of price was important * * * and that they had lost business to certain competitors who enjoyed lower control prices * * *" we think it is equally significant that other manufacturers who paid the higher prices testified that they did not lose business as a result of paying such higher control prices, and that they considered other factors of far greater importance in determining the price of the completed burner. They referred to such matters as manufacturing methods, overhead, distribution costs, service, advertising, as having an important bearing on comparative prices in addition to the costs of the component parts.

In further proof of its contention that the price of controls was not

Prices Charged Oil Burner Manufacturers by M-H for Controls		Range of Prices Charged Wholesalers by Oil Burner Manufacturers for Burners	
		Low	High
Bracket 1	$17.35	$50.00	$111.00
Bracket 2	16.45	45.00	96.20
Bracket 3	15.90	47.50	102.00
Bracket 3a	15.35	52.50	89.00
Bracket 4	14.00	61.70	100.00
Bracket 4a	14.25	55.00	101.25
Bracket 5	13.75	45.00	114.50

the vital factor in arriving at burner prices and in fact had very little relation to it, M-H submitted a table derived from the findings of a nationwide survey showing the range of prices charged by its customers in each price bracket for the year 1941. From this survey, it will be noted that the highest price charged for burners, $114.50, was by a customer having the advantage of the lowest price bracket for M-H controls, and that a customer in the next-to-highest price bracket sold its burner for the lowest price, $45. Many variations can be made from these facts. All seem to add up to the one fact that there is little, if any, relationship between the prices of the controls and the prices of the burners into which the controls are built, hence that the evidence does not support the Commission's finding that "changes in the price of * * * controls resulted in corresponding changes in the price of completed burners."

Reference was made in the general finding quoted above to Quiet Heet as one of the manufacturers enjoying lower control prices to which other manufacturers lost an undetermined volume of business. There is no question on this record but that Quiet Heet, entering the field in 1936, very soon became the largest producer in the industry, and by 1941 was able to sell its burners at the lowest price. The Commission attributed this to the fact that it bought its controls from M-H for the lowest price. We think this is to ignore the vast discrepancy between the range of prices for controls and that for the finished burners. The fact was, as established by the evidence, that Quiet Heet entered the field with entirely different theories of production and distribution from those of its already established competitors. Its proprietor testified that he "started out to merchandise it on a volume basis, effecting certain economies, making a few shortcuts here and there and trimming down my overhead and operating costs to the minimum." Among those economies were the elimination of all field service which was one of the heavy items of expense of the higher price manufacturers, reduction of advertising costs to a minimum by its own use of printed postcards to the trade and by charging dealers for all advertising matter furnished to them, and adoption of cheaper packaging methods and materials. It was this type of economies that enabled Quiet Heet to sell its burner in 1941 for $68.50 less than its highest price competitor who paid the same price for the control, and for $66 less than its next highest price competitor who paid only $3.60 more for its controls, as shown in [the accompanying] table. . . .

Part of the fallacy of the Commission's position lies in its analysis of the competitive situation between the various manufacturers. This is reflected in its order where it refers to manufacturers "who in fact compete in the sale and distribution of such furnace controls," as if the controls themselves were the article of merchandise they dealt in instead of the burners of which the controls were only one part. It may be true that if the manufacturers were generally selling controls as such, a differential of 2 or 3 dollars in the price they paid for them would have a substantial effect on the price obtained. Under such circumstances a finding that a competitve advantage in purchase price paid would necessarily give rise to a competitive advantage in sale price would perhaps be justified. But where the controls were used in the manufacture of burners, the cost of which was determined by many other factors—cost of other materials and parts, service, advertising, to mention only a few—it cannot be said that discriminatory price differentials substantially injure competition or that there is any reasonable probability or even possibility that they will do so.[49]

The Commission's appeal to the Supreme Court was rejected on the technical ground that the petition was not filed within the period allowed by law. Hence, the circuit court's decision that Honeywell's volume discounts were not injurious became final. In dissenting from the Supreme

[49] 191 F. 2d 790-92.

Court's ruling as to procedure, Mr. Justice Black commented upon the substance of the case in a way that echoed the decision in the Morton case:

> The end result of what the Court does today is to leave standing a Court of Appeals decree which I think is so clearly wrong that it could well be reversed without argument. . . . The Court of Appeals held that there was no evidence at all to substantiate the Commission finding that a quantity-discount pricing system of Minneapolis-Honeywell resulted in price discriminations that violated Section 2(a) of the Robinson-Patman Act. But there was evidence before the Commission that some customers of Minnneapolis-Honeywell were given substantially bigger discounts on purchases than those given their competitors. And the Commission found that these variations were not justified by any differences in costs of manufacture, sale, or delivery. We have emphasized that such a showing amply supports a Commission cease and desist order. . . . The Court of Appeals here failed to follow our holding in the Morton Salt case. For this reason also it should be reversed.[50]

In concurring with this dissent, Mr. Justice Douglas noted that he did not believe "the merits of the case are as clear as Mr. Justice Black indicates."

The Supreme Court's opinion in the Morton Salt case established the interpretation of injury to competition in the volume- and quantity-discount cases; and after the Minneapolis-Honeywell decision the Seventh Circuit, too, adopted it. In deciding the Edelmann case in 1956, this court said:

> . . . The record . . . shows substantial discriminations in price; that the purchasers of petitioner's products sold in a market where competition was keen; that these purchasers operated on small profit margins; that many of the purchasers found it expedient to enter into group buying arrangements for the purpose of aggregating their purchases and thereby obtaining higher discounts than they would otherwise receive. . . . On the basis of the above facts the Commission found what appears reasonable and obvious: that the competitive opportunities of the less favored purchasers were injured when they had to pay substantially more for petitioner's products than their competitors had to pay.[51]

[50] *FTC* v. *Minneapolis-Honeywell Regulator Co.,* 344 U.S. 206, 213-14.
[51] *E. Edelmann & Co.* v. *FTC,* 239 F. 2d 152, 155.

Similar interpretations of injury to competition in the secondary line have been expressed by the Seventh Circuit in three other volume-discount cases and by the Eighth Circuit in one.[52] The legal meaning of the concept is now well established.

According to the view at first expressed by the Seventh Circuit, a decision as to whether or not competition may be damaged requires an examination of relevant data on volume of business, diversion of business, profits, and similar matters bearing on the competitive fortunes of those in the market. The concept adopted by the Supreme Court in the Morton case, and now generally accepted, dispenses with such information. To show injury in the secondary line, there is need only to show that the favored and disfavored customers were in competition with one another and that the amount of the price difference was substantial, either as a part of the sale price or as a part of the profit margin or in the aggregate saving that it made available to the favored customers. From substantiality in relation to sales price, the Commission can infer differences in resale price and diversion of trade or significant differences in operating profit. From substantiality in relation to operating margin, the Commission can infer an effect on profits. From substantiality in the total benefit obtained through discrimination, the Commission can infer a significant addition to the funds available for sales promotion, and consequent diversion of trade. It is not necessary to ascertain by examination of the facts that changes in business practice or diversion of trade actually occurred. Since the facts as to each commodity can be considered separately without regard to the importance of that commodity in the customer's total business, injury to competition among customers may be discovered by inference, even when the commodity is so small a part of the customer's sales volume that the customer is aware of no injury. Evidence that disfavored customers are prospering is not relevant, for competition is held to be injured even if the effect is merely to retard the growth of those who are disfavored or to retard the decline of those who are favored. Prevention of competition is sufficient to satisfy the statute, and no evidence that competitors are numerous or strong can disprove the claim that, but for discrimination, they might have been more numerous and stronger. Thus inference rises superior to evidence when there is a conflict between the two.

[52] *Whitaker Cable Corp.* v. *FTC*, 239 F. 2d 253; *C. E. Niehoff & Co.* v. *FTC*, 241 F. 2d 37; *P. and D. Manufacturing Co., Inc.* v. *FTC*, 245 F. 2d 281; *Moog Industries, Inc.* v. *FTC*, 238 F. 2d 43.

The contrast was dramatically presented by the Commission's decision in a recent case against Moog Industries.[53] The opinion of Commissioner Secrest, for the majority, noted that Moog's argument that there was no injury was "based largely on the fact that respondent's customers testified generally that they had not been injured by reason of the higher prices paid by them as compared with prices paid by their competitors in the same trading area." It commented that on cross-examination these witnesses admitted that their view was based on the fact that they and their competitors followed Moog's suggested resale prices. The majority thought that equality of resale price did not dispose of the question of injury in view of the fact that higher profit margins might permit better service and more sales effort. It found evidence of the probability of injury in the fact that distributors thought taking the 2 per cent cash discount was essential to their business, though the discount was less than Moog's volume discounts; and in the fact that the profit margins of distributors were low. "The dealers' financial life depends on the aggregate of small margins of profits made on a number of individual automotive items. . . . With over-all net profit so low, discounts to favored customers, ranging up to 19%, could well mean the difference between commercial life and death if these discounts were extended to a sufficient number of items purchased by a distributor."[54]

Commissioner Mason's dissenting opinion said that:

Every witness called positively denied he suffered any competitive injury from the challenged discounts or rebates—a position they all stoutly maintained in spite of the badgering the prosecutor gave them for ruining the Government's case. . . . To top all of this, the Government was finally forced to concede that if all other jobber witnesses who received the lesser discounts were to be summoned to the stand, they, too, would deny they had been injured. . . . Justice requires that we give precedence to direct evidence over inferences.[55]

On appeal, the Eighth Circuit sustained the Commission's order on November 5, 1956. As to the question of injury, it said "It was shown and found that two or more of petitioner's purchasers did business in each trade area and were, consequently, competitors therein. Through operation of the applicable cumulative annual rebate schedule, some

[53] Docket 5723, decided April 29, 1955.
[54] 51 FTC 939, 947.
[55] *Ibid.*, p. 953.

were charged higher prices than others. This constitutes an adequate evidentiary basis to support the Commission's finding that the price discriminations may substantially injure competition."[56] The testimony of customers that they had not been injured and the stipulation that all other customers, if called, would testify similarly, were discredited by the court on the grounds:

> First, that the Commission's findings were not based upon non-permissible inferences, but upon proven facts and inferences properly to be drawn therefrom, and second, a number of these witnesses were large buyers or members of groups, and thus received high rebates and were benefited by the plan, and, third, their answers were conclusion contrary to simple mathematics. . . . A witness cannot be allowed by conclusions to deny a mathematical fact, and all the testimony of these jobbers, on this score, amounts to—if they understood the facts—is that they are not objecting.[57]

Ambiguity of the Findings About Injury

Because of these characteristics of the approach to problems of injury in volume-discount cases, the records of the cases cannot be used to determine in which instances the effect of the discrimination was merely to establish an advantage for certain buyers and in which instances there was a further effect of reducing the vigor of competition on the buying side of the market, the selling side of the market, or both. It is obvious that in a number of the situations in which some kind of injury to competition in the primary line was found—notably those involving Jacobs, Dentists' Supply, Morton Salt, National Lead, Ferro Enamel, Standard Brands, Anheuser-Busch, American Optical, Bausch & Lomb, and Minneapolis-Honeywell, there was substantial concentration of control on the sellers' side of the market. But such companies as Simmons,[58] Benrus, Ubiko, Early and Daniel, Kentucky Chemical, Sealed Power, Aeration Processes, Life Savers, Holtite, Jacques Kreisler, F. & V., and Central Soya were not dominant ones. It is obvious, too, that on the

[56] *Moog Industries* v. *FTC*, 238 F. 2d 43, 50.

[57] *Ibid.*, pp. 50-51. A similar, though less sharp, clash of inference and testimony, with similar decisions and dissents at the Commission level and similar decisions on appeal, characterized Docket 5722, *Whitaker Cable Corp.*, and Docket 5913, *P. and D. Manufacturing Co.*

[58] Simmons' volume of sales was about 20 per cent of that of the industry.

buyers' side of the market, the discriminations that had to do with biscuits, salt, bakers yeast, Life Savers, ice cream mix, and rubber footwear
constituted particular instances of the pervasive advantages for chain
stores and other powerful buyers which the act was designed to curb. It
is not clear that problems as to the power of great buyers were reflected
in the discriminations pertaining to optical goods, locks, bedding, temperature controls, dental supplies, shoe findings, jewelry, animal feed,
and men's hats. Had the Commission undertaken, or been required by
law to undertake, a more substantial analysis of the competitive impact
of discounts for volume or quantity, there might or might not have
appeared in these cases problems of competition similar to, though
smaller than, those visible in the first group of cases.

It is noteworthy, too, that the Commission consistently assumed, without challenge from respondents, that the full amount of the price difference in favor of the larger buyer was available to him as an advantage
in buying. An observer might wonder if the purchase of larger amounts
did not sometimes entail expenses for storage, insurance, and the like,
greater than would have been incurred in buying smaller amounts. So
far as this may have been so, a part of the discount received by the
buyer presumably compensated him for an additional expense, and only
the remainder gave him any competitive advantage. But apparently
neither the Commission nor the respondents considered an examination
of the buyer's expenditures relevant to the problem of injury.

Cost Justification

Although sellers were legally permitted to justify volume or quantity
discounts by showing that these concessions made only due allowance
for differences in cost, this kind of justification was infrequently attempted in the 49 cases in which the Commission has issued orders
against such discounts, and was even less frequently successful. In most
of the cases the Commission's findings make no reference to costs. In
5 cases there is a statement that the discrimination was not cost-justified,
but these cases were not tried, and the findings indicate that the Commission was merely inferring from the pattern of the case that a cost
defense would have been impossible. In 7 cases there was a serious
proffer of a cost defense. In 2 of the 7, the defense was accepted as to
part of the discriminations; in the other cases it was totally rejected.

In some instances, the discrimination was of a kind to which a cost defense probably could not be applied. In the book cases customers buying the same amounts were found to have been differently treated. In the Minneapolis-Honeywell case, the Commission found that the volume discount was granted to some customers by giving them credit for purchases placed directly with Honeywell by persons to whom they resold. In the National Biscuit case, as well as in others, the Commission found that the volume discount was allowed to corporate and voluntary chains on the basis of the aggregate purchases made by the various parts of the organization, even though the goods were neither ordered through a central office nor delivered to it. In the Minneapolis-Honeywell case and in some others, it found that the discount appropriate to a stated volume was allowed to buyers whose purchases did not actually reach that volume. Such discounts could not be justified by a mere showing that when the stated volume was achieved the cost savings were as great as the price difference.[59]

Apart from such anomalies, the infrequency with which cost defenses were offered may have been due, as is often said in comments about the Robinson-Patman Act, to the difficulty and expense encountered in assembling cost information pertinent to price difference between customers who buy in different amounts. It may have been due also to a belief by sellers that whatever cost differences might be found could not be great enough to cover the discriminatory price differences. The justification of a volume discount by a difference in cost was peculiarly difficult, and the Commission was predisposed to reject it except where differences in volume reflected differences in the size of individual purchases. The Commission's opinion in the Master Lock case said:

> The additional discount of 5 per cent offered by the respondent to customers whose annual purchases generally exceeded $10,000 was apparently predicated on the belief that the orders received from this customer group were both larger and fewer in number, in proportion to their purchases, and therefore cost the respondent less per dollar of sales to bill, pack, and ship, than the orders received from customers whose annual purchases usually amounted to less than $10,000. This belief, however, is frequently not supported by the facts. On the contrary, not only do customers in the last named group frequently place

[59] In the Minneapolis-Honeywell case, the cost defense was developed after reclassifying customers and costs in accord with the actual rather than the imputed volumes bought.

a smaller percentage of orders amounting to less than $5 each than do the customers allowed the additional discounts, but they frequently also place a larger percentage of orders exceeding $100 each than do customers accorded additional discounts. Furthermore, the average size of the individual order received by sellers from customers granted an extra discount is frequently less than the average size of the individual order received from customers not granted that discount.

Aside from differences in methods of sale and delivery, savings in the cost of serving different customers result from the differences in the size of the orders placed by such customers, irrespective of their aggregate purchases for a given period of time. Large orders are usually assembled, priced, packed, billed, and delivered at a lower cost per dollar of sales than small orders. In the instant case there is no evidence that the respondent employed different methods of sale and delivery in serving the customers not accorded the 5 per cent discount than it used in serving those receiving the said discount, nor that it cost the respondent less per dollar of sales to make shipments to the first named group than to the group last named.[60]

In three of the seven instances in which the Commission considered a cost defense supporting quantity or volume discounts, the findings disposed of the matter without extended discussion. In the Morton Salt case, the Commission found in a single sentence that Morton had not shown its discounts to be cost-justified.[61]

In the National Lead case, cost defenses for quantity discounts were minor parts of a case primarily concerned with price fixing and territorial price discrimination. Price differences discriminating against purchases in quantities less than a carload were in question; and the Com-

[60] 27 FTC 991-92. Docket 3386, *Master Lock Co.* No cost defense was submitted in this case, which was decided on the basis of an admission answer. The Commission's statement, therefore, is to be regarded as dictum, *i.e.,* comment not necessary to the decision of the particular case.

[61] William Warmack, who worked on the case for the Commission, subsequently described the cost defense as "mere office calculations." He said, "No functional cost survey and analysis of any kind was ever made and, for the most part, the costs were separated on the basis of the number of invoices." He said Morton presented no evidence to show that this method gave reasonably accurate results. See William J. Warmack, "Cost-Accounting Problems Under the Robinson-Patman Act," *Robinson-Patman Act Symposium* (1947), p. 110. The defense offered by Morton and the challenge of it by the Commission's staff has been analyzed in detail in Herbert F. Taggart, *Cost Justification* (1959), pp. 170-86. Professor Taggart's book is the first detailed study of efforts at cost justification under the statutes. Unfortunately, it became available so late in the writing of this book that only superficial use of it has been possible here.

mission found that the price differences substantially exceeded the differences in transportation charges that could be used to justify them. Apparently no issue arose as to whether there were other differences in cost pertinent to the purchase of small quantities.[62]

In the case concerned with rubber and canvas footwear, an elaborate cost study for the year 1940 was included in the stipulation of facts on which the Commission's decision was based. The Commission set forth its conclusions on cost in its findings, but not the analysis on which they were based. It found that portions of the discount structure were cost-justified; that for three discount categories cost differences failed to cover price differences by amounts so small as to be unimportant; but that for four discount categories the price differences exceeded the cost differences by substantial amounts—between 4 and 5 per cent. Accordingly, the cost defense was rejected.[63]

In the cases involving Standard Brands, International Salt, Minneapolis-Honeywell, and Niehoff, the cost defense was more fully discussed.

In the International Salt case, the respondent sought to justify both a quantity discount and a volume discount on table salt by showing cost differences.[64] The justification for the quantity discount was based on the argument that the average cost of making a sale was $5.62, and that in applying this cost to sales involving different quantities, International Salt would save 5 cents per case or more in selling 100 cases at one time as compared with selling 55 cases or less at one time. The Commission rejected this argument on the ground that International refused to make sales of less than two tons (the equivalent of 74 cases) and that, therefore, the cost saving computed from smaller quantities was irrelevant. Moreover, the Commission held that International had not shown that the

[62] See 49 FTC 864-65, 869.
[63] See Docket 4972, *U. S. Rubber Co.*, 46 FTC 998. The stipulations in the case have been analyzed in Taggart, *Cost Justification*, pp. 284-339. After two supplemental stipulations involving three and one-half years of work and negotiation, counsel on both sides apparently agreed on the amounts of price and cost differences. Since the Commission adopted their conclusions without setting forth any cost analysis in its findings, the thinking that underlay the findings retained the status of work by a professional staff. It was not given the authority and usefulness as a precedent that attaches to a Commission decision. The cost study in this case is supposed to have involved an expenditure of $250,000. See John Parkany, "Federal Trade Commission Enforcement of the Robinson-Patman Act, 1946-52," (doctoral dissertation, Columbia University, 1956), p. 256.
[64] Docket 4307, *International Salt Co.* The cost defense is analyzed in Taggart, *Cost Justification*, pp. 140-69.

average cost of making a sale was properly applicable to all sales regardless of their size.

The justification by International of its volume discount was based on a comparison of the cost of selling to A. & P. with the cost of selling to all other purchasers. The Commission rejected this comparison on the ground that "by combining the costs of selling to all purchasers other than A. & P. regardless of the customers' volumes of purchases, methods of purchasing or whether purchasing at respondents' highest or lowest price, respondents have made an analysis which is incapable of establishing the differences in costs of sales as between respondents' purchasers who received this . . . discount and those who did not."[65] The Commission also noted that the record did not show the propriety of some of the assumptions used in allocating costs, such as the assumption that the duration of calls by salesmen was uniform regardless of the buyer.

The cost justification submitted by Standard Brands was rejected after elaborate analysis.[66] Although Standard sold a long line of bakery and grocery products, the discrimination involved in the case had to do only with bakers yeast and foil yeast. The segregation of the appropriate costs was a major problem. For managerial purposes, Standard had long estimated costs by applying various predetermined percentages to dollar sales. In preparing its cost study, Standard analyzed various classes of traceable costs in order to determine how they should be divided between bakery products and grocery products. The division of these costs between the two classes of products was sharply different from that which would have resulted from the use of the predetermined percentages. However, instead of using the new ratios developed for traceable costs as a basis for the allocation of the residual expenses, Standard allocated the residual expenses inversely, so that after they had been added to the traceable costs, the division of the total still conformed to the predetermined percentages. The predetermined percentages were also used in deciding what portion of the cost of bakery products should be assigned to bakers yeast. The costs of yeast, as thus computed, were then allocated among volume brackets on the basis of sample studies of various categories of costs. For example, the computed total for route selling and delivery was allocated according to the time spent at the premises of customers during a six-day period. The total costs for each volume

[65] 49 FTC 154.

[66] Docket 2986, *Standard Brands, Inc.* For a detailed analysis of the cost defense see Taggart, *Cost Justification*, pp. 39-80.

242 THE PRICE DISCRIMINATION LAW

bracket were converted into an estimated cost per pound sold to the customers in that volume bracket during a selected month.

The Commission rejected this analysis primarily on the ground that the use of predetermined percentages inconsistent with the percentages appropriate to traceable costs gave allocations of aggregate cost that were merely arbitrary.[67] Whereas only 36 per cent of the traceable cost was allocated to bakery products, 52 per cent of the residual cost was so allocated. Moreover, the sales and cost totals used in the analysis pertained to the entire country; yet the resulting costs were offered to justify a volume-discount schedule that applied to only a part of the country, and no effort was made to justify four other price schedules applicable to other parts of the country.

In the Minneapolis-Honeywell case, the Commission accepted a cost-justification covering five out of the eight volume classes in the discount schedule.[68] To prepare this justification, Honeywell had reallocated the costs applicable to customers who had received off-scale discounts (about 43 per cent of all manufacturing costs used in the study) so that these costs appeared in the discount bracket representing the number of units actually purchased.[69] But Honeywell offered no justification covering the three volume classes that received the largest discounts, though by dollar volume more than 55 per cent of its sales were made at those discounts. The Commission's order was directed at these larger discounts and at off-scale selling.

In the Niehoff case, the respondent submitted a cost justification for volume discounts on automotive supplies.[70] The findings disclose with unusual clarity the type of data submitted and the basis for the Commission's decision. The justification was based on an analysis of advertising expense, "direct sales expense on a per account basis," and time and cost studies of 17 orders by an industrial engineer "on a per order basis showing the cost of processing orders of various dollar size through the 21 steps each order must traverse from receipt to shipment."[71]

[67] The Commission also doubted the accuracy of the methods of allocation used in apportioning costs of solicitation and service.

[68] The defense has been analyzed in Taggart, *Cost Justification*, pp. 257-83.

[69] According to the vice-chairman of Honeywell's Board of Directors the study took from 4 to 8 accountants and analysts almost 9 months, and to repeat it at frequent intervals would be prohibitively expensive. See *A Study of the Antitrust Laws*, Hearings before the Senate Committee on the Judiciary, 84 Cong. 1 sess., Pt. 3, p. 1337.

[70] It has been analyzed in Taggart, *Cost Justification*, pp. 399-428.

[71] 51 FTC 1134.

The information obtained on cost for orders of different sizes was reduced to a graph from which the cost of filling orders of other sizes was inferred by extrapolation. Procedure from this point was as follows: ". . . Respondent then takes any customer in any discount bracket, totals his year's net billings and divides by the number of orders, to ascertain the average size order over the year, and multiplies this by the total processing cost per dollar of net billing applicable to that size order to obtain the actual processing cost of that customer's business." The hearing examiner rejected this procedure as fallacious because:

> Respondent's discounts are not granted on a quantity per order basis but upon an annually cumulated volume basis. If each customer's order was in exactly the same amount each time, this method might be acceptable, but a customer buying $15,000 annually of respondent's products might well send in as a substantial part of that volume a number of small and high cost orders, whereas contrariwise $500 of annual purchases could well be in two orders of $250 each. . . . There is no showing of the number of orders received over the year 1951 from each of the 17 customers whose single orders were cost analyzed, nor any showing of their individual amounts, and hence it is impossible to tell how many orders varied precipitately from the average and hence how much actual cost variance there may have been.[72]

Most of Nichoff's analysis of advertising expense was also rejected. Niehoff had allocated the total equally to each account, and had then treated the allocated sum as a lump of cost to be attributed to the customer's volume of purchases, with the effect that as that volume increased, the cost per dollar of sales declined. The hearing examiner accepted this procedure for one item—catalog expense[73]—the effect of which was insufficient to justify the price differences. He thought that the effectiveness of other types of advertising expense—primarily in trade papers and for printed matter—could not be measured by any customer's volume, and hence could only be allocated "on a per dollar of sales basis, which, of course, furnishes no cost justification for differing prices as between customers."[74]

Niehoff's analysis of direct sales expense was rejected completely. It was based on the contention that salesmen made the same number of calls on each jobber, and consisted in the allocation of direct selling

[72] *Ibid.*, pp. 1135-36.
[73] This amounted to $32,389 of the total of $100,437 of advertising expense.
[74] 51 FTC 1137.

expense equally to each customer, with a subsequent treatment of the lump-sum allocations in the same way as for advertising expense. The testimony of the one salesman, the hearing examiner found, refuted the contention that different jobbers received the same number of calls, and thus destroyed the basis for the allocation of expense.[75] Moreover, this testimony indicated that a considerable portion of total time was spent in calls on prospective customers, which the hearing examiner thought should not be allocated on a per-customer basis.

In reviewing the case, the Commission rejected the hearing examiner's conclusion that Niehoff's catalogs were equally distributed to jobbers buying different amounts, and therefore rejected his acceptance of the partial cost justification based on allocation of expense for catalogs. Otherwise the Commission accepted the hearing examiner's analysis of the cost defense.[76]

In two private cases, *Russellville Canning Company* v. *American Can Co.* and *Bruce's Juices* v. *American Can Co.,*[77] cost defenses have received careful judicial review. In both cases, the defense was offered to justify a volume-discount schedule under which American Can granted discounts of from 1 to 5 per cent on annual purchases valued at from $500,000 to $7 million; and the maximum discount was received by only three customers (Stokely, Libby, McNeill, & Libby, and California Packing Co.). In the Bruce's Juices case, the lower court rejected the cost defense because (1) it grouped customers in broad classes instead of showing the actual cost of serving individual customers; (2) many of the costs were pertinent to volume delivered to particular plants rather than to the aggregate volume delivered to all plants, which was the basis for the discounts; and (3) certain costs were arbitrarily allocated. In affirming the decision of the lower court, the Fifth Circuit did not discuss the cost defense in detail, but said that any system of discounts under which 98

[75] Calls on particular jobbers in 1949 varied from none to seven, with a considerable number of jobbers receiving from one call to four.

[76] Docket 5768, *C. E. Niehoff and Co.,* Initial Decision by Frank Hier, Hearing Examiner, July 6, 1954, and Opinion of the Commission by Commissioner Secrest, May 17, 1955.

[77] The decisions in the Bruce's Juices case appear in 87 F. Supp. 985 and 187 F. 2d 919; the Russellville decisions in 87 F. Supp. 484 and 191 F. 2d 38. In the Russellville case, a cost defense was offered not only for volume discounts but also for a charge of violation of Sec. 2(e). It is discussed above, p. 204. The cost aspects of both cases are analyzed in Taggart, *Cost Justification,* pp. 466-93.

per cent of the customers qualify for no discount whatever imposes a heavy burden of justification on its proponent.

In the Russellville case, the lower court rejected the cost defense on similar grounds:

> A literal interpretation of Section 2(a) would appear to call for a consideration of the sales costs to individual customers and to individual plants of customers who operate more than one. It is difficult to see in what other manner price differentials can be limited to the sphere of actual costs. . . . If a system whereby all of the small customers are lumped together in one group solely because of their quantity buying ability . . . is justifiable, then the Congress has done a futile thing in enacting this legislation, for, obviously, it has failed to correct the recognized evil whereby "a large buyer could secure a competitive advantage over a small buyer solely because of the large buyer's quantity purchasing ability." . . . Defendant . . . set up the system [of classification for discounts] and then conducted studies for the test period to justify it (or to allocate costs already known), never changed it, and in fact, during the period of its dealings with plaintiff no study of costs whatsoever in regard to its discount system was made. This, in the opinion of the court, could not meet the most liberal "good faith cost study test."[78]

The Eighth Circuit, however, thought the standard of the lower court for costs too rigid. In its opinion American Can had shown care and good faith in developing cost information: The volume-discount schedule had been adopted after the passage of the Robinson-Patman Act following consultation with a former district judge, a former Solicitor General of the United States, and an investigator for the Federal Trade Commission. When American Can's auditing department reported that the cost records were not sufficient to show the costs of selling to customers grouped according to the volume they bought, the schedule was based on the judgment of a vice-president in charge of sales, and the relation of cost to it was studied by an audit running from April 1, 1937 to December 31, 1941. The study showed that the schedule was cost-justified. Though one experienced accounting witness testified that the study was "crazy" because it failed to consider individual differences, placed customers in too few classes, and ignored the influence of location, another testified that it was well conceived and carefully operated. When the dis-

---

[78] 87 F. Supp. 484, 495-96.

counts were revised in 1946, the new ones were justified by the old cost study. After summarizing the standards of adequacy implicit in the lower court's decision, the Eighth Circuit said the law did not show a congressional intent to require so much.

> If a manufacturer granting quantity discounts is required to establish and to continuously maintain a cost accounting system which will record the expenses incurred in selling every individual customer and all of the data which the plaintiff deems essential, the burden, expense and assumption of risk involved would seem to preclude the granting of quantity discounts, at least until the approval of the plan by the Federal Trade Commission had been secured. . . . If . . . the system was adopted in good faith and the cost study during the test period of more than four years was honestly maintained, and reflected with substantial accuracy the differences in selling costs as between the customers in Class C and those in Classes A and B, we think the court's conclusion that the justification was inadequate because it was not continued beyond the test period, did not reflect cost differences as between individual customers, and failed to take into consideration conjectural geographical differences in selling costs and other matters which might be thought to have some speculative bearing on such cost differences, was not justified.[79]

The court remanded the case for a new trial, which did not take place because the case was settled by a payment from American Can to Russellville.[80]

Meeting a Competitor's Prices

In most of the quantity-discount and volume-discount cases, there was no effort to justify the concessions on the ground that they had been made in good faith to meet the equally low price of a competitor. This defense was not available in 2 cases in which the discrimination was a part of a conspiracy among sellers. It was offered in only 9 cases—those

---

[79] 191 F. 2d 38, 59.

[80] Bruce's Juices won its suit against American Can and received damages. In a public statement by Congressman Wright Patman, a former executive of an unnamed company is quoted as saying that the cost of fighting a suit against American Can contributed in large measure to the destruction of his company. Details contained in the letter indicate that the company was Bruce's Juices. See *To Amend Section 2 of the Clayton Act,* Hearings before the Senate Committee on the Judiciary, 85 Cong. 1 sess., Pt. 2, p. 1017.

against Standard Brands, International Salt, Morton Salt, and Minneap-
olis-Honeywell, and 5 more recently decided against Whitaker Cable,
Moog Industries, C. E. Niehoff, E. Edelmann, and Standard Motor
Products. The Commission rejected it in each case.

In the Standard Brands case, the defense of meeting competition was
offered only to justify off-scale selling. The Commission conceded that
some off-scale prices had been made to customers who reported lower
offers from competitors. However, the Commission found that these were
not mere particular instances of price cutting. Rather, Standard had
maintained a general policy whereby subordinates could sell below
scale within fixed limits, with no requirement that they confine themselves to meeting a competitive price. Moreover, Standard's goodwill
enabled it to secure more for its yeast than competitors. The Commission thought "that competitive and other considerations were the bases
of its [Standard's] general price policy pursued in a process of outstrip-
ping competitors," but that "it was not shown that the price situations in
which respondents found themselves were not of their own making."[81]

In the Morton Salt case an effort was made to justify certain special
off-scale discounts as adjustments to meet competition. The Commission
found in general terms that the evidence submitted was too vague and
indefinite to show that the long-continued discriminations were made in
good faith.

In the International Salt case the defense that competition had been
met in good faith was offered to justify the volume discount accorded to
those who bought more than $50,000 per year. The Commission rejected
the defense on two grounds. The first was that, although in 1936 International had altered the amount of the discount and the requirements
for receiving it "to conform with what they understood to be the pricing
practices of their competitors," this fact was not important because "the
practice of granting discounts on the basis of the total annual requirements of a purchaser regardless of from whom they were purchased was
employed by respondents or their wholly owned subsidiaries prior to
that date." Hence International was not departing from a nondiscriminatory pricing scale but was continuing to apply the discriminatory pricing
standard it had previously adopted. The second ground was that International's failure to attempt to eliminate or lessen the amount of discrimination for eight years after 1940, when the Commission's com-

[81] 30 FTC 1136.

plaint brought "the illegal nature of this discount" to International's attention, was inconsistent with good faith. The second ground for the decision seems to mean that a discount that is lawful because granted in good faith to meet a competitor's price may become unlawful, so far as this type of justification is concerned, merely because the Commission has chosen to challenge it and the respondent has refused to yield without controversy.[82]

In the Minneapolis-Honeywell case, in which discounts for five out of the eight volume brackets were found to be cost-justified, the discounts for the other three brackets, and the prices for off-scale sales, Honeywell contended, were offered in good faith to meet the prices of competitors. Honeywell submitted evidence on competitive offers covering 22 accounts where sales had been made off-scale. The Commission pointed out that this body of evidence did not apply to 54 other accounts involved in off-scale selling or to other recipients of the three largest discounts. As to the justification of the highest volume brackets, the Commission found that only 4 of the 22 companies for which Honeywell submitted evidence of competitive offers had made purchases that would qualify them for the brackets in question; that 2 of these companies had received low prices not to meet a competitor's price but to induce the buyer to cease charging a high premium for oil burners that were equipped with Honeywell controls; that apparently 1 of them had received low prices in recognition of its ability to make controls for itself; and that 1 of them had received a low price after Honeywell learned that this customer had made a large number of oil burners equipped with controls supplied by a competitor, even though Honeywell did not yet know the price this competitor had charged. The Commission also noted that in practically all of the 22 instances, Honeywell had followed its regular practice of submitting a year's contract in December of the previous year, when it had no knowledge about the prices that would be charged by competitors. The defense of meeting competition was not accepted for any of the 22 accounts, and was considered clearly inadequate to justify other off-scale sales or the highest volume brackets.[83]

[82] 49 FTC 153-55.

[83] The vice-chairman of Honeywell's board of directors later testified, "All that a concern like Honeywell can do is to use its best business judgment as to the character of the information that comes in to it from the field as to competitors' prices." See *A Study of the Antitrust Laws,* Hearing before the Senate Committee on the Judiciary, 84 Cong. 1 sess., Pt. 3, p. 1338.

In these cases the Commission consistently expressed the view that the defense of meeting a competitor's price can be used only to justify a particular price quotation to a particular customer on the basis of a reasonable belief that he has received that same quotation from another source. If the seller quotes a price lower than his competitor, or if he quotes a low price in anticipation of similar action by his competitor or in the belief that the competitor's past prices will prevail in the future, he has, in the Commission's opinion, stepped beyond the limits of the good-faith defense. He cannot use the defense to justify a general and systematic concession to a whole class of his customers. Nor can he justify a volume or quantity discount structure on the basis of a competitor's practice if what he attempts to defend is merely a modification of an earlier unlawful structure of discounts that he had established on his own initiative.

The limiting effect of these interpretations is clearly demonstrated in five recent contested cases against manufacturers of automobile parts and accessories.[84] These manufacturers contended that their volume or quantity-discount schedules, or portions thereof, had been adopted in good faith to meet the similar schedules of competitors. In the Moog case, for example, the executive vice president of the respondent company testified that in examining the discount schedule of Wausau Motor Parts Company, a competitor:

> We would try to evaluate the effect of Wausau on our market, how close we would have to come to meeting the competitive offer and how far away we should stay because of certain pitfalls which it may lead us into, and upon examination of this we would use our own good judgment and experience to try and work this thing in with all of the others and come out with a contract and a schedule which we feel would earn us the greatest amount of profit and lose us the smallest number of customers and attract the most.[85]

In the Niehoff case, the president of the respondent manufacturer testified that Niehoff's adoption of a volume-discount plan was forced on it by the adoption of similar plans by competitors; that Niehoff's prices were higher, on the average, than those of its competitors, though lower

---

[84] Docket 5721, *Standard Motor Products, Inc.;* Docket 5722, *Whitaker Cable Corp.;* Docket 5723, *Moog Industries;* Docket 5768, *C. E. Niehoff and Co.;* Docket 5770, *E. Edelmann and Co.*

[85] 51 FTC 941-42.

in some instances, particularly where the competitor's product enjoyed special prestige; and that to quote a single price on each product and then reduce prices in each particular instance would be impossible because so much discretion could not be given to salesmen and because approval of recommendations by salesmen would be hopelessly expensive and time-consuming. Standard Motor Products defended its discounts on the aggregate volume of buying groups on the ground that:

> In each instance competitors of appellant approached the group at their organizational meetings and offered to sell an ignition line at a greater discount or rebate (a lower price) than appellant was selling its customers who were about to become members of such "group." Appellant's customers . . . told appellant's representatives that if appellant did not meet the price offered by its competitors, it would lose their business. In each instance . . . appellant authorized a sales representative to make an offer to the group of a price as low as but never lower than the price offered by competitors. . . .[86]

Circumstances such as these were found insufficient to show that the respondents had met the equally low prices of competitors in good faith.[87] In the Whitaker and Moog cases, the defense was rejected on the ground that the discounts expressed a pricing practice of long standing, not the meeting of particular price reductions in particular situations. In the Standard Motor Products case, this reason was reinforced by two others—that the respondent knew the competing offers were unlawful, since they were available on pooled purchases rather than the purchases of individual customers; and that in meeting these offers Standard Motor Products acted aggressively rather than defensively, since it not only held its own customers but got new business at the reduced price from other members of the buying group. In the Edelmann case, though the price schedule had been set in the light of those of Edelmann's two chief competitors, Edelmann had set prices sometimes higher and sometimes lower than its rivals, constituting a continuing nationwide system, related not to existing but to future competition, and designed "to come

---

[86] Docket 5721-1. Brief of Appellant on Appeal from the Initial Decision and Order, p. 8.

[87] Prior to the decisions, the Supreme Court had considered the defense of meeting competition in two cases, one against *A. E. Staley Manufacturing Co.* (Docket 3803), and the other against *Standard Oil Company of Indiana* (Docket 4389). The court's statements about the scope of the defense had a substantial effect on these decisions. See below, pp. 319-22.

close enough to the pricing systems of its two principal competitors to allow it to retain most of its customers and perhaps gain a few more." In the Niehoff case, too, the defense failed because the price reductions were not temporary, localized, individualized, and defensive, but constituted "a nation wide pricing system which inevitably spawns systematic and continuing price discriminations" and "cannot be wholly defensive." The program was "geared generally to competing for business and not specifically for meeting competing prices."[88]

In the latter case the hearing examiner was impressed by Niehoff's showing that, in selling more than 3,000 items in small quantities in competition with 30 or 40 competitors, price reductions in individual localized instances were impracticable. "These," he said, "are indeed persuasive facts and make out a hardship case." But as "low man of the judicial totem pole" he felt constrained to follow the guiding cases.[89] Neither the Commission nor the circuit court pursued the implied suggestion that the interpretation that makes the defense of meeting competition inapplicable to pricing systems might properly be modified.

Effect of the Commission's Orders

In the present study an effort has been made to ascertain the effect of the proceedings against volume and quantity discounts by interviews with persons affected. Such a study has been made for 13 of the volume-discount cases, 1 of the quantity-discount cases, and 2 of the cases involving both volume and quantity discounts.[90]

In considering the cases that have been studied, it is convenient to distinguish four different groups.

First is the case against Minneapolis-Honeywell, in which the Commission's order regarding price discrimination was reversed on appeal. Thereafter Minneapolis-Honeywell continued to grant volume discounts. Whereas before the case the discounts had been based on the previous

---

[88] 51 FTC 998, 1131, 1146.

[89] *Ibid.*, p. 1131.

[90] Since the sample for study was selected in 1955, no case was included in which the Commission's decision was rendered after December 31, 1954. This fact accounts for the omission of the interesting group of automobile parts cases for which the decisions have been summarized in earlier pages. Seven cases were not studied because of their recency. Of the earlier group, the study omitted 19 volume-discount cases and 7 quantity-discount cases.

year's purchases, they are now based on the average of the previous three years. Off-scale selling has been substantially reduced. Any departure from scale must be approved by a vice-president, and there are few such approvals.[91] The volume-discount schedule has been changed, as appears in the following tables.

Volume-Discount Schedules in 1941[a]

Annual Volume (Sets)[b]	Aggregate Net Prices per Set	Discount as Percentage Below Highest Aggregate Net Price per Set
50– 349	$17.35	—
350– 999	16.45	*5.19*
1,000–2,499	15.90	*8.36*
2,500–4,999	15.35	*11.33*
5,000–7,499	14.90	*14.12*
7,500–9,999	14.25	*17.87*
10,000 and up	13.75	*23.05*

[a] Source: 44 FTC 379.

[b] Volumes shown hereon are for sets only and are not for separate units. Respondent's automatic temperature controls in all 5 years were priced on a unit basis irrespective of whether purchased by units or by sets, and the several manufacturers' price brackets were similar for those contracting to purchase sets and those contracting to purchase units, the minimum number of units necessary to reach a particular bracket being three times the minimum number of sets necessary to reach that bracket. For example, bracket 1 prices applied to a customer contracting to purchase either 50 sets or 150 units. 44 FTC 379.

Volume-Discount Schedules in 1956[a]

Annual Volume (Sets)	Aggregate Net Prices per Set	Discount as Percentage Below Highest Aggregate Net Price per Set
50– 2,999	$28.40	—
3,000– 7,499	27.20	*4.23*
7,500–14,999	26.20	*7.75*
15,000 and up	25.55	*10.04*

[a] Source: from interviews.

Minneapolis-Honeywell has enlarged the size of the lower volume brackets and begun the top bracket with a larger volume. It has slightly

[91] The vice-chairman of Honeywell's board of directors has commented, "I do not see how any businessman can tell whether his competitor's price is lawful." See *A Study of the Antitrust Laws,* Hearings, Pt. 3, p. 1346.

reduced the price concessions to the smaller buyers and substantially reduced them to the larger buyers. The change was apparently due to the cost study that was made for the defense of the price-discrimination case. Quantity discounts for jobbers, which were formerly available alongside the volume discounts for manufacturers, are no longer given, though the case had little to do with this change.[92]

The same volume discounts are available to furnace manufacturers and oil burner manufacturers. Hence furnace manufacturers usually buy controls direct from the maker for installation in the furnace instead of obtaining them as a part of an oil burner. This change has developed partly because in the middle 1930's oil furnaces, which typically had been conversions of other furnaces, began to be designed and manufactured especially for oil heating. However, a part of the responsibility for the change is attributed to the price discrimination case by one of Minneapolis-Honeywell's customers, whose sales of controls for oil heating fell about 92 per cent because of it. According to the vice-chairman of Honeywell's board of directors, a number of competing producers of controls, large and small, have entered the industry since the case, and Honeywell's percentage of the market is smaller than during the proceeding.[93]

The second kind of case involved discrimination as one aspect of a broad conspiracy among sellers. The frit case had involved a conspiracy to fix prices, which had included the establishment of a uniform scale of volume discounts based on the total volume bought from all sellers. The National Lead case was concerned with price fixing through a zone-price formula but pertained also to discrimination, not justified by cost, between buyers of carloads and buyers in smaller quantities.

The main purpose of the orders in these cases was to terminate the conspiracies. Whether this purpose was achieved lies outside the scope of the present study. There was agreement among those who were interviewed that volume discounts are no longer given by producers of frit. One producer of lead pigments apparently offers no quantity discounts. In the lead case, zone pricing overshadowed the quantity discounts, and no further information has been obtained about the latter.

The third kind of case is that involving H. C. Brill Company. The discriminations involved in this case arose from contracts with three

[92] *Ibid.,* pp. 1338-46.
[93] *Ibid.*

chain stores under which Brill, a maker of preparations for home-made ice cream, was to grant rebates of from 1 to 3 per cent if annual purchases attained specified totals of from $5,000 to more than $30,000. Under these contracts American Stores received nothing because its purchases were too small; Kroger received $3.53; and A. & P. received $410.12. The findings in the case imply that the arrangement was new, and do not indicate that it was renewed or that similar contracts were made with other customers. Thus there is reason to infer that the Commission's order had no effect on Brill's general method of doing business. No further light has been shed on the matter by interviews.

The remaining 12 cases are of the fourth kind.[94] In all of them the Commission issued orders designed to terminate persistent price concessions to large buyers in circumstances in which these concessions had been individually made by particular sellers. The cases differ in various respects. In some there was a simple division between the large buyer and the small; in others, a schedule of as many as eleven classes of size. Concessions to chain stores were conspicuous in the discriminations as to salt and biscuits, but not in the discriminations as to locks and dental supplies. The discriminating seller was a dominant concern in the sale of industrial chucks, yeast, and optical goods but not in the sale of bedding or hats. The tire case included private brand discounts and illegal advertising allowances; the two salt cases included both quantity and volume discounts, and one of them involved illegal advertising allowances as well; the Hubinger case included territorial discriminations; the hat case included illegal advertising allowances; while the other six cases had only volume discounts. The discount practice was important to Morton in the sale of salt, whereas it was of diminishing significance to Jacobs in the sale of industrial chucks, and Simmons was beginning to doubt its success in the sale of bedding. In spite of such differences, however, all of the cases were alike in the fact that discounts based on the amount bought expressed a single seller's response to the incentives and pressures that bore on his merchandising policies and created problems in his relations to his competitors and in the competitive relations among his customers.

[94] In the Hubinger case, the problems of territorial discrimination and a special concession to one customer overshadowed that of volume discounts. No information is available about the effect of the order on the latter type of discrimination.

After the Commission's orders, volume discounts were abandoned by respondents in the cases involving table salt, bedding,[95] optical goods, locks, and industrial chucks. Morton abandoned them for salt with considerable fear that it would be handicapped through the use of similar discounts by competitors not subject to the Commission's order, but International promptly did likewise without waiting for the order in its case, and within six months salt companies had generally eliminated similar discounts. Jacobs did not object strongly to their abandonment for industrial chucks, since they had been adopted, while the company was growing, for the sake of increasing volume and thereby permitting lower costs, and the need was less than in prior years. Indeed, Jacobs had already abandoned similar discounts in sales to distributors and had actually instituted a program of gradually reducing discounts to customers who were manufacturers. Doubting that volume discounts were accomplishing their purpose of selling more Simmons products to buying syndicates, Simmons accepted the Commission's order as a protection against the demand of its customers.

For dental supplies, volume discounts by the manufacturer on a more generous scale continued for a time in a form that the Commission later found to be a violation of its order; but the more enduring change was the substitution of volume discounts by dealers for volume discounts by Dentists' Supply. On July 1, 1943, a few weeks before the Commission's order, Dentists' Supply abandoned its previous volume discounts and instead recommended to dealers that they adopt a suggested volume-discount scale. The proposed discounts were easier to get than the former ones; indeed, whereas the maximum discount under the old plan could be obtained by few dental laboratories, the higher maximum under the

[95] Simmons now grants a quantity discount up to a maximum of 3 per cent, but no volume discount. However, shipments are made from the factory only if the order is 10,000 pounds or more and on an f.o.b. plant basis. Smaller orders are filled from Simmons' own warehouses. The dealer incurs higher charges on shipments purchased through these warehouses because of handling, storage expenses, and the freight cost from factory to warehouse. If the dealer is located at a considerable distance from Simmons' nearest warehouse, an additional freight charge to the dealer's store is absorbed. The price structure described above does not apply to sales of private brand merchandise that Simmons makes for its mail order customers to their individual specifications. In such cases all shipments are normally made in carload quantities, f.o.b. Simmons' various manufacturing locations.

new plan was attainable by many, as indicated in the accompanying table.[96]

Annual Volume	Percentage Discount	Net Payment
$ 111.11	10	$ 100
375.00	20	300
800.00	25	600
1,714.68	30	1,200

Dealers generally adopted this scale, and were still using it during interviews for this study. In practice, however, some of them apply it, not to annual purchases of teeth made by Dentists' Supply, but to aggregate purchases of teeth made by all manufacturers; and at least one of them concedes the largest discount to buyers who buy less than the specified minimum.

Until January 1, 1950, Dentists' Supply operated a retail outlet in New York City under the name Dentsply. This outlet made contracts with dentists and dental laboratories providing for volume discounts. Until 1948, discounts were applied to the amounts specified in each contract at the percentages of the suggested resale price list; thereafter dentists received similar volume-discount contracts, and dental laboratories received 20 per cent regardless of volume. Non-contract purchasers received no cumulative discounts but were given discounts in accord with the volume-discount scale on single purchases of the specified amounts. In 1951 the Commission began a compliance investigation of these activities; but in 1953, although it found that its order had been violated, it closed the proceeding without action because the violation had ceased: Denstply had been sold to S. S. White Dental Manufacturing Company more than a year before the investigation began.[97]

[96] See Docket 4915, *Dentists' Supply Co. of New York,* Trial Examiner's Report upon the Investigation of Alleged Violation of the Commission's Order to Cease and Desist, Oct. 1, 1951. Under the plan condemned by the Commission, purchasers were placed in five volume brackets depending on the value of teeth bought from dealers in a year. The boundaries of the classes were $1,000, $2,500, $5,000, and $10,000. For purchasers who bought more than $1,000, Dentists' Supply gave "bonus" teeth worth, at retail prices, 10, 15, 20, and 25 per cent, respectively, of the minimum volume in the successive brackets.

Under the new plan dealers were to give discounts up to 30 per cent on smaller annual purchases.

[97] The hearing examiner reported that in suggesting volume discounts to dealers, Dentists' Supply had violated a part of the order which forbade it to require or arrange that its dealers give the discounts it was forbidden to give. The Commission found that this part of the order had not been violated, but did not explain the reason for rejecting the conclusion of the hearing examiner.

For hats, rubber tires, packaged biscuits and yeast, modified schedules of volume discounts have been used by the respondents since the Commission's order. The relevant portion of the order in the Stetson case was directed narrowly at the practices followed by Stetson at the time of the case.[98] Stetson had 10 discount brackets, with discounts running as high as 8 per cent. After the case it reduced the number of brackets to 5 and the maximum discount to 5 per cent in the belief, based on cost studies that it had made, that the new discount structure could be cost-justified. The number of customers receiving discounts was tripled or quadrupled. Under the new plan, the orders of the units of a chain store can be pooled only if they are placed at one time by a central buying office that receives the bills and pays them.

In the tire case, volume discounts were apparently regarded as less important than cost-plus contracts on private brands[99] and commissions to oil companies.[100] However, they were covered by the Commission's findings and order. In June 1939 the compliance report of U. S. Rubber set forth a new volume-discount schedule for sales to distributors, requiring volumes larger than before to earn discounts smaller than before. There were 4 discount brackets, ranging from 1 to 2.5 per cent, on annual purchases ranging from minima of $15,000 to $50,000 and over. Similar discount schedules were adopted by other tire manufacturers. In later years, however, U. S. Rubber changed the applicable discounts, apparently following price changes made by others.

The decree as to National Biscuit Company, entered by consent in 1944, was directed at a discount structure under which few received discounts. Before the case, the customers of the company were divided into five classes according to their aggregate monthly purchases. Each class was subdivided according to the average purchase per store owned by the particular customer. Customers buying $150,000 or more per month received discounts varying from 3.5 to 4.5 per cent according to the average purchase per store. Those buying from $10,000 to $150,000 received discounts varying from 3 per cent to 4.5 per cent. Those buying from $5,000 to $10,000 received discounts varying from

---

[98] Stetson was forbidden to continue its existing discriminations, to grant varying discounts "in the manner and under the circumstances found in paragraph 5 of the aforesaid findings of facts," and to discriminate otherwise "in any manner or degree substantially similar" or "in any other manner resulting in price discriminations substantially equal in amount to the aforesaid discriminations." (41 FTC 254.) The Stetson case also included advertising allowances. See above p. 185.

[99] See below, pp. 463, 471-72.

[100] See above, p. 178.

2 to 3 per cent. Those buying from $750 to $5,000 received discounts varying from 1 to 2.5 per cent. In the first quarter of 1944, only 213 customers received volume discounts.

Under the new discount structure, discounts were much more widely available. There were four monthly volume classes, with boundaries at $250, $5,000, and $10,000. Each class had three subdivisions based on average store purchases, with boundaries at $25 and $50. Discounts to buyers with a monthly volume of less than $250 ranged from 0 to 1.5 per cent according to the average purchase per store, with some discount available to any store that bought as much as $25 per month. In the next volume bracket, the range was from 1 to 2.5 per cent; in the next, from 2 to 3.5 per cent; and in the highest, from 3 to 4.5 per cent. A pooling privilege was made available to members of voluntary chains and co-operatives, to be exercised at the option of each member. In 1944 more than 41,000 additional retailers received discounts aggregating an additional $250,000. By 1949 the aggregate additional discounts had risen to $660,000 and the number of additional qualifying retailers to 82,000.

In 1949 the Compliance Division of the Commission challenged continued use by Nabisco of discounts based on aggregate volume.[101] An argument over the meaning of the order against Nabisco was concluded by modification of the order in 1954 over protest of the company.[102] In the meantime, for various commercial reasons, Nabisco again changed its discount schedule on January 1, 1954. In the new schedule discounts were based primarily on monthly purchases per store rather than aggregate volume. There were five classes of store purchases, with boundaries at $20, $35, $50, and $75, with discounts for purchases of more than $20 at discount rates of 1 per cent, 1.5 per cent, 2 per cent, and 3 per cent. An additional discount of 1 per cent was granted for an aggregate monthly

[101] The Nabisco order was like the Stetson order in that it forbade discriminations substantially similar to those found in the case.

[102] One paragraph of the original order had forbidden Nabisco "from otherwise discriminating in price between purchasers of bakery packaged food products of like grade and quality, in any manner or degree substantially similar to the manner and degree of the discriminations referred to in paragraph 4 of the aforesaid findings as to the facts, or in any other manner resulting in price discriminations substantially equal in amount to the aforesaid discriminations, except as permitted by Section 2 of the Clayton Act as amended." (38 FTC 222). For this paragraph the new order substituted a prohibition "from otherwise discriminating in price between purchasers of bakery packaged food products of like grade and quality where said purchasers in fact compete in the sale and distribution of such products." 50 FTC 937.

volume exceeding $500.[103] The purchases of members of voluntary chains and co-operatives could be pooled, at the member's option, for purposes of computing this additional discount and paying it to the headquarters of the group. Under the new schedule 227,491 customers received discounts in the first quarter of 1954.[104]

During the present study, Nabisco's latest discount structure was being discussed with the Commission. In September 1956, Nabisco supplied, at the Commission's request, an additional compliance report. In this report, Nabisco defended the 1 per cent volume discount, which it said was the only feature of the discount structure that was under challenge. It argued that, since the corporate chains have the larger stores, elimination of the headquarters discount would give them an advantage, whereas independents can associate themselves in voluntary groups and obtain the headquarters discount as readily as corporate chains. It also argued that the amount of the headquarters discount would have been so small for the stores that did not receive it that its absence could not have injured competition.[105] In support of this contention, it submitted an analysis of the purchases of these stores that indicated that if they had received the headquarters discount in April 1955, 76 per cent of them would have received less than 24 cents per store; only 3 per cent of them would have received more than $1.30 per store; and only one half of 1 per cent would have received as much as $3.79 per store. On September 30, 1958, the Commission was still considering the matter.

The order against Standard Brands also resulted in a modified schedule of volume discounts. Two classes of product were involved in the case. On foil yeast, Standard had allowed a discount of 3 cents per dozen to customers buying 300 or more pieces per month. It reduced the discount to 1.5 cents per dozen and made it available both to independents and to the separate units of corporate, voluntary, and co-operative chains. In the new form, Standard believed that the allowance could be cost-justified.

For the other product, bakers yeast, there had been 5 volume-discount

[103] In addition, Nabisco now offered a 1 per cent advertising allowance and a 1 per cent promotional allowance, each available regardless of volume to all customers who undertook to perform specified advertising and promotional services.

[104] In 1950 Nabisco had 467,827 customers.

[105] Nabisco has also asserted that its present discount structure is amply cost-justified by a cost study made in 1949 but has not chosen to submit the evidence as to cost or to rest its case on this ground.

schedules applicable to different territories. Under the most important one, which had 11 volume classes, the buyer of less than 150 pounds per month paid 25 cents per pound, while the buyer of more than 50,000 pounds paid 14 cents. After the order, a new schedule reduced the number of volume classes to 9 and established the lower limit of the largest volume class at 2,500 pounds per month. Prices to the smallest buyers ranged, according to geographical location, from 21 to 24 cents per pound; prices to the largest buyers, from 12 to 15 cents. Whereas the maximum price spread in the previous schedule had been 11 cents a pound, the maximum in the new schedule was 9 cents.[106] However, the volumes pertinent to the new schedule could not be computed by pooling the purchases from different yeast makers nor by pooling the purchases from Standard Brands by different bakeries be-

[106] The prices were as follows:

STANDARD BRANDS' PRICES FOR BAKERS YEAST, EFFECTIVE IN MAY, 1940
(Cents per pound)

Pounds per Month	Schedule A	Schedule B	Schedule C	Schedule D
1– 99	21	22	23	24
100– 249	18	19	20	21
250– 449	16	17	18	19
450– 699	15	16	17	18
700– 999	14	15	16	17
1,000–1,399	$13\frac{1}{2}$	$14\frac{1}{2}$	$15\frac{1}{2}$	$16\frac{1}{4}$
1,400–1,899	13	14	15	16
1,900–2,499	$12\frac{1}{2}$	$13\frac{1}{2}$	$14\frac{1}{2}$	$15\frac{1}{2}$
2,500 and up	12	13	14	15

Source: Standard Brands Compliance Report.

These prices applied to all bakery plants in the following areas:
Schedule A: Buffalo, Chicago, Cincinnati, Cleveland, Kansas City, New England, New York, Philadelphia, St. Louis, and Washington Divisions; Norton, Virginia; Nashville, Chattanooga, Johnson City, and Knoxville, Tennessee; Bowling Green, Kentucky; Texarkana, Arkansas; all of Oklahoma—with the exception of Calumet, Sault Sainte Marie, Manistee, Petosky, and Traverse City, Michigan; Bismarck and Minot, North Dakota; Rapid City, South Dakota; and Greenville, Mississippi.
Schedule B: Birmingham, Dallas, California, and Seattle Divisions; Calumet, Sault Sainte Marie, Manistee, Petosky, and Traverse City, Michigan; Bismarck and Minot, North Dakota; Rapid City, South Dakota; Greenville, Mississippi—with the exception of Norton, Virginia; Nashville, Chattanooga, Johnson City, and Knoxville, Tennessee; Bowling Green, Kentucky; Key West, Florida; Roswell, New Mexico; Texarkana, Arkansas; El Paso, Texas; Boise, Idaho; Kalispel, Montana; Alaska; and the states of Oklahoma, Arizona, and New Mexico.
Schedule C: Rocky Mountain Division, States of Arizona (California Division) and New Mexico (California Division); Boise, Idaho; Kalispel, Montana; El Paso, Texas.
Schedule D: Key West, Florida; Alaska.

longing to a corporate or voluntary chain. The discounts were applicable to the amount bought from Standard Brands by each separate plant or warehouse. Off-scale prices were to be quoted only to meet competitors' prices.

After more than four years under the new schedule, Standard Brands modified its discounts in July 1944 and January 1945. The first modification consisted in extending the territorial limits of the schedules with the lower prices. The second was a general revision under which the number of volume brackets was reduced from 9 to 7 and the number of territorial schedules from 4 to 3. Although the two largest volume brackets covered the same volumes as before, the others were changed so that a given volume would place a customer higher in the schedule. The maximum price spread continued to be 9 cents, but the level of prices was reduced, the range for the smallest purchases being from 20 to 23 cents and for the largest from 11 to 14 cents.[107]

Apparently as a result of these changes, the Commission began a compliance investigation as to whether or not Standard Brands had violated the Commission's cease and desist order and as to whether or not it was selling bakers yeast at unreasonably low prices for the purpose of destroying competition. The second part of the inquiry was dropped in 1950. At the same time the Commission decided that Standard Brands had violated the order by selling at volume discounts that injured competition, by permitting buyers to pool their purchases, and by off-scale pricing. Thereupon it requested affirmance and enforcement of its order by the Court of Appeals.

The evidence in the Commission's hearing as to compliance consisted primarily of testimony by other yeast producers that Standard's price reduction had caused them distress by making it necessary for them to reduce prices and by reducing the sales of some of them. Standard, which

[107] Source: 46 FTC 1488.

Pounds per Month	Schedule A	Schedule B	Schedule C
1– 49	20	21	23
50– 99	18	19	21
100– 449	15	16	18
450– 999	13	14	16
1,000–1,899	12	13	15
1,900–2,499	11½	12½	14½
2,500 and up	11	12	14

Schedule A: The United States—except certain Rocky Mountain, Southeastern and Southwestern territories.

Schedule B: The remainder of the United States.

Schedule C: Alaska.

had originally explained the price reductions as measures to pass on economies achieved in making and distributing yeast, now explained them as defensive acts evoked by losses of business to competitors who were selling at lower prices.[108] From the price and volume data obtained by the Commission, it appears that before the revision of 1945, Standard Brands encountered lower prices in every volume bracket. In the most important zone[109] comparative prices as tabulated by the Commission were as indicated in the accompanying table.[110]

Comparative Prices of Bakers Yeast

(Cents per pound)

Pounds per Month	Standard Brands	Anheuser-Busch	National Grain Yeast	Red Star Yeast	Federal Yeast	A. M. Richter Sons
1– 50	21	20	18	20	20	18
50– 100	21	18	16	18	18	17
100– 150	18	18	16	18	16	16
150– 250	18	16	15	16	15	15
250– 450	16	15	14	15	14	14
450– 500	15	15	14	15	14	14
500– 700	15	14	13	14	13	13
700– 750	14	14	13	14	13	13
750–1,000	14	14	13	13.5	13	13
1,000–1,400	13.5	13.5	12.5	13	12.5	12.5
1,400–1,500	13	13	12.5	13	12.5	12.5
1,500–1,900	13	13	12	12.5	12	12
1,900–2,000	12.5	12.5	12	12.5	12	12
2,000–2,500	12.5	12.5	12	12	12	12
2,500–3,000	12	12	11.5	12	11.5	11.5
3,000–3,500	12	12	11.5	11.5	11.5	11.5
3,500–4,000	12	12	11.5	11.5	11.5	11
4,000 and up	12	12	11	11	11	11

[108] The Commission's tabulations of sales showed, however, that Standard's per cent of industry sales was remarkably steady—about 57 per cent—from 1941 to 1945, and that its poundage increased nearly 13 per cent during the period. Of its rivals in the most important zone, National Grain Yeast, Federal Yeast, Atlantic Yeast, Calumet Yeast, and A. M. Richter had declined in percentage of industry sales, and the last four also in poundage.

[109] A separate tabulation for the West Coast showed that Peerless Yeast and Consumers Yeast, Standard's two Western competitors, quoted the same prices as Standard (though in two or three instances Consumers Yeast had reduced prices one cent to large buyers).

[110] 46 FTC 1491. The tabulation did not include prices for Capital Yeast, which sold in Massachusetts, Connecticut, and New Hampshire; Atlantic Yeast, which

No competitor quoted a price higher than Standard. Standard's largest competitor quoted lower prices on most volumes below 700 pounds per month, equal prices on higher volumes. Because of differences in the locations of the boundaries of volume brackets, Red Star's prices equaled Standard's on certain transitional volumes, but were generally lower. The other three competitors were consistently lower. For volumes below 700 pounds per month the maximum differential was commonly more than a cent a pound, with extremes of 3 cents for volumes between 150 and 250 pounds and 5 cents for volumes between 50 and 100 pounds. For volumes above 700 pounds, the differential was characteristically one cent or one-half cent.

In the most important zone,[111] the changes in January 1945 set Standard's prices for some volumes below those of the lowest competitors included in the Commission's tabulation and for other volumes at the level of the lowest of these competitors.[112] After competitors had altered their prices in the light of Standard's new schedule, most of the differentials below Standard's prices in the most important zone had been eliminated.[113] Except where the boundaries of volume-discount classes

---

sold in the New York metropolitan area; and Calumet Yeast & Grain Products, which sold from Chicago to South Bend. Capital Yeast and Atlantic Yeast each sold slightly more than 1 per cent of the industry's volume in 1945 and Calumet only one tenth of 1 per cent. Richter, however, was even smaller than Calumet. Prices for Atlantic and Calumet are not available, but those for Capital are given in the public record (Docket 2986-1-4, p. 615). They were as follows:

Pounds	Cents
1 - 49	15
50- 249	14
250- 624	13
625-1,249	12
1,250-1,874	11.5
1,875-2,499	10.5
2,500 and up	10

Why they were not included in the Commission's tabulation was not stated. It is notable that they were much lower than those the Commission used.

[111] On the West Coast the changes consistently set new low levels. Standard's new West Coast prices were below those of West Coast competitors by 3 cents for volumes of 50-250 pounds, 2 cents for volumes of 450-700 pounds, 1½ cents for volumes of 1,000 to 1,400 pounds and 1 cent for all other volumes.

[112] Standard's prices were lower by ½ cent for volumes from 1,000 to 1,500 and from 1,900 to 4,000 pounds per month; by 1 cent for volumes of from 100 to 150 pounds and from 450 to 500 pounds. They equaled the prices of the lowest competitor for volumes from 150 to 250 pounds, from 500 to 1,000 pounds, from 1,500 to 1,900 pounds, and over 4,000 pounds. For volumes below 100 pounds and from 250 to 450 pounds there were still lower prices than Standard's.

[113] On the West Coast, however, Consumers Yeast and Peerless had set prices 1 cent per pound below Standard for all volumes.

were not quite identical, no competitor quoted a higher price than Standard for any volume. In the most important zone, lower prices were quoted only by two small competitors, Richter and Capital, by National Grain Yeast on volumes below 450 pounds per month, and by Federal Yeast on volumes above 20,000 pounds per month. The 1945 prices are shown in the accompanying table.[114]

Prices of Bakers Yeast, 1945
(Cents per pound)

Pounds per Month	Standard Brands	An-heuser-Busch	National Grain Yeast	Red Star Yeast	Federal Yeast	A. M. Richter Sons	Capital Yeast
1– 50	20	20	18	20	18	18	15
50– 100	18	18	16	18	16	17	14
100– 250	15	15	15	15	15	15	14
250– 450	15	15	14	15	14	14	13
450– 500	13	13	13	13	13	14	13
500– 625	13	13	13	13	13	13	13
625– 1,000	13	13	13	13	13	13	12
1,000– 1,250	12	12	12	12	12	12	12
1,250– 1,500	12	12	12	12	12	12	11.5
1,500– 1,875	12	12	12	12	12	11.5	11.5
1,875– 1,900	12	12	12	12	12	11.5	10.5
1,900– 2,500	11.5	11.5	11.5	11.5	11.5	11.5	10.5
2,500–20,000	11	11	11	11	11	11	10
20,000 lbs. up	11	11	11	11	10	11	10

In March 1947, during the compliance hearings, Standard announced a new price schedule and requested that in the light of it the investigation be dropped without prejudice. In this schedule the seven-volume brackets were reduced to six by combining the two smallest volume classes.[115]

[114] Docket 2986-1-4, p. 616. Volume classes were established by some companies to end in 9 (e.g. 1-49) and by others to end in zero (e.g. 1-50). These differences have been ignored.

[115] The schedule was as follows:

Pounds per Month	Cents per Pound
1– 99	19
100– 449	15
450– 999	14
1,000–1,899	13
1,900–2,499	12.5
2,500 and up	12

Source: Trial Examiner's Report on Investigation of Compliance with Cease and Desist Order (Apr. 14, 1948), p. 27.

Prices for the four largest classes were one cent higher than before. The price for the next class was unchanged, and the price for the new lowest class was, respectively, a cent higher and a cent lower than the prices for the two classes that had been merged in this class. As a result of the change, the maximum spread in prices was reduced from 9 cents to 7 cents.[116] The Commission did not accede to Standard's request that, because of the revision, the investigation be dropped.

The compliance investigation also contained evidence as to pooling and off-scale selling. The former consisted in the fact that for seven months in 1945, Standard had granted a volume discount on the combined purchases of two Boston bakeries. As to the latter, the Commission found that in the New York metropolitan area scale prices were consistently observed in sales to only 15 out of more that 242 accounts during 1945 and the first two months of 1946. Most, but not all, of the off-scale sales were made by allowing a discount on a buyer's total purchases rather than his purchases from Standard.[117] Standard explained that:

> The sales representative first attempted to get all the business of the customer at respondent's scale price. If the customer was unwilling to give the respondent all of the business, then the sales representative tried for a part of the business at respondent's scale price for that part. If the customer refused . . . the sales representative then quoted an off-scale price if he was satisfied that that price was not lower than the price being charged by a competitor to that customer, and not lower than respondent's scale price for the total business of the customer.[118]

Standard's instructions to its sales representatives provided that, except with the approval of the home office, off-scale prices could not be quoted where no competitor was actually selling. After August 31, 1945, no off-scale price could be quoted to a customer who used only Standard yeast because the home office was unable to determine the authenticity of claims as to competitors' price offers.

On October 4, 1946, apparently as a result of the compliance investigation, instructions regarding off-scale selling were tightened by a requirement that customers who bought less than the amount justifying the

[116] The new schedule applied to the most important area, subject to differentials of 1 cent and 3 cents for other areas.
[117] 46 FTC 1494.
[118] Docket 2986. Brief for Respondent (June 21, 1948), p. 29.

price must be promptly advised that the appropriate higher price would be charged unless the amount of the purchase was promptly increased to the proper figure. The new instructions also provided that the district manager must approve all off-scale prices. The Commission took the position that, since Standard's prices were traditionally higher than those of its competitors, and the price reductions by competitors were efforts to restore the price differentials that prevailed before Standard's price reduction, Standard's action in meeting these price cuts was not in good faith.[119]

In 1951 the Second Circuit affirmed the order against Standard Brands, found that the parts of it concerned with pooling and off-scale selling had been violated, and issued its own order enforcing these parts.[120] It rejected the claim of the Commission that the order in regard to volume discounts had been violated; for the order had been issued on the ground that these discounts injured competition in the secondary line, and the

---

[119] Some of Standard's price reductions had set prices lower than those of competitors, and these did more than meet "the equally low price" of a competitor. But the Commission did not emphasize this. It denied the good faith of Standard because of the level of the price rather than the nature of the discrimination; in effect, it used an attack on discrimination to cloak a finding that Standard's prices were unduly low. It ignored the fact that the price changes of 1945 reduced prices to the smaller buyers more than to the larger and thus reduced the discrimination. It said, "For more than 9 years prior to January 2, 1945, respondent consistently sold bakers' yeast at prices higher than those of most of its competitors and yet retained more than 57 per cent of the total volume of said yeast sold throughout the United States. A competitive situation or condition was thus established under which most competitors of respondent could normally expect to sell and did sell bakers' yeast at prices slightly below those of respondent. Also, buyers normally expected to purchase, and did purchase, said product from respondent at prices slightly in excess of those paid most of its competitors. Under these conditions it was unnecessary for respondent to meet or match exactly a lower price of a competitor in order to retain business or to get new business. By adoption of its price scales of January 2, 1945, respondent overturned the conditions of 9 years' standing and initiated discriminatory prices in many instances lower than the prices of its competitors and thereby forced them to lower their prices to an extent which threatened their ability to survive. By thereafter selling below the prices thus established, in some instances respondent in fact put into effect still larger price differentials resulting in still broader discriminations than those found to exist under said price scale. In view of the foregoing, the Commission is of the opinion that the respondent did not in good faith meet the equally low prices of competitors after January 1945 but abandoned its former policy of making higher prices than its competitors for one of underselling them on a discriminatory basis." 46 FTC 1495.

[120] *FTC v. Standard Brands, Inc.,* 189 F. 2d 510.

damage to competition, which the Commission saw in the revised discounts, was in the primary line to Standard's competitors, rather than in the secondary line to its customers.[121] The Commission has not subsequently instituted a new proceeding addressed to the problem in the primary line; and thus the case has created no obstacle to the maintenance by Standard Brands of a price policy that will not permit price differentials by its competitors.

In a new certificate of compliance filed after the order of the Court, Standard Brands announced that it would avoid pooling and would eliminate all off-scale selling so that it would obtain "its scale price in every case regardless of competitive status or price." To police this policy, Standard now employs a full-time supervisor and maintains extra accounting records.

The consensus in the interviews about bakers yeast is that volume discounts have become much less substantial, and that the maximum discount on 2,500 pounds per month can be obtained by most plants. Bakers whose purchases range from 4,000 pounds a month to more than 500,000 say that they pay 15.5 or 16 cents per pound. One buyer, taking between 50,000 and 75,000 pounds per month, says that it pays a price of from 12 to 13 cents per pound. The smaller yeast manufacturers, some of which established themselves by selling below the price of Standard Brands, now generally charge about the same prices as Standard, though one of them sells for less. One of them says that to reduce prices to attract trade is useless, since Standard Brands will promptly meet the reduction locally.

[121] The relevant part of the Commission's order forbade Standard from discriminating in price by selling bakers yeast at different prices based on the total quantity or volume purchased over a period of time where the effect might be the damage to competition contemplated in the law. The language of the order as to damage was approximately identical with that of Sec. 2(a) of the act. The Court found that the evidence "sustains the Commission's findings of substantial lessening of competition between Standard Brands and some of its competitors," but held that this did not prove violation of the order. In the initial proceedings, the Commission had made no findings concerning injury to Standard's competitors. Nor had the complaint charged such injury. "The order, therefore, must be read in the light of the complaint and the findings accompanying the order. Consequently, the findings made in connection with the violation hearings of reduction of competition with Standard Brands' competitors do not show a violation of clause (2) of the order. . . . This seeming formalism is desirable in fairness to respondent, since . . . [if a new case should be based upon this kind of injury] it may be able to offer evidence proving that its actions were not unlawful vis-à-vis its own competitors." 189 F. 2d 510, 513.

Effects on Competitors

Competitors of the respondents in the various volume-discount cases met the subsequent changes in discounts in widely different ways. In the salt industry, producers generally followed Morton's lead in eliminating volume discounts. In the tire industry, competitors followed the modified discount schedule of U. S. Rubber, at least temporarily. At the time of the hat case, Stetson was the only hat maker using a volume-discount schedule, so that change in that schedule did not create a disparity in competitive practice. In optical supplies there were parallel cases and parallel orders for the two large producers—American Optical Company and Bausch & Lomb. In yeast, Standard Brands and the other yeast producers jockeyed for position with substantial similarity, though not identity, of volume classes and discount percentages.

In other industries, however, concerns not subject to the orders continued to offer discounts that were forbidden to the respondents in the cases. The order against Master Lock resulted in a reduction of discounts and the elimination of freight allowances.[122] Since the competitors of Master Lock allow freight, many distributors have a smaller margin on the products of Master Lock than on competing products.[123] In the bedding industry certain manufacturers still use volume discounts running as high as 10 per cent. For biscuits, some makers have discounts larger than Nabisco's.

Effects on Prices

Information on the effect of the volume- and quantity-discount cases on the level of prices and on the prosperity of those affected is fragmentary. What there is, however, indicates that the effects in different cases have been diverse and that there has been no clear trend in the results.

[122] This company was required to cease and desist "from continuing to practice the discrimination in price adjudged illegal in the aforesaid findings and conclusions or from directly or indirectly in any other manner discriminating in price by paying or granting freight allowances or discounts, the effect whereof may be. . . ." 27 FTC 993.

[123] One distributor says that loss of discounts from Master Lock and from many other suppliers has forced him to reduce his sales territory from 31 states to 16 or 17 and to reduce his sales force from 226 to 141.

In some instances, the revisions required by the order of the Commission were made by increasing the prices to those who had previously paid least. The order in regard to Master Lock reduced the distributive margins of concerns that had formerly bought advantageously. Elimination of volume discounts by Simmons protected it from demands of buyers and apparently increased its net realization without loss of customers. In the tire industry, concessions to large distributors were reduced.[124] In the salt industry, concessions to the larger buyers of table salt ended, and these buyers then paid more. Particular customers who have been interviewed subsequently obtained private label salt to sell at low prices, but sold relatively little of it to replace Morton because their customers demanded the Morton brand. One buyer, who had bought Morton salt through a buying group in order to obtain the volume discount, bought direct from Morton when no such discount was available.

In other cases, however, the change that followed the order made low prices more widely available. The volume discounts quoted by distributors of dental supplies were more generous than those previously quoted by the manufacturer. The successive revisions of the discount structure of National Biscuit made some discount available to more than 227,000 distributors, whereas before the case only 213 had received discounts. In the first revised discount structure, the discounts remained as high as before but were received by more customers. In the second, the amount of the maximum discount was reduced, but the effect of this action was more than offset for most customers by the greater ease with which a substantial discount could be obtained. In the case of yeast, the successive revisions of the discount structure by Standard Brands were accompanied by price reductions so large that the Commission and the Second Circuit thought that they injured competition between Standard and its rivals. In the case of industrial chucks, the change in the price structure that was brought about by the order raised prices to approximately 16 per cent of the customers and reduced them to approximately 84 per cent. Jacobs' new price structure resulted in approximately the same revenue that had been realized before the change.

The immediate impact of the orders is the only part of their effect on prices that can be ascertained, but it may be the least significant part. If there were changes in the intensity of competition, the availability of

---

[124] Though this was true of volume discounts, cost-plus contracts for resale under private brands continued.

supplies, the chances to enter the field or stay in it, and similar matters, the immediate effect of readjustments in the price structure may have been offset or more than offset by changes in the price level reflecting these influences. Even under the most favorable circumstances, the persons directly concerned with a market are unlikely to know the origin of the forces playing on them. During the period covered by this study, the opportunity to disentangle the effects of the Commission's orders about volume and quantity discounts was particularly small. A great depression came to an end and was succeeded by a great war, and this was then followed by an armed peace interrupted by an undeclared war in Korea. Changes in the purchasing power of the economy and in the relative demand for various kind of goods over-shadowed the alterations that were required by legal process.

9 / *Quantity Limits*

ALTHOUGH THE ROBINSON-PATMAN Act is based on the general principle that price discriminations otherwise unlawful are permitted where the differences in price merely reflect differences in cost, an exception to the application of this principle to quantity and volume discounts appears in the statute. The provision concerning costs contains a proviso that, after investigation and hearing, the Federal Trade Commission may "fix and establish quantity limits, and revise the same as it finds necessary, as to particular commodities or classes of commodities where it finds that available purchasers in greater quantities are so few as to render differentials on account thereof unjustly discriminatory or promotive of monopoly in any line of commerce; and the foregoing shall then not be construed to permit differentials based on differences in quantities greater than those so fixed and established."[1] Thus the Commission is empowered to issue an order limiting the cost defense where the fewness of those who can invoke it results in unjust discrimination or tendency toward monopoly. The fixation of a quantity limit would make no change in the law applicable to price differences between quantities less than that specified in the quantity-limit rule. However, it would invalidate the cost defense in so far as the differences in cost arose from a quantity greater than that specified in the rule.

An effort to promulgate a quantity-limit rule has been made in only one instance, that of rubber tires sold in the replacement market. The project apparently originated in a conference in May 1947, between members of the Small Business Committee of the House of Representatives and officials of the Federal Trade Commission and the Department of Justice. At this conference, replying to questions from members of the committee, the officials of the antitrust agencies agreed that discriminations in the tire industry appeared to be damaging to competition. However, they expressed considerable doubt that the discriminations

[1] 49 Stat. 1526.

could be stopped under existing law; and they did not desire to propose new legislation. After a suggestion by an official of the Commission that the quantity-limit proviso might be useful, the members of the committee who were present requested that the possibilities of a quantity-limit order be explored and were assured that the Commission would do so.[2]

Thereafter the Commission undertook a broad investigation of the rubber tire industry to lay a basis for the proposed rule making. Questionnaires to tire manufacturers were issued in July 1947, January 1948, and February 1948. In general, manufacturers were asked to provide, for the year 1947, figures as to their sales of tires and tubes and the prices charged, and to state separately for each purchaser who bought more than $100,000 per year, the amount that he bought and the prices that he paid. Twenty-one manufacturers supplied such information. An unspecified number of small buyers of replacement tires and tubes were asked to make reports naming their principal competitors and supplying information on the nature of the competition. The information obtained in the various reports was treated as confidential by the Commission. Indeed, it has not even been used in unidentified form as the basis for a report on conditions in the distribution of tires. It was used, however, as a basis for factual findings in the consideration of a quantity-limit rule.

On September 28, 1949, the Commission promulgated a proposed quantity limit for replacement rubber tires and gave interested parties a specified time within which to file "data, views, and argument" concerning it. Under this rule, the maximum limit to which a cost defense might be applied was a carload of 20,000 pounds. The information underlying the rule was set forth in less than 1½ pages of the Federal Register.[3] It consisted of, first, a table showing the volume of tires bought in 1947 from manufacturers of different sizes, and the relative prices paid, by groups of replacement buyers classified according to the amount of their total purchases; second, a brief analysis of the competition encountered by distributors of replacement tires, supporting the conclusion that certain large distributors, national and local, were the principal competitors of many smaller distributors; third, selected quotations from the reports by small distributors, indicating that large competitors sold tires below the prices and even below the costs of the small concerns; fourth, computations of imputed operating expenses and profits for the small enterprises

[2] Information from a participant in the conference.
[3] Pp. 6044-46.

and their larger competitors; and fifth, brief comments on the relation of the data to the proposed carload limit.

The computations of costs and profits were made by applying to "the generally prevailing list or consumer price" figures on gross margin, operating expenses, and net profit that were "in line with average percentage figures for those items according to what appears to be a reliable source." The comments on carload quantities began by conceding that the large manufacturers had said they could not furnish the needed information, and then concluded, "on the basis of information from other sources," that in 1947, among purchasers with an annual volume of less than $35,000 (constituting about ⅔ of all purchasers), "there were practically none available as purchasers of carloads and no substantial number available as purchasers of truckloads."

The table, which provided the only specific information from a well-authenticated source, is set forth in full on page 274.

On the basis of this summary statement of the grounds for a quantity-limit rule, interested persons were given an opportunity to file information, argument, and alternative proposals. In January and early February 1950, legal and economic statements and supporting studies were filed by the leading tire manufacturers, the National Association of Independent Tire Dealers, Montgomery Ward, and various others.[4]

[4] See Federal Trade Commission, File No. 203-1, "In the Matter of an Investigation of the Rubber Tire Industry," Data, Views and Argument Submitted on Behalf of United States Rubber Company, Jan. 19, 1950 (together with four supplementary studies entitled Gross Margins and Net Profits of Tire Dealers, 1923-1948, by Warren W. Leigh, December 1949; Concentration and Price Trends in the Rubber Tire Industry 1930-1947, by Ralph C. Epstein, December 1949; Automotive Tire Sales by Distribution Channels, by Warren W. Leigh, Dec. 30, 1948, Bureau of Business Research, University of Akron; and "Unjustly Discriminatory or Promotive of Monopoly" Defined and Applied to Tire Distribution, by Wroe Alderson and Robert E. Sessions, Jan. 2, 1950); Data, Views and Argument Submitted by the B. F. Goodrich Company in Opposition to the Establishment by the Federal Trade Commission of a Quantity Limit; Supplemental Data, Views and Argument Submitted by the B. F. Goodrich Company; Data, Views and Argument of the Goodyear Tire and Rubber Company, Inc., Jan. 19, 1950; Brief of the Firestone Tire and Rubber Company in Opposition to Proposed Quantity Limit for Replacement Rubber Tires; Economic Brief of the Firestone Tire and Rubber Company in Opposition to Proposed Quantity Limit for Replacement Rubber Tires, Jan. 19, 1950; Presentation by the National Association of Independent Tire Dealers, Inc. See also subsequent Rebuttal Data, Views and Argument of the Goodyear Tire and Rubber Company, Feb. 6, 1950; Rebuttal Data, Views and Argument Submitted by the B. F. Goodrich Company in Opposition to the Establishment by the

Replacement Motor Vehicle Tires and Tubes, 1947[a]

Volume Brackets	Purchasers		Purchases (Tires and Tubes)						Prices (Tires Only, as of Dec. 31, 1947)			
	Number	Per Cent of Total	Amount		Distribution by Size of Manufacturer (Per Cent Purchased From)				Price Indices		Price Differentials (Per Cent under Highest Price)	
			Dollar Volume (000 Omitted)	Per Cent of Total	7 Largest Manufacturers	7 Next Largest Manufacturers	7 Smallest Manufacturers		Passenger[b]	Truck[c]	Passenger	Truck
Under $100,000 {Smallest}	47,247	98.027	$435,658	52.4	84.2	12.0	3.8		100.0	100.0	—	—
Under $100,000 {Largest}									84.0	79.5	16.0	20.5
$100,000 to $600,000	888	1.842	155,492	18.7	85.1	12.7	2.2		81.5	77.0	18.5	23.0
$600,000 to $5,000,000	52	.108	70,822	8.5	86.4	13.2	.4		74.0	68.0	26.0	32.0
$5,000,000 to $25,000,000	9	.019	83,785	10.1	88.0	10.0	2.0		71.5	60.0	28.5	40.0
$25,000,000 to $50,000,000	2	.004	86,208	10.3	97.3	2.7	0		69.5	61.5	30.5	38.5
Total	48,198	100.000	831,965	100.0	86.3	11.1	2.6		—	—	—	—

[a] Source: 21 manufacturers' reports to FTC, as published in *Federal Register*, 1949, p. 6045. Purchasers, purchases, and prices by volume brackets; distribution of bracket purchases by size of manufacturer.

[b] Passenger tires: 6.00×16, 4 ply black.

[c] Truck tires: 7.50×20, 10 ply rayon.

In four days of oral argument in February, statements were made on behalf of seven tire manufactures, Montgomery Ward, The National Federation of Independent Business, and the National Association of Independent Tire Dealers. Since the hearings did not include sworn testimony, cross-examination or other efforts to examine contested questions of fact, the record of the case abounds in conflicting allegations that cannot be resolved from the record itself.[5]

Federal Trade Commission of a Quantity Limit; Rebuttal by United States Rubber Company of Data, Views and Argument Submitted by Other Interested Persons, Feb. 6, 1950; Rebuttal by the National Association of Independent Tire Dealers, Inc.

[5] In a dissent from the quantity-limit rule promulgated by the Commission, Commissioner Mason subsequently described the procedure as follows:

"Comprehensive and carefully analyzed summaries of the data submitted to the Commission in response to its mail inquiries were never made a part of the public record. Instead, the factual information was disclosed to interested parties only in the form of a notice of hearing and an attached factual appendix, which together filled less than two pages of the Federal Register. The allegations of fact contained in the appendix consisted partly of ultimate conclusions as to the facts and partly of summary statements, primarily statistical in nature, unaccompanied by explanations of the types of data relied upon and the statistical methods used in developing those summaries. Except in this document the information upon which the majority has relied was not exposed to public criticism or supplementation.

"The result of this cursory method of disclosing the factual basis for the proposed rule was that interested parties who opposed the rule did not have an adequate opportunity to examine and criticize the Commission's allegations of fact and the Commission was thereby deprived of an adequate testing of these allegations. The statements submitted by interested parties prior to the public hearing and the arguments made at the public hearing undertook to challenge the Commission's statistical methods and conclusions as to such matters as the total number of customers and the total amount of replacement tire sales; the classes and class boundaries appropriate to a classification of customers according to the volume of their purchases; the average prices paid by purchasers in each volume class; the availability of carload purchasers; the profits and margins of various classes of distributors; and other similar matters. In the absence of knowledge about the statistical methods used by the Commission and about the character of the basic data, the critics were forced to rely upon their guesses as to what the Commission probably did and were often incorrect in these guesses. What the Commission had actually done was not exposed in a way which provided the benefit of informed criticism.

"One example will serve to illustrate this characteristic of the public record. The Commission's statement in the Federal Register indicated that the 21 tire manufacturers from whom it had obtained data had a total of 48,198 customers for replacement tires. The four largest manufacturers employed an agent to compile the figures of their own sales into aggregates, and found that after eliminating duplications, these four companies alone had more than 50,000 customers. Thereupon they challenged the validity of the Commission's report of slightly more than 48,000 customers for 21 manufacturers. The fact is that the reports received by

The hearing was followed by a long period of internal discussion within the Commission. Some light has been thrown on the process by comment in dissent to the quantity-limit rule. Commissioner Mason said:

. . . The Commission limited its further consideration of conflicting factual statements to staff memoranda that did not resolve them. For example, the Commission's brief statement in the Federal Register contained a table indicating the percentage of total purchases of tires and tubes by buyers in each volume bracket, which was bought, respectively, from the seven largest manufacturers, the seven manufacturers intermediate in size, and the seven smallest manufacturers. Upon the basis of those figures, it was argued on behalf of the rule that there was an affinity between the largest distributors and the largest manufacturers. This point was challenged on behalf of the four largest manufacturers on the basis of a computation of their own aggregate sales to customers in the various volume brackets, from which they concluded that they sold a smaller percentage of the requirements

the Commission from these 21 manufacturers aggregated about 90,000 purchasers of replacement tires, but that the data available to the Commission did not include the names of purchasers with annual dollar volumes of less than $100,000, and that the Commission reduced the figure of 90,000 to slightly more than 48,000 on the basis of an estimate of the number of duplications among the smaller purchasers, this estimate being derived from certain dealer reports to the Commission as to the number of manufacturers from whom they bought and from certain estimates current in the tire industry as to the percentage of dealers who buy from more than one manufacturer. Since the participants in the public hearing were not informed that the figure 48,198 was an estimate, much less how the estimate had been made, their comments as to whether or not the estimate was reasonable and as to the effect of any error which it might contain upon the proposed rule were not and could not be of a kind that assisted the Commission in reaching a decision.

"Interested parties who objected to the Commission's proposed rule made formal demand that the Commission give them an opportunity to introduce evidence which they believed would demonstrate the undesirability of the rule. While the Commission permitted them to file 'data, views, and argument,' it did not grant the request that the allegations of fact contained in the documents filed be subjected to the processes of verification and cross-examination which convert such allegations into credible evidence, nor did it establish any alternative procedure sufficient to test the reliability of these allegations. Interested parties argued that, in the absence of the right to introduce evidence and prove its validity, the Commission must treat as facts all statements of fact as to which offers of proof were made. Interpreting the proceeding as legislative, the Commission has not done this; but the majority, without establishing alternative procedures for testing the factual allegations for which such offers of proof were made, has rejected or ignored allegations which, if correct, would demonstrate that there is no need for any quantity-limit rule and that the rule now promulgated is objectionable." FTC, File No. 203-1, Minority Findings of Commissioner Mason, pp. 12-14.

of the larger customers than of the smaller customers, and that, therefore, the opposite statistical result which appeared in the Commission's
figures for the seven largest manufacturers must be due to the smallest
three of that seven. Neither the computation by these manufacturers
nor their conclusion from it was challenged by the Commission's
spokesmen at the public hearing. The computation by the four manufacturers was subsequently challenged, however, in a staff memorandum to the Commission which contained further computations of
the Commission's data purporting to show that the results for the
largest four manufacturers were the same as those that the Commission had shown for the largest seven and were diametrically opposite
to those shown by the manufacturers' computations. Thus, the Commission had before it a direct contradiction between two different
computations of data supplied by the same four manufacturers, without any explanation of the origin or character of the contradiction.
This fact was brought to the Commission's attention in another staff
memorandum. However, the Commission did nothing toward further
clarification of the matter, and the majority, in its published statement,
has accepted the original computation presented on behalf of the
Commission in the Federal Register. It has thus disregarded the alternative computation presented by the four manufacturers without taking steps to determine which of the two sets of figures is correct.

This illustration is representative of various respects in which the
staff memoranda, by which the Commission carried the debate upon
the facts beyond the results of the public hearing, consisted merely in
reiteration of positions taken by the Commission's staff, sometimes
with and sometimes without additional supporting data. The majority
of the Commission has made no effort to test the truth of allegations
of fact submitted by interested parties except by comparing them with
allegations of fact submitted by the Commission's staff; and in these
comparisons the majority has apparently assumed that wherever there
is a conflict of such allegations, the Commission's staff is necessarily
correct. Thus the procedure has been inadequate to enable the Commission to determine wisely where the truth lies.

Had the majority relied upon the public record alone, they could
not have made their findings and promulgated their rule; for insofar as
that record is concerned, the weight of evidence supports those who
object to the rule and appears to discredit the meager factual statements which the Commission included in the Federal Register as its
basis for action. By accepting statements of fact that are not in the
public record, the majority manages to make a prima facie case for
disregarding many of the apparently significant criticisms that appear
in the public record, and for re-establishing the apparent validity of
some of the conclusions of fact upon which they rely. But whether
these reaffirmations of the case for the rule would, in their turn, stand

the test of criticism, nobody knows. For this reason, the procedure has been an arbitrary acceptance of the factual allegations that tend to prove the case for the rule and an arbitrary rejection of the factual allegations that tend to disprove it.[6]

On December 31, 1951, the Commission promulgated a rule that on and after April 7, 1952, "the quantity limit as to replacement tires and tubes made of natural or synthetic rubber for use on motor vehicles as a class of commodity is 20,000 pounds ordered at one time for delivery at one time." In support of the rule, the Commission found that available purchasers "in the greater quantities of annual dollar volumes of $600,000 or more," were so few as to render differentials on account thereof unjustly discriminatory and promotive of monopoly in the lines of commerce in which both the sellers and the buyers were respectively engaged. It also found that the carload quantity of 20,000 pounds ordered at one time for delivery at one time was "the reasonable maximum as to which there will be a sufficient number of available purchasers so as not to render such a maximum differential unjustly discriminatory against purchasers in smaller quantities and promotive of monopoly," and that the fixation of such a quantity limit was reasonably necessary.[7] In support of the first finding, the Commission said that the differentials on the greater quantities bought by the large purchasers were in fact on account of quantity even though they did not take the form of quantity discounts, since unusually large volumes were involved and were material to the arrangements. It held that purchases in the volume bracket from $100,000 to $600,000 might well be considered to be one of the "greater quantities" but that there could be no doubt that the quantities in the three larger volume brackets were properly so classified. It held that the injustice of the discriminations for the 63 buyers in the three largest brackets was shown by the fact that these buyers could resell at prices approximating the purchase cost of the smallest buyers and that the monopolistic tendency of the larger price differentials was shown by the fact that the traditional dealer-distributor group, which had sold about 90 per cent of all replacement tires in 1926, made only 48 per cent of such sales in 1941, recovered to 52 per cent during the war, but had slipped to slightly less than 52 per cent in 1947. Buyers in

[6] *Ibid.*, pp. 14-15.
[7] FTC, File No. 203-1, Findings, Order, and Statement of Basis and Purpose, pp. 1-2.

these largest brackets were said to be on the average 163, 1,121, and 5,150 times larger than the average buyer in the smallest bracket. A monopolistic tendency on the selling side of the market was found in that the concentration of sales was greater in sales to the larger buyers than in sales to the smaller ones, and in that there had been a substantial decline in the number of tire manufacturers between 1926 and 1947, which probably continued after 1947.

The finding that the carload quantity limit was the appropriate remedy rested in part on the analogous use of a carload limit by the Interstate Commerce Commission. The Commission held that discounts based on volume over a period of time are arbitrary and probably would accelerate the trend toward monopoly, and that the available purchasers of multiple carloads were objectionably few. It supported the latter finding by an analysis of the carload purchases of a representative group of dealers with annual dollar volumes ranging up to about $350,000 in 1947. This analysis showed that in the volume bracket ranging from $35,000 to $100,000, the percentage of total purchases that was made in carload quantities increased from about 25 by purchasers who bought the smaller amount to about 40 for purchasers who bought the larger amount, and that in the higher bracket ranging from $100,000 to $350,000, the percentage of carload purchases ranged from about 50 for the smaller purchasers to about 75 for the larger ones. Carload purchases were made by about 25 per cent of the dealers whose volumes exceeded $100,000 and by only about 5 per cent of the dealers whose volumes were less than that amount. These relationships were held to justify a broad inference "that all of the few purchasers with annual volumes of $600,000 and over should be able to buy all or substantially all of their requirements in carload lots of 20,000 pounds, and that they alone could buy in multiple carload quantities in any substantial degree," and that "the overwhelming majority of additional carload purchases will be made by some but substantially less than all of the purchasers with annual volumes between $100,000 and $600,000." From these inferences, the Commission argued:

It being necessary to have as available purchasers of the quantity fixed by the limit some of those with annual volumes in the $100,000 to $600,000 bracket so as to eliminate the objectionable fewness, the quantity established by the rule determines how many there should be, not precisely by naming an annual volume somewhere between

$100,000 and $600,000, that would be arbitrary in its inclusion and exclusion, but flexibly by establishing the quantity ordered at one time, for delivery at one time which is not beyond reach of purchasers generally in that volume bracket and as to which there are obvious savings in handling and delivery costs.[8]

Commissioner Mason dissented from the quantity-limit order in an opinion that emphasized the insufficiency of the factual finding. He said that although the quantity limit rule was intended for use only in unusual situations, the Commission had sought to cope with problems in the tire industry in only one proceeding under the Robinson-Patman Act prior to invoking the rule, and had concluded that this proceeding had been relatively ineffectual though it had made no field investigation to determine the effect of its order or to ascertain the facts as to compliance with the law by other tire manufacturers. He criticized the quantity-limit proceeding on the ground that the case in support of the rule had not been exposed to adequate public analysis and that the allegations of fact made by opponents of the rule had been rejected arbitrarily without determining their strength or weakness. He insisted that the rule was irrelevant to the proceeding and to the alleged facts, since the Commission's findings of fewness had to do with volume discounts, while the rule had to do with carload quantities in spite of the fact that "there is substantially nothing before the Commission that bears upon the effect of single purchases in quantities greater than a carload."[9]

He thought that under the guise of fixing a quantity limit, the Commission was seeking to force a revolution in the basis on which discounts were granted in the tire industry. He pointed out, for example, that

[8] *Ibid.*, p. 9.

[9] *Ibid.*, pp. 15-16. In regard to the argument of the Commission concerning a correlation between carload purchases and annual volume, he said: "The critical annual volume, according to findings made by the majority, is $600,000, not $350,000. The Commission has no information whatever as to the relation between carload purchases and annual volumes above $350,000. Moreover, the showing is that at all annual volumes between $35,000 and $350,000, some purchases are made in carload quantities or larger and some purchases in less than carloads. The majority does not indicate what effect upon competition may be anticipated with changing proportions of carload purchases. They offer neither fact nor finding to indicate what proportion of carload purchases is to be regarded as sufficient to make a purchaser a carload buyer; consequently, they offer no guidance as to the number of buyers in quantities greater than carload. Yet if the statutory requirements are met, these buyers in larger quantities must be so few that these larger quantities cannot safely be allowed to become a basis for discounts."

Firestone Tire and Rubber Company made its lowest price available to any buyer who took an annual volume of $250,000 a year, and that though this volume was substantially less than the $600,000 selected as the critical volume figure, the effect of the Commission's order would be to require Firestone to revise its discount structure and abandon all its volume discounts. "Firestone is not found to be doing anything harmful but is nevertheless required to reform." He criticized the Commission's concept of fewness, asserting that a number small enough to endanger competition is of the order of 3, 6, or 9, rather than 63. He also said that the Commission's figures on price differentials were exaggerated in that they made no allowance for differences in the basis of price quotations such as the fact that the prices paid by mass distributors did not include transportation charges. Noting that the public hearing contained expressions of fear lest the proposed order jeopardize the business of specialized tube manufacturers, co-operatives, and the smallest tire dealers, he expressed regret that the Commission did not make an investigation "solid enough to permit an evaluation both of the alleged dangers of not promulgating the rule and of the alleged dangers that would follow if the rule were promulgated."[10]

Petitions for declaratory judgments against the rule were filed by various affected persons and were denied by the district court for lack of jurisdiction and for failure to state a claim as to which relief was authorized. Cases brought by 14 manufacturers, 35 independent tire dealers, and 12 private brand distributors were consolidated by the Court of Appeals for the District of Columbia in an opinion rendered July 16, 1953.[11] The Court held that the complaints alleged a kind of damage from the application of the rule that, if proved, would justify injunctive relief, and remanded the case to the district court for consideration on the merits. On September 7, 1955, the district court gave summary judgment against the rule.[12] The decision was affirmed by the Circuit Court for the District of Columbia on February 28, 1957.[13] The matter was not appealed to the Supreme Court.[14]

[10] Ibid., pp. 16, 22.

[11] B. F. Goodrich v. FTC, 208 F. 2d 829.

[12] B. F. Goodrich v. FTC. et al., 134 F. Supp. 39.

[13] FTC v. B. F. Goodrich Co. et. al., 242 F. 2d 31

[14] The Federal Trade Commission asked the Solicitor General, who controls such appeals, to appeal the decision, but he refused to do so. See Price Discrimination, the Robinson-Patman Act and Related Matters, Hearings before the House Select Committee on Small Business, 84 Cong. 1 sess., Pt. 1, pp. 304-06.

The ground for judicial decision against the rule was that the Commission's findings of fact did not support it. The court of appeals said that the Commission:

> . . . chose to make a finding concerning the paucity of available purchasers in quantities greater than a certain annual dollar volume, and then fixed a quantity limit in terms of a carload. Even though the Commission's accompanying Statement may have indicated its belief that available buyers in quantities greater than a carload are so few as to give it authority under the quantity-limit proviso (which appellees seriously question) the Commission did not purport to base its order on that belief.[15]

Hence there was no finding of fewness or of jeopardy to competition that was relevant to the rule actually promulgated. Therefore the quantity limit for replacement rubber tires was set aside.

The Commission has instituted no other proceeding in contemplation of a quantity limit rule. The record of the tire case supports the suggestion that if it should do so it should first seriously consider a substantial change in the procedures by which such a rule is promulgated.

Since the effects of the quantity-limit rule must be to deprive the public of the benefits of economies that might be reflected in prices and price differences, it is important that the showing of injustice or monopolistic tendencies on which the rule is based should be solidly grounded. Something more is required than the jeopardy to competition which, in an ordinary proceeding under the Robinson-Patman Act, permits an order only if the discrimination is not cost-justified. As the circumstances are unusual, they may not be difficult to prove; but nevertheless, they should be proved solidly. Since the rule is to be applied to an entire industry or commodity, the scope of the proof should be sufficient to establish the nature of the economic relationships and tendencies within the area to be covered.

The procedure used in the tire case did not produce such proof. Most of the data, views, and arguments submitted by interested parties and most of the discussion of this material at public hearings were designed to make a case against the issuance of the rule. Since there was neither sworn testimony nor cross-examination, the strength of the case is often difficult to appraise. Taken at face value, however, it constitutes an impressive showing against the proposed quantity limit. The case for the

[15] 242 F. 2d 31, 36.

quantity limit consists chiefly of materials obtained by the Commission during its investigation. These materials, however, were never submitted for the public record, and hence there was no opportunity for those affected by the Commission's conclusions to subject the ground for those conclusions to well-directed attack.

What the Commission relied on was a series of summary statements that might well justify an investigation but, until proved, could not properly justify an order. Most of these statements were statistical in character and appeared in the table that has been reproduced herein. The underlying statistics on which the table was based were not made available to the public, and in various respects—for example, as to the number of purchasers, the distribution of large company sales among classes of purchasers, and the size of price differentials—the statistical adequacy and accuracy of the table was responsibly challenged. In the findings by which the order was supported, statements based on the table were supplemented by little else in the way of factual information. Percentage figures were given to show the trend of the sales of dealer-distributors as part of total sales, the trend of concentration in manufacturing and the relationship of volume to purchase in carloads for dealers with from $35,000 to $350,000 of volume. Underlying data were not submitted nor analyzed in detail on these matters, so that there remained considerable room for doubt regarding the adequacy of the findings and their interpretation.

Since the promulgation of a quantity-limit rule may be interpreted as legislative rather than judicial in its character, one need not demand that the procedure in considering the rule satisfy all the requirements of judicial due process. Indeed, it would be difficult, if not impossible, to permit every interested party to submit evidence and engage in cross-examination, as might be appropriate in a judicial proceeding. Nevertheless, greater precautions are needed than were used in the tire case. When a law is adopted by the Congress, the exposure of the proposal to a large number of lawmakers representing diverse interests affords practical assurance that no single view on the facts or the pertinent considerations will prevail without being exposed to all relevant and some irrelevant attacks. In a quantity-limit proceeding, however, a proposed rule developed by the Commission's staff is the product of relatively few persons who share a common attitude toward the enforcement of the law. Unless their investigations and interpretations of facts and policy are exposed to outside criticism more fully than was the case in the proceeding concerned with rubber tires, there can be no assurance that error and bias have been eliminated from the action of the Commission.

In the light of the proposed rule about tires, the quantity-limit provision of the law must be regarded as seriously defective. The principle that steps shall be taken to prevent monopoly, even at some sacrifice of efficiency, is consistent with Section 2 of the Sherman Act and with the basic thinking on which that act rests. So long as public policy forbids monopolization without providing for any cost defense, it can properly permit a public body to avert a tendency toward monopoly by some curtailment of the available cost defenses. But in such cases the cost of preserving competition is high; and it should be paid only reluctantly, in the face of a strong showing that nothing else will accomplish the result. In the tire case the evidence was slight, the diagnosis slighter, and the exploration of possible alternatives substantially nonexistent. The Congress had included in the law a provision authorizing the Commission to fix quantity limits not only when they were promotive of monopoly but also when they were "unjustly discriminatory"; and, apparently relying on this phrase, the Commission approached the fixation of a quantity limit with tests of damage to competition scarcely more severe and with standards of proof less rigorous than those it used in an ordinary proceeding against discriminatory volume discounts. Yet the discretion entrusted to the Commission in such a quasi-legislative proceeding is so great that if the order had been reasonably related to annual volumes of purchase rather than to carload quantities, the courts might have affirmed it. A tightening of the provision that conveys power to issue such orders is imperative.

But the provision is also unduly narrow. It was written with quantity (and perhaps volume) discounts in mind. It is so worded as to be inapplicable to cost justifications based on the method of sale rather than the quantity sold. Hence it is inapplicable to many functional discounts, territorial discriminations, and arbitrary concessions to selected enterprises, however monopolistic the consequences of such discriminations may be. Moreover, it has little bearing on the defense that competition was met in good faith. It might lead to denial of the good faith of a seller who reduced his price to meet a price openly based on a quantity in excess of a quantity limit that had been fixed. Otherwise, however, a discrimination that can be justified as meeting competition in good faith can be assailed no more readily if it is promotive of monopoly than if it merely impairs the competitive opportunities of disfavored customers.

If the law is to include special precautions to forestall imminent monopoly, they should be applicable to all the kinds of discrimination to which the statute applies and should rise superior to every type of defense by which monopolistic tendencies can be protected.[16]

[16] With three members expressing dissent, the Attorney General's Committee expressed the opinion that the quantity-limit proviso is objectionable, not only because it singled out quantity discounts, but also because it ineptly sanctions "a crude form of price-fixing by administrative fiat where competition should safeguard the public interest." The committee noted that "arrangements to impede competing distributive techniques have long been viewed as unreasonable restraints of trade." (*Report of the Attorney General's National Committee to Study the Antitrust Laws,* March 31, 1955, p. 177.) Presumably this comment means that the Committee regards Sec. 2 of the Sherman Act as sufficient to cope with discriminations having monopolistic effects that cannot be reached under the Robinson-Patman Act. If the quantity-limit provision were tightened and broadened, as is here suggested, a part of the basis for the Committee's criticism would be removed. The significant remaining issue would be whether or not there is advantage, where monopoly is imminent, in outlawing discrimination not only when it has a monopolistic purpose, but also where, regardless of purpose, it probably will create a monopoly.

10 / *Functional Discounts*

THE ROBINSON-PATMAN ACT does not explicitly mention functional discounts, that is, discounts granted not because of the characteristics of the transaction but because of the buyer's status as wholesaler, retailer, educational institution, or member of a similarly identified class. The legislative history of the act indicates that specific attention was given to the question of functional discounts, but affords little basis for an understanding of the way in which the Congress finally determined that the broader provisions of the act should bear on them.[1] Both in the House and in the Senate, a paragraph was included in the bill as reported from the judiciary committees that explicitly authorized allowances based on the buyer's status as wholesaler, retailer, or manufacturer; and in the bill as reported to the House there was an additional provision that the status of an intermediary distributor should be determined by his method of selling rather than by his method of buying. Farm organizations protested this requirement on the ground that it would prevent the receipt of wholesale discounts by farmers' co-operatives. In the House the functional discount provision was eliminated before the bill was approved; but the Senate retained it in passing the bill. The conference committee eliminated it entirely. Neither the conference reports nor subsequent discussion thereof by the two houses stated the ground for the deletion nor the status of functional discounts under the amended bill. It is arguable that the Congress thought that a difference in price between functional classes was so appropriate that it could not be interpreted as a discrimination; or that the Congress believed that absence of competition between functional classes would deprive a price discrimination between them of

[1] Section 2(c) pertains explicitly to allowances for one type of functional intermediary, the broker. Section 2(d) explicitly recognizes the possibility that intermediary distributors may render sales services to sellers and be compensated for them, and Section 2(e) similarly recognizes the possibility that the seller may render selling service to his distributor. Section 2(a) contemplates the possibility that discrimination may injure competition or prevent it in resale markets as well as among direct buyers.

286

injurious effect; or that the Congress intended functional discriminations to undergo the same tests of legality as to injury, cost justification, and good faith as were to be applied to other discriminations. Whatever the congressional intent, the language of Section 2(a) of the statute applies as readily to functional discounts as to any other kind of price difference, since it prohibits broadly all discriminations in price that adversely affect competition and cannot be justified in the specified ways.

At first glance, it may appear that concerns performing different functions are not in competition with one another and that, therefore, discrimination among them cannot hurt competition. However, damage to competition might result from functional discounts at three competitive levels. First, a seller might use such discounts for a discriminatory attack on his competitors and thereby injure competition in the primary line. Second, two or more functional classes of distributors might be differentiated by characteristics that did not prevent them from competing for the same customers, and discrimination among them might adversely affect that competition. Third, though the functional classes receiving the discounts might operate at different distributive levels, as do wholesalers and retailers, the customers of one class might be in competition with the members of the other, as retailers who buy from wholesalers are in competition with retailers who buy directly from the manufacturer; and the relative size of the functional discounts might be such as to affect the relative opportunity of those customers. The statute applies whenever competition is damaged by discrimination in any of these ways, regardless of the purposes that may underlie the discount structure. It applies not only if the vigor of competition in the market may be reduced by the discrimination but also if there may be injury to competition with the seller or with the favored customers. A discrimination is unlawful if all or part of a disfavored class of customers may be injured.

The strict logic of the statutory language suggests that illegality may be even wider. Discriminations are unlawful if they prevent competition as well as if they damage it. Where functional groups do not compete with each other, their failure to do so is often due to the nature of the discount structure. Legal considerations aside,[2] wholesalers do not sell at retail because they do not wish to; but retailers, whether or not they wish

---

[2] Under the Robinson-Patman Act a wholesaler selling at retail cannot lawfully receive his wholesale discount on the portion of his goods thus sold, if competition with others is thereby injured; and therefore has increased incentive to stay out of the retail market.

to sell at wholesale, refrain from doing so because the retailer's discount
is too small to enable him to compete with those who receive the wholesaler's discount. Thus the competition of retailers with wholesalers is prevented by the discount structure. Had the Commission applied to functional discounts a conception of injury as broad as it has used in some
of the volume-discount cases, it might have concluded that substantially
all discounts designed to distinguish successive levels of distribution are
unlawful. In practice, however, no such interpretation has been made or
appears probable.

Scope of the Functional Discount Cases

The Commission has issued orders in 33 cases involving functional
discounts. Twelve of these cases were tried, and in 5 the decision was
appealed. The orders in the other 21 cases rested on consent, admission
answers, or stipulations of fact accompanied by a waiver of most or all
of the trial procedure. Eleven of the cases, including the important one
against General Foods, were decided in 1955, 1956, and 1957, too late
to be included in the sample of cases chosen for special study.[3] In this
book they are included in statistical summaries; and where relevant the
findings, orders, and appellate decisions in them are discussed; but no
effort has been made to ascertain the effect of the orders on subsequent
business practice. Of the 22 remaining cases, 15 have been specifically
studied.[4]

In some of the 15 cases studied, the significance of the functional

[3] These are Docket 5722, *Whitaker Cable Corp.;* Docket 5770, *E. Edelmann
and Co.;* Docket 5897, *Doubleday and Co.;* Docket 5989, *Fruitvale Canning Co.;*
Docket 6018, *General Foods Corp.;* Docket 6052, *P. Sorenson Mfg. Co., Inc.;*
Docket 6480, *Thomas Y. Crowell Co.;* Docket 6654, *Sealed Power Corp.;* Docket
6743, *Grove Laboratories;* Docket 6747, *Topps Chewing Gum;* Docket 6748,
Philadelphia Chewing Gum Corp.

[4] The omitted cases are Docket 3263, *Agricultural Laboratories;* Docket 3264,
Hansen Inoculator; Docket 3265, *Urbana Laboratories;* Docket 3266, *Nitragin
Co.;* Docket 5049, *American Art Clay Co.;* Docket 4972, *U.S. Rubber Co.;*
Docket 5579, *F. and V. Manufacturing Co.* The first four of these were companion cases concerned with the sale of seed inoculants and feeds at discounts
to split-function jobbers and to farm bureaus. The fifth was a companion case to
those against *American Crayon* (Docket 4142) and *Binney & Smith* (Docket
4143), which have been studied. The sixth, concerned with rubber and canvas
footwear, involved reservation of the highest quantity discounts for national and
regional chain and mail-order customers to whom sales were made directly by
factory sales executives. The last had to do with jobber discounts on jewelry
granted to chain retailers.

aspect was not sharply brought out. In 2 instances discriminatory functional discounts were associated with a price-fixing conspiracy, which received primary attention.[5] Moreover, in certain cases the functional discount plan was so devised and administered that it was closely related to volume discounts (the window-glass case and the yeast case) or to unsystematic price variation (the Nutrine and Curtiss Candy cases). Since the legal issues on which decision turned did not depend on the exact nature of the functional relationships nor on the purpose and setting of the classifications that were used, information on these points was less than adequate even in some of the cases that were tried. Only in the Standard Oil case, the Ruberoid case, and the three spark plug cases were functional discounts made the center of attention in a proceeding that was fully contested.[6] In the spark plus cases, moreover, attention was focused primarily on the significance of the relation between prices for original equipment and for replacement, an issue that was decided in favor of the respondent companies; and consequently, the significance of the complicated discriminations in the replacement market was brought out in summary fashion.

The limited attention that has been given to functional discounts under the statute is surprising, for the problems that might evoke inquiry are widespread. Intermediary distributors frequently experiment with enlargement or curtailment of their functions and thereby obtain larger or smaller discounts without ceasing to compete with concerns of a different functional scope. Many manufacturers sell at more than one distributive level and thus raise problems as to the effect of their price differentials on the relations between direct and indirect customers. That such distributive practices give rise to widespread complaint is evident in the trade press and in legislative hearings. More of the price-discrimination cases probably would be concerned with such matters but for inherent difficulties in applying the Robinson-Patman Act to the relevant problems. The nature of these difficulties will appear below.

Varieties of Functional Discounts

For purposes of this discussion, the functional classification of customers should be understood to include all ways of grouping customers

---

[5] Docket 3154, *Pittsburgh Plate Glass Co.,* and Docket 3161, *Golf Ball Manufacturers Association.*

[6] In Ruberoid, however, the nature of the problem is not clearly stated in the findings; to understand it one must read the appellate decision.

that are based on differences in the characteristics of the customers themselves rather than in the nature or magnitude or other characteristics of the sellers' transactions with those customers. Thus, a buyer may be classified as a wholesaler because he characteristically buys at one distributive level and sells at another, and he may enjoy this classification whether he buys in large quantities or small and whether his purchases in a given period of time are greater or smaller than those of buyers differently classified. Where such a principle of classification is used, there is no difficulty in identifying price concessions as functional discounts. There are, however, perplexing cases in which a functional discount is difficult to distinguish from a transactional discount.[7] The functional class may be defined, not by its place in a sequence of distributive operations, but by characteristics closely related to the volume of purchases by its members. Where chain stores are recognized as a functional class, for example, the concerns included in the class probably buy on the average, or even without exception, substantially more in a given period of time than the concerns not included. A chain is likely to be defined as an enterprise possessing at least a stated number of retail outlets, and the limitation imposed by this definition is likely to make the class resemble even more closely a group that buys in large volume. Nevertheless, structural or operational characteristics, rather than the amount bought, determine membership in the class.

Sellers may classify their customers either vertically or horizontally. Vertical classifications distinguish concerns operating at successive levels of distribution, such as wholesalers and retailers. Often, however, there is a difference in the vertical extent of the functions performed by different distributors, and in such instances the seller may classify his distributors either by the level at which they buy or by the level at which they sell. Thus a chain store buying from a manufacturer, as wholesalers buy, and selling to the consumer, as retailers sell, may be classified as a wholesaler because of its buying operations or as a retailer because of its sell-

---

[7] Among the cases not explicitly studied, the footwear case (Docket 4972, *U.S. Rubber Co.*) is an unusually good example. In a quantity-discount schedule, discounts up to 8 per cent were provided for customers who bought from the sales force of the manufacturer's branches; 13 per cent or better was provided for customers who bought no larger amounts from the sales executives of the branch; and more than 18 per cent was given to national chains and mail-order houses that bought directly from the factory wholesale division. For a time there was also a special 15 per cent discount on certain goods available to national and regional chains and mail-order houses.

ing operations. In horizontal classifications, distributors may be segregated by various types of differences, such as the scope of their coverage of the market, the nature of their activities, and the types of customers with whom they are in contact. In a classification by scope, for example, national chains may be distinguished from regional chains, local chains, and unit stores. In classification by activity, concerns maintaining a warehouse that carries a full stock of merchandise may be distinguished from concerns that place orders with the manufacturer for direct shipment to their customers. In a classification by contacts, concerns selling to schools may be distinguished from concerns selling to distributors. Similarly, classification may be based on the use to which the buyer puts the goods. Thus purchases for resale may be distinguished from purchases for consumption or for further manufacture.

In an elaborate system of customer classification, several principles of classification may be employed simultaneously, either as supplements to one another or as alternatives used in separate parts of the market. Consequently, if the Commission's functional discount cases were grouped according to the nature of the functional classes that received discounts, some of the cases would fall into more than one group.

The functional discounts that have been involved in the Commission's cases rested on several principles of classification of customers. In one instance, the seller maintained several price lists, which were apparently used as instruments of negotiation. Salesmen unable to make a sale at a higher price were free to offer a lower price contained in a different price list and to explain the offer as derived from a decision that the customer properly belonged in the class to which the price list containing the new offer was applicable. In such a program, the definitions of the customer classes necessarily remained vague, and the seller used no objective principle of classification. The price lists for candy involved in the Nutrine case were used in this way. It appears probable that Namsco's two price lists were also used as a basis for preferential treatment of concerns that could demand lower prices. Curtiss apparently had a price list for use by its salesmen in selling to jobbers, small chains, and small vending-machine operators, but granted other prices in direct sales from the factory to variety syndicates, large chains, and large vending-machine operators. Such opportunistic classifications of customers are as vulnerable under the statute as any other methods of sporadic price concession.

Closely related to this form of customer classification was one in which the customer classes were designed to give rough recognition to differences in the buying power of different kinds of buyers. So far as there is any coherent meaning in the customer classes in the Nutrine and Curtiss cases, and probably in the Namsco case, it is of this kind. Nutrine's price lists applied to eastern syndicate accounts, national syndicate accounts, small syndicate accounts, and small retail accounts. Curtiss used different prices for general sales, sales to syndicate stores, and sales to several specifically named large purchasers. The manufacturers involved in the Golf Ball case made a special price to members of the Professional Golfers Association in recognition of their group bargaining power and their strategic control of the sale of golfers' supplies at important golf clubs. Similarly, Caradine Hat Company granted price concessions to members of buying organizations. In the sale of spark plugs, Champion and Electric Auto-Lite recognized as classes of buyers such powerful concerns as automobile companies buying plugs for resale in the replacement market. Champion also quoted a special price to operators of large fleets of motor cars. In view of the purpose of the statute to curb the powerful buyer, customer classifications designed to recognize buying power are obviously vulnerable at law.

In several cases the classification of customers was based on the scope of their activities or the extent of their coverage of the market. This principle was loosely invoked in Nutrine's customer classification, already referred to, and appeared to underlie the customer classification that was used by Curtiss. Since there is a close relation between the extent of the buyer's market coverage and his buying power, classification on the basis of coverage cannot be clearly distinguished from classification on the basis of buying power.

Some customer classes were based on the nature of the customer's buying operations. Ruberoid sold roofing to concerns that bought in wholesale quantities even though these concerns might be engaged as "applicators" in installing the material as well as in selling it at wholesale. Similarly, the Standard Oil Company of Indiana recognized as jobbers four gasoline distributors in Detroit because they took delivery from tank cars in wholesale quantities and had satisfactory credit ratings, without regard to the fact that they resold partly or wholly through their own filling stations.[8] Since the method of buying does not determine the level

---

[8] Standard contended, and the courts eventually agreed, that the discounts to these concerns were made in good faith to meet the equally low prices of competitors. This point is pertinent to the legal questions involved but does not affect

at which the customer resells, this kind of customer classification is vulnerable under the statute in any instance in which the resale takes place in competition with concerns not eligible for the discount.

By contrast, in selling paint, Lowe and Lucas (subsidiaries of Sherwin-Williams) sought to base their distributors' discount on the fact that the recipients resold the paint to retailers. The classification of the customer was made to depend on his method of sale rather than his method of purchase. This kind of classification is consistent with the concern expressed in the act as to injury to resellers; it created a problem not because of its principle but because of the laxity with which the plan was carried out.

The amount of service the customer provided to the seller and the amount of preference he showed for the seller's goods were made bases for classification in the spark plug cases. Champion gave a special discount to distributors who undertook to do certain promotional work and to co-operate in maintaining Champion's distributive policies. General Motors created a customer class for distributors who handled A. C. spark plugs and oil filter cartridges on an exclusive basis and performed certain other services. Electric Auto-Lite divided jobbers into four or five classes, of which one was allowed to buy direct while the others bought through intermediaries. One of the obligations of the direct buyer was active promotion to specified types of customers. For a time there were four classes of indirect jobbers, designated as contract jobbers, service jobbers, wholesale jobbers, and local jobbers. Later there were three classes, designated as registered jobbers, contract jobbers, and service jobbers. Where classifications depend on promotional activity, extent of the stock carried, exclusive purchase, and similar matters, customers falling into different classes are likely to be in direct competition with one another, and consequently variation in the discounts they receive is vulnerable under the law.

---

the fact that the form of the concession consisted in according to these customers a jobber's status and thereby making them eligible for a jobber's discount. According to Standard's attorney, "Standard was most meticulous in refusing, even in the face of lower competitive offers, to give a customer the 1½¢ lower tank car price unless the customer owned bulk storage facilities and transportation facilities, actually took delivery in tank car quantities, and assumed the entire wholesaling function." See Statement of Hammond E. Chaffetz on Behalf of Standard Oil Company (Indiana) in Opposition to H. R. 1840 and S. 11 and in Support of S. 780, in *To Amend Section 2 of the Clayton Act*, Hearings before the Senate Committee on the Judiciary, 84 Cong. 2 sess. (1956), pp. 456-57.

In one case, classification of customers was apparently used as a rough equivalent for a volume discount.[9] In the sale of window glass, concerns that bought from the factory were divided into two groups, known, respectively, as quantity buyers and carload buyers. The former group included those buyers that bought a minimum of from 3,000 to 5,000 fifty-foot boxes for stock annually. The problems of discrimination raised by this kind of classification are approximately the same as those that would be raised by a volume-discount structure in which the boundaries of the volume brackets corresponded to the amounts used in defining customer classes.[10]

Problems of Discrimination
Raised by Such Discounts

Five types of legal problems have been raised in the functional discount cases. The simplest of these has had to do with incorrect use of the seller's customer classifications, so that concerns received the functional discount without being eligible for it.[11] Such inaccuracies are inherent, of course, in the use of customer classes as negotiating devices, such as was found in the Nutrine and Curtiss cases. Indeed, Nutrine had classified particular customers in one group for the purchase of certain items, while classifying the same buyers in a different group for the purchase of other items. In selling paint, Lowe and Lucas professed to give wholesale discounts on paint that was resold to retailers but not on paint that was resold to consumers. However, when customers were engaged in a mixed wholesale-retail business, the sellers accepted the estimates of these customers as to the portion of the business that was wholesale and thus granted wholesale discounts on larger parts of the

[9] See above, footnote 5, p. 289.

[10] There is, nevertheless, a difference between the two types of discount structure. When the seller uses volume discounts, a customer may move readily from one volume bracket to another with changes in the amount he buys. When the seller bases a customer classification on volume, reclassification is likely to be infrequent, and the discount appropriate to the buyer's classification may, therefore, fail to reflect his current or recent volume.

[11] Among the cases not explicitly studied, that against *F. & V. Manufacturing Co.* (Docket 5579) was concerned with the practice of giving chain retailers jobbers' discounts of from 12 to 20 per cent on jewelry, regardless of the amount they bought.

total than were justified by the facts.[12] In the cases in which there was misclassification, problems of injury arose over the difference in treatment between the concern that was misclassified and the other concerns in the class to which it properly belonged.

Closely related to misclassification, but more common, was the problem created by concerns with divided functions—for example, concerns doing both a wholesale and a retail business. This was the heart of the difficulty in the paint case. It was also a major problem in the cases involving American Oil Company, Ruberoid, and Standard Oil Company of Indiana.

American Oil Company made an agreement with the owner of a fleet of taxicabs by which it would sell gasoline at a discount for use in these cabs. The gasoline was delivered to a filling station operated by the customer, and the discount was obtained on gasoline resold to the general public as well as on that consumed by the fleet. In selling to wholesalers of roofing materials, Ruberoid did not require them to segregate for discount purposes the part of what they bought that would be resold to retailers from that which would be used in their contracting business or sold in their affiliated retail establishments. Of the four "jobbers" who obtained gasoline from Standard Oil Company of Indiana in Detroit at tank-car prices, three resold partly to retailers and partly through their own filling stations, and one resold wholly through its own stations. No problems arose on the propriety of a discount on the portion resold at wholesale.[13] However, the Commission challenged the provision of the same discount for the remainder. It saw injury to competition in the fact that the favored buyers enjoyed a wider operating margin than other retailers and in the fact that one of them passed on a part of the low purchase price by cutting the retail price.

In two of the cases studied, there was a problem of discrimination in the fact that more than one rate of discount was provided for customers in the same customer class. American Crayon recognized a class known as multiple-discount customers, of whom some received a 5 per cent discount not available to distributors generally, while others received

---

[12] Lucas attempted to persuade its customers to submit certified statements of the amount of their wholesale sales but accepted unverified estimates from concerns that refused to submit certified ones.

[13] Nevertheless, a part of the finding of injury was concerned with such resale. See below, footnote 28, pp. 305-06.

10 per cent.[14] Binney & Smith recognized a similar group known as competitive distributors, some of whom received a special discount of 10 per cent, while the rest for a time received a special discount of 5 per cent (later raised to 10 per cent). The basis for the difference does not appear clearly in the record of either case. In selling candy, Curtiss accomplished a somewhat similar result, according to the Commission's findings, by making free deals and special promotional offers available for limited periods of time to selected groups of customers, while the same concessions were not available to others, even in the same customer class. In this part of the case, the Commission treated each special concession as an instance of discriminatory pricing, without specifically determining to what extent equivalent concessions subsequently became available to the disfavored groups.

These three types of discrimination are, of course, not central to the use of functional discounts. They can be avoided by care in defining functional classes and in assigning customers to them, by uniform treatment of the customers in any one class, and by assigning to two or more classes the customers whose business does not fall wholly within a single class.

A more significant problem was posed by the cases in which different functional classes were in competition with one another. Where the classification was based on the size or scope of the buyer or on the amount that he bought, competition between concerns falling into different functional classes was almost inevitable. Similarly, there was likely to be competition between concerns rendering the seller different degrees of service or giving his products different degrees of preference. Competition between classes was possible though not inevitable where the classification was based on the nature of the buyer's buying operations. The only principle of classification that did not invite issues as to competition between customer classes was that in which customers were classified according to the level of the distributive process at which they resold.

In the spark plug field, the eventual replacement market was served largely by retailers. Sales to these retailers were made by automobile manufacturers, by oil companies, and by jobbers, and in some instances, also by the distributor and the plug manufacturer. Sales to the jobbers were made by warehouse distributors and plug manufacturers and (in

---

[14] In addition, some received 15 per cent, and some two successive discounts of 10 per cent, on purchases of "Prong" tempera.

the case of Auto-Lite plugs sold to small jobbers) by large jobbers. Sales to the larger consumers of plugs who operated motor fleets were made by distributors or jobbers. Not all of these complexities appeared in the schedule of any one manufacturer; but in each instance warehouse distributors, jobbers, automobile manufacturers, and oil companies, sepa rately classified for discount purposes, were in competition with one another for certain classes of business.

Similarly, in the sale of golf balls, professional golfers who belonged to the Association competed with retail stores in selling balls to the public. In the sale of candy to the consumer, large and small syndicates, local retailers, and vending-machine operators competed. Members of group-buying organizations competed with nonmembers to sell the straw hats involved in the Caradine case. Multiple-discount and competitive distributors of school supplies competed with other distributors in sales to retailers.

Where functional classes occupied successive stages of the distributive process, a different kind of problem arose. It is exemplified by the spark plug cases and the Detroit gasoline case. The simple channel for the sale of A. C. spark plugs was from the plug maker to the warehouse distributor, from him to the jobber, and from the jobber to the retail dealer or the operator of a fleet of automobiles. General Motors, however, sold not only to warehouse distributors but also to large jobbers and to such retailing organizations as mail-order houses and oil and rubber companies that operated retail establishments. Similarly, the warehouse distributor sold not only to the jobber but also to selected large dealers, retail chains, and fleet accounts. Manufacturer, warehouse distributor, and jobber all sold at the dealer level. Manufacturer and warehouse distributor both sold at the jobber level.

The pattern of distribution by the other two spark plug manufacturers was similar, though less complicated. Electric Auto-Lite sold plugs not only to the warehouse distributor but also directly to certain jobbers. Champion sold directly to certain automobile manufacturers that resold replacement plugs to dealers and to certain oil companies that operated retail establishments and may thus be regarded as selling not only at the distributor level but also at the jobber level.

The prices quoted by the manufacturers were such as to pre-empt the business of the customers to whom they chose to sell direct, and to give those customers a buying advantage over others at the same level who bought indirectly through intermediaries. In thus selling at different prices to classes of customers at different vertical levels, the manufacturers prevented competition by their distributors for the business of certain customers, and reduced the competitive opportunity of the indirect buyers in their competition with the direct buyers.[15]

In the Detroit gasoline case, most of the direct-buying retailers were not the favored customers but the disfavored ones. Standard Oil sold at its tank-car price (1.5 cents lower than the tank-wagon price paid by retailers) to four companies—Citrin-Kolb, Wayne, Stikeman, and Ned's.[16] Although these customers were classified as jobbers, the first three sold at retail from 6.5 to 29.4 per cent of their purchases, and the fourth sold wholly at retail. During three years, Citrin-Kolb resold to one retailer customer for a cent less per gallon than the tank-wagon price and to another for one-half cent less. For a short time it also gave to customers of one of its own retail filling stations discount cards entitling the holder to a reduction of two cents per gallon in the retail price. Ned's resold to the public at cut prices. Its practices included, from time to time, the issue of trading stamps worth two cents a gallon, redeemable in merchandise or gasoline; the grant of commercial discounts varying from one to two cents per gallon; general sale to the public at two cents less than the prevailing retail price; and the use of various undercover discounts and premiums. The Commission found that the price reductions to the four companies had given them a competitive advantage over other sellers at retail and had facilitated price cutting by two of them that diverted business. It also found that the discrimination had permitted Citrin-Kolb to resell to a retailer at cut prices and had thus permitted Citrin-Kolb's customer to reduce his retail prices and to divert business to the injury of his competitors, some of whom were customers of Standard Oil. The discriminatory relationships included in this pattern were of three kinds, according to the Commission's findings. First, there was a discrimination in price between certain favored retailers who combined wholesaling and retailing functions and other retailers to whom Standard sold at the retail level. Second, there was a discrimination in price between the favored retailers and other retailers to whom the favored buyers, acting as jobbers, supplied Standard's gasoline at tank-wagon prices. Third, there was a discrimination between Citrin-

[15] They also controlled resale prices to different classes of indirect buyers and thus established differences in the competitive opportunity of these classes.

[16] For a time the price reduction to Ned's was only ½ cent.

Kolb's two favored retailer customers and other retailers, including both direct and indirect buyers.[17]

Kinds of Injury to Competition Found

In every case concerned with functional discounts, the Commission found (or alleged in a case settled without substantive findings) a probability of injury to competition in the secondary line.[18] In more than half the cases—17 out of 33—it also found (or alleged)[19] a probability of injury in the primary line. In both lines of commerce, the finding in most cases included both impairment of competition between the seller or the beneficiary and his competitors and reduction of competition in the market. In the secondary line, the finding (or allegation) rested on these dual probabilities of injury in 27 cases,[20] and solely on injury to a class of competitors in 6 cases. In the primary line, both forms of injury were found (or alleged) in 14 cases, injury only to a class of competitors in 1 case, and injury only to market competition in 2 cases. In 12 cases—1 in the primary line, 3 in the secondary line, and 8 in both lines—the Commission also found (or alleged) that the discrimination tended to create a monopoly.

As in the volume-discount cases, the findings of injury frequently were not explained or were explained in a way insufficient to show

[17] For the basis for this finding, see footnote 28, pp. 305-06.

[18] For discussion of the various types of injury to competition, see pp. 215-36.

[19] Five of the cases were settled by consent procedure without substantive findings. In these instances, the allegations of the complaints have been used as the only available evidence of the scope of injury as seen by the Commission. In four of the five cases, all three types of injury were alleged in both the primary line and the secondary line. In the fifth case (Docket 6743, *Grove Laboratories*), no injury was alleged in the primary line but all three kinds of injury were alleged in the secondary line.

[20] In one case, Docket 4556, *Curtiss Candy Co.,* the language of one passage in the findings might be interpreted to cover the narrow and broad types of injury in the secondary line of commerce, with no injury in the primary line, while that of another seems to say that there was only the narrow type of injury, but in both lines of commerce. The latter has been accepted for purposes of this summary.

In Docket 3154, *Pittsburgh Plate Glass Co.,* the language is also ambiguous. It clearly finds the narrow type of injury in the secondary line of commerce. In addition, it finds the broad type of injury to competition and a tendency to create a monopoly; but whether in the primary line, the secondary line, or both, is not clear. In the summary given here, these broader findings are also assumed to be applicable to the secondary line.

why the narrow injury to particular groups of enterprises was found to involve a broad impairment of market competition. In 16 cases[21] the conclusion as to injury was reached with nothing alleged or found to support it except a statement of the nature of the discrimination and a finding that the enterprises involved were in competition with one another. In 3 cases the only further relevant information consisted of illustrations of the effect of the discrimination on the relative buying prices of particular competing customers. Explanations, varying in clarity and scope, were given in the other 14 cases.

Injury in the Primary Line

The lack of a stated basis for the finding is most conspicuous for injuries in the primary line of commerce. In only one of the 17 cases in which such injury was found (or alleged) was there any statement as to the grounds for the finding. This was the case against Sealed Power Corporation (Docket 6654), in which the Commission's complaint said that competing sellers who did not offer comparable group buying privileges to jobbers had lost substantial amounts of business to Sealed Power.[22]

In five cases, however, in which the Commission limited its findings of injury to the secondary line, an explanation was given for the refusal to find a harmful effect in the primary line also. Three of these were companion cases in which the Commission had charged that price discrimination on spark plugs hurt competition not only among buyers of plugs but also among plug manufacturers. As to the latter type of injury, the supporting argument was that in selling plugs at low prices, sometimes below cost, to automobile manufacturers for original equipment in automobiles, respondents had excluded the smaller plug makers from the original equipment market; and that the loss of the prestige

[21] In two of these, Docket 3154, *Pittsburgh Plate Glass Co.*, and Docket 3161, *Golf Ball Manufacturers Association*, discrimination was a part of a price-fixing program; and the damage to competition from the discrimination was merged in the obvious damage done by the conspiracy. In four others, in which the proceedings resulted in consent orders, the findings contain nothing explicit except a statement that the complaint may be used in construing the decree; and hence the Commission's concept of injury and the basis for it can only be ascertained from the complaint.

[22] Since the case ended in a consent order, without findings of fact, no further light was thrown on this statement.

that went with use in original equipment had the effect of excluding the small plug makers from large parts of the replacement market also. Rejecting this argument, the Commission confined its findings of injury to the secondary line and its order to sales for the replacement market. It saw persuasive evidence that lack of prestige had adversely affected the sales of small plug makers in the replacement market, but found, without further explanation, that this conclusion was not "supported by the greater weight of all the evidence." It also saw "some evidence" that these plug makers had been unable to sell plugs for original equipment because they "were either unable or unwilling" to sell as cheaply as the respondents. But it found that in buying plugs automobile manufacturers consider not only price but also such factors as quality, public acceptance, the maker's ability to supply requirements, and the availability of the plugs and service for them throughout the United States. It saw in the record no evidence of undue mortality or undue loss of business by small plug manufacturers attributable to the discriminatory prices on original equipment plugs.[23]

In the fourth case, against E. Edelmann and Company (Docket 5770), the hearing examiner decided that, though competition in the secondary line was endangered by the discrimination, the evidence did not demonstrate the probability of injury in the primary line. The evidence on diversion of trade was fragmentary and showed loss as well as acquisition of customers; competitors had similar discriminatory arrangements; the two most important competitors were larger than the respondent; one competitor had grown steadily; the respondent had grown less rapidly than the industry; and, though accurate figures on shares of the relevant business were not available, respondent's sales of about $1,600,000 were about .07 per cent of the national sales of all automotive products. In sustaining the hearing examiner, the Commission's opinion said that evidence bearing on relative position in the industry is material in considering effects in the primary line and manifestly had been considered in his decision.

In the fifth case, against Namsco (Docket 5771), in finding injury in the secondary line of commerce, the hearing examiner found the evi-

---

[23] This aspect of the matter is discussed most fully in the decision in the case against *Champion Spark Plug Company* (Docket 3977), on which the foregoing comments rely. The more concise statements in the other two decisions, which were released on the same day, express the same general point of view, both directly and by reference to the Champion decision.

dence as to injury to competition in the primary line sparse and contradictory. He thought it showed, at most, a desire to get business from competitors, but not success in doing so.

It is noteworthy that injury in the primary line was found in only one case that was tried, and that of the five cases in which a proposal for such a finding was explicitly rejected, four were tried, while the fifth, a companion case to two that were tried, was settled by a stipulation that made its disposition rest on the decision in the tried cases. Question arises whether the other findings of injury in the primary line were based on differences in the relevant circumstances or merely expressed a tendency to exaggerate findings of damage where the issue was not contested.

The inexplicable incidence of these findings is illustrated by the cases against American Crayon and Binney & Smith. In both cases the order rested on stipulations of fact. The findings indicate that the discriminations by both companies in selling school supplies were similar. In each case the Commission found that these discriminations were capable of producing both the narrow and broad types of injury to competition in the primary line of commerce and the narrow type of injury in the secondary line. In the Binney & Smith case, but not in the American Crayon case, a probability of the broad type of injury in the secondary line and a tendency to monopoly in the primary line were also found. No explanation was given for the differences.

Injury in the Secondary Line

Explanation of the findings was given in 13 of the 33 cases in which the Commission found (or alleged) injury in the secondary line. There was no explanation, however, in the 11 cases in which the Commission found (or alleged) a tendency to monopoly in the secondary line, or in most of the 27 cases in which it found (or alleged) effects on market competition as well as on classes of competitors. Of the 13 cases in which findings of injury in the secondary line were explained, 10 involved both the broad and narrow types of injury, 3 the narrow type only. Among the 10 cases in which the broad type was found, the explanation of the injury in 9 cases consisted in a summary of evidence that indicated diversion of business from one group of customers to another or adverse effect on the profits of the disfavored buyers, without further demonstration that the vigor of competition in the market had been or probably would be affected. The diversion was not shown to differ in character or in severity from that found in the other two cases in which its effect was found to be the narrow type of injury but not the broad one. In the tenth case, the bigness of the favored buyers was emphasized. As in the volume- and quantity-discount cases, the Commission did not say how it distinguished the cases in which it saw a tendency toward monopoly, nor why it found a probability that competition in the market would be lessened in some cases and not in others.

In considering problems of injury to competition in the secondary line by functional discounts, the Commission has used concepts similar in many respects to those applied in the volume-discount cases. A substantial price difference between concerns that are in competition with one another is regarded as inherently injurious, because it enhances the operating margins of some of the competitors and can then be used for sales promotion, enhancement of service, expansion, or price reduction.[24]

[24] The nature of the Commission's thinking about injury in the secondary line appears clearly in the decision in the Namsco case (Docket 5771). The Commission found that the profits of jobbers are small—for example, 3.74 per cent for one jobber—and that the aggregate profit is made up of small profits on many items, among which Namsco products, though slow moving, are essential. It said, "With net margins of profit as narrow as they are among respondent's customers, where 2 per cent of cost of acquisition may account for more than half of that margin, it follows inescapably that the price preference found . . . even though only one out of a number of lines handled, contribute directly and powerfully to that jobber's business, health, and his ability to compete." The Commission thought that since Namsco suggested resale prices, which were generally observed, the price concession had not resulted in price cutting in resale. Methods of competition, however, included provision of additional service, additional salesmen, larger and more varied stocks of goods, branch houses, proximity to the customer, etc. "The institution or expansion of these competitive aids depends directly on operating profit margin, a major factor in which, on this record, is cost of merchandise purchased. From the above, it is concluded, therefore, that respondent's discrimination in price between customers competing in the resale of its products has had and may have the effect of substantially lessening competition among its customers so competitively engaged and of injuring and preventing competition among them." 49 FTC 1169.

In the interviews concerning this case, it was noteworthy that scarcely any of those interviewed, whether they had been favored or disfavored customers, regarded the discriminations as unusual or injurious. In this respect they agreed with disfavored customers who testified in other automobile parts cases that the discriminations against them were not injurious. Those interviewed described a market in which pricing has the characteristics of an Oriental bazaar, and in which

Where price cutting has actually occurred, it has been attributed to the buying advantage and has been regarded as a means to divert trade from competitors. Proof of an advantage in operating margins or of diversion of trade leads directly to the conclusion that competition may be or has been injured, sometimes only between favored and disfavored customers, but usually in the market sense also.[25]

In one respect, however, the concept includes something new—the preclusionary effect of price reductions by which sellers favor buyers at one level of distribution as compared with buyers at another level. Curtiss, for example, gave preferential prices to large vending machine operators, which enabled them to expand their candy business. Jobbers who bought from Curtiss could not sell to these vending machine customers, and found that, because of vending machine competition, their retailer customers could buy less than before. Similar effects were found in the replacement markets for spark plugs.

However, the application of the concept of injury to cases in which competition has arisen because of sale at more than one distributive level has been unavoidably awkward. If a manufacturer sells directly to some retailers while others must buy through wholesalers, the injury to

discrimination is the established method of competition rather than an excrescence on the competitive process. In this market, numerous sellers produce many different items, not only because of the varying makes, models, and years of the cars to which the equipment is to be attached, but also because of the rapidly changing preferences of ultimate consumers, many of whom buy accessories or replacements that have temporarily become a fad. The popularity of a product is subject to rapid change, and price changes to take account of changing popularity are frequent. The persons interviewed did not regard Namsco's pricing methods as unusual. They said that similar discounts were common and that when one seller discontinued them customers switched to a competitor. Nevertheless, they thought the popularity of a particular manufacturer's product was more important than the price charged for it.

[25] In one case, against *E. Edelmann and Company* (Docket 5770), the hearing examiner found injury in spite of testimony by three jobbers denying it and in spite of statistics showing that the number of wholesalers and their volume of business had increased rapidly and that many of them were small. As to the statistics, he found that the growth of the wholesale business might be due to extraneous influences such as war and inflation, and that the existence of many small jobbers did not demonstrate their business health nor prove that they were not suffering injuries less than fatal. As to the testimony, he said that the witnesses were not objective, since they were beneficiaries of discriminatory price reductions from other suppliers, which they thought would be affected by the decision; and that their denial of an injurious effect, which rested on the fact that uniform resale prices were observed, ignored the significance of differences in the service distributors could provide.

competition at the retail level arises through a difference between the prices paid by retailers who buy directly and those who buy indirectly, but the price paid by those who buy indirectly is that charged by the wholesaler, not that charged by the manufacturer.[26] If the manufacturer is not held responsible for the wholesaler's price in the resale market, a difference between the manufacturer's price to wholesalers and to direct-buying retailers will not be regarded as injurious to competition in the secondary line of commerce because his wholesaler and retailer customers are not in competition with one another. But the statute applies to discriminations that injure competition, not only with favored customers, but also with the customers of these customers.[27] If this provision, or the surveillance exercised by the manufacturer over resale by wholesalers, is sufficient to establish the manufacturer's responsibility for the wholesaler's resale price, problems of injury may arise in the competition of direct buyers with indirect buyers. So far as this is so, a delicate balance appears to be required between prices charged to retailers in different channels of distribution. In the Curtiss case direct sales by the manufacturer gave the direct buyers an advantage over indirect buyers, which was regarded as injurious to competition. In the gasoline case, however, the passing on of a part of its jobber buying advantage by Citrin-Kolb in resale to a retailer was held to be injurious to competition because it placed retailers who bought direct at a disadvantage.[28] Considered together, the two findings appear to rest on the

[26] See *Krug* v. *International Telephone and Telegraph Corp. et al.*, 142 F. Supp. 230.

[27] Discriminations may be unlawful if they "injure, destroy, or prevent competition with any person who either grants or knowingly receives the benefit of such discrimination, or with customers of either of them." Robinson-Patman Act, Sec. 2(a), 41 Stat. 1526.

[28] In the particular case the finding as to the third type of discrimination is anomalous. The Commission made no general challenge of the propriety of the jobber price in its application to the portion of the purchases of the four favored customers that was resold to retailers, which constituted the larger part of the purchases of three of them. Nevertheless, the Commission found that Citrin-Kolb's resale to two dealers at cut rates was due to the discriminations in price that it received. In the Commission's brief on appeal before the circuit court (In the U. S. Court of Appeals for the 7th Circuit, *Standard Oil Company, Petitioner*, v. *F.T.C.*, No. 9215, Brief for Respondent, December 20, 1948, pp. 91-96), the part of the order that was intended to cope with this situation was defended on the ground that if Standard "sells to wholesalers in tank car quantities at 1½ c. or more a gallon below the price it charges retailers in the same territory, and if the wholesaler then passes along a part of his wholesale margin to his retailer customers, selling to them below the tank-wagon price paid by petitioner's direct

principle that the manufacturer should maintain such a relation between his wholesale prices and his retail prices that the wholesalers' retail prices will be the same as his own.

If such a requirement were clearly recognized, it would place on the manufacturer the duty of policing the resale prices of his wholesale distributors if his customers are in competition with their customers. It would also place on him an obligation to establish between his whole-

---

retailer-customers, the resulting competitive injury is the same as if petitioner sold directly to retailers at discriminatory prices. The competitive advantage thus obtained by the favored dealers' customers directly results from the lower price charged the favored dealers, and violates the Clayton Act, as amended. . . ." This appears to say that a discount to a jobber is a discrimination, that it injures competition wherever any part of it is passed on, that its mere existence is to be held responsible for any passing on that occurs, and that, as the grantor of the jobbing discrimination, Standard is responsible for the injury.

In holding Standard responsible for the consequences that even an otherwise unchallenged wholesale price may have in retail markets, the argument is peculiar to the particular case; and had its implications been accepted, the Commission would necessarily have examined the wholesale transactions of all four jobbers, not only for injury in the form of lower resale prices, but also for injury in the form of services to the retailer more favorable than those rendered by Standard in direct sales to other retailers. (Indeed, the brief suggested the propriety of this by saying, "Whether the favored dealer passes along part of his wholesale margin to his retailer-customers by cutting the tank-wagon price, by . . . himself advertising the retail outlets which bear his insignia, by charging low rentals to lessee operators, or by any other means, the result is a competitive advantage to the wholesaler's customers which results from his ability to buy at tank-car prices. . . .")

By failing to apply the theory fully, the Commission deprived its case of consistency. Nevertheless, the finding illustrates a significant part of the Commission's view of injury, for if there had been any discrimination among jobbers that gave benefit to Citrin-Kolb, or if the price to jobbers had been so low as to invite price-cutting in resale, the finding as to injury in resale would have been consistent with the Commission's general position.

The sweep of the position taken by the Commission in this case was apparently due to belief that Standard's distributors, wholesale and retail, were under Standard's control. The brief that has been quoted argued that the order imposed no policing duties upon Standard because Standard already "polices both the favored dealers and the retailers." When the case reached the court of appeals for the second time, the Commission's argument (In the U. S. Court of Appeals for the 7th Circuit, *Standard Oil Company, Petitioner* v. *F.T.C.,* No. 11409, Brief for the Respondent, undated, p. 44) was explicitly based on Standard's control of distribution: "If petitioner's retail customers were free to shift their patronage to a reseller who offered prices lower than those charged by petitioner, they could avoid competitive injury by so doing. However, petitioner's retail customers cannot do this. They are a captive market, made so by the short term leases and contracts heretofore described."

sale and retail price a differential for the wholesaler that is neither so large that it encourages the wholesaler to cut prices in reselling nor so small that it encourages the wholesaler to resell for more than the manufacturer charges at retail. In the Standard Oil case, the Commission accepted the logic of this argument by including in its modified cease and desist order a provision requiring Standard Oil to cease discriminating:

> . . . by selling such gasoline to any jobber or wholesaler at a price lower than the price which respondent charges its retailer-customers who in fact compete in the sale and distribution of such gasoline with the retailer-customers of such jobbers or wholesalers, where such jobber or wholesaler resells such gasoline to any of its said retailer-customers at less than respondent's posted tank-wagon price or directly or indirectly grants to any such retailer-customer any discounts, rebates, allowances, services, or facilities having the net effect of a reduction in price to the retailer.[29]

In commenting on this part of the order, the Seventh Circuit said:

> To avoid the force of this paragraph, the petitioner may do one of two things. First, discontinue selling to wholesalers at a price different than that made to retailers. The petitioner's three largest competitors in Detroit have found it agreeable to do so. The petitioner argues that this is an elimination of wholesalers. If this be true, it is elimination only where their existence cannot be justified except on the exploitation of a differential in price not justified by any cost savings to obtain that price. This does not impress us as either illegal, unwarranted, or unjust.
>
> Secondly, the petitioner may under the right to choose its customers refuse to sell to wholesalers who sell to retailers below the price the petitioner makes to its own retailers. The petitioner does not have to make price-control agreements with any one. It has only to govern its own conduct to avoid the impact of an unlawful discrimination. . . . The petitioner has no control and can have no control over the price of the gasoline after it is sold to the wholesalers. The latter may put any price on it they may choose. They may give it away if they like. The petitioner should not be required to police its wholesalers and sell

[29] 43 FTC 58. The entire order was subject to provisos that none of its prohibitions should be taken as inhibiting price differentials that were not found to have a tendency to injure competition, or as preventing price differentials that made only due allowance for differences in cost. In addition, it provided that the prohibitions of the order should not inhibit "a lower price to jobbers than to retailers where respondent thereby makes only due allowance for its differences in cost of manufacture, sale or delivery resulting from the differing methods or quantities in which such gasoline is to such purchasers sold or delivered." *Ibid.*

to them at the petitioner's peril. The petitioner should be liable if it sells to a wholesaler it knows or ought to have known is engaging in or intends to engage in the competitive practices condemned by this proceeding.

Accordingly, the court directed that the Commission's order be modified so that the prohibition applied only to sales to wholesalers at a lower price "where such jobber or wholesaler, to the knowledge of the respondent or under such circumstances as are reasonably calculated to impute knowledge to the respondent, resells such gasoline or intends to resell the same" in the specified way.[30]

The decision of the circuit court was reversed by the Supreme Court on grounds pertaining to the defense of meeting competition, without consideration of the point here under discussion. Thereupon the case was remanded to the Commission to examine the question whether Standard's price concessions had been made in good faith to meet competition. Finding that they had not, the Commission issued a new order in 1953. In this order, the same principle of responsibility as to the jobber's resale price was asserted, but in language focused on the retail price rather than the wholesale price. Standard was forbidden from discriminating "by selling such gasoline to any retailer at a price known by respondent to be higher than the price at which any wholesaler-purchaser is reselling such gasoline to any retailer who competes with such direct retailer-customer of respondent, where respondent is selling to such wholesaler at a price lower than respondent's price to such direct retailer-customer."[31]

The semantic changes in the Commission's order were apparently intended to emphasize the possibility of reducing prices to direct-buying retailers rather than, as in the previous order, the possibility of increasing prices to jobbers. To both versions, however, the analysis of the Seventh Circuit is equally applicable: Standard could cease to sell to jobbers (or to retailers). Alternatively, where a jobber reduced a retail price in

---

[30] 173 F. 2d 210, 217. It is noteworthy, however, that in two private suits the courts have refused to award damages for injuries suffered by distributors from narrow differences between prices at successive distributive levels. See *Jarrett* v. *Pittsburgh Plate Glass Co.*, 131 F. 2d 674 and *Klein* v. *Lionel Corp.*, 237 F. 2d 13.

[31] 49 FTC 956. The modification had been made earlier but rejected by the circuit court because, during the pendency of the previous appeal, the Commission was without jurisdiction. Prior to the change there had been vigorous questions about this part of the order by members of the Supreme Court during the argument of the case. See 19 *U.S. Law Week* 3102.

a way that might injure competition, Standard had the alternative of refusing to sell to the jobber or altering the relation between its own prices to jobbers and retailers sufficiently to bring retail prices into line. In asserting that the order did not require Standard to police the jobber's resale price, the Court meant only that Standard was not required to engage in detective work or overtly coerce jobbers. In the economic sense, however, a policy of refusing to sell to price-cutters, a policy of penalizing price cuts by making the price-cutter pay more, and a policy of retaliating against price cuts by competing more sharply against the price-cutter's customers are merely alternative methods of controlling prices. Thus the Commission's order imposed on Standard duties of resale price control, with the alternative of abstaining wholly from sale to one of the two classes of customers. Whereas (apart from the Miller-Tydings and McGuire acts) the broad policy of the antitrust laws has been to prohibit resale price maintenance as anti-competitive, the concept of injury to competition under the Robinson-Patman Act, when applied to discriminations in favor of jobbers, was interpreted in a way that encouraged resale price maintenance.

The case was subsequently appealed once more. The Seventh Circuit decided against the Commission in an opinion concerned wholly with the defense of meeting competition and including no comment as to this matter. To the Supreme Court the Commission announced its intention not to seek affirmance of this part of the order. Its brief said that its purpose had been to relieve:

> . . . what in essence was a "captive market" situation—that is, the inability of the "non-jobber" customers to obtain, either from Standard or from the wholesaler "jobbers," preferential prices which the wholesaler "jobbers" were granting in some instances to their sub-dealers. On the other hand, it was not the purpose of the Commission to require Standard to eliminate legitimate functional pricing or to make it responsible for the pricing practices of its wholesaler "jobbers."

Because of the problems necessarily involved, and in order to reconcile administrative interpretation with broader antitrust policies, the Commission had concluded that its purpose could be better served by other means, such as a proceeding under the Federal Trade Commission Act or under Section 3 of the Clayton Act.[32]

[32] In the Supreme Court of the United States, October Term, 1957, *FTC* v. *Standard Oil Company*, Reply Brief for the FTC, November 1957, pp. 31-32.

The difficulties of an effort to maintain appropriate price relationships between successive distributive levels have not been confined to the Standard Oil case, though in no other case have they been so explicitly recognized. Injury at both the earlier and later stages of distribution appeared in discrimination between distributive levels in the spark plug cases. The orthodox channel of distribution was from manufacturer to warehouse distributor to jobber to dealer to consumer. Some of the discriminations were found to favor warehouse distributors over jobbers when the two competed in sales to dealers or large consumers. These involved relationships similar to those of the Standard Oil case. Other discriminations were found to favor jobber chains over warehouse distributors. These were the reverse of those in the Standard Oil case: they favored the second level of distribution over the first. There were also discriminations that favored automobile companies and oil companies over warehouse distributors; and since these concerns resold primarily to dealers, and thereby may be regarded as operating at the jobber level, the discriminations in their favor may also be regarded as the reverse of those in the Standard Oil case. Thus the spark plug pattern of distribution included concessions to buyers at successive levels of distribution, some of which gave advantage to the intermediary nearer to the manufacturer while others gave advantage to the intermediary nearer to the consumer. The Commission saw injury at each distributive level through the difference in price between different classes of competing intermediaries and through the difference in price between direct and indirect buyers.

The orders in all three cases included passages forbidding the manufacturer to discriminate (1) by selling to any direct purchaser at a higher price than to a competing direct purchaser; and (2) by selling to any indirect purchaser at a higher price than to any other competing direct or indirect purchaser.[33] The latter part of the order clearly applies to price relationships at successive levels of distribution wherever direct and indirect purchasers are in competition.

Injuries such as those in the Standard Oil and spark plug cases arose because the spread between the seller's prices at different distributive levels was either so wide as to permit favored distributors at higher levels

---

[33] Under accepted rules of interpretation, these orders, like all others concerned with discrimination, carry the implied qualification that they do not prevent cost-justified price differences nor price concessions made in good faith to meet the equally low price of a competitor. See *FTC* v. *Ruberoid Co.,* 343 U.S. 470.

of distribution to resell at cut prices at lower levels, or else so narrow as to prevent these higher level distributors from reselling as cheaply as the lower level customers could buy direct. Where injury arises from both conditions, as in the Champion case, the readjustment involves both increases and decreases in the price differences. Where the differences are thought to be unduly narrow, as in sales to large fleets in the Champion case, the purpose of a corrective order is presumably to increase the functional price difference either by lowering the price to disfavored intermediaries or by raising it in direct sales by the seller or his favored customer. Nevertheless, if control over indirect buyers is not exercised, both the statute and the order in the spark plug cases make it possible for the seller to end such an unlawful discrimination, not by increasing the difference, but by eliminating it entirely. Sale to consumers or dealers at the same price as to jobbing intermediaries would, of course, enhance the relevant types of injury to the point where destruction of the spark plug business of these intermediaries became probable. Yet sale to all at a uniform price, regardless of their place in the channels of distribution, would end the discrimination and thus be lawful.[34] Binney & Smith, for example, was found by the Commission to have sold school supplies at a uniform price to jobbers and large retail chains. This price uniformity, though obviously injurious to jobbers, was not questioned by the Commission.[35]

The basic difficulty in such situations lies in the fact that the concept of discrimination as price difference is inappropriate in considering the competitive effect of the relative prices established by a seller in his sales at successive levels of distribution. The law should not attempt to provide a standard of propriety for the relationships among these prices.[36]

[34] In an early case against Bird & Son, the Commission's complaint was based on the fact that Bird sold floor coverings to Montgomery Ward and other mail-order houses at jobber prices, while charging other retailers as much as 14 and 18 per cent more. When the Robinson-Patman Act became law, Bird had nearly completed a revision of its marketing plan by which it ceased to sell to retailers other than mail-order houses and sold to its jobber and mail-order customers at uniform net prices. The Commission found in this new arrangement no discrimination in price and thought the statute permits discrimination in choosing customers. Since the transitional discriminations were negligible in the volume of business they affected and were cost justified, it dismissed the complaint. See 25 FTC 548-54.
[35] See Hearing Examiner's Report on Compliance, November 4, 1952.
[36] Cf. Report of the Attorney General's National Committee to Study the Antitrust Laws (March 31, 1955), p. 208: "The Committee recommends, therefore, that

If it does so, however, the standard must necessarily be concerned with appropriate differences rather than with the elimination of differences. Excessive and insufficient differences must be equally open to challenge. The effect would necessarily be to fix distributors' margins, a result directly contrary to the policy of the Sherman Act. Though startling, the resale price portion of the order in the Standard Oil case expressed the logic underlying the application of the law to vertical price relationships. In the spark plug cases, the extension of the orders to cover the relations between prices to direct and indirect buyers has a similar tendency.

It is noteworthy that the Commission has applied the concept of discrimination to vertical price relationships chiefly in cases in which, as in the Standard Oil case and the spark plug cases, the manufacturer controlled resale prices or was believed to exercise some other kind of control over distributors; and that only in the Standard Oil case did the Commission clearly apply the remedies of vertical control over prices that are logically appropriate to this part of the law. The concepts of controlled distributive margins are antithetical to the Commission's point of view as a guardian of the antitrust laws. They have been accepted by the Commission reluctantly where they appeared to be inescapable. Hence they have been applied in few cases, and then sometimes, as in the spark plug cases, in language that does not make their import unmistakable. No general alarm has developed in the business community about the legality of vertical price differences. Instead, the Commission's occasional proceedings against injuries found in such differences have been attributed, not to the concepts of the statute, but to the Commission's wrong-headedness. It is not surprising that from

---

suppliers granting functional discounts either to single-function or to integrated buyers should not be held responsible for any consequences of their customers' pricing tactics. Price cutting at the resale level is not in fact, and should not be held in law, 'the effect of' a differential that merely accords due recognition and reimbursement for actual marketing functions. . . . On the other hand, the law should tolerate no subterfuge. . . . Only to the extent that a buyer *actually* performs certain functions, assuming all the risk, investment, and costs involved, should he legally qualify for a functional discount. Hence a distributor should be eligible for a discount corresponding to any part of the function he actually performs on that part of the goods for which he performs it."

In this suggestion the committee apparently envisaged the subdivision of functional discounts into parts applicable to various activities, and contemplated that the Commission should try to determine in each particular instance whether the activities for which payment was made were actually performed. To the present writer, such an effort appears to be impracticable. If feasible, however, it would require surveillance over prices and distributive activities more pervasive than anything yet undertaken.

time to time the Commission has been unable to avoid finding injurious discrimination between direct and indirect customers nor to avoid corrective orders that sought to define the gap between prices at successive levels of distribution. Rather, it is surprising that the statutory provision by which a seller is held responsible for injury among the customers of his customers has not forced the Commission to undertake this type of proceeding more frequently.

The failure of the Congress to cope with the problem either by excluding it from the application of the statute or by applying a rule suited to its peculiar nature has left the Commission an impossible job in this type of case. The general concepts of injury under Section 2(a) can be applied without unusual difficulty to functional discounts that establish price differences among customers competing at the same distributive level; but they cannot be applied successfully to the price differentials that divide one distributive level from the next.

Cost Justification

In five of the functional discount cases in which there were trials and one in which there was a stipulation of facts, an effort was made to justify the discounts, or some of them, by differences in costs. Cost defenses were offered as to candy in the Curtiss case, gasoline in the Standard Oil case, spark plugs in the Champion case, books in the Doubleday case, footwear in the U. S. Rubber case, and canned food in the Fruitvale case.[37]

The cost defense in the footwear case has been discussed in the chapter on quantity and volume discounts. Doubleday presented no accounting analysis, and admitted that it had never analyzed its cost of selling trade books to any purchaser and had never made a detailed cost study to justify its price differences. Such a study, it thought, was impossible or impractical because of Doubleday's "widespread and varied operations and the complexities involved." On the basis of these admissions, the cost defense was rejected. In the Fruitvale case the hearing examiner rejected the cost defense summarily by saying that the buyers who paid the higher prices frequently bought more at one time than their favored competitors.

---

[37] In another case, that against General Motors, cost justification was alleged in the respondent's answer, but no effort was made to prove it. The Commission's findings said that the record did not establish such justification.

In the other three cases, rejection of the cost defense was accompanied by an analysis setting forth the nature of the inadequacies therein.

Champion's cost defense did not apply generally to the vertical price differences that have been discussed in considering the problem of injury. It was offered only in justification of special prices quoted to Atlas Supply Company and Socony Vacuum Oil Company.[38] Champion sought to show that these prices were justified by differences between the cost of selling to these two customers and the cost of selling to distributors generally. The Commission objected to the lumping together of 485 other distributors, in disregard of the probable variations of sales expense among them. It pointed out that one of these customers was Cities Service Oil Company, as to which there was reason to believe that Champion's sales effort was probably less than in sales to Atlas and Socony. The Commission also noted that the record established slight basis for justification of some of the procedures used in computing and allocating costs.

The Commission's objections to the cost defense by Curtiss were similar.[39] Curtiss sought to justify its special prices to vending-machine operators, and to this end compared the costs of selling to them and the average cost of selling to all other customers, who bought about 95 per cent of Curtiss' five-cent candy bars. The Commission rejected this use of an average for a group of concerns that differed greatly in size, character, and prices paid. It also criticized the substitution of arbitrarily estimated average prices and of computed prices (derived by applying production figures to dollar sales) for the actual prices charged to different classes of customers. It found that many of the items of cost used in the analysis were allocated on the basis of dollar sales because the books did not permit allocation "on an actual operative basis" and because no cost survey had been made.

In the gasoline case, Standard submitted two different cost justifications, one pertinent to a price concession of ½ cent per gallon made to Ned's between 1936 and 1938, and the other pertinent to the discount of 1½ cents per gallon available to the other three favored buyers and to Ned's from 1938 onward.[40]

[38] This cost defense is analyzed in Herbert F. Taggart, *Cost Justification* (1959), pp. 112-39.

[39] *Cf. ibid.*, pp. 237-56.

[40] *Cf. ibid.*, pp. 187-236.

Thomas E. Sunderland, General Counsel of Standard Oil Company (Indiana), commented on his company's cost defense on September 15, 1949, in a speech

The Commission rejected the first of these defenses on the ground that all customers other than Ned's had been improperly grouped together in disregard of significant differences; that the methods of delivery to Ned's and to others had been presumed to be consistently different, contrary to fact; that Ned's had not been assigned any share of various categories of cost, especially the cost of Standard's advertising of gasoline, that properly should have been allocated partly to it; and that the costs attributed to others had been improperly padded by including Standard's landlord expenses as owner of filling stations and the cost of portions of salesmen's time that were not devoted to Detroit customers.

The broader cost defense sought to justify jobber discounts by comparing the costs of tank-wagon deliveries in the Detroit metropolitan area with the costs of selling to jobbers found in a survey in the Kansas-Oklahoma field. The Commission rejected the Kansas-Oklahoma survey on the ground that conditions in that field were not comparable with those in Detroit and that there were substantial inconsistencies in the handling of different categories of cost. The Commission also rejected the analysis of tank-wagon costs in Detroit on the ground that it included figures for other types of sale and delivery. An effort by Standard to improve the Detroit figures by appropriate segregation and allocation of items that would distinguish the jobber channel from other channels was also rejected, on the grounds that the costs in serving dealers had been padded by including irrelevant categories of cost (such as cost of serving outlying rural sections and landlord expenses) and that there

---

entitled "Is It Illegal to Meet Competition in Good Faith under the Robinson-Patman Law?" He has authorized the writer to quote a revised version of his remarks, as follows:

"Standard made a good faith effort to demonstrate that the difference between the tank car price at which it sold to the Detroit jobbers and the tank wagon price at which it sold to dealers was justified by differences in the cost of serving the two classes of customers. Since, however, the lower tank car price had been granted to the jobbers in response to competitive offers rather than as a result of cost accounting studies, it could not be expected that Standard's cost savings would be exactly equal to the jobber margin. Although Standard's cost studies made for purposes of the case showed that all but a small portion of the difference could be justified, the Federal Trade Commission held this to be insufficient proof. Standard's experience indicates that it is unlikely that a supplier will ever be able to justify a jobber margin through proof of the supplier's cost savings, for savings in cost are neither the sole motivation for jobber distribution nor the measure by which the margin is determined. The jobber margin is set by competition in a free market, and sellers must meet these lower competitive offers or lose their jobber customers."

were inconsistencies and improprieties in the methods of allocation used. (For example, no portion of consumer advertising was allocated to the jobber channel.)

Apart from the footwear case, in which the Commission's findings as to cost are too general to be evaluated, the condemnation of these cost defenses is persuasive. Incommensurables were classed together and questionable methods of allocation were used. However, the defects appear to be attributable in part to the inadequacy of the underlying cost information and the magnitude of the task of focusing this information on the relevant price differences. As to both Curtiss and Standard Oil, the Commission found that the books of account did not permit allocations of costs satisfactory for the purpose.

Moreover, to constitute an adequate defense, the costs must have been offered in sufficient detail to justify every injurious price difference. In the spark plug cases, this would have required justification of differences among from three to five categories of distributors plus several categories of direct-buying fleet owners. In the Curtiss case, it would have required the justification of three categories of discount to vending-machine operators against one another and also against prices to several other categories of distributors; the justification of the price differences among these other categories; and the justification of a wide variety of special deals. In the gasoline case only two discounts needed to be justified, and one of these had been available to only one customer for only two years. However, the amount of these discounts would have had to be covered by cost differences applicable to each of the various types of nondiscount customers whose operations were different enough that Standard incurred significantly different costs in serving them. Thus, even in this case, a variety of separate cost comparisons would have been necessary. It is a formidable task to develop a successful cost defense for a functional discount structure where there are numerous functional classes or where there is such diversity in the way business is done with different groups of buyers as to preclude the simplification of the cost problem by throwing all buyers into a small number of groups for purposes of cost allocation.

It is interesting to note that differences in the costs incurred by different classes of buyers were not considered in any of the cases.[41] Such

[41] In the Standard Oil case, Citrin-Kolb tried to introduce evidence of its costs, but the proffer was rejected. Apparently the proffer had two purposes: to show lack of competitive injury and to show that Standard must have saved what Citrin-

differences could not have been used in direct justification of price differences, since the law makes the cost defense available only where the price concession is justified by an appropriate difference in the seller's cost. However, where functional discounts were based on differences in the activities or services performed by buyers, the effect of these differences on buyers' costs appears to be directly relevant to the question whether or not the discounts were injurious. In the Standard Oil case, for example, it is obvious that the four concerns receiving the jobbers' discount performed functions, such as the bulk storage of gasoline, that were not performed by the ordinary filling-station operator. If these additional functions had cost the big buyers as much as 1.5 cents per gallon, the discount granted by Standard would have had no effect in reducing the net cost of the gasoline sold at retail by the large buyers. An extra 1.5 cents in the price paid by some customers would have been equivalent to an extra 1.5 cents in the cost incurred by other customers. Thus, a full exploration of the likelihood of injury through price difference appears to necessitate a consideration of the question of the cost differences among customers that are systematically related to the price difference. Though such costs are not explicitly covered by the Commission's findings, what is said as to injury appears to rest on a presumption that the extra services performed by favored classes of distributors required no substantial extra expenditures. Apparently, this presumption was not vigorously challenged in any of the functional discount cases that were tried.[42]

Kolb spent. The evidence was objected to as irrelevant, but excluded as incompetent. See Transcript, pp. 1234-39, and *To Amend Section 2 of the Clayton Act,* Hearings (1956), p. 463.

[42] In the spark plug cases, though service franchises were involved, no question appears to have been raised as to costs incurred by the distributor. In two recent cases (Docket 5897, *Doubleday and Company* and Docket 6018, *General Foods Corporation*), efforts were made to justify price concessions to distributors as compensation for services received. In the General Foods case, the hearing examiner analyzed the contention as, in effect, a cost defense, and said: "The fact that some customers have greater business costs than others has never been accepted as justification for price differentials. Respondent states in its brief that 'the ICWD's added cost of doing business is, as a result of Respondent's ICWD program, passed backwards, to Respondent, rather than forward, to the ICWD customer.' This is exactly what the law says cannot be done." (Docket 6018, Opinion of the Commission, mimeo., p. 12.) In appealing the decision to the Commission, General Foods argued that the concessions were actually payments for sales services of the kind contemplated by Section 2(d); but the Commission found that they did not have this character.

Meeting Competition in Good Faith

The defense that price concessions were made in good faith to meet a competitor's equally low prices was offered in four of the functional discount cases that have been studied—those involving Champion, General Motors, Standard Oil, and Namsco.[43] The question of meeting com-

---

In the Doubleday case, preferential prices had been charged three concerns classified as jobbers—American News Company, Baker & Taylor, and A. C. Mc-Clurg & Co. The contention was that Doubleday received valuable service and would have incurred expense if the favored distributor had not performed it. The hearing examiner rejected the argument on the ground that the law does not contemplate that the seller shall pay for what the distributor does to sell his own merchandise. In reviewing the decision, the Commission held that no reasonable relation had been shown between the amount of the discounts and the value of the services. However, by a vote of 3 to 2, it rejected the hearing examiner's statement of the applicable legal principle. The two dissenting Commissioners (Secrest and Mead) thought that what the buyer did in resale was not a service for which the seller could pay. The opinion for the Commission (written by Howrey, with Mason concurring and Gwynne concurring in the result) said, "It is possible . . . for a seller to shift to customers a number of distributional functions which the seller himself ordinarily performs. Such functions should, in our opinion, be recognized and reimbursed." (Docket 5897, Opinion of the Commission, mimeo., p. 5.) Subsequently, in answer to protests, Commissioner Gwynne disclaimed the views as to functional discounts expressed by the opinion, called attention to the fact that two other Commissioners had dissented on this point, and said that the decision did not represent a change in the Commission's views about functional discounts. (See release by the National Building Material Dealers Association, February 3, 1956, which quotes in full Mr. Gwynne's letter to Senator Charles E. Potter.)

In neither case was the issue raised whether, after defraying his additional costs, the favored buyer had a net advantage that might produce injurious results.

[43] The defense of meeting competition was also offered in four cases recently decided, those against *Whitaker Cable Corporation* (Docket 5722), *E. Edelmann and Company* (Docket 5770), *Doubleday and Company* (Docket 5897), and *Fruitvale Canning Co.* (Docket 5989). The first two companies submitted the defense for both volume discounts and functional discounts, and the argument as to both was commingled. For both companies, the matter has been discussed in the chapter on quantity and volume discounts, pp. 250-51.

Doubleday's defense of meeting competition was rejected by the hearing examiner on the ground that Doubleday had not shown "what prices respondent claims to have met, whether they were equally low, to whom they were extended, when and under what conditions" and that there was no showing that the concessions thus justified were "temporary, localized, individualized, defensive rather than aggressive and not part of a pricing system," and given to meet a competitor's price that was lawful. The Commission confirmed the decision without comment as to this matter. (Docket 5897, Initial Decision, filed January 7, 1955, p. 27.)

In the Fruitvale case, the hearing examiner rejected the defense of meeting

petition in good faith was not raised in the cases that were not tried nor in the Curtiss and Ruberoid cases.

In the General Motors case, the Commission found broadly that the evidence in the record did not show that price differentials were made in good faith to meet competition. No analysis of the evidence was supplied to support this finding. In the Namsco case, the evidence relevant to meeting competition consisted of a few statements in letters that the Commission regarded as "sparse, lacking in detail, contradictory, and neither substantial nor sufficient evidence." In the Champion case, the defense of meeting competition was offered only with reference to the price concessions to Atlas Supply Company and Socony Vacuum Oil Company. The Commission rejected it on the ground that Champion sold to Atlas in substantially the same manner as before the effective date of the Robinson-Patman Act; that Champion had not reduced prices to Atlas to meet certain verbal offers from other spark plug manufacturers; that Champion had reduced prices below those of A. C. Spark Plug Company, the only other concern from which Atlas actually bought; and that Champion had reduced its prices to Socony more than a year after the last offer from any other company.

The gasoline case provided a test of the significance of the defense of meeting competition. Standard contended that all of the concessions at issue in the case had been made to meet rival offers and that the favored customers could always have bought comparable gasoline at prices equally low or lower. Instead of determining the merit of this claim, the Commission (Commissioner Mason dissenting) concluded as a matter of law that:

> . . . It is not material whether the discriminations in price granted by the respondent to the said four dealers were made to meet equally low prices of competitors . . . because . . . this does not constitute a defense in the face of affirmative proof that the effect of the discrimination was to injure, destroy and prevent competition with the retail stations operated by the said named dealers and with stations operated by their retailer-customers.

Prior to June 19, 1936, the effective date of the Robinson-Patman amendment, Section 2 of the Clayton Act declared discriminations in

---

competition on the ground that, since Fruitvale's price to favored customers was sometimes higher than the prices of its competitors, "price was clearly not the deciding factor." The Commission quoted this finding with approval, and added that in some instances the prices charged to favored customers were lower than competitors' prices.

price to be unlawful when the effect of such discriminations may be substantially to lessen competition or create a monopoly, with provisos permitting, among other things, discriminations in price "in the same or different communities made in good faith to meet competition." Under that proviso a discrimination in price made in good faith to meet competition might under proper circumstances have been a complete defense to a charge of unlawful price discrimination.

In framing the Robinson-Patman Act Congress recognized that the provision in Section 2 of the Clayton Act permitting discriminations in good faith to meet competition was indefinite and uncertain and had the effect of weakening Section 2. Consequently Congress discarded the proviso in Section 2 which made the meeting of competition in good faith a complete or absolute justification and made price differences due to differences in cost, market changes and marketability of the goods the only absolute justifications now available to a respondent charged with unlawful price discrimination. Section 2(a) of the Clayton Act as amended by the Robinson-Patman Act contains no reference to lower prices made in good faith to meet competition. That matter was covered by Congress through a proviso in Section 2(b), and such proviso was "intended to operate only as a rule of evidence in a proceeding before the Federal Trade Commission."

A *prima facie* case of violation of Section 2(a) may be established by proving (1) jurisdiction, (2) goods of like grade and quality, and (3) discrimination in price. Discrimination in price here was shown by proving a difference in the prices charged competing customers. Based upon the *prima facie* case thus shown the Commission may draw from such *prima facie* case a rebuttable presumption that the effect of such discrimination may be to substantially lessen competition or tend to create a monopoly or to injure, destroy or prevent competition. The burden then shifts to the respondent.

In rebuttal of the *prima facie* case the respondent under Section 2(b) may show that the respondent's lower price was made in good faith to meet an equally low price of a competitor. However, such a showing is not an absolute defense to a charge of unlawful discrimination and proof of meeting a competitor's equally low price can be availed of only to the extent it may rebut the *prima facie* case.

. . . If proof of good faith in meeting an equally low price of a competitor is made, the Commission could no longer rely upon its *prima facie* case, but must show by additional and affirmative evidence that the effect of the discrimination may be to substantially lessen competition. . . . Where such injurious effect on competition is affirmatively proved, the proof made as to meeting an equally low price of a competitor under the proviso of Section 2(b) does not constitute a substantive justification or defense.[44]

---

[44] 41 FTC 281-83.

The Commission supported this interpretation of the law by analyzing the legislative history to show that, whereas the original Clayton Act had made meeting competition a substantive defense, the Robinson-Patman Act had referred to it only in the procedural section. The Commission also argued that a limit to the right to meet competition was necessarily implied in the purposes of the law.

> The provision for a showing of good faith to meet an equally low price of a competitor cannot be construed as a *carte blanche* exemption to a respondent to engage in discriminations in price which have the adverse effects on competition proscribed under Section 2(a). Such a construction would constitute recognition of the soundness of the principle that one competitor's violation of law justified its violation by another. It would also justify discrimination by a chain organization to meet the equally low price of a single unit competitor who had not discriminated at all as well as discrimination to meet the price of any competitor whose discrimination is lawful because justified by cost differences. It would defeat the substantive purposes and requirements of Section 2(a) in such situations as well as in the present case, where discrimination to meet the equally low prices of a competitor has produced the adverse effects on competition which it was the main purpose of the section and of the Act to prevent.[45]

Judicial review of the gasoline case centered on this construction of the statute. The Seventh Circuit assumed that the evidence of Standard's good faith was conclusive, and from its own analysis of the legislative history reached the same conclusion as the Commission regarding the inconclusiveness of the defense that competition had been met in good faith. The Court pointed to the fact that Standard's good faith had to do with the quality of its relations to its own competitors, whereas the injury found by the Commission pertained to the competition among Standard's customers. "Whereas here the discrimination is between purchasers who are in competition, and the competition which is alleged and proved to be injured is among the retail customers of the favored purchasers and other retailers, the fact that the seller's discriminatory price was made to meet his own competition is not controlling."[46]

The Supreme Court divided five to three, with one justice not participating. Mr. Justice Burton's majority opinion reversed the Commission and the circuit court and held that a showing that competition was met

[45] *Ibid.*, p. 283.
[46] 173 F. 2d 210, 216.

in good faith was a complete defense. Since the Commission had not decided whether Standard's good faith was actually proved, the case was remanded to the Commission to make appropriate findings on this point and thereafter to reconsider the decision.

The majority opinion rested partly on the view that the validity of the defense of meeting competition had already been recognized in previous cases and partly on the argument that the right to meet competition is central to the preservation of competition itself.

> We need not now reconcile, in its entirety, the economic theory which underlies the Robinson-Patman Act with that of the Sherman and Clayton Acts. It is enough to say that Congress did not seek by the Robinson-Patman Act either to abolish competition or so radically to curtail it that a seller would have no substantial right of self-defense against a price raid by a competitor. For example, if a large customer requests his seller to meet a temptingly lower price offered to him by one of his seller's competitors, the seller may well find it essential, as a matter of business survival, to meet that price rather than to lose the customer. It might be that this customer is the seller's only available market for the major portion of the seller's product, and that the loss of this customer would result in forcing a much higher unit cost and higher sales price upon the seller's other customers. There is nothing to show a congressional purpose, in such a situation, to compel the seller to choose only between ruinously cutting its prices to all its customers to match the price offered to one, or refusing to meet the competition and then ruinously raising its prices to its remaining customers to cover increased unit costs. There is, on the other hand, plain language and established practice which permits a seller, through Section 2(b), to retain a customer by realistically meeting in good faith the price offered to that customer, without necessarily changing the seller's price to its other customers. . . . It must have been obvious to Congress that any price reduction to any dealer may always affect competition at that dealer's level as well as at the dealer's resale level, whether or not the reduction to the dealer is discriminatory. Likewise it must have been obvious to Congress that any price reductions initiated by a seller's competitor would, if not met by the seller, affect competition at the beneficiary's level or among the beneficiary's customers just as much as if those reductions had been met by the seller. The proviso in Section 2(b), as interpreted by the Commission, would not be available when there was or might be an injury to competition at a resale level. So interpreted, the proviso would have such little, if any, applicability as to be practically meaningless.[47]

[47] 340 U.S. 231, 249-50.

The minority of the Supreme Court found in the legislative history support for the Commission's interpretation of the law, and regarded the majority's view as a nullification of the amendment as to meeting competition, which the Congress had included in the Robinson-Patman Act. To make meeting competition a complete defense, it thought, would defeat the congressional purpose.

> . . . Adoption of petitioner's position would permit a seller of nationally distributed goods to discriminate in favor of large chain retailers, for the seller could give to the large retailer a price lower than that charged to small retailers, and could then completely justify its discrimination by showing that the large retailer had first obtained the same low price from a local low-cost producer of competitive goods. This is the very type of competition that Congress sought to remedy.[48]

In its revised decision, the Commission found that Standard's concessions had not been made in good faith. It admitted that Standard had had substantial reasons for believing that "if it ceased granting tank-car prices to Citrin-Kolb, Wayne, and Stikeman and continued to refuse the tank-car price to Ned's Auto Supply Company it would lose these accounts"; for the first three "had already been recognized as entitled to the tank-car price under the commonly accepted standards of the industry," and Ned's "had achieved a volume of distribution which brought it within the range where it was likely to be so recognized by a major oil company at any time." In spite of this admission, the Commission denied Standard's good faith on three principal grounds—first, that, since Standard knew or should have known that the concessions could not be cost-justified and "continually created the probability of injury to competition between retail dealers," it had a duty to review the price policy it was following when the Robinson-Patman Act took effect and bring that policy into conformity with the new statute, but had made no real attempt to do so; second, that the discriminations were "not the result of departures from a nondiscriminatory price scale," but were made in accord with Standard's usual practice of granting the tank-car price to buyers in bulk who had adequate storage facilities and credit; and third, that Standard knew that its major competitors granted tank-car prices on substantially the

[48] Ibid., p. 263.

same basis, so that if the grant by any one of them was held to be in good faith, the same defense would apply to all the others and all would be relieved of any need to establish nondiscriminatory prices. The Commission said it did not believe "that the statute provides a means of effectively insulating any particular pricing pattern from attack or that it guarantees that so long as a pricing pattern in effect prior to 1936 remains undisturbed price discriminations made pursuant to that pattern may be lawfully continued."[49]

Two commissioners dissented from the finding. Commissioner Mason, who had dissented from the original finding, referred to that dissent. Commissioner Carretta, in a long analysis of the evidence, concluded that in the years preceding the complaint Standard had lost four of its seven jobbers in Detroit but had later recovered one of them, Stikeman, and that Standard's four favored customers were qualified to receive jobber prices according to the commonly accepted standards of the industry. He found evidence of Standard's good faith in the slowness and reluctance with which it reduced its price to Ned's and in the fact that various offers had been received by the other three favored customers.[50]

The conclusion of the Commission that the price concessions lacked good faith was rejected by the Seventh Circuit in a second review in May 1956.[51] The Court held that, since the defense of meeting competition was preserved in the Robinson-Patman Act, a concern whose price concessions were made in good faith to meet a competitor's prices had no obligation to withdraw or revise them when that act was passed; and that knowledge that the concessions might injure competition and were not cost-justified was irrelevant to the question whether these concessions had been made to meet a competitor's price. It rejected as incorrect the finding of the Commission that the discriminations were not the result of departures from a nondiscriminatory price scale, and concluded that "the record affirmatively demonstrates to the contrary." In support of this view, it pointed out that only four customers in Detroit obtained the concession and that bargaining and haggling preceded the grant, for example in the case of Ned's. It found no logic in the Commission's objection to the probable reciprocal use of the defense of meeting competition by the major oil companies, both because the situa-

[49] 49 FTC 952-54.
[50] Ibid., pp. 956-80.
[51] 233 F. 2d 649.

tion had not yet arisen and because "It is strange reasoning that one seller should be deprived of the defense provided in 2(b) because some other seller might also invoke its protection." The broad scope of good faith as seen by the Court was clearly expressed in the statement, "We think that a seller must be permitted in the exercise of a sound judgment to determine when and under what circumstances it will reduce its price in order to meet that of a competitor, and a right to require that a purchaser be possessed of the facilities for storing, handling, and distributing the product."[52]

In January 1958 the Supreme Court sustained the decision of the circuit court in favor of Standard Oil Company of Indiana by a vote of 5 to 4.[53] The majority opinion was obviously designed to settle the proceeding on the narrowest possible grounds. The court dismissed the argument of the Commission that Standard and its competitors had reciprocally adopted a discriminatory pricing system on the ground that the Commission had not incorporated in the case a showing of such action by Standard's competitors, that the Commission had dismissed parallel cases against some of the competitors, and that the findings in the Standard case indicated disparities of pricing practice inconsistent with the argument of the Commission. Noting that both sides were agreed that discrimination by Standard pursuant to a pricing system would preclude a finding of good faith, the court treated the case as dependent solely on a factual issue as to whether the price concessions in Detroit expressed such a pricing system. Holding that the court of appeals had fairly assessed the record on this question of fact, the majority sustained the appellate decision on the well-established ground that, where there has been no arbitrary and unreasonable assessment of the facts, the judgment of a lower court on such matters will not be overturned. The opinion made no reference to the statement of the appellate court that the respondent's knowledge regarding the injurious nature of the discrimination was irrelevant to the question of good faith. The controversy over whether Standard had a duty to withdraw or revise its price concessions after the passage of the Robinson-Patman Act was brushed aside by the statement that the crucial question was why the price concessions were continued after 1936 and that the appellate court had appropriately found that the maintenance of the concessions was due to efforts by competitors to lure the favored customers away. Thus

[52] *Ibid.*, pp. 654-55.
[53] *FTC* v. *Standard Oil Co.*, 78 S. Ct. 369.

the opinion left open a question as to the conditions under which revision of price concessions originally lawful might have been requisite to good faith in the absence of such efforts by competitors.

The minority opinion found in the record proof of the Commission's conclusion that Standard had adopted a discriminatory pricing system like that of its competitors and held that this circumstance was inconsistent with Standard's good faith. It declared that good faith exists only where a respondent meets a lawful lower price and is absent when a respondent merely matches a predatory pricing system or meets a competitor's pirating offers. Moreover, it denied Standard's good faith on the ground that Standard had arbitrarily defined the recipients of its favors as jobbers without reference to the function they performed or the cost of serving them; that the definition amounted to a device to give big retailers one price and small ones another; and that good faith could not rest on such a plainly deceptive contrivance.

The issue as to Standard's good faith is closely related to the breadth of the competitive problem involved in the Standard case. The Commission's complaint, findings, and order all pertained to the distribution of gasoline in Detroit, and the analysis of Standard's good faith, both by the Commission and by the circuit court, was confined to this segment of the gasoline market. With the case thus conceived, the substantive economic question has to do with the vigor of competition among the gasoline distributors in Detroit. In effect, Standard was charged with sabotage of its own direct-buying retail outlets for the benefit of its favored jobbers and their customers, and the Commission's order sought to eliminate that sabotage.

Thus conceived, the case is unrealistic. In 1940, less than 19 per cent of the gasoline Standard sold in the Detroit area moved to retailers through intermediaries. In 1953, 20 per cent did so. Standard's reliance on jobbing channels was decidedly less than that of certain other major oil companies that sold in the area.[54] It is difficult to believe that Standard chose to damage the dealers, on whom it chiefly relied, for the sake of others who handled a minor part of the volume.

Commentators on the case have offered several hypotheses to explain

[54] In 1940, Socony Vacuum sold nearly 82 per cent to intermediaries; Gulf, nearly 47 per cent; and Texas, more than 44 per cent. In 1953, the corresponding percentages for these three companies were, roughly, 36, 48, and 38. See Note by Norman M. Gold and Richard P. McGrath, "Functional Discounts Under the Robinson-Patman Act; the Standard Oil Case," 67 Harvard Law Review 294, 314.

Standard's price policy. Standard declares that Detroit was a dumping ground for excess gasoline, that falling consumption had led to a pitched battle for sales, and that it was defending itself against raids by competitors.[55] In general, this explanation is supported by John McGee in the most thorough analysis of the case that has yet been printed.[56] However, other interpretations have been given. According to one view, Standard wished to use the competition of a few retail price cutters to keep retailers' margins low and obtain for itself as large a share as possible of the consumer price.[57] According to another interpretation, the major oil companies had been maintaining tank-wagon prices by tacit or overt agreement; but some of them had failed to observe the agreement and Standard reduced prices to retaliate. A third hypothesis em-

[55] Statement of Hammond E. Chaffetz, *To Amend Section 2 of the Clayton Act,* Hearings (1956), pp. 453-54.

[56] John S. McGee, "Price Discrimination and Competitive Effects: The Standard Oil of Indiana Case," 23 *University of Chicago Law Review* 398-473. McGee's analysis is that the opening of the East Texas field in 1930 greatly increased the supply of gasoline; that the combined effect of the depression and the larger supply was a sustained fall in prices; that the Detroit market was in peculiar difficulty because refining capacity in Michigan was growing, and in 1938, when national consumption of gasoline was rising, Michigan consumption was falling; that cut-rate chains of filling stations and jobbers of gasoline not supplied by the major refiners became important and rapidly growing factors in the Detroit market in the latter part of the 1930's, with the share of the latter increasing from 6.8 per cent of the market in 1936 to 15.2 per cent in 1939; that price reductions in tank-wagon prices and at retail were prevalent in Detroit, with the latter exceeding the former; that much and perhaps most of the price competition took the form of what the law regards as discriminatory concessions; that grant of the status of jobber was one of the techniques by which refiners, including the major companies, competed for the business of the larger distributors; that Standard had lost four jobbers, one through business failure and three through lower prices granted by Shell and Gulf in 1933 and 1934; that Standard's concessions to the four favored concerns were a part of the process by which the stronger distributors obtained lower prices in a disorderly market; and that during the period covered by the case Standard barely managed to hold its share of the Detroit market (17.1 per cent in 1936, 17.4 per cent in 1937, 16.4 per cent in 1938, 17.4 per cent in 1939, 16.2 per cent in 1940). McGee sees in the discrimination not only a "symptom of competitive vigor" but also an effective bar to the various efforts made by organized retailers to fix prices by cartelization. However, he thinks "that the declining price level injured some gasoline retailers as well as refiners. And, to the extent that price discrimination was the device through which price cutting was effectuated, price discrimination must carry some of the blame for these injuries." *Ibid.,* p. 463.

[57] In the United States Court of Appeals for the Seventh Circuit, *Standard Oil Company, Petitioner,* v. *FTC,* No. 11,409, Brief on Behalf of National Congress of Petroleum Retailers, Inc., and Retail Gasoline Dealers Association of Michigan, Inc., *Amici Curiae,* undated, pp. 7-11.

phasizes the point that independent refiners were becoming important in the Detroit area by selling gasoline below the price of the advertised major brands, and interprets Standard's price cuts as efforts to exclude independent refiners or to limit their share of the market by meeting their prices, and to do so in a way that would place as much as possible of the burden of price reduction on Standard's dealers in the form of reduced margins rather than on Standard in the form of reduced tank-wagon prices.[58]

To varying degrees, these different theories can be and have been supported by bits of evidence selected from the trial record and other sources; but since the proceeding did not rest on any of the theories, there was no adequate presentation of the evidence pro and con, and it is impossible to establish conclusively from the record the truth or falsity of the various opinions. It is reasonable to suppose that Standard's policies in Detroit did not stand alone, but were related to its general distributive and pricing policies.[59] It is also reasonable to suppose that these general policies, and local departures from them, if any, were substantially influenced by the strategic relationship of the major oil companies to one another and to independent suppliers. The major oil refiners have been repeatedly involved in antitrust proceedings concerned with problems of conspiracy, monopolization, and vertical price control; and Standard of Indiana has been involved along with others in some of these cases. The question of Standard's good faith in price reductions in Detroit may be approached, as the circuit court apparently thought it should be, by simply determining whether Standard's customers, before receiving low prices from Standard, had received equally low offers from others. If the criterion of good faith is to be so narrow, the Commission's

---

[58] The second and third hypotheses are advanced jointly in Bernard Weisberg, "Price Discrimination in Gasoline Marketing: the Detroit Jobbers Case," 19 *University of Chicago Law Review* 61-64. The third also appears in a letter by Commissioner Kern of the Federal Trade Commission on March 1, 1956 (see *Congressional Record*, Vol. 102, Pt. 4, 84 Cong. 2 sess., p. 5390), and in an article by Robert A. Wallace and Paul H. Douglas, "Antitrust Policies and the New Attack on the Federal Trade Commission," 19 *University of Chicago Law Review* 24-26. Various errors of fact in the article by Wallace and Douglas are analyzed in the article by McGee.

[59] Indeed, price policy in Detroit, for Standard and others, has been affected by such broad considerations as the increase in water shipment of gasoline at low prices, the lowering of the charges on the Great Lakes pipeline, the development of new refineries near Detroit, and similar factors.

finding as to good faith was obviously wrong. The question of good faith may also be approached, as the Commission sought to approach it, by considering the implications of Standard's entire course of conduct. But if this is the basis for judgment, the Commission's attack on the problem was unduly narrow. In such an analysis, the problem of good faith (like the problem of injury) should be considered in the light of Standard's place in gasoline manufacture and distribution and its relation to other gasoline manufacturers and distributors, not merely in the light of the history of particular price concessions.

The Supreme Court's decision that meeting competition was a complete defense had a substantial effect on the Commission's selection of cases. In July 1954, the general counsel of the National Congress of Petroleum Retailers sent to the Commission, on behalf of service stations in Jackson, Mississippi, a complaint that the Texas Company was allowing a one-cent discount to its stations in Jackson that was not available to other retailers in the vicinity. In August, the director of the Commission's Bureau of Investigation replied that in practically all similar instances that had been investigated:

> . . . It has been established that the complained-of discriminatory pricing practices were being followed in connection with local gasoline price wars which were the outgrowth of efforts of the major oil companies to meet competition of dealers selling nonbranded gasoline at reduced prices. Under such circumstances no corrective action has been taken by the Commission because of the defense available to the sellers under Section 2(b). . . . A seller is within his legal rights in confining his price reductions to dealers in the vicinity of the dealer or dealers whose competition he seeks to meet, even though such action results in injury to customers to whom similar reductions are not made available.[60]

During the progress of the Standard Oil case the validity of the defense of meeting competition was widely debated in the trade and legal press and in Congress. As appears in the chapter on territorial price discrimination by formula, the status of the right to meet competition in good faith was crucially important in the basing-point cases. The decision in the gasoline case was a central subject of debate during the effort to modify the Robinson-Patman Act with respect to delivered pricing formulas. Subsequently, the controversy over meeting competition fo-

[60] Quoted in *To Amend Section 2 of the Clayton Act,* Hearings (1956), p. 89.

cused on a series of bills designed to cover that particular subject.[61] Congressional committees considering the proposed legislation obtained repeated statements from the Commission as to what the Commission thought was the existing status of the defense of meeting competition and what it thought that status should be. The Commission repeatedly changed its views, primarily because the balance of opinion was altered as the membership of the Commission changed.[62]

Until the Supreme Court announced its decision that meeting competition in good faith was a complete defense, proposals to amend the law (incorporated in the basing-point proposals) were intended to establish the conclusiveness of the defense clearly by new legislation. After the court decision, similar proposals continued to be offered, but in addition groups desiring to strengthen the Robinson-Patman Act offered proposals to amend the law to limit the defense. The status of the current controversy and the nature of the issues involved are discussed in Chapter 17.

Results of the Functional Discount Cases

Little evidence is available on the effect of the Commission's action against discriminatory functional discounts in most of the cases that have been studied. The Nutrine case was decided late in 1939. In January 1940 Nutrine vainly asked the Commission to postpone the effective date of its price-discrimination order for ninety days or more. The request was supported by a statement that each of five identified competitors was currently engaged in price discrimination and that Nutrine had requested that parallel cases be brought against them, thus far in vain.

> Before the Federal Trade Commission issued its order in this case, your respondent endeavored to put into effect a price plan which it was advised was strictly in accord with the several provisions of Section 2 of the Clayton Act. For instance, a one-price plan was tried. This plan failed because competitors of your respondent, knowing of

[61] See S. 719 and H. R. 2820, 82 Cong.; S. 540, S. 1353, S. 1357, S. 1377, S. 1752, S. 3646, H. R. 635, H. R. 4170, H. R. 5848, H. R. 8190, H. R. 8191, 83 Cong.; S. 11, S. 780, H. R. 11, H. R. 89, H. R. 1840, H. R. 2577, H. R. 2611, H. R. 2690, H. R. 2850, H. R. 3949, H. R. 4824, H. R. 9487, H. R. 10619, 84 Cong. After the Eighty-fourth Congress, attention focused on the companion bills S. 11 and H. R. 11.

[62] See below, Chap. 17, pp. 576-80.

such a price plan, used through their sales representatives and sent out by mail, price lists that contained prices that were lower than what was being quoted in your respondent's list.

Your respondent endeavored to prepare and have available to the sales representatives price lists that would meet the competition of the competitors. This meant doing business at a small profit because of the one-price plan. Your respondent's competitors used their lower price lists on only selected and choice accounts.

Your respondent then endeavored to meet this competition by permitting sales representatives to meet competition as they found it. First, your respondent's officers endeavored to pass upon the advisability and justification for such price concessions. It was found that this was impractical, because retail dealers buying candy would not wait two or three days to ascertain if their order had been accepted. The amount of sales was too small to justify telegraphic communications between the salesmen and the officers.

It is respectfully submitted that if your respondent grants unto its sales representatives the right to meet competition without the consent of the officers that such a plan would lead to further chaos and perhaps eventually to further discrimination. . . .

It is a belief of this respondent that if it is forced to immediately put into effect a price plan in conformity with the Federal Trade Commission's order to cease and desist, that it will suffer a large loss in business, that it will be compelled to decrease its sales staff and further, that it will suffer an irreparable injury. . . . It is indeed a hardship for one company to be ordered to do something by the Commission which order involves a practice indulged in by practically all other competitors long prior to the time that the others are proceeded against. . . . As soon as this competitive situation is cleared up, it will not be a difficult task to institute and use a one-price plan or such price plans that will meet with the requirements of the Commission's order.

This respondent has close to ten thousand dealer accounts. Some dealers buy as low as $15.00 and others over $20,000.00 per year. Classification of these accounts has been attempted. As soon as the classification has been completed, it is found that some competitor has placed the account on a better classification. Eventually it was found that the list of exceptions was greater than the original classification and eventually the same confusion existed as was before. . . .[63]

Nutrine went out of business in 1951. In the present study, no one has been found to supply a reliable account of its practices and fortunes in the decade between the order and the disappearance of the company.

[63] Docket 3756, Motion to Postpone Effective Date of Order, January 1940, pp. 1-3.

In the American Oil case, in which a discount available to certain chains of taxicabs was also granted on sales of gasoline at retail by a filling station that supplied the chains, American Oil professed to be unaware of the fact that discount gasoline was being diverted to the retail market. When it discovered the diversion, it altered the contract so that General Finance Company, which represented the taxicab fleets, paid the regular price on all gasoline and subsequently received a rebate on the portion it certified had been supplied to its taxis. This plan took effect before the Commission's order. At the time of the compliance reports, American had substituted a plan under which it charged the dealer price on gasoline delivered to the General Finance Company's filling station and the commercial consumer price on gasoline delivered to its garage for use in its taxicabs. General Finance Company ceased operating in the early 1940's. None of the taxicab companies participating in this scheme receives a special discount at the present time from American Oil. In general, these companies do not resell gasoline to the public; but at the time of the interviews one of them did so.[64] As a general policy, American continues to make special prices in competitive circumstances to owners of fleets of motor cars on gasoline supplied for consumption in these fleets, but not for resale.

The golf ball case resulted in the stoppage of price concessions by manufacturers to members of the Professional Golfers Association. Apparently, the manufacturers welcomed this change. Special brands are now produced for sale through professional golfers, but in quality and price these are identical with the brands sold through other channels. The attitudes of manufacturers toward professional golfers are now expressed, not in discounts and advertising allowances, but in the degree of reliance placed on professional golfers as distributors of golf balls. In this respect there is considerable diversity. Of five manufacturers about whom information is available, one sells exclusively and one primarily through professional golfers, while three sell chiefly through other channels. The Professional Golfers Association has been negotiating with manufacturers in an effort to devise a lawful and acceptable way by which it can obtain royalties for the use of its PGA trademark.[65]

The order in the straw hat case resulted in a discontinuance of special discounts to buying groups by Caradine and in Caradine's loss of the business of buying groups to competitors through price competition.

[64] This company subsequently ceased to buy from American.
[65] See above, pp. 177-78.

Caradine's employees have decreased from 700 to 150 and the sales volume from $5,000,000 to less than $2,000,000, but this decline is attributed to a decrease in the manufacture of harvest hats and to Caradine's higher wage scale. At present Caradine quotes different prices to jobbers, chains, and retailers. The Commission recently investigated compliance with the order and has not raised question about the existing price structure. Egyptian Retailers Association, which formerly had one hundred general stores as members, was put out of business, according to its former secretary, by the loss of discounts in situations in which the change in pricing practices was attributable to the Robinson-Patman Act. This opinion was expressed in discussion of the Caradine case, but there is no indication that Caradine's business was regarded as an important part of the loss.

In the window glass case, the effect of the Commission's order cannot readily be disentangled from that of other developments. A consent decree was entered under the Sherman Act against many of the same companies in 1948, and the practices covered by that decree included many of those against which the Commission's order was directed.[66] Moreover, in the Commission case and the Sherman Act case, the issue of discrimination had been subordinate to that of conspiracy in restraint of trade. Members of the industry now discuss what they have done since the 1948 decree, rather than since the Commission's order .

The Commission's order of 1937 forbade the respondent manufacturers and distributors from conspiring to prevent any distributor from buying from any of the manufacturers on terms not generally accorded to others or to add any amount to the manufacturer's price for window glass in carload lots for direct shipment. The Commission also ordered the distributors to cease inducing the manufacturers to discriminate. It ordered the manufacturers, individually, to cease discriminating between carload lot purchasers to whom shipment was made direct from the factory, but provided specifically that the order did not prevent manufacturers' jobbing warehouses "from selling carload lots on a brokerage basis at prices commonly obtained" by independent jobbers. The 1948 decree under the Sherman Act included provisions forbidding the defendants to conspire to fix price differentials or discounts or to discriminate against or refuse to sell to jobbers, distributors, or dealers.

[66] District Court for the Northern District of Ohio, Western Division, Civil Action No. 5239, *U.S.* v. *Libbey-Owens-Ford Glass Co., et al.,* Final Judgment, Oct. 30, 1948.

It also prohibited them individually from refusing to sell or discriminating in filling orders for pool cars or because the buyer had not been previously listed as a quantity buyer, and from selling at unreasonably low or discriminatory prices for the purpose of destroying a competitor or suppressing competition. Under other provisions of the decree, Pittsburgh Plate Glass and Libbey-Owens-Ford were required to increase the number of establishments allowed to buy at factory prices by 10 per cent.

There is general agreement among the manufacturers and distributors interviewed that sales from the factory are now made by manufacturers in carload lots at a uniform price, while manufacturers' warehouses sell at a higher uniform warehouse price. Between 1937 and 1948 the number of customers to whom one manufacturer sold window glass at the factory increased 124 per cent. In the five years following 1948, this manufacturer increased the number of establishments that bought flat glass[67] at the factory by more than 31 per cent. Some distributors have found that their manufacturing supplier has taken away a part of their carload sales to large buyers and, by extending his jobbing warehouse sales, has also taken some of their business in less than carload quantities.

Discrimination still exists, but in a form apparently not forbidden by the order or by the consent decree. Certain manufacturers refuse to supply carload lots from the factory to some customers who wish to buy there. When these customers buy at the manufacturer's warehouse at the warehouse price, or from an independent distributor, they pay more than their competitors who are permitted to buy at the factory. Some independent distributors reduce this disadvantage for their customers by giving discounts on carload purchases. The difference in the manufacturer's price is presumably justified by the cost difference associated with the different method of selling. Thus selection of customers has taken the place of a factory price differential as the method of discrimination.

It is doubtful that, from the point of view of those concerns that are excluded from factory buying, the change is any improvement. One purpose of the distinction between quantity buyers and carload buyers in the window glass industry was apparently to divide the market between manufacturers and distributors. The quantity buyer had an incentive to buy at the factory. The carload buyer who bought at the factory did

[67] Flat glass includes not only window glass but also plate glass and certain glass specialties.

worse rather than better than if he bought from the distributor. Since this arrangement was a part of a general conspiracy, it was uniform for all participants; but in the absence of conspiracy, the individual manufacturers may still wish to adopt policies on the number of distributors they will use and on the character of the business they will refer to their distributors. Where such a vertical division of the market is undertaken by a manufacturer through selection of his customers and refusal to sell to certain kinds of customers, the Robinson-Patman Act does not forbid it.[68] However, a policy of refusal to sell may seem to sellers and buyers unduly rigid in failing to take account of recurrent unusual situations in which the buyer has special need to buy at the factory and the manufacturer is especially willing to let him do so. Flexibility can be introduced if the division of the market is achieved by discounts rather than by refusal to sell. In such a discount policy certain classes of customers are discouraged from buying at the factory through disadvantageous prices but are allowed to buy there whenever they are willing to pay a premium for the privilege. But to base the program on price differences is to engage in price discrimination that probably is unlawful. In the present state of the law, the harsher measure is permitted, while the gentler one is forbidden.

The Standard Oil case was finally won by Standard Oil, but was still pending on appeal during field study of the case for this book. Standard continued to grant lower prices to its four customers in Detroit. Whereas the differential was a cent and a half per gallon when the case began,

[68] See *Chicago Seating Co. v. Karpen*, 177 F. 2d 863. See also Docket 6018, *General Foods Corporation*. On February 15, 1956, the Commission confirmed an initial decision by its hearing examiner by which, though General Foods was found to have discriminated illegally in price, no unlawful discrimination was found in the fact that some customers were allowed to buy direct from the manufacturer while some of their competitors were required to buy through wholesalers at substantially higher prices. This part of the decision followed from a finding that the indirect buyers were not customers of General Foods but of the wholesalers from whom they bought. The present practice as to window glass is not exactly analogous, however, since warehouse sales of window glass are made by the manufacturer, not the wholesaler. It is noteworthy that a recent case (Docket 6743, *Grove Laboratories*) included a complaint under the Federal Trade Commission Act charging that the seller had followed an unfair practice in requiring some of its customers to buy specified minimum quantities while others were allowed to buy in any quantity. The case resulted in a consent order against the practice on December 2, 1957. The situation differed from that in window glass in that there was no segregation of customers by place of purchase like the segregation of window glass buyers into those who buy at the factory and those who buy at warehouses.

during the present study it was about three cents per gallon. The difference in methods of delivery that had originally seemed to bear some relation to the price differential was no longer characteristic of the market. With the development of large tank trucks, tank-car delivery had become infrequent, and jobbers usually took delivery at the seller's terminal in tank trucks, which carried the gasoline direct to retailers' stations. The industry's definition of a jobber had come to be a concern that serviced twelve or more filling stations.

There have been changes in the structure and size of the jobbers. Stikeman has become a wholly owned subsidiary of Wayne. Ned's was sold in 1954 to Firestone Tire and Rubber Company. During the case Ned's ceased to buy direct from Standard, but instead bought through Merchants Petroleum Service, an intermediary organized by the owners of Ned's expressly to supply Ned's with gasoline. Thus, in form, Ned's bought as a retailer through a jobber that did no retail business. The same method of purchase continued after the acquisition of Ned's by Firestone.

Recurrent price cutting still takes place in Detroit, typically initiated by concerns that obtain their gasoline from other sources than Standard. During the present study, low prices were being offered by two large distributors whose gasoline comes from independent refineries. The predominant opinion among those interviewed[69] was that price cutting on gasoline is primarily the result of overbuilding of filling stations, fostered by suppliers who are seeking an advantageous distributive position; that when retailers are too numerous, some of them compete for gallonage by price reductions; and that suppliers participate in the price wars, often by localized price reductions, in an effort to maintain their place in the market by protecting their distributive outlets.

In 1955 the House Committee on the Judiciary sought to ascertain the magnitude of the problem of competition between jobbers and direct-buying retailers in the gasoline industry by an inquiry addressed to 19 major oil companies.[70] Standard of Indiana replied that it sold 4.15 per

---

[69] One producer, however, doubts that filling stations have been overbuilt. It has reduced, over-all, the number of its own stations. It points out that gasoline consumption has increased and that new stations have often been established to serve newly developed neighborhoods; and says that in its opinion volume per station is generally higher than in the prewar period.

[70] The correspondence appears in *Price Discrimination, the Robinson-Patman Act and Related Matters,* Hearings before the House Select Committee on Small Business, 84 Cong. 1 sess., Pt. 3, Appendix, pp. 1251-66.

cent of its volume to 32 jobbers who competed with retailers. There were comparable replies from 12 other companies.[71] Of these, 3 reported no such sales.[72] For the other companies, the number of such jobbers varied from 2 to 113 and the volume sold to them from 1 to 10 per cent of the seller's total. Among the 10 companies that made such sales, Standard of Indiana ranked fourth in the percentage of volume thus sold and tied for fifth in the number of such jobber customers. In an accompanying letter, Standard said:

. . . The jobber is becoming increasingly an important factor in the distribution of petroleum products. In our marketing territory the number of jobbers has been increasing and they have also been increasing their share of the market. No supplying company can ignore this phenomenon. While sometimes it is practicable to distribute only through jobbers in some areas and only through retailers in others, this is not always feasible . . . choice is limited by the opportunities available and the competitive pressures that are encountered.[73]

After the Ruberoid order had been sustained on appeal, Ruberoid applied throughout the country a program it had adopted in New Orleans, the place where the discrimination had taken place, during the pendency of the case. Under this plan, wholesalers were to receive a functional discount of 6 per cent, and concerns that combined wholesaling with other kinds of business were to buy at the price paid by retailers, to make monthly written certification of the amount of their wholesale sales, and to receive the wholesale discount as a rebate on the amount certified. This plan proved unworkable because it was not adopted by Ruberoid's competitors, was resented by customers, and was found to result in inaccuracy and falsification.[74]

[71] In addition, Shell reported that it made such sales to "very few" jobbers and that the percentage of its volume involved was "infinitesimal."

[72] Sun Oil sold to jobbers, but not in territory where they competed with its retailers. Standard Oil of Ohio sold to jobbers through a separate corporation, using brands different from those it sold to retailers. Standard of California gave no details.

[73] Ibid., p. 1254.

[74] Statement of Cyrus Austin, Counsel for the Ruberoid Company of New York City, in A Study of the Antitrust Laws, Hearings before the Senate Committee on the Judiciary, 84 Cong. 1 sess. Pt. 3, pp. 1205-07.

Commenting on this kind of problem, the vice-chairman of Minneapolis-Honeywell told a Senate committee, "In this day of multiple-function distributors it is becoming harder and harder for a manufacturer like Honeywell to sort out its customers and to determine the extent to which various types of customers are

Ruberoid then substituted a one-price policy. Where there was no problem of split function, Ruberoid sold to all buyers at a uniform carload or truck-load price, except that it granted a functional discount to authorized wholesalers on carloads and truckloads invoiced to the wholesaler but shipped direct to the retailer or roofing contractor. Where a wholesaler had split functions, he received the wholesale discount on all his purchases, but the same discount was given to all retailers in the same trading area who bought direct from Ruberoid. Thus discrimination was eliminated from Ruberoid's pricing. However, inequality continued at the retail level, since the direct-buying retailers paid less than the retailers who bought through wholesalers, most of whom bought in quantities less than a carload or truckload. Since, where there are split-function wholesalers, retailers who buy carloads or truckloads now buy directly from Ruberoid at the same price as wholesalers, wholesalers in such areas who had large retailer customers have lost them.

In the Sherwin-Williams case the part of the order applicable to functional discounts directed Lowe and Lucas to cease granting distributors' discounts on the portion of the purchases that the distributors resold at retail. As a result, distributors were required to submit records of their wholesale and retail sales or affidavits as to the amounts involved. There appears to have been no other direct effect on functional discounts. However, largely as a result of the case, Sherwin-Williams substantially changed its distributive practices. It undertook a program of merchandising through its own retail stores, and now has about 2,000 such stores. Its trade sales pass in large part through this channel. This development may be responsible for the fact that the large paint manufacturers now sell paint directly to dealers on a uniform-price basis.[75]

---

entitled to particular trade discounts. . . . In the past we have had to ask ourselves and our counsel whether the Robinson-Patman Act requires us to attempt to police what our customers do with controls purchased from us in order to make sure that they are not sold in competition with other customers in a different trade classification. I am told by counsel . . . that a seller in our position may be subject to legal risks if it does not check up on customers' pricing tactics—and also subject to legal risks under other statutes if he does so." See *ibid.*, p. 1338.

Similarly the counsel for the National Standard Parts Association testified that, according to a survey in a trade publication, wholesalers of automobile parts do about 13 to 15 per cent of their business at retail. He commented, "I don't know how anybody can police that, unless we get so much paper business that you won't have time to sell merchandise." *Ibid.*, p. 1268.

[75] The Commission's order also required Sherwin-Williams to cease pooling and

Namsco is a manufacturer of automotive equipment, such as hub caps and wheel discs. Like other such manufacturers, it sells to various types of buyers, including independent distributors of automotive supplies, co-operatives, fleet operators, repairmen, rebuilders, and automobile manufacturers who sell replacement parts to their dealers. The Commission found that Namsco had quoted less than its usual jobber prices to three groups of customers. First, it sold to eight special accounts at discounts of from 10 to 17 per cent below the jobbers' price. Second, for three years, beginning in 1947, it granted five co-operative organizations discounts of from 5 to 10 per cent below jobbers' prices. Third, beginning in May 1949, it issued a white list with prices below jobbers' prices by as much as 33⅓ per cent, and used this white list in selling to 104 buyers. Most of those who bought from the white list were jobbers affiliated with chain-store outlets from which the largest volume of purchases was obtained. The ostensible purpose of the white list was to retain the business of these buyers "because of competitive prices."

After the Commission's order, Namsco apparently established a new price schedule intermediate between its previous high and low prices. Some of the larger customers say that by earning the quantity discounts and promotional allowances available in the new schedule, they obtained terms comparable with those previously available. Several of the smaller customers had never heard of the case. No one interviewed thought that the case had changed the character of pricing in the automotive parts industry. The industry was described as one in which higgling and special deals have a pervasive character, as in an Oriental bazaar. There was apparently little desire for relief from the types of concessions that Namsco had granted.[76] However, several of those interviewed were concerned about the sale of replacement parts under the private labels of large distributors. There was also general concern about the sale of parts by filling stations affiliated with oil companies and by automobile dealers. Such distributors were described as a captive market. One dealer even suggested that the Commission's cases against small automotive

---

cumulating orders and thus bringing certain customers within quantity-discount brackets for which they could not otherwise qualify. Though the continuance of existing schedules of volume and quantity discounts was not forbidden, Sherwin-Williams subsequently discontinued its volume discounts entirely, retaining only a carload discount.

[76] See footnote 24, pp. 303-04.

parts makers had been fomented by an automobile manufacturer in order to weaken independent producers.[77]

After the order against Binney & Smith, which was issued in 1940, this company established a uniform price for all retail chains and jobbers.[78] Five years later, however, it granted a functional discount to a new class of "school-discount customers," of whom there were 43 in 1952. These were concerns that sold chiefly the products of Binney & Smith's competitors but received frequent orders from schools for Binney & Smith brands. The discount was available on goods to be resold to schools in return for an undertaking to carry a representative stock of Binney & Smith products, to bid on these products where there was call for merchandise made by Binney & Smith, and to give them prominent display in catalogues.[79] In 1951 the Commission undertook a compliance investigation, which was completed in 1953. It found that the allowance available to school-discount customers violated the order.[80] Binney & Smith consented to the Commission's petition that the order be enforced by the Second Circuit, and in August 1954 the Court accordingly affirmed and enforced the order. Binney & Smith has refused to grant an interview as to subsequent developments. According to various customers, distributors who sell to schools are now on an equal basis and the discounts available to others are generally uniform.

In the parallel case against American Crayon, there was also a compliance investigation. The Commission found that the discount available to educational promotional distributors on products they resold to

---

[77] The counsel for the National Standard Parts Association told a Senate committee that the orders in the automobile parts cases had not stopped General Motors, Ford, and Chrysler from getting discounts. He said the orders are against manufacturers who do not sell to the major vehicle manufacturers, and that they apply to the relationships among independent concerns. See *A Study of the Antitrust Laws,* Hearings, Pt. 3, p. 1252.

[78] It continued its promotional allowance to school distributors, which is discussed on pp. 186-90.

[79] In spite of the resemblance between the requirements for this discount and the promotional allowance available to school distributors, the Commission treated the former as a discount to be appraised under Section 2(a), while it continued to regard the latter as a promotional allowance subject to the requirements of Section 2(d). The reason for the distinction was apparently that the Commission did not think that the requirements as to services by school-discount customers were made and applied in good faith.

[80] The promotional allowance was also found to be violative of the order. See above, pp. 186-88.

schools had been granted to two customers on certain purchases that were resold to retail dealers or in retail stores. However, the action had been contrary to American Crayon's policy, had involved no substantial amount of goods, and had been stopped when it came to the attention of executives. Accordingly, the Commission decided that it did not justify further proceedings. But the Commission found significant violations of the part of the order applicable to promotional allowances. Its petition for enforcement of the order because of this violation became involved in legal complexities, as a result of which the order was not finally affirmed and enforced until February 1957. In the course of these difficulties, the part of the order that pertained to functional discounts was temporarily set aside, but later reinstated.[81] As in the case of Binney & Smith, discounts appear to be generally uniform. But little specific information is available.

Information about the prices of candy after the Curtiss case is fragmentary, vague, and conflicting. In general terms, one customer asserts that Curtiss has reformed, another that its aggressiveness has decreased, and a third does not agree. Nothing specific is available as to the present policy toward functional classification of customers.

The available information about the distribution of spark plugs after the orders in the spark plug cases is incomplete. At least one automobile company now buys replacement plugs under a private label, but the terms of purchase by automobile companies have not been ascertained.[82] At least one oil company receives a 10 per cent promotional allowance. No more has been ascertained about the terms on which oil companies buy. As to the rest of the distribution structure, the pattern is clearer.

The practices alleged in the General Motors complaint were discontinued in 1940 after the Commission had issued a complaint against them. The Commission's order under a revised complaint issued in 1948 was based on the possibility that abandoned practices might be resumed.

[81] See above, pp. 186-88.

[82] The manager of the legal department of Electric Auto-Lite told a Senate committee that at the time of the complaint a warehouse distributor paid, for plugs to be resold to registered jobbers, nearly 1 cent per replacement plug more than vehicle manufacturers paid for the same plugs; but that in 1953, at the time of Auto-Lite's compliance report, a warehouse distributor buying for resale to registered jobbers paid a fraction of a cent less per plug for most plugs than a vehicle manufacturer. See *A Study of the Antitrust Laws*, Hearings, Pt. 3, pp. 1379-80.

From General Motors' contentions and the Commission's rulings in the case, it appears that after January 1941, prices of A. C. plugs were uniform to wholesale accounts and direct sale to jobbers was discontinued. During the pendency of the proceeding, discrimination was eliminated from prices to fleet owners, and the distinction in prices between national distributors and warehouse distributors was abandoned.

In 1953, the year in which the orders were issued, Electric Auto-Lite was selling directly (except for sales to vehicle manufacturers) only to warehouse distributors and direct jobbers, to both of whom the price was the same. Registered jobbers, though required to buy through warehouse distributors, paid the same price; and on such sales a margin for the warehouse distributor was rebated by the manufacturer. Contract jobbers, however, bought from warehouse distributors or direct jobbers at a price per plug five cents higher.[83] Sales to fleet accounts were made by registered jobbers only.

Further adjustments in these distributive patterns took place subsequently. The manager of Auto-Lite's legal department told a Senate committee in 1955 that Auto-Lite sold plugs to warehouse distributors for 34.5 cents per plug (less 2 per cent for prompt payment). Warehouse distributors resold to wholesale jobbers at the same price and to registered jobbers at 37 cents per plug, reported these sales to Auto-Lite, and received a commission of 18 per cent on the first type of sale and 14 per cent on the second. Jobbers then sold to dealers at resale prices suggested by Auto-Lite. The difference of 2.5 cents in the prices to the two classes of jobbers was said to be justified by a cost difference of 3.1 cents found in a cost study for the midwestern division for the first quarter of 1955.[84] Auto-Lite sold directly to manufacturers of engines and vehicles (chiefly Chrysler) at net prices slightly higher than those paid by warehouse dis-

[83] The manager of Auto-Lite's legal department told a Senate committee in 1955 that elimination of the 5 per cent commission formerly available to warehouse distributors on sales to contract jobbers and service jobbers had the effect of allowing registered jobbers to compete for this business. Eventually, however, the service jobber classification was discontinued. *Ibid.*, p. 1382.

[84] The difference in cost was attributed to the registered jobbers' practice of buying in small lots. Eighty per cent of the time of the division was found to be used in selling replacement plugs and 82 per cent of the dollar volume to be derived from such plugs. Accordingly, 80 per cent of the advertising and selling expense was allocated to such sales, and the hours spent in promoting sales and the number of plugs sold were computed separately for wholesale jobbers and registered jobbers; and from these totals, sales costs per plug were computed for sales to each class. *Ibid.*, pp. 1379-83.

tributors for plugs resold to wholesale jobbers[85] and slightly lower than those paid by warehouse distributors for plugs resold to registered jobbers. On the average, the price to warehouse distributors was a fraction of a cent lower than to vehicle makers.

The price difference between vehicle manufacturer and warehouse distributor prevailed for only a few months. By subsequent changes, the price to vehicle manufacturers became the same as to the warehouse distributor.

By 1956, all manufacturers had established less varied channels of distribution. They now sell to distributors, but not to jobbers. Though some of them make contracts with large fleet owners, these contracts provide for purchase from jobbers on stated terms. Apparently, distributors sell to jobbers, jobbers to dealers and fleet accounts, and dealers to consumers. There was general agreement among the dealers in automotive supplies who were interviewed that the fleet business has been growing, that their sales of spark plugs have been diminishing, and that they carry plugs chiefly as a convenience to their customers.

At the time of the interviews, the distributors of one of the plugs paid slightly more than 31 cents per plug and resold to jobbers at 39 cents. Plugs for large fleet accounts were sold by the jobber at 41 cents, and on such sales the jobber received a further discount of 10 per cent. The jobber sold to small fleets and to the dealer in lots of 50 plugs at 53 cents, with higher prices to dealers for smaller quantities. The consumer usually paid the list price of 93 cents.

With minor differences in the intermediate prices and discounts, it appears, so far as information is available, that this pattern was also followed in distributing the plugs of the other two manufacturers. The general effect has been to regularize the prices and discounts of each manufacturer at each distributive level and to eliminate competition for business between concerns operating at different levels. However, uniformity of discounts for a given plug at a given level is not complete. Concerns dealing in one of the plugs at the jobber level appear to be classified into national accounts and others, with a special discount for the former.

In the autumn of 1955, the Federal Trade Commission undertook an investigation of compliance with the order against Champion and appointed a hearing examiner to conduct the investigation. In the summer

[85] Apparently the difference in the price was partly due to the fact that the warehouse distributor received a 2 per cent discount for prompt payment not available to the vehicle maker.

of 1958, no hearings had yet been held. In response to inquiry, the Commission's Division of Compliance indicated that it had raised questions about compliance with the spark plug orders by all of the manufacturers, had obtained supplementary reports of compliance, thought satisfactory changes in practice had been made, and would submit the reports to the Commission. However, it withheld information on the nature of the objection to the practices prevailing in 1955 and as to the nature of the changes made subsequently.

The Effect of Proceedings Against
Discriminatory Functional Discounts

This meager information as to the consequences of the functional discount cases supplies a slender basis for conclusion on the broad effects of this part of the statute. What follows rests primarily on inference from the cases themselves and from the logical relation between the concepts of the law and the problems pertaining to the functional classification of customers.

Students of marketing generally agree that progress in distribution has lagged behind progress in manufacturing, that distributive methods are often wasteful, and that the opportunities to improve the efficiency of distribution are substantial. Accordingly, it is important to encourage rather than discourage experiment with distributive methods and distributive channels. Among the possibilities that might be explored are change in the number of successive intermediate distributors and in the vertical extension of each, change in the kind and amount of distributive service rendered, and change in the number and variety of different distributive channels used. Prior to experiment, it would be rash to assert that the best system of distribution for industry generally or for a particular industry would be attained by an increase or decrease in vertical integration, by greater or less specialization in distributive function, by uniform or diverse methods of distribution. What is needed is opportunity to try various methods in competition with one another.

The tendency of the law is to make experiment with methods of distribution perilous. A seller whose prices are differentiated to recognize differences in the scope and character of the distributive services performed by different distributors is in jeopardy if those distributors compete with one another or if, but for that price difference, they might do so. A seller who uses more than one channel of distribution to reach a particular market is in jeopardy if his prices differ from channel to channel in such a way that the difference can reach down to the market on which the channels converge. A seller who sells at two or more levels of distribution, or who encourages his distributors to do so, incurs heavy responsibilities as to the maintenance of price relationships designed to prevent the different degrees and kinds of vertical integration from having any impact price-wise at lower distributive levels. A seller who uses functional discounts to reach some parts of his market while he sells direct, without functional discounts, to other parts of it, is in jeopardy unless the parts can be clearly segregated, without competitive overlap. A uniform price to all comers and its corollary, a uniform method of distribution, provides safety. Complexity, diversity, and experiment create danger.

The danger in experimentation is central rather than peripheral, for the purpose of experiment should be to find cheaper or more effective methods of distribution in order that those that are more expensive or less effective may be abandoned. The elimination or substantial curtailment of the activities of some kinds of distributors would be a probable consequence of successful experiment. A change in distributive methods might reduce, increase, or leave unchanged the vigor of the competitive forces that shape the market. But it probably would harm a class of distributors. Since such harm is sufficient to make a discrimination unlawful under the statute, experiment with methods of distribution is likely to be illegal except where cost savings can be shown to justify it. The economies attained by an experiment are often not immediate and are often difficult to segregate and prove. Hence, in spite of the possibility of cost justification, the law is likely to retard experiment.

To say this is not to deny that the functional classification of customers can be used as a device for discrimination that injures competition in the market sense and that unfairly handicaps particular distributors. Weak buyers can be placed in one functional class and strong buyers in another. Carefully devised functional classification can provide a rough equivalent for a volume-discount structure. Functional discrimination can be practiced for a monopolistic purpose and with monopolistic effect. Discriminatory discounts can obscure the relative efficiency of different methods of distribution and lead to the survival of the favored rather than the efficient.[86]

[86] The Attorney General's Committee failed to recognize the difficulties presented by these possibilities; and, with two members dissenting, it recommended "that suppliers granting functional discounts either to single function or to integrated

But the protections against such developments that are provided by the present law have serious gaps. Two of the most serious are (a) that the seller who is not free to charge certain classes of distributors a higher price is free to refuse to sell to them; and (b) that the seller who may not give a direct-buying retailer a part of a wholesale discount is free to adopt a one-price policy and give him all of it. Moreover, if the direct buyer receives a partial discount that is held to be injurious, cost justification becomes easier if the discount is larger and hence more injurious. The price difference to be justified is that of the seller, that is, the difference between the price to the favored retailer and the price to the wholesaler. If the favored retailer receives a small discount, the price difference is large; as the discount increases, the price difference becomes smaller and less cost difference is needed to justify it.

The Detroit Gasoline case illustrates some of these opposing possibilities. If the analysis by the Federal Trade Commission of the issues in the case is accepted, the proceeding may well have tended to retard the development of efficient methods of distributing gasoline. It is widely asserted that there are too many filling stations and that in consequence the charge for moving gasoline from the retailer's storage tank into an automobile is too large. Reduction in the number of retail gasoline distributors and increase in their average volume may be desirable. Delivery in tank-car or tank-truck quantities to distributors who combine wholesaling and retailing functions may be a means of achieving such results. If there is an ultimate economic advantage in reshaping urban gasoline distribution along lines similar to Ned's, it is, nevertheless, improbable that this advantage will show itself immediately as a reduction in Standard's distributive costs equal to or greater than the jobber discount obtained by Ned's. It is also difficult to segregate a manufacturer's costs in a way that will supply legal proof of the amount of the saving.

---

buyers should not be held responsible for any consequences of their customers' pricing tactics," provided the buyers actually performed the functions for which the discounts were granted. (*Report of the Attorney General's National Committee*, p. 208.) The recommendation apparently pertained only to discounts recognizing successive levels of distributive activity, and thus covered less than is here considered to be included in functional discounts. Nevertheless, it was apparently intended to apply to such discounts regardless of either their magnitude or their lack of uniformity as compensation for the same function. In effect, it proposed to recognize no possibility of damage to competition in the secondary line of commerce from such discounts.

Thus a move in the right direction may lack cost justification and be obviously injurious to many established retailers.

If, however, one accepts the analysis of some observers, the possibility of greater local efficiency in distributing gasoline, if present at all, is incidental to a broad strategy of discrimination designed to consolidate the position of the major gasoline companies against threats of independent competition or to re-establish collusive pricing by retaliation against chiselers. Under either of these hypotheses, the adverse effect on competition is clear, and the chance that the process of distribution will be rationalized is remote.

This writer doubts that the law of price discrimination is a satisfactory instrument with which to approach these functional problems. As in antitrust policy generally, the danger to competition in the market sense should be given more weight than possibilities for greater efficiency if there is actual conflict between the two. However, there is peculiar need to avoid insistence on a quiet life for particular classes of distributors, even if the failure to do so makes the fate of distributive concerns depend not on their individual efficiency but on the place they happen to occupy in a changing system of distribution.[87] The narrow concept of injury to competition is inappropriate in appraising the impact of changes in distributive channels. Moreover, where channels of distribution are changing, the effect of the change on competition in the market sense cannot be understood without analysis of the forces at work at two or more levels, including the selling side of the market as well as the buying side. The principal advantage of the law of price discrimination in the policy of price discrimination, as compared with the Sherman Act, is that it isolates a relatively small body of facts and permits action about

[87] The Attorney General's Committee, with two dissents, commented, "In our view, to relate discounts or prices solely to the purchaser's resale activities without recognition of his buying functions thwarts competition and efficiency in marketing. It compels affirmative discrimination *against* a substantial class of distributors, and hence serves as a penalty on integration. If a businessman actually fulfills the wholesale function by relieving his suppliers of risk, storage, transportation, administration, etc., his performance, his capital investment, and the saving to his suppliers, are unaffected by whether he also performs the retailing function, or any number of other functions. A legal rule disqualifying him from discounts recognizing wholesaling functions actually performed compels him to render these functions free of charge. . . . Whether distributive efficiency would be fostered by non-integration, symmetrical integration, or scrambled functions, or some amalgam of all three, should not be determined by the Federal Trade Commission but by the competitive market." *Ibid.*, pp. 207-08.

them before their ultimate ramifications are explored. In considering the impact of changes in distributive methods, this characteristic is, on balance, a defect. Sound public policy calls for more comprehensive analysis. The information necessary to a case under the Sherman Act is requisite to intelligent handling of a case under the Robinson-Patman Act, and, this being so, the broader proceeding is likely to be better focused and more effective.

11 / *Territorial Discrimination by Price Formulas*

PROCEEDINGS UNDER THE Robinson-Patman Act against territorial price discrimination have constituted only one segment of a complicated pattern of government policy and political controversy concerned with territorial pricing formulas. Unlike other activities under the Robinson-Patman Act, they cannot be readily understood if considered in isolation.

When the Robinson-Patman Act was passed, territorial price discrimination had long been at the center of government thinking about discriminatory aspects of public policy toward monopolies. Discriminatory local price cutting was thought to be one of the principal means by which a monopoly position was attained; and the protection of small competitors from such tactics was a principal purpose of the provision against price discrimination that was included in the Clayton Act of 1914. Subsequently, territorial discrimination came to be regarded as objectionable because it repressed economic development in areas that were discriminated against. By the time the Robinson-Patman Act was passed, both of these grounds for concern, though still present, had been overshadowed by a third, the belief that the use of basing-point pricing formulas, which were characteristically discriminatory, was a principal means by which price-fixing conspiracies were achieved in certain major industries. There had been proposals that the dangers of such formulas should be averted by a legal requirement that all goods be priced f.o.b. mill. Thus proceedings against territorial price discrimination under the Robinson-Patman Act were regarded as relevant to problems of price-fixing conspiracy, locational opportunity, monopolistic suppression of rivals, and the possibility that public policy might establish fixed requirements in regard to permissible pricing formulas. Since public opinion was united on some of these matters and divided on others, the cases were variously interpreted as obvious applications of existing law and controversial efforts to evolve new law. Eventually their controversial aspects evoked the only major political battle that has been produced by the Robinson-Patman Act. By this battle, though the words of the statute were not changed, the spirit of its application was altered.

To understand the cases concerned with territorial price discrimination, therefore, we must examine not only the facts and decisions in these cases but also the evolution of public policy prior to the Robinson-Patman Act and the struggle over proposed amendment of the law after the principal cases were decided.

Policy Toward Territorial Discrimination
Before the Robinson-Patman Act

The practice of charging different prices in different localities aroused concern at an early stage in the development of the antitrust laws. The rise of the great trusts, which were regarded as the major targets of the Sherman Act, was thought to be facilitated by local price-cutting, by which the prices charged by a trust in the territory adjacent to a small competitor were set lower than the prices charged elsewhere.[1] Nourished by its higher prices in noncompetitive territory, the trust could lose money, if necessary, in competitive territory in order to discipline or destroy its competitor. Selecting one competitor after another as its target, it could extend its control by a series of local price wars. Attack on such local price-cutting was conspicuous in early Sherman Act cases. To prevent local price-cutting when it produced monopolistic results was one of the principal purposes of the Congress in enacting the Clayton Act in 1914. That the law of price discrimination incorporated in Section 2 of this act was intended to control local price-cutting was probably the clearest point in its interpretation.

[1] In 1907, the Commission of Corporations reported that the Standard Oil Company charges "a price which is proportionate to the extent of its monopoly in a given place, and reduces prices in proportion to the degree of competition which it may meet." (See *Report of the Commissioner of Corporations on the Petroleum Industry*, Pt. 2, pp. xxxviii, xxxix, 451.) Louis Brandeis, not yet a Supreme Court justice, testified in 1914 that except for railroad rebates such local price discrimination was the most powerful of Standard's weapons. (See *To Prevent Discrimination in Prices and to Provide for Publicity of Prices to Dealers and the Public,* Hearings before the House Committee on Interstate and Foreign Commerce on H.R. 13305, 63 Cong. 2 and 3 sess., 1914, pp. 4-5.) Evidence of Standard's discrimination was a significant part of the antitrust case against Standard Oil decided in 1911. See *Standard Oil Co. of New Jersey* v. *U.S.,* 173 F. 170 and 221 U.S. 1.

Concern over territorial price differences is also apparent in the antitrust legislation of many of the states. South Carolina enacted a general state law on the subject in 1902, followed by Nebraska in 1905, Missouri, Tennessee, and South Dakota in 1907, Louisiana and Oklahoma in 1908, Wyoming in 1911, Massachusetts in 1912, and Idaho and Wisconsin in 1913. Other similar statutes in various states pertained to particular commodities, such as milk. Central in these statutes was an effort to prevent concerns from establishing different prices in different parts of the state for the purpose of injuring the business of a competitor.[2] Some of the laws forbade sellers from discriminating in prices among localities for this purpose; others, apparently concerned primarily with agricultural commodities, forbade buyers from discriminating by localities in purchase prices; and others extended the prohibition to cover both purchase and sale.[3] In practically all instances, however, the statute

[2] See Works Progress Administration, *State Antitrust Laws*, Marketing Laws Survey, Vol. 1. The Missouri Law, as revised in 1932, provides, "Any person . . . engaged in the production, manufacture, purchase, sale, or distribution of any commodity . . . in general use that intentionally, for the purpose of destroying the competition of any regular, established dealer of such commodity, or to prevent the competition of any person, who in good faith intends and attempts to become such dealer, shall discriminate between different . . . localities . . . by purchasing such commodity . . . at a higher price . . . in one . . . locality . . . than is paid for the same commodity . . . by the said person . . . in another . . . locality . . . or by selling such commodity . . . in one . . . locality . . . at a lower price . . . than such commodity . . . is sold for by said person . . . in another . . . locality . . . after making due allowance for the difference, if any, in the grade or quality and in the actual cost of transportation from the point of purchase to the point of manufacture or storage, or from the point of production, manufacture, or storage to the place of sale or distribution . . . shall be deemed guilty of unfair discrimination which is hereby prohibited and declared unlawful." *Ibid.*, pp. 387-88.

[3] But for the emphasis on purpose, the laws that sought to avoid discrimination by both buyers and sellers would have presented major conceptual difficulties. Common sense might have suggested that, for a seller, nondiscriminatory prices would be those that gave him a uniform realization at his place of business after deducting transportation expense. Similarly, common sense might have suggested that, for a buyer, nondiscriminatory buying prices would be those that resulted in uniform delivered costs at his place of business. But where sellers and buyers were at various distances from one another, these two common sense standards could not be simultaneously met. Suppose that the transportation charge from seller A to buyer B is 50 cents and to buyer C is 60 cents, while the transportation charge from seller D to buyer B is 55 cents and to buyer C is 45 cents. Seller A can get a uniform realization at his mill if his delivered price to C is ten cents higher than to B. If A's mill realization is $1, his delivered price to C is $1.60 and to B $1.50. If C is to have a nondiscriminatory buying price, his payment to D, on a delivered basis, must also be $1.60, which will give D a mill realization of $1.15. If B is to

was concerned with injury to the competitors of the person who engaged in the discrimination, rather than with injury to those with whom that person dealt.[4] The concept of injury was similar in this respect to the concept of injury in the primary line in cases under the Robinson-Patman Act.

Although most of the legal proceedings of the federal government concerned with territorial discrimination prior to the Robinson-Patman Act rested on charges that the discriminating seller was injuring his competitors, one important case was developed on a different theory. This was the Federal Trade Commission's proceeding against United States Steel Corporation, instituted in 1920 and decided by the Commission in 1924. The Commission charged that the corporation and its subsidiaries had discriminated in a way that reduced competition not only with them but also with their favored customers. The discrimination was found to be unlawful both under the price discrimination provisions of the Clayton Act and under the provisions of the Federal Trade Commission Act concerned with unfair methods of competition.

Emphasis was placed in the Commission's findings on the effect of the discriminations among customers. United States Steel Corporation and other steel producers had quoted delivered prices consisting, with certain exceptions, of a base price at Pittsburgh plus the cost of transportation from Pittsburgh to the customer. Thus, though the Gary works of United States Steel were adjacent to Chicago, delivered prices in Chicago included a transportation cost from Pittsburgh amounting to about $7.60 per ton. Similar "phantom freight" was incorporated in the delivered prices prevailing at other western points. The Commission found that because of these discriminations the markets of the western fabricators were circumscribed. For example:

> Chicago fabricators of steel buildings and bridges are unable to compete east of Chicago against the Pittsburgh fabricators on straight,

---

have a nondiscriminatory buying price, he must pay D $1.50 delivered, which will give D a mill realization of 95 cents. But with varying mill realizations on sales to different customers, D's prices will then be discriminatory. There is no way in which the two sellers and the two buyers can simultaneously maintain nondiscriminatory prices. Since the state laws were designed to cope with the activities of powerful concerns expressing a predatory purpose, rather than to prevent discrimination generally, the conception of discrimination was not made precise, and difficulties of the kind illustrated did not arise.

[4] Though the general purpose of some of the laws was apparently to protect farmers, the method used, as in the Missouri law, was usually to forbid discriminations in buying that were intended to injure competing buyers.

competitive structural steel work. Pittsburgh fabricators, on the other hand, compete on an equality in Chicago with Chicago fabricators. . . . Nowhere in the United States does the Chicago fabricator have an advantage over the Pittsburgh fabricator. In only a very limited territory can he compete on an equality. . . . In the case of the manufacturers of heavy drop forgings and screw-machine products, and other products where there is a heavy steel waste entailed in the manufacturing process, the Pittsburgh manufacturer has a very substantial advantage over the Chicago manufacturer right in the city of Chicago. . . . A number of steel consumers in the West have either been obliged to put up or contemplate putting up plants in the Pittsburgh district because of the Pittsburgh Plus prices on steel; others cannot afford to do so. The fabricators generally in the West have shown that their plants have not expanded materially for a number of years.[5]

The Commission's findings in this case treated the discrimination against western fabricators as an unfair method of competition primarily on the ground that the disadvantaged buyers were prevented "from competing on an equality or from competing at all."[6] The Commission found also that the Pittsburgh-plus system substantially lessened competition among steel producers, since it was a price-fixing device by which producers assured "an absolutely uniform price at any given point." In the Commission's view price competition among steel producers would bring about f.o.b. mill prices, and such prices did in fact prevail during periods of competition in the industry.

Accordingly, the Commission ordered United States Steel Corporation to cease selling its rolled-steel products at Pittsburgh-plus prices; to cease selling them on any other basing point than that where they were made or shipped; to cease selling them without indicating on the invoices or contracts the amount of the price f.o.b. shipping point and the amount of the transportation charge; and, in general, to cease unlawful discrimination. Without admitting the validity of the Commission's order, the corporation filed a compliance statement saying that it would conform "in so far as it is practicable to do so." In fact, it established a Chicago base price two dollars higher than the Pittsburgh price, and in later years gradually added additional basing points.[7] The Commission did not challenge the corporation's qualified acceptance of the order.

[5] 8 FTC 21-25.

[6] A second ground was that the sellers thus obtained a decisive advantage over those of their customers with whom they competed for fabricating business.

[7] Testifying before a Senate committee in 1936, Robert Gregg, Vice President of United States Steel, was asked, "In other words, what you are saying is this:

The Pittsburgh-plus case was significant in the development of thinking about territorial price discrimination. It not only focused attention on competition in the secondary line but also expressed dramatically the idea that such competition is damaged when buyers are systematically deprived of the advantages of their location. It coupled the finding of injury in the secondary line with the finding that the discriminations through which this injury developed were price-fixing devices. It equated competition in the steel industry with the existence of an f.o.b. mill price structure. Since the case was not appealed until 1938, the various conceptual elements in the decision attained influence in later thinking about territorial price discrimination without having been subjected to judicial review.[8] The extravagance of the discriminatory pattern against which the order was directed and the severity of the handicaps that this pattern imposed on certain fabricators, together with the monopolistic reputation that United States Steel Corporation had acquired from congressional investigations and from inconclusive prosecution under the Sherman Act, predisposed observers to sympathize with the Commission's purpose and to accept its analysis.

That you are complying not with the order issued by the Federal Trade Commission but that you are complying with the statement which you filed with the Federal Trade Commission?" He replied, "That is correct." This filed statement, after saying that rolled-steel products would not be sold on any other basing point than that where they were manufactured or from which they were shipped, continued, "Sales from manufacturing plants, fabricating plants, and warehouses will be made f.o.b. plant or warehouse, or at delivered prices, as occasion may offer. In all cases of sales at delivered prices the contract of sale or the invoice will clearly and distinctly indicate how much is charged for the steel products sold f.o.b. the producing or shipping point and how much is charged for the actual transportation of such products, if any, from such producing or shipping point to destination. All f.o.b. selling prices, whether at the mills, warehouses, or fabricating plants, and all delivered prices, will be nondiscriminatory within the meaning of the second section of the Clayton Act, but will be subject to the variations permitted by said act." See *To Prevent Uniform Delivered Prices,* Hearing Before the Senate Committee on Interstate Commerce, 74 Cong. 2 sess. (1936), pp. 212, 208-09.

[8] U. S. Steel appealed the case in 1938 after the Federal Trade Commission Act had been amended in such a way that failure to appeal within sixty days would have made the order final and subject to civil penalties if violated. In 1948, after the Supreme Court's decision in the cement case (see below, pp. 388-89), U. S. Steel changed to a method of selling f.o.b. mill. On this ground and on the ground that the future of price formulas for steel would be decided in a conspiracy case that the Commission had brought against the steel industry, U. S. Steel withdrew its objections to the 1924 order and consented to a court decree, issued by the Third Circuit on October 5, 1948, affirming and enforcing the order.

Attention Shifts from Discrimination
to Price-Fixing

No other proceeding was instituted against territorial price discrimination by formula before the Robinson-Patman Act.[9] Territorial pricing formulas were involved in several conspiracy cases under the Sherman Act, but in no case were of central significance. In the Standard Sanitary case,[10] decided against the defendants in 1912, zone prices were fixed under a patent agreement; but the price fixing was overt, and the case turned on the legal status of price fixing in the light of the underlying patents. In the American Linseed Oil case,[11] decided against the defendants in 1923, price differentials between zones had been agreed on, but the case turned on the legal significance of a comprehensive system of price reporting and subsequent collusive policing of the reported prices. In the cement and maple flooring cases,[12] both decided in favor of the defendants in 1925, the defendants had made use of basing-point systems; but consideration of these systems was central to neither case. In the cement case the allegation was joint activity, largely statistical, tending to fix prices, of which the compilation of freight rate books to be used in computing transportation costs from basing points was a part; but the court found that uniformity of trade practices had not been shown and that, though prices tended to be uniform because the product was standardized, price change was frequent. In the maple flooring case, a freight rate book for use in a basing-point system was also involved; but the freight computations from the single base at Cadillac, Michigan, were regarded by the court as approximations of actual rates from sellers' plants, and the standardization of freight charges was treated as a minor part of collective computation of the cost of maple flooring, the significance of which was central to the case. Only in the Sugar Institute case, in which a verdict for the government was rendered in 1936 was a territorial formula explicity condemned and forbidden under the Sherman Act. Though the case focused on agreed price reporting, one of the many joint activities of the defendants had been to agree on the maintenance of a delivered price system. This was condemned by the lower court as

---

[9] Only one other order concerned territorial discrimination, that against Pittsburgh Coal Co., 8 FTC 480. The discrimination condemned in this case was a difference in the price of coal between the Twin Cities and Duluth.

[10] 226 U.S. 20.

[11] 262 U.S. 371.

[12] 268 U.S. 588 and 268 U.S. 563.

restraint of trade.[13] A portion of the decree in the case forbade concerted determination of transportation charges, concerted limitation of
freight absorption, and agreement upon a system of delivered prices or
on refusal to sell f.o.b. refinery. This part of the decision was not appealed.

In the interval between the Pittsburgh-plus decision in 1924 and
the passage of the Robinson-Patman Act in 1936, a series of public
reports by the Federal Trade Commission and others confirmed the bad
reputation that the Pittsburgh-plus case had given to basing-point systems. In these reports, though such systems were treated as discriminatory, emphasis was increasingly placed on their price-fixing aspects. In
1931 Frank A. Fetter, past president of the American Economic Association, summarized his studies of the application of the antitrust laws
in a book entitled *The Masquerade of Monopoly,* which attracted wide
attention. His thesis was that discriminatory territorial pricing practices,
and particularly basing-point pricing formulas, had constituted the devices by which powerful business interests had fixed prices and suppressed their smaller competitors; and that failure to understand these
pricing methods had been responsible for much of the ineffectiveness
of judicial proceedings against these powerful interests. In 1927, the
Federal Trade Commission undertook a broad inquiry into f.o.b. mill
pricing, uniform delivered pricing (either country-wide or by zones), and
basing-point pricing, intended to "discover the causes for the adoption
of these various methods and their relation, if any, to the matter of
competition, differences in prices, price levels, and cross-freighting or
other needless costs." In 1932, the Commission published the first report
derived from this inquiry, which had to do with the basing-point formula
in the cement industry.[14] In the divergence of mill-net realizations, the
uniformity of the delivered prices quoted by different sellers, and the
inflexibility of prices, the Commission saw evidence that the multiple
basing-point system of the industry was not operating in accord with
normal competitive processes. It found that the system resulted in
unnecessary cross-hauling, the elimination of which might have saved
as much as $42,000,000 in 1927. In 1933, this report was supplemented
by a report on the cement industry prepared in response to a Senate

[13] 297 U.S. 553; 15 F. Supp. 817.

[14] Federal Trade Commission, *Report on Price Bases Inquiry, The Basing-Point
Formula and Cement Prices* (1932), p. xiii.

resolution. Prominent among the report's conclusions was the statement that:

> The multiple basing-point pricing system as developed by the cement industry has a tendency to lessen price competition. The system forms the basis for arriving at uniform delivered prices of cement and destroys the value of calling for sealed bids by the Government and other large purchasers. . . . Price competition in the cement industry might be restored in large measure if each manufacturer in submitting bids would quote an f.o.b. mill price, based on his own operations and independent of any knowledge or information as to how competitors probably will arrive at the prices they will submit.[15]

The Commission's belief that basing-point pricing involves price fixing became stronger during the NRA period. Under NRA the steel industry obtained temporary approval of a code that specifically provided for a multiple basing-point system. In February 1934, a Senate resolution directed the Commission to investigate the code and report to the Senate. In March the Commission reported that the code "in effect declares unfair and unlawful the practice of f.o.b. mill-base pricing which the Commission assumed to be fair competition. But more than this, it requires important steel producers to violate the Commission's order and permits all to ignore it."[16] Treating the code as an instrument of price fixing, the Commission said:

> When highly organized groups of competitors establish and maintain an elaborate and complicated price formula, composed of numerous subordinate formulas which are themselves elaborate and complicated, when they incorporate in the master formula arbitrary factors such as common basing points and delivery charges other than the actual, thus arriving at identical delivered prices, it is a conserva-

---

[15] *Cement Industry*, S. Doc. 71, 73 Cong. 1 sess., p. xvi.

[16] Donald Richberg, general counsel for the National Recovery Administration, later testified: "We were not passing upon those operations as legal or illegal. We felt that they were entirely open to attack by the Federal Government if, in the course of the operations, it appeared that they were being conducted on an illegal basis. We did not approve of the conditions of the code in detail as being ideal or even proper. We took the position that we would allow a 90-day trial period of the code in the hope thereby of gaining all the labor benefits, and in the meantime adequately informing ourselves regarding these highly debatable questions." See *To Prevent Uniform Delivered Prices*, Hearing, p. 85 and *Practices of the Steel Industry Under the Code*, S. Doc. 159, 73 Cong. 2 sess. (1934), p. 64.

tive conclusion that they have thereby simply arrived at the goal and object which motivated the initial step and each succeeding step in the process.[17]

Meanwhile, the steel code had been extended for a further trial period of about six months. It was again extended in May 1934. At the time of the second extension, certain changes were made in the code, and an executive order by the President emphasized the continuing doubts of the administration as to the propriety of the program. The President said that the changes, "while alleviating some of the inequities in the existing system, illustrate the desirability of working toward the end of having prices quoted on the basis of areas of production and the eventual establishment of basing points coincident with all such areas, as well as the elimination of artificial transportation charges in price quotations." He directed the Federal Trade Commission and the NRA to study the operation of the code and to report their recommendations within six months.[18] Finding themselves unable to collaborate, the two agencies made separate reports. The Federal Trade Commission reported in November, "The diagnosis which the Commission makes is that the basing-point system not only permits and encourages price fixing, but that it is price fixing."[19] The Commission recommended that the Code be changed to eliminate provisions that expressly sanctioned the multiple basing-point system or aided price fixing or related to the regulation of production or new capacity, so that the activities of the industry would be open to legal attack on the ground that they violated the antitrust laws.

The report of the NRA was prepared by a committee of four persons, who signed it in their personal capacity.[20] They concluded that the basing-point system:

> . . . does not tend to as serviceable a form of competition as a system in which there is more incentive for a producer to lower his base price as a means of extending his sales area, rather than doing

[17] Ibid., p. 45.
[18] Gustav Seidler, Jr., "The Control of Geographic Price Relations Under Codes of Fair Competition," Work Materials No. 86, NRA Division of Review, 1936 (mimeo.), pp. 22-23.
[19] Federal Trade Commission, Report to the President with Respect to the Basing-Point System in the Iron and Steel Industry (1935), p. 35.
[20] They were R. W. Shannon, Deputy Administrator of the Code; Burr Tracy Ansell; M. P. Sharpe; and J. M. Clark (the latter a former president of the American Economic Association).

this by merely absorbing freights and discriminating. We have seen that there are wastes of competitive cross-hauling, which must ultimately be charged to the consumers, and that certain purchasers are burdened with artificial freights.

As to the relation of basing-point systems to price fixing, they said that:

> ... So far as understandings may exist, the basing-point system facilitates them, but is not of sufficiently decisive importance in that respect so that the success or failure of efforts to reach price understandings hinges on whether the basing-point system is or is not in force. . . . The abolishing of the basing-point system would temporarily make such understandings more difficult to reach and make effective, but by itself would in all probability have no lasting effect in preventing them.

Accordingly, they recommended that a base be established near every group of mills and that a limit be set on permissible freight absorption, and that unless such modifications could be brought about with reasonable speed, consideration be given to abandonment of the provisions of the code concerned with prices.[21] Decisions as to further action on the steel code had not been reached when the Schechter decision terminated the National Industrial Recovery Act.

The last of the Federal Trade Commission's reports concerning basing points prior to the enactment of the Robinson-Patman Act were made in 1936. In that year the Commission submitted to the Congress a brief summary of a study of the zone-price formula in the range-boiler industry.[22] In the same year the President directed the Commission to study identical bids on sheet-steel piling that had been received on three different projects of the Public Works Administration and to submit a report with recommendations. The Commission reported that the bids had been collusive and that identical bidding was fundamental in the relationships among steel producers. "Their pricing system meticulously meets every requirement of a program closing every loophole for even slight divergencies in delivered prices. Such a closely articulated system would be wholly impossible without collusion." The Commission recommended

---

[21] "Report of the N.R.A. on the Operation of the Basing-Point System in the Iron and Steel Industry," Nov. 30, 1934, pp. 172, 136-37, 173-74. (mimeo.).

[22] Most of this study was made in 1933, but work on it was suspended during the NRA period. See "Study of Zone-Price Formula in Range Boiler Industry," mimeographed release by the Commission, March 30, 1936.

that the matter be referred to the Attorney General, that evidence of identical bidding be assembled by the purchasing officials of the Federal Government, and that "the President give consideration to recommending to Congress the enactment of legislation making unlawful such organized systems of delivered prices as frustrate price competition." The last recommendation followed a reference to bills pending in both Houses of Congress that "would make the operation of noncompetitive basing-point systems unlawful per se." The Commission saw distinct advantage in such legislation because it would render unnecessary the separate investigation of a great number of industries. "If in but one case the Supreme Court upheld the validity of the statute, it is believed that the artificial character of such basing-point systems would aid in their collapse. There would be a strong sentiment on the part of many members of the industry to return to price competition rather than defy an Act of Congress and await action by the Department of Justice or by this Commission."[23]

After NRA, Senator Burton K. Wheeler held hearings in 1936 on a bill entitled "The Anti-Basing-Point Act." This bill would have added to the Clayton Act provisions making it unlawful (1) to add to the shipping-point price of any commodity a charge for delivery to the destination "other than the actual cost of delivery through such agency as the purchaser may elect to specify"; (2) to enter into an agreement to use a system whereby prices were charged including any amount measured by any transportation rates not actually defrayed in the delivery of the commodity; (3) to quote a delivered price without stating what portion of it was actually transportation cost and without giving the buyer the option of taking delivery at the shipping point with the actual transportation cost deducted. In hearings on the bill, Senator Wheeler expressed the view that there was no intention to forbid reductions of price to meet competition through the quotation of various prices at the mill. The bill was not reported by the committee.[24]

In the Temporary National Economic Committee, the controversy over basing points was renewed. The Federal Trade Commission submitted a memorandum reiterating its charge that the basing-point system in the steel industry suppressed competition. Professor Fetter and members of the Commission's staff testified before the committee. United

---

[23] Federal Trade Commission, "Report to the President on Steel Sheet Piling," June 10, 1936, duplicated, pp. 18, 41-42.

[24] *To Prevent Uniform Delivered Prices*, Hearing, pp. 1-2, 333, 437, 447-48.

States Steel Corporation counterattacked with two long memoranda defending the use of basing-point pricing. These evoked a long rejoinder by two members of the Commission's staff and further testimony before the committee. The committee's final report included a declaration, adopted unanimously, that basing-point systems "are used in many industries as an effective device for eliminating price competition." The committee apparently assumed that such arrangements were unlawful, but commented that to eliminate them under existing law would involve a costly process of separate prosecutions in many industries that would place a heavy burden on antitrust enforcement. It therefore recommended that Congress enact legislation "declaring such pricing systems to be illegal" but providing "for a brief period of time for industries to divest themselves of this monopolistic practice."[25]

In summary, in the years before the Robinson-Patman Act became law, public attention to territorial pricing systems had been focused almost entirely on basing-point systems in the steel and cement industries. These systems had been repeatedly challenged. The Pittsburgh-plus arrangement had been adjudged by the Federal Trade Commission to be unlawfully discriminatory and destructive of price competition. Though the cement and maple flooring industries had escaped conviction in antitrust proceedings in spite of their basing-point arrangements, the cases involving them had turned on trade-association activities rather than on basing-point pricing practices. In public reports the Federal Trade Commission had repeatedly condemned the multiple basing-point systems that prevailed in the cement industry and that had been established in the steel industry after the Pittsburgh-plus case. Even NRA had questioned the fairness of the basing-point arrangements for steel and had pressed the industry to modify its practices in the direction of f.o.b. mill pricing with freight absorption. Influential economists, led by Professor Fetter, thought basing-point pricing the most important weapon of monopoly in many industries. Other distinguished economists, such as Professor Clark, disagreed: they variously saw the system as a minor aid to price fixing, as an inevitable expression of monopolistic tendencies inherent in the concentration of economic power, or as the natural expression of competition over distance in mass-production industries. Few, if any of them, however, thought it an institution to be defended and extolled. The alternatives of public policy envisaged in statements by congressmen and government officials who had considered the matter after the end of NRA were either to attack basing-point pricing in a series of proceedings under existing law or to enact new legislation striking directly at such practices. The latter course had been recommended by the Temporary National Economic Committee. In view of the fact that this committee included persons from both parties in both Houses of Congress, as well as officials of the Departments of Justice, Labor, Commerce, and the Treasury, the Federal Trade Commission, and the Securities and Exchange Commission, its views may be regarded as a fair reflection of governmental attitudes.

In the growing hostility to basing-point systems, the center of attention had gradually shifted from price discrimination to price fixing. The later reports of the Federal Trade Commission continued to condemn basing-point pricing because it handicapped buyers in some localities, but gave diminishing attention to this type of criticism. There was also little emphasis on Professor Fetter's point that the system facilitated the growth of big companies at the expense of small ones. The principal charge was that the basing-point formula provided an effective device by which prices could be harmonized and price competition eliminated. As the rationale underlying this charge was developed, members of the staff of the Federal Trade Commission came to believe that it was applicable not only to basing-point pricing but to all precise formulas for the determination of territorial pricing relationships. The attack on basing-point formulas was broadened to cover zone pricing and systematic freight equalization also.

It is noteworthy, however, that problems in regard to territorial price relationships had been discussed entirely in a setting of conspiracy or of monopoly power. Though proposals had been made for legislation outlawing basing-point systems and requiring f.o.b. mill pricing, there had been no broad study of industrial practice in the establishment of territorial pricing patterns. The ideas about damage to competition in the secondary line from territorial price differences had been developed in a conspiracy setting and had not been applied to commercial markets thought to be characterized by neither conspiracy nor monopoly. Similarly, the analysis of the significance of f.o.b. mill pricing as an alternative to delivered pricing had been developed in the study of industries in which the shift from the former to the latter had been an aspect of price fixing. Generalizations had been formulated about the relation among territorial discrimination, price fixing, monopoly, the advantages of location, and pricing formulas. These generalizations were supported by logical analysis and illustrated by particular investigations; but they had outrun the data on which they were based. They had resulted in proposals for laws applicable to the whole business community, without specific inquiry as to their pertinence to more than a segment of that community.

Proposals to outlaw the basing-point system similar to those in the Wheeler bill were presented during congressional consideration of the Robinson-Patman Act. A definition of price avowedly intended to require f.o.b. mill pricing was inserted in the draft law by the House Judiciary Committee but deleted during subsequent debate on the floor of the House.[26] Though the law as finally enacted contained no reference to basing-point pricing, its language was capable of being applied to problems of territorial price discrimination.

Frequency of Legal Action Against Price Fixing by Formula

Thereafter, as before, however, the Commission's main concern in considering territorial pricing formulas was their use for purposes of price fixing. Between July 1, 1936 and June 30, 1955 the Commission issued orders against price fixing in 46 cases in which it found a delivered pricing method important enough to be specified in the findings or in the order.[27] Twenty-two of these cases were concerned with zone pricing, 9 with basing-point systems, 5 with systems of freight equalization, 5 with uniform delivered pricing, and 5 with more than one kind of

---

[26] See above, p. 44. The decision was made without a record vote at the request of the House Judiciary Committee, which, finding opposition to the provision by some members of the Rules Committee, decided not to jeopardize the main purpose of the Robinson-Patman bill. In the brief debate several members expressed opposition to a requirement that goods be priced f.o.b. mill, saying that it would prevent volume production and raise costs, would be ruinous to small-town industry located far from markets, and would handicap American producers in competing with foreigners. Others, some of whom favored legislation against basing-point pricing, thought the matter not germane to the Robinson-Patman bill, and favored separate legislation to deal with it. See *Congressional Record,* Vol. 80, Pt. 8, 74 Cong. 2 sess., p. 8223.

[27] For a list of the cases, see App. A, Table 6.

delivered price formula.[28] In 41 of the 46 cases, there was no finding of violation of the Robinson-Patman Act.[29] Fourteen of the 46 cases were appealed, of which only 2 included a finding of price discrimination. In

[28] As used here, the term *uniform delivered pricing* means charging the same delivered price at all destinations; the term *zone pricing* includes all those systems the effect of which is to establish two or more territorial zones between which delivered prices are different and within any one of which delivered prices at all destinations are identical; a *single basing point system* is one in which delivered prices are computed as though goods originated at a single point of origin, and consist of the price at that point plus freight from that point to the destination; a *multiple basing point system* is one in which delivered prices are computed as though goods originated at two or more points of origin, but with some points of production not treated as basing points; and a *freight-equalization system* is like a multiple basing point system except that all points of production are basing points. In multiple basing point and freight equalization systems, the basing point used in computing a delivered price at a given destination is the one which results in the lowest delivered price; and all sellers quote that price even if, in doing so, they fail to cover all of their actual delivery expense. Such failure is described as *absorbing freight*. In basing point systems, single and multiple, shipments from points of production that are not treated as basing points may result, particularly at nearby destinations, in expenditures for freight that are less than the computed freight charges from the applicable basing point. The excess of the transportation charge collected from the buyer over the transportation expense actually incurred is described as *phantom freight*. (The term phantom freight is also applied to excess charges due to use of a more expensive method of transportation in computing freight than in shipping the goods.) In basing point systems, computed freight costs are greater than actual freight expenditures at some destinations, less at others; that is, there is both phantom freight and freight absorption. In a freight-equalization system, there is freight absorption, but no phantom freight.

[29] Six situations involved charges of both price fixing and discrimination, those concerning the *Chain Institute* (Docket 4878), *United Fence Manufacturers Association* (Docket 3305), the *Cement Institute* (Docket 3167), the corn products manufacturers, *Corn Products Refining Co., et al.* (Docket 5502), the manufacturers of lead pigments, *National Lead Co., et al.* (Docket 5253), and the makers of frit, *Ferro Enamel Corp., et al.* (Docket 5155). In the Chain Institute case the discrimination charge was dismissed. In the frit case the freight-equalization system involved in the price fixing scheme was unrelated to the volume discounts that were attacked under the Robinson-Patman Act. In the fence case the respondents did not contest the proceeding, and the order covered both price fixing and discrimination found in the price fixing formula. In the cement case, an order covering both price fixing by formula and the discrimination inherent in the formula was sustained by the Supreme Court. In the lead case, the Commission found both price fixing by zone formulas and discrimination between zones, though a part of the complaint having to do with discrimination within zones was dismissed. In the corn products case, the proceeding concerned with conspiracy followed a series of discrimination cases in which orders had been issued against individual respondents and was based on the findings in those cases.

11 instances the findings of violation by the Commission were sustained by the courts.

In proceeding against conspiratorial use of delivered pricing formulas, the Commission did not customarily charge that the respondents had violated the Robinson-Patman Act, even though it thought that the prices fixed in their conspiracy were discriminatory. It often brought cases charging conspiracy only, found that the conspiracy involved discrimination, and included in its order a requirement that the respondents cease agreeing to discriminate.[30] When conspiracy was involved, the law of price discrimination played a subordinate role.

Frequency of Legal Action Against Territorial Discrimination

Before December 31, 1957, the Commission issued orders against territorial price discrimination in 19 cases.[31] These cases fall into two

[30] For example, in two cases concerned with clay products (Dockets 5467 and 5468, *Structural Clay Products, Inc., et al.*), the Commission charged and found conspiracies to fix prices according to zone-pricing formulas. Its orders included a prohibition of joint action to discriminate in ways that matched delivered prices and deprived buyers of the advantage of locations near a plant. (See 44 FTC 892 and 906.) In another clay products case (Docket 5483, *Clay Products Association Inc., et al.*) a charge of discrimination was dismissed, but in a consent order under the charge of conspiracy the Commission similarly ordered the respondents not to engage in a common course of action by which they discriminated for the purpose or with the effect of matching prices. (See 47 FTC 1256.) In the Chain Institute case a charge of price discrimination was dismissed, and an order was issued against conspiracy by formula pricing. A part of the order required each corporation individually to cease selling at prices determined in accord with a single basing-point system, a freight-equalization system, or a zone system for the purpose or with the effect of matching the delivered price quotations or delivered prices of other sellers and thereby preventing purchasers from finding any advantage in price in dealing with one seller as against another. The order was sustained on appeal. See 49 FTC 1041 and 246 F. 2d 231.

[31] This summary omits various cases in which territorial price differences existed but were not explicitly attacked by the Commission. For example, in the *Standard Brands* case (Docket 2986) the Commission proceeded against volume-discount schedules that differed from one section of the country to another. It mentioned as one of the grounds for rejecting Standard Brands' cost defense the fact that the data on which the cost computations rested had a different territorial coverage than the price schedule to which the cost defense was applied. Nevertheless, nothing in the Commission's analysis of the case suggests that it was concerned about differences in the prices paid by buyers at different locations. See 29 FTC 121; 30 FTC 1117; 46 FTC 1485; and 47 FTC 1831.

groups, one containing 11 in which the discrimination consisted in adherence to a territorial pricing formula, and the other containing 8 in which no such formula was found. It will be convenient to consider the formula cases first, and to defer to a later chapter consideration of the others.

Among the 11 cases that had to do with discrimination by formula, 4 were conspiracy cases that included a count concerned with territorial discrimination. In 2 of them, the Commission's order was appealed and sustained by the courts. The 7 others were cases against individual manufacturers of corn products, all of whom were subsequently included in the corn products conspiracy case. Two of the individual corn products cases were also appealed, and in both instances the Commission was sustained by the courts.

Thus, in basing-point and zone-pricing cases, charges of price discrimination played a subordinate role in a legal attack focused on price fixing conspiracy. Only in the corn products industry was the law of price discrimination used separately against territorial pricing formulas; and even in this industry the Commission believed that a price fixing conspiracy lay in the background, and eventually proceeded against that conspiracy.

Three types of delivered pricing formulas have been attacked as discriminatory—uniform delivered pricing, zone pricing, and basing-point pricing.

Uniform Delivered Prices

In two cases the Commission has challenged uniform delivered pricing as discriminatory, but in only one of the two has it issued an order against the practice. In 1938 the Commission charged that, in 14 states in which they controlled more than 90 per cent of the total sales, United Fence

---

Similarly, in the case against *Aeration Processes* (Docket 6152), the Commission's order was concerned with different volume-discount schedules applicable to different territories in New England. The order was issued, without a contest, by the consent of the respondents; and neither the findings nor the terms of the order are explicit enough to indicate whether the Commission's attack had to do with the volume discounts alone or with the territorial price differences also. See 50 FTC 994.

Various cases in which there were territorially limited concessions to particular buyers, incidental to more comprehensive discriminations, have not been regarded as cases concerned with territorial discrimination. An instance is the *Curtiss* case (Docket 4556), in which some of the special deals offered by Curtiss were territorially restricted. See 44 FTC 237.

Manufacturers Association and its members had conspired to fix prices by quoting uniform delivered prices to all customers at every destination in those states. The respondents admitted all of the material allegations of the complaint. The Commission found that the conspiracy violated the Federal Trade Commission Act and that the quotation of the uniform delivered price constituted unlawful price discrimination under the Robinson-Patman Act. The latter conclusion rested on the opinion that the net receipt at the mill constituted the price in each sale and that, therefore, a uniform delivered price was actually a series of different mill prices on sales to different destinations, with the lowest prices available to the customers to whom shipment was most expensive. Through this discrimination, the Commission said, the conspirators achieved identity in delivered prices, refrained from trying by price competition to hold the most profitable business near their own plants in return for the privilege of selling on equal terms in the high net-return areas of other producers, nullified the influence of varying costs and varying local conditions of supply and demand on prices, deprived of effect on prices the advantages of the most efficient and best-located concerns, and deprived consumers located near points of production of the locational advantages that they would normally enjoy. Lessening of market competition and a tendency to create a monopoly were found to be the effects. The order in the case included provisions requiring the respondents to cease promoting or facilitating discrimination in realized prices at point of shipment through any agreement to sell at identical delivered prices or any agreement resulting in the quotation of identical prices at any common destination by respondents variously located.[32]

The United Fence Manufacturers Association has not been in existence for at least ten years. One of the largest producers now sells f.o.b. its producing plants. Information is not available on the territorial pricing practices of other producers.

[32] The part of this case concerned with price discrimination apparently made no impression on either the Commission or its critics. Persons who expressed the Commission's views during the political controversy following the Supreme Court's decision in the cement case were apparently not informed about this case. Although critics of the Commission were trying to prove that the Commission regarded variation in net mill realization as discrimination, they apparently made no reference to the United Fence decision. The Commission wrote to Senator Kefauver on January 18, 1950 that "There has never been a case in which this Commission or the courts have found the use of this type of pricing [uniform delivered or so-called 'postage stamp' pricing] to constitute illegal discrimination in price." See *Congressional Record*, Vol. 96, Pt. 4, 81 Cong. 2 sess., p. 4498.

In the National Lead case, in which uniform delivered prices were also challenged as discriminatory, the issue was vigorously contested, and the Commission eventually dismissed this part of the complaint. The case involved conspiracy to fix prices by the use of a zone-pricing system. The complaint charged that there was unlawful discrimination in the difference of delivered prices to customers in different zones and also in the uniformity of delivered prices to customers in the same zone at different distances from the seller's factory door. The latter type of discrimination was said to consist of the quotation of uniform delivered prices to customers so located that there were substantial differences in the costs of delivery to them.

The Commission found that the respondents had fixed prices and discriminated in price through zone-price differentials. However, it dismissed the further charge that the uniform delivered price within a zone was discriminatory. It said:

> The allegations are in effect that each of the respondents sells its products in accordance with a zone delivered pricing method and practice, but the alleged discriminations relied on as constituting injury to competition are the differences in the net prices received by each of the respondents at its mill. Thus, the complaint does not clearly show that the alleged unlawful discriminations as between purchasers of the respondents' products who are located in the same zone occur as the result of differences made in actual prices at which the respondents sell their products. For this reason, the Commission is of the opinion that this charge of the complaint should not be further considered.[33]

The apparent contradiction between the results of the fence case and the lead case may be explained in various ways. It is possible that an earlier attitude had been reconsidered by the Commission in the light of the fact that the Supreme Court had included in its opinion in the Staley case[34] a dictum that there was no discrimination in a uniform delivered price. However, there was no indication in the public statements

[33] 49 FTC 871. The Attorney General's Committee has interpreted this statement and one of similar import in the *Chain Institute* case (Docket 4878) as expressions of a policy that, in determining discrimination, price shall always mean delivered price—thus reversing the position taken in the cement and other cases. But the decisions do not explicitly announce such a policy, nor disclaim an intention to treat mill realizations as prices when mill prices are the "actual prices at which the respondents sell their products."

[34] See below, p. 385.

of the Commission after the Staley case that it intended to compare delivered costs in order to detect discriminations in circumstances in which sales were actually made at the seller's place of business. It is possible that the terms of sale were such in the fence industry as to justify the Commission in finding that sales were actually made at the mill and realizations there were actually the prices, even though the industry used the forms of delivered pricing; and that the facts in the lead case were such as to require the conclusion that sales were actually made at the delivery point and that the amounts charged there were actually the prices.[35] If so, obviously there was price difference in the first instance and not in the second. Though such an interpretation leaves the decisions of the Commission self-consistent, it must arouse in the observer an uneasy feeling that identities of substances were obscured by minor technical differences in selling relationships.

Other interpretations are even less satisfactory. The first case was not contested; the second was. The Commission may have decided the first case without fully realizing its implications. The first case was decided at a time when few voices were raised in support of delivered pricing by formula and the latter shortly after protest, aroused by the Commission's decisions in territorial pricing cases, had almost resulted in amendment

---

[35] A contract may be so drawn that the sale takes place either at the mill or at the customer's place of business, and so that the price does or does not include transportation costs. Since under the law a uniform price raises no question of discrimination, a price structure in which there were varying mill realizations from uniform payments by all customers could be interpreted as discriminatory if prices were mill prices and nondiscriminatory if prices were delivered prices. If the concept of price differed from case to case so that in each case price had the meaning it would have in commercial law, similar territorial price structures might be considered discriminatory in some instances and not in others.

Except for price structures in which the amounts paid at all destinations are uniform or the amounts received at the mill are uniform, price differences are present in both mill prices and delivered prices, so that the difference between the two concepts of price is unimportant in identifying discriminations. The more general importance of the concept of price springs from the fact that the defense of meeting competition is available only in meeting the equally low price of a competitor. To meet a competitor's delivered price may be to obtain a mill realization higher or lower than the competitor's mill realization; therefore the concept of price is conceptually important in setting limits for this type of defense. However, this issue arose in neither the fence case nor the lead case. In fact, no case has been presented to the Commission in which (1) a decision about territorial discrimination depended on the adequacy of the defense of meeting competition and (2) the validity of this defense depended on the concept of price that was used.

of the Robinson-Patman Act and the Federal Trade Commission Act. Between the two decisions there was an interval of 15 years, during which the personnel of the Commission changed. When interpretations of the law vary with the personalities of those who decide, the political pressures to which they are exposed, or the recalcitrance of those who are accused, the variation must be regarded as a weakness in the legal system.

Zone Prices

The Commission has issued an order under the Robinson-Patman Act against discrimination in zone pricing in only one instance, the National Lead case already mentioned. It found that sellers had established four sets of zones for three classes of lead products. For one class of products the United States was divided into two zones with a price differential of 25 cents per 100 pounds. For another class a similar two-zone system was used on shipments in carload quantities, and a four-zone system, with a range of 75 cents in zone prices, on smaller shipments. For a third class there were seven zones, with a difference of one dollar per 100 pounds between the lowest and highest zone prices. Analysis of the location of customers demonstrated that there were often substantial price differences between buyers who were near each other on opposite sides of zone boundaries, and that in some instances customers located in different zones competed against one another over wide areas. The zone-price differences were found to be important in relation to the profit margins of various customers. Injury in both the narrow and the broad sense was found among both sellers and buyers, and likewise a tendency to create a monopoly among both.

The order of the Commission forbade the respondents from agreeing on a zone-price system or any other system resulting in identical price quotations. It also forbade them individually from selling at zone prices for the purpose or with the effect of systematically matching delivered prices and from discriminating by selling at different zone prices to buyers in different zones who were in competition with one another in resale. The prohibition as to the matching of delivered prices was relevant to the conspiracy that violated the Federal Trade Commission Act. The prohibition as to price differences between competing buyers was relevant to the discrimination that violated the Robinson-Patman Act. Either prohibition of individual conduct, taken alone, made continued use of a zone system by a single company very difficult. But the legal implications of the two prohibitions were different. Since conspiracy was not material to the violation of the Robinson-Patman Act, an order under that statute not limited to conspiracy raised no legal issues. Its pertinence was not challenged on appeal. The similar order against individual conduct under the Federal Trade Commission Act resulted in a dissent at the Commission level, was set aside by the court of appeals, and was restored by the Supreme Court.[36]

On appeal, the Seventh Circuit not only modified the order as indicated above, but also dismissed the charge of discrimination as to dry white lead on the ground that there was no competition between the buyers in the premium zone and those in the par zone. It sustained the findings of the Commission of unlawful discrimination in the zone differentials for white lead-in-oil and lead oxides.[37] The Supreme Court reviewed the case only with reference to the Commission's right to issue an order against individual conduct in matching delivered prices by use of a zone system, which it sustained.[38]

[36] The majority of the Commission explained that the relevant part of the order was necessary to make the elimination of conspiracy effective, since without it "the momentum of the system, so firmly and maturely established, might last for some time." Commissioner Mason dissented on the grounds that the Commission did not have the broad injunctive powers of a court of equity and that to prohibit zone pricing without conspiracy was to make "one man's legal price illegal merely because others follow." (See 49 FTC 884-91.) In December 1955, the Seventh Circuit set aside this part of the order on the ground that under the Federal Trade Commission Act the Commission's condemnation of the use of zone prices had been directed at conspiracy and did not justify an order concerned with pricing by individual concerns. In February 1957, the Supreme Court sustained the Commission's original order in this respect. Relying on a statement in the Commission's opinion that after competition was restored the respondents would be free to show that this prohibition was no longer necessary or desirable, Mr. Justice Clark described the controversial requirement as temporary and pointed out that it was directed only at zone pricing that resulted in identical prices among competitors—that is, in which competitors used zones that were in whole or in part identical and prices that were identical in such zones. He also said that the order does not destroy the right of any of the respondents to meet a competitor's prices in good faith. It is not clear, however, how one respondent can meet the zone prices of another without in fact establishing, in the territory where both do business, the identity of zones and prices against which the order is directed.
[37] 227 F. 2d 825.
[38] 352 U.S. 419-31.

During the case, the pricing practices of the industry in selling lead oxides were substantially changed. National Lead established prices f.o.b. plant on December 1, 1952, before the Commission's decision in the case. Eagle-Picher also established f.o.b. plant prices. In 1957, four months after the Supreme Court decision, the Glidden Company was quoting mill prices, but with a differential in their level at different plants. One customer indicates that his costs have been substantially reduced by his ability to buy lead oxide at a shipper's nearby plant with relatively little freight expense. Freight has been absorbed or equalized to meet competition under the new method of quotation, and substantial identity of delivered prices has continued to exist.

Basing-Point Prices:
Cases Against Single Companies

The proceedings of the Commission against price discriminations in basing-point systems fall into two classes. In the first class are seven cases, all pertaining to corn products, each of which was concerned with discriminatory use of the basing-point system by a single corn products manufacturer. In the second class are two cases, involving corn products and cement, in which the charge of price discrimination was associated with a conspiracy charge. The conspiracy case for corn products consolidated the cases against individual companies and added the element of price fixing to the element of discrimination that had been present in those cases. The conspiracy charge as to cement treated the multiple basing-point pricing formula as the means by which, simultaneously, competition was set aside and discrimination was established.

All of the cases against individual manufacturers of corn products were instituted in 1939, and all of the cease and desist orders in these cases were issued between September 1940 and June 1942. Although the cases covered certain supplementary types of discrimination, they were focused primarily on the use by the industry of the basing-point system.[39]

---

[39] The case against *Penick and Ford* (Docket 3802) had to do only with territorial price differences. In the cases against *Staley* (Docket 3803) and *Clinton* (Docket 3800) the Commission found not only such differences but also discriminatory "booking," that is, filling orders for certain preferred customers at the former price after others were required to pay an increased price. In the case

Corn syrup was manufactured in ten plants owned by eight companies, all located within four hundred miles of one another.[40] Corn Products Refining Company, the largest producer, had three plants, at Chicago, near Peoria, and at Kansas City. These plants had about 45 per cent of the total corn-grinding capacity of the eight producers. The other plants, listed in order of size, were located at Decatur, Illinois (the Staley Company); Roby, Indiana (American Maize Products Company); Cedar Rapids, Iowa (Penick and Ford, Ltd.); Clinton, Iowa (the Clinton Company); Granite City, Illinois (Union Starch and Refining Company); Keokuk, Iowa (the Hubinger Company); and St. Louis, Missouri (Anheuser-Busch, Inc.). Orders against territorial discrimination were issued for all of these companies but American Maize Products.[41] In

---

against *Union Starch* (Docket 3804), territorial discrimination was accompanied by discriminatory price differences on sales in containers of different sizes. In the case against *Anheuser-Busch* (Docket 3798), where there was discrimination as to containers as well as territorial discrimination, different customers were found to have paid different prices for containers of the same size. These five cases were concerned only with the prices of corn syrup. The case against *Hubinger* (Docket 3801) covered both corn syrup and gluten feed. Hubinger's discrimination on the former involved territorial price differences, booking, and special discounts to two customers; on the latter, nine contracts for the sale of a stipulated monthly amount at a special price. The case against *Corn Products Refining Company* (Docket 3633) was the most complicated. It covered corn syrup, gluten feed, and corn starch. For the first it involved territorial discrimination, booking, and container differentials; for the second, territorial discrimination and special prices to six purchasers; for the third, special prices to two purchasers and exclusive dealing contracts with two in violation of Section 3 of the Clayton Act.

On March 15, 1941, the Commission issued an order in an eighth case, in which territorial discrimination was not included. This was a proceeding against *American Maize Products* (Docket 3805) on charges of booking and discriminatory container differentials. (See 32 FTC 901.) A complaint against a ninth company (Docket 3799, *Piel Brothers Starch Co.*) was issued, but dismissed because the concern was in process of liquidation. Piel's plant was sold in 1939 to National Starch Co. See Bernard Shull, "Price Discrimination in the Corn Products-Confectionery Industrial Pattern" (doctoral dissertation, University of Wisconsin, 1957), p. 133.

[40] In addition to those listed, there are three companies, National Starch Products Co. of Indianapolis, Huron Milling Co. of Harbor Beach, Michigan, and Keever Starch Co. of Columbus, Ohio and East Chicago, Illinois, which, at the time of the proceedings, were not producers of corn syrup. *Ibid.*, pp. 86, 102.

[41] An order was also issued in a case against *American Maize Products* (Docket 3805), but the discriminations found did not include territorial price differences. Presumably the reason was that the company's plant at Roby, Indiana, is within the Chicago switching district, so that its sales of corn syrup were characteristically f.o.b. mill.

each instance the seller had quoted delivered prices consisting of the price at Chicago plus rail freight to the destination.[42]

The Kansas City plant of Corn Products Refining Company quoted in Kansas City a price equivalent to the price at the Chicago plant plus the freight from Chicago to Kansas City. Similar phantom freight was included in its delivered prices throughout the area in which the freight cost from Chicago was greater than the freight cost from Kansas City. In a few sales in which customers in Chicago were supplied from the Kansas City plant, they paid the Chicago price, and freight from Kansas City was absorbed. Deliveries from the Chicago plant to all destinations provided uniform mill realizations. Deliveries from the Kansas City plant were at prices including varying amounts of phantom freight or freight absorption, which produced varying realizations at the mill. All customers who were nearer freight-wise to Kansas City than to Chicago were deprived of the benefit of their location near the Kansas City plant. The Commission found that in August 1939 the delivered price of $2.49 for glucose at Kansas City included phantom freight of 40 cents per hundred pounds; at Fort Smith, Arkansas, 20 cents; at Lincoln, Nebraska, 32 cents; at San Antonio, 19 cents; and at Denver, 10 cents. The Commission found that candy manufacturers who bought glucose in various localities were in competition with one another and that the difference in the cost of the raw material gave an advantage to Chicago manufacturers. A small difference in the resale price was sufficient to divert the business of chain stores and other large buyers of candy. In consequence, the difference in raw material costs had a significant effect either on operating margins or on volume of sales. Some of the candy manufacturers who were located outside Chicago before the construction and operation of the Kansas City plant had subsequently relocated in Chicago. The Commission concluded that, in selling from Kansas City on a Chicago base,

[42] The formal findings described the nature of the pricing practice with different degrees of particularity. In the case against Corn Products Refining Company, the method of pricing was explicitly described. In the Clinton, Hubinger, and Staley cases, delivered prices based on Chicago were compared with delivery costs from the factory of the respondent. In the Anheuser-Busch case, without computation of freight costs in the findings, the Commission found that prices based on Chicago did not reflect cost differences. In the Union Starch case, freight charges were not computed in the findings, and there was no reference to cost; but the use of a Chicago base was found. In the case against Penick and Ford, even the use of a Chicago base was not mentioned: The Commission found that delivered prices at various places differed to an extent not shown to be cost-justified.

Corn Products Refining had discriminated in a way that had the capacity to injure competition in the primary line of commerce in both the broad and the narrow sense, tended to create a monopoly in that line of commerce, and also had the capacity to lessen competition substantially in the secondary line of commerce.[43]

During the trial of the Corn Products case, orders were issued against four of the other companies. After the Commission had introduced some evidence against Anheuser-Busch, Union Starch, and Hubinger, additional evidence was placed in the record by stipulation, and the respondents waived their rights to present testimony, briefs, and argument. An order was issued against Anheuser-Busch on September 25, 1940, against Union Starch on December 11, 1940, and against Hubinger on April 3, 1941. Meanwhile, Penick and Ford had stipulated the facts required for the proceeding against it and had consented to the entry of an order by the Commission based on the stipulation, without further formalities of testimony, briefs, or argument. An order was issued on November 29, 1940. On March 17, 1942, the day after the decision of the Commission in the case against Corn Products Refining, an order was also issued against the Clinton Company. In this case the facts had been stipulated, but in legal brief and oral argument Clinton had contested the Commission's interpretation of them and the propriety of an order. On June 10, 1942, an order was issued against Staley. Like that against Clinton, it was based on a stipulation of facts followed by a dispute as to their legal significance, but though Staley filed a brief, it did not request oral argument.

The case against all six respondents was that, though their plants were not in Chicago, their delivered prices had been computed on a Chicago

---

[43] The price structure antedated the opening of the Kansas City plant in 1922. Presumably, the plant was built because the seller was attracted by the opportunity to convert some freight expense into profit. In the absence of conspiracy, one might expect that this advantage to the seller would be subject to erosion through the competition of other nearby plants, then existing or to be erected, such as Hubinger's plant at Keokuk, Iowa; and one might envisage the possibility that the temporary receipt of phantom freight was not injurious to competition among buyers but, instead, a useful incentive to bring plants nearer to the more distant consuming centers and thus eventually reduce the buying disadvantage of the buyers who had previously been remote from centers of production. Since there was conspiracy in the corn products industry, the advantages of sellers were not thus eroded. The Commission, which was aware of the conspiracy, did not consider in its findings as to injury to competition the possibility of such a result.

base. In consequence, the patterns of phantom freight and freight absorption in their price structures were similar to those in the sales by the Kansas City plant of Corn Products Refining Company, and the variations in realizations at the plant were also similar. In each case the Commission found injury to competition in the fact that the candy manufacturers paying the higher prices and competing with others more favored must choose between an unsatisfactory profit margin and a loss in volume of sales. In the Clinton case, this finding was supplemented by a statement that because of the discrimination, disfavored mixers of table syrup were unable to sell their products in areas in which their freight advantage, as compared with Chicago mixers, was less than the discrimination against them on glucose. The finding in the Staley case also covered injury to makers of table syrup as well as candy, but emphasized the effect of difference in cost on prices and operating margins rather than on the territorial breadth of the market.[44]

In spite of the generally similar nature of the discriminations, the findings of injury varied widely in the six cases. Special discounts on corn syrup by Hubinger to two purchasers were found to have the capacity to produce both the narrow and broad types of injury in the primary line of commerce, and to tend to create a monopoly in that line as well. Except as to these discounts, all the effects found were on competition among buyers. For Hubinger, Anheuser-Busch, Penick and Ford, and Union Starch, these effects included both the narrow and broad types of injury to competition and also a tendency to monopoly. For Clinton and Staley, however, only the narrow type of injury in the secondary line was found.[45] There was no explanation of these differences in the findings. Except for Corn Products Refining, which was the leading producer,

[44] Subsequent analysis of statistics for the confectionery industry by Shull, "Price Discrimination in the Corn Products-Confectionery Industrial Pattern," pp. 147-52, indicated that during the operation of the single basing-point system "significant increases in the relative importance of Chicago as a candy manufacturing center took place" and that "in the years following the abandonment of the single basing-point system, the rate of increase in the relative importance of Chicago diminished greatly, at first, and then decreased absolutely." Data for two other centers, St. Louis and Kansas City, indicated that the relative importance of these cities fell while the single basing point was in use.

[45] It is noteworthy that, although the violations found in the case against American Maize Products were limited to discriminations in booking and in differential charges for containers (of which the former was also found in the cases against Clinton and Staley), the injury found in the American Maize case included all three types of harm to competition in the secondary line—a more impressive finding than against Clinton and Staley.

Clinton and Staley had been the only companies to contest the issuance of an order against them.

The price discriminations found in the four corn products cases in which the findings contain computations of territorial price differences were analyzed by the Commission as though, in using a Chicago basing point, the outlying producers were obtaining phantom freight or absorbing freight in amounts measured, at each destination, by the difference between the published freight rate from Chicago and the published freight rate from the seller's plant. In fact, this was not so. Producers of corn products, like fabricators in various other industries, enjoyed the benefit of fabrication-in-transit privileges in paying freight.[46] The facts of the matter were briefly brought out in the testimony in the Hubinger case,[47] but Hubinger accepted an order without briefs or argument, and

[46] In the findings of the case against Corn Products Refining Company, milling in transit is mentioned as the basis for minor deviations from prices f.o.b. Chicago in sales by the Chicago mill. The matter is not further explained. See 34 FTC 861.

[47] According to the record in this case, Hubinger was able to use the fabrication-in-transit privilege in sales to points as scattered as Chicago, St. Louis, Kansas City, Oklahoma City, and Fort Worth. The effect was a substantial reduction in the freight charge on corn syrup. "For example, the local Keokuk-to-Chicago rate is 18 cents. We receive corn from a central Iowa point located on the Rock Island rails, paying an average of 19 cents to Keokuk. The corn rate from this point of origin to Chicago would be 24 cents. When this corn is originally received at Keokuk, we pay the 19-cent rate, manufacture it into corn syrup, unmixed, and then when we ship it to Chicago by the Rock Island, we would not pay the 18-cent rate, but we apply our milling-in-transit application, using the point of origin of corn to Chicago rate, 24 cents, less than the 19-cent corn rate, or a balance of 5 cents, plus an out-of-line charge of 1 cent. . . .

"Q. Suppose . . . you bought corn and had it shipped in and milled it and shipped it back in the same direction; do you get milling in transit on that back haul?

"A. Well, from Alexander, Missouri, five miles down here, we have a back haul going south.

"Q. In other words, it comes out and goes right back down again?

"A. That is it. . . . We protect the through corn rate to points in Chicago, the Chicago switching district, Peoria, and St. Louis. All of other points west of us is on the through-product rate, and on points east of Chicago it is on the balance of the corn rate up to Chicago or Chicago pro rate point, plus the commodity rate beyond. . . .

"Q. But if you had bought it in some other place and direction and you were sending it towards the southwest, let us say you were sending it to St. Joseph or Kansas City or Oklahoma City, or something of that kind, what would the rate be?

"A. That would be the through established commodity rate from point of origin to final destination, less the corn rate paid into Keokuk. . . . Like we receive corn, we will say, from Estherville, Iowa. Estherville, Iowa, to Kansas City, the corn rate would be about 16 cents, but the corn syrup, unmixed, rate would be a 31-

this part of the record apparently did not influence the analysis by the Commission.

By fabrication in transit, the outlying mills west of Chicago, and perhaps others, could deliver corn syrup in Chicago at a total transportation cost for corn and corn syrup approximately equal to that incurred by Corn Products Refining Company for corn delivered in Chicago, provided the corn bought by these mills originated at the same points as that bought by Corn Products Refining Company. In quoting a Chicago base price on Chicago sales, therefore, these companies probably were not absorbing significant amounts of freight. At some intermediate points the computed freight from Chicago on the finished product may well have exceeded the actual amount of the in-transit payment from the point of shipment.

Shipments in a direction away from Chicago incurred charges from the point of origin of the corn to the destination of the corn syrup at the commodity rate rather than the corn rate, and thus the net saving to the mill from the fabrication-in-transit privilege varied with the rail distances the shipment traversed as raw material and as finished product.[48] Moreover, there were complications because the privileges extended by the different railroads were not identical and because the freight reduction could not be claimed in some instances in which the corn was moved by one railroad and the syrup by another. An *a priori* determination of the pattern of phantom freight and freight absorption is not possible; specific analysis of the payments made to railroads on various shipments would

---

cent rate, and the corn rate from Estherville to Keokuk, we will say, 20.5 cents. So, in reality, we would pay about 10.5 cents to Kansas City.

"Q. That is a 31-cent rate which would be the rate on glucose from Estherville to Kansas City?

"A. Yes.

"Q. Less the 20.5-cent rate, which would be the Estherville to Keokuk rate?

"A. Correct." (Docket 3801. Official Report of Proceedings Before the Federal Trade Commission, June 20, 1940, original transcript, pp. 104, 106, 110-11.)

[48] The commodity rate is higher than the corn rate. On the shipment of corn to the mill, the commodity rate resulted in the payment of a freight premium. On the shipment of syrup from the mill to the destination, the payment of the remainder of the through commodity rate from the point of origin of the corn resulted in a freight saving as compared with the commodity rate for the shorter haul. The longer the inward shipment, the greater the premium. The greater the difference between long- and short-haul commodity rates, the greater the saving. The advantage in the fabrication-in-transit privilege consisted in the excess of the saving over the premium.

be necessary.[49] Hence, it is not possible to determine *a priori* to what extent mill net realizations varied on shipments to different destinations. The illustrations on which the Commission rested its conclusions are almost certainly invalid. Nevertheless, it is clear that the pricing pattern involved substantial amounts of phantom freight and freight absorption. But neither the findings nor the trial records contain enough information to show the pattern of these or the amounts involved.

In six of these seven cases, it appears from the findings that no question arose as to the absorption of freight in good faith to meet a competitor's prices. As the largest concern in the industry and the one that had established the Chicago base price, Corn Products Refining Company was in no position to raise this issue. Anheuser-Busch, Penick and Ford, Union Starch, and Hubinger accepted the Commission's orders without arguing the legal questions that might be involved. Though Clinton argued the case, it apparently raised other points, for the findings contain nothing as to meeting competition.

Staley, however, defended its pricing system on the ground that it had merely accepted the price structure it found in the industry and that it had no alternative other than to meet the prices of its competitors.[50] The Commission agreed that the Chicago base was already in use when Staley began to sell glucose and that Staley had adopted the practice of selling at the same delivered prices as its competitors. "Respondents have consistently followed the prices for glucose announced by their competitors according to the pricing formula stated; that is, Chicago base plus freight to destination, except in certain instances when respondents have been the first to announce a change in the price of glucose, and in such instances they have announced prices in accord with the pricing formula therefore [sic] in use by their competitors and themselves."[51] There was, however, no more explicit finding as to the bearing of these facts on Staley's defense that competition had been met in good faith.

[49] Persons in the industry who were interviewed were unwilling to discuss the fabrication-in-transit system or to make available a comprehensive study of it which had been made for the industry. Their reticence about the matter may account for their failure to criticize the Commission's analysis during the legal proceedings.

[50] As to the supplementary charges of discrimination in the effective date of price changes, the Commission rejected this contention because no real effort had been made to determine whether other sellers had made similar discriminatory offers. Suspicion and the verbal statements of salesmen had been relied on.

[51] 34 FTC 1369.

*Court Decisions in the
Basing-Point Cases*

Appeals were filed by Corn Products Refining Company and Staley, but not by the other companies. The Seventh Circuit upheld the view of the Commission that the prices of Corn Products Refining Company were illegally discriminatory. Judge Lindley's opinion said:

> In so far as the delivery price includes for freight more than the actual cost of transportation it measures a definite discrimination forbidden by statute. . . . The inclusion of a fictional cost of delivery, having no justification in fact, in itself suggests, upon the part of the manufacturer, arbitrary fixation of prices discriminating illegally as between competitive customers. Systematic price discrimination is irreconcilable with free, active competition. . . . We think it irrefutable from the facts that resulting substantial loss is reasonably likely to accrue to purchasers in the less favorably located communities.

He rejected the defendant's contention that the Robinson-Patman Act was not intended to cover basing-point systems. He interpreted the legislative history as expressing disagreement among members of Congress, with neither condemnation nor approval of basing-point pricing by the Congress as a whole. He added, "As we read the Act, it does not grant exemption from discrimination merely because the facts fall within certain formulae. The real question is, do the discriminations inherently have the condemned probable effect upon competition?"[52]

The Staley case was considered by the Seventh Circuit and returned to the Commission on the ground that the findings of the Commission were inadequate. Judge Minton's opinion said that the Commission seemed to think that the proof of discrimination led automatically to the conclusion that competition was injured but that this was incorrect: the injury must be set forth in a finding supported by evidence. He also directed the Commission to consider further Staley's claim that its discriminations were made in good faith to meet competitors' prices.[53]

A modified decision against Staley[54] was issued by the Commission on

[52] 144 F. 2d 211, 215-16. The court also confirmed the Commission's findings and order as to all other aspects of the case except as to discrimination in container differentials. As to this, it saw no basis for an inference that price differences for containers of different sizes violated the law. *Ibid.*, p. 220.

[53] 135 F. 2d 453.

[54] Federal Trade Commission, *Statutes and Decisions*, Vol. 4, 1944-48 (1951), p. 705.

September 13, 1943. It contained findings of injury similar to those in the other corn products cases summarized above.[55] It rejected Staley's claim of good faith in meeting competition territorially because (1) Staley had sometimes taken the lead in lowering or raising prices; (2) in some places use of the basing-point system meant that Staley discriminated by quoting prices higher than they would have been if nondiscriminatory, so that, in effect, it "discriminated in price to meet the higher price of a competitor"; (3) discrimination was an integral part of Staley's pricing system, through which identical delivered prices were quoted and Staley's locational advantage in its home market was surrendered in return for a reciprocal surrender of similar advantage by competitors; (4) matching prices and thereby destroying competition was the purpose of the system. Staley's good faith in its booking practices was denied because Staley had relied on salesmen's reports of customers' statements about competitors' prices though it had reason to know that some of these statements were false. The burden of proof as to good faith was on Staley, not the Commission, the Commission decided, and that burden had not been successfully carried; but had the Commission been required to prove bad faith, it would have taken notice of a consent decree in 1932 following a charge that corn products manufacturers had fixed prices in violation of the Sherman Act.[56]

When the case reached the Seventh Circuit for the second time, Judge Minton's opinion sustained the Commission's finding of injury largely because the respondents had stipulated that:

> . . . The higher prices paid for such syrup by such candy manufacturers located as aforesaid other than in the City of Chicago, Illinois, contribute to a greater or lesser degree in their having higher raw material costs than those candy manufacturers located in Chicago, Illinois, the degree in each instance depending upon the difference in price and the proportion of such syrup used in the candies manufactured; . . . that the lower profits of these candy manufacturers paying higher prices for such syrup diminishes their incentive or desire to compete with

---

[55] Users of glucose were said to employ it as an important raw material in producing products sold under competition so keen that a fraction of a cent in price difference would divert business. Disfavored customers were said, therefore, to face the alternative of impaired profits if they met the prices of their favored rivals and impaired volume if they did not do so. They were also said to be deterred from entering business at the disfavored locations.

[56] *U.S.* v. *Corn Derivatives Institute*, Equity 11634, Northern District of Illinois, 1932.

those candy manufacturers paying the lower prices for such syrup and may deter potential new candy manufacturers from entering the industry in cities where they would pay the higher syrup costs.[57]

However, Judge Minton rejected the finding of the Commission on good faith. He was not impressed by the fact that on several occasions Staley had taken the lead in changing delivered prices.

> The fact that the companies were first in the field with a price is not controlling. The question here is: Were they first in the field to use the basing point pricing system? It is the use of the system that is complained of. The evidence and stipulations are all to the contrary. The companies' competitors were using the system when the companies entered the field. The companies merely followed the system and practices which had been established by their competitors. That this was done in good faith is not questioned in the evidence.

He gave weight to the point that the bulk of Staley's business was in the Chicago market and that to get into Chicago Staley found it necessary to absorb freight from Decatur.[58] Accordingly he set the Commission's order aside.

Two judges were not in accord with all of Judge Minton's opinion, but for different reasons. Judge Major, who agreed that the order should be set aside, thought the Commission had failed to prove price discrimination because, in passing the Robinson-Patman Act, the Congress did not intend to outlaw the basing-point system,[59] and because in various cases, such as the first cement case, the legality of that system had been recognized. He did not take issue with Judge Minton's view that Staley had

[57] 144 F. 2d 221, 223n-24n.
[58] *Ibid.*, p. 225.
[59] As reported by the House Judiciary Committee, the Robinson-Patman bill contained a passage defining price as the vendor's realization after deducting transportation cost. The committee report said that the purpose was to eliminate the basing-point or delivered-price method of sale and to require the use of f.o.b. mill method. This passage was deleted from the bill by unanimous consent, apparently because certain members of the Rules Committee opposed it. See *Congressional Record*, Vol. 80, Pt. 8, 74 Cong. 2 sess., p. 8223. In the debate, some members defended the basing-point pricing practice, and others said that it should be dealt with by separate legislation. In the debates in the Senate, Senator Borah said that the bill would have no effect on the basing-point system, and Senator Van Nuys, who was in charge of the bill, agreed that this was correct; but in the exchange of comment the basing-point system was so loosely described as to obscure the meaning of the remarks. See above, pp. 26-27, and below, footnote 2, pp. 439-40.

acted in good faith, but thought there was no need to decide the merits of such a defense.[60] Judge Evans agreed with Judge Minton that the Commission had shown injurious discrimination within the meaning of the law, but rejected his conclusions as to good faith and therefore dissented from the decision. Judge Evans thought that in adhering to the basing-point system, Staley was not merely quoting a lower price:

> . . . Staley did not want "to stir up the animals" by starting a price war. He accepted the status quo—a status quo which followed a practice which "substantially lessened competition and tended to create a monopoly," and which was, no doubt, satisfactory to one about to enter the field. But the satisfaction was not over the fact that it was to be permitted to "lower prices," but over the fact that said practice tended to lessen competition.

Moreover, Staley adhered to the basing-point system generally and not merely in Chicago where it encountered the competition of Corn Products Refining Company. Judge Evans could see no good faith in the addition of phantom freight to the prices of goods sold at Decatur. Moreover, he thought that good faith could never be attributed to a seller who discriminated in such a way as substantially to lessen competition and tend to create a monopoly.[61]

The Supreme Court decided the Corn Products and Staley cases on the same day in co-ordinated opinions, both written by the Chief Justice. After holding that territorial price discrimination is covered by the statute, he decided that neither the legislative history of the Robinson-Patman Act nor judicial decisions gave any immunity to basing-point systems. He found in the legislative history an indication that Congress, unwilling to require f.o.b. factory pricing and thus make all basing-point systems automatically unlawful, had left the legality of such systems to be determined under the general prohibitions of the Robinson-Patman Act. In the maple-flooring and cement cases that had been decided under the Sherman Act in 1925, he said, the question at issue had been not price discrimination but price fixing. Moreover, in maple flooring the basing points had been so near the points of production as to make their effect on transportation charges trivial, and manufacturers had been will-

[60] 144 F. 2d 221, 227-31. He expressed the same opinion more briefly in dissent in the Corn Products case. See ibid., pp. 211, 221.

[61] Ibid., pp. 221, 225-26.

ing to sell at the mill on request. In the cement industry basing points had been near production points and had involved freight absorption rather than phantom freight. He specifically disclaimed any intention to decide the question whether such a system—that is, one of mill pricing with systematic freight equalization—is permissible under the price discrimination law.

He found ample support for the Commission's inference of injury to competition in the findings that glucose is a principal ingredient of low-priced candy and that differences of fractions of a cent in the price of such candy are enough to divert business. He noted the finding of the Commission that certan manufacturers had moved to Chicago from the phantom-freight area.[62]

In the Staley case Chief Justice Stone held that, in changing the wording of the law so that respondent is authorized to rebut the Commission's case by showing that he met the price of a competitor in good faith, the Congress had intended to make the defense "a matter of evidence in each case, raising a question of fact as to whether the competition justified the discrimination." He treated as "startling" Staley's contention that a seller may justify a basing point delivered price system, which is otherwise outlawed by Section 2, because other competitors are in part violating the law by maintaining a like system. He rejected this interpretation on the ground that the statute does not concern itself with pricing systems but places emphasis on individual competitive situations. The test of good faith "presupposes that the person charged with violating the Act would, by his normal, nondiscriminatory pricing methods, have reached a price so high that he could reduce it in order to meet the competitor's equally low price." By this test he found that Staley's basing-point system lacked good faith, for Staley had never attempted to establish its own non-discriminatory price system but had "slavishly followed in the first instance a pricing policy" that resulted in systematic discriminations. Moreover, Staley had taken advantage of the system to maintain high prices where it could charge phantom freight, and its purpose in using basing-point pricing had not been to meet the low Chicago prices but "to establish elsewhere the artificially high prices whose discriminatory effect permeates respondents' entire pricing system."

Staley had argued that the delivered price at Decatur could be regarded as a base price and the lower realizations from delivered prices at all other

[62] 324 U.S. 726.

points as instances of price reduction to meet competition. The court rejected this view both as an interpretation of past conduct and as a possibility in future price adjustment. ". . . we must reject respondents' argument that the Commission's order could be rendered nugatory, by respondents' establishing such a high factory price as always to admit of reductions in order to meet the prices of competitors who are using a Chicago basing-point system. For we think it could not be said that this practical continuation of the present discriminatory basing-point system would be in good faith." However, the Chief Justice disclaimed the intention to prevent Staley from absorbing freight where the factory price plus actual freight was higher than competitors' prices. He also said that it did not follow from the opinion that sellers were forbidden to maintain a uniform delivered price by absorbing freight, "for in that event there is no discrimination in price."[63]

Basing-Point Prices: Cases Involving Joint Action

In the corn products conspiracy case, the Commission found that the manufacturers of corn products had collaborated through their associations in a price agreement maintained through the use of basing-point and zone-pricing systems. The Commission's findings of price discrimination by the individual companies were used in this case as a part of the evidence of agreement and also as a basis for a comprehensive finding of price discrimination. The respondents were then ordered to cease agreeing to establish zone-pricing systems, identical delivered prices, basing-point systems, or any systems of quoting or charging prices, or agreeing not to sell corn derivatives f.o.b. point of production. They were individually ordered not to act in a way that helped maintain any such agreement and not to discriminate in price in a way injurious to competition except as justified by the provisos of the statute.[64] The case added a prohibition of conspiracy to the prohibitions of price discrimination contained in the orders against the individual companies, and applied to American Maize Products and National Starch Products as well as to the other manufacturers who had been involved in the previous basing-point

[63] *Ibid.,* pp. 746, 753-57.
[64] The language of the order as to price discrimination is a close paraphrase of the language of the Robinson-Patman Act.

cases.[65] Otherwise, it did little to change the situation established by the corn products cases that have been discussed above.

When the group of corn products cases is considered as a whole, it is evident that discriminations on corn syrup, and the proceedings against them, were related to competition in two different and, indeed, opposite ways. Territorial discrimination by formula was the form taken by a concert of action about prices, and attack on it was an attack on the conspiracy. But the price agreement had been loosened and in part defeated by off-scale selling by at least five companies through such devices as discriminatory booking of orders at the old prices and special concessions to a few favored customers. Attack on these practices, standing alone, would have strengthened the conspiracy. In proceeding against both types of practice at once, the Commission sought to terminate the conspiracy and also to substitute nondiscriminatory forms of competition for the existing discriminatory forms.

The case against the Cement Institute was primarily concerned with price fixing through the general use of a multiple basing-point system.[66]

[65] American Maize Products and National Starch Products were among the respondents and were made subject to the order. Thus, though the previous order against American Maize had not covered use of the basing-point system, and there had been no previous case against National Starch, both were forbidden, along with the other companies, to take part in the collective maintenance of a territorial pricing formula. Since the part of the order concerned with discrimination was general, the effect presumably was to forbid American Maize and National Starch to discriminate territorially, as the others had been found to do.

[66] Relevant to the cement case are two proceedings against individual cement companies for price discriminations that had a territorial effect though they did not concern price differences between localities. The cases are Docket 5670, *Ideal Cement Company, et al.*, (47 FTC 221) and Docket 5671, *Monolith Portland Cement Company, et al.*, (47 FTC 1292). In each the Commission found that the seller had sold at the plant to purchasers who transported cement from the point of sale by motor carrier at prices 20 cents per barrel higher than to purchasers who transported it by rail, and that the effect might be to reduce competition in the secondary line in both the narrow and broad senses. According to the answers of the respondent companies, soon after the decision in the cement conspiracy case one producer abandoned the price differential and adopted a policy of selling at a uniform price regardless of the method of transportation, but only in carload lots in a single loading operation (though in more than one vehicle if desired). Six or seven months later the other producer also abandoned the differential, provided a carload quantity was loaded. In each case, the differential had been abandoned before the complaint. The respondents filed admission answers and accepted orders preventing resumption of similar discriminations.

Trucking differentials similar to those condemned in these cases were common

However, the Commission charged and found that the basing-point pricing formula entailed discrimination. The actual prices of cement were the mill-net realizations, which differed with the location of the customer. ". . . The discrimination in mill nets by each respondent seller forms a systematic pattern that is the mathematical counterpart of the delivered-price pattern resulting from the multiple basing-point delivered-price system, which system is an expression of the effort of each respondent seller to match the delivered prices of other respondent sellers."[67] The difference in mill-net prices inherent in the system was found by the Commission to injure competition among the respondents in both the narrow and broad senses and to tend to create a monopoly among them. In other words, the conspiracy itself constituted the impairment of competition which, in the Commission's findings, made the discrimination unlawful.[68]

Voluminous evidence of conspiracy was summarized in the Commission's findings in the cement case. It included not only evidence derived from the characteristics of the multiple basing-point system but also evidence of assorted activities in establishing and perfecting the system and enforcing conformity to it by recalcitrant producers. For proof that the system was unlawfully discriminatory, the Commission relied on findings that the mill-net realizations of sellers from customers variously located differed commonly by from 25 to 50 cents a barrel and in extreme

---

in the cement industry and other industries where delivered prices were computed by formulas based on rail freight. These differentials helped prevent buyers from evading prices that included phantom freight by furnishing their own transportation. They helped avert differentials in delivered prices based on varying charges for transportation. Thus they were useful adjuncts to conspiracies that relied upon pricing formulas and to the territorial discriminations associated therewith. They also helped sellers to avoid, or receive payment for, the trouble and expense of loading trucks at plants that were better equipped to load railroad cars. However, a trucking differential limited to the amount that could be cost-justified might have been ineffective in accomplishing the purposes that such differentials often served; and in any event, its amount would have varied from plant to plant and would have been difficult to determine. In both of the cases under discussion, the respondent said that it believed the differential had been cost-justified, and in both it said that proof would have been expensive and would not be undertaken.

[67] 37 FTC 254-55.

[68] The respondents contended that they had met competition in good faith. The function of this allegation was primarily to explain identity in prices as the result of competition rather than conspiracy. In finding that there had been price fixing, the Commission and the courts necessarily rejected the claim and made it unavailable as a defense against a finding of discrimination.

instances by more than one dollar a barrel, with the higher realizations from the customers nearer the mill. That the sellers recognized mill nets as the true prices of cement was said by the Commission to be established from the evidence, but the Commission noted that if delivered prices were considered the true prices, there would still be discriminations reflecting a plan to bring about identity in the delivered prices of different sellers.[69]

The cement order was important for its effect on the public and on the political status of the Commission's policy toward basing points. In appellate review and in public discussion, it became the occasion for a reconsideration of problems raised by various other orders dealing with basing points, the defense of meeting competition, and similar matters. Although the case had to do with a price-fixing conspiracy, judicial review of that case discussed the application of the Corn Products and Staley decisions to the individual use of basing-point formulas. In the Seventh Circuit, Judge Major interpreted these decisions to mean that the collection of phantom freight results in unlawful discrimination, but held that ". . . those decisions did not hold that freight absorption was discriminatory; in fact, that question was expressly left open." He thought the Supreme Court had recognized "that a seller may absorb freight when done in good faith to meet an equally low price of a competitor, even though a uniform delivered price at all points of delivery might result."[70]

The Supreme Court overturned this judgment. Speaking for the Court, Mr. Justice Black said:

> In the Corn Products case, the Court, in holding illegal a single basing-point system, specifically reserved decision upon the legality under the Clayton Act of a multiple basing point price system, but only in view of the "good faith" proviso. . . . The latter case [Staley] held that a seller could not justify the adoption of a competitor's basing point price system under Section 2(b) as a good faith attempt to meet the latter's equally low price. Thus the combined effect of the two cases was to forbid the adoption for sales purposes of any basing point pricing system.

Reiterating the distinction between systematic discrimination and price reduction in individual competitive situations, Mr. Justice Black rejected the defense of meeting competition in the cement case on the ground that

[69] 37 FTC 254-57.
[70] 157 F. 2d 533, 560-61.

each respondent sold some cement at prices determined by the basing-point formula and governed by other base mills and thus adopted a discriminatory pricing system. In these circumstances he saw no difference in good faith between collecting phantom freight and absorbing freight. He held that the defense did not mean that Section 2(b) "permits a seller to use a sales system which constantly results in his getting more money for like goods from some customers than he does from others."[71]

The Supreme Court decided the Corn Products and Staley cases in April 1945. It decided the cement case in April 1948. Although the opinions in the first two cases had apparently invalidated all basing-point pricing in which there was substantial phantom freight, they had provoked relatively little protest in the business community. Presumably, the statements disclaiming decision as to multiple basing-point systems, approving uniform delivered prices as nondiscriminatory, and disclaiming an intention to invalidate freight absorption were thought sufficient to permit a wide variety of delivered price systems. In the cement case, however, the court had said that all basing-point systems are unlawful and had explicitly rejected the idea that systematic freight absorption could be regarded as meeting competition in good faith. The decision was widely interpreted as a declaration that all systems of pricing other than f.o.b. mill were unlawful, and that a concern using an f.o.b. mill system could depart from it only sporadically by absorbing freight in specific situations.[72] The result was a political controversy over proposals to amend the Federal Trade Commission Act and the Clayton Act, which is summarized in the next chapter.

[71] 333 U.S. 683, 723-25.

[72] Belief that the decision called for comprehensive changes in business practice was strengthened by a news release issued by the Commission on April 28, 1948. It characterized the portions of the Supreme Court's decision that concerned price discrimination as a reaffirmation of the principles of the glucose cases "that price discrimination in a basing point system involves freight absorption as well as phantom freight, and that the law does not exempt the one any more than the other if competition is injured or destroyed. Both now stand clearly condemned as instruments of unlawful price discrimination. . . ." After quoting Mr. Justice Black's statement that the combined effect of the decisions was to forbid adoption of any basing-point system, the release said: "Hope is expressed that industry in general, and organized industry in particular, will avail itself of the opportunity now presented to conform voluntarily to the law as determined by the Supreme Court in the Cement case. . . ." See Study of Pricing Methods, Hearings before the Senate Committee on Interstate and Foreign Commerce, 80 Cong. 2 sess., Nov. 9-Dec. 8, 1948, pp. 444-45.

Effects of the Orders in
Basing-Point Cases

Although there was no amendment of the statutes, the impact of the orders of the Commission in the corn products and cement cases was substantially affected by developments during the controversy. In defending its position, the Federal Trade Commission declared repeatedly that it did not think delivered pricing or freight absorption inherently illegal and that it thought the right to meet competition in good faith should be guaranteed by law. The strong congressional support for amendment of the law made clear that if the statute were not conservatively applied in these respects, a change in the law was probable. While the controversy was going on, the Supreme Court decided in the case against Standard Oil Company of Indiana[73] that good faith in meeting competition is a complete defense against a charge of price discrimination. In the order in the corn products conspiracy case, the Commission specifically disclaimed any intent to interfere with individual competitive freight absorption. Accordingly, the concerns subject to the corn products and cement orders interpreted these orders in the light of the whole situation, including the shadings that law and administrative policy had acquired during the political controversy.

After the orders against the individual companies, the manufacturers of corn syrup abandoned their use of a single basing point.[74] According to answers filed to the complaint in the conspiracy case, each of them substituted a system of mill pricing with freight equalization in selling carload quantities and zone pricing in selling packaged derivatives.[75]

[73] See above, pp. 319-33.

[74] *Cf.* Simon N. Whitney, *Antitrust Policies—American Experience in Twenty Industries* (1958), Vol. 2, pp. 272-78, 281-83.

[75] The orders against individual producers of corn products had been issued in 1940, 1941, and 1942, and the appeals by Corn Products Refining and Staley had been decided in 1945. The complaint in the corn products conspiracy case was issued in June 1947, and the order in November 1950. Hence one might expect that the findings in the case would throw light on the changes in the industry after the earlier orders took effect. But this is not so. Although the findings state that the Commission made an exhaustive survey of the sales of five large-volume corn derivatives from 1941 through 1947, all specific information included in the findings has to do with January 1942, when the orders against Corn Products Refining, Clinton, and Staley had not yet been issued. Statements in the findings as to pricing formulas pertain to "most of the period covered by the complaint," the

Staley, and perhaps others, did not absorb freight during a period of shortage immediately following the change;[76] but when a buyers' market returned in the late 1940's, freight equalization became general.

In general outline, the freight-equalization system is still followed. A base price is quoted at each mill. It is, in several instances, the same as the Chicago price of Corn Products Refining Company. For Hubinger, however, it was 7 cents lower in mid-March 1957,[77] and for Staley 9 cents lower. For the Kansas City plant of Corn Products Refining, it was apparently 5 or 6 cents higher. Delivered prices are computed by adding rail freight from the mill, and where the result is a difference in the delivered prices quoted by different sellers, enough freight is absorbed to meet the lowest delivered price resulting from use of the

---

time of "the closing of the record" in the cases against the individual companies and January 1942. The Commission says that "at a more recent date" than the date covered by the findings in the earlier cases producers shifted to a multiple basing-point system on corn syrup unmixed (47 FTC 646). It also says that (presumably at the more recent date also) a zone system was used for gloss starch, and a mixed basing-point and zone system for golden corn syrup. (Ibid., pp. 652-53.) These statements are illustrated, however, by tabulations for January 1942. Information from other sources indicates that changes in pricing methods were not made by all companies prior to that date, but were not complete for syrup until 1945, and for starch until 1948.

The Commission said that "throughout most of the period" from 1938 through January 1947, "each respondent has generally quoted the same delivered cost to a buyer at a given destination as the other respondents." (Ibid., p. 656.) Though pertinent to a price-fixing charge, this finding tells nothing about the nature of any discrimination that was involved. The meagerness of the findings is undoubtedly due to the fact that the case was decided on the basis of agreed stipulations of fact.

[76] E. K. Scheiter, vice president of Staley, told a Senate committee in 1948 that after the decision his company sold at a mill price plus freight without deviation; that as a result its delivered prices were higher than those of competitors in certain markets —for example, 14 cents per 100 lbs. higher on corn syrup and 16 cents per 100 lbs. higher on starch in Chicago; that when customers protested after the war, Staley tried to meet competition by reductions in mill prices; that in meeting competition where Staley was high, these reductions set Staley's new prices lower than competitors' prices in markets on the Eastern seaboard; that competitors then defended these markets by reductions that again excluded Staley from Chicago and other markets; and that therefore Staley resumed freight absorption to Chicago and St. Louis and west of the Mississippi. See Study of Pricing Methods, Hearings, pp. 614-16.

[77] For Hubinger the difference may have reflected a 7-cent switching charge incurred on sales in Chicago. However, there was no such differential at Roby, Indiana, Clinton or Cedar Rapids, Iowa, or St. Louis.

f.o.b. mill formula.[78] Phantom freight has been eliminated, though on some shipments the published freight from the mill is probably lower than the actual freight expense under the milling-in-transit privilege.

This change has not altered the competitive situation in and around Chicago. Corn Products Refining Company has continued to sell there at its mill price plus freight. Other shippers absorb enough freight to meet the prices of Corn Products Refining in the Chicago market.

The plant prices of other companies were set lower than the former delivered prices in the same localities.[79] Buyers in adjacent territory obtained corn products more cheaply. With nearly the same mill price in Kansas City as in Chicago, Corn Products Refining Company now quotes lower delivered prices than before southward and westward of Kansas City, as well as northward for a limited distance.

Under the new pricing system, customers are permitted to buy at the plant, and some do so. Delivered prices on shipments from the plant are computed on the basis of rail freight. Prices are published.

Because of the changes in prices and freight rates since the inception of the case, no direct comparison of delivered prices now with those previously prevailing would be useful. However, the effect of the change in various markets is apparent in the differentials between delivered prices in those markets and in Chicago before the case and today.[80]

---

[78] The general counsel of Corn Products Refining Company told a Senate committee, "Each company in our industry prices from its own plant and meets competition. . . . we are the lowest price in Chicago. So everybody is meeting our competition. Because of the way the freight works, one of our competitors is lower on the Eastern seaboard by a penny or two, I forget what. We meet his competition, and we get actual evidence of that competition. We do not calculate his freight rates and meet that. We go out and find his prices. We are meeting prices." See *A Study of the Antitrust Laws,* Hearings Before the Senate Committee on the Judiciary, 84 Cong. 1 sess., Pt. 3, pp. 1091-92.

[79] One producer denies that there was price change to any customer. Others interviewed say the contrary unanimously.

[80] Comparisons in the ensuing list cover prices at destinations south and west of Chicago for which information as to prices in 1939 was provided in the Commission's findings. Most of these destinations are so located relative to points of production that the establishment of mill prices at additional mills might be expected to change delivered prices appreciably. No such effect was to be expected at more remote destinations. In cities on the East Coast, which are major markets for corn products, the local delivered prices appear to have been substantially higher in 1957, relative to the Chicago price, than in 1939, primarily because increases in transportation costs were larger for longer hauls. Presumably the price differences at the points in the list were also affected by changes in transportation costs.

The following table, based on one manufacturer's 1957 prices, provides such a comparison for tank car quantities of 43-degree Baume unmixed corn syrup.

Location	Difference in Cents per 100 lbs. from Chicago Price on 8/1/39	Difference in Cents per 100 lbs. from Chicago Price on 2/14/57
Decatur, Ill.	+18	− 9
Centralia, Ill.	+18	+18
St. Louis, Mo.	+18	+ 8
Davenport, Iowa	+18	+17
St. Joseph, Mo.	+40	+20
Kansas City, Mo.	+40	+ 6
Little Rock, Ark.	+60	+42
Alexandria, La.	+61	+67
Shreveport, La.	+71	+64
Dallas, Texas	+80	+61

Freight absorptions by any producer in reaching these markets may be estimated by comparing the actual delivered price with the delivered price that would result from the addition of full rail freight to the mill price. Since most of the cities listed are south and west of Staley's plant, an effort has been made to compute Staley's freight absorption in reaching them. The result is as follows:

Location	Actual Price 2/14/57	Decatur Price Plus Freight from Decatur 2/14/57	Staley's Freight Absorption
Chicago, Ill.	$5.47	$5.75	−28
Decatur, Ill.	5.38	5.38	0
Centralia, Ill.	5.65	5.65	0
St. Louis, Mo.	5.55	5.65	−10
Davenport, Iowa	5.64	5.81	− 17
St. Joseph, Mo.	5.67	5.80	−13
Kansas City, Mo.	5.53	5.79	−26
Little Rock, Ark.	5.89	5.91	− 2
Alexandria, La.	6.14	6.18	− 4
Shreveport, La.	6.11	6.12	− 1
Dallas, Texas	6.08	6.26	−18

Producers of corn products find it more difficult than before to know the prices that are being quoted by their competitors. One of them says that he is consequently less flexible in responding to the price changes that others may initiate. Another says, however, that all firms respond immediately to price changes because when prices are out of line someone immediately loses so much business that he must change his price.[81] Customers say that delivered prices are always uniform or that price differences last only a day or two. However, there is some disagreement as to the extent of leadership in changing prices. One customer says that the last four price changes were initiated by four different companies. One producer estimates that Corn Products Refining takes the lead in initiating price changes about six times out of ten and that it is more likely to be the leader upward than downward. Another producer, who did not initiate price changes before the case, sometimes does so now either upward or downward. A producer asserts that Corn Products Refining has ceased to be price leader, but not because of the case. However, according to a customer, Corn Products Refining is usually the price leader. This is also the opinion of the general counsel of Corn Products Refining.[82] One producer is regarded by several of the persons interviewed as the only one in the industry likely to make disorderly price reductions by such tactics as cutting the price on clear syrup under the pretense that it is off-color.

Price changes in 1956 are said by customers to have been unusual in character. Early in the year Union Starch began to allow its customers to date their invoices several months ahead and to deduct a storage allowance of from 10 to 15 cents per 100 pounds. Corn Products Refining Company countered in March with a price reduction of 25 cents, which was met by Union. Thereafter Union gave up the storage-allowance plan. After a brief effort in May to restore prices, Corn Products continued a substantial reduction throughout the summer, with other companies following suit. An effort by Corn Products to raise prices in mid-September was unsuccessful when some of the smaller producers did not conform.

In meeting competition, the corn products manufacturers appear to place varying emphasis on evidence of competitive price offers. One

[81] Information regarding the "booking" practice is fragmentary and contradictory. According to certain producers it has been discontinued. According to certain purchasers, it continues in a modified and nonselective form.

[82] He told a Senate committee: ". . . If the price of bulk products was changed . . . the chances are we would be the price leader." To the question whether other companies generally followed this company's prices, he replied, "I would say generally that is so. I will tell you, our competitors like for us to raise the price when it has to be raised, and they like to lower the price, so they get credit for lowering the price." To the question whether competitors sometimes take the lead in price reduction, he replied, "Yes, sir, that is correct." See *A Study of the Antitrust Laws,* Hearings, Pt. 3, pp. 1082-83.

company makes specific inquiry as to what competitors are charging. Another candidly computes the delivered price it must meet by adding to competitors' mill prices the published freight rates from competitors' plants.

The reduction in relative delivered prices at Middle Western and Southern destinations has improved the position of outlying candy manufacturers. One says that he can sell further north than before. Two others note that they pay lower prices because freight is computed from a nearer point. The magnitude of these results is difficult to estimate. In mentioning his advantage, one of these manufacturers said that the difference in cost is not great enough to influence sales. A supplier estimates that in particular areas the case brought about price reductions of from 5 to 7 per cent and that, on the average, the reduction was from 1 to 2 per cent. There is general agreement among candy manufacturers, however, that what is gained or lost through differentials in the cost of glucose is unimportant as compared with other locational factors. The greatest advantages of the Chicago candy makers are reported to be their advantages in buying sugar, derived from their ability to buy it at rates based on water shipment, and their freight advantages in shipping candy to distant points, which are derived from pool-car rates quoted from Chicago. The latter are so important that candy makers as far distant as Oklahoma find it advantageous to make shipments to Los Angeles via Chicago rather than direct.[83]

After the Supreme Court had sustained the decision of the Commission in the cement case, the basing-point system was rapidly abandoned in the cement industry.[84] Nearly every mill became a point of price quotation. For a time, most mills adopted the practice of determining destination prices by adding full freight to their mill prices, even when, as a result, their delivered prices were higher than those of their competitors.[85] Three incentives may have contributed to the adoption of this

[82] A candy maker west of Chicago estimates that his cost on a shipment to Los Angeles via Chicago is $2.75 per hundred pounds lower than if he shipped direct. The cost of his short haul to Chicago is nearly half as great as the cost from Chicago to Los Angeles.

[84] Cf. Whitney, Antitrust Policies, Vol. 2, pp. 302-08, 310-11, 316-18.

[85] After analyzing the compliance reports filed by 55 respondents' companies, the Commission said that 37 either reported that they were absorbing freight or reserved the right to do so; 3 regarded the order as preventing any freight absorption; 2 reported that they were selling f.o.b. mill without freight absorption; 2 said that they were selling at a uniform f.o.b. mill price but made no statement as to freight absorption; 6 reported that they were selling at f.o.b. mill prices but made

practice. First, the sellers may have believed that the effect of the decision in this and other basing-point cases was to require them to sell f.o.b. mill with full freight added, or at least to make any other course of action legally hazardous. Second, various members of the industry were participating in efforts to amend the law as it applied to delivered pricing systems, and they may have believed that an increase in delivered prices attributed to the Commission's order in the cement case would persuade their customers of the desirability of legislation. Third, and probably most important, the Supreme Court's decision in 1948 coincided with an acute shortage of cement. As the shortage had developed, producers had become generally aware that they could sell their output near their own mills more profitably than in markets they reached by freight absorption; but they had been unwilling to abandon their customers who were remote from their mills, and they had seen no way of raising prices to these customers that was consistent with the multiple basing-point system. The assertion that the Commission's order required the addition of full freight to mill prices provided an excuse for raising the prices to distant buyers or ceasing to sell to them. The requirements of the law rather than the decisions of sellers could be held responsible for the change.

The general practice of unqualified f.o.b. mill selling did not outlast the shortage. As soon as sellers began to need the business of distant buyers, they began to absorb freight to get it. They found it easier to do

---

no statement as to the uniformity of those prices or as to freight absorption; and 5 gave no information as to their prices. (See letter to Senator Paul Douglas, March 20, 1950, *Congressional Record*, Vol. 96, Pt. 6, 81 Cong. 2 sess., p. 7855.) In spite of the frequency with which the right to absorb freight was asserted in these reports, contemporary comment indicated that most sales were being made without freight absorption.

In hearings held by a Senate committee in 1948, executives of three cement companies made statements, and a letter from a fourth was introduced into the record. A vice-president of Hercules Cement Corp. and the President of Nazareth Cement Co., both from the Lehigh Valley, said that their companies were selling f.o.b. mill without absorbing freight and that in consequence their prices in important urban markets were from 19 to 28 cents higher, on a delivered basis, than those of their nearest competitors. (*Study of Pricing Methods*, Hearings, pp. 841, 777.) The president of Marquette Cement Manufacturing Co., a Chicago concern, said that his company continued to sell in carload quantities at delivered prices and to absorb freight to meet lower delivered prices. (*Ibid.*, pp. 856-62.) A letter from the president of Spokane Portland Cement Company said that his company intended to meet competition by adjusting invoices where it received proof that a competitor had quoted a lower price. (*Ibid.*, p. 1281.)

so because in the meanwhile the Federal Trade Commission had repeatedly disclaimed the opinion that either the law or the orders in
basing-point cases required f.o.b. mill pricing or forbade freight absorption and because the Supreme Court had decided in 1951 in the case
against Standard Oil Company of Indiana that meeting competition in
good faith is a complete defense to a charge of price discrimination.

Such information as is available indicates that freight absorption is
now widespread.[86] However, those who have been interviewed assert
that the industry has not adopted systematic equalization of mill-based
prices. One says that his company meets prices where a dealer or buyer
confirms in writing the statement that he has a lower price offer, but
sometimes will not meet a competitor's price because markets are tight
or sales nearer home are more profitable. Another says he meets prices
where he finds his company cannot sell without doing so. A third meets
prices on the basis of salesmen's reports. A fourth demands better evidence than before that competition exists, but on a tight market does
not always meet a competitor's price. Another "absorbs freight selectively," and places a maximum limit on the amount of freight absorption
from each plant, the limit varying from nothing to 20 cents per barrel.
According to one customer in a market served by two groups of mills,
most of those that are more distant freight-wise refuse to absorb a
freight differential of more than 25 cents. He nevertheless buys from
the higher priced mills, sometimes because there is a shortage and sometimes because for certain uses he prefers the color of their cement.

The methods of handling delivery charges exhibit significant differences from those prevailing before the order. Not only are mill prices
generally quoted,[87] but various sellers allow buyers to take delivery at
the mill if they choose to do so. Buyers are also allowed by some sellers
to take delivery at destinations other than those at which the buyers are
located. In one instance the buyer may choose to receive his cement
at any point, except that if he buys through a dealer he may not accept
delivery in the territory of another dealer.

There is appreciable but not universal acceptance of forms of transportation other than rail, both for actual shipment and for price quo-

[86] Particular concerns interviewed absorb freight on from 1 to 60 per cent of
their sales. The amounts absorbed apparently range as high, in extreme cases, as
69 cents per barrel.

[87] In the case of one company there is reason to think that an equalized delivered price is computed first and a mill price is then derived from it.

tation.[88] In 1948 about 17 per cent of the cement sold was shipped by truck. In 1954 more than 30 per cent was thus shipped.[89] One company ships mostly by truck and in such sales bases its transportation charges on truck shipment where before the case it used a published rail handbook. A second shipped nothing by truck in one year, and a third of the output of one of its plants by truck in the following year. Some companies quote delivered prices in such a way as to show the division between plant price and transportation charge.

With these changes in methods of price quotation, phantom freight apparently has disappeared, and there is an increased difficulty in knowing the price of a competitor. One government agency now finds that bids on cement show some variation, though not by significant amounts.[90]

The quotation of mill prices as well as destination prices has provided a new opportunity for government agencies and others buying large amounts. One government agency now asks for quotations both at the plant and at the delivery point. It finds that the latter usually reflect actual transportation expenses. It can specify both routing and means of transport, and is thus able to compute the cheapest transportation and to save money in certain cases by buying at the plant.

From reservations that appeared in some of the interviews, it seems probable that in some parts of the country sellers whose business is largely intrastate regard this fact as significant and do not apply to their intrastate sales all of the changes that they have made in their pricing practices.

Very little information is available about the effect of these changes on the levels of prices, mill realizations, and profits. One company as-

[88] In 1953-54, Samuel M. Loescher tried to ascertain the extent of willingness to let customers buy at the mill for truck delivery. He found that only 25 mills allowed uncontrolled trucking, 36 allowed trucking under controls, and 88 allowed only rail shipment. See Loescher, "Inert Antitrust Administration: Formula Pricing and the Cement Industry," *Yale Law Journal*, Nov. 5, 1955, p. 20.

[89] Figures compiled by Whitney (*Antitrust Policies*, Vol. 2, p. 308) from *Minerals Yearbook* of the Bureau of Mines. The increase had begun before the cement decision.

[90] It is noteworthy that in dropping a civil suit in Denver that involved the cement industry the Department of Justice announced that after the Supreme Court decision substantial variation had come to exist on bids for government cement contracts. However, the Twentieth Century Fund found in 1954 that, of 29 state highway commissioners who supplied answers as to their purchases of cement, only 7 reported receiving bids that varied in amount. See Whitney, *Antitrust Policies*, Vol. 2, p. 305.

serts that it did not change the level of its quoted prices in making the adjustments required by the order. One says that its sales volume, which had been increasing, stood practically still for two years after the Supreme Court decision but thereafter resumed its increase. In the financial statements of five other companies, the upward trend of sales and profits appears to have been uninterrupted by the Supreme Court decision in four cases, whereas in the fifth there was a drop in net income in the year after the decision.

From the interviews with cement manufacturers, it appears that no significant difficulties were encountered in modifying sales practices along the lines described above. All who absorbed freight on any appreciable amount of their sales were emphatic, however, in describing the continuance of freight absorption as indispensable to the operation of their enterprises.

12 / *The Political Controversy Over Delivered Pricing*

THE DECISION OF THE SUPREME COURT in the cement case apparently produced consternation in the steel industry. On the day after that decision, Irving S. Olds, Chairman of the Board of United States Steel Corporation was reported to have said that there were two alternatives—to seek remedial legislation or to educate the Supreme Court.[1] By early June, leaders of the industry apparently had decided to try to amend the law.[2] On July 7, United States Steel Corporation led the industry in adopting an f.o.b. mill pricing pattern, the general effect of which was to raise delivered prices.[3] Freight absorption was ended without reduction of mill prices; and in a short time, the level of mill prices was raised. Contemporary comment viewed the change as an influence that would induce consumers of steel to urge Congress to amend the law.[4] By midsummer, executives and salesmen of certain steel companies were urging their customers to support amendatory legislation.[5] There were indications that steel users who did not share the

[1] *New York Journal of Commerce,* April 28, 1948.

[2] *Steel Trade Press,* June 6, 1948; *New York Times,* June 6, 1948.

[3] At points where delivered prices had included phantom freight, the change reduced prices. Where freight had been absorbed, delivered prices rose. Since, on the average, the industry had absorbed freight, the level of price on a delivered basis was higher than before. There was no change in base prices at the time; but these were soon increased also.

[4] *Wall Street Journal,* July 8, 1948; *New York Journal of Commerce,* July 8, 1948; *Iron Age,* August 17, 1948. Senator Myers of Pennsylvania subsequently said on the floor of the Senate, "It was a good time for the steel industry, from the standpoint of its own profits, to adopt such a policy [pricing f.o.b. mill] whether the policy was in fact one which would be required by the force of law in subsequent Supreme Court decisions. Steel was still scarce, and there was a terrific seller's market. By converting to mill net pricing, the freight costs, which steel had been absorbing out of profits, were passed on in full to the consumer, and the profit per unit of steel rose accordingly." *Congressional Record,* Vol. 95, Pt. 8, 81 Cong. 1 sess., p. 11174.

[5] In July, Ben Morrell, President of Jones & Laughlin, wrote to every customer, "We urge our customers and all others interested in the welfare of the country, to

400

steel industry's opinion were reluctant to express their views for fear that their access to steel would be adversely affected.[6] The support of local unions was sought by the companies through predictions that otherwise plants would be wholly or partly shut down and men would be laid off.[7]

Efforts were made to organize groups throughout the country to protest against the existing law and demand its amendment.[8] An early result of the agitation was the Senate's passage of a resolution to investi-

---

give serious consideration to this matter. We believe that they will conclude, as we have, that prompt action by the Congress is essential if we are to have the vigorous competition in this country which has been so fundamental to our national development." (*Ibid.*, Pt. 5, p. 7026, Pt. 9, pp. 11356-57.) In August, E. T. Weir of National Steel was reported by the *New York Journal of Commerce* to have written a similar letter: "There is no time to be lost. The quicker action is taken, the quicker relief can be secured. A great deal of work must be done. Since the type of Congress we had during the 1930's refused to do what the Supreme Court has done, there is every reason to expect that the type of Congress to be elected in November will act to reverse the Court." *Ibid.*, Pt. 5, p. 7026. See also *Steel,* September 13, 1948; *New York Times,* report of comment by the President of Youngstown Sheet and Tube Company, September 21, 1948; *Congressional Record,* Vol. 95, Pt. 5, p. 7027; *ibid.,* Pt. 9, 11347.

[6] On October 14, 1948, the *New York Times* reported that at the National Hardware Show certain hardware manufacturers said that their costs had been reduced by the adoption of f.o.b. mill pricing, but asked that their names be kept confidential "because of possible loss of steel allocations" or of "trade reprisals." *Ibid.*, Pt. 5, p. 7027.

[7] *Competitive Absorption of Transportation Costs,* Hearings before the Senate Committee on Interstate and Foreign Commerce, 81 Cong. 1 sess. (1949), p. 187, testimony of Otis Brubaker, Director of Research, United Steel Workers of America, CIO.

[8] In October 1948, a public relations firm was employed at a fee of $11,000 per month to undertake a campaign. Money was furnished by a "National Competition Committee," organized in Pittsburgh, to which 52 business enterprises there and elsewhere subscribed sums of from $250 to $1,000. Six field men were employed to form "grassroot" organizations in various cities. However, some of the subscribers objected to the fact that the employed firm had registered under the Lobbying Act. Moreover, the *Toledo Blade* found out about the organization and printed a story about it. Therefore, according to the vice-president of the public relations firm, the work was terminated after a meeting on December 7, 1948. In December the *Rocky Mountain News* also found out about the undertaking. According to a news story in that paper, with a date-line of December 22, an interview with an official of the public relations firm indicated that the work was currently going forward. See *Price Discrimination, the Robinson-Patman Act and Related Matters,* Hearings before the House Select Committee on Small Business, 84 Cong. 1 sess., Pt. 1 (1956), pp. 113-24. See also *Congressional Record,* Vol. 95, Pt. 5, pp. 7025-31; Pt. 9, p. 11347.

gate the problem through a subcommittee of the Committee on Inter-state and Foreign Commerce.[9]

After three days of hearings on the resolution at which members of the Federal Trade Commission and of its staff testified,[10] the resolution was adopted June 10, 1948. Formal investigatory hearings were held in November and December of the same year, but no report was sub-mitted until February 1949, after the introduction of proposals for amendatory legislation. The subcommittee in charge of the hearings spent its time partly in negotiations with the Federal Trade Commission, looking toward the possibility of an agreed settlement of the controver-sial questions, and partly in an effort, by public hearings, to formulate the issue before the public and to criticize the alternative formulation offered by the Federal Trade Commission.[11]

Scope of the Attack on Existing Law

Any serious effort to amend the law in order to overcome the effect of the Commission's decisions and the opinions of the court pertaining to basing-point and zone-pricing cases was necessarily concerned with both the Federal Trade Commission Act and the Robinson-Patman Act. Most of the Commission's cases had been concerned with price-fixing conspiracies violative of the Federal Trade Commission Act. The prin-ciples established in these cases could not be overturned unless some-thing could be done to change the concept of conspiracy, the rules of evidence by which conspiracy could be proved, or the scope of the Com-mission's orders. In a case pending on appeal at the time the contro-versy began, the Commission had extended its attack under the Federal Trade Commission Act by charging and finding that the individual use of a basing-point system, in the knowledge that the others in the industry were using it and that the effect would be to eliminate price competition, was a violation of the statute.[12] This interpretation of the law, which

[9] S. Res. 241, 80 Cong. 2 sess., *Congressional Record,* Vol. 94, 80 Cong. 2 sess., Pt. 6, p. 7949.
[10] *Study of Methods of Competition in Commerce and Impact of Legislation and Government Regulations on American Consumers,* Hearings before the Senate Committee on Interstate and Foreign Commerce, 80 Cong. 2 sess. (1948).
[11] *Study of Pricing Methods,* Hearings before the Senate Committee on Interstate and Foreign Commerce, 80 Cong. 2 sess. (1948), pp. 1011-12.
[12] Docket 4452, *Rigid Steel Conduit Association.* This case had two counts. Under the first the Commission charged and found that producers of rigid steel

came to be called the doctrine of conscious parallelism, was an obvious point for attack. Other matters that were singled out for criticism with reference to the interpretation of the law of conspiracy were the Com-

---

conduit had conspired to fix prices by use of a basing-point system. Under the second count, the Commission charged and found that the same producers, individually, had violated the Federal Trade Commission Act by using a basing-point system concurrently with others. Under the first count, the respondents were ordered to cease any planned common course of action to use a basing-point system or any other formula that produced uniform delivered prices. Under the second count each company, individually, was ordered to cease using a basing-point system, or selling at prices that systematically reflected "the inclusion of a transportation factor greater or less than the actual cost of transportation," for the purpose or with the effect of "systematically matching delivered-price quotations with other of said respondents or producing the equivalent of such matched delivered prices through systematic discriminations in the mill nets received. . . ." (38 FTC 595.) Two respondents who were acquitted under the first count were found in violation under the second, and were subjected to this part of the order.

On appeal the Seventh Circuit sustained the Commission. As to the second count, the court said: "Each conduit seller knows that each of the other sellers is using the basing-point formula; each knows that by using it he will be able to quote identical delivered prices and thus present a condition of matched prices under which purchasers are isolated and deprived of choice among sellers so far as price advantage is concerned. Each seller must systematically increase or decrease his mill net price for customers at numerous destinations in order to match the delivered prices of his competitors. Each seller consciously intends not to attempt the exclusion of any competition from his natural freight advantage territory by reducing the price, and in effect invites the others to share the available business at matched prices in his natural market in return for a reciprocal invitation." The Court then said that the legal question was the same as that of the cement case, citing in support of this statement a dictum of the Supreme Court's cement decision to the effect that the Commission has jurisdiction over individual conduct which falls short of violating the Sherman Act. The court then concluded, "In the light of that opinion, we cannot say that the Commission was wrong in concluding that the individual use of the basing-point method as here used does constitute an unfair method of competition." 168 F. 2d 175, 181.

The Supreme Court divided four to four on the case and wrote no opinion. The effect of its action was to confirm the court below without further clarifying the law relevant to the matter.

Critics of the decision had difficulty in seeing how a group of companies could be simultaneously engaged in conspiracy, as found in count one, and in individual action falling short of conspiracy, as found in count two. The independent status of count two, they thought, was made clear by the fact that two respondents were found in violation under that count alone. They thought the decision meant that any seller violated the law when he quoted a delivered price identical with that of any other seller.

To the Commission, count two had been primarily a device to permit the issuance of an order covering more than the maintenance of a planned common course of action. Where a basing-point system had become well established, continued use

mission's use of identity in delivered prices as proof of conspiracy, the Commission's interpretation of patterns of reciprocal freight absorption as conspiratorial rather than as innocent efforts to meet competition in

---

of it was capable of continuing the effects of the conspiracy; yet there was difficulty in proving that this continued use was collective rather than individual. The Commission doubted that it had power to make an order, based on a finding of conspiracy, that would require companies individually to abandon the pricing formula they had conspired to establish. Hence it extended its findings to cover the individual as well as the joint action of the respondents.

Though this was the primary purpose, members of the Commission's staff undoubtedly hoped that if their view of the law was sustained, they would subsequently be able to attack industry-wide use of basing-point formulas without incurring the burden of proving that the use had been conspiratorial. So far as the present writer is aware, however, no responsible participant in the case thought of count two as applicable to individual conduct that fell short of participation in a systematic industry-wide pricing formula.

When the Commission's decision came under attack, the Commission sought to allay the fear that the principle in question was intended to apply generally to identical prices. In a notice to the staff issued on October 12, 1948 ("In re: Commission Policy Toward Geographic Pricing Practices," in Senate Committee on Interstate and Foreign Commerce, *Study of Federal Trade Commission Views on Freight Absorption,* 81 Cong. 2 sess., Committee Print (1950), pp. 16-17), it said: "In the Rigid Steel Conduit case, the Commission found, and the circuit court agreed, that adherence to an industry-wide basing-point formula, with the knowledge that other concerns are adhering to it also, constitutes in itself a violation of the Federal Trade Commission Act by the individual adhering companies when price competition is thereby eliminated. It would have been possible to describe this state of facts as a price conspiracy on the principle that, when a number of enterprises follow a parallel course of action in the knowledge and contemplation of the fact that all are acting alike, they have, in effect, formed an agreement. Instead of phrasing its charge in this way, the Commission chose to rely on the obvious fact that the economic effect of identical prices achieved through conscious parallel action is the same as that of similar prices achieved through overt collusion, and, for this reason, the Commission treated the conscious parallelism of action as violation of the Federal Trade Commission Act. Should the Supreme Court sustain the Commission's view, the effect will be to simplify proof in basing-point cases, but to expose to proceedings under the Federal Trade Commission Act only courses of action which might be regarded as collusive or destructive of price competition."

Subsequently, the Commission made further efforts to define its position. On February 11, 1949, in answering written questions, Commissioner Davis submitted to the Senate Committee on Interstate and Foreign Commerce statements, approved by a majority of the Commission, that identical prices can result from competition as well as from conspiracy, that the precedents of the cement and conduit cases were "applicable only in 'conspiracy situations,' " and that the order in the conduit case was not intended to require f.o.b. mill selling, but was intended "to have the practical effect of preventing the respondents in that proceeding from continuing to use the basing-point pricing system which had been established and maintained by conspiracy, or from substituting for it the industry-wide

good faith, and the Commission's effort to require that pricing formulas that had been used for conspiracy purposes be abandoned lest the conspiracy continue tacitly by continued general observance of the formulas.

In two important cases, those against Staley and Corn Products Refining, the Commission and the courts had found that basing-point formulas violated the Robinson-Patman Act apart from any finding of conspiracy. An attack on the existing law as applied to pricing formulas required, necessarily, an effort to change the Robinson-Patman Act as well as the Federal Trade Commission Act. Since in all formulas except selling f.o.b. mill there was a clear discrepancy between the variation in transportation charges and the variation in delivered prices, problems pertaining to the cost defense could not be regarded as relevant to proposed amendment of the law. With this exception, however, attack was possible as to each of the major legal concepts pertaining to Section 2(a). The Commission had found differences in prices in the fact that the seller realized different amounts at the mill in sales to different destinations. It was possible to challenge the concept that the price was the realization at the mill and to propose the alternative view that the price was

---

use of any other pricing formula which produced the same result, and thus nullifying the effect of the proceeding." He explained the legal theory of count two as covering "a practice followed by each of a group of sellers with knowledge by each that the same practice is being followed by all other members of the group, as well as with knowledge of the results of the common use of the practice, and that those results are in fact the restraint and suppression of competition." He said that the two respondents who were included in the findings and order under the second count only might have been subjected to the first count also; that since "in practical effect" the second count was equivalent to conspiracy, he saw no inconsistency in subjecting them to the second count only; and that the proof of their participation "conformed more precisely to the second count than to the first count." (*Competitive Absorption of Transportation Costs,* Hearings, p. 270.) Finally, in July 1949, in denying a motion to reopen and modify the order in the conduit case, the Commission said, "The Commission does not consider that the order in its present form prohibits the independent practice of freight absorption or selling at delivered prices by individual sellers. What the questioned portion of the order does prohibit is the continuance of the basing-point, delivered-price system, found to have been the subject of conspiracy, or any variation thereof which might be accomplished through the practices specified . . . when done, as stated in the order, 'for the purpose or with the effect of systematically matching delivered price quotations.' " (Docket 4452, Order Denying Motion to Reopen and Modify, July 7, 1949.) Commissioner Mason did not dissent from the Commission's action, but subsequently dissented from an order denying motion to reopen and modify order to cease and desist. *Ibid.,* May 11, 1956.

the delivered price and that the relevant price differences were those between delivered prices.[13] The Commission's concept of injury to competition in the territorial price discrimination case had been based, in large part, if not wholly, on the view that the buyer was deprived of his natural advantages of location. Since the Commission saw conspiracy in the background in all of these cases, it had found no difficulty in challenging concerted efforts to pre-empt such advantages for sellers. The view that, apart from conspiracy, the buyer rather than the seller should enjoy the advantages of location and should be guaranteed that enjoyment by law was open to challenge. But the most important challenge had to do with the defense that competition had been met in good faith. In the Staley case the Supreme Court had found that this could be done in individual competitive situations but not systematically. In a case concerned with functional discounts rather than with territorial price discrimination, that against Standard Oil Company of Indiana, the Commission had found that where the fact of injury to competition is positively shown, the defense that competition has been met in good faith is not adequate. This latter finding was pending on appeal at the time of the controversy. It was possible to attack the law as to territorial price discrimination both by insisting that the meeting of competition in good faith should be a complete defense and by insisting that this defense should be available not only in individual competitive situations but where the practice was used systematically and even where it was used reciprocally by two or more sellers.

It is noteworthy that the lines of attack on the law of conspiracy and those on the law of price discrimination were intertwined. Formulas for freight equalization, in which every producing point is a basing point,

---

[13] The question whether the price was the mill realization or the cost of the goods at the customer's place of business was significant in two ways:

(1) A uniform delivered price could not be challenged as discriminatory, whereas the varying mill realizations from such a price structure could be challenged. This point, however, was of limited significance, since in basing-point, freight-equalization, and zone-price systems, price differences appeared in both mill realizations and delivered prices.

(2) In any delivered pricing system, sale at the same delivered price as a competitor could be described as meeting that competitor's equally low price and thus might be defended under the provisions of Section 2(b). However, a seller who absorbed freight to meet a delivered price was likely to realize less at the mill than the concern whose price he was meeting. If mill realizations were prices, therefore, he could be held to have sold below his competitor's price, and thus to have stepped beyond the limits of good faith in meeting competition.

could be described as arrangements by which all sellers reciprocally and systematically met competition in territory adjacent to other sellers. Anything that could be done to establish the legality of such practices under either statute was likely to influence the interpretation of the other statute as well.[14]

As the controversy over the status of basing-point pricing developed, it became a focus for expression of discontent as to other aspects of the law that were thought to have relevance to this controversy. Reference has already been made to the conduit case and the case against Standard Oil Company of Indiana. Two other cases were brought into the discussion. In one, that against Morton Salt Company, a majority of the Supreme Court had interpreted the statutory language "the effect may be" to mean that there was a reasonable *possibility* of the specified effect, and this interpretation had been emphasized by a dissent in which the traditional interpretation of reasonable *probabilty* had been supported as an alternative. Though the Federal Trade Commission had made no use of the concept of reasonable possibility, and members of its staff had publicly indicated that they saw no need for the new concept, the apparent effect of the decision in diminishing the burden of proof as to injury to competition was considered pertinent to the basing-point controversy and was emphasized therein. Similarly, in the Moss case[15] an appellate court had interpreted the Robinson-Patman Act to mean that the Commission need only show a price difference in order to establish a prima-facie case of violation of the law. Although in all cases, including the Moss case, the Commission had consistently interpreted the law to mean that it must show not only that there were price differences but that they probably would be injurious to competition, this court decision also caused alarm and was invoked during the basing-point controversy as a basis for argument that the Commission might challenge any seller

[14] In *Iron Age*, Eugene Hardy wrote on October 7, 1948 (p. 114) that leaders in the steel industry thought Congress would be unwilling to legalize the basing-point system explicitly and that therefore legislation "to relieve the Commission of its weapons of attack on delivered pricing is receiving active consideration in steel circles." He mentioned as possibilities: forbidding the Federal Trade Commission to issue an order to cease a method of pricing not inherently unlawful, even if that method was part of a conspiracy; and making a clear legislative statement that any seller was privileged to meet competition as frequently and systematically as he wished and "without regard to whether or not his competitors may be similarly meeting his and each other's prices." See speech by Senator Morse, *Congressional Record*, Vol. 95, Pt. 5, p. 7031.
[15] See below, pp. 480-81.

under the Robinson-Patman Act merely because his mill realizations differed in different sales.

Formulation of the Lines of Attack

The assembly of these complex conceptual elements into a program for advocacy of new legislation[16] was probably influenced and certainly illustrated by a confidential memorandum prepared by three attorneys engaged in practice before the Commission.[17] Congressional hearings concerned with the controversy bore so many resemblances to the strategy outlined in the memorandum as to suggest that, directly or indirectly, the proposals of the memorandum became available to members of Congress and helped to organize their thinking.[18]

The memorandum reads in part as follows:

> In considering what should be the objective, it is wise to remember that certain things, no matter how logically they may be defended will never be politically popular because they just do not look right. One of these is the kind of so-called phantom freight which results from the Pittsburgh-plus system or from the existence of non-basing-point mills in a multiple-basing point system. The public just will not stomach the thought of a buyer in Chicago buying from a Chicago factory and being forced to pay freight from Pittsburgh.
>
> Another thing which is politically difficult to defend is the type of zone system in which, for example, the lowest price is charged in the East, a higher price in the Middle West, a still higher price in the Far West, and a still higher price on the Pacific coast, when there are mills located in all or most of those zones. Such a system is merely a modification of the Pittsburgh-plus, and will be so recognized without diffi-

[16] Cf. Earl Latham, The Group Basis of Politics; A Study in Basing Point Legislation (1952). Cf. also Howard R. Horrow, "Business Reactions to Court Decisions Against Basing Point Pricing Methods" (doctoral dissertation, University of Illinois, 1951).

[17] "Suggested Program to Reestablish the Legality of Delivered-Price Marketing Methods." The authors of the memorandum were George Lamb, Sumner Kittelle, and Fraser Hilder. See Price Discrimination, the Robinson-Patman Act and Related Matters, Hearings, pp. 478-96.

[18] Mr. Lamb testified that a number of copies were given to various industries and that it was possible he had given a copy to the counsel of the Senate committee that conducted hearings on the matter. William Simon, who had been counsel of the committee, testified (ibid., pp. 180-81) that in 1948 George Lamb had presented him with a document that was to be used as educational material, but that Simon did not read it.

culty by the man in the street if he takes any interest in the subject at all. . . .

The type of delivered pricing method perhaps most easily defended is that in which each manufacturer sells at a price f.o.b. his factory and, when selling in a territory closer to a competitor's plant, gives the buyer an allowance to equalize his freight cost with the freight from such competitor's plant. This method of selling is the result of natural growth and the way in which that growth takes place from the establishment of the first plant in an industry until the opening of the most recent plant can be demonstrated simply and dramatically in a manner which the opponents of delivered pricing find hard to attack.

Paradoxically, because when analyzed it involves phantom freight, the so-called universal delivered price method (one price delivered anywhere in the United States) can also be defended politically, because of its commonness. The man in the street knows that chewing gum and Palm Beach suits have been sold that way for generations and he sees nothing inequitable or sinister about it. . . .

The basic objective of industry, stated broadly . . . will be to preserve the freedom of each businessman to choose and use, in his own sole discretion, any delivered pricing method which does not involve discrimination in delivered prices which he cannot justify (a) by cost differences or (b) by the meeting (when, where, and as often as he wishes) of competitors' delivered prices. . . .

If the opponents of delivered pricing can persuade the subcommittee that the Commission only wants to prohibit price conspiracies and that it has no intention of outlawing the individual use of delivered pricing apart from conspiracy or price discrimination, they may steer the subcommittee away from the real issue and into a general review of the antitrust laws. The hearings then will be turned into another TNEC which will accomplish nothing.

The question of conspiracy and the question of discriminatory prices must be met squarely. This does not mean that business should ask that either price fixing or price discrimination be legalized, for that would mean quick political death to the entire effort to relegalize delivered pricing. It is the Commission's false theories regarding conspiracy and price discrimination in their relation to delivered pricing which must be met squarely and exposed. . . .

Framing of the issues for the subcommittee can best be accomplished by a preliminary brief. . . . The brief should show, for example, that delivered pricing does not and cannot, of itself, result in price fixing; that price competition can and does exist under delivered pricing methods; that under straight f.o.b. mill pricing there would be less, not more, price competition than under delivered pricing methods because the latter enables more sellers to compete in more markets, while the former restricts each seller to a narrow market. . . .

The brief should show that, in actual cases (e.g., the Chain Institute case, now pending), it is the theory of the Commission's attorneys that, if there is any evidence of price fixing, it is necessary to prohibit all delivered pricing methods in the industry in order to get rid of the price fixing, despite the fact that the delivered pricing methods grew naturally without collusion. . . . In this connection, the brief would show how little evidence the Commission needs to prove a conspiracy to fix prices; how it relies upon mere price uniformity from time to time plus the common use of a delivered pricing method, plus membership in a trade association; how the mere fact that each competitor knows that the others are using a delivered pricing method is stressed by the Commission as evidence that they conspired to use it, despite the fact that such knowledge would be impossible to avoid by any businessman who was alert.

. . . If, having found such conspiracies, the Commission is free (as recent court decisions indicate) to prohibit not only the alleged conspiracy itself but also all further use of that delivered pricing method or any other method of pricing except f.o.b. mill, it will be ridiculous to pretend that, as a practical matter, the Commission does not intend to force all or most of American business into the f.o.b. mill pattern. . . .

The issues should also be defined and framed, in the brief for the subcommittee, on the question of price discrimination. The meaning of this term as used by the Commission should be clearly described, and it should be demonstrated how the Commission has tried to reinsert into the statute a definition of price that was specifically rejected by Congress. The brief should also show how the Commission is attempting to whittle away to nothing the right of a seller to meet his competitor's lower prices in given market areas. It should show the fallacy of the Commission's theory that because the meeting of competition sometimes produces price uniformity, it should be abolished, i.e., that if permitting a seller to compete in a competitor's territory results in price uniformity, such right to compete should be taken away and each seller given a virtual monopoly of its own territory. . . .

Since the Commission's chief attack on delivered prices has been through the medium of alleged "conspiracies," it might appear desirable at first blush to curtail the Commission's fact-finding powers or grant businessmen latitude in the matter of price agreements. Political considerations dictate, however, that any such attempt would make the proposed legislation far less palatable to Congress than if it were addressed solely to the merits of delivered pricing.

No effective bill to relegalize delivered pricing can refer to it by that name or even by the names "basing-point system," "zone system," etc. Such language would require exhaustive definition which might merely challenge the ingenuity of the Federal Trade Commission's attorneys to misconstrue it as they did the Robinson-Patman Act. The solution is to immobilize the "tools" which the Commission uses in its attack on delivered pricing, namely, the legal concepts that—

(1) "Price" under the Robinson-Patman Act means "mill net return:"

(2) It is unlawful to meet competition by absorbing freight systematically, and the defense of meeting competition is not an absolute defense to a charge of discrimination in any event;

(3) If there has been any agreement among competitors to use a delivered pricing method, or even an agreement on prices without reference to the delivered pricing method, it is proper for the Commission to prohibit not only the unlawful agreement but also all further use of that delivered pricing method. (In the Rigid Steel Conduit case, the order went further and prohibited not only the particular delivered pricing method in the industry but all others, leaving straight f.o.b. mill pricing as the sole alternative.) . . .

Generally speaking, the proposed bill should amend the Robinson-Patman Act (both the civil sections enforced by the Commission and the criminal section enforced by the Department of Justice) so that—

(1) "Price" will be defined to mean the delivered price; and

(2) It will be clearly stated that any seller is privileged to make a lower price to one customer than to another to meet a competitor's equally low or lower price to the second customer, and to do so—

(a) as frequently and "systematically" as he wishes;

(b) in any territory or marketing area that he wishes; and

(c) without regard to whether or not his competitors may be similarly meeting his and each other's prices.

To prevent the Commission from declaring that, even though these definitions and provisions apply to the Robinson-Patman Act they do not prohibit continued attacks on delivered pricing under the Federal Trade Commission Act, the latter statute should also be amended to provide that nothing in it may be construed to prohibit any price discrimination which is not unlawful under the Robinson-Patman Act. The Sherman Act should be amended similarly.

Thus far the legislation would immobilize two of the Federal Trade Commission's three "tools" of attack on delivered pricing. The third should be approached through amendments to both the Federal Trade Commission and Sherman Acts to the effect that no cease and desist order or injunction issued under either statute in a case where any agreement, understanding, combination, conspiracy, or agreed common course of action in restraint of trade has been found shall prohibit, or be construed to prohibit, the individual and independent use by any party to such agreement, understanding, etc., of any business practice or method of pricing or selling not in itself unlawful, regardless of whether or not such practice or method was the subject of each agreement, understanding, etc.

It will be noticed that this type of legislative provision does not legalize conspiracies or price-fixing agreements. It would not relieve an industry which had been ordered to stop conspiring from the necessity of changing those business practices found to have been agreed upon in order to break the chain of conspiracy. But it would not permit the Commission to continue its present practice of edging industries step by step into the corner of f.o.b. mill pricing as their sole available method of selling.

Legislation of this type would not legalize all types of delivered pricing. It would not, for example, legalize a single basing point system such as "Pittsburgh-plus," nor would it legalize the phantom freight collected by a nonbasing point mill in a multiple-basing point system. It would not legalize certain types of zone-pricing systems. It would, however, permit the two most important types of delivered pricing methods, namely, (i) the multiple-basing point system where every factory sells f.o.b. mill, absorbing freight when necessary to meet competition in other mills' territories, and (ii) the universal delivered price method. In addition, it would legalize such variants of the above methods as the maximum freight allowance (e.g., buyer's actual freight allowed up to 30 cents per hundredweight).

Serious consideration should be given to countering any move by the opposition to draw the hearings out unduly by proposing that legislation of the type herein described be enacted on a stopgap or temporary basis to preserve the status quo pending the results of a more exhaustive study.[19]

Character of the Defense of the Law

Defenders of the existing law met the attack on it, as Mr. Lamb predicted, by insisting that the central concepts of the laws of conspiracy and price discrimination were at issue,[20] that possibly the purpose and certainly the effect of legislation would be to weaken or destroy the effectiveness of the basic prohibitions contained in these laws, and that the cases that had aroused alarm had consisted merely in attacks on conspiracy or

[19] *Price Discrimination, the Robinson-Patman Act and Related Matters,* Hearings, pp. 479-88.

[20] See, for example, *Study of Methods of Competition in Commerce . . . ,* Hearings, testimony of Commissioners William A. Ayres, Ewin L. Davis and Robert E. Freer, pp. 2-32; testimony of William T. Kelley, general counsel, pp. 74-79; and Walter B. Wooden, assistant general counsel, pp. 35-40.

on injurious price discriminations. They pointed out that the industries involved in the cases on which attention was focused—cement, steel, and corn products—had questionable records under the antitrust laws,[21] and that the practices used in these industries had been basing-point pricing with the quotation of phantom freight. They repudiated the idea that either law or the policy of the Federal Trade Commission condemned delivered prices or freight absorption as such.

In stating these views, the majority in the Federal Trade Commission found it necessary to consider for the first time the possible meaning of concepts that had been employed in basing-point cases if they were to be

[21] Corn Products Refining Company, formed by a series of mergers, which gave it at one time 100 per cent of the glucose business and 64 per cent of the starch business, was ordered dissolved in a case under the Sherman Act in 1916 and in 1919 withdrew its appeal in the case and accepted a decree by which it was required to sell two old glucose mills and its interest in Penick and Ford. In 1925 a complaint against the company alleging unfair methods of competition was dismissed by the Federal Trade Commission by a vote of 3 to 2. In a suit under the Sherman Act, instituted in 1932, the Corn Derivatives Institute was dissolved by consent decree. See Simon N. Whitney, *Antitrust Policies—American Experience in Twenty Industries* (1958), Vol. 2, pp. 258-65, and Bernard Shull, "Price-Discrimination in the Corn Products-Confectionery Industrial Pattern" (doctoral dissertation, University of Wisconsin, 1957), pp. 78, 83.

In 1917, 2 cement producers pleaded guilty and 7 others pleaded *nolo contendere* to charges of price fixing and allocating territory on the West Coast. In 1924, a decree was issued against conspiracy to fix the prices of cement in the Rocky Mountain area, and a similar decree was issued against 6 companies in another case. In 1921, a criminal prosecution of 18 cement producers for price fixing ended in a hung jury; and in 1925, in a companion civil case, the Supreme Court reversed a conviction by a lower court. See Whitney, *Antitrust Policies,* Vol. 2, pp. 289-95.

The U.S. Steel Corporation was severely criticized as monopolistic in a report by the United States Commissioner of Corporations in 1911-13 and in hearings by the Stanley Committee in 1911. A suit to dissolve it was won by the company by a 4 to 3 decision of the Supreme Court in 1920. In 1924, the company was subjected to the Commission's order in the Pittsburgh-plus case. Various steel producers were involved in civil and criminal cases concerned with price fixing on stainless steel, which ended in pleas of *nolo contendere* in 1945 and a consent decree in 1948; a civil case concerned with price fixing on bolts and nuts, which ended in a consent decree in 1931; a case concerned with conspiracy to sell certain types of tin plate only for export, which ended in acceptance of a Federal Trade Commission order to cease and desist in 1936; and in the Commission's rigid steel conduit case. A complaint by the Commission charging that the whole steel industry had conspired to fix prices by use of a basing-point formula had been issued in 1947. In addition, various mergers and interlocking relationships had been challenged by the Government under the antitrust laws and the Hepburn Act, but without success. See *ibid.,* Vol. 1, pp. 257-77.

applied generally to American industry. In some instances the majority thought that these concepts were being misinterpreted in public discussion and sought to correct the interpretation by explicit public statement. In other instances, an effort was made to diminish the significance or circumscribe the application of concepts that had been adopted in conspiracy situations without full awareness of their implications for other types of situations.

The Commission did not retreat from the position it had taken on conspiracy. However, it interpreted its decision in Count 2 of the conduit case as applicable only to conspiracy situations, and, in effect though not explicitly, repudiated the idea that the doctrine of conscious parallelism might be applied where no finding of conspiracy could be made.[22]

The Commission's major efforts to define its position anew were made with reference to the Robinson-Patman Act.[23] It said that it had found price discrimination in differences in mill realizations because, in the particular industries as to which it had made such decisions, the prices charged were prices at the mill. It said, however, that it was ready to recognize either a mill price or a delivered price as the applicable price in a particular instance, and that in the price discrimination law, as in the general law of sales, the term *price* had whatever meaning was appropriate to the actual arrangements between the parties. The Commission explicitly and repeatedly repudiated the view that it saw anything

[22] See footnote 12, pp. 402-05.

[23] The Commission's most significant public statements were: "Notice to the Staff in re Commission Policy Toward Geographic Pricing Practices," Oct. 14, 1948, printed in Senate Committee on Interstate and Foreign Commerce, *Study of Federal Trade Commission Views on Freight Absorption,* pp. 15-21; letter from D. C. Daniel, Secretary, Federal Trade Commission, to B. C. Davis, Jr., Secretary, Chamber of Commerce of the State of New York, Jan. 12, 1949, printed in *ibid.,* pp. 21-22, and in *Competitive Absorption of Transportation Costs,* Hearings, pp. 278-80; and letter from Commissioner Ewin L. Davis to Senator Edwin C. Johnson, Feb. 11, 1949, enclosing answers to 54 questions submitted by Senator Johnson. The answers to the questions are printed in *Study of Federal Trade Commission Views on Freight Absorption,* pp. 23-32; the letter and the answers in *Competitive Absorption of Transportation Costs,* Hearings, pp. 267-78. The Commission also regarded as important an order of July 7, 1949, denying a motion to reopen and modify its cease and desist order in the conduit case, and a release of June 10, 1950, concerning a proposed cease and desist order in the corn products conspiracy case. Both are printed in *Study of Federal Trade Commission Views on Freight Absorption,* pp. 32-34. Clarifying statements were also made in speeches by commissioners and members of the staff;—for example, in speeches by Commissioner Freer before the New England Counsel, Sept. 18, 1948, the Sales Executive Club of New York on Dec. 7, 1948, and in the City

inherently unlawful in delivered pricing or in freight absorption,[24] but insisted that both practices, like all other innocent pricing practices, should be fully subject to legal remedies if they became part of a scheme of price fixing or price discrimination. Similarly, the Commission explicitly repudiated any intent to force sellers to adopt f.o.b. mill pricing formulas.[25]

The Commission's statements as to the relation of the advantages of location to concepts of injury under the price discrimination law were necessarily less categorical. The idea that the buyer had a right to the advantages of location had been built into the previous cases against a background of conspiracy, and the Commission had not developed a

Club of Denver on Dec. 28, 1948. Note also answers to questions asked in 1950 by the so-called Watch-Dog Subcommittee of the Senate Committee on Interstate and Foreign Commerce (see below, pp. 430-32).

[24] With the approval of Commissioners Ferguson and Ayres, Commissioner Davis wrote, in reply to questions by the subcommittee of the Senate Interstate Commerce Committee, "When used in a manner which is not illegal under present law, freight absorption may permit interpenetration of markets and tend to promote competition. . . . Freight absorption may be an innocent or even beneficial practice. It may be harmful, not only when it is incident to a conspiracy, but also when it is an instrument for a monopolistic purpose or when it produces price discriminations that injure competition. The law should not and does not either expressly condemn or expressly sanction freight absorption, but should and does treat it like other trade practices, which, in the absence of conspiracy, are lawful unless they have an unlawful purpose or effect." Senate Committee on Interstate and Foreign Commerce, *Study of Federal Trade Commission Views on Freight Absorption*, pp. 27-28.

To an inquiry from the Secretary of the Chamber of Commerce of the State of New York, the Commission replied that "the law permits a single enterprise to use any pricing practice it may choose, including the quotation of delivered prices computed from one or more basing points, unless that practice involves price discriminations which injure competition within the meaning of the Clayton Act." *Ibid.*, p. 21.

[25] In reply to questions from the Secretary of the Chamber of Commerce of the State of New York, on Jan. 12, 1948, the Commission said, "The Commission does not advocate the imposition of a requirement that business enterprises price their goods f.o.b. mill or that they use any other form of geographic pricing practice. In the Commission's opinion, one of the principal virtues of the antitrust laws is the fact that they maintain freedom of choice and variety of behavior among businessmen, forbidding only the specific practices and conditions which have been condemned by law as destructive of competition." *Ibid.*, p. 22.

Similarly, in replying to questions from the Senate committee, Commissioner Davis wrote, "The basing-point decisions leave every businessman free to use any pricing method he chooses, so long as it is not one which eliminates or injures competition. I presume that pricing practices will continue to vary from industry to industry and from company to company. . . ." *Ibid.*, p. 30.

clear concept of injury appropriate to territorial price discrimination that did not occur in a conspiratorial setting.[26] In a policy statement addressed to the staff, the Commission interpreted its conclusions that there had been injury to competition among buyers in its major territorial cases against Staley and Corn Products Refining as based on findings that there were "very substantial price differences upon products which were of great importance to the business of these customers and that, as a consequence of these price differences, injurious effects had appeared in the volume and profits of the concerns paying the high prices." However, it said:

> There are strong reasons why the concept of injury adopted by the Court in the Morton Salt case should not be applied automatically to discriminations arising under geographic pricing systems in which purchasers paying different prices are differently located and the price differences generally diminish as the distances diminish between purchasers' locations. In these circumstances, competition between purchasers paying significantly different prices may occur in quite limited areas or only along the fringes of trade territories. Seeming advantages in price may be materially affected by disadvantages of location. These and other considerations make it clear that in geographical price discriminations inferences of injury to competition drawn merely from the existence of price differences between purchasers who compete in some degree would have no sound basis. The minimum determination of injury should be based upon ascertained facts that afford substantial probability that the discriminations, if continued, will result

---

[26] The general nature of the Commission's thinking appears in a statement by Commissioner Davis, addressed specifically to the effect of the basing-point cases on industrial concentration. "Under the basing-point system, consumers located at a base could buy the commodity more cheaply than anywhere else, and consumers located near a nonbase producer could obtain no price advantage from their location. Therefore, there was a tendency for consumers to concentrate at basing points, so far as the advantage of cheaper buying was not offset by other disadvantages. Where the basing-point system is abandoned, a consumer who wants advantage from location near a producer is equally likely to get it by locating at the former base or near any of the producers who were formerly not at a base. Thus the tendency of the change is toward a greater dispersion of consuming plants.

"Under the basing-point system, a producer who was located far from a base enjoyed the advantage of phantom freight upon sales in his local market, and some small producers have sought out new locations in order to get this advantage. But such a nonbase producer obtained a profit advantage only in nearby markets. He was under a severe handicap in selling toward the base. The producer located at the base, however, was able to sell throughout the base area

in injury to competition . . . the concept of injury applied in this field must be appropriate to the particular problem and not based merely upon analogy to concepts elsewhere.[27]

Thus, without explicitly repudiating the view that the buyer has the right to the advantages of location, the Commission indicated its intention to examine the effect of territorial discrimination in particular instances rather than to draw inferences based merely on the nature of the price differences. Subsequently, in replying to questions from a Senate Committee, Commissioner Mead wrote: "The Commission does not consider that either buyers or sellers have a legal right to exclusive benefit from the advantages of location. Buyers and sellers alike have a right to seek to enjoy those advantages by competitive bargaining and to be protected from conspiracies, monopolies, or unlawful discriminations that deprive them of the opportunity to benefit from such advantages."[28]

The Capehart Bill

Legislative developments during the basing-point controversy can be conveniently divided into four stages. In the first stage, a subcommittee of the Senate Committee on Interstate and Foreign Commerce held investigatory hearings into the policies of the Federal Trade Commission and the impact of existing law, and a bill was introduced designed to amend the law drastically.[29] These hearings had the focus proposed in the memorandum quoted above; that is, they were based on the assumption that the questions at issue were mandatory f.o.b. mill pricing and prohibited freight absorption and were concerned with the exploration

---

without absorbing freight or encountering a price lower than his own, and thus managed to share the local markets of the nonbase producers. Nonbase producers tended to remain small, and most production continued to be concentrated at basing points. Where the basing-point system is abandoned, artificial handicaps upon the growth of nonbase producers may be expected to disappear, and special opportunity for basing-point producers to sell throughout the basing-point area may be expected to disappear also. The tendency of the change is to reduce the relative importance of basing-point centers of production and thus to disperse productive capacity." *Ibid.*, p. 30.

[27] *Ibid.*, p. 20.

[28] See *Competitive Freight Absorption*, S. Rept. 2627, 81 Cong. 2 sess. (1950), p. 19. The statement had been reviewed, without "desire to express any disagreement," by Commissioners Ayres, Carson, and Spingarn.

[29] *Study of Pricing Methods*, Hearings Before the Senate Committee on Interstate and Foreign Commerce, 80 Cong. 2 sess. (1948).

of the effect of such requirements.[30] Before a public report was made on the hearings, the senators principally responsible for them introduced a bill to amend the law.[31]

[30] The subcommittee reported in March 1949. It "wholeheartedly and un-equivocally approved" the condemnation by the Supreme Court of the conspiracy found in the cement case. But it thought that the dicta of the cement decision, the decision of the circuit court in the conduit case (see above, footnote 12, pp. 402-05) and the activities of the Federal Trade Commission (which it interpreted as efforts to bring about mandatory f.o.b. mill pricing) had created uncertainty "as to whether the individual practice, by competing sellers of absorbing freight to compete in distant markets, was illegal." Unless freight absorption was permissible, it reported, "there is no escape from required selling at exclusively f.o.b. mill or factory prices, and uniform delivered prices are thus likewise illegal." Though the committee noted that the Federal Trade Commission had repeatedly issued statements disavowing any effort to condemn freight absorption or delivered pricing as such, it commented that "The duration and extent of the Commission's adherence to the views most recently expressed . . . is, of course, not known at this time." The committee thought that Congress "must find legislative means by which to make certain that all conspiracies to fix prices are effectively outlawed and at the same time safeguard to buyers and sellers the right to use freight absorption and delivered pricing practices when they choose to do business on those terms." See *Study of Federal Trade Commission Pricing Policies,* S. Doc. 27, 81 Cong. 1 sess. (1949), pp. 4-5, 63, 64.

[31] The bill, S. 236, appears in S. Doc. 27, pp. 73-77, in two versions, as introduced, and as amended after criticism. In the original version, it contained a preamble much of which was vague but which included a declaration of policy "to prohibit the requiring of the sale of products at f.o.b. factory or mill prices, where buyer and seller do not choose to transact business on such terms." The Federal Trade Commission Act was to be amended by inserting a declaration that:

"Any pricing practice employed pursuant to an agreement or conspiracy among two or more sellers shall be an unfair method of competition, but no pricing practice employed by any seller in the absence of any agreement or conspiracy with any other seller shall be deemed an unfair method of competition or an unfair act or practice in commerce within the meaning of this section because it involves (1) the charging of uniform delivered prices for goods of like grade and quality to all purchasers without regard to the place of delivery, or (2) the charging of uniform delivered prices for goods of like grade and quality to all purchasers for delivery within any geographical zone, or (3) the absorption (in whole or in part), allowance (in whole or in part), or averaging (in whole or in part) by such seller of transportation charges for the delivery of any goods, or results in delivered prices similar or identical to those charged by any other seller for goods of like grade and quality: *Provided,* That nothing contained in this sentence shall render lawful any act or practice in commerce otherwise unlawful because of fraud, deception, or coercion."

By a further amendment of the Federal Trade Commission Act, the Commission was to be empowered, in cases of conspiracy involving a delivered pricing system, to order the participants (a) to establish mill prices and (b) to give buyers the option

This bill encountered criticism from various government agencies,[32] particularly from the Federal Trade Commission, the majority of the members of which expressed the view that it would seriously weaken existing laws. After an effort to reach agreement with the Commission on the text of a proposed revision, the sponsors of the bill ceased to press for its enactment.[33]

---

of purchasing at those prices or at delivered prices not higher, but possibly lower, than those mill prices plus actual transportation costs.

The procedural section of the Robinson-Patman Act was to be amended by providing that upon proof of discrimination

". . . the person thus charged may rebut the prima-facie case thus made, and may establish that the seller's prices or practices are lawful, by showing that the lower price, or the furnishing of such services or facilities, to any purchaser or purchasers was made in good faith to meet the competitive price of any competitor or the services or facilities furnished by such competitor: *Provided,* That this defense shall not be available when the seller is acting pursuant to any agreement or conspiracy with any other seller. Any such lower price charged in good faith to permit such sellers effectively to compete may be less than the competitive price being met if such differential is customary in the general price relationship of the respective products or otherwise justified by the competitive situation of the two or more sellers. Competition may be met in good faith, and in the absence of conspiracy, by the charging by any seller of lower prices to meet competition in any or all markets, regularly, customarily, or systematically, with or without prior announcement. Unless such justification shall be affirmatively shown in any proceeding before the Commission, the Commission is authorized to issue an order terminating the discrimination."

For purposes of the Robinson-Patman Act, "price" was to be defined as "the price fixed by contract, expressed or implied, between buyer and seller"; "to lessen competition," or "to injure or prevent competition," was to mean "as to buyers, a result which materially threatens the ability of any buyer to compete with any other buyer or buyers in the resale of any commodity or in the sale of any product manufactured from such commodity, and as to sellers, a result which materially threatens the ability of any seller to continue to compete with any other seller or sellers in the sale of the commodity"; and "may be" was to mean "reasonable probability."

[32] The Department of Justice opposed the bill both by letter and in testimony by the Assistant Attorney General in charge of the Antitrust Division. The Secretary of Agriculture opposed it by letter. The Secretary of Commerce expressed sympathy with the general purpose, but advised caution in considering some of the provisions and suggested the desirability of awaiting the pending decision on the appeal of the conduit case. See *Competitive Absorption of Transportation Costs,* Hearings, pp. 4-6, 74-89, 319-21, 323.

[33] The original bill was criticized in testimony by Joseph E. Sheehy, Chairman of the Commission's Planning Council, and Robert Dawkins, special legal assistant to the Commission, on Jan. 25, 1949. (See *ibid.* pp. 89-109.) Thereafter, negotiations for a compromise bill were undertaken. (See S. Doc. 27, pp. 69-70.) The na-

The Moratorium Bill

The second stage consisted of an effort to enact a proposal for a so-called moratorium, which would have provided that for a period of

ture of the negotiations was publicly disclosed, in part, by the release of a letter from Commissioner Ewin L. Davis to Senator Edwin C. Johnson, dated Feb. 17, 1949 (Federal Trade Commission, mimeographed). In this letter, Commissioner Davis, speaking for a majority of the Commission, said:

"As the draft [the redraft of S. 236] now stands, it provides that neither uniform delivered pricing nor freight absorption through which delivered prices become identical shall be a violation of this statute in the absence of a conspiracy. A proviso states that the draft is not intended to change the present law respecting conspiracy or to affect the Commission's right to receive and consider evidence relevant to charges of conspiracy. Of course, price identities among competitors are sometimes innocent and sometimes the result of conspiracies. My feeling as to this amendment is that by singling out identity of delivered prices as a substantively innocent matter, without regard to characteristics such as persistence of identity in point of time or successive changes, a presumption is established against such identities as evidence of conspiracy even where the accompanying circumstances under which the identities appear justify an inference of conspiracy. It is possible, but not certain, that the proviso to this part of the amendment is sufficient to remove this presumption. However, I cannot be sure on this point, particularly in view of the fact that the General Counsel of your Committee objected to language, proposed for inclusion in the proviso, which would clearly have prevented any such presumption. As the draft is now worded, I am confident that the point in question would result in extensive litigation. . . .

"The second passage which concerns me greatly is the proviso . . . under which the Commission would be foreclosed from finding from the circumstances set forth in the proviso that price reductions had not been made in good faith to meet the price of a competitor. I am in sympathy with the purpose of making the meeting of competitors' prices in good faith a complete defense against charges of price discrimination. However, I deplore any effort to circumscribe the concept of 'good faith' itself, whether by singling out possible elements in it or otherwise. . . . An effort has been made to render this part of the proposed amendment harmless by specifying that good faith 'shall not be denied solely' because of the attributes of sellers' pricing practices. It appears probable, however, that to name these particular attributes is to give them a peculiar status and require the Commission to eliminate them from the entire body of circumstances accompanying a transaction before it considers whether these circumstances spell out good faith. I am not certain that this would be the result, but I feel confident that respondents would make this argument and that the Commission and the business community would be confronted by a long period of uncertainty in the law until the doubt could be removed by litigation. The general counsel of your Committee would not entertain a proposal that this possibility be eliminated by deleting the language which circumscribes 'good faith' and thus leaving the Commission free to determine the presence or absence of good faith from all the circumstances, subject to the usual court review." See letter to Senator Johnson from D. C.

somewhat more than a year the relevant statutes should not be interpreted to prevent sellers from quoting and selling at delivered prices nor from absorbing freight for the purpose of engaging in competition in good faith.[34] The announced purpose, as foreshadowed in Mr. Lamb's memorandum quoted above, was to prevent the challenged applications of law during a period long enough to enable Congress to examine the situation carefully and determine whether permanent legislation was needed. The proposal received widespread support in the Senate, was favorably reported, and was believed by observers to be assured of passage if it came to a vote. It was criticized by the majority of the Federal Trade Commission both on the ground it would create a period of un-

---

Daniel, Secretary of the Federal Trade Commission, March 1, 1949, in *Competitive Absorption of Transportation Costs,* Hearings, pp. 329-34.

When agreement between the sponsors of the bill and the Commission could not be reached, the sponsors reverted to a version more unsatisfactory to the majority of the Commission than that which had been under discussion.

[34] The text of the bill, as introduced, is set forth in S. Doc. 27, p. 77. It began with a declaration that:

"Because of widespread uncertainty resulting from recent administrative and judicial constructions of the Federal Trade Commission Act, as amended, and the Clayton Act, as amended, the Congress hereby declares that it is the sound and traditional policy of the United States that contracts, combinations, conspiracies, or monopolistic practices in restraint of trade are inimical to the public interest in maintaining a free, private, competitive enterprise system; but that it has not been the intent of the Congress to deprive individual companies of the right to use delivered price systems or to absorb freight to meet competition in any or all markets, provided such activities are carried on independently and in good faith, and not through any combination or conspiracy in violation of the Sherman Act, as amended."

It then provided that:

"Until the expiration of two years after the enactment of this Act, the Federal Trade Commission Act, as amended, and the Clayton Act, as amended, shall not be construed as depriving individual companies, in the absence of conspiracy or combination or other agreement in restraint of trade, of the right to independently use delivered price systems or to absorb freight to meet competition in any and all markets."

Provision was made that the bill should not affect "any proceeding pending in any Federal court of the United States on February 1, 1949."

As reported to the Senate, this bill had been changed by deleting the preamble, setting July 1, 1950 as the terminal date, and substituting the phrase "quote and sell at delivered prices" for the phrase "use delivered price systems."

Hearings on this bill were published under the title, *Pricing Practices— Moratorium,* Hearings Before the Senate Committee on the Judiciary, 81 Cong. 1 sess. (1949).

certainty as to the eventual rules of law and on the ground that it foreshadowed undesirable legislation.[35]

The O'Mahoney Bill: Purposes and Provisions

The third stage involved the drafting, presentation, and passage by
the Senate of a substitute bill offered by Senator O'Mahoney. This bill
was drafted by three employees of the Federal Trade Commission in the
hope of forestalling the moratorium bill or more undesirable permanent
legislation.[36] It was designed to re-enact existing law, as interpreted by
the Commission, except as to matters in which changes in the law were
regarded favorably by the Commission, and, as to those matters, to be
consistent with the views of the Commission. Senator O'Mahoney's
sponsorship of the bill was significant because he was widely known as
an ardent supporter of the antitrust policy and as an opponent of basing-
point systems. He introduced his bill on the day before the moratorium
bill came to debate in the Senate, and during debate offered it as a
substitute. After brief discussion, and amendments that were apparently
intended to be minor, his bill was passed by the Senate.

As introduced, the bill amended both the Federal Trade Commission

[35] See letter from D. C. Daniel, Secretary of the Commission, to Edwin C. Johnson, Chairman of the Trade Practices Subcommittee, March 1, 1949, printed in
Competitive Absorption of Transportation Costs, Hearings, pp. 335-37. Commissioner Lowell Mason, however, approved the bill. *Ibid.* pp. 337-38.

[36] Commissioner James M. Mead described the preparation of the bill in a
letter to Senator Edwin C. Johnson on November 20, 1950, as follows:
"The Commission is informed that subsequently, after the introduction of proposed moratorium legislation and shortly before the beginning of debate thereon,
Corwin Edwards, of the Commission's staff, was asked for a draft of legislation
which would incorporate various explanations and interpretations of the law that
had been made publicly by Commissioners or by members of its staff and that
would not impair the effectiveness of the antitrust laws. He consulted Messrs.
Dawkins and Sheehy of the Commission's staff, and these three persons prepared
a draft which endeavored to conform to the foregoing specifications. In general
principle it was not greatly different from suggestions that Mr. Dawkins had previously made to Mr. Simon [in the negotiations over revision of S. 236].
"The position of these staff members was precisely what it had always been:
namely, that legislation on this matter was neither necessary nor desirable. They
were informed, however, that a bill to replace the moratorium bill would be
introduced and they believed that it probably would be enacted; and they thought
the draft prepared by them would minimize the difficulties which, in their opinion,
were inherent in legislation on the subject.
"The draft as submitted was introduced as the amendment to S. 1008, then
pending." See S. Rept. 2627, p. 21.

Act and the Robinson-Patman Act. To the former it added a provision that:

> It shall not be an unfair method of competition or an unfair or deceptive act or practice for a seller, acting independently, to quote or sell at delivered prices or to absorb freight; provided, that this shall not make lawful any combination, conspiracy, or agreement; or any monopolistic, oppressive, deceptive, or fraudulent practice, or other practice violative of law, carried out by or involving the use of delivered prices or freight absorption.[37]

This amendment was intended to be declaratory of existing law.

To Section 2(a) of the Robinson-Patman Act the bill added the provision that:

> It shall not be an unlawful discrimination in price for a seller, acting independently, A. to quote or sell at delivered prices if such prices are identical at different delivery points or if differences between such prices are not such that their effect upon competition may be that prohibited by this section; or B. to absorb freight to meet the equally low price of a competitor in good faith, and this may include the maintenance, above or below the price of such competitor, of a differential in price which such seller customarily maintains.[38]

This amendment was intended to give statutory effect to the dictum of the Supreme Court in the Staley case that uniform delivered prices involved no discrimination, and to preclude decisions (like that of the Commission in the United Fence case, which, however, the authors did not have explicitly in mind) that such prices were discriminatory so far as they resulted in varying mill realizations. It was also intended to remove any fear that independent freight absorption to meet competition in good faith would be held unlawful. This was thought to be consistent with a further amendment pertaining to the defense of meeting competition generally, which is discussed below. The amendment had the further purpose to clarify the status of meeting competition by freight absorption in cases in which there was a customary differential between the prices of competitors, a matter as to which existing law was silent.[39]

Section 2(b) of the Robinson-Patman Act was to be amended in two

[37] S. 1974. *Congressional Record,* Vol. 95, Pt. 5, p. 7033.

[38] *Ibid.*

[39] On recommendation by the House Judiciary Committee, the House added a similar amendment to the provision of the bill which made meeting competition in good faith a complete defense, so that the maintenance of customary differentials was sanctioned not only for freight absorption but also for other types of price concessions.

respects: first, provision was made that the Commission's prima-facie case must include a showing of the probable effect on competition (in accord with the Commission's practice but contrary to the decision of the circuit court in the Moss case). Second, respondents were authorized to "justify" a discrimination by showing that they had met competition in good faith (whereas in existing law they were merely authorized to make such a showing in rebuttal, with uncertain legal effects). This provision changed existing law as interpreted by the Commission (but not as subsequently interpreted by the Supreme Court), but was consistent with a public statement by the Commission that such a rule of law would be desirable, and was also consistent with the views of the Antitrust Division of the Department of Justice.

The bill included definitions of *"price," "delivered price," "absorb freight," and "the effect may be."* The purpose of the second and third definitions was merely to give explicit meaning to new legal terms. The purpose of the definition of price—which gave price the same meaning as in commercial law applicable to the transaction—was to give the term the meaning that had been attributed to it in explanatory statements by the Federal Trade Commission, and to remove the fear that the Commission might insist that the mill realization should always be regarded as the price. The purpose of the definition of "the effect may be" was to remove fears that the Commission might rely on the views of a majority of the Supreme Court, expressed in the Morton Salt case and emphasized by a dissent, that this term meant that there was a reasonable *possibility* rather than a reasonable *probability* of the relevant effect. The Commission had consistently used the term to mean reasonable probability, and, with some embarrassment, had sought to minimize the significance of this portion of the decision of the court.

Before its passage in the Senate, the bill was amended in several respects.[40] Only two or three of the changes were significant. These are discussed below in connection with further legislative history of the bill.

The O'Mahoney Bill: Legislative History

The fourth stage covers the further consideration of the O'Mahoney bill, S. 1008.[41] Consideration of the Senate bill by the House, and sub-

[40] The text of the bill [S. 1008] as it passed the Senate appears in *Congressional Record,* Vol. 95, Pt. 6, p. 7092.

[41] Originally introduced as S. 1974, the O'Mahoney bill acquired the new number when it was substituted for the moratorium bill, S. 1008.

sequently of the House version by the Senate, developed sharp controversy along three lines. First, those who most strongly advocated new legislation sought to accomplish at least a part of their purpose by amendments that affected the nature of proof in price discrimination cases. Second, supporters of the policy of the Robinson-Patman Act bitterly opposed the inclusion in the bill of a provision that would reduce the applicability of the price discrimination law to discriminations made in good faith to meet competition.[42] Third, there was disagreement about the meaning and effect of the proposed amendment of the Federal Trade Commission Act; some saw it as a declaration of existing law, others as a change that would restore the legality of basing-point systems.

The effort to weaken the existing law by seemingly minor changes in the bill consisted primarily of a proposal to change the definition of "the effect may be." In the initial debate in the Senate, the bearing of this language on the provisions of the Administrative Procedures Act was discussed, and the definition was amended to provide that the phrase should mean that there "is substantial and probative evidence of the specified effect." The change of verb from "may be" to "is" was interpreted by the Federal Trade Commission as substituting for the test of probability the requirement that an injurious effect must have already developed. Accordingly, the Commission asked the House Judiciary Committee to substitute the language of the original O'Mahoney bill. This was done, and the House passed the bill with this change. However, the conferees rejected the House amendment and defined "the effect may be" to mean "that there is reliable, probative and substantial evidence of the specified effect." The conferees sought to limit the impact of the change by explaining that it applied only to the portions of the Clayton Act that were amended by the bill, not to the meaning of the phrase in the Clayton Act generally. Fearing that the change would seriously alter burdens of proof both under the bill and generally under the Clayton Act, Senator O'Mahoney successfully urged that the Senate send the bill back to conference. The Department of Justice concurred in the interpretation of the Federal Trade Commission of the effect of the amendment. In the second conference, the language of the original

[42] In the House of Representatives, after Representative Wright Patman had vainly tried to persuade the Judiciary Committee to hold extensive hearings, hearings were held by his Committee on Small Business. They were published under the title, *Small Business Objections on Basing Point Legislation, particularly S. 1008*, Hearings before the House Select Committee on Small Business, 81 Cong. 1 sess. (1949).

O'Mahoney bill was restored, and the definition was thus once more limited to its original purpose—rejection of the test of reasonable possibility announced by the majority of the Supreme Court in the Morton Salt case.

As introduced, the O'Mahoney bill provided that a showing that competition was met in good faith should be a justification for a price discrimination otherwise unlawful. On the floor of the Senate, Senator Kefauver offered an amendment, hastily drafted, to make the defense of meeting competition inapplicable where the effect "will be to substantially lessen competition."[43] This amendment was accepted by Senator O'Mahoney and included in the bill at it passed the Senate. In the House of Representatives, a controversy developed as to the status of the defense of meeting competition. The House Judiciary Committee proposed to delete the Kefauver amendment. In debate, however, the House adopted a proposal by Representative Carroll making the defense of meeting competition inapplicable where the effect "may be" that prohibited by the law of price discrimination. This amendment was included both in the provision authorizing freight absorption and in the procedural provision as to defense under the Robinson-Patman Act. With these amendments, the bill passed the House. Though some members of the Senate were anxious to accept the House version in order to assure the adoption of the Carroll amendments, a majority decided to send the bill to conference. In conference, the first of the two Carroll amendments was changed so that the applicable verb was "will be" (as in the original Kefauver amendment) instead of "may be," and the second Carroll amendment was deleted entirely. Instead of the latter, the conferees inserted new language saying that the provision authorizing the defense of meeting competition "shall not make lawful any combination, conspiracy, or collusive agreement or any monopolistic, oppressive, deceptive or fraudulent practice." Though these changes were bitterly opposed in debate, the House adopted the conference report. In the Senate, too, there was strong opposition. Primarily because of the definition of "the effect may be," discussed above, the bill was sent back to conference, from which it emerged with no change in the language about meeting competition. This language remained in the bill as it finally passed both Houses.

Though sabotage of the definition of "the effect may be" had been

[43] *Congressional Record,* Vol. 95, Pt. 6, pp. 7070-71.

averted, the changes in the Carroll amendments had introduced new difficulties both as to the burden of proof and as to the interpretation of the law. Individual absorption of freight was to be lawful except where its effect "will be" to substantially lessen competition. Thus the exception was made to depend on a certainty rather than a probability. Moreover, since this modified version of the Carroll amendment applied to freight absorption only, and was not applicable to the defense of meeting competition generally, the effect was to establish an inconsistency between the treatment of freight absorption and the treatment of other forms of price concession. For discrimination other than freight absorption, the right to meet competition was no longer limited by the Carroll amendment, but instead was qualified by the statement that the authorization to do so did not make lawful "any combination, conspiracy, collusive agreement, or monopolistic, oppressive, deceptive or fraudulent practice." Since such agreements and practices were inconsistent with the good faith that must be shown by those who offered the defense of meeting competition, the reference to them could be interpreted as a mere restatement of the requirement that competition must be met in good faith. Thus interpreted, the reference did nothing to reduce the scope of the defense. Whether or not the interpretation was correct, the exact meaning of the defense, as thus qualified, could be determined only after exploratory litigation.

When the bill first passed the Senate, the Federal Trade Commission was alarmed only by the definition of "the effect may be." It indicated to the House Judiciary Committee that it had no objection to the enactment of the bill with or without the Kefauver amendment.[44] After the first conference report, both the Commission and the Department of Justice opposed the bill. The Department's opposition was centered solely on the definition of "the effect may be," although the Department noted an inconsistency between the provision regarding freight absorption and the provision regarding meeting competition generally. The majority of the Commission said that the bill would weaken if not destroy the effectiveness of the Robinson-Patman Act. Though the problem as to the definition of "the effect may be" was removed by the second conference report, the difficulties in the remaining amendments were un-

[44] See letter from Commissioner Ewin L. Davis to Congressman Francis E. Walter, June 9, 1949, printed in *Clarification of Pricing Practices*, Hearings before the House Committee on the Judiciary, 81 Cong. 1 sess. (1949), pp. 60-62.

changed, and the Commission continued to oppose the bill.[45] Bitter opposition also continued to be expressed by various members of Congress. Most of it centered on the problems of meeting competition under the Robinson-Patman Act.

However, particularly in the Senate, some of the opponents believed that the proposed changes in the Federal Trade Commission Act were not harmless, but, in practice, would sanction the revival of basing-point systems of price fixing. Senator Paul Douglas of Illinois, for example, said in the debate of May 26:

> The bill . . . permits an individual firm to carry out each and every feature of the basing-point system, namely, to insist upon delivered prices and, therefore, to prevent the buyer from buying steel or cement or corn syrup, or whatever the product might be, at the mill of the seller, and compelling him to accept it at its own mill with the freight added. . . . It permits him to absorb freight, and it permits him to meet the prices of competitors. Those are the three essential features of the basing-point system itself. If we legalize each and every one of them, we legalize the basing-point system and permit individual firms to arrive at an identity of prices. They can argue that they have never met together to conspire. . . .[46]

He suggested that a proper title for the bill would be "A bill to weaken the antitrust laws of the United States."[47]

After considering the interpretation of the bill contained in the report of the House Judiciary Committee, the majority of the Commission, too, came to believe that there was serious danger of such a result. In debate, in the Senate, the phrase "or other practices violative of law" had been deleted from the amendment to the Federal Trade Commission Act, and the word "collusive" had been inserted, so that the proviso to this amendment said that the amendment did not make lawful "any combination, conspiracy, or collusive agreement; or any monopolistic, oppressive, deceptive, or fraudulent practice, carried out by or involv-

---

[45] Commissioner Mead subsequently wrote: "In the course of its passage through the Congress it acquired amendments and a legislative history which materially changed its meaning and gave prospect of confusion more serious than that alleged to exist in the present law. For this reason, staff members, including those who participated in the drafting of the bill in its original form, advised the Commission that enactment of the bill as reported from conference would have unfortunate consequences." See S. Rept. 2627, p. 21.

[46] *Congressional Record*, Vol. 96, Pt. 6, 81 Cong. 2 sess., p. 7818.

[47] *Ibid.*, p. 7851.

ing the use of delivered prices or freight absorption." In accepting these changes, Senator O'Mahoney had indicated in debate that they did not alter the meaning of the bill. The report of the House Judiciary Committee, however, interpreted this part of the bill by quoting with approval a statement by the Assistant Attorney General in charge of the Antitrust Division that the words "monopolistic, oppressive, deceptive, or fraudulent practice" were concerned with efforts to drive a competitor out of business. The report said that the Supreme Court's action in the conduit case "required the committee to take positive action" and that the committee did not intend to enlarge the jurisdiction of the Federal Trade Commission in any manner. There was no corresponding statement repudiating an intention to reduce the jurisdiction of the Commission. Thus the report implied that the proviso should be narrowly interpreted.[48]

Commissioner Mead later wrote:

The progress of the bill was so rapid that the Commission did not have opportunity at this time [when the bill was before the House] to analyze the effect of the report of the House Judiciary Committee upon the probable judicial interpretation of the first section of the bill. When there was time for this analysis, the Commission came to believe that, whereas the language of Section 1, as amended on the floor of the Senate, was harmless under the interpretation given to that amendment by Senator O'Mahoney, who sponsored the bill in the Senate, the interpretation included in the report of the House Judiciary Committee would probably result in an unfortunate curtailment of the scope of the Federal Trade Commission Act as applied to monopolistic schemes that might be worked out through the use of freight absorption or delivered pricing as devices. In view of the fact that this was the only committee report and that committee reports take precedence over comments on the floor in ascertaining the meaning of a statute, the Commission thought this danger was serious.[49]

In the House of Representatives, a motion to recommit the second conference report was defeated 175 to 204 on March 14, 1950, and the

[48] See *Clarification of Pricing Practices*, H. Rept. 869, 81 Cong. 1 sess. (1949). In opening the House debate on behalf of the Judiciary Committee, Representative Walter indicated the meaning he found in the bill by saying, "Of course there is opposition to this measure. That opposition comes from those who would make unlawful the basing-point system. That opposition comes from those who believe the Supreme Court outlawed the basing-point system." See *Congressional Record*, Vol. 95, Pt. 7, p. 8993.
[49] See S. Rept. 2627, p. 22.

report was then accepted by a voice vote. In the Senate the report was accepted on June 4 by a vote of 43 to 27.

On June 16, 1950, the President vetoed the bill.[50] His veto message said that the bill would obscure rather than clarify the law and that members of Congress were widely disagreed as to its meaning. He saw a danger that the eventual interpretation of the bill would reduce the protection provided by the antitrust laws. He noted that much of the earlier uncertainty over the meaning of the law had been removed by discussion, and that it was now clear that there was no bar to freight absorption or delivered pricing as such.

The Watch-Dog Committee

During the latter stages of the consideration of the bill, the majorities that it commanded in both Houses were so small that an effort to override the veto was clearly impracticable. Instead, on June 22, the Senate Committee on Interstate and Foreign Commerce appointed a so-called watch-dog subcommittee to maintain continuing surveillance over the activities of the Federal Trade Commission with reference to delivered pricing. In appointing the subcommittee, the chairman of the committee said that shifts in the position of the Federal Trade Commission during the basing-point discussion had destroyed public confidence and required continued close day-by-day watchfulness.[51] The subcommittee obtained from the Commission and from individual commissioners' answers to questionnaires about various aspects of the Commission's policies; held a hearing at which two commissioners were questioned intensively; and, in December 1950, published a report.[52] It said that the

---

[50] *Congressional Record,* Vol. 96, Pt. 7, p. 8721.

[51] *Ibid.,* Pt. 16, p. A4620.

[52] Answers to 15 questions by Commissioner James M. Mead, on behalf of the Commission, with a letter of dissent by Commissioner Lowell B. Mason, both dated August 14, 1950, were published in a committee print, Senate Committee on Interstate and Foreign Commerce, *Study of Federal Trade Commission Views on Freight Absorption.* Commissioner Ayres answered a separate questionnaire on September 15, 1950. On August 24, 25, and 29, Commissioners Mead and Carson were examined orally in a public hearing. Thereafter another questionnaire, containing 36 questions, was sent to the Commission in September and answered by Commissioner Mead on November 20. The answers by Commissioner Mead in November and the Watch-Dog Committee's report appear in S. Rept. 2627.

Commission had given the committee "lengthy, involved, vague, and sometimes conflicting responses"; that "it does not seem possible that the Commission can, or will, clarify the law as to competitive freight absorption"; that the Committee was unable to determine "when freight absorption is discrimination" or "when and under what circumstances the Federal Trade Commission regards freight absorption as constituting an injury to competition"; that, although the Commission had said freight absorption is not forbidden by the Federal Trade Commission Act in the absence of conspiracy, the committee could not find out whether this view was in any way qualified by phrases of uncertain meaning, such as "tacit connivance." The report ended with a recommendation that Congress "clarify the right of sellers to *competitive* freight absorption."

The Committee directed its staff to prepare a bill. Subsequently, various bills[53] were introduced by Senator McCarran, Senator Capehart, Congressman Walter, and others. A bill by Senator McCarran (sponsored also by Senators Johnson, O'Conor, Wherry, and Bricker) was passed by the Senate on August 2, 1951, by a vote of 42 to 34.[54] It was favorably reported by the House Judiciary Committee on July 2, 1952, but did not pass the House. It did not seek to amend the Federal Trade Commission Act nor to legislate explicitly as to the status of delivered prices or basing-point pricing under the Robinson-Patman Act. It provided only that meeting a competitor's equally low price in good faith (or the equally extensive services or facilities furnished by a competitor) should be a complete defense to a charge of discrimination, subject to the proviso that good faith should be deemed absent if the seller knew or should have known that the price, service, or facility accorded by the competitor was unlawful.[55] Though introduced in the Eighty-third and Eighty-fourth Congresses[56] the bill did not again emerge from committee.

---

[53] In the Eighty-second Congress, S. 719, H.R. 2820; in the Eighty-third Congress, S. 540, S. 1377, H.R. 4170; in the Eighty-fourth Congress, S. 780.

[54] *Congressional Record*, Vol. 97, Pt. 7, 82 Cong. 1 sess., pp. 9362-9401.

[55] S. 719. The text of the bill appears in *Study of Monopoly Power*, Hearings before the House Committee on the Judiciary, 82 Cong. 1 sess., Pt. 5 (1951), p. 2.

On January 8, 1951, the Supreme Court had decided in the case against Standard Oil Co. of Indiana that meeting competition in good faith is a complete defense to a charge of price discrimination.

[56] S. 540 and S. 780.

In 1954 Senator Capehart introduced a bill[57] with the joint purpose
to guarantee that meeting competition in good faith should be a complete
defense to a charge of price discrimination and to guarantee the right
to absorb freight. The bill would have included in Section 2(b) of the
Robinson-Patman Act a provision "That it shall not be a violation of
this act for a seller, acting independently, to sell at delivered prices, or
to absorb freight to meet in good faith an equally low price of a competitor." This provision was limited by a declaration that conspiracies
and attempts to monopolize were not in good faith. It was extended,
however, by a provision that what it permitted should not be prohibited
under Section 5 of the Federal Trade Commission Act. At the President's suggestion, the Bureau of the Budget had worked with Senator
Capehart on the bill. According to a letter from the director of that
bureau, changes made in the bill (which was a rewritten version of
S.1377, introduced by Senator Capehart in 1953) had been agreed upon
by the Bureau of the Budget, the Chairman of the Federal Trade Commission, the Assistant Attorney General in charge of the Antitrust Division, and representatives of the Secretary of Commerce and the Council of Economic Advisers; and the bill was in accord with the program
of the President.[58] In spite of this impressive support, however, the Judiciary Committee decided on August 2, 1954, to postpone action on the
bill indefinitely. In 1956 Senator Capehart was still sponsoring it, but
interest had shifted to bills designed to broaden the price discrimination
law by reducing the scope of the defense of meeting competition.[59]

Effect of the Controversy on
Commission Policy

The political struggle over delivered pricing had the effect of substantially reducing the emphasis placed by the Federal Trade Commission on proceedings concerned with territorial pricing formulas. At the
time of the cement decision by the Supreme Court, nine cases were pending in which the Commission subsequently decided that such formulas
had contributed to violations of law. Four of these cases were con-

[57] S. 3646, introduced June 22, 1954.
[58] See *Congressional Record,* Vol. 100, Pt. 7, 83 Cong. 2 sess., p. 8562.
[59] *To Amend Section 2 of the Clayton Act,* Hearings before the Senate Committee on the Judiciary, 84 Cong. 2 sess. (1956), statement of Senator Capehart,
p. 630.

cerned with conspiracy alone;[60] five both with conspiracy and with price discrimination.[61] In a tenth case, one count of the complaint had to do with unsystematic local price discrimination for the purpose of destroying competitors.[62] Three of the four cases that were concerned with conspiracy alone and the case that was concerned with unsystematic local price cutting resulted in orders to cease and desist before the political controversy had come to focus—two in May 1948, one in June 1948, and one in August 1948.[63] In 1950, during the controversy, an order was issued in the corn products case. After the controversy, orders were issued in the other five pending cases—in 1951 in cases against Clay Products Association and Clay Sewer Pipe Association; in 1951 in the case against American Iron and Steel Institute; and in 1953 in the cases involving the Chain Institute and National Lead. In three of the four cases involving price discrimination, the discrimination charge was dismissed, and the Commission's order was addressed only to the conspiracy charge. In the clay products case, the Commission explained that a difference in actual prices, presumably meaning delivered prices as distinguished from mill realizations, was not clearly shown.[64] In the fourth case involving discrimination, that against National Lead, the Commission issued its sole order against price discrimination. It found that the price differentials between zones were unlawful, but dismissed the part of the charge concerned with variation in mill realizations on sales to different destinations within a zone.

The five orders under the conspiracy charge did not demonstrate con-

[60] They were 1 against Crown Manufacturers Association, instituted in 1941; 2 against Structural Clay Products Institute, et al., begun in 1946; and 1 against American Iron and Steel Institute, begun in 1947.

[61] They were those against the Chain Institute, begun in 1945; National Lead Company, et al., begun in 1946; Clay Products Association, begun in 1947; Clay Sewer Pipe Association, begun in 1947; and Corn Products Refining Company, et al., begun in 1947 as a culmination of the discrimination cases against the individual corn products manufacturers.

[62] This was a case against Pure Carbonic, Inc., et al., begun in 1945.

[63] These were, respectively, the two cases involving Structural Clay Products, that involving Pure Carbonic, and that involving Crown Manufacturers Association. In the Pure Carbonic case, the count charging price discrimination was withdrawn, without prejudice to its later renewal, as one of the conditions of an agreed settlement.

[64] Both in this case and in the clay sewer pipe case, the findings of conspiracy included conspiracy to discriminate, and the order against conspiracy forbade agreement to discriminate. The effect of dismissal of the price discrimination charge was omission of an order against discrimination by the companies acting individually.

THE PRICE DISCRIMINATION LAW

tinued zeal in attacking territorial pricing formulas. In the three cases involving zone pricing and in one of the two basing-point cases, condemnation of the pricing formula was not indispensable to prove that the law had been violated; for there had been a comprehensive conspiracy, which could be shown by correspondence, adherence to common price lists, and similar evidence. In the other case, that against American Iron and Steel Institute, the basing-point formula was of central importance. The terms of the decision were negotiated with the respondents, and a consent order was entered. The findings described the basing-point system in the industry, set forth the collective activities in connection therewith, and concluded that, taken together, the acts and practices found "have tended to lessen competition, are oppressive to the public interest and unfair within the intent and meaning of the Federal Trade Commission Act" and "if not checked, would unduly suppress competition." However, no formal finding of conspiracy was made. Thus, with the consent of the steel industry, the findings echoed the view underlying the second count of the conduit case, that use of a basing-point system might violate the Federal Trade Commission Act even if it fell short of conspiracy.

The order in the case, however, was directed at conspiracy. It forbade the respondents collectively to enter into or carry out a planned common course of action to fix prices, exchange price lists, compile freight rates, sell in accord with formulas that produce identical delivered prices, or fail to quote f.o.b. mill prices. It forbade them individually to contribute to the operation of any planned common course of action by any such means. The order included provisos reminiscent of the political controversy that had recently ended. They said "that the Federal Trade Commission is not considering evidence of uniformity of prices or any element thereof of two or more sellers at any destination or destinations alone and without more as showing a violation of law," and that the Commission "is not acting to prohibit or interfere with delivered pricing or freight absorption as such when innocently and independently pursued, regularly or otherwise, with the result of promoting competition."[65]

[65] 48 FTC 154. The text of the complaint, findings, and order, have been reprinted in *Administered Prices,* Hearings before the Senate Committee on the Judiciary, 85 Cong. 1 sess., Pt. 4, Steel, pp. 1305-25. In subsequent Senate hearings, the counsel of the Judiciary Committee's Subcommittee on Antitrust and

After the political controversy, there was a marked decrease in the number of new cases concerned with territorial pricing formulas. Charges of conscious parallelism like that of count two of the conduit case have not been made in any subsequent case. Two complaints charging conspiracy in the use of a zone-pricing system and one charging conspiracy in the use of a basing-point system were issued in 1949; one complaint charging conspiracy in the use of a zone-pricing system and one charging conspiracy in the use of a freight-equalization plan combined with a basing point for sales west of the Mississippi were issued in 1951, and two complaints charging conspiracy in the use of zone-pricing systems were issued in 1953 and 1954, respectively.[66] In each case the pattern of the price agreement was comprehensive, and the analysis of the territorial formula was not crucial to the proof of violation. Orders, including prohibitions against agreement on the delivered pricing methods, were issued in 2 of the cases in 1950, in 1 in 1952, in 2 in 1953, in 1 in 1955 and in 1 in 1956. Until December 31, 1957, there was no other order concerned with conspiratorial aspects of territorial price variation.[67]

Even less activity has been shown about discriminatory aspects of basing-point and zone-pricing formulas. From the Supreme Court's cement decision in 1948 through 1955, no order under the Robinson-Patman Act struck at territorial price discrimination apart from conspiracy. From June 1956 to December 31, 1957, there were five orders

---

Monopoly said that the effect of this proceeding and of the previous basing-point cases was the offer of an f.o.b. mill price at every point where steel was produced, but that after the order identical prices and matched bids continued to exist in the industry. Roger Blough, Chairman of the Board of United States Steel, offered explanatory material, which became the basis of inconclusive controversy. *Ibid.*, Pt. 2, pp. 276-79, 354; Pt. 3, pp. 956-65.

[66] The cases were those involving the *Fir Door Institute*, 47 FTC 395; the *Malleable Chain Manufacturers Institute*, 48 FTC 1163; the *Douglas Fir Plywood Association*, 47 FTC 416; *Sayles Finishing Plants, Inc., et al.*, 49 FTC 1427. *Blotting Paper Manufacturers Association, et al.*, 50 FTC 364; *Barnes Metal Products Co., et al.*, 51 FTC 706; and *Cordage Institute*, Docket 5848, decision not yet printed in FTC Decisions in September 1958.

[67] Two such cases were pending, however, in 1958. One, against manufacturers of multi-wall paper shipping sacks, charged that they had fixed prices by a formula that included sale at zone delivered prices. (Docket 6476, *St. Regis Paper Co., et al.*, complaint Dec. 7, 1955.) The other, against manufacturers of tackless stripping used in installing carpets, charged that they had conspired to fix resale prices by zones. (Docket 6943, *The Roberts Co.*, complaint Nov. 18, 1957.)

against territorial discrimination, none of which applied to basing-point or zone formulas.[68]

It is difficult to disentangle the effects of the basing-point controversy from other influences, such as changes in the personnel of the Federal Trade Commission and changes in the political complexion of the administration. It appears, however, that there have been substantial changes in the Commission's application of the law, whatever may be the explanation of these changes. It is possible, of course, that the vulnerability of price fixing by territorial formula and of price discrimination that includes phantom freight was so thoroughly publicized during the controversy that businessmen have abandoned such practices. In so far as this is not the case, however, one must conclude that the Commission has shown less zeal and persistence in exploring this type of problem.

Few of the controversial issues about delivered pricing that were hotly debated from 1948 to 1950 are considered vital today. The Attorney General's National Committee to Study the Antitrust Laws, source of the latest effort to formulate a consensus of experts on antitrust issues, reported in 1955 that delivered pricing "standing alone is wholly equivocal; its business significance derives from the market context in which it appears."[69] But the committee recognized that "where sellers desire to suppress price competition, a strictly enforced compulsory 'delivered' pricing formula among all industry members can materially contribute to success" by easing "the task of policing and supervision which is indispensable to the success of any collusive stabilization." The committee

[68] Docket 6327, *Maryland Baking Co.;* Docket 6331, *Anheuser-Busch, Inc.;* Docket 6383, *American Brake Shoe Co.;* Docket 6639, *Arkansas City Cooperative Milk Association, et al.;* Docket 6737, *The Borden Co., et al.* These cases are discussed below in Chap. 13.

A sixth case, Docket 6152, *Aeration Processes,* involved certain territorial price variations as well as volume discounts and the pooling of purchases for discount purposes. Since the case resulted in a consent order on June 16, 1954, the findings reproduce the information in the complaint. The injury is said to have consisted in the fact that retailers ceased to buy goods from competitors—a result presumably due to volume-discount arrangements rather than territorial difference. The order forbids price discrimination when the seller is in competition with any other seller, and thus could apply to territorial as well as other discriminations. However, the case throws no light on the problem of price variation by localities.

[69] *Report of the Attorney General's National Committee to Study the Antitrust Laws* (March 31, 1955), p. 215.

endorsed proceedings against conspiratorial use of such systems.[70] But it thought that the Robinson-Patman Act should be used against territorial discrimination only when there were significant disparities in delivered prices. It opposed use of the price discrimination law in conspiracy situations, which it thought should be challenged only under the Sherman Act. Resort to conspiracy proceedings alone in such instances would, it thought, focus attention on the central problem, "devitalization of the competitive process through collusion among the discriminators," and would minimize the problem of preserving in the laws about discrimination an effective right for concerns not engaged in conspiracy to meet competition in distant markets. Several members opposed the recommendation on the grounds that the Robinson-Patman Act is properly applicable to impairment of competition among sellers and that overt acts to enforce a delivered-price conspiracy may be hard to find when sellers are few.

In the light of the cases, it appears that much might be lost if conspiracy by price formula were attacked only under the Sherman Act. Most of the cases have arisen under the Federal Trade Commission Act and have been sponsored by the Federal Trade Commission, not the Department of Justice. However, it appears that little would be lost if such arrangements were attacked as conspiracies rather than as price discriminations. Except in the corn products cases, the Commission has never proceeded against a pricing formula as discriminatory without simultaneously charging that it was conspiratorial; and in the corn products industry a conspiracy proceeding became the summation of the cases against the individual producers. There has been no instance in which the Commission has resorted to a discrimination case because it could not establish a conspiracy case. The function of the price discrimination charges[71] has been to enable the Commission to issue orders by which enterprises were forbidden not only to conspire to use a price formula, but also to use the formula individually. So long as the Commission appeared to be precluded from attacking a conspiracy by orders that governed the conduct of individual companies, orders based on charges of price discrimination were useful supplements to conspiracy

[70] A majority of its members, however, condemned the effort in the Rigid Steel Conduit case to reach parallel use of delivered pricing formulas that fell short of conspiracy. *Ibid.*, pp. 216-21.

[71] This was also the function of the second count of the Rigid Steel Conduit case.

orders; for the effect of a formula established by conspiracy could be maintained if the formula continued to be used through the momentum of trade custom. But in the National Lead case, the Supreme Court decided that the Commission's orders in conspiracy cases might apply to the practices of individual participating companies.[72] With this decision, the need to supplement a charge of conspiracy disappeared. No case has yet arisen in which the Commission was willing to rely on discrimination charges alone to terminate the use of a price-fixing territorial formula. But even before the National Lead case, cases were frequent in which the Commission relied solely on conspiracy charges to attack a formula and to support an order against collusive discrimination. With the greater scope given by the National Lead decision, the incentive to approach the problem in this way is enhanced.

[72] In the Chain Institute case the court of appeals affirmed and enforced a similar order. See *Chain Institute* v. *FTC*, 246 F. 2d 231.

13 / Territorial Discrimination Without Industry-Wide Formula

IN EIGHT CASES the Federal Trade Commission has issued orders against territorial price discrimination without finding that any territorial pricing formula was involved. None of these cases was accompanied by charges or findings of price-fixing conspiracy. In 4 of the 8 cases the orders were issued in 1957.[1] Apparently, other similar orders are probable in cases not yet decided. Whereas the use of the Robinson-Patman Act against territorial pricing formulas appears to have ended, its use against unsystematic territorial price variation is apparently becoming more vigorous. These cases and certain related private suits will be discussed in this chapter.

The cases with which this chapter is concerned have to do with local price reductions by a concern selling over a wide area, but competing with concerns that sell in a smaller territory. The pattern of such local price cutting is similar to that which has long been attacked in proceedings under the Sherman Act; but among the Commission's cases are some against sellers who neither have a monopoly nor can reasonably be said to seek one. The question raised, therefore, is the appropriate scope of a rule against local price cutting. Two issues are involved: First, what kind of a showing of damage to competition is needed to support an attack on price differences between one locality and another?[2] Second, where such damage has been found, how much restric-

---

[1] The other four were issued in 1939, 1941, 1953, and 1955, respectively.

[2] It is interesting to note that applicability of the law to territorial price variation was debated during consideration of the Robinson-Patman bill by the House of Representatives. On May 25, 1936, a joint letter from the American Farm Bureau Federation, the National Grange, the Northwest Farmers Union Legislative Committee, the Farmers National Grain Corporation, and the National Cooperative Milk Producers Federation expressed various objections to the bill (see above, footnote 8, p. 25), one of which was that Sec. 2(a) might be so interpreted "that different prices could not be charged by the same seller in different markets." It

439

tion on the seller's freedom to compete by price reduction may properly be imposed to prevent further damage?

Of the orders of the Federal Trade Commission that have raised this problem, 3 were issued before the end of 1953, 5 after November 15, 1955. Two of the 3 earlier cases were included among those specifically studied.[3] One of these involved the use of the Robinson-Patman Act against a predatory attack on a business rival designed to establish and consolidate monopoly power. In this instance, the Robinson-Patman Act was used with a purpose similar to that of the early Sherman Act cases.

The Earlier Cases

Chicory was processed by only three companies—Muller, Franck, and Schanzer. Muller and Franck were controlled by the same family interest, had interlocking offices, and did a complementary business, with Franck chiefly engaged in selling packaged chicory to retailers and Muller chiefly selling bulk chicory to coffee roasters. The only other company, Schanzer, was originally an importer and subsequently began to produce domestically because of a higher tariff and the devaluation

---

asked to have the matter clarified. In debate in the House, Congressmen Patman, Miller, and Boileau said the bill could not be so interpreted. After reading the relevant passage from the letter, Mr. Boileau asked Mr. Miller, who was spokesman for the majority of the Judiciary Committee, "Is it the gentleman's opinion that their fears in this respect are without foundation?" Mr. Miller replied, "They are entirely unfounded." On the other hand, Congressman Celler, a member of the Judiciary Committee who opposed the bill, said, "I say that you cannot make, under the bill, a different price for the same goods of the same quality in a different locality." See *Congressional Record*, Vol. 80, Pt. 8, 74 Cong. 2 sess., pp. 8230-33.

[3] The one not studied was Docket 3740, *Metz Brothers Baking Co.* On September 16, 1938, Metz reduced prices below the prices of other bakers in southwest Minnesota and northwest, southeast, and central South Dakota. Thereafter, its prices for a 24-ounce loaf of bread were 8 cents in these areas, as compared with 10 cents in northwest Iowa. Metz admitted the material allegations of the complaint, and the Commission found, without stating its grounds, that the discrimination produced both the broad and the narrow types of damage to competition in the primary line and tended to create a monopoly in that line. The findings do not provide information about the occasion for or purpose of the price change, the size of Metz, the size or number of Metz's competitors, or the effect of the price change on relative sales by Metz and its competitors. Presumably the pattern of the discrimination and the problems raised thereby were similar to those of the Page Dairy case, discussed below (pp. 442-45). The complaint, findings, and order appear in 30 FTC 268.

of the dollar. Muller's plant was in Michigan in the heart of the chicory-growing area, Franck's in New York, and Schanzer's in New Orleans, the principal chicory market, which consumed about 75 per cent of all domestic chicory. All of the plants depended either on the Michigan area or on imports from overseas for their supplies of raw chicory. Schanzer was a comparatively small company, with a net worth of $71,000 in 1937 as compared with about $2,000,000 for Muller and Franck combined.

The Commission found that Muller and Franck had reduced prices to Schanzer's customers, often below cost,[4] in an effort to destroy Schanzer's business. The findings take note of no regularity in the geographic structure of the prices of Muller and Franck, and contain details which indicate that discounts were granted opportunistically in areas where they would have the greatest effect in diverting business from Schanzer and that there were also other opportunistic discriminations among customers.[5] The defense rested on the contention that, with unimportant exceptions, Franck had sold f.o.b. New York and New Orleans and Muller f.o.b. these points plus f.o.b. its factory in Port Huron, Michigan; and that since New Orleans was a principal coffee center and the principal center for the importation of chicory,[6] the reduction of the price there was to be expected. This contention, however, is not inconsistent with the Commission's finding that the prices of Muller and Franck in Schanzer's home market of New Orleans were lower, in spite of higher freight costs, than in most of the territory that was freight-wise nearer to their factories. The Commission's findings of a purpose to destroy Schanzer were based not only on the territorial variation in prices but also on the history of price changes, on various efforts to handicap Schanzer, and on documents in which the Muller executives described their own strategy. After trying to match the aggressive pricing of Muller and Franck, Schanzer raised prices in January 1937.

[4] In the year ending June 30, 1937, the Commission found Muller lost on the average 8 cents per hundred pounds on granulated chicory, but lost from 66 cents to $1.11 per hundred pounds on sales in New Orleans. Franck's sales of granulated chicory were profitable as a whole in spite of sales at or below cost to its two largest New Orleans customers during much of the year.

[5] For example, Franck had made special concessions to its two largest customers for granulated chicory, who together took 75 per cent of its total sales of that product in 1936 and 87 per cent in 1937.

[6] The Commission found that about 75 per cent of Franck's output and 40 per cent of Muller's were sold in New Orleans trade territory. See 33 FTC 24ff.

Muller and Franck increased their sales from 1936 to 1937 by more than 872,000 pounds, while Schanzer's sales fell by more than 860,000 pounds,[7] which was more than 37 per cent of Schanzer's 1936 total.

The case was pending on appeal during the early part of the war, and in consequence the price of chicory was set by O.P.A. at a level based on Muller's prices. Thereafter Schanzer ceased to sell chicory except in 8-ounce packages, and protests by coffee roasters resulted in an increase in the price ceiling. The Commission's order was affirmed on appeal during the period of wartime regulation. Muller then discontinued its New Orleans base price and sold chicory in that area f.o.b. Port Huron. Since the chicory root for Schanzer's factory came from Michigan, this change of practice, in effect, equalized prices in New Orleans, except as there were different freight rates on the processed chicory shipped by Muller and the dried root shipped to Schanzer's factory. In the postwar period the tariff on chicory was substantially reduced, and the labor costs of domestic production rose substantially, so that foreign imports supplied the principal competition for Muller and Schanzer alike. Schanzer resumed importation of foreign chicory root; and both Schanzer and Muller absorbed freight on domestic chicory in an effort to meet foreign prices in the New Orleans market. After 1954, the growing of domestic chicory practically ceased, and domestic producers depended wholly on imported dried root. There is no indication of current efforts by Muller and Franck to drive Schanzer out of business. Schanzer now operates with imported root, and has maintained its proportion of the domestic business.

The second case involving unsystematic territorial price variation had no such overtones of industry-wide monopoly. It was concerned with the practice of a large regional dairy in varying its prices from one locality to another in recognition of the varying kinds and amounts of competition encountered in different local markets. The territory covered by the case is served by small local dairies, larger regional dairies, and branches of the largest national dairies. Page Dairy, of Toledo, Ohio, respondent in this case,[8] bought milk in both Indiana and Ohio, in territory covered by two Federal milk marketing orders, and sold not

----

[7] This is the finding of the Court of Appeals (142 F. 2d 511, 518). The Commission found, more generally, that in 1937 Schanzer lost 650,000 pounds, or more than 25 per cent of its volume. The source of the discrepancy has not been ascertained.

[8] Docket 5974.

only in Ohio but also to retailers in northeastern Indiana and south-eastern Michigan in competition with both regional and local dairies. It charged higher prices in Ohio than in Indiana and Michigan, and charged less by one or two cents per quart in some Indiana towns than in the other towns in Indiana and Michigan in which it made sales. The impact of price competition of Page Dairy was felt not only in price variations by locality but also in the fact that the company did not fol-low the general practice of charging a premium of one cent per quart for homogenization[9] and that it took the lead in making price reduc-tions on large containers. At four places in Indiana and one in Michi-gan, Page Dairy offered homogenized vitamin D milk in half-gallon cartons while competitors offered it only in quart cartons at prices higher by from one-half to 2.5 cents per quart. In five other towns, competitors, too, sold in half-gallon cartons, but in one of these five localities the prices by Page Dairy were lower by a cent per quart and in another by a cent and a half. Some of the competitors of the com-pany introduced the half-gallon container only to meet its competition.

The Commission found that price discriminations by Page Dairy had the reasonable probability of injuring competition with the company in the narrow sense or of substantially lessening competition or tending to create a monopoly in the primary line of commerce.[10] The finding of injury was supported by a statement of the price differences; a statement that the retailer's gross margin of profit on milk is narrow, so that dif-ferences in price readily divert purchases; and a finding that, as a result of the pricing practices, some buyers had discontinued or curtailed their purchases from competitors of Page.

From the trial record it appears that before the complaint against Page Dairy, other dairies had made an unsuccessful effort to draw it into an agreement to fix prices. The Commission's witnesses all agreed that the practice of quoting different prices in different localities was general in the area. It is a reasonable inference that the competitors of the company brought its prices to the Commission's attention, not be-cause the local discrimination was unusual, but because Page Dairy was a price-cutter and would not co-operate with other dairies.

The Commission's order in 1953 required Page Dairy to cease selling

---

[9] Instead, Page charged a premium of one cent per quart for milk containing vitamin D. For a time some vitamin D milk was not so labeled and was sold without the premium. Later the premium was charged for all vitamin D milk.

[10] The findings have the alternative form "or." See 50 FTC 395.

to any buyer at a lower price than to any other buyer where it was in competition with any other seller.[11] The immediate effect of the order was a price increase by Page Dairy, as a result of which various dairies that had been troubled by price competition of the company felt that their problems had been met. Page Dairy grants discounts of from 3 to 6 per cent based on the size of average daily deliveries, which its discount sheet says are cost-justified. Some of its competitors do not offer similar discounts. There is general agreement that price cutting is still common, but that Page Dairy is no longer the most formidable price-cutter. Some producers accuse others of secret price concessions and unjustified local price cutting. There appears to be little doubt that sale in different localities at different prices is still common among dairies in the area that are not confined to a single locality. Presumably, those who make local price reductions would justify the differentials as due to meeting competition in good faith.

Changes in market practices have reduced some of the pressures that were evident in the Page Dairy case. Vitamin D is now generally provided in milk, and price differences based on it are no longer a problem. The two-quart container is much more common and the gallon glass bottle has appeared, so that the advantages of the company in the provision of milk in large cartons have been whittled away. There has been a rapid reduction in the number of small bottling plants, primarily because a relatively large operation is more economical.[12] Consequently, there are fewer local processors in situations so precarious that they cannot endure price competition.

Nevertheless, the basic problem raised by the Page Dairy case persists, though in less aggravated form. So long as the milk produced by farmers in adjacent territories is subject to different milk marketing orders, there will be differences in the price at which dairy companies can obtain milk, and there will be a tendency for the larger ones to buy, so far as they can, in the cheapest markets. Differences in the purchase price of milk offset transportation costs sufficiently to provide an

[11] Since Page operated only in Toledo and nearby territory, the order applied to the region covered by the Commission's investigation and findings.

[12] One small processor estimates that his own processing costs are $1.50 per hundredweight, while those of a large urban competitor are about $1.00. He estimates that from 1954 to 1956 about 55 small processors have ceased operating or disappeared by merger in 20 counties of northeastern Indiana; and that of the 30 dairies in the Fort Wayne area 5 or 6 are left.

incentive to carry milk considerable distances.[13] The economies of large-scale processing will continue to facilitate the elimination of small dairies and the invasion of the milk markets of small towns by urban dairy companies.[14] These inherent pressures on the small-town dairies do not arise from discrimination, but a large dairy selling throughout a wide area can enhance its own profits and increase the handicap suffered by some of the small dairies by quoting its lowest prices where it encounters the largest amounts of local competition or where it crosses the path of another large urban dairy. Since the small local dairy cannot reach far into other localities, its problem, when it encounters local price discrimination, is akin to that of the victim of monopolistic price cutting, whether or not the big dairy company that discriminates has any significant degree of monopoly power in the area as a whole. Presumably, the Commission's case against Page Dairy was intended to remove this kind of pressure by requiring the company to adopt a uniform price throughout its marketing area (except as prices to outlying customers might be increased to reflect transportation expense). If so, the Commission did not succeed, through the example of the Page Dairy case, in inducing large dairies in the area to discontinue the adjustment of their local prices to the competition locally encountered.

The problem of territorial price differences was raised in a different form in a private suit by Russellville Canning Company against American Can Company, other aspects of which have been discussed in previous chapters. Russellville Canning Company and several other canners operated plants in the Ozarks, obtained cans from American Can Company's plant at Terre Haute, Indiana, and paid freight, not f.o.b. the factory, but f.o.b. the factory of a competing can manufacturer in St. Louis. Under this arrangement, the freight cost to Russellville and its competitors was the same. Complaints that Ozark canners were at a locational disadvantage induced American Can, beginning in 1941, to compute freight from its warehouse at Fort Smith, Arkansas, rather than from St. Louis; however, most cans were still shipped direct to the customer from Terre Haute. Under the new plan, all Ozark customers paid less freight

[13] In Angola, Indiana, where Page buys milk, the buying price is 17 cents per 100 pounds below that in Toledo. The differential is an offset to the cost of hauling the milk to Toledo for processing and back to Indiana for sale.

[14] The introduction of the paper container has assisted the large dairies. Since paper is lighter, a truck can carry more milk, and delivery at a distance is cheaper. Since carton processing machines are expensive, small dairies cannot afford them.

than before, but Russellville paid more than its Ozark competitors. Russellville protested, and after 1944 insisted on paying the amount specified in its contract, which provided for freight from St. Louis, rather than the lesser amount acceptable to American Can. It sued for damages, not only because of the freight differential, but also because of American Can's volume discounts and because of a special allowance given by American Can to one customer.[15] The lower court found that the warehouse at Fort Smith was not the actual source of supply and that the freight differentials were injurious discriminations damaging to Russellville.[16] The court of appeals agreed that, if injurious, the differentials were unlawful. However, it saw no damage to Russellville. It thought the reduced charges had benefited all of the Ozark canners and that: "What the plaintiff really complains of is not that it was damaged by such freight equalization, but that it was not benefited by it to the same extent as some of its local competitors."[17] The suit was privately settled by a payment from American Can to Russellville before the issues in the case had been finally adjudicated.

Recent Cases: The Facts

In each of the five recent cases in which the Commission has issued orders, the discrimination consisted in setting a lower price in one or two cities or areas than the same seller maintained elsewhere.

A consent order was issued against American Brake Shoe Company on November 15, 1955.[18] Consequently, the nature of the discrimination can be ascertained only from the complaint by the Commission. From this it appears that before 1949 American Brake Shoe was the only manufacturer of railroad car journal bearings selling in Virginia, North Carolina, Georgia, and Florida. In that year a new regional manu-

[15] See above, pages 203-05 and 244-46.

[16] 87 F. Supp. 484.

[17] 191 F. 2d 55. In the Bruce's Juices case, the court found that one of the discriminations by American Can Company was the requirement that Bruce pay full freight from the factory for a particular size of small cans, while two competitors of Bruce received the benefits of lower freight rates under a freight-equalization plan from which Bruce was excluded. This was found to be unlawful. However, the difference arose from discrimination against a particular customer, not from different prices or pricing practices in different localities. See 187 F. 2d 919.

[18] Docket 6383, American Brake Shoe Co.

facturer appeared there. American Brake Shoe then reduced its prices
to a level as low as its new competitor in these southeastern states, without corresponding reductions elsewhere. The competitor made a further
reduction to the largest purchaser, and after a year's delay American
Brake Shoe not only met this concession but beat it by a few cents,
quoting a price below its own cost of manufacture and sale. Prices were
increased by American Brake Shoe in other parts of the country in
1952 without any change in prices in the southeastern states. During
the period when the competitor's price was lower, the competitor took
away from American Brake Shoe 95 per cent of the business of the
largest purchaser; after beating that price,[19] American Brake Shoe recovered more than half of the loss. The complaint saw in the situation
a tendency toward monopoly and both the broad and the narrow types
of damage to competition in the primary lines of commerce. The Commission ordered American Brake Shoe to cease selling bearings to any
purchaser in a trade area at prices different from those charged to other
purchasers in the same area where it was in competition with any other
seller for such sales. However, the order did not prohibit the quotation
of lower prices in the southeast than in other parts of the country.

The discrimination by Maryland Baking Company had the avowed
purpose of putting a competitor out of business.[20] The respondent, a
nationwide enterprise, had only one relatively small competitor in the
sales of cones for ice cream in the metropolitan areas of Washington
and Baltimore. The competitor, formerly a producer of rolled sugar cones
only, began to produce cake cones as well. This enlargement of its
business was met by Maryland Baking Company by a large reduction
in the price of rolled sugar cones, which accounted for only about 1.5
per cent of Maryland Baking's total sales.[21] Sales of rolled sugar cones
by Maryland Baking tripled in volume. In spite of a price reduction, the
competitor's business in such cones fell from about 91 per cent of the

---

[19] In 1952 American Brake Shoe quoted a price 6 cents lower, but nevertheless
continued to lose the business of the favored customer, and sold only 1 per cent
of his requirements. In 1953 it quoted 10 cents lower than its competitor and also
gave a cash discount. In that year it sold 41 per cent of the buyer's requirements.
With the same price differential, it sold 58 per cent in 1954.

[20] Docket 6327, *Maryland Baking Co.*

[21] In May or June 1951, Maryland Baking reduced the price of rolled sugar
cones from $6.66 per thousand to $5.00 per thousand, while it was selling them
in the Philadelphia metropolitan area, Delaware, and New Jersey for $7.16. The
competitor subsequently reduced its price to distributors from $6.80 to $6.00.

market in 1950 to about 58 per cent in 1953-54. It held the remaining business partly by selling direct to retail outlets as it lost jobber customers. By selling chocolate-coated rolled sugar cones to ice cream manufacturers, however, it managed to increase its total business. The Commission found both the broad and narrow types of injury in the primary line of commerce. It ordered Maryland Baking to cease selling cones to any purchaser at a higher price than to another where it was in competition with another seller in sales to the purchaser receiving the lower price. The order was not limited to rolled sugar cones or to the metropolitan areas over which the case arose. Maryland Baking appealed, primarily on the ground that the order was too broad, alleging that thereby its prices were put in a strait jacket throughout the country. The Commission proposed to meet this objection by changing the order so that different prices were forbidden only where the lower price "undercuts the price at which the purchaser charged the lower price may purchase ice cream cones of like grade and quality from another seller."[22] The Fourth Circuit affirmed the order as thus modified, interpreting it "to forbid discrimination in prices within any area in the United States in which the company is doing business, but not to require uniform prices throughout the country nor to forbid the company's making prices in good faith to meet competition."[23]

The discrimination by Anheuser-Busch consisted in two price reductions on beer in St. Louis County, Missouri, without corresponding reductions elsewhere in the country.[24] Anheuser-Busch, one of the largest brewers, sells a premium beer throughout the United States, and produces from 7 to 8 per cent of the national output of beer. In St. Louis its principal competitors are three regional brewers, Falstaff, Griesedieck Western, and Griesedieck Brothers. Sales in the St. Louis area constituted, respectively, 14 per cent, 25 per cent, and 24 per cent of the total sales of these competing companies, and only 3.5 per cent of the sales of Anheuser-Busch. Before 1954, Anheuser-Busch beer sold in St. Louis at a premium of 58 cents per case, and was outsold there by each of the three regional brewers. In January 1954, Anheuser-Busch reduced the differential to 33 cents, and in June eliminated it entirely. On neither occasion did it reduce prices elsewhere. In March 1955, as a result of

[22] Cited in *Maryland Baking Co.* v. *FTC*, 243 F. 2d 716.
[23] *Ibid.*
[24] Docket 6331, *Anheuser-Busch, Inc.*

a price increase by Anheuser-Busch, followed by smaller increases by the others, a differential of 30 cents was restored. By that time Griese-dieck Western's sales had dropped from about 39 per cent of the total for the area to about 23 per cent; Falstaff's sales, which had been between 29 and 30 per cent with an upward trend, had dropped by about one third of one per cent; and Griesedieck Brothers' sales had dropped from over 14 per cent to less than 5 per cent.[25] Anheuser-Busch had increased its share of the market from 12.5 per cent to more than 39 per cent. Within three or four months after the differential was restored, Falstaff's percentage of sales in the area grew and the percentages of the other two competitors increased, though not to the previous figures, while Anheuser-Busch fell back to about 21 per cent.

The Commission found both the broad and the narrow injury to competition in the primary line of commerce and also a tendency to create a monopoly in that line. It ordered Anheuser-Busch not to discriminate by reducing prices in any market in which it is in competition with any other seller without proportionally reducing prices everywhere.[26]

It should be noted that, although Anheuser-Busch sold its beer at various prices in various market areas, these price differences were not made a part of the case. The attack was focused only on the change in these differences that resulted from the price reduction in St. Louis; and by forbidding price reductions that were not proportional (where competition was present), the order not only accepted the differences in price from area to area, but substantially limited the right of Anheuser-Busch to reduce them in the future.

The Borden case also concerned local discrimination.[27] Since there was a consent order, the facts can be determined only from the allegations of the complaint. On this basis, it appears that two subsidiaries of the Borden Company sold fluid milk in the area in and around Wilmington, Delaware, at prices from 2½ to 3¾ cents per quart below those at which they sold in Pennsylvania and New Jersey and also granted cash discounts of 2 per cent to some purchasers that were not available to others. Injury of both the broad and narrow types was alleged in both

---

[25] There was evidence that the sales of the two Griesedieck companies had been falling for other reasons, but during the period in question the decline was accentuated.

[26] Docket 6331, *Anheuser-Busch, Inc.*, Opinion and Order Sept. 10, 1957.

[27] Docket 6737, *The Borden Co. et al.*, complaint March 8, 1957, order Nov. 13, 1957.

the primary and secondary lines of commerce, as well as a tendency to monopoly in both lines. No information was supplied as to the number and strength of Borden's competitors nor as to the basis for asserting damage to competition among buyers. Borden's subsidiaries were ordered not to sell fluid milk to one buyer more cheaply than another engaged in the same line of commerce (1) where the lower price undercuts the price at which the buyer may buy from another seller; or (2) where any buyer not receiving the benefit of the lower price competes in resale with the buyer who receives it. Borden was ordered not to participate in any such conduct by them.

The case against Arkansas City Cooperative Milk Association was like the Borden case, and, like it, resulted in a consent order.[28] On the basis of the complaint, it appears that the co-operative sold fluid milk wholesale in Arkansas City at prices from one to three cents per quart lower than elsewhere in Kansas and Oklahoma. It competed in the wholesale market with an independent dairy located in Arkansas City. It also sold milk at retail in Arkansas City in competition with two local dairies, and in 1954 reduced its retail prices there by 13 cents per gallon, delivered, to a price lower than its competitors' prices for milk sold cash-and-carry. The complaint alleged both the broad and the narrow types of injury in both the primary and secondary lines of commerce, as well as a tendency to create a monopoly in both lines. The scope of the Commission's order was the same as in the Borden case.

Because there were consent orders in the cases against Borden and Arkansas City Cooperative Milk Association, and because the complaints in these cases are silent about matters important to the problem of injury, one cannot be sure of the relevant facts in these cases. Nevertheless, the findings of injury in the five cases differ considerably in their apparent grounds and in their persuasiveness. The cases against American Brake Shoe and Maryland Baking contain the elements of a charge under the Sherman Act: A large seller with a monopoly position acts to preserve his monopoly by discriminatory local price cutting against a small local competitor, with considerable effect on the competitor's sales and with slight effect on his own profits.

The injury in the case against Anheuser-Busch was less severe. It was not clear that the company tried to destroy its competitors in St. Louis or

[28] Docket 6639, *Arkansas City Cooperative Milk Association, Inc., et al.*, complaint Sept. 24, 1956, order Sept. 4, 1957.

that their business existence was at stake. One of the three held its own under the attack by Anheuser-Busch, and was injured only in the sense that its share of the market stopped increasing. The St. Louis market was only a part of the sales area of each of the competitors, though a much smaller part for Anheuser-Busch than for the others. The action of the company went no further than to eliminate a price differential between its beer and the beer of its competitors, under the protection of which the competitors had previously outsold Anheuser-Busch in St. Louis. Whereas a purpose to weaken competition pervaded the first two cases, it is possible to impute to Anheuser-Busch such purposes as experiment with a new price policy, attainment of a better balance of sales in different areas, or maintenance of the volume of production in the St. Louis plant.

The basis for the finding of injury in the primary line of commerce in the Borden case was apparently still narrower. Borden is nationally a very large company; but markets for fluid milk are regional rather than national, and there is no showing of the extent of competition with the Borden subsidiaries in Wilmington, in Pennsylvania, and in New Jersey. Information as to injury consists only in a statement of the price differences. Yet every kind of injury recognized by the statute is alleged on both the selling side of the market and the buying side, and through the process of consent settlement the allegations become, in practical effect, findings.

The Arkansas City case is the culmination of this series of progressively more ambitious proceedings. Like the Borden case, it was settled by consent; and it is the same as the Borden case in the breadth of its concept of injury. The order is based, however, on local price reductions in a small town in Kansas. Though the size of Arkansas City Cooperative is not stated, obviously it was not great, except, perhaps as a share of a market in a relatively small area. We are told that there were two other local retailers and one other local wholesaler of fluid milk; but we know nothing of the number or character of nonlocal competitors of the Arkansas City Cooperative nor of the extent of the market served by the local concerns mentioned. It may be that there were no other sellers who did business state-wide and that the local sellers were dependent wholly on local business. It may be that the co-operative had an unusual degree of power. But even if there was danger that it might come to dominate the market, this danger presumably was limited by the possibility that nearby sellers might invade its territory. The case seems to condemn local price cutting in terms that would be applicable to every concern that sells in more than one locality and encounters any competitor whose market has a smaller territorial extent.

The Theory of Injury

The theory of injury to competition underlying these cases was stated in a recent speech by the director of the Commission's Bureau of Litigation.

> The basic theory underlying the intent of Congress in declaring "area" price discriminations to be violations of the law is generally that of preventing predatory use of market subsidization. In other words, the law hits at the practice of throttling local competition by lowering prices in one geographic area while maintaining higher prices in other areas. It seeks to prevent a large seller, with an interstate treasury, from subsidizing a diminution or complete elimination of profits occasioned by discriminatory price cutting in one area, by maintaining —or perhaps raising—its normal profitable pricing structure in other areas. . . . The precise market share of the discriminator on a nationwide basis is not controlling in making any determination of its ability, by area price discrimination, to injure or destroy its local competitors. The over-all size of the seller is significant, however, in that it enables it to engage in area price discrimination without fear of monetary loss to itself. Thus, even though the low prices in one area may eliminate or materially reduce the seller's profits in that area, it can withstand the absence or diminution of profits there because of the benefits of its higher prices in other areas. Likewise, the precise concentration of the injured competitor's sales in the area of the challenged price discriminations is not and cannot be a determining factor as to the existence or nonexistence of competitive injury. The area of the price discrimination must represent, however, a substantial portion of the over-all sales of the injured competitors. . . . There is no requirement in the Robinson-Patman Act, of course, that the injury involved in area price cases be confined to purely local competition; competition on the regional, or even the national, level may be just as effectively injured or lessened by area price discrimination. It is also important to note that the Robinson-Patman Amendment does not include as an element of a violation any predatory intention by the seller. . . .[29]

[29] "Area Price Discrimination," remarks of Joseph E. Sheehy, Director, Bureau of Litigation, Federal Trade Commission, before the Association of General Counsel, Cleveland, Ohio, Oct. 23, 1957 (mimeo.), pp. 2-3. Mr. Sheehy's duty is

From this it appears that disparity in the size and territorial scope of competitors is sufficient to justify a finding that a local price reduction by the larger in any area important to the smaller rests on subsidization and is injurious to competition. However, in two cases[30] in which such differences in size were present, the Commission has dismissed a charge of territorial price discrimination. In a case against General Foods, concerned with a free deal on pectin products on the West Coast that was not available elsewhere in the United States, lack of injury to competition was found by a majority of the Commission in spite of the fact that General Foods dominated the West Coast market and was the major seller nationally. Similarly, one-cent deals in various areas by the Purex Corporation were not found to be illegally discriminatory. In both cases, absence of a demonstrated causal connection between the deals and loss of sales by competitors was the chief reason for dismissal.[31] In cases

---

to direct the prosecution of the cases; but he has no part in the Commission's decisions. He warned his audience that he was expressing his personal views and not the official views of the Commission.

[30] Docket 5675, *General Foods Corp.*, dismissed April 13, 1954; Docket 6008, *Purex Corp., Ltd.*, dismissed Aug. 24, 1954.

[31] In the Purex case the hearing examiner found that if there was any difference between the broad and narrow concepts of injury it was slight, since the Commission had expressed the belief that either must be substantial (51 FTC 116). However, he ruled that mere proof that there were price differences and that there was competition was not prima facie proof of injury to competition in the primary line. (*Ibid.*, p. 167.) Since his decision was not appealed to the Commission, these opinions were not reviewed. In the General Foods case, the hearing examiner held that, in cases of injury to competition in the primary line from territorial discrimination, the important question was "not whether a particular seller may have lost business but rather whether competition in the area in question has been or is likely to be substantially injured. In short, whether there is a substantial tendency toward monopoly." Though the Commission confirmed his dismissal of the case, it rejected this standard. Commissioner Gwynne's opinion said: "We do not believe the law makes the distinction between competitive injury to sellers and competitive injury to their customers that the above statement would seem to indicate. Both sellers and customers are equally under the protection of Section 2(a). The test is the same in either case. The standard for determining the unlawfulness of an unjustified price discrimination, namely, the substantiality of the effects reasonably probable, is the same whether the competitive injury occurs at the seller level or at the customer level. . . . Under differing circumstances the proof necessary to establish injury or even to make out a prima facie case will differ." See 50 FTC 887.

Though in 1939 General Foods had more than 75 per cent of the national market for liquid pectin and 40 per cent of the national market for powdered pectin,

concerned with territorial discrimination, unlike cases concerned with volume discounts, loss of sales by competitors apparently must be proved rather than inferred and hence must be found in the past rather than predicted in the future. In this respect, in the words of the director of the Commission's Bureau of Litigation: "There is no such thing as a 'per se' violation possible in area price discrimination."[32] However, if there is disparity in the scale of operations and if a local price cut reduces the sales of a competitor, the Commission apparently will conclude that competition has been injured.[33] Since for most commodities in most markets concerns of different sizes and territorial extent are in competition with one another, this conception of injury means that local price reductions large enough to attract purchasers are pervasively in jeopardy.

The Scope of Corrective Orders

The scope of the orders in the five recent cases is startling. Even in the case against American Brake Shoe, where the order is narrowest, the

---

deals on the West Coast avowedly intended to get more business there and limit the eastward spread of western competition were held to be lawful because the evidence did not prove injury. There was evidence as to three competitors of General Foods. The sales of two had increased during the period of the deals (one to an extent that the hearing examiner thought almost incredible). Though the sales of the third had fallen, the decline appeared to be due to influences other than the deals. The hearing examiner recognized the possibility that, but for the deals, these competitors would have done better, but regarded such an inference, unsupported by evidence, as in "the realm of conjecture and speculation."

In a dissenting opinion, Commissioner Mead said that the discrimination was an attempt to retain dominance of the market, and pointed out that in 1939, the last year before the special deals began, General Foods had 46.1 per cent of the market in the Pacific Northwest and 55.7 per cent of the market in the Pacific Southwest, whereas in 1942, the last year for which regional figures were available, its percentages were 62.5 and 69.1 respectively. See 50 FTC 897.

[32] Sheehy, "Area Price Discrimination," p. 11.

[33] On April 8, 1957, the Commission issued a complaint against the Amalgamated Sugar Company, charging that it discriminated illegally by reducing the price of sugar in Utah only. Amalgamated had an annual sales volume of about $46 million. The allegations of the complaint were that about 3.3 per cent of Amalgamated's sales were made in Utah, as compared with 9.2 per cent, 69.2 per cent and 25.4 per cent for its three chief competitors, and that the price reductions were sufficient to divert trade unless met. From these facts, the Commission inferred all three types of injury in the primary line. The case ended in a consent order in 1958 (Docket 6768).

restriction imposed by it exceeds that which was relevant to the facts of the case or appropriate to prevent the exercise of differential power. Whether, outside the southeastern area, American Brake Shoe has a monopoly or competes with other enterprises large or small was not found by the Commission. No allegation about its position in other regions was included in the complaint. Yet in any area in which it has a competitor, even one larger and more powerful than itself, it is required to keep its prices uniform. Every price difference by it within any area is presumed to be harmful to competition, regardless of the number of its competitors or the territorial scope and size of their business. However, since price differences between areas are permitted, the restriction tends to apply more severely to competition with small competitors than with large ones.

As to the primary line of commerce, the orders against Maryland Baking, Borden Company, and Arkansas City Cooperative are alike. They provide that where the seller has a competitor, he may not undercut that competitor's price if he sells at a higher price to anyone else. The orders are not limited to situations in which competitors are few and weak; they apply even where there are many competitors and where, as compared with the seller, one or more competitors may cover as much or more territory and may be as strong or stronger. Since the subsidiaries of Borden Company operate only in the Wilmington area, the order in the Borden case is applicable in their market territory rather than in all areas where the company sells. Within that territory, however, it applies regardless of the character of the competition locally encountered. Arkansas City Cooperative is forbidden to take the initiative in reducing milk prices below those of a competitor anywhere in Kansas or Oklahoma unless its prices are uniform throughout that territory. Maryland Baking Company must quote uniform prices throughout the nation or refrain not only from quoting prices lower than its small localized competitors but also from quoting prices lower than any large competitors that may exist now or may subsequently come to exist. The order is not, like that against American Brake Shoe, applicable region by region. If Maryland Baking Company charges a higher price in Florida, it may not in Oregon undersell a competitor, even a powerful one doing a nationwide business.

In each case there was, of course, need to issue an order broad enough to prevent the respondent from using the same tactics on someone else. But there was also need to avoid undue restriction on price competition.

The problem in all three cases should have been to devise an order that would be applicable only in the situations in which selective price reductions were dangerous to competition. Instead, the presumption seems to have been that if a seller has ever used predatory price competition anywhere, any differential price reduction by him anywhere else is necessarily predatory. By giving the orders undue scope, the Commission created the possibility that the effect of the cases, on balance, will be to endanger competition rather than to protect it.

The restriction on Anheuser-Busch is even more sweeping. Hereafter the company may not reduce a price in any place where it has a competitor, whether that competitor is a local concern or another national enterprise like Anheuser-Busch, without reducing prices proportionately everywhere. Since it has only 8 per cent of the national market and presumably has national competitors, if not local ones, everywhere that it sells, the practical effect of the order is to make all price reductions by the company national in scope. The restriction is not limited to underselling nor to reductions that introduce new differences into the price structure; it requires Anheuser-Busch to maintain premium prices in all markets if they are maintained in any, and to preserve its present structure of territorial price differences. Price reduction in a single area is forbidden even if in that area the prices of the company are unusually high, so that to reduce prices there would bring it closer to uniformity of delivered prices or of net realizations at the producing point. The principle of the order in this case is opposite to that of the orders against Maryland Baking Company, Borden Company, and the Arkansas City Cooperative. For the latter three, the prerequisite to a local price reduction below the price level of a competitor is uniformity of territorial prices. For Anheuser-Busch, the prerequisite to any price reduction is maintenance of the existing lack of uniformity.

Under well-established rules of interpretation, each of these orders is subject to two implied qualifications: first, that it does not prevent price differences that merely make due allowance for differences in cost; and second, that it does not prevent price reductions made in good faith to meet the equally low price of a competitor. Under the first qualification, relative prices in different places can be adjusted as transportation costs change. Under the second, retaliatory price cutting is permitted where initiatory price cutting is forbidden.

But neither of these reductions of the scope of the orders is sufficient to alter the startling impact of what is left. The principle expressed in the Maryland Baking Company, Borden Company, and Arkansas City cases appears to be that, having violated the Robinson-Patman Act by local price cutting in a single locality against a competitor weak enough to be hurt thereby, a seller may not thereafter compete in price anywhere, even against competitors powerful enough to protect themselves, unless he either sells at a uniform price in all territorial markets or never undersells a competitor. The Anheuser-Busch case suggests a third possibility —price competition limited to proportional reduction of his prices throughout his sales territory. As such restrictions are imposed on more sellers, their effect can only be to reduce the vigor of price competition and the flexibility of price adjustment.

Though the Commission's interest in territorial discrimination was for years incidental to its desire to prevent discriminatory formulas from being the instruments of schemes to reduce price competition, the orders against territorial discrimination in its latest cases go so far in correcting discrimination that they may be themselves the means of reducing price competition. In these orders, the Commission has lent unnecessary support to the opinion that there is a conflict between the policy of the Robinson-Patman Act and that of the Sherman Act.

Judicial Review

It should be noted that the position taken by the Commission in the cases under discussion has not yet been fully reviewed by the courts. The cases against Metz Brothers, American Brake Shoe, Borden Company, and Arkansas City Cooperative resulted in admission answers or consent orders. The order against Page Dairy was not appealed. In April 1959, the Seventh Circuit set aside the order in the Anheuser-Busch case. The court declared that Anheuser-Busch was under attack for price reduction in St. Louis, not for differentials in price between St. Louis and other markets; and that such reductions might violate Section 3, under which the Commission had no jurisdiction, but not Section 2(a).[34] Presumably

---

[34] *Anheuser-Busch, Inc.* v. *FTC*, CCH, *Trade Cases 1959*, par. 69330. The court also commented that (a) the price differentials between markets did not constitute discriminations under Sec. 2(a), and (b) if any relief was appropriate, it would be for customers in other markets, not for competitors in St. Louis.

the case will be appealed to the Supreme Court. The orders against Muller and Maryland Baking Company have been reviewed by the courts; but in each there was evidence of a predatory attack on the sole competitor in the market. Thus neither case supplied a test of the bearing of the law of price discrimination on territorial price differences or local price reductions where the problem of injury arose, not from the seller's monopolistic purpose, but from difference in territorial scope between the seller and his competitors.

Some light has been thrown on this type of situation by court decisions in three private suits in which there was a charge that discrimination had injured competition in the primary line of commerce.[35] One of these cases turned on a finding that the purpose of the discriminator had been to destroy his competitor. Hence it throws more light on the breadth of Federal jurisdiction than on the nature of injury to competition. Moore, a baker in Santa Rosa, New Mexico, suffered there from the competition of Mead's Fine Bread Company, a baker selling over a wider area. By a threat to move to another town, Moore induced merchants in Santa Rosa to agree to buy from him exclusively. Mead retaliated by cutting in half the price of bread in Santa Rosa without making price reductions elsewhere. Moore's business was destroyed, and Moore sued. Moore's prior effort at exclusion was held not to justify the discrimination; and the injury both to Moore and to local competition was clear. In spite of the local character of the sales involved, the Supreme Court found a basis for Federal action in the fact that Mead's business was interstate and the local price cuts were supported by resources derived from interstate commerce and from higher prices in interstate sales. "If this method of competition were approved," said the court, "the pattern for growth of monopoly would be simple."[36]

In a second private case, *National Nut Company of California* v. *Kelling Nut Company,* the court decided that a complaint of local underselling was sufficient to constitute a charge of illegal discrimination: "A practice of underselling plaintiff in certain territory where plaintiff has an established business and maintaining a higher level of prices in other localities where competition with plaintiff or other companies is not so

---

[35] Since the question of injury in the Russellville case, discussed above, pertained to the secondary line of commerce, the decision in this case is not relevant to the issue.

[36] *Moore* v. *Mead's Fine Bread Co.,* 348 U.S. 115, 119.

keen is a practice condemned by the antitrust laws." However, the court also held that "different prices might be charged for the same article in different trade territories and still not tend to lessen or eliminate competition or create a monopoly. The differential in price might be justified by different conditions in the different trade territories."[37] The effect of the decision was merely to permit trial of the case on its merits by the lower court; and the decision merely meant that under some circumstances local underselling might be illegal.

More directly in point is the third private case, *Balian Ice Cream Company* v. *Arden Farms Company*. The decision presents a sharp contrast to that of the Commission in the Anheuser-Busch case. The discrimination against which the suit was directed arose through a reduction by Arden Farms of the prices of bulk and packaged ice cream in and around Los Angeles and consisted in sale in that area at lower prices than elsewhere. Competing local ice cream manufacturers sued under the Sherman Act, Section 3 of the Clayton Act, Section 2(a) of the Robinson-Patman Act, and California state law. Thus the courts found it necessary to relate the facts not only to charges of unlawful price discrimination but also to charges of sale at unreasonably low prices and of an attempt to monopolize. Shooting at several targets at once, the decisions in the case did not always make clear which of their shafts were directed at the issue of price discrimination.

The district court found that the share of Arden Farms of the market in the Los Angeles area had fallen from 23 per cent in 1946 to 18 per cent in 1949; that a leading competitor was underselling Arden Farms by 24 cents per gallon, and that in November 1949, Arden Farms not only reduced prices but also curtailed advertising, laid sales people off, and made other economies. Nevertheless, Arden Farms held only 17 per cent of the market in 1950. Its profit on ice cream, which had been $260,000 in the Los Angeles area in 1949, was $240,000 in 1950. One competitor went out of business for reasons not connected with the price reduction. The other plaintiffs, who had increased their percentage of the market from 11 in 1946 to 13 in 1949, had the same percentage in 1950.

Although these findings supported a conclusion that competition had not been injured, the court gave extended attention to the question whether Arden Farms had met competition in good faith:

[37] 61 F. Supp. 76, 81-82.

. . . In reducing his price to meet competition, the seller has a choice of policy. (a) If it involves a particular customer, he may, in an endeavor to keep him, underbid the price. (b) If it involves several customers in an area, he may reduce the price to his customers within the area. (c) If he is confronted, as were the defendants in this case, by various competitors, each of whom, in his own way, offered what are euphemistically known in the trade as "inducements"—by which are meant gratuities, rebates in kind, and other "deviations" from listed prices, to the same or to different customers—he is justified in taking what the Supreme Court in the case just cited [Standard Oil] considered an extreme measure, i.e., to reduce his prices in the whole locality. In this manner, a price set-up full of discrimination, which his competitors seek to freeze, is turned into a general reduction. Equality thus succeeds discrimination. I know of no principle of law which condemns such act. To the contrary, reason and good sense warrant the conclusion that such course is sound legally, as well as economically. Otherwise, under the guise of fighting monopolistic practices, we would be sanctioning them by perpetuating partial discrimination.[38]

In affirming the decision of the district court, the Ninth Circuit likewise emphasized the question of meeting competition, though it also denied that the discrimination was injurious. It said that proof of the lawfulness of the prices Arden Farms claimed to meet was not incumbent on the company. It added:

The implication of the arguments of plaintiffs is that prices can never be lowered by a concern, which does any interstate business, in one area if it fails to make a corresponding cut in every locality where it does business. . . . The assumption suggested above would ring the death knell of competition. Even if it were shown that Arden undercut the prices of poorer quality products, it would not be unfair if the general purpose were to eliminate improper rebates and special concessions made by its competitors. . . .[39]

The court also distinguished between injury from price reduction and injury from discrimination:

There was absolutely no evidence in the record that the differentials as to sales in commerce or in other areas had any relation to any injury

[38] *Balian Ice Cream Co. et al.* v. *Arden Farms Co. et al.,* 104 F. Supp. 796, 802.
[39] *Balian Ice Cream Co. et al.* v. *Arden Farms Co. et al.,* 231 F. 2d 356.

or damage which plaintiffs may have sustained. . . . Arden was doing business in a number of largely disconnected, homogeneous, competitive areas. There simply was no reason for uniformity of price throughout these areas.[40]

The Supreme Court denied certiorari in March 1956.[41]

[40] *Ibid.* p. 367.

[41] The denial of certiorari (along with the circuit court decision in the second appeal of the Standard Oil case) was regarded by Commissioners Anderson and Secrest as a threat to enforcement of the Robinson-Patman Act, in consequence of which they became advocates rather than opponents of a congressional limitation of the right to meet competition. In testifying before a congressional committee, Commissioners Gwynne and Kern disagreed as to the significance of the Balian decision. Commissioner Gwynne thought the case contained "some unfortunate language by way of dictum," but that the decision rested on the court's finding that the facts did not show damage to competition. Commissioner Kern thought that there was "an undoubted injury to competition," that the court had accepted the defense of meeting competition without requiring proof of the specific meeting of individual lower prices, and that in denying certiorari the Supreme Court had accepted as good faith the meeting of a general competitive situation. (See *To Amend Section 2 of the Clayton Act,* Hearings before the Senate Committee on the Judiciary, 84 Cong. 2 sess., 1956, pp. 236-37.) A similar discussion took place in *To Amend Section 2 of the Clayton Act,* Hearings before the Senate Committee on the Judiciary, 85 Cong. 1 sess., Pt. 1 (1957), pp. 644-45.

It is noteworthy that the Commission's decision in the Anheuser-Busch case was rendered more than a year after the denial of certiorari in the Balian case.

14 / *Miscellaneous Types of Discrimination*

PROCEEDINGS UNDER the Robinson-Patman Act have involved several types of discrimination not based on the quantity or volume purchased, on the customer's functional classification, or on the place of delivery. Of these, three are significant enough to deserve discussion.

Discounts for Exclusive Dealing

The first is a price concession offered to induce the buyer to deal exclusively with the seller. In several instances, a price discrimination was accompanied by exclusive dealing,[1] and in some of these price concessions were conditioned on the buyer's willingness to make an exclusive dealing arrangement.

In the Corn Products Refining case the Commission found that a price reduction on corn starch had been made to two purchasers in contracts for exclusive dealing, but condemned these contracts under Section 3 of the Clayton Act rather than under the Robinson-Patman Act. In the Champion case the company's discounts to distributors of spark plugs were found to be conditioned on services to Champion that made exclusive dealing necessary even though it was not specifically required. Until 1941 Champion had also given price concessions to certain operators of commercial fleets provided they bought Champion plugs exclusively. In the General Motors case discounts to distributors of spark plugs were found to be explicitly conditioned on exclusive dealing. In the Curtiss case, which rested on Section 3 of the Clayton Act as well as

[1] Docket 3050, *Christmas Club;* Docket 3633, *Corn Products Refining Co.;* Docket 3977, *Champion Spark Plug Co.;* Docket 4556, *Curtiss Candy Co.;* Docket 4920, *Minneapolis-Honeywell Regulator Co.;* Docket 4933, *Automatic Canteen Co. of America;* Docket 5620, *General Motors Corp.;* Docket 5436, *Draper Corp.*

the price discrimination law, one of the price concessions was a 10 per cent rebate to concessionaires at baseball parks and similar places for purchase of Curtiss five-cent candy bars exclusively. In each of these cases there were other important discriminations not associated with exclusive dealing.

The exclusive dealing practice was central in one of the cases not selected for study, that against the Draper Corporation.[2] This corporation, manufacturer of bobbins, shuttles, and repair and replacement parts for looms, gave its customers a 5 per cent discount on condition that they would not purchase or use such products from its competitors. The Commission found the practice to be in violation of Section 3 of the Clayton Act and also of the Robinson-Patman Act. Both the narrow and broad types of injury to competition were found in the primary line, and also a tendency to create a monopoly in that line, presumably because of the inherent tendency of such a discount to divert trade from other producers. The Commission ordered the discontinuance of such discounts.

Private Brand Allowances

A second type of discrimination was based on sale of goods for resale under private brands. Such discrimination appeared clearly in three cases, those against United States Rubber Company, Hansen Inoculator Company, and Whitaker Cable Corporation.[3] Amid other discriminations found in the U. S. Rubber case, Montgomery Ward, Atlas, Western Auto Supply, and Arkansas Fuel Oil Company paid U. S. Rubber less for tires to be resold under private brands than was paid by other customers for tires bearing the brand of U. S. Rubber.[4] On automotive cable products, Whitaker Cable Company granted not only functional and volume discounts, but also discounts of varying amounts on private brand purchases by American Oil, Phillips Petroleum, Sun Oil, and Goodyear Tire & Rubber companies. Whereas jobbers paid from 5 to 20 per cent less than the jobbers list price, these private brand buyers paid from 20 to 35 per cent less. Hansen sold commercial inoculants under one buyer's

[2] Docket 5436. See 43 FTC 480.
[3] For the *U. S. Rubber* case (Docket 3685) see 28 FTC 1489; for the *Hansen Inoculator* case (Docket 3264) see 26 FTC 303; for the *Whitaker Cable* case (Docket 5722) see 51 FTC 938.
[4] Other portions of this case have been discussed in the chapters on proportionality and volume discounts. See above, pp. 178-79, 257.

private brand at 15 cents while it sold its own brand to that buyer's competitors at 24 cents.

The private brand allowance has a deceptive appearance of regularity since it establishes a clear distinction between buyers of private brands and buyers of the manufacturer's brands. In fact, however, there is likely to be, as in the Hansen case, arbitrary selection of the particular buyer to whom private brand sales are made, and there may be, as in the Whitaker case, variation in the private brand discount. Although private brand buyers are usually large, and the allowance, therefore, has the effect of giving preference to large buyers, not all large buyers obtain the allowance nor do all get it on equal terms. Arbitrary distinctions are made between buyers who may be comparable in size and in the quantities they buy. In the Whitaker case, for example, Sun Oil received a maximum allowance of 28.5 per cent, while the allowance to American Oil and Phillips Petroleum was 20 per cent.

Varieties of Unsystematic Concessions

The most common form of price concession other than those discussed in previous chapters consists in unsystematic price reductions to particular customers. Unlike the concessions previously discussed, discrimination of this kind rests on no avowed principle, follows no avowed pattern, and often involves concessions so heterogeneous that no pattern can be imputed to it by the observer.

Unsystematic concessions that take the form of departures from a systematic discount schedule have been frequent in Robinson-Patman cases. Some of them have been mentioned in discussing the systematic discriminations to which they pertain. In general, they have involved the selection of particular customers for discounts or allowances to which these customers would not have been eligible under the company's ostensible price schedule. From Standard Brands, customers obtained volume discounts based on their predicted volume of purchase when in fact they did not buy the requisite amount. In various cases, the Commission found that the privilege of pooling purchases in order to qualify for volume discounts was extended to selected buyers or selected classes of buyers. In the Sherwin-Williams case, the Commission found that discounts were based on cumulated and aggregated purchases in instances in which single purchases would not justify the price concession. In this case, too, it appeared that customers of Lowe and Lucas were allowed to estimate the proportion of their business that was conducted at wholesale and hence eligible for the wholesale discount, and that these estimates typically and variously exceeded the proportion eligible. In the case against Nutrine, it was found that salesmen were allowed to determine the classification of individual customers, and that principles of classification were so loosely applied as to place the same customer in one class for one type of candy and in a different class for another type of candy. In the Minneapolis-Honeywell case, 76 customers were found to have bought off-scale in 1941.

In some instances, special price concessions were the result of imprecise practice in applying the applicable discount schedule. When quantity or volume discounts were based on past sales, or functional discounts on estimates by customers, the inevitable result was that similarity in purchases made or in functions performed would be accompanied by difference in prices paid. The ostensibly uniform application of an imprecise standard produced a varying result.

In other instances, the departure from the systematic schedule consisted in special concessions deliberately made to particular buyers. These buyers were given larger discounts than usual or permitted to take unearned discounts or given the benefit of low prices after prices to their competitors had been increased. Presumably, such concessions reflected either a judgment that the buyer's business was unusually important because of its volume or for other reasons, or else a judgment that there was unusual risk of losing this business. The concessions probably (but not certainly) rested on the exploitation of exceptional buying power such as it was the purpose of the statute to prevent.

In various instances, discrimination in favor of a particular buyer either stood alone or had been superimposed on other patterns of discrimination. The finding of discrimination in the case against Hollywood Hat Company[5] rested solely on price reductions granted to one large West Coast buyer in the felt hat buying season of 1936. The case against Florida Citrus Canners Cooperative[6] turned solely on an option for the purchase of a large quantity of canned citrus juice which was given to A. & P. in 1946. In the Benrus case[7] the Commission found that volume

---

[5] Docket 3020, *Hollywood Hat Co.*, 25 FTC 555. The company was also found to have misrepresented its products in violation of the Federal Trade Commission Act.

[6] Docket 5640, *Florida Citrus Canners Cooperative*, 49 FTC 37.

[7] Docket 5969, *Benrus Watch Co.*, 49 FTC 476.

discounts were generally available, with a maximum of 8 per cent for annual purchases of more than $75,000, but that the largest buyer received a flat discount of 14½ per cent. In the American Brake Shoe case,[8] which had to do with territorial discrimination against a new competitor, the largest buyer in the territory where prices were cut was found to have received a special price of $5.90 on bearings that were being sold to others in the area at cut prices of $7.00 and to others outside the area at $8.65. Companion cases against Pittsburgh Plate Glass Company and Libbey-Owens-Ford[9] were based on findings that the former company had sold automobile safety glass to Ford and the latter had sold it to General Motors at prices lower than to distributors and dealers. The price to Ford was found to be from 32 to 48 per cent below the price to distributors and from 59 to 67 per cent below the price to dealers. The amount of the concession to General Motors was not stated. In the Champion case a part of the discrimination on spark plugs for the replacement market consisted of special low prices to Atlas and Socony-Vacuum and to the automobile manufacturers, with the price to Ford below the price to other automobile companies. In the companion case against General Motors, a part of the discrimination consisted in special prices to International Harvester, Allis-Chalmers, and Goodrich. In the case against Corn Products Refining Company, the territorial discriminations found were accompanied by special prices to six purchasers of gluten feed and two purchasers of corn starch and by permission for some customers to enjoy "booking" privileges, that is, to continue to pay low prices for a time after a general price increase. In the companion Hubinger case, nine buyers were found to have paid special prices for gluten feed and two buyers special prices for corn syrup, and there were similar booking privileges. Booking privileges were also found in the companion cases against Clinton and Staley. In the Namsco case, eight special accounts and five co-operatives were found to have received exceptional discounts of varying amounts on automobile parts.

Apart from off-scale selling and isolated price concessions, unsystematic price discrimination has appeared in cases under the Robinson-Patman Act in two forms: (a) selective application of orderly price

---

[8] Docket 6383, *American Brake Shoe Co.*, decided Nov. 15, 1955; decision available only in mimeographed form.

[9] Docket 6699, *Pittsburgh Plate Glass Co.*, decided April 19, 1957; Docket 6700, *Libbey-Owens-Ford Glass Co.*, decided May 22, 1957. Both decisions were available only in mimeographed form when this study was made.

schedules, and (b) grant of concessions that expressed no orderly principle.

Selective Application of Price Schedules

Selective application of price schedules consists in making a schedule of discounts available to selected customers, while other customers, who could meet the ostensible requirements for the discounts or who are excluded on no clearly stated grounds, are provided with a less generous schedule or with no discounts at all. Such a pattern has appeared frequently. In selling spark plugs, for example, Champion allowed certain jobbers to buy direct at lower prices than jobbers who bought through distributors, and selected certain commercial fleets for more favorable treatment than others. General Motors sold directly at preferential prices to selected jobbers and contract dealers and selected chains of jobbers. Electric Auto-Lite assigned jobbers selectively among several classes of customers. In selling automobile parts, Namsco sold to some customers from a blue list while it sold to others from a white list at prices as much as one third lower. In the Holtite case, the Commission found that rubber heels and soles and shoe findings had been sold to some customers at volume discounts varying from 1 to 20 per cent while they had been sold to others at volume discounts varying from 1 to 50 per cent.[10] In the Life Savers case, some corporate chains, but not all, were found to have received a volume discount of 10 per cent; and some of the recipients had received it on sales made to their unit stores, whereas others had received it on sales to central warehouses.[11] In the Brill case, the Commission found that Brill had made a volume discount contract with three corporate chains, but there was no showing that the same contract was available to others.[12] In the U. S. Rubber case, in addition to the private brand concessions mentioned above, volume discount schedules were similarly found to have been made available to a selected group of oil companies, large dealers and undesignated others.[13]

Selective use of orderly schedules appeared most clearly in five cases in which it was the sole basis for the Commission's orders.[14] These cases

[10] Docket 5828, *Holtite Manufacturing Co.*, 50 FTC 379.
[11] Docket 4571, *Life Savers Corp.*, 34 FTC 472.
[12] Docket 3299, *H. C. Brill Co.*, 26 FTC 666.
[13] Docket 3685, *U. S. Rubber Co.*, 28 FTC 1489.
[14] See above, pp. 210-11.

had to do with quantity discounts by book publishers, dependent on the number of copies of a single title bought at one time. Houghton Mifflin Company used two quantity discount schedules, one providing discounts from list price of from 40 to 46 per cent, while the other provided discounts of from 43 to 48 per cent on the same quantities. Little, Brown & Company also used two schedules, one with discounts of from 40 to 47 per cent, with the maximum at 5,000 copies, the other with discounts of from 43 to 50 per cent, with the maximum at 25,000 copies. Harper & Brothers also used two schedules. In one, discounts varied from 41 to 43 per cent, in the other, from 43 to 44 per cent; in each the maximum discount was available for a purchase of 250 copies; but one schedule had three brackets, while the other had two. Random House and Simon and Schuster granted a basic discount of 43 per cent regardless of volume. The former allowed some of its customers volume discounts, ranging up to 49½ per cent for 5,000 copies, that were not available to others. The latter also made volume discounts available to a portion of its customers, at rates of from 46 to 50 per cent.

Catch-as-Catch-Can Pricing

In addition to isolated concessions, special concessions superimposed on orderly price structures, and selective application of orderly schedules, such as have been described above, the Commission has found discriminations that consisted of *ad hoc* concessions expressing no orderly principle. How many cases have been of this type is uncertain; for in some instances the Commission's findings tell little about the structure of the discrimination, and concessions may appear to have been without order because their pattern is not described.[15] Taking the findings at their face value, however, 16 cases have been concerned solely with discriminations of this haphazard character. Seven of these are among the cases that have been studied.[16] They will be discussed below, along with the case against

---

[15] In the case against *Williams and Wilkins* (Docket 3844), for example, the Commission found only that sales had been made to competing customers at different prices. In view of the practices of the book trade, it is possible that the discriminations took the form of quantity discounts. Similarly, though the findings against National Grain Yeast disclose no pricing pattern, there is reason to believe, from other sources, that its discriminations consisted of volume discounts like those of Standard Brands.

[16] The findings supply little information about the other cases. In Docket 3050, *Christmas Club,* which involved violation of the Federal Trade Commission Act

Florida Citrus Canners Cooperative, in which there was a price concession to a single large buyer, and the case against U. S. Rubber, in which special prices were made available to buyers who resold under private brands.

In most of the cases that have been studied, little effort was made by respondents to defend themselves. In only two of the nine was the Commission's order preceded by a trial, and in these two the trial was abbreviated.[17] Because of the general failure to contest the proceedings, little is known about the underlying motives of the respondents, and in many instances the findings are too brief and general to make clear who

---

and of Sec. 3 of the Clayton Act as well as Sec. 2(a) of the Robinson-Patman Act, the finding as to price discrimination consists merely in the statement that the savings systems provided by Christmas Club were furnished to banks for varying percentages of the deposits obtained through their use. (See 25 FTC 1116.) In Docket 4344, *Vonnegut Hardware Co.,* the finding is merely the bald statement that fire-exit latches were sold to some unnamed customers at discounts of 40 per cent and to others at discounts of 50 per cent. (See 32 FTC 512.) In Docket 3844, *Williams and Wilkins,* the Commission found that medical books were sold to buyers, who were neither identified nor described, at discounts ranging from 20 to 35 per cent. (See 29 FTC 678.) The findings in the case against *Walter H. Johnson Candy Co.* (Docket 4677) illustrate the discriminations found by saying that Automatic Canteen bought candy bars at $2.03 per 100, while unnamed other vending machine operators paid prices of $2.25, $2.40, and $2.50, and jobbers paid 64 cents for packs of 24 bars; but they provide no further information. (See 44 FTC 1021.) In Docket 6039 the Commission found that Western Grain Company had sold corn meal and other grain products to unnamed purchasers at varying prices, without ascertainable pattern in the price differences, and illustrated the finding by listing the prices charged in various localities on certain dates. (See 49 FTC 983.) In Docket 6198, *Frank F. Taylor Co.,* in which, under a consent order, the complaint supplies the only information about the discriminatory practices in the sale of baby-walkers and velocipedes, it appears that favored purchasers such as unnamed mail-order and chain automobile companies were charged flat prices, regardless of volume bought, while others paid higher prices under a volume-discount schedule the terms of which are not given. (See 51 FTC 51.) The case against *Republic Yeast* (Docket 4367) is a companion to two that were studied, against *National Grain Yeast* (Docket 3903) and *Federal Yeast* (Docket 3926). (See 33 FTC 701.) The cases against *Unity Stamp Co.* (Docket 5048) and *Adolph Gottscho* (Docket 5517) are, except for the poverty of details included in the findings, companion cases to two cases that have been studied, the *Moss* case (Docket 4405) and the *Krengel Manufacturing Co.* case (Docket 5516). See 44 FTC 199 and 46 FTC 100.

[17] In one, that against Krengel, the respondent submitted no evidence. In the other, against Moss, a portion of the facts was stipulated. In the Krengel case, the respondent submitted no brief and did not argue the case orally. In the Moss case, there was no oral argument, but a brief was submitted.

received the price concessions and who did not. There is a possibility that in some of the cases the lack of an identifiable pattern is due to the incompleteness of the record rather than to the unsystematic nature of the discriminations.

In two of these cases, the price concessions were clearly related to the size and power of large buyers. In the case against Florida Citrus Canners Cooperative (Docket 5640), a special price to A. & P. was involved. In the spring of 1946, when prices on citrus juices were low because the largest citrus crop in the history of Florida had appeared when government purchases had almost ceased, the co-operative gave A. & P. an option on 750,000 cases of juice at a price approximately equal to the market. The contract gave A. & P. the right to spread its purchase over several months. Shortly thereafter, the market price began to rise. A. & P. exercised its option at various dates in March and April, during which the differential between its buying price and the buying price currently available to its competitors became progressively larger. In March, the differential on various types of juice was from 0 per cent to 7.7 per cent. By the end of April, it ranged from 25.4 per cent to 30 per cent. The aggregate advantage enjoyed by A. & P. is estimated at about $600,000. A. & P. resold considerable portions of what it bought at prices below the buying prices of other retailers. The Commission found that the arrangement was injurious to competition in both the primary and secondary lines, both in the market sense and in the narrow sense of injury to a class of competitors. It also found that any substantial discrimination might have the same effects even though the price differential was less than 1½ per cent.[18]

After the order against Florida Citrus Canners, the co-operative adopted precautions to avoid further violation of the statute and to define prompt delivery as meaning delivery within a fifteen-day period. Sales to A. & P. were continued, but at the going market prices, whether or not the product bore the private label of A. & P. Compliance with the order was made easier because, subsequent to 1946, conditions of accumulating surplus and sagging prices, such as had been encountered in the spring of that year, did not recur; and because, as the number of

---

[18] The case illustrates a weakness of legal action against price discriminations in industries in which prices change frequently. The discriminatory situation existed for a few months in 1946. The Commission's complaint was issued in February 1949; its order in July 1952. By the time of the order, conditions in the sale of citrus juice had changed substantially.

canners of Florida citrus juice fell from about 65 to about 25, prices became more stable.

In the case against U. S. Rubber, the Commission found that (in addition to making concessions on private brand tires) the company had made special prices on its own brands to certain volume buyers, including oil companies, large dealers, and unnamed others, and that through its retail stores it had given special price concessions to certain large commercial accounts.[19] In addition, it had paid to certain oil companies—Socony Vacuum, American Oil, Pan-American Petroleum, and Tide-Water Associated Oil—commissions of 7½ per cent on its sales to filling stations affiliated with these oil companies. In the discriminations on private brands, the Commission found all recognized types of injury to competition—both the narrow and broad types in both the primary and secondary lines of commerce and a tendency to create a monopoly in both lines. In the special concessions to commercial accounts, it found the probability of injury in the narrow sense to competing retailers. In the concessions to other large buyers, it found the probability of the narrow type of injury to competition among buyers and of both the broad and narrow types of injury and a tendency toward monopoly among tire manufacturers.

The order in the case was directed at practices that had prevailed prior to the Robinson-Patman Act. The occasion for the part of it concerned with price discrimination (as contrasted with payments for sales effort) was in dispute between the company and the Commission as to the adequacy of voluntary correctives the company had applied after the act was passed. U. S. Rubber Company had established a subsidiary known as U. S. Tire Dealers Corporation, primarily for the purpose of finding a lawful way to continue its private brand business. It sold tires to private brand volume buyers and to the subsidiary corporation at a uniform factory cost plus a uniform percentage for profit. All sales of U. S. brand tires to dealers were made through the subsidiary corporation, and after defraying the cost of doing business, the subsidiary refunded to the dealers their proportionate share of any excess over cost that it had accumulated at the end of each year. The obvious purpose was to make the price difference between U. S. Rubber's brand and the private brands automatically

[19] No details were given in the Commission's findings. From another source it appears that one large buyer received, successively, 50 per cent trade discount, 5 per cent franchise discount, 17½ per cent distributor discount, and 2½ per cent bonus for purchase of an annual volume of more than $50,000.

equivalent to the difference in cost. Though the Commission accepted the principle of this plan, it challenged the allocation of costs which, of course, affected the ultimate price paid for U. S. brand tires. Particularly, it insisted that the cost of U. S. brand tires be computed separately and that no interest payments by the subsidiary to the parent company be included in costs. These adjustments were made by U. S. Rubber and set forth in the company's compliance report in 1939. In addition, at the request of the Commission, a portion of the company's advertising cost was charged to original equipment sales.[20] Price lists to distributors were revised by increasing the number of volume brackets and reducing the size of the various volume discounts.[21] During the pendency of the case, the operation of company stores and direct sale to commercial accounts had been ended. The effect of the various changes was to reduce the price differentials among distributors and dealers and to terminate the operation of retail stores by the company. The basic pattern of pricing to private brand owners was not affected. Private brand owners continued to purchase on a cost-plus basis. Prices of U. S. Rubber brands to dealers and distributors continued to be higher by amounts computed to express a cost differential. The differential was changed by certain modifications in the method of computing costs. Though the subsidiary of U. S. Rubber has been dissolved, the method of basing price differentials on differences in cost is still used.

In the other cases involving unsystematic discrimination, there is no such clear relation between the discounts and the power of big buyers. Sellers have used catch-as-catch-can pricing for a variety of reasons or for no ascertainable reason.

In the case against National Numbering Machine (Docket 3889), the Commission found that machines had been sold to various buyers at prices differing from $5.00 to $8.00 per machine. Three hundred machines had been sold to one buyer at a price of $5.00, one hundred machines to another buyer at a price of $6.00, and machines in quantities of five or less to other unnamed buyers at prices ranging from $6.00 to

---

[20] In addition, the then operating sales subsidiary of U. S. Rubber for U. S. brand tires discontinued payment of its 7½ per cent commission to those oil companies to which it sold tires for resale, but continued to pay similar commissions to other oil companies. See above pp. 178-79.

[21] The volume discounts shown in the compliance report were 1 per cent above $15,000; 1½ per cent above $25,000; 2 per cent above $35,000; and 2½ per cent above $50,000. Apparently there was no change in the maximum discount. The previous discount schedule is not available.

$8.00. The buyer paying the lower price had resold machines at $7.50 and $8.50. Though the findings contained no information about the size of the respondent or of the favored buyers, and no further information about the nature of competition in the industry, the Commission found that these price differences were injurious to competition in both the primary and secondary lines of commerce in both the broad and narrow senses; and that they tended to create a monopoly in both the primary and secondary lines. It ordered the respondent to cease making the same or substantially similar discriminations among competing customers unless they made only due allowance for differences in cost. No information is available as to the effect of the order.

In the case against C. F. Sauer Company (Docket 3646), the Commission found a variety of price concessions on salad dressings, spices, and similar products. From the complaint it appears that these grew out of the use of three price lists, each of which was used in selling to selected customers. Sauer apparently regarded mayonnaise as its most important product, from which Sauer derived most of its volume in sales to its jobber customers. Salad dressing was not offered through Sauer's salesmen and was quoted to jobbers at prohibitive prices, but was sold to chain stores. Mayonnaise was sold at about the same price to everyone, with a slight price advantage to jobbers, while on salad dressing certain chains paid lower prices than the jobbers. On various products the differences in the prices quoted to individual customers ranged from 5 per cent to 25 per cent. Price discriminations were accompanied by selective advertising allowances at varying rates.[22] Concessions and allowances became available by decisions made by the head of the Sauer Company. Among the matters that appeared to be influential in these decisions were the volume of the customer's purchases and the size of his order, the distance of the customer from Sauer's factory, the number and location of the customer's stores, the intensity of competition, the level of the competitor's price, the business already done by Sauer's brands in the locality, and the potential for further business. Sauer's favored customers apparently cut prices to levels comparable with the buying prices of some of the others. Sauer endeavored to cope with the problem by negotiating a satisfactory resale price, but in vain.[23] In the controversy that ensued,

[22] See above, p. 176.

[23] In the description of Sauer's practices, information derived from the Commission's findings has been supplemented from the complaint, from the docket record, and from interviews.

complaints were made to the Federal Trade Commission, and some customers refused to pay their debts to Sauer.[24] The Commission found that the discrimination was injurious to the disfavored customers in the narrow sense.

After the case, higher prices were charged to the formerly favored buyers. There is apparently an orderly price structure; the available information does not make clear whether this structure includes only small quantity discounts or also certain volume discounts.[25] The former head of the company is now dead, and customers appeared to be agreed that since his death, the operation of the concern has been less capricious.

The case against Booth Fisheries (Docket 4883) pertained to the sale of frozen fish in a limited area in South Dakota. The area was one of small volume and little competition, in which much of the product was sold by truckers on commission. Since the respondent filed an admission answer, the facts can be ascertained only from the Commission's findings. These list sales of several types of frozen fish to specified customers during specified periods of time at differing prices. In particular instances the price difference was large enough to permit resale at prices lower than the buying prices of the disfavored customers. Although price stability is more possible for frozen fish than for fresh fish, the lack of complete identity in the dates at which different prices were quoted raises a question in the reader's mind whether any part of the price differences reflected price change through time. The Commission found that the discrimination was harmful to competition in the secondary line in both the narrow and broad senses. The reasoning on which the latter conclusion was based was not set forth. Booth was ordered to cease discriminating among competing purchasers where the effects might be injurious to competition, unless the discrimination was cost-justified or was justified by changing market conditions.

As a result of the case, Booth tightened its supervision of salesmen and established limits on the authority to make price concessions that was entrusted to peddlers who sold on commission. It now requires that concessions regarded as consequential be made only after consulting the

[24] Enclosure of the wrong invoice to a customer led to discovery of the differentials. Two customers then refused to pay except at the lower price. For a time commercial dealings between them and Sauer were severed.

[25] Sauer sells a variety of products, including spices, extracts, mayonnaise, and relishes. Apparently conflicting information was obtained as to the details of Sauer's price structure, probably because the different terms applicable to various types of products were not adequately distinguished by informants.

main office. Attorneys for the company review sales from time to time and discuss the meaning of the law with salesmen. Little information could be obtained as to the effect of this new supervision on prices actually prevailing in the market. Six of the eight grocers whose purchases are known to have been involved in the case are now out of business. One of the others, who had complained to the Commission about Booth's prices, says that the Commission's action was too slow to protect him. "If I had waited for the government to act, I would have been out of business. . . . The government cannot hold an umbrella over business. Their help is too little and too late, and it does not get at the fundamental cause of the problem." After analyzing his own margins, he went out of the grocery business and concentrates on the retailing of meat, though he continues to buy Booth's fish. He thinks he now buys advantageously because he "can store large quantities" in his freezer.

Three parallel cases were brought by the Commission against National Grain Yeast (Docket 3903), Federal Yeast Corporation (Docket 3926), and Republic Yeast Corporation (Docket 4367). Of these, the first two have been studied.[26] Each of the two cases was disposed of by an admission answer and a stipulation of facts. In each, the Commission found, on the basis of stipulation, that the respondent had quoted to its customers prices that differed in some instances by 7 per cent and more, and that it had given some customers free yeast in quantities sufficient to produce differences of 5 per cent or more in the cost of yeast. In addition, cash discounts of 1 per cent or 2 per cent had been given to some customers but not to others who paid in the same way and at the same time.[27] In the case against National Grain Yeast, the complaint illustrated the discrimination by comparing the prices paid by two bakers on Long Island and two in the Bronx in 1937.[28] The aggregate advantage of the low

---

[26] In the Republic Yeast case the Commission found, on the basis of an admission answer, that Republic Yeast had sold bakers yeast at prices varying from 10 to 14 cents per pound, and had given some customers free yeast in amounts of from 20 to 1,121 pounds, thereby making price concessions up to a maximum of 5.8 cents per pound. Republic Yeast had also given cash discounts to some and withheld them from others who paid as promptly. See 33 FTC 701.

[27] Though the case as to price discrimination was the same for both companies, the proceeding against National Grain Yeast was also concerned with unlawful payment of brokerage and commercial bribery, which were not parts of the case against Federal Yeast.

[28] In each case, in stipulating the facts on which the Commission decided the case, the respondent neither admitted nor denied the truth of the specific illustrations.

price to the favored baker of the two on Long Island was $3,628 and to the favored one of the two in the Bronx, $819. In the complaint against Federal Yeast, one similar illustration was given, in which a New York baker enjoyed an aggregate advantage of $1,050. In each case the complaint also supplied one illustration of the provision of free yeast. In November 1936, National Grain Yeast had given 290 pounds of yeast to a customer in the Bronx who bought 350 pounds; in December 1936, Federal Yeast had given 115 pounds to a customer in New York who bought 1,171 pounds. In each instance, another buyer of a similar amount had received no free yeast.

In each case, the stipulation of facts included the conclusion that the savings in cost to the favored customers were "material and vital factors of competition." The Commission then found in each case that the discrimination had the capacity to injure market competition in the primary line and competition between favored and disfavored customers in the secondary line. It ordered the respondents to stop discriminations that might be injurious except where they were cost-justified.

The Commission's finding that discrimination might injure competition in the primary line is surprising. Both companies were among the smaller members of an industry in which Standard Brands and Anheuser-Busch, with about 57 per cent and 17 per cent of the total sales respectively,[29] were the dominant producers. National Grain Yeast was the third largest yeast maker, with slightly more than 10 per cent of the total output of bakers yeast in 1941. Federal Yeast, fourth largest, produced less than 5 per cent of the total in that year. Price cutting was one of the principal means by which the small companies competed against the large ones. The prices of both companies were consistently lower than those of Standard Brands. Among price concessions by National Grain Yeast, one was to a chain baker whose business was principally responsible for the growth in volume of sales by National Grain Yeast. The Commission's findings as to injury in the primary line were not explained.

Information as to the effects of the orders against the two yeast companies is limited. It appears that National Grain Yeast follows a schedule of volume discounts similar to those of Standard Brands, with the largest discount available for purchases of 2,500 pounds per month. Federal Yeast supplied information in an interview but would not authorize

[29] These were the percentages of the total output of bakers yeast produced by the two companies in 1941.

public use of it. Price concessions in the yeast industry are said by others to take the form of free samples, the substitution of eggs and other ingredients for yeast, and increases in the strength of the yeast. Whether such types of concessions are made by the two respondent companies has not been ascertained.

In four cases, the Commission found that competition among manufacturers of rubber stamps had been injured by price discrimination.[30] Two of these have been studied. There are said to be more than 70 such manufacturers in New York City alone. The respondent in one of the two cases studied, Samuel H. Moss, Inc. (Docket 4405) employed about 19 persons. The respondent in the other case, Krengel Manufacturing Company (Docket 5516), employed about 10 persons. The Commission's findings contain no information about the number of companies or the distribution of business, either in the country generally or in New York City.

The Krengel case was tried, but the respondent did not submit evidence, briefs, or oral argument. According to the Commission's findings and the underlying evidence introduced by the Commission, about 10 per cent to 15 per cent of Krengel's stamp business was done at preferential prices. Among the beneficiaries of discrimination were 6 companies that had enjoyed low prices for 20 years or more, 3 that had enjoyed low prices from a subsidiary before Krengel acquired it, 1 to whom low prices were quoted to meet competition, and 6 others who obtained concessions for unspecified reasons. Concessions varied from one customer to another, with a range, where percentages were specified, from 29 per cent to as much as 60 per cent of the retail list price. The beneficiaries were large companies, and, in general, they were the buyers of the larger

[30] The case against *Unity Stamp Co.* (Docket 5048) was decided on the basis of an admission answer. The Commission found that the company's prices on three-inch stamps varied from 4 cents to 35 cents, with an additional charge for each extra line, and on two-inch stamps, from 4 cents to 15 cents, with similar additional charges. No other information was supplied by the findings. Nevertheless, the Commission found that the discrimination might be expected to hurt competition in both the narrow and broad senses in the primary line, and that it tended to create a monopoly in that line. See 44 FTC 199.

The case against *Adolph Gottscho* (Docket 5517) was decided even more summarily. After an admission answer, the Commission found, without further detail, that Gottscho charged some buyers higher prices than others, and on this basis concluded not only that the discrimination might be expected to injure competition in the primary line in the narrow and broad senses but also that it tended to create a monopoly in that line. See 46 FTC 100.

volumes. Nevertheless, the concessions apparently had not been granted in recognition of volume.[31] In the case of three of its customers, Krengel explained that because it valued their business on other products "we just work along with the rubber stamp part which is negligible." As to another, it explained that it had tried to raise the price but had lost the business until it made the old allowance available once more.

The Commission introduced evidence by six witnesses to the effect that their policy was not to buy stamps at higher prices than other customers, and that price would be an important factor in determining from whom they bought. It also submitted evidence by five witnesses representing other stamp manufacturers to the effect that they could not profitably sell stamps at the reduced prices quoted by Krengel. Two of these witnesses testified that they had lost most of the business of the Radio Corporation of America and of Eclipse Pioneer Corporation because of price cutting.[32] A witness from RCA agreed that the business of this company had been transferred because of price inducements. The Commission summarized the evidence as follows:[33]

> . . . The record discloses that one very substantial account was practically lost to respondents by one of their competitors because of such competitor's inability to meet respondents' low, discriminatory prices. In addition to this specific instance, there is testimony from three other competitors of respondents to the effect that it was not possible to manufacture and sell rubber stamps profitably at the discriminatory prices granted by respondents to their favored customers. The evidence further shows that price is one of the principal factors governing purchases of rubber stamps. The Commission therefore concludes and finds that the effect of respondents' discriminations in price has been and may be substantially to lessen, destroy, and prevent competition between respondents and their competitors in the sale and distribution of rubber stamps in commerce as aforesaid.[33]

[31] For example, during the first six months of 1941, Krengel sold stamps below list price to Bell Telephone Laboratories, Mutual Life Insurance, Socony-Vacuum, Cities Service, Sears Roebuck, Eclipse Pioneer, American Express, Railway Express, New York Central, Central Railroad of New Jersey, and New York, Ontario and Western Railroad. Three of these purchasers bought fewer than 120 stamps during the period, and among them was one that bought 56 and one that bought 10. Four purchasers that bought 120 stamps or more made purchases at list prices.

[32] Eclipse Pioneer bought 142 out of a total of more than 12,500 stamps sold by Krengel during the first six months of 1941. No information is available about the size of Krengel's sales to RCA.

[33] 46 FTC 80.

The facts in the Moss case were similar.[34] Moss's price for a one-line stamp, two inches long, varied from 4 cents to 15 cents, and for a one-line stamp three inches long, from 4 cents to 30 cents. The charge to General Electric for a three-inch stamp was 4 cents for the first line, plus 1 cent for each additional line; to the New Haven Railroad, 4 cents plus 4 cents for each additional line; to Prudential Insurance, 6 cents plus 2 cents for each additional line; to Oxweld Acetylene Company and Linde Air Products Company, 10 cents plus 7 cents for each additional line; to American Air Lines, 13 cents plus 13 cents for each additional line; and to various other companies, other prices. The Commission found that the discriminatory prices had diverted the American Air Lines business from Martin and Company of Chicago, the Linde Air Products business from Martin and Company and from A. F. Cordray Company of San Francisco, the Oxweld Acetylene business from Universal Stamp and Stationery Company of Newark, the business of the New Haven Railroad from Spencer Stamp Works of Springfield, Mass., the business of the New Britain National Bank from the Hartford Stamp Works of Hartford, Conn., and the business of General Electric from Massey and Company. Massey tried to meet Moss's price but found it below cost and discontinued the stamp business. The Commission concluded:

> Such acts and practices of the respondent have the capacity and tendency to induce the purchase of respondent's rubber stamps by various users thereof and have tended to, and do, divert trade to the respondent from its competitors. The lower prices at which respondent offered for sale and sold its rubber stamps to users thereof to induce the purchase of respondent's rubber stamps in preference to those of its competitors had a substantially injurious effect upon competition in the sale and distribution of rubber stamps in commerce between and among the various States of the United States, and in some instances respondent's prices were such that competitors could not meet such prices without suffering a loss on such business and in one instance a competitor was forced out of business as a result of such acts and practices of the respondent.[35]

[34] Apparently the Moss case was based partly on complaint by Unity Stamp Co., which testified that Moss offered stamps to customers of Unity Stamp Co. at prices of from 5 to 7 cents per line, whereas Unity Stamp Co. had been charging from 10 to 20 cents. The company lost some customers and held others by meeting Moss's offers, though it believed Moss's prices to be unlawful. Unity Stamp Co. was also subjected to an order for its discrimination. See above, footnote 30, p. 477.

[35] This competitor, Massey and Company, lost the stamp business of General Electric, which was about 90 per cent of its volume, when Moss bid 4 cents per

Therefore, the Commission decided, Moss's discrimination not only injured competition in the primary line in both the narrow and the broad sense, but also tended to create a monopoly.[36]

In both cases the Commission found that the diversion of trade from one competitor to another by discriminatory pricing was injurious to competition among sellers, even though the sellers were numerous and there was no evidence to show that the beneficiaries of the diverted trade were large, dominant, or capable of attaining through their price discriminations a sustained growth that threatened to make them dominant. The principle underlying the Commission's decisions appears to be that competition among sellers is necessarily injured by discrimination that diverts trade.

The Commission's decision in the Moss case was appealed. In March 1945, the second circuit sustained the decision. Its opinion held that the Commission had merely shown that lower prices were made to some customers than to others, but that this showing was sufficient to shift the burden of proof to the respondent and that the respondent "did not prove affirmatively that the discrimination did not lessen competition or tend to prevent it." Thus the court did not regard the Commission's evidence as sufficient to show damage to competition; it thought that such a showing was not necessary but that the respondent must instead show the absence of the damage.[37] The court said that discrimination was unlawful only in case it lessened or tended to prevent competition with the merchant who engaged in the practice, but that this provision "no doubt means that the lower price must prevent, or tend to prevent, competitors from taking business away from the merchant which they might have got had the merchant not lowered his price below that which he was charging elsewhere."[38]

---

line. Two years later Massey regained the General Electric account by meeting Moss's price; but this price was below Massey's cost, and Massey ceased to make rubber stamps.

[36] 36 FTC 648-49.

[37] This interpretation rested, presumably, on the language of Sec. 2(b), to the effect that when the Commission has proved "that there has been discrimination in price or services or facilities furnished, the burden of rebutting the prima-facie case thus made by showing justification shall be upon the person charged with a violation of this section." The Commission had consistently assumed that it had the duty to prove not only that there had been a discrimination, but also that the discrimination was potentially injurious to competition. Indeed, the court's decision to the contrary in the Moss case was regarded as embarrassing by the Commission.

[38] 148 F. 2d 378, 379. Moss subsequently moved to modify the court's order enforcing the Commission's order. This motion was denied on June 3, 1946, though

The effect of the court's decision in the Moss case was paradoxical. By an interpretation of the law as to the burden of proof, which the Commission did not request and has not subsequently invoked, the court sustained an order that, in its opinion, did not prove the injury requisite to a violation of law. The more important question, the meaning of injury to competition in the primary line, was beclouded rather than clarified by the decision. A literal reading of the findings of the Commission and the opinion of the Court indicates that the court's concept of injury to competition is even broader than that of the Commission. The Commission found such injury in diversion of trade *to* the discriminating seller *from* his competitors. The court said that such injury presumably arose where the lower price prevented, or tended to prevent, diversion of trade *from* the discriminating seller *to* his competitors. In other words, the Commission found injury in the acquisition of more customers by aggressive price cutting, whereas the court saw it even in the retention of existing customers by defensive price cutting. Thus the interpretation of the Commission appears to be included within that of the court. Yet the Commission's evidence, apparently conclusive in showing that trade had been diverted, was not regarded by the court as adequate to demonstrate that competition had been injured; and the court sustained the order of the Commission only on the basis of a belief that when the Commission had proved the existence of discriminatory price differences, it need not prove injury but might leave disproof to the respondent. This aspect of the decision raises question whether the court meant what it seemed to say about the meaning of injury. If its statement of the law is to be taken at face value, it is of major importance.[39]

---

minor changes in the wording of the order were made for purposes of clarification. (See 155 F. 2d 1016.) After receiving a brief from the Acting Solicitor General, which repudiated the court's reasoning as to burden of proof but argued that the judgment should not be upset because the court had given the wrong reasons for it, the Supreme Court denied a petition for a writ of certiorari. See Robert B. Dawkins, "Defenses Available in Cases of Geographic Price Discrimination," 37 *Georgetown Law Journal* 223-24. The same view as to burden of proof was expressed again by the same court in a later decision. See *FTC* v. *Standard Brands*, 189 F. 2d 510.

[39] On April 27, 1954, in dismissing a case against General Foods (Docket 5675) for a lack of injurious effect, the Commission discussed the court's opinion in the Moss case and the conflicting court opinion in the Staley case, and flatly declared "the burden of proof to establish injury to competition is on counsel supporting the complaint." (See 50 FTC 889.) The principle announced by the Commission is consistent not only with the Staley decision, but also with the position taken by the Seventh Circuit in the Minneapolis-Honeywell case and by the Tenth Circuit in *Mead's Fine Bread* v. *Moore*, 208 F. 2d 777.

In any event, the policy of the Commission, as expressed in the Moss and Krengel Company cases, is of similar significance, though of smaller sweep. Since discriminatory price concessions typically have the effect of diverting business (or of retaining business that would otherwise have been diverted), the principle adopted in these cases means that any discrimination large enough to serve as an effective inducement to buy is unlawful in the absence of one of the statutory justifications. In effect, price differences are held to be injurious to competition among sellers per se, and hence usable only where they are retaliatory or cost-justified.

The effect of the order on Krengel Manufacturing Company has been a substantial loss of business. Its sales of stamps fell so much after the case that the company added new lines of business. A smaller proportion of its business than before is in rubber stamps. Only four of the more than 70 firms that make stamps in New York are subject to the Commission's orders—Krengel Manufacturing Company, Samuel H. Moss, Unity Stamp Company, and Adolph Gottscho. For Krengel Company to make a discriminatory price reduction is to violate the Commision's order. A similar discriminatory reduction by most of its competitors violates no order, though it may possibly be a violation of the statute. As to the effect of the order on the prices of the company, the customers who were interviewed are not in agreement. One, which regards rubber stamps as so unimportant that they are bought "by the office boys," says that because of the trouble caused by the case it has quit buying from Krengel Company and lets the office boys buy from anybody else.

Interviews about the effects of the Moss case were obtained with four of the six competitors whose loss of business to Moss had been put in evidence. To all of them, the case had been relatively unimportant. One said that his business with a small customer had been affected by the discrimination, and that he had regretted being drawn into the case. One said that he was induced to testify by being told by the government that discrimination had been responsible for loss of a good account (which

---

The placing of the burden of proof is presumably more important where the injury to competition is thought to be in the primary line of commerce than where injuries in the secondary line of commerce are in question. As to the latter, the Supreme Court found in the Morton Salt case that the Commission "need only prove that a seller had charged one purchaser a higher price for like goods than he had charged one or more of the purchaser's competitors." (334 U. S. 45.) Whether such a showing is sufficient because it proves injury or because the Commission is not required to prove injury is unimportant in this type of case; but it may be important in a case concerned with competition in the primary line if more than a mere price difference is required to prove injury in that competition.

according to the figures he supplied, constituted about one ninth of his business); but that he had never troubled to ask why he lost the account, had refused to testify until a hearing was scheduled nearby, and did not care much about the account. During the interview he recalled with surprise that he recovered the account in the year after the case. A third said that he had been affected less than competitors located in New York and that the two good customers he had lost were lost partly because their offices had moved to New York. The fourth competitor did not directly comment on the importance of the case, but said that the account he had lost had constituted about one per cent of his business. He did not succeed in selling to this account after the case.

Apparently, the change in business conditions that accompanied the Second World War terminated the price cutting that had prevailed previously. A price schedule for rubber stamps is now set forth in Moore Price Services Bulletin. The only manufacturer's price list that has been obtained does not conform to the Moore list. But according to another manufacturer, the producers of stamps generally use the same scale of quantity discounts, providing for reductions of 5 per cent on purchases of more than $15, 10 per cent for more than $25, 15 per cent for more than $35, 20 per cent for more than $50, 25 per cent for more than $65, and 30 per cent for more than $85. These are the discounts shown in the Moore Bulletin. This manufacturer no longer troubles to issue his own catalog, but consults the Moore Bulletin instead. One customer comments that the stamp manufacturers do not seem to him to be competing very vigorously. No specific information is available on the extent to which these developments are due to the orders of the Commission.

The cases of unsystematic price discrimination and private brand discrimination that have been reviewed have shed little further light on the cost defense in price discrimination cases. Only in the case involving United States Rubber do problems of cost appear to have been seriously considered. In other instances, the selective nature of the discrimination apparently precluded any successful cost defense. In the U. S. Rubber case, the new feature is the use of a uniform sales price at the level paid by the most favored customers and the segregation of the further costs of distribution incurred in selling to other customers, so that when the surplus above the segregated additional costs is refunded to the buyer, the price differentials and cost differentials will automatically correspond. It is surprising that there has not been further experiment with such devices.

The treatment of the concept of injury to competition in these cases is noteworthy in several respects. Injury in the secondary line was found in all of the cases studied except those against Moss and Krengel Company. In the numbering machine, tire, fish, and citrus juice cases, the injury consisted not only in impairing the competitive opportunities of disfavored buyers, but also in damaging competition in the market; and in the first two of these cases it included a tendency to create a monopoly among buyers. Yet the evidence produced to justify findings of damage to market competition or tendency to monopoly among buyers was scant. Large and powerful buyers benefited from the discriminations by U. S. Rubber and Florida Citrus Canners. But in the case against National Numbering Machine, the only evidence of any injury to competition in the secondary line was the price differences themselves. Such differences, which were thought to justify only a finding of injury in the narrow sense in the two yeast cases, were thought in the numbering machine case to justify a finding of injury in the market sense and a finding of tendency toward monopoly as well. In the Booth Fisheries case, there was evidence that the disfavored customers were exposed to price competition that made it impossible for them to sell profitably, at least at particular times and places. Though nothing in the findings indicated the frequency, scope, and severity of such results or the number and relative size of the competitors, this evidence was used as the basis for a finding of damage to competition in the market sense as well as in the narrower sense.

Even more striking is the Commission's handling of the concept of injury in the primary line. Such competition was found to be injured in the market sense in seven cases, those involving U. S. Rubber, Florida Citrus Canners, National Numbering Machine, National Grain Yeast, Federal Yeast, Moss, and Krengel Company. Except in the yeast cases, the Commission also found injury in the narrower sense. In three instances—U. S. Rubber, National Numbering Machine, and Moss—it found a tendency toward monopoly. U. S. Rubber was a powerful manufacturer, and Florida Citrus Canners, a substantial co-operative. It is hard to envisage monopoly or dominance of the market, however, in the image of National Numbering Machine, Moss, Krengel Company, National Yeast, or Federal Yeast. The findings in the case against National Numbering Machine consisted solely in the price differences, unsupported by findings as to the size and power of National Numbering Machine, the size and power of its competitors, or the proportion of the market that it served, or even by a showing that the discriminations had diverted trade from its competitors. In the cases against National Grain Yeast and Federal Yeast, the only findings of evidence in addition to a similar showing of price differences was respondents' admission that the savings were "material and vital factors of competition." Yet both concerns operated in an industry in which two other companies made approximately 75 per cent of the sales. In the cases against Moss and Krengel Company, two small rubber stamp manufacturers, employing respectively about 19 and about 10 persons and engaged in business in a city served by at least 70 local competitors plus competitors from other cities, were found to injure competition in the primary line by discriminations through which they diverted certain accounts from their competitors. The discrimination by Moss was found to tend toward monopoly, though that by Krengel Company was not. The findings were supported by a showing that one competitor had found the rubber stamp business unprofitable and abandoned it and that several did not believe they could sell profitably at the discriminatory low prices charged by the respondents. There was no showing, however, that the number of competitors was being or probably would be substantially reduced or that the market share, size, or power of the respondents was being or probably would be substantially increased.

Thus the cases concerned with injury to competition in the primary line appear to rest on the opinion that discrimination, even by a small company in a large market, has the capacity to damage market competition and even to create monopoly if it has the capacity to divert trade. Indeed, the cases appear to go further, by inferring the necessary diversion of trade if the differences in price are substantial. The logical consequence of such a principle is the outlawry of competition that takes the form of specific price concessions. The appearance of industry-wide price lists and industry-wide discount sheets, such as are said to have developed in the rubber stamp industry, cannot be regarded as a surprising sequel.

15 / *Receipt of Unlawful Concessions*

SINCE THE PRINCIPAL PURPOSE of the Robinson-Patman Act was to reduce the buying advantages of the powerful buyer, specific curbs on buying power were to be expected in the statute. Nevertheless, Section 2(a), having to do with discounts and allowances injurious to competition, and Sections 2(d) and 2(e), having to do with proportionality of payments and services, were so written that they apply to the sellers of goods but not to the buyers thereof. Though Section 2(c), the brokerage provision, pertains equally to buyers and sellers, the other substantive provisions that have been discussed in previous chapters pertain to sellers only. At a late stage in the consideration of the proposed law, the Congress reduced this one-sidedness by adopting, as an amendment to the bill, Section 2(f), which is specifically concerned with buyers' conduct. Thus it became unlawful for any buyer knowingly to induce or receive a discrimination forbidden by the statute.

Since the term "discrimination" as used in this part of the law is not self-explanatory, question arises as to the scope of the liability thus established for buyers. Does the prohibition extend only to the receipt of the discounts and allowances forbidden in Section 2(a) or does it extend also to the receipt of the disproportional payments and services forbidden in Sections 2(d) and 2(e)? The question has not been explicitly decided either in judicial review or in a formal conclusion of law by the Federal Trade Commission. Interpretation of the statute in this respect must rest on inference from the language and structure of the act itself and from the behavior of the Commission in administering it.

Both the language of the act and the structure thereof suggest that Section 2(f) is to be regarded as the counterpart of Section 2(a) but not as the counterpart of Sections 2(d) and 2(e). Section 2(f) forbids the inducement or receipt of an illegal "discrimination in price." Section 2(a) forbids sellers to discriminate in price in particular circumstances. Both

486

the words and the underlying concepts are parallel. What is forbidden in Section 2(d), however, is disproportionality in payments for services and in Section 2(e) a discrimination in the provision of services. To regard Section 2(f) as the counterpart of these prohibitions would require that the term "price" be interpreted to include not only payment for service but performance of service. Such a stretch of the concept of price is not plausible. Moreover, since Section 2(c), applicable to brokerage commissions, carries its own prohibitions as to the practices of the buyer, this fact negates any broad presumption that the Congress intended the provision as to buying practices in Section 2(f) to be the comprehensive equivalent of the provisions as to selling practices contained in all previous parts of the statute.

In administering the law, the Federal Trade Commission has not interpreted Section 2(f) as though it applied to buyers who receive the benefit of violations of Sections 2(d) and 2(e). It is true that in two cases involving Miami Wholesale Drug Company and Atlantic City Wholesale Drug Company (Dockets 3377 and 4957), the Commission proceeded against buyers who had received payments for advertising. In each case, however, the Commission found that the so-called advertising payments had been subterfuges through which the buyers had received discounts on their purchase prices and that the effect of these discounts had been to impair competition in ways forbidden by Section 2(a). In a recent series of cases in the food industries, the Commission issued 11 complaints against suppliers of grocery products, charging that they had made disproportionate advertising allowances in violation of Section 2(d). The Commission then issued 2 corollary complaints against Food Fair Stores and Giant Food Shopping Center on the theory that these two companies had unlawfully induced and received the allowances. Instead of proceeding in these two cases under Section 2(f) of the Robinson-Patman Act, however, the Commission brought the complaints under Section 5 of the Federal Trade Commission Act, alleging that the receipt of the advertising allowances hurt the buyers' competitors and obstructed and prevented competition and therefore constituted an unfair method of competition forbidden by Section 5.[1] If it had thought that proof of disproportionality, which it was offering in the cases against the sellers under Section 2(d) of the Robinson-Patman Act, was sufficient to convict

[1] For a discussion of the Food Fair and Giant cases, see footnote 25, p. 165.

the buyers of receiving unlawful payments under Section 2(f), the Commission presumably would not have assumed the additional burden of proving that the buyers' conduct was detrimental to competition and therefore unfair.

In forbidding the knowing inducement or receipt of unlawful discriminations, the Congress made Section 2(f) dependent on Section 2(a). Only if the seller's conduct is illegal under the standards of Section 2(a) can the buyer's acts be illegal under the standards of Section 2(f). The buyer's violation is derivative from the seller's violation, and proof in a case against the buyer must include facts sufficient to establish a case against the seller as well. Whatever weaknesses and ambiguities exist in Section 2(a) are thus imported into Section 2(f) also. If, however, the Commission wishes to proceed against a buyer, it must add to its case further evidence showing that the buyer induced or received the discrimination and that he did so knowingly. Thus, the burden on the Commission under Section 2(f) is necessarily greater than under Section 2(a).

Because of this burden a comprehensive attack on discrimination is more difficult in a case against a buyer than in a case against the seller. If a seller's price structure includes discriminations affecting many buyers, a sample of these discriminations, derived from the seller's records, can be used as a basis for an order requiring that similar discriminations be abandoned as to all buyers. But if a powerful buyer obtains discounts from many sellers, receipt of these discounts is unlawful only in the instances in which the discriminations by the sellers are unlawful; and therefore, even though evidence is limited to a sample, specific proof of illegality on the part of a number of sellers must be introduced into the case if there is to be a basis for a broad order against the buyer. There may be economy of time and effort in a proceeding against a large seller, but there cannot be similar economy in a proceeding against a large buyer. Similarly, if a buyer is ordered not to receive unlawful price concessions, it is probable that the question whether he is complying with the order cannot be answered from his records alone, without examining the records of his suppliers.

Therefore, in spite of the fact that the powerful buyer is the target of the law and is subject to explicit prohibitions, the design of the statute makes it inevitable that the attack on buying shall be, in practice, primarily an attack on the seller's conduct. The effect of the law on buyers is chiefly an indirect consequence of the proceedings against sellers.

Relative Ineffectiveness of Cases
Against Buyers

This one-sidedness is evident in the record of the Commission's proceedings in cases in which legal action was instituted against buyers and sellers who participated in the same discriminations. In three instances in which the relation of buyer and seller to one another was intimate, the Commission proceeded jointly against them and issued cease and desist orders in uncontested cases. In the other instances of proceedings on both sides of the market, the record has been one of greater and quicker success by the Commission in cases against buyers than in cases against sellers. Before the end of 1957 there had been six situations in which closely related cases were brought against buyers and sellers. One, having to do with the purchase and sale of corn syrup, resulted in eight cases against corn syrup manufacturers and two cases against buyers of corn syrup. Orders against the eight sellers were issued first; the order against one of the buyers was issued after decision by the court of appeals, and the order against the other buyer after decision by the Supreme Court, in the case against the principal seller. In the case against one of the buyers, attention was focused chiefly on the concern's discriminatory selling practices in resale markets.

The second situation had to do with discriminatory prices on candy. An investigation of the relations between a large buyer and its suppliers resulted in 35 complaints against sellers and one against the buyer.[2] The proceeding against one seller was not contested and resulted in an order. A proceeding against a second seller was dropped because the respondent discontinued business. In the other 33 cases against sellers, the Commission's complaints were based on a novel theory that a discount in price is also a disproportionate payment and a disproportionate service because it facilitates resale and hence violates Sections 2(d) and 2(e) as well as 2(a). Before trial the Commission disclaimed this theory and dismissed all 33 complaints as improperly drawn. Instead of issuing new complaints covering only Section 2(a), it took no further action against the respondents. An order was issued against the large buyer, but after the Supreme Court had rejected it and remanded the case to the Commission for further consideration under a different interpreta-

---

[2] The Commission also issued orders in three earlier proceedings against sellers and one against a buyer. These apparently were not connected with the group of cases discussed here.

tion of the law as to burden of proof, the Commission dismissed the case. Thus the final product of the investigation was one order against a seller.

The third situation had to do with discrimination in the sale of canned fruit. At the time of the decision as to burden of proof, mentioned above, proceedings were pending against a seller for discriminating in price and against each of two chain stores for receiving the discrimination. The cases against the chains were dismissed; the case against the seller resulted in a cease and desist order.

The fourth situation had to do with a joint proceeding against a manufacturer of radio tubes and a radio producer who bought them. After the decision as to burden of proof, mentioned above, the charge against the buyer was dismissed. Later the seller's discriminations were found to have been cost-justified.

The fifth and sixth situations had to do with discriminations on automobile supplies. In one, proceedings were undertaken against four manufacturers for granting discriminations and one distributor for receiving them. In the other, there were proceedings against four manufacturers and two distributors. Orders were issued against one of the manufacturers in 1953, four in 1955, one in 1957, and one in 1958. The case against one was dismissed in 1955 because the respondent was no longer engaged in the relevant line of business. Though the complaints against the three buyers were issued before four of those against sellers, all three of them were still undecided on August 1, 1958.

In the aggregate, these situations resulted in charges against 53 sellers and 9 buyers. Seventeen sellers were subjected to orders. Of the others, 33 were involved in the fiasco in the candy industry, 2 were out of business, and 1 provided cost justification. Orders were issued against 2 buyers, and decision as to 3 others was still pending in 1958. The other 4 proceedings against buyers were dropped because of the difficulties presented by the Supreme Court's interpretation of the law as to burden of proof. Of the 6 discriminatory situations, 5 resulted in one or more orders against sellers; 1 resulted in orders against buyers, with the result still uncertain in 2 others.

Extent of the Use of Section 2(f)

In spite of the difficulties inherent in the use of Section 2(f), the Commission has issued 12 orders in cases involving this section.

As in the cases against sellers, the Commission's findings of damage to competition in these cases differ greatly in clarity, scope, and persuasiveness. In every case the Commission found injury to the competitive opportunities of disfavored buyers and also a substantial lessening of competition among buyers.[3] It found a tendency to create a monopoly among buyers in 7 cases. Listed from the most persuasive to the least, 2 of these involved a conspiracy of buyers and sellers; 1, the buying practices of one of the two largest distributors of surgical supplies; 1, the buying practices of the largest distributor of candy through vending machines; 1, the buying practices of a large candy manufacturer that competed with other companies of comparable size; and 2, the buying practices of local wholesalers of drugs in Miami and Atlantic City.

In the primary line, the Commission found the narrow type of injury in 5 cases, the broad type in 6, and a tendency to create a monopoly in 3. A tendency to monopoly among sellers was found in 1 of the cases involving conspiracy, and in the candy cases involving Brach and Automatic Canteen (but not in the one involving Curtiss). Substantial lessening of competition in the market sense was found in 1 conspiracy case, in the 3 candy cases, and among the unnamed suppliers of goods in the cases against Associated Merchandising Corporation and National Tea Company. Yet only the narrow effect was found in the primary line in the buying practices of Atlas, the buying agent for five of the Standard Oil companies, and no effect at all in the primary line was found in the buying practices of Aloe, one of the two largest surgical supply distributors.

Cases of Incidental Discrimination

Ten of the 12 cases under Section 2(f) have been specifically studied.[4] In 3 of the 10 cases the proceeding was directed against sellers and

[3] In one case (Docket 3154, *Pittsburgh Plate Glass Co.*), findings of injury are ambiguous. The Commission clearly finds the narrow type of injury in the secondary line. In finding the broad type of injury and a tendency to monopoly, it uses language that is not clear. The findings are here interpreted to apply to the secondary line of commerce only.

[4] The cases not especially studied are Docket 3377, *Miami Wholesale Drug Co.* and Docket 5648, *National Tea Co.* The former was like the case against *Atlantic City Wholesale Drug Co.*, Docket 4957. A wholesale druggist induced suppliers of drug products to place advertisements in a magazine he issued and to pay for the advertising by credits on merchandise he bought. The Commission found that the publication had no advertising value, but was used as a subterfuge to get price concessions of as much as 33⅓ to 50 per cent; and that these concessions (1) en-

buyers jointly, and the charge that the buyers had received the unlawful discrimination was coupled with the charge that the sellers had granted it.

This was true in the case of Pittsburgh Plate Glass Company, which has already been discussed. The discrimination consisted in a classification of distributors into quantity buyers and carlot buyers, of whom the former were eligible for a special discount. The price structure had been evolved in a conspiracy participated in by the glass manufacturers and a national association of glass distributors. The charge against the distributors under Section 2(f) received no special attention in the case, particularly since the recipients assented to the entry of an order without trial. The Commission found in the discrimination the probability of a substantial lessening of competition in the primary line of commerce, together with both the narrow and broad types of injury and a tendency to create a monopoly in the secondary line.

Similarly, in the golf ball case, the grant of a discount by the manufacturers and its receipt by members of the Professional Golfers Association were both aspects of a collective agreement among sellers and buyers. As in the glass case, the charge under Section 2(f) was overshadowed by the conspiracy, and the order was entered without trial. Injury to competition was found in both the broad and the narrow sense in both the primary and secondary lines of commerce. A tendency to create a monopoly was also found in each line.

In the third case, which pertained to a contract for sale of gasoline by the American Oil Company for use in taxicabs controlled by General Finance Company, seller and buyer were both subjected to the order. Here, too, the case was not contested, and the issuance of an order against the buyer was regarded as a simple extension of the case against

---

abled the favored wholesaler to sell to other wholesalers at prices lower than competing wholesalers could obtain goods from suppliers and (2) enabled him and his wholesaler customers to sell to retailers at lower prices than those at which other wholesalers could profitably resell. Narrow and broad injury to competition and a tendency to monopoly were found in the secondary line of commerce.

The case against National Tea was based on that company's use of 500,000 coupon books with a cash value of $2.7 million in the autumn of 1948. The coupons were redeemed by the company in merchandise at their cash value, and unnamed suppliers of the merchandise then rebated the cash value of the coupons to National Tea. The Commission found both the broad and the narrow injury to competition in both the primary and secondary lines of commerce.

Both cases were decided on the basis of admission answers.

the seller. The Commission found both the narrow and the broad types of injury to competition in the secondary line of commerce.

In 1 of the other 7 cases, that against Curtiss Candy Company, the complaint against the respondent covered selling practices as well as buying practices, with primary attention to the former. Curtiss was probably the largest producer of candy bars, with total sales of about $14 million, of which about $8 million was bars.[5] The Commission found that Curtiss had discriminated in price, provided disproportionate sales services, and made disproportionate payments for service in its sale of candy, and had induced manufacturers of glucose to grant it discriminatory prices. The buying practices included in the case pertained to the same discriminations that the Commission had condemned in a series of proceedings directed at the various manufacturers of corn syrup. The Commission found in these discriminations a substantial lessening of competition in the primary line of commerce and both the broad and narrow types of injury in the secondary line. Perhaps because these offenses had already been covered in the cases against sellers, the attention of the Commission and the respondent centered on Curtiss' selling practices. Though the case was tried, the decision cast little light on the significance of Section 2(f).

Cases Against Buyers Who Lacked Dominant Power

In the remaining 6 cases attention was centered on the buying practices of the respondents. In 5 of these cases the sole charge was violation of Section 2(f). In 1 case this charge was coupled with a charge that respondents had conspired in violation of the Federal Trade Commission Act and that they had received unlawful brokerage in violation of Section 2(c). It is in this group of cases that one must seek the meaning of the law against discrimination as applied to buyers.

One of the cases, against E. J. Brach Candy Company, pertained to buying practices similar to those of Curtiss. Brach is the largest producer of a general line of candy, with a sales volume of nearly $8 million in 1938.[6] The Commission found that Brach had induced dis-

[5] Bernard Shull, "Price Discrimination in the Corn Products-Confectionery Industrial Pattern" (doctoral dissertation, University of Wisconsin, 1957), pp. 194, 204.

[6] *Ibid.*, p. 193.

criminations in the price of glucose by persuading the corn products manufacturers to let it continue to pay the old price after a price increase, by making arbitrary deductions from invoices, by falsely claiming that it had received lower price offers, and by placing excessive orders in anticipation of price increases and subsequently obtaining extensions in the time within which delivery was to be made. The effect, the Commission found, was substantially to lessen competition and to tend to create a monopoly in both the primary and secondary lines of commerce and also to injure competition in the narrow sense in the secondary line. The practices of sellers in granting such concessions had been a part of the subject matter of the corn products cases. The Commission's order against Brach forbade one candy manufacturer to receive from the corn products producers discriminatory benefits these producers were already individually forbidden to grant.[7] Brach vainly sought modification of the order on the ground that it

> . . . insures the continuation of the prevailing practice of the several manufacturers of corn glucose to quote prices identical in each instance. . . . The order as it now stands prohibits the respondent in this case from protecting itself and the industry as against such monopolistic practice, and consequently the general public is denied the right of a competitive price in the purchase of corn glucose . . . whereas the practice of respondent in purchasing at the lowest price obtainable tended to keep open competition in the sale of glucose.[8]

In a case against Atlantic City Wholesale Drug Company, the Commission used Section 2(f) to terminate quasi-fraudulent methods of chiseling, in which it found, in the secondary line of commerce, not only the narrow and broad types of injury to competition, but also a tendency to create a monopoly. The company published a magazine, for which it solicited advertising from its manufacturing suppliers. It charged the manufacturer varying amounts for the advertising, to be paid in the form of deductions from the purchase price of goods it bought. It refused to buy from manufacturers who would not advertise. Apparently, it printed less than 200 copies of the magazine, mailed most of them to its advertisers, and gave the rest to various druggists. One of the suppliers

---

[7] The order, like all but one of the orders against the glucose manufacturers, applied not merely to the particular forms of discrimination found, but also to any other unlawful discrimination on glucose.

[8] Docket 4548. Motion to vacate, modify or clarify order, undated, p. 1.

who participated in the plan found that on his first small shipment the deduction for advertising was more than one third of the invoice price and that the advertisement promoted the wholesaler rather than the supplier's product. He therefore discontinued the arrangement. Another supplier, located in the Far West, granted a 20 per cent discount as an advertising allowance in the hope that it would help him develop a market in the New York area, but discontinued the concession when the Commission's proceeding began. As a result of the Commission's order, the magazine and the associated program of advertising concessions were discontinued.

Cases Against Powerful Buyers

Apart from the cases of conspiracy mentioned above, the cases thus far discussed were not concerned with buyers who clearly possessed power greater than that of the sellers with whom they dealt. The remaining four cases raise in various forms the problem of the powerful buyer.

The case against Atlas Supply Company was directed against a joint buying subsidiary that had been established by the Standard Oil companies of New Jersey, Ohio, California, Indiana, and Kentucky. These companies, successors to the Standard Oil Company that was dissolved as an unlawful monopoly in 1911, had organized Atlas in 1929 to buy tires, batteries, and other automotive parts and accessories for resale. The products were resold under the Atlas brand through the filling stations that sold the gasoline of the various companies. According to one of the participating companies, Atlas was organized chiefly because the companies discovered by experiment that their business would benefit from a private brand advertised nationally. Since the market territories of the participants overlapped significantly only in Texas and Utah, the joint undertaking was not difficult.

Atlas established specifications for tires and batteries, advertised them under the Atlas brand, and acted as purchasing agent for the companies that controlled it. It bought tires at first only from United States Rubber Company, but subsequently used Goodrich as a supplier also. It bought batteries principally from Auto-Lite Battery Corporation but also from three other suppliers. It purchased fan belts and radiator hose from Raybestos-Manhattan, and electric lamps and related products from General Electric and Westinghouse. The joint buying power of the participating oil companies was used in some instances to induce suppliers to sell at substantial discounts and in other instances to establish Atlas as a suppliers' agent receiving commissions on sales to the oil companies. As examples of discriminatory prices, the Commission's complaint mentions the purchase of tires and tubes from United States Rubber at cost plus 6 per cent, while competing distributors paid more; the purchase of batteries from Auto-Lite at prices 25 per cent below those paid by competing distributors; and the purchase of fan belts and radiator hose from Raybestos at prices 28 per cent below those paid by competing distributors. The complaint says that, in distributing electric lamps for General Electric and Westinghouse, Atlas purported to act as their agent and received commissions.

Following the arrangement there was a rapid increase in the sales of tires, batteries, and accessories by the participating oil companies. In 1929 and previously, these companies had negligible percentages of the sales of such products. By 1949 they made about 10 per cent of the total replacement sales in the United States. Apparently, they used their buying advantage to resell the products at a discount. The policy of one of them during this period was to pass a part of its discount advantage to its customers so that these would come back to buy gasoline, but to avoid deep discounts because this created ill-will for its supplier and because it wished to break even in distributing the products.

The Commission charged Atlas with unlawful receipt of brokerage in violation of Section 2(c) and with unlawful receipt of price concessions in violation of Section 2(f). The case was disposed of by answers in which respondents admitted the allegations of fact, waived hearings, and consented to the Commission's order. The Commission found in the discriminations the narrow type of injury to competition in the primary line of commerce and both the narrow and broad types of injury in the secondary line. In the order the buyers were required to cease receiving brokerage, knowingly inducing or accepting discriminations in price where they were competing with other customers of the seller or where the seller was competing with other sellers, or using their combined purchasing power to obtain preferential prices. However, the order did not seek to prevent continued use of the Atlas private brand or the continued existence of Atlas Supply Company under the joint control of the five gasoline companies.

As a result of the case, Atlas discontinued its buying activities. It continues to establish specifications for commodities bearing the Atlas brand, to inspect and test such commodities, to advertise the brand nationally, and to license the participating gasoline companies to use the brand. Whereas before the case Atlas operated at a profit and paid dividends to its stockholders in proportion to their purchases of the products on which the profits were earned, after the order it ceased to make profits; instead it charged license fees for the use of its brand computed to cover its operating costs. Participating gasoline companies now buy their private-label tires, batteries, and accessories directly from the producers, and may use different suppliers. One buys tires from United States Rubber, Goodyear, and Firestone. Another buys from United States Rubber and has been negotiating with another supplier.

The change has imposed new buying expenses on the gasoline companies. One of them set up a new buying department consisting of six clerks and two supervisors. Another has established a purchasing department for tires, batteries, and accessories, and has attached to this department a legal staff, part of which was transferred from Atlas.[9] When one company is offered special deals by suppliers, it inquires as to the general availability of the prices, sometimes insists on paying more than has been asked, and sometimes rejects a small supplier's advantageous offer because the size of the transaction would not justify the effort that would be necessary to ascertain whether or not the price is generally available. The change has increased its administrative and legal overhead costs.

In buying tires, the individual gasoline companies have continued to use cost-plus contracts. According to one of them, sales expense is not regarded as a cost factor in these contracts. This same company says that the Commission has looked askance at the arrangement but that

[9] The employment of new personnel by the gasoline companies was accompanied, of course, by elimination of the purchasing activities formerly carried on by Atlas. Though information is not available with which to compare the numbers of persons involved and the relative costs, it is reasonable to suppose that decentralized buying in five offices requires more people and greater expense than had been required for centralized buying in one office. Whether or not the economic cost of the buying activities was increased in this sense, there can be no doubt that the monetary cost was increased to the gasoline companies. Previously, Atlas carried the buying expense, paid for it out of special price concessions, and transmitted a dividend to the buyers. Subsequently, the buyers not only lost the dividend but also incurred the buying expense.

the company believes that the delivered cost to the dealer, after allowance for the intermediary's cost of advertising and distribution, "is not far away from the dealer's cost via other distribution channels."

The effect of the order on price levels cannot be ascertained, for the case began three weeks before the beginning of the Korean conflict, and the order was issued in July 1951, during a period of general price increases. One respondent thinks that individual buying may be responsible for some increase in purchase prices. Another asserts that the purchase prices of the relevant products went up, but that this was to be expected when rubber prices were high and lead was being allocated.

Whatever the effect on prices, there is no indication that the case has prevented the continued growth of the gasoline companies as distributors of tires, batteries, and accessories. Figures as to sales of these commodities were obtained for only one of the respondent companies. This company's sales of tires and tubes in 1955 were 200 per cent of 1949 and 120 per cent of 1952. Its sales of batteries in 1955 were 171 per cent of 1949 and 120 per cent of 1952. Its sales of other accessories were 240 per cent of 1949 and 200 per cent of 1952. This rate of growth appears to have been substantially greater than that of the aggregate sales of dealers in tires, batteries, and accessories.[10]

A second case involving a buying group was directed against Associated Merchandising Corporation. This organization represented 21 concerns operating 22 large department stores, which, in 1941, had aggregate sales of about $425 million. Among them were such concerns as Filene's of Boston, Bloomingdale's of New York, Strawbridge and Clothier of Philadelphia, J. L. Hudson of Detroit, Stix, Baer and Fuller of St. Louis, and Bullock's of Los Angeles. About one fourth of the purchases of the goods sold by the participants were made through or with the aid of Associated Merchandising. The Commission found that Associated Merchandising had induced suppliers to give it rebates based on the annual purchases of the members and had distributed these rebates to the member stores in proportion to their respective purchases, and that Associated Merchandising claimed that its members saved from 6 to 7 per cent per year through the arrangement. Manufacturers par-

---

[10] Figures for the entire industry, as reported in various editions of U. S. Bureau of the Census, *Statistical Abstract of the United States,* are not sufficiently comparable to permit a direct comparison of the rates of increase. However, so far as any inference can be drawn from them, the increases for the industry appear to have been smaller.

ticipating in the plan, the Commission found, were given preference in buying; their products were featured in the selling efforts of the participating stores. Among suppliers and among buyers, the Commission found both the narrow and broad types of injury to competition.

After negotiation between the Commission and the respondent, the Commission's order was entered without a trial. Thereafter, Associated Merchandising continued to furnish buying services to affiliated stores as their buying agent and to supply them with market information and operating statistics. In its buying function, it locates wanted merchandise for the stores and bargains with suppliers on behalf of its clients, subject to the order's requirement that neither it nor its principals may induce or receive a discrimination in price. The agency relationship was limited so as to provide, in purchasing operations, representation of individual stores but not collective representation. A new concern, Aimcee Wholesale Corporation, organized and owned by Associated, was set up to do a general wholesaling business. It buys department-store merchandise from suppliers and resells both to the member stores and to others. "More than a majority" of its sales are made to the affiliated stores, but in the aggregate constitute about 5 per cent of the total purchases of those stores. The affiliated stores now buy a part of their merchandise direct, a part through Aimcee as wholesaler, and a part through Associated as agent. Preferred sources of supply are no longer specified. Aimcee Wholesale Corporation often places quantity orders for a particular commodity and resells the same to AMC affiliates and to others. Information is not available with which to appraise the effect of the changes on the relative prices of the goods received by the affiliated stores and by their competitors.

An order under Section 2(f) was also issued against a powerful individual buyer of surgical equipment and supplies, A. S. Aloe Company. Aloe was one of the largest retail dealers in surgical products, with places of business in St. Louis, Kansas City, and Los Angeles, and with more than 100 traveling salesmen. The Commission found that 15 manufacturers had sold at prices giving Aloe an advantage over certain of its competitors, which ranged, on different items, from 5.3 per cent to as much as 44.4 per cent. Aloe's advantage was 10 per cent or more on 54 of the 61 products listed; 20 per cent or more on 26 products; and 30 per cent or more on 13 products. These buying advantages contributed, the Commission thought, to Aloe's ability to issue elaborate catalogs, to employ a large staff of salesmen, to pay its salesmen well enough to enable them to make excessive private trade-in allowances,[11] to present free goods to the heads of medical departments, to sell on liberal credit terms, and to quote special discounts. The Commission found that Aloe was well informed as to the higher prices paid by its competitors and that it constantly pressed for preferential buying prices. The result, the Commission found, was not only both the narrow and broad types of injury to competition in the secondary line of commerce, but also a tendency to create a monopoly in that line.

As a result of the Commission's order, Aloe found it necessary to pay higher prices. The impact of the order, which was issued in 1941, was reinforced by the fact that after 1939 most surgical instruments were sold under resale-price contracts. With the enlargement of the market during the Second World War, prices moved upward. Aloe now asks its suppliers to guarantee that the prices it pays are generally available to others who buy the same quantity in the same market. In practice, however, other buyers do not generally take the same quantity. Moreover, Aloe has partially avoided the effect of the order by manufacturing certain items for itself. It has also established regional branches, which operate on an intrastate basis. According to various competitors and suppliers, Aloe continues to have a price advantage in buying. One supplier estimates this advantage at 10 per cent. Another says that Aloe obtains an advantage not available to others on about 30 per cent of its orders, which are delivered to Aloe in St. Louis for stock. On these orders Aloe pays the freight from St. Louis to destination. It is noteworthy that in 1952 the Commission entered an order against members of the American Surgical Trade Association, including Aloe, after finding that they had tried to promote resale price maintenance and the establishment of uniform terms of sale by procedures that included complaints against price cutting, discussion of prices at district meetings, exclusion of firms from the association for not observing published prices, and diversion of trade from nonmembers.[12]

Underlying the play of competitive tactics is a change in market channels. Hospitals are buying an increased portion of their surgical supplies direct from manufacturers rather than through dealers. Hospital purchases are often made after submission of sealed bids. Aloe and the other large surgical supply dealer, American Hospital Supply Company,

[11] Used surgical products that were traded-in became the property of the salesmen, and the trade-in allowance was charged against the salesman's commission.
[12] *American Surgical Trade Association et al.*, 49 FTC 334.

sometimes bid for such business on a cost-plus basis. In spite of the tendency of hospitals to buy direct, the number of surgical supply dealers has apparently been increasing.

Of the 12 Commission orders under Section 2(f), 8 were issued in cases that did not go to trial. Moreover, in one of the cases tried, that against Brach, the respondent admitted most of the material allegations of the complaint, and the trial was limited to evidence on a few of the less important issues. Three cases were fully tried, those against Curtiss, Atlantic City Wholesale Drug, and Automatic Canteen. In the Curtiss case the issues under Section 2(f) were collateral to other problems of price discrimination and received little attention. In the Atlantic City Wholesale Drug case, the discrimination consisted in practices that could not survive when disclosed. Prior to the case against Automatic Canteen Company, there was no proceeding under Section 2(f) that raised important contested issues as to the legal and economic significance of the buyers' search for price concessions.

The Automatic Canteen Case

Automatic Canteen Company of America is engaged in leasing automatic vending machines to distributors and in buying and selling commodities to be sold through these machines. Although it deals in cigarettes and various other commodities, its principal business is in candy, chewing gum, nuts, and other confectionery products. In 1946 it owned more than 87,000 machines for the sale of candy and leased most of these to 83 distributors with territories in 33 states and the District of Columbia. In addition, the company owned nearly 63,000 machines for the sale of chewing gum, and nearly 80,000 machines for the sale of nuts. In its fiscal year ending in 1945, its sales of merchandise amounted to nearly $13 million, and its income from machine rentals and similar sources to nearly $900,000. During the previous decade it had experienced rapid and sustained growth.[13]

The Commission found that Automatic Canteen Company had made exclusive-dealing arrangements with its distributors in violation of Section 3 of the Clayton Act and had knowingly induced and received dis-

---

[13] In 1936 merchandise sales were $1,937,000 and rentals and other operating income $127,000. The peak of merchandise sales was $14,739,000 in 1943; that for rentals and other operating income, $1,074,000 in 1944. Net income before taxes reached a peak of $2,167,000 in 1942 but had fallen to $1,458,000 in 1945.

criminations in the prices of candy, gum, nuts, and other confectionery items in violation of Section 2(f) of the Robinson-Patman Act. Automatic Canteen had informed suppliers of the prices and terms it would accept without inquiry as to whether comparable price concessions would be offered to other customers or could be justified on a cost basis. It had refused to buy from certain candy makers unless prices were reduced below those paid by other customers. In some cases it had sought to persuade suppliers that designated amounts would be saved on sales to it and would justify designated price reductions. Thus in 1939 it had written to Curtiss Candy Company claiming that savings would amount to 27 per cent, and in 1937 to W. F. Schrafft & Sons claiming that savings would amount to between 21 and 25 per cent.[14] From 80 of its 115 suppliers Automatic Canteen Company had obtained price concessions that gave it an advantage over its competitors ranging from slightly less than 1.2 per cent to slightly more than 33 per cent.[15] The Commission concluded that the aggregate amount of the preferential discounts was nearly equal to the gross profits of the company, and cited as an example Wrigley's gum. The advantage to the company in buying

[14] In both instances the savings were itemized. For Curtiss they consisted of 6 per cent in freight, 7 per cent in sales cost, 5 per cent in eliminating 24-count cartons, 8 per cent in eliminating free deals and samples, and 1 per cent in eliminating returns and allowances. For Schrafft, savings on the same items were estimated as 5 to 7 per cent, 7 per cent, 5 per cent, more than 2 per cent, and between 1 and 2 per cent, respectively. In addition, the letter to Schrafft claimed a saving of from 1 to 2 per cent on shipping containers.

[15] The investigation resulted in complaints not only against Automatic Canteen as buyer but also against 35 manufacturers of candy and chewing gum. In these cases, the seller was charged not only with granting unlawful discriminations in violation of Sec. 2(a) but also with violating Secs. 2(d) and (e). In most of them he was accused of violating Sec. 2(c) also. The charges as to the first three types of violation consisted in different interpretations of the same discriminations and, if sustained, would have had the effect of depriving the respondents of the possibility that they might have exculpated themselves by proving cost justification or the meeting of competition in good faith. Upon reconsideration, the Commission decided that the alleged offenses were properly to be considered violations of Sec. 2(a) and that the duplicate charges under the other sections were improper. Accordingly, in 1948 and 1949 it dismissed all the complaints, reserving the right to institute other cases appropriately limited. In fact, it never did so. Thus the Commission's only orders against sellers of candy were three previously issued (Docket 3756, *Nutrine Candy Co.,* Docket 4556, *Curtiss Candy Co.,* and Docket 4571, *Life Savers Corp.*) and one against *Walter H. Johnson Candy Co.* (Docket 4677) in which the charge under Sec. 2(a) stood alone. The Commission's grounds for dismissing the other cases were stated in an opinion in Docket 5605, *New England Confectionery Co.,* 46 FTC 1041.

prices from Wrigley from 1937 to 1945 aggregated $3,947,000, while its gross profit on the gum was $4,091,000.

The Commission found that the discriminations in favor of Automatic Canteen Company damaged competition among both manufacturers and distributors of confectionery and among manufacturers, owners, and lessees of vending machines. The company obtained extra profits that permitted it to provide additional services to its lessees and to pay, or enable the lessees to pay, higher commissions for preferred vending machine locations. Trade was diverted to the lessees of the company from candy retailers and other vending machine operators. Trade was diverted to the company from competing jobbers and from other owners of vending machines. Trade was diverted from manufacturers of vending machines who sold to the competitors of Automatic Canteen Company and from candy manufacturers who relied on the jobbing trade or on other vending machines for their outlets. These groups could avoid diversion of trade only by sale at low prices or provision of additional service damaging to their profits. The effect was the narrow type of injury, a substantial lessening of competition, and a tendency to create a monopoly among manufacturers of candy, manufacturers of vending machines, distributors of candy, and operators of vending machines.

The Commission ordered Automatic Canteen Company to abandon its exclusive-dealing arrangements and to cease inducing or receiving prices lower than the seller charged other customers where there was a competitive relationship either between the company and these customers or between the seller and other sellers who sought to do business with the company. However, the order provided that the company was not precluded from defending itself against a charge of violation by showing that the lower price made only due allowance for differences in cost.

Underlying the efforts of Automatic Canteen Company to obtain lower prices were various peculiarities in buying methods that probably had some effect in reducing the costs of the seller. The company was the first to persuade manufacturers that sales to vending-machine operators should be made in 100-count unprinted corrugated cartons rather than in the customary 24-count display cartons. It also bought in many cases f.o.b. the manufacturer's plant or delivered at a conveniently located central warehouse, whereas most customers bought candy on a delivered basis. Automatic Canteen was not interested in the special deals and free samples, common in the candy industry, that reduced the income or increased the expense of manufacturers in selling to the candy trade.

The evidence on behalf of the Commission is rich with instances in which the company emphasized, in its negotiations with suppliers, the possibilities of savings from these and other characteristics of its purchases. The record also contains scattered passages supporting the view that Automatic Canteen Company exaggerated the magnitude of these savings. However, the relation between the discrimination and the cost differences was not explicitly explored. The Commission's attorneys presented their case on the theory that when they had shown an injurious discrimination, the respondent had the burden of offering whatever cost defense it thought relevant. Automatic Canteen chose not to submit evidence on cost, on the ground that the Commission had proved no violation of law unless it proved that the discriminations were not only injurious but also illegal and that, therefore, the Commission had the duty of showing that the discriminations were not cost-justified.[16]

Adopting the views of its attorneys, the Commission found that Automatic Canteen Company had made no attempt to show that the price differentials made only due allowance for cost, and did not further explore the question of cost justification. In an accompanying opinion, after citing the decision of the Supreme Court in the Morton Salt case that a concern discriminating in price has the burden of showing cost justification, Commissioner Mason said: "Certainly, the same burden rests upon one who is shown to have knowingly induced or received a discrimination in price in violation of sub-section f." Similarly, after citing the Staley decision, he said, that Automatic Canteen had made no effort to show that the discriminatory prices were made in good faith to meet the prices of competitors and that the burden of presenting this defense rested on the company.[17]

Automatic Canteen Company appealed the Commission's decision on the theory that the Commission had failed to prove the illegality of the discriminations by failing to show that they were not justified by differences in cost.[18] The Court of Appeals affirmed the Commission's

---

[16] Indeed, Automatic Canteen chose to submit no evidence on any point. It entered into a stipulation consenting to the issuance of an order by the Commission without briefs and argument, provided that order was limited in scope and stringency in accord with a draft that had been prepared by the Commission's attorney. The order was issued pursuant to this stipulation.

[17] 46 FTC 896.

[18] Since it was the theory of Automatic Canteen that the Commission must show the illegality of a price difference by disproving the validity of the available justifications of such a difference, the logic of the position of the company presumably required the Commission to disprove not only the cost defense but also the

decision on the ground that Section 2(b) of the Robinson-Patman Act explicitly states that when the Commission has proved a discrimination in price "the burden of rebutting the prima facie case thus made by showing justification shall be upon the person charged with a violation of this section."[19]

Before the Supreme Court, the Commission argued that Automatic Canteen Company could have provided a cost defense if it had chosen to do so.

> Both general knowledge and the evidence of the present record refute the assertion of unavailability to petitioner of evidence of its sellers' costs. Large buyers are not so naive. . . . From petitioner's correspondence with W. F. Schrafft and Sons Corporation, . . . it will be noted that petitioner claimed that certain items of cost savings in definite amounts resulted from its methods of purchase and delivery. . . . The seller's reply . . . furnished its appraisal of petitioner's claimed cost savings in relation to actual costs. Similar discussions of particular items of cost occurred during petitioner's oral negotiations with many other sellers. . . .
>
> Even if the seller had said nothing whatever about his costs, still petitioner would not have been helpless. An examination of the items of savings claimed by petitioner will show this. Within a narrow margin of possible error the costs of shipping containers and the difference in carton costs on 24-count and 100-count packages can be ascertained by the buyer. The free deals referred to were public knowledge in the trade, and their terms were readily available to petitioner. The amount of the returns, allowances, and samples might vary considerably among sellers, but knowledge of the general policy of the particular seller in this area would afford a reasonable guide. Freight costs are available through published tariffs. The extent of any savings in sales costs is the least available of any of these items, but general knowledge of the trade affords a basis for approximating this, if a margin for safety be allowed in the estimates.
>
> It should also be observed that if a seller is willing to negotiate a lower price with a buyer based on cost savings, such negotiations can only be conducted on the basis of identified savings and their amounts. This process alone will inform the buyer of the seller's position on costs. . . .[20]

---

defense of meeting competition and any other available defenses. In fact, however, Automatic Canteen focused its attention on the cost defense, and only this part of the problem was explicitly considered in the appellate decisions.

[19] 194 F. 2d 433, 437.

[20] *Automatic Canteen Co. of America* v. *FTC*, Brief for the Federal Trade Commission, in the Supreme Court, December 1952, pp. 41-43.

To this Automatic Canteen Company replied: "It is absurd to assume that when a buyer, in the bargaining process, tells the seller that he thinks he should have a lower price based on cost savings, the seller will immediately give him a cost analysis."[21]

The Supreme Court reversed the court below and returned the case to the Commission for further action. Mr. Justice Frankfurter's opinion on behalf of the majority of the Court rested on the view that a cost defense is an intricate matter, requiring information that the buyer does not possess and that the seller would be willing to furnish to the buyer only if there were a degree of collaboration between the two that might well offend antitrust policy. Emphasizing the unwisdom of exposing a buyer who engaged in any bargaining over price to the risk that he might thus become attainted with law violations of which he had no knowledge, the opinion held that Section 2(f) makes it unlawful "only to induce or receive prices known to be prohibited discriminations" and "that a buyer is not liable under Section 2(f) if the lower prices he induces are either within one of the seller's defenses such as the cost justification or not known by him not to be within one of those defenses." After characterizing as ambiguous the statutory language as to burden of proof, the opinion said, "we think the fact that the buyer does not have the required information, and for good reason should not be required to obtain it, has controlling importance. . . . Certainly the Commission with its broad power of investigation and subpoena, prior to the filing of a complaint, is on a better footing to obtain this information than the buyer."[22]

Having thus decided that Automatic Canteen Company was guilty only if the discriminations were not justified by costs and that the Commission had the burden of showing this lack of justification, the court suggested possibilities as to ways in which the Commission might find it convenient to proceed. In many instances, the court thought, the Commission might "find it not inconvenient to join the offending seller in the proceedings." Moreover,

> . . . Trade experience in a particular situation can afford a sufficient degree of knowledge to provide a basis for prosecution. By way of example, a buyer who knows that he buys in the same quantities as his competitor and is served by the seller in the same manner or with

[21] Reply Brief by Automatic Canteen Co., pp. 7-8.
[22] 346 U.S. 61, 74, 78-79.

the same amount of exertion as the other buyer can fairly be charged with notice that a substantial price differential cannot be justified. The Commission need only show, to establish its prima facie case, that the buyer knew that the methods by which he was served and quantities in which he purchased were the same as in the case of his competitor. If the methods or quantities differ, the Commission must only show that such differences could not give rise to sufficient savings in the cost of manufacture, sale or delivery to justify the price differential, and that the buyer, knowing these were the only differences, should have known that they could not give rise to sufficient cost savings. The showing of knowledge, of course, will depend to some extent on the size of the discrepancy between cost differential and price differential, so that the two questions are not isolated. A showing that the cost differences are very small compared with the price differential and could not reasonably have been thought to justify the price difference should be sufficient.[23]

Three justices dissented. The dissenting opinion, written by Mr. Justice Douglas, said:

> The Congress plainly endeavored to curb the buyer in the kind of activities disclosed by this record. As the House Report reveals, the line sought to be drawn was between those who incidentally receive discriminatory prices and those who actively solicit and negotiate them. . . .
> The Court disregards this history. The Court's construction not only requires the Commission to show that the price discriminations

---

[23] *Ibid.*, pp. 79-80. This passage presents a striking contrast to one that appears earlier in the same opinion, when Mr. Justice Frankfurter was deciding whether it was reasonable to expect Automatic Canteen Company to offer a cost defense: "The elusiveness of cost data, which apparently cannot be obtained from ordinary business records, is reflected in proceedings against sellers . . . whenever costs have been in issue, the Commission has not been content with accounting estimates; a study seems to be required, involving perhaps stop-watch studies of time spent by some personnel such as salesmen and truck drivers, numerical counts of invoices or bills and in some instances of the number of items or entries on such records, or other such quantitative measurement of the operation of a business. . . . The Commission argues that knowledge generally available to the buyer from published data or experience in the trade could be used by petitioner to make a reasonable showing of his sellers' costs. There was no suggestion in the Commission's opinion, however, that it would take a different attitude toward cost showings by a buyer than it has taken with respect to sellers, and 'general knowledge of the trade,' to use the Commission's phrase, unsupported by factual analysis has as yet been far from acceptable, and indeed has been strongly reproved by Commission accountants, as the basis for cost showings in other proceedings before the Commission." *Ibid.*, pp. 68-69.

were not justified; it also makes the Commission prove what lay in the buyer's mind. . . . Where, as here, the buyer undertakes to bludgeon sellers into prices that give him a competitive advantage, there is no unfairness in making him show that the privileges he demanded had cost justifications. This buyer over and again held itself out as a cost expert. (Footnote reads: A reading of the record leaves no doubt that petitioner knew in numerous instances that it was squeezing a price from the seller which was less than the seller's costs.) I would hold it to its professions. Since it was the coercive influence, there is no unfairness in making it go forward with evidence to rebut the Commission's prima facie case.[24]

In the light of the Supreme Court opinion, the majority of the Federal Trade Commission dismissed the Automatic Canteen case on the ground that a review of the record did not disclose evidence of probative value that would warrant the finding that the prices received by Automatic Canteen Company were not cost-justified. Though the record showed that the company had considerable knowledge of the costs of sellers, "this knowledge was not related in the record to specific sellers and specific price situations." The majority of the Commission thought that if the matter was to be considered further the proper remedy was a new proceeding rather than a continuation of the old case. Commissioner Mead dissented. In his opinion the case should have been reargued and, if necessary, reopened for the taking of further evidence. He pointed out that the question whether or not Automatic Canteen Company had violated the law had not been settled and that considerable delay was inherent in the development of a new proceeding.[25]

The order dismissing the price discrimination charge was issued January 12, 1955. On August 1, 1958, no subsequent complaint had been issued.

Having won the price discrimination part of the case, Automatic Canteen Company was under no obligation to abandon its search for price concessions. Certain suppliers say that they no longer give special discounts to the company. Some of them, however, say that they quote lower prices to vending machine companies generally, and justify these by the economies associated with different methods of packing and selling. Certain competing vending-machine operators believe that the company now enjoys a price advantage, which one of them estimates as of from 2 to 4 per cent.

[24] *Ibid.*, p. 85.
[25] 51 FTC 574-82.

Meanwhile, Automatic Canteen Company has developed a new source of income. Through an advertising agency it sells advertising service that consists in placing a "Vendkard" on its vending machines. Though at first used by Automatic Canteen Company only, the Vendkard is now used by certain other vending-machine operators also. The charge for a Vendkard is said to be 20 cents per machine per week for a unit period of four weeks. This indicates that in a four-week period Automatic Canteen receives 68 cents per card after deducting the 15 per cent commission of the advertising agency. In bargaining with suppliers, the company seeks to sell Vendkard advertising. One of the manufacturers interviewed sells to the company without using Vendkards.

Automatic Canteen Company has continued to grow rapidly. Valued at retail prices, its merchandise sales amounted to nearly $29 million in 1946 (of which nearly $27 million was candy and penny goods), $67 million in 1953, and $112 million in 1955 (of which slightly more than $38 million was candy and penny goods).[26] However, this growth has not given the company a monopoly of sales through vending machines nor of candy through vending machines. According to the magazine "Vend," the dollar sales by the vending machine industry were about $1 billion in 1949 and about $1.6 billion in 1954; and the dollar sales of candy in units of five cents or more by vending machines were $126 million in the former year and $300 million in the latter.[27] One vending-machine operator, whose business is declining, thinks that competitors of Automatic Canteen are gradually fading out and that the size of the company provides decisive advantages in the ability to move machines from bad spots to good ones, to place orders for the slack season, and to make nationwide contracts with the central offices of great national companies. However, another vending-machine operator attributes his success partly to anger aroused in candy manufactures by the bargaining tactics of Automatic Canteen.

The candy and chewing gum manufacturers who were interviewed supplied only fragmentary information. Of the 10 who were most communicative, 3 had sold little to Automatic Canteen Company. Of the other 7, 6 said that the company received a smaller percentage of their

---

[26] The figure for 1955 includes the sales of Rowe, a maker of vending equipment that was acquired in that year.

[27] Estimates by the National Automatic Merchandising Association are available only since 1953. They are lower than those by Vend. For total dollar sales in 1953 and 1954 they are $1,318 million and $1,410 million, as against Vend's $1,536 million and $1,600 million. For candy sales for the same years, they are $211 million and $222 million, as against Vend's $276 million and $300 million.

output after the case. In 3 instances this was attributed to causes related neither to the case nor to price policy, and in 1 instance it was unexplained. In 1 instance the producer thought the loss of sales to Automatic Canteen was related to his withdrawal of special concessions, and in 1 to his refusal to buy Vendkard advertising. Five of the producers indicated that they had withdrawn special concessions that they formerly had given to Automatic Canteen Company. Most of them said that they currently sold at uniform prices or at prices varying only by differentials between 24-count and 100-count packages, freight payments on large shipments, or uniformly applied quantity, volume, or functional discounts. One said that he frequently quoted reduced prices to meet competition. The interviews with manufacturers do not indicate that any of those interviewed is dependent on Automatic Canteen for a decisive proportion of its sales or regards sale to Automatic Canteen as indispensable to its business success.

After the decision in the Automatic Canteen case the Federal Trade Commission re-examined pending cases in which violation of Section 2(f) was alleged. In 1953, cases against Safeway Stores and Kroger, and against Philco as buyer in a proceeding against it and Sylvania Electric Products, were dismissed because the evidence supporting the complaint was not adequate to prove "the degree of knowledge on the part of the respondent" required by the Supreme Court decision. In 1955, a case against Crown Zellerbach Corporation was dismissed on similar grounds.[28] However, in 1954, the Commission refused to dismiss complaints against Borden-Aichlen Auto Supply Company (Docket 5766) and D. & N. Auto Parts Company (Docket 5767), in each of which a violation of Section 2(f) was alleged. In both complaints the Commission had charged that the defendants knowingly induced discriminatory prices; and the Commission held that evidence should be presented in an effort to meet the standards of the Supreme Court decision. A similar complaint against American Motor Specialties Company (Docket 5724) was also pending.[29] From the Supreme Court decision in the Automatic

---

[28] Hearings in the Crown Zellerbach case had been held before the Supreme Court's decision in the Automatic Canteen case. Cost aspects of the proceeding are analyzed in Herbert F. Taggart, *Cost Justification* (1959), pp. 518-26.

[29] Initial decisions were rendered against most of the respondents by the hearing examiner in July 1958. In each case he found that a buying group had been organized for the purpose of obtaining lower prices; that after receiving price offers the group decided on sale of the products of one manufacturer for each line of goods (though members of the group were individually free to sell com-

Canteen case in 1953 to September 1, 1958, the Commission issued only two cease and desist orders based on charges of violation of Section 2(f). In April 1958, in a proceeding decided by the consent of the respondent, the Commission issued an order parallel to that of the American Oil case discussed above, against a manufacturer that sold gasoline at a discount for use in taxicabs and the taxicab companies that diverted the gasoline to the general retail market.[30] In August 1958, another consent order was issued against a group of distributors of automotive supplies in a case similar to those against Borden-Aichlen, D. & N. Auto Parts Company, and American Motor Specialties.[31]

An Appraisal of Section 2(f)

The existing state of the law as to violations by buyers cannot be satisfactory to the Federal Trade Commission, to defendants named in complaints, to weak buyers seeking protection against powerful competitors, or to sellers who are pressed for price reductions. The burden placed on the Commission under the law as now interpreted is a forbidding one. The Commission must show not only that there has been a discrimination having the capacity to injure competition but also that this discrimination cannot be justified under the cost defense that would be available to a

---

peting lines if they wished to do so); that members received volume rebates based on their total purchases, and greater than their individual purchases would justify; that orders were sent to sellers by individual members or by the group office; that shipments were made to members direct; that payment was made to the seller by the group office for all members; and that, though warned by decisions in the Whitaker, Moog, Edelmann, Niehoff, P. & D., and Sorensen cases that group rebates were unlawful, the respondents had not changed their procedures. In two of the three cases, the groups had distributed the products of some of the sellers against whom these earlier orders were directed. Two of the groups had submitted evidence that their members relied on suppliers' statements as to cost justification. This evidence was rejected on the ground that members knew that allowances were not based on particular sales but on combined group purchases and therefore were related to other factors than costs. In all three cases the conclusion was that since shipments were made directly to each member, each knew or should have known that the group rebates could not be cost-justified. Final orders against Borden-Aichlen and D. & N. were issued on Feb. 24, 1959, and against American Motor Specialties on March 12, 1959. In each case the Commission affirmed the hearing examiner's decision.

[30] Docket 6698, *Shell Oil Company et al.*, decided April 2, 1958.

[31] Docket 6837, *Warehouse Distributors, Inc. et al.*, decided Aug. 14, 1958.

seller in a case against him.[32] Thus the Commission must prove that there are no differences in cost adequate to account for the discrimination. The establishment of a cost defense has been inherently difficult for sellers who had unlimited access to their own cost records. Special studies of costs have appeared to be needed in most cases. But the difficulty for the Commission in proving the impossibility of a cost defense is necessarily greater than the difficulty for a seller in proving a cost justification. The Commission is an outsider with access to cost records only by use of its inquisitorial powers. If the records are inadequate, the Commission can neither prove its case nor make the seller improve his cost accounting. Whereas a seller developing a defense need make special studies only to support the hypotheses he chooses to offer—presumably those most favorable to him—the Commission cannot disprove the possibility of a cost defense except by proving the inadequacy of every plausible hypothesis of cost justification.

Moreover, it is not enough for the Commission to show that the seller's discriminations are not justified by cost. It must also show that the buyer knew or had reason to know of this lack of justification. Since an expansion of the buyer's knowledge enhances the buyer's risks, it is obvious that concerns pursuing an aggressive buying policy will be complacent about their ignorance and will avoid acts that might have the effect of reducing it.

But even if the Commission proves that there was a lack of cost justification that was known to the buyer, it may not have met the burden imposed on the law-enforcement agency by the Supreme Court. Since the price discrimination would be lawful if it were made in good faith to meet the equally low price of a competitor, it is possible that the Com-

[32] There has been difference of opinion among commentators as to whether the decision in the Automatic Canteen case imposes the full burden of proof about costs on the Commission in all cases against buyers. According to one view, this is the effect. (See Cyrus Austin, *Price Discrimination and Related Problems Under the Robinson-Patman Act*, rev. ed., 1953, p. 145; Abe Fortas, "Affirmative Legal Defenses," *CCH Antitrust Law Symposium* (1954), pp. 187, 200; W. H. S. Stevens, "Defense of Meeting the Lower Price of a Competitor," *Lectures on Federal Antitrust Laws*, 1954, pp. 129, 138.) According to another view, if the buyer can be shown to know the seller's costs, the burden of proof as to cost reverts to him. (See Notes, 29 *Indiana Law School Journal* 236, 240, 247, 249, 250, 1954; H. Thomas Austern, "Dealing with Uncertainties," *CCH Antitrust Law Symposium*, 1954, pp. 343, 359.) The former view has been accepted here. If, as a matter of law, the latter view is correct, we are not likely to discover the fact, for buyers will avoid obtaining knowledge that might have such consequences.

mission must also prove that the seller did not reduce prices in good faith to meet competition.[33] If it carries this burden, presumably it must, first, examine the price offers available to the buyer at the time of the discrimination; second, examine the seller's awareness of these price offers and the considerations as to the motives of the seller that bear on the good faith of the seller's decision to meet the offers; third, show that, in the light of the absence of offers, the seller's ignorance of the offers, or the purpose and strategy of the seller, the price concessions made by the seller were not made in good faith to meet competition; and fourth, prove that the buyer knew of this lack of good faith or should have known of it. The complexities of this burden of proof are clear. An aggressive buyer who uses the price offers of one seller to obtain dis-

---

[33] The Supreme Court's decision in the Automatic Canteen Co. case rested on the general principle that the buyer's receipt of a discrimination is unlawful only if the seller acted unlawfully in granting it, and specifically on the view that the Commission carries the burden of showing the absence of the cost justification that would make the seller's action lawful. If the decision is to be interpreted as meaning that the Commission must prove the absence of all circumstances that might make the seller's discrimination lawful, the burden of proof as to meeting competition in good faith rests on the Commission.

However, the argument of the Automatic Canteen Co. was centered on cost justification, not on meeting competition; and the court stressed the difficulty the company would have in obtaining cost information if the burden of proof were placed on it. Thus the decision can be interpreted to mean that the Commission carries the burden of proof only about matters concerning which the buyer cannot reasonably be expected to have access to information. If this is the applicable rule, it is not certain who carries the burden of proof as to meeting competition. On the one hand, the buyer knows what competing price offers he has received. On the other hand, the good faith of the seller in meeting competition depends, not only on the offer of equally low prices by competitors, but also on such matters as the seller's purposes; the breadth, frequency, and duration of the seller's price concessions; and the lawfulness of the prices the seller has chosen to meet. (See below, pp. 551-67.) As to these matters, the buyer is not likely to be adequately informed. Thus it is possible that the Commission may be required, on grounds analogous to those of the decision in the Automatic Canteen case, to carry some or all of the burden of proof about the meeting of competition in good faith.

The Attorney General's National Committee to Study the Antitrust Laws discussed the case on the presumption that a balance of convenience will be sought by the courts as to all the relevant questions. It found in the court's opinion indication that the buyer might carry the burden of proof as to meeting competition in good faith. It speculated that he might also carry the burden as to his knowledge of injury in the secondary line, while the Commission might carry it as to the buyer's knowledge of injury in the primary line. It concluded, however, that the "precise application" of the rule of convenience to concrete cases "cannot yet be told." See *Report of the Attorney General's National Committee to Study the Antitrust Laws* (March 31, 1955), p. 197.

criminatory concessions from another has done something to protect himself in the very process of negotiating for such a concession; for he has given the seller knowledge of competitive offers and has thus laid the groundwork for a successful claim that the seller met competition in good faith. In doing so, he has also erected an obstacle to the Commission's success in proving that he knowingly received an unlawful discrimination. The circumstances that may demonstrate the seller's lack of good faith are many, including, for example, collusion in price making and the pursuit of a monopolistic purpose. In some instances the Commission may need to demonstrate that buyers had guilty knowledge of circumstances in the behavior of sellers that precluded these sellers from the use of the defense of meeting competition in good faith.

It may be that the Commission must also demonstrate the insufficiency of other possible defenses—for example, the defense that prices differed through time because of changing market circumstances. Here, as in the case of cost and good faith, if the burden is on the Commission, it will require not merely that such defenses as the buyer may advance be refuted, but that all the plausible defenses be disproved in order to establish conclusively the illegality of the discrimination the buyer received. It is unnecessary to explore each possible defense in detail in order to establish the conclusion that, under such a burden, a proceeding under Section 2(f) would often be extravagantly wasteful of the Commission's resources.

The Supreme Court's suggestion that the Commission bring joint proceedings against buyers and sellers does not dispose of these difficulties. In proving a violation by a seller, the Commission need merely show that there has been an injurious price discrimination, and may limit itself thereafter to disproving such defenses as the seller offers and supports by persuasive evidence. In proving a violation against a buyer, the Commission, so far as it carries the burden of proof, must disprove each defense that would be adequate if established. If, in a joint proceeding, a seller chose to accept an order without a contest,[34] this decision, which might have been made merely to avoid the expenses and risks of litigation, could scarcely be regarded as conclusive against the buyer and certainly could not be regarded as proving guilty knowledge on the part of the buyer. If, in a given case, a seller chose not to present a cost defense but

---

[34] Of 117 cases in which orders under Sec. 2(a) were issued before Dec. 31, 1957, 86 were decided without trial on the basis of admission answers, stipulations of fact, or consent procedures.

to rely instead on the argument that his discrimination was not injurious or that he had merely met competition in good faith, presumably his selection of his grounds for defense would not relieve the Commission of the duty of proving, in its case against the buyer, the absence of cost justification and the buyer's knowledge thereof. Moreover, if the seller offered a cost defense that the Commission found to be inadequate because of weaknesses in his accounting data, the seller's failure to prove cost justification would not automatically enable the Commission to prove an absence of cost justification; for, had better accounting data been available, they might have shown the necessary cost differences. Ignorance of cost differences strengthens the case against the seller but weakens the case against the buyer. So long as the tests of violation for buyers and sellers are widely different, an effort to proceed jointly against both is as likely to complicate as to simplify the Commission's task.[35]

In removing the incentive for the Commission to direct its proceedings against buyers, the existing interpretation of the law has no doubt given comfort to the aggressive buyer. However, when the Commission undertakes such a proceeding, the respondent buyer must be troubled by certain portions of the majority opinion of the Supreme Court in the Automatic Canteen case. The court suggested that the Commission might be able to prove knowledge of lack of cost justification merely from trade experience. It suggested that a prima facie case might be established by showing that the buyer knew that the methods used and the quantity purchased were the same as those for a competitor who paid a higher price. It also suggested that if the methods or quantities differed, a showing might be made (presumably from trade knowledge and without examination of the seller's records) that the cost differences attributable to these methods or quantities must have been small as compared to the price differences. Thus the court invited the Commission to rely on common belief about the nature of costs or on loose analogies to similar factual situations rather than on a close examination of the books of account, supplemented where necessary by a specific study of activities and the related expenditures. The incentive for the Commission to accept the invitation is inherent in the heavy burdens of proof the Commission must carry if it rejects such loose standards of evidence. If the Commission should adopt such short-cuts, a successful proceeding under Section 2(f) might again come to seem feasible. However, there would

---

[35] Cf. Mark S. Massel and R. James Gormley, "Business Methods and Antitrust Policy: The Automatic Canteen Case," 1 *Antitrust Bulletin* 467-78.

be legitimate ground for alarm among aggressive buyers if the legality of their conduct were to be determined by such estimates. The basis for alarm would be at its maximum if the Commission should use such estimates not only as to large price differences but also as to differences of 2, 3, and 5 per cent such as have sometimes been found unlawful in proceedings against sellers.

From the point of view of the weak buyer, the present situation is highly unsatisfactory. His powerful and aggressive competitor remains free to obtain price concessions, including concessions that the seller has no right to make, so long as in doing so the powerful buyer avoids knowledge that the seller's action is illegal. When a buyer like Automatic Canteen obtains concessions from 80 different suppliers in a single industry, there is no simple way by which this aggressive behavior can be stopped through a single lawsuit. Separate proceedings probably must be brought against each seller until the cumulative impact of the orders induces a general change in pricing practices.

From the point of view of a seller confronted by a strong buyer, the situation is also unsatisfactory. Even though the buyer's aggressiveness has given rise to the price reductions that have come under attack, the seller rather than the buyer must bear the burden of litigation and suffer the restriction of a corrective order.

From the point of view of the public interest, the appropriate line of policy is difficult to determine. A vigorous search for low prices is an important aspect of a competitive economy. Pressure on sellers for price reductions is a necessary counterthrust against the continuous incentive to make higher profits by charging more. If a buyer incurs legal risk whenever he obtains a price that he knows is not generally available, bargaining on the buying side of the market is likely to be substantially weakened. If the buyer is required to make an intelligent judgment as to the legality of the seller's sales practices, on pain of violating the law when he makes a mistake, a duty is imposed on him in the course of business that is not always easy of performance by qualified tribunals after extensive legal proceedings.

Yet the central purpose of the Robinson-Patman Act is to curb the advantages obtained by powerful and aggressive buyers. Where discriminatory pricing originates in the activities of such a buyer, an attack on it through legal proceedings against the sellers who are victims of his power is roundabout and ineffective.

If the purposes of the law are taken for granted, the basic difficulty in the present statute consists in the fact that it attacks the buyer over the seller's shoulder. He should be held responsible, not for participating in the seller's misconduct, but for his own acts and policies. The relevant questions are whether he possesses undue power and exercises undue pressure. The standards for measuring excesses of buying power and buying pressure have not been formulated, and no one can formulate them satisfactorily in a few simple phrases produced by a few moments' thought.[36] But the standards implicit in the present law are not satisfactory. If several sellers have made concessions to a particular buyer, so that most of them are merely meeting the competition of others in good faith, this fact suggests the existence of undue buying power and undue pressure more persuasively than if a single concession had been made by a single seller. But whether buying power is excessive and buying pressure undue cannot be ascertained merely by examining the good faith of sellers who cut prices nor by discovering whether price reductions, usually made by sellers who are imperfectly informed about their own costs, can be subsequently shown to be cost-justified.

Until the law of price discrimination defines the buying practices that it condemns in such a way that they can be identified by an examination of the buyer's conduct and of the setting in which it took place, without reference to the internal details of the policies of sellers, the application of this part of the law must continue to be ineffective and often inappropriate, and to have a dubious significance in public policy.

[36] See below, pp. 642-43, 649-52.

16 / *The Nature of Injury to Competition*

THE CENTRAL PROHIBITION of the Robinson-Patman Act, that concerned with price discrimination by sellers, forbids discriminations that have a capacity to injure competition. For this reason the breadth of the idea of injury that has been invoked under the statute is crucial in determining the meaning of the law.

The Distinction Between
Broad and Narrow Injury

Two substantially different concepts of injury to competition appear in the language of Section 2(a). The first is set forth in words borrowed from the Clayton Act: "where the effect . . . may be substantially to lessen competition or tend to create a monopoly in any line of commerce." This language has been interpreted not only in earlier price discrimination cases but also in cases concerned with exclusive dealing and tying arrangements. Its meaning with reference to any of these practices has been found in the effect of the practice in reducing the vigor of rivalry in the market and thus impairing the protections which that rivalry is expected to provide for the buyers and sellers of goods. There is thought to be a spectrum of possibilities as to competition, ranging from the impersonal and atomized competition of a perfectly competitive market to complete control by a monopoly or monopsony. Harmful discrimination is envisaged as a type of discriminatory pricing that results in a significant shift toward the monopoly end of the spectrum. Such a shift is thought to be significant when it brings about a material change in the degree of competitive protection enjoyed by those engaged in the market.

The second type of injury appears in the statute in the language: ". . . where the effect . . . may be . . . to injure, destroy, or prevent competition with any person who either grants or knowingly receives the benefit of such discrimination, or with customers of either of them. . . ." This language is novel in the Robinson-Patman Act.[1]

Its meaning is indicated, however, by interpretative statements offered by sponsors of the statute during congressional debates prior to enactment. The authors of the bill were concerned with the possibility that a discriminating seller might destroy a rival or that favored customers might be enabled through price discrimination to drive out disfavored customers, without thereby substantially reducing the competitive pro-

[1] Defects in the wording of the new provision have enhanced the difficulty of interpreting it. Of the three verbs, "injure, destroy, or prevent," one, "destroy," is concerned with such comprehensive damage that it appears to cover much less ground than the traditional verb, "lessen"; another, "injure," carries no clear implication as to the scope of the damage it is intended to cover, though since the reference is to injury rather than substantial injury, the intent presumably was to invoke the law against lesser degrees of damage than are involved in the "substantial" lessening of competition; and the third, "prevent," extends the statute by covering not only effects on competition already existing but also effects on nonexistent competition that might arise but for discriminatory pricing. The application of these verbs to competition with a person who grants a discrimination covers new ground so far as the concept of injury is more inclusive than that in the traditional language; this competition is offered by competitors of the seller and, under the traditional language, discrimination became unlawful when it might substantially lessen such competition or when it tended to give the seller a monopoly, but not when it had lesser effects. The application of the new verbs to any person who knowingly receives the benefit of a discrimination was intended by the Congress, and has been interpreted by the Commission and the courts, to invoke a concept of competitive injury different from the traditional one, as is more fully set forth in the text. The application of this provision only where there are knowing beneficiaries appears to be inadvertent; for if a seller knowingly injures his disfavored customers, there is no intelligible reason why the state of knowledge of the favored customers should be crucial in decisions as to whether or not the disfavored ones are to be legally protected from the effects of the seller's policies. Finally, the extension of the new concept to cover competition with the customers of either the seller or his knowing beneficiary is ill-conceived. Apparently, the intent was to make the statute apply in protection of the customers of disfavored buyers who compete with the customers of favored buyers. This has been accomplished. However, the phrase "either of them" includes the seller also; and competition with the customers of the seller is indistinguishable from competition with the seller's favored beneficiary, already covered in a previous phrase. So far as this competition is concerned, the new language is meaningless unless it is interpreted in a way to permit evasion of the limitation imposed by the word "knowingly."

The apparent intent of the Congress, and the current interpretation of the statute, would be more clearly conveyed if the new wording were as follows: ". . . where the effect . . . may be . . . to prevent or lessen competition with any person who grants a discrimination or with any person who receives the benefit of such discrimination or with the customers of the latter."

tections enjoyed by consumers in resale markets. Conceivably, a discriminating seller might replace his victim, or every disfavored customer might be replaced by a favored customer, and the new rivals might compete among themselves as vigorously as their predecessors had previously done. In such circumstances the buyer in resale markets might be protected by competition as fully as before, and there might be neither a tendency toward a monopoly nor a substantial lessening of market competition. Nevertheless, competition by the victims of discrimination would have been not only lessened but eliminated. The effect of the discrimination would have been to injure or to destroy and would subsequently be to prevent competition with the discriminating seller or his favored customers or both. The sponsors of the bill declared explicitly that the purpose of the new language was to prohibit discriminations having such effects.

With respect to competition in the primary line of commerce, the difference between the two concepts of injury is apparent. The first concept is concerned with market competition, the second with the impact of one seller's practices on others. The first is invoked to prevent damage to competition akin to that resulting from predatory practices by would-be monopolists. The second may be invoked even where there is no such damage. Indeed, as the Samuel H. Moss and Krengel Manufacturing Company cases demonstrate, it may be interpreted to mean that price discrimination may not be used by one seller to divert trade from competitors or to protect himself from such diversion.

With reference to competition in the secondary line of commerce, the difference between the two concepts of injury is equally apparent. The first concept is concerned with market effects, the second with effects on particular groups within the market. The first is invoked to prevent damage to competition similar in kind, though perhaps not in degree, to that which is the concern of the entire body of antitrust legislation. The second may be invoked even where there is no such damage. Its purpose is to prevent price discrimination from becoming a means by which a disfavored group or class of buyers is deprived of opportunity in resale markets, whether or not there is a further effect on the competitiveness of these resale markets.

Critics of the Robinson-Patman Act have frequently characterized it as concerned primarily with the protection of competitors (as distinguished from the protection of competition). This characterization is incorrect in two respects. First, it ignores the fact that the statute applies to the reduction of market competition as well as to injury to groups of competitors. Second, it attributes to the statute an effort to protect individual competitors, whereas neither the statutory language nor the subsequent cases need to be interpreted as concerned with the protection of individuals. The new concept of injury pertains to injury suffered by classes or groups of competitors, not by competitors individually. The object in view is to preserve the business opportunities of buyers and sellers from damage by price discriminations, not to preserve single competitors from damage from all sources. Nevertheless, it is broadly true that illegality under the Robinson-Patman Act is to be found not only in injury to market competition but also in injury to a class of competitors that affects their competitive opportunities. In this respect the law extends beyond the traditional scope of antitrust legislation and invokes standards of fairness that are not implicit in the effort to maintain a competitive economy.

The statute is so framed, however, that one cannot tell to what extent the Commission may have used it to protect classes of competitors where there was no damage to market competition. Either injury to a group of competitors or injury to market competition is sufficient to violate the law; and when the Commission proves one type of injury, it does not need to prove the other. One cannot safely infer, therefore, that where no effect on market competition was found, it did not exist. In particular instances, the facts have been sufficiently disclosed to justify an inference as to the scope of the damage actually existing. In many cases, however, what has been disclosed supplies an insufficient basis for an intelligent guess.

For convenience, the traditional concept of lessening competition that is found also in the Clayton Act and is an expression of the general policy of the antitrust laws is referred to in this book as the broad concept of injury or as the concept of injury in the market sense. The new concept that is concerned with injury to the competitive opportunities of classes of enterprises is referred to as the narrow concept or as the concept of injury to a class.

A major question arises as to the effect of invoking the narrow concept of injury in the Robinson-Patman Act. To what extent does it result in proceedings different in kind and number from those that would have been brought if the law had been concerned only with injury in the market sense? Have two clearly distinguishable types of proceeding developed to express the two concepts of injury? So far as the proceedings have covered additional ground because of the narrow concept, has this extension reinforced and consolidated, been irrelevant to, or been inconsistent with the traditional task of maintaining competition in the market? In considering these questions, competition among sellers and competition among buyers must be separately discussed, since the effect on the one may have differed from the effect on the other.

Before the Robinson-Patman Act, cases under the Clayton Act and the Sherman Act had made clear the way in which price discrimination can substantially reduce market competition in the primary line. A large seller, in contact with many customers and many geographical markets, could make selective price reductions on the particular parts of his business in which he encountered the competition of a more specialized (and usually smaller) seller. Because these reductions applied to a smaller percentage of his business than of the business of the specialized competitor, he could use them to weaken or destroy his rival without substantial loss to himself. By repeating this process with one rival after another, he could reduce the number of his competitors, intimidate the rest until they accepted his leadership, and enlarge his percentage of the market. Damage to competition appeared as the discriminating concern acquired a percentage of the market that gave it dominance and pointed toward monopoly, as competitors became fewer, and as the independence of action of the smaller and more specialized concerns diminished.[2]

Though the cases had been less concerned with injury to competition in the secondary line, the concept of such injury that appeared in them was similar to that of injury in the primary line. The buying advantage enjoyed by a powerful buyer was thought to give him, in resale markets, an ability to reduce prices that could be used to enlarge his share of the market, to weaken or destroy his competitors, and to subject competitors who were not destroyed to his leadership. His price reductions in resale markets were not necessarily selective, since he was not a discriminator but a beneficiary of discrimination. The damage done to competition,

[2] In a recent article John McGee has challenged the view that this practice was significantly used by the old Standard Oil trust, and has argued that such a practice would be unprofitable to a large company. He argues persuasively that other means of establishing monopoly power, such as merger with competitors, are more advantageous to the would-be monopolist. In the opinion of the present writer, however, he seriously underestimates the effect of such predatory tactics in improving the terms on which a powerful enterprise can acquire its competitors' properties, in making other enterprises amenable to the leadership of the powerful enterprise, and in discouraging new entrants into an industry. See John McGee, "Predatory Price Cutting: The Standard Oil (N.J.) Case," 1 *Journal of Law and Economics* 137 (October 1958).

however, was akin to that produced in the primary line by selective pricing.

In the application of the concept of injury to competition in the market sense, the problems encountered have to do with the degree of effect that shall be considered injurious. Discriminations may differ in scope, frequency, and severity, and may be applied in different circumstances. They may produce different degrees of growth for the discriminating concern or for the beneficiary of the discrimination, different degrees of loss of business for injured sellers and buyers, and different degrees of impairment of the independence of those who are jeopardized or hurt. Controversial questions necessarily arise as to the extent of the movement in such directions that shall be regarded as substantial enough to require use of the prohibitions of the statute. Except for such matters of degree, however, the concepts are clear, both as to their nature and as to their economic significance.

No such clarity was to be expected in the application of the new and untried concept of injury to a class of competitors. Since the Congress had not made price discrimination unlawful *per se* nor forbidden all discriminations by competing sellers nor all discriminations among competing customers, it was to be presumed that some discriminations might exist without producing injury in the narrow sense. However, it was reasonable to suppose that a discriminating seller made a price concession for the purpose of getting or retaining business that he would otherwise lose, and that when he made a sale at a discriminatory price, some competitor lost that sale. Similarly, it was reasonable to suppose that any buyer who benefited from a discrimination was thereby enabled either to resell at a lower price or to incur more business expense or to make more profit, which he might use for expansion, than if he had enjoyed no such buying advantage; and it was apparent that, whichever form the benefit took, it constituted a differential advantage over his competitors who paid more for the goods. Thus the meaning of injury to a class of competitors was not self-evident. There was need to distinguish between the injury to competitors that is an automatic consequence of competition and the injury that constitutes a loss of competitive opportunity. Since the test of effect had been invoked instead of a *per se* rule, this distinction could not be found in a simple assumption that any discrimination necessarily entailed the prohibited type of injury. To determine the nature of the test of injury was the most challenging task presented by the statute.

Injury in the Primary Line of Commerce

Damage to competition in the primary line of commerce has been found by the Commission (or alleged in cases settled by consent without findings) in 63 per cent of the cases in which orders have been issued under Section 2(a). The most common finding (or allegation) in these cases has been the probability of a substantial lessening of competition in the market. This was found (or alleged) in 72 out of the 74 cases involving injury in the primary line. A narrow injury to competing sellers has been found (or alleged) in 58 cases and a tendency to create a monopoly in 54 cases.

In 16 cases the Commission found no injury except in the primary line. Three of these were conspiracy cases,[3] and 2 involved not only price discrimination but also exclusive dealing.[4] Of the other 11 cases, 2 involved local price cutting by a dominant concern against a sole competitor,[5] 1 involved price reductions by a nationwide producer in a single city,[6] 2 involved selective territorial price reductions over a wider area by enterprises of moderate size,[7] and 6 involved volume discounts or haphazard price reductions by which small producers obtained business from their competitors.[8] In all of these cases the Commission alleged or found damage to market competition, and in all but 3 it alleged or found a tendency to create a monopoly.[9] The Commission's willingness to issue

[3] Docket 3167, *Cement Institute;* Docket 3305, *United Fence Manufacturers Association;* Docket 5502, *Corn Products Refining Co. et al.* The first and last were tried, the second disposed of by an admission answer.

[4] Docket 3050, *Christmas Club;* Docket 5436, *Draper Corp.* Neither of these cases was tried.

[5] Docket 6327, *Maryland Baking Co.;* Docket 6383, *American Brake Shoe Co.* The former case was tried; the latter resulted in a consent order.

[6] Docket 6331, *Anheuser-Busch, Inc.* This case was tried.

[7] Docket 3740, *Metz Brothers Baking Co.;* Docket 5974, *Page Dairy Co.* In the first there was an admission answer; the second was tried.

[8] Docket 4405, *Samuel H. Moss, Inc.;* Docket 5048, *Unity Stamp Co.;* Docket 5516, *Krengel Manufacturing Co.;* Docket 5517, *Adolph Gottscho, Inc.;* Docket 6152, *Aeration Processes, Inc.;* Docket 6370, *Magnesium Co. of America.* Only two of these cases were tried, those against Moss and Krengel.

[9] In 2 of the cases there were no findings as to injury because a consent settlement was made without findings; therefore the complaint is the only record of the Commission's view of injury. Of the other 13 cases, 5 were tried and 8 were decided on the basis of admission answers or consent processes that resulted in findings by the Commission. The three cases in which there were no findings as to monopoly were those involving Krengel Manufacturing Co., Corn Products Refining Co., and Maryland Baking Co., all of which were tried.

orders based solely on injury in the primary line increased with time. In five successive groups of 62 orders, the number directed at such injury only was, successively, 4, 1, 3, 3, and 5. If, however, the cases in which there was conspiracy or exclusive dealing are deleted from the list, the numbers are 1, 1, 1, 3, and 5. Of the 6 cases concerned with price reductions by small producers to get business, 1 fell in the second group, 1 in the third group, 2 in the fourth group, and 2 in the fifth group.

If one disregards the findings on injury except in the cases that went to trial, a smaller proportion of cases involved injury in the primary line; but otherwise the showing is similar. Thirty-three cases involving violations of Section 2(a) were tried. Among these, 16, or about 48.5 per cent, resulted in findings of injury in the primary line. The broad type of injury was found in all 16 cases, the narrow type in 12, and a tendency toward monopoly in 12.

In 6 cases the Commission found no injury except in the primary line. One of these was a conspiracy case; 3 involved selective territorial price reductions; and 2 involved haphazard price reductions by small enterprises to get business from competitors. In 4 of the cases all three types of injury were found; but in 1 of the territorial cases and 1 of the cases involving haphazard price cutting by a small concern, there were no findings of a tendency toward monopoly. Four of the 6 cases fell in the last two of the five equal groups of price discrimination orders.

As is indicated at length in the chapters that discuss particular types of discrimination, most of the findings of injury to competition in the primary line are not explained, and there are frequent instances in which different types of injury have been found in circumstances that apparently were parallel. Findings of a tendency to monopoly have been made not only as to discriminations by large dominant companies but also as to the discriminatory practices of various small competitors that produce rubber stamps, seed inoculants, and the like. Although the Commission has distinguished among the various concepts of damage in the primary line by finding sometimes one and sometimes another type, one cannot escape the conclusion that the meaning of the broad and monopolistic effects on competition has been debased in practice. Since the narrow type of injury makes a discrimination just as unlawful as a broader type of injury, there has been no incentive to consider carefully what degree of injury is present in a particular instance. The danger of reduced market competition or of monopoly has been perceived more readily from less persuasive facts than it would have been in proceedings under Section 3 of the Clayton Act.

Injury to competition in the primary line has been characteristically found by the Commission where the discriminations originated in a conspiracy among sellers. It has also been found in a number of cases in which a single seller had a monopoly position or had a clear purpose to achieve monopoly or was discriminating against his only competitor. In these instances the finding that competition was endangered added nothing to the concepts of the antitrust laws.

In most instances in which the Commission's findings were explained, however, damage to competition in the primary line was inferred from the fact that discrimination resulted or probably would result in diversion of trade to the discriminating seller from his competitors.[10] In certain cases, such as those against the optical companies, the discriminating seller was among the largest concerns in the industry, and those who lost or probably would lose business to him included most of the smaller companies. Bigness, however, was not requisite to this type of finding. In the yeast industry, the Commission saw damage to market competition in discrimination not only by the largest seller but also by relatively small ones that competed with him. In the rubber stamp industry, it saw such damage, and even a tendency to monopoly, in a catch-as-catch-can struggle for business through discriminatory pricing by various small producers who had many competitors of comparable size.

Moreover, the finding of injury in the primary line has not depended on the magnitude of the diversion of trade. In certain instances—for example the case against Sealed Power—a substantial amount of diversion was found. In other instances, such as the cases against National Numbering Machine, National Grain Yeast, and Federal Yeast, diversion of trade was inferred from a price difference, and the inference was regarded as sufficient to support a further inference of damage to competition among sellers. In the Minneapolis-Honeywell case, the Commission (though not the circuit court) treated such an inference as strong enough to overcome an impressive body of evidence that Honeywell's competitors were competing successfully. In the Yale and Towne case,

---

[10] ". . . the Commission has placed major emphasis on whether the discriminatory prices have caused or may cause a diversion of business." See Edward F. Howrey (former Chairman of the Commission), "Some Facets of the Robinson-Patman Act," address before the National Confectioners' Association, June 13, 1957 (mimeo.).

however, the Commission rejected its attorney's contention that this type of inference was sufficient for decision and said that it was not always conclusive when there was other evidence to overcome it. From the cases in which injury in the primary line was not found, it is apparent that an inference of diversion of trade in the primary line from a discriminatory price difference may be overcome (1) by evidence that price is relevantly unimportant in the thinking of purchasers, (2) by evidence that trade was not actually diverted or that there was substantial loss of customers to competitors as well as gain from them, and (3) by evidence of such facts as the smallness of the discriminating seller, the lag of his sales behind those of his competitors, the widespread use of comparable discriminatory practices, and the existence of vigorous competition. It appears, however, that the Commission finds the third group of circumstances less persuasive than the first two.

In summary, the Commission's general position is that competition is injured when trade is diverted from competitors by discrimination; that this diversion may be inferred from price differences alone; but that the inference, though persuasive, is not conclusive in the face of affirmative proof that it did not take place or that it is improbable because of the unimportance of price, the smallness of the seller, or the existence of off-setting competitors' discriminations, or in the face of abundant evidence that competition remains vigorous and competitors successful.

In cases involving territorial price discrimination, a slightly different standard has developed. Diversion of trade is thought sufficient to produce injury to competition in the primary line provided the discriminating seller covers a wider territory than his competitor, and provided the market in which he discriminates supplies a substantial portion of his competitor's sales. However, in territorial cases there is unwillingness to infer diversion of trade from the mere fact of a price difference. Evidence that trade has been diverted is regarded as essential. Moreover, while the Commission's views of injury in the primary line have been accepted by the courts in discrimination cases generally, a difference of opinion appears to be developing between the Commission and the courts as to territorial discrimination. The Seventh Circuit set aside the order in the Anheuser-Busch case. The Balian case suggests that the courts may wish to examine such questions as whether the amount of business diverted was enough to affect competition, what the motives of the seller were in discriminating, and whether the local price reductions could have been made only because of the seller's resources in other markets.

The Commission's view of damage to competition in the primary line, as summarized above, tends in itself to jeopardize competition. Competition among sellers is a struggle for customers. Where it exists, diversion of purchases from one competitor to another is inevitable. Indeed, the ability of sellers to retain their clientele or even their respective percentages of total sales would be regarded in a Sherman Act case as indicative of an absence of competition. In so far as there is price competition, diversion of trade springs from incentives provided by price cutting. In this respect there is no difference between the diversion that results from a competitive reduction of the price level and a discriminatory price reduction. To regard any diversion of trade as injury to competition is to treat the central characteristic of price competition as injurious to competition itself where it results from a discriminatory price change rather than a general one.

In practice this means that injury to competition in the primary line is found because competitors are injured by price cutting. The question whether there was discrimination is considered in order to determine whether the Commission has jurisdiction under the statute. Once discrimination is found, however, no effort is made to distinguish between injury that results from discrimination and injury that results from competition. The discrimination is seen as the cause of the injury not only where the discrimination could take place only because the discriminating seller has resources in markets not affected by the price cutting, but also where, as in the rubber stamp cases, the resources of the discriminating seller are as fully involved in cutting prices as those of his competitors. That competitors have been injured is regarded as sufficient to make a case; and they have been injured whenever the price cutting has had any effect on their sales. The practical result of such a standard is to outlaw all price discriminations that are large enough to accomplish anything for the seller who undertakes them.

In the case of territorial discriminations, the broad sweep of this concept is slightly reduced by the requirement that, if injury is to be found, the discriminating seller must have a larger territorial scope than his rivals and must engage in discrimination in a market important to those rivals. However, a seller who markets his goods over a wide area encounters typically, in parts of that area, competitors who have a smaller territorial scope. These smaller competitors necessarily attribute relatively great importance to the localized segments of the market within which their sales are confined. The practical meaning of the Commission's territorial standard of injury, therefore, is that, except in the unusual circumstance in which a large seller encounters no competitors who are territorially smaller, he may not make price reductions applicable to only part of his territorial market even if he can make these reductions without subsidizing them from the income he obtains elsewhere.

The effect of the Commission's standard of injury is to outlaw price competition based on differential pricing—for large sellers when the differentials are territorial and for all sellers when the differentials take other forms—except as the price differences can be justified by cost differences or by meeting competition. But competition can be lawfully met only after someone else has first reduced the price and only when the reduction goes no further than to meet him. Thus the right to meet competition protects no one in taking the initiative in making price reductions. Price reductions large enough to have a competitive impact can be initiated under this concept of injury only when they are cost justified. This comes dangerously close to a general prohibition of all downward price movements except general ones.

The Commission apparently arrived at this interpretation of the statute in an effort to apply in the primary line of commerce concepts of injury analogous to those that it was using in the secondary line. It has specifically held that the narrow test of injury can be applied to sellers as well as buyers and that the test is the same on either side of the market.[11] In doing so it has allowed the formal logic of language to rise superior to an analysis of the differences between buying and selling relationships. In the secondary line, injuries to competition arise among concerns all of whom are customers of the seller. The vigor of the competitive relationships among these concerns is affected by the seller's price policies, but these policies are not themselves a part of the competition that is affected. In the primary line, however, the competition that may be injured is the competition in which the seller is engaged, and the seller's freedom to continue to engage in competition may be impaired if injury is so conceived as to impair it. Indeed, it is clear that competitors will be injured by competition as well as by perversions thereof. There is, therefore, a need to introduce in the primary line distinctions between types of injury that have no meaning when applied to the secondary line.

[11] In the General Foods case, see above, footnote 31, pp. 453-54.

The need for these distinctions is evident in the fact that corrective orders against injury in the primary line are stricter than against injury in the secondary line. An order applicable to injury in the secondary line usually directs a seller not to discriminate among competing buyers. It leaves him free to set different prices and make unrelated price changes in selling to buyers who do not compete with one another. In many cases, therefore, the order does little to curb the seller's freedom to differentiate his prices in different localities, to different functional classes of customers, and to buyers who make different use of the product. An order directed against injury in the primary line, however, usually requires the seller not to sell in competition with any competitor at a lower price than he quotes elsewhere. Sometimes the prohibition applies only when the lower price is below the competitor's price. The order may also require the seller not to make a price reduction by which he undersells the competitor (or even any price reduction at all) unless the reduction applies to all his business. Such an order is not limited to segments of the seller's market within which buyers compete. It is as pervasive as competition itself. It is directed explicitly at the tactics by which the seller takes his part in competition.

The Commission does not make any consistent distinction between its concepts of injury in the primary line and in the secondary line. In failing to do so, it has sought to restrict the competition of sellers unwisely. The logical meaning of its standards of injury is that, except where price competition is too weak to divert trade or discrimination can be justified by cost or by meeting competition, there shall be no price reductions other than general ones and no price structures other than sale at a single uniform price. Except under these narrow conditions, the competitive process of diverting trade from competitors by price competition becomes in itself an injury to competition. The Commission has been too devoted to the competitive ideal to adopt such a standard explicitly or to apply it consistently. This fact probably accounts for the many ambiguities and inconsistencies in its findings about injury in the primary line. Nevertheless, the underlying rationale of its decisions has been such that, when vigorously urged to proceed in situations of haphazard price competition like that of the rubber stamp industry, the Commission has perceived no defensible way of refusing to do so.

Escape from this uncomfortable position can be found only by adopting the standard announced by the hearing examiner but rejected by the Commission in the General Foods case. Use of the narrow concept of

injury in the primary line necessarily has anticompetitive effects. Whatever may be the proper scope of the law as to damage to competition in
the secondary line of commerce, discrimination should be forbidden because of effects in the primary line only if those effects are great enough
to be harmful to competition in the market sense.[12] The law of discrimination should be applied with the same care as the law against
predatory price cutting. The fact that one or more sellers were hurt should
be regarded as irrelevant unless there is also a showing that, in view of
the power or the purposes of the discriminating seller or the weakness of
his competitors, a continuance of the discrimination would be inconsistent with a continuance of market competition itself.

Injury in the Secondary Line of Commerce

The concept of injury in the secondary line of commerce has been used
by the Commission more frequently than that of injury in the primary
line. Among the 117 cases that resulted in orders under Section 2(a),
101, or about 86 per cent, were based wholly or partly on findings of
injury to competition among buyers. Forty-three, or about 37 per cent,
were based solely on this type of injury. As in the primary line, the Commission often failed to explain its findings, sometimes made findings that
were apparently inconsistent, and sometimes found market effects in a
way suggesting that the concepts of damage to market competition and of
tendency to create a monopoly had been debased. However, these characteristics were less apparent in the secondary line than in the primary
line. Findings of the narrow type of injury were most common: they
appeared in 98 cases, or about 84 per cent of the total. The broad type
of injury was found in 73 cases, about 62 per cent, and a tendency to
create a monopoly in 39 cases, about 33 per cent.

Among the 33 cases that were tried, 27, or about 82 per cent, were

[12] The Attorney General's National Committee to Study the Antitrust Laws
commented, "For the essence of competition is a contest for trade among business
rivals in which some must gain while others lose, to the ultimate benefit of the
consuming public. Incidental hardships on individual businessmen in the normal
course of commercial events can be checked by a price discrimination statute
only at the serious risks of stifling the competitive process itself." (*Report of the
Attorney General's National Committee to Study the Antitrust Laws*, March 31,
1955, p. 164.) The committee's discussion of injury mingles comment relevant to
the primary and secondary lines; apparently the committee did not consider the
question whether different standards were appropriate in the two lines.

based wholly or partly on findings of injury in the secondary line. In 19, or about 57.6 per cent, only this type of injury was found. The narrow type of injury was found in 25 cases, the broad type in 22, and a tendency toward monopoly in 6—about 76, 67, and 18 per cent, respectively, of the total number of cases tried. It is noteworthy that findings of a tendency toward monopoly were substantially less frequent in the tried cases than in the other cases.

One conception of damage to competition among buyers runs through most of the cases: damage is perceived in any substantial difference in the prices charged to competing buyers. The substantiality of a price difference is to be shown through proof (1) that the price difference is large enough to affect significantly the buyer's profit margin in reselling, (2) that if the price difference were reflected in resale prices it would significantly affect the buying decisions of customers in resale markets, or (3) that the price difference provides, for the favored buyer, an aggregate saving large enough to be used for significant business purposes. Where the discrimination is substantial by any of these tests, an inference that the discrimination is injurious to the class of customers that does not receive it is thought to be inescapable. With a substantial saving from price concessions, the favored buyer can engage in intensive sales effort, offer services to customers, expand his business, or otherwise improve his competitive position. With a buying advantage substantial in its capacity to affect market behavior or profits, he can divert trade to himself by reducing his resale prices. The disfavored rival is necessarily hurt: If he reduces prices to meet competition, his profits are diminished. If he does not reduce prices when his favored competitor does so, his sales are diminished; and if he encounters no enhancement of price competition, he suffers the effects of the favored buyer's intensified sales effort and accelerated expansion.

Injury along one or more of these lines is regarded as obvious, and will be inferred from a substantial price difference. The inference supporting it is not to be refuted by evidence that the disfavored buyers show no signs of serious damage. The fortunes of distributors are regarded as the result of various influences, of which price discrimination is only one. Injury from price discrimination is perceived not only where the injurious effect of the discrimination overrides all other influences but also where it diminishes the advantages that the disfavored buyers would otherwise have enjoyed.

Where buying advantages large enough to be injurious are found, there is an unstated assumption that they are obtained without offsetting expense. Although a preferential price may have been conditioned on purchase of a larger amount or performance of an enlarged distributive function, the costs of the favored buyer are not examined to ascertain the extent to which he obtains a net advantage. Instead the full amount of the price difference is assumed to be available to the buyer for competitive purposes.

Willingness to infer injury from substantial price difference has hardened with time. In recent cases[13]—but with the Yale and Towne case as an exception—the inference has risen superior to evidence that the disfavored customers have grown and prospered,[14] to evidence that the beneficiaries of the discrimination were small and weak,[15] and to unanimous statements by the disfavored customers that they were not injured.[16]

An alternative view of injury was adopted by the Seventh Circuit in the Minneapolis-Honeywell case. Here the court looked to the facts of the market for evidence that the competitive standing of favored customers had been substantially improved or that the competitive position of disfavored customers had been substantially worsened. It was concerned with such questions as whether disfavored customers were making substantial profits on the resale of the goods and whether or not their volume of business was declining in absolute amount or in percentage of the total. If there was no evidence of such effects, it thought there was no injury to the disfavored customers. Although this view prevailed in the Honeywell case (in which, on procedural grounds, the Supreme Court denied certiorari), the Supreme Court rejected it in the Morton Salt case. The Seventh Circuit subsequently abandoned it, and it now has no standing.[17]

---

[13] The cases in question have to do with automobile parts. Findings of injury were based on price differences which, in some instances, ran as high as 19 per cent; upon inference that the discounts must be important, since some buyers joined buying groups to get them; and upon testimony that cash discounts amounting to about 2 per cent were necessary to business success. The most striking examples of these cases are Docket 5768, *C. E. Niehoff & Co.* Docket 5721, *Standard Motor Products, Inc.*; and Docket 5723, *Moog Industries, Inc.*

[14] The Niehoff case.

[15] The Standard Motor Products case.

[16] The Moog case.

[17] This interpretation differs sharply from that presented by the Attorney-General's Committee in its report in March 1955. Relying heavily on the Commission's decision in Docket 5675, *General Foods,* in which a complaint was dismissed in April 1954, the Attorney General's Committee thought that this decision marked "the formal demise of the 'presumptive injury' rule." It thought that,

The central concept of injury has been supplemented by two others, applicable respectively to functional and territorial discriminations. In the functional discount cases injury has been seen in preclusive price differences that give an advantage to direct buyers over indirect buyers or to indirect buyers over direct buyers. A part of the injury in such cases arises from different buying prices for competitors operating at the same distributive level and is similar in character to the injury already described. Another part, however, may consist in the exclusion of certain classes of distributors from certain classes of sales, that is, in a shift in the channels of distribution. Within limits that are not wholly clear or consistent, the Commission has seen injury in such changes. Where price relationships at two or more levels of distribution have been involved in the concept of injury, the injury has arisen from the seller's failure to preserve appropriate differentials between the successive levels rather than from his failure to maintain an equality of price. Consequently, there has been an embarrassing tendency for the activities of the Commission about functional discounts to point toward the freezing of distributive channels, the maintenance of resales prices, or both.

Though the Commission's general conception of injury has been used in the territorial discrimination cases, it has been supplemented from time to time by the idea that buyers are injured when they are deprived of the natural advantages of their location. This idea had been fore-

---

realistically interpreted, the narrow concept of injury could ensure compatibility with basic antitrust standards. It said that "the courts have tended to abandon prior misinterpretations of the Act, in favor of the workable principles exemplified by the Minneapolis-Honeywell case." Recommending that "analysis of the statutory 'injury' center on the vigor of competition in the market rather than hardship to individual businessmen," it said, "we believe that criteria of competitive effect which focus exclusively on individual competitors' sales or profits rather than the health of the competitive process literally go beyond the terms of the law." (*Report of the Attorney General's National Committee*, pp. 162-65.) However, the committee thought that the law should be interpreted to prevent "deliberate price slashes for the purpose of destroying even a single competitor"; it regarded such predatory price cutting "as a practice which inevitably frustrates competition." *Ibid.*, p. 165.

Within two months after the publication of the committee's report, the Commission issued its decisions in the Niehoff, Standard Motor Products, and Moog cases, drawing inferences of injury in spite of the smallness of favored customers, the prosperity of disfavored customers, and the unanimous testimony of the latter that they were not injured. The courts subsequently sustained these decisions. The General Foods decision now appears to be, not an indication of a trend, but an exception to one.

shadowed prior to the Robinson-Patman Act by the famous Pittsburgh-plus case, in which the Commission found that United States Steel Corporation had discriminated illegally in price by establishing a delivered-price structure through which steel produced far from Pittsburgh was sold at the Pittsburgh price plus freight from Pittsburgh to the destination. The Commission had found that Middle Western fabricators, paying prices that included this phantom freight, could not compete against Eastern fabricators in Eastern markets, enjoyed no price advantage in Western markets, and had often found it impossible to expand their sales as the Western markets grew in size. A similar loss of the advantages of location was found by the Commission to have created injury in the secondary line in the United Fence case, although the findings were set forth in general terms and without explicit detail. In the case against the Clinton Company, the Commission explicitly found that the mixers of table syrup whose locations subjected them to higher prices for glucose were thus confined to a smaller market area than that which their freight advantage in shipping syrup to contiguous territory would otherwise have given them.

Although these are the only instances in which the findings concerning territorial price discrimination have made explicit reference to the advantage of location, the concept expressed in these cases underlies the other findings of injury in the secondary line in the cases concerned with pricing formulas. The reduction in profit margins that the Commission has seen as injurious in such cases has been measured in terms of the phantom freight paid. A customer located near the mill door of a seller has been found to suffer a discriminatory price increase when he buys at delivered prices equal to those quoted by a distant seller and including transportation charges from the distant seller's place of business. The amount of discrimination has been conceived as the part of the price that would not have been paid if the buyer had been granted the full advantages of his location near his source of supply. Not the absolute difference in delivered prices, but the part of the difference not accounted for by the difference in transportation cost to suppliers has been regarded as the discriminatory price differential. Thus the Commission's concept of injury in the secondary line in the cases concerned with pricing formulas has rested on the view that the buyer has a right to the advantages of location and that, when his expenses increase because this right is denied, his competitive opportunities are thereby reduced.

However, a conflicting view is equally persuasive. Sellers, like buyers, may have locations with differing advantages. It is economically desirable that sellers as well as buyers shall have incentives to locate themselves in the best places and shall derive rewards from doing so. When a seller and a buyer are adjacent to each other, it is obvious that transportation costs in transactions between them can be minimized; but the seller, like the buyer, has a persuasive claim to enjoyment of the profits derived from the proximity. It is true that if buyers could not hope for the advantages of location they would have no incentive to establish their places of business near their sources of supply. It is equally true that if sellers could not hope to enjoy these advantages they would have no incentive to establish producing establishments near consuming markets. The statement that the seller should enjoy the advantages of location is inherently as persuasive as the statement that the buyer should do so.

The Commission's concern over the buyer's loss of these advantages was appropriate in the cases in which it was expressed. In the cement, glucose, and fence industries, as well as in the steel industry at the time of the Pittsburgh-plus case, the Commission found that the discriminatory pattern had been established by conspiracy. The sellers had preempted the advantages of location by joint action that gave them dominant power. Sellers and buyers had not enjoyed an equal opportunity to bargain for these advantages; instead, the interests of one side of the market had been made to prevail. The Commission properly saw this result as a perversion of the competitive process. Though, in analyzing the cases, it used language implying that the right of buyers to the advantages of location was absolute in all circumstances, it did not issue complaints and orders in price discrimination cases based on such a view and divorced from a setting of conspiracy.

Thus, though the Commission's expression of its views was not tenable, its proceedings in this field were appropriate. The Commission's formulation of this concept of injury developed in cases of conspiracy and is properly to be interpreted as a corollary of the view that buyers as well as sellers should have an opportunity to strive for these advantages without being foreclosed from receiving them. When political controversy raised question as to how far the idea was applicable to situations other than conspiracy, the Commission gave it this interpretation. The meaning of injury to competition in the secondary line arising from territorial discrimination has been imperfectly explored; for in proceeding against discrimination by individual sellers through territorial pricing formulas, the Commission has acted only where there was a conspiracy in the background, and in proceeding against local price reductions without formula, the Commission has given little attention to injuries in the secondary line.[18] However, there appears to be no reason to believe that the right to locational advantages will be asserted by the Commission except in a conspiracy setting.

If the views of the Seventh Circuit in the Honeywell case as to the nature of injury in the secondary line had been generally adopted, the distinction between the broad and narrow concepts of injury would have been minimized. Injury to competition in the narrow sense would have been perceived only where there were market changes similar to, though perhaps smaller than, those that might demonstrate injury in the broad sense—expansion of the market share of the favored buyer and impairment of the position of his competitors as a group. Although it is conceivable that a number of favored buyers might have grown at the expense of a number of disfavored buyers, without change in the balance of competitive forces relevant to market competition, such a neat adjustment would have been improbable. In the usual case, the aggrandizement of the favored buyer would have been anticompetitive in its tendency.

The establishment of the Commission's view with the Supreme Court's approval maximized the disparity between the two standards of injury. Proof of injury in the narrow sense required only a showing that a price difference was substantial in relation to buying habits or to profit margins or that the aggregate revenue from a price difference was substantial in relation to aggregate operating revenues or aggregate profits. Under this test of injury, the only discriminations that remained lawful were discriminations between noncompeting customers and discriminations that were minimal both in the amount of the price concession and in the volume of business to which it applied. That a considerable proportion of such injuries in the narrow sense would involve no injury to competition in the broad sense was probable.

The gap between the two concepts of injury was further widened, at least in cases involving quantity and volume discounts, by another char-

[18] Such injury has been found in this type of case only in the proceeding against *E. B. Muller & Co.* (Docket 3224), where the attention was primarily on the damage to Muller's competitor. It was alleged in the cases against the *Borden Co.* and *Arkansas City Cooperative* (Dockets 6737 and 6639), but since these cases resulted in consent decrees there were no findings as to the matter.

acteristic of the new concept. This was the fact that the concept was applied to single products even where the injury pertained to a class of customers engaged in marketing a wide variety of products. The Morton Salt case supplies a clear example. The disfavored customers whose competitive opportunities were found to be injured were distributors of grocery products. Under the market concept of injury, the questions relevant to their status would have been whether any distributor was acquiring such power as to dominate the rest. Under the narrow concept, the relevant question was whether any concern enjoyed, in the purchase of salt, an advantage that had a significant effect on its resale prices, profit margins, or business income. Since salt was a relatively unimportant item in a wholesale grocer's volume of business, it would have been difficult to show that the discrimination on it jeopardized the survival or the independence or substantially affected the business income of the disfavored wholesalers. However, injury to the competitive opportunities of these wholesalers was adequately shown from the mere fact that, in reselling salt at the same price as their favored competitors, they necessarily obtained from salt small profits or none. Had the narrow concept of injury not been applied product by product, it would have been inapplicable to all of the low-volume items handled by wholesale grocers, even though, through a series of discriminations cumulative in effect, the disfavored wholesalers might have suffered a substantial aggregate disadvantage. In applying the concept of injury to one product at a time, however, the Commission and the Supreme Court perceived injury to competitive opportunity even in effects so small that, standing alone, they probably would not have significantly altered the market behavior or the gross or net revenues of the supposedly injured group.

The scope given to the new concept of injury in the Morton Salt case was explicitly justified by the Supreme Court on the ground that without it cumulative effects would go uncurbed. A question necessarily arises as to whether or not the scope of the concept of injury to a class of competitors should vary from one context to another with changes in the probability that there will be such cumulative effects. This question is peculiarly pertinent to the cases concerned with territorial price differences. In territorial discriminations advantages may not be cumulative. The advantage enjoyed as a buyer by a processor in one locality over a processor in another is the summation of the territorial price differences on the various materials and components that enter into his assembly costs.

A buying advantage on one material may be offset by a disadvantage on another. When the territorial price differences for a particular material are considered separately, any offsetting disadvantages for the favored buyer are necessarily disregarded. Competitors with equal assembly costs may be considered injured, one by a territorial disadvantage on one material, the other by an offsetting disadvantage on another material. Unlawful injury may be found in each instance, though the existence, prosperity, and independence of neither competitor is jeopardized.

In a policy statement about territorial price discrimination during the basing-point controversy, the Commission apparently was concerned about such possibilities. It explicitly said that concepts of injury developed in the quantity- and volume-discount cases should not be applied uncritically to territorial price relationships because there were peculiarities in the impact of such relationships on competing buyers. One of these peculiarities was the improbability of cumulative effect. However, in the corn products cases, the Commission analyzed the injury that candy makers incurred from differential prices on glucose without attempting to consider whether the disadvantages derived from the price differences were enhanced or offset by the price differences encountered in buying other supplies. Indeed, the Commission apparently assumed that price differences on glucose were wholly responsible for such local advantages and disadvantages as were shown by the fact that certain candy manufacturers moved to Chicago.[19]

Although the narrow concept of injury has developed in such a way that its difference from the broad concept has been maximized, the decisions of the Federal Trade Commission and most of the decisions of the courts have consistently ignored the difference between the two concepts.[20] In the statute, price discrimination becomes equally unlawful

[19] The interviews for this book indicated persuasively that the principal advantages of Chicago as a candy-making center are the availability of pool car rates for outgoing shipments of candy and the cheapness of cane sugar obtained by water shipments. The advantages in the price of glucose are real but apparently less important.

[20] In one case, *Victor N. Alexander* v. *The Texas Co.*, 149 F. Supp. 37, decided in 1957, a court distinguished sharply between the concepts of injury. It said "that statute prohibits price discrimination only where it has produced one or more of the three anticompetitive consequences it is intended to prevent. The effect of the alleged discrimination must be (1) substantially to lessen competition or (2) tend to create a monopoly, or (3) to injure, destroy, or prevent competition, among sellers, buyers or their customers . . . it is perfectly clear that the results

whether it results in the broad injury or the narrow injury. The same defenses are applicable to discriminations producing either kind of injury, and the same remedial powers are available if a violation of law is found. There is, therefore, no incentive for the Commission to distinguish sharply between the two kinds of injury nor for the respondents to insist on such a distinction. Whatever type of injury can be most conveniently proved is likely to become the basis of the Commission's case. Since a showing of injury to a class of competitors is usually easier than a showing of injury to competition in the market, efficiency and economy in law enforcement suggest emphasis on the narrow concept rather than the broad one.

Moreover, the lack of a legal distinction between the two types of injury has encouraged the Commission and the courts to fail to distinguish clearly between them and at times to use the two concepts interchangeably without reference to their differing significance. In 1957, the chairman of the Commission told a Senate committee that although lessening competition or tending to create a monopoly involved different competitive effects from injury to competition with the beneficiary of a discrimination, ". . . the decisions of the Commission and the courts have not spelled out the dividing line between them, in fact, we can almost conclude that each shades into the other to such an extent that such a line cannot for practical purposes be drawn."[21] Confusion between the two concepts is promoted by the fact that injury must be demonstrated, not by abstract reasoning, but by testimony or other evidence

---

of the defendant's alleged price discrimination did not fall within the first or second of these categories. This Court judicially notices, and the record shows, that plaintiff was merely one of 19 Texaco dealers in the Shreveport-Bossier City area between August 12, and November 18, 1955. At that time there also were more than 200 other gasoline service stations, handling many competitive brands of petroleum products, in the area. Whatever consequences the alleged price discrimination may have had upon plaintiff's business would have been almost infinitesimal in their effect upon the over-all service station business of the area; and any such small-scale discrimination could not (1) have substantially lessened competition in interstate commerce or (2) have tended to create a monopoly of such commerce in the area, within the meaning of the statute. It is possible, although not shown by the complaint, that defendant's alleged price discrimination may have come within the third category by injuring, destroying or preventing competition between plaintiff and the 12 dealers who are said to have been given cheaper prices. Plaintiff has not alleged that this was so."

[21] *To Amend Section 2 of the Clayton Act,* Hearings before the Senate Committee on the Judiciary, 84 Cong. 2 sess. (1956), p. 635.

capable of being submitted in a judicial proceeding. In a communication to the Congress during the basing-point controversy,[22] the Commission said:

> In most circumstances there is a difference between protecting individual competitors against injury from price discrimination and protecting competition against injury by price discriminations. . . . As a practical matter, the question of injury to competition is examined by ascertaining what effect, if any, the seller's discriminations in price have upon his competitors in competing with him, or have among his customers and their customers in competing among themselves and with others. . . .

The Commission has frequently found, in general terms, that a class of intermediate distributors was injured and then drawn the conclusion that the discrimination involved both the narrow and the broad type of injury, without stating any reason for believing that the damage to a class of competitors also constituted damage to competition in the market.

Though, in the absence of a distinction in legal meaning, the blending of the two concepts is understandable, it has had the effect of making the Commission's findings insufficient to show the relation between market competition and the price discriminations found. On the one hand, where the Commission has found only the narrow type of injury, there is no certainty that the broad type of injury could not also have been found if it had been worth looking for. On the other hand, in widening the interpretation of injury to a class of competitors, the Commission has, by analogy or by sloppiness, also widened the interpretation of injury to market competition, to the point where the latter concept, as now used by the Commission, has no clear meaning.

The most difficult and controversial question of policy raised by the Robinson-Patman Act is to what extent and under what safeguards the law should seek to assure equality in the competitive position of buyers. This question can be adequately discussed, however, only after considering not only the problems associated with the narrow concept of injury but also those that arise as to the right to meet competition and as to cost justification. Further consideration of it will be deferred, therefore, to the final chapter of this book.

[22] Senate Committee on Interstate and Foreign Commerce, *Study of Federal Trade Commission Views on Freight Absorption.* Committee Print. 81 Cong. 2 sess. (1950), pp. 9, 12.

A significant weakness of the concept of injury to competition, as it is set forth in the statute and has been applied in the cases, lies in the fact that any of the various types of injury to competition (in the absence of justification on such grounds as cost or meeting competition in good faith) conclusively establishes the illegality of a discrimination regardless of the collateral effects that may be associated therewith. Thus a discrimination may be unlawful because of injury to competition among sellers, among buyers, or among the buyer's customers, and because of either the narrow or the broad type of injury. The previous discussion of the meaning of injury in these various respects has raised question whether the full force of the law should be used against all of the relationships that have been held to be injurious. This question has to do with the propriety of the standard of injury at each of the points at which that standard is applied.

There is, however, a second relevant problem that has to do with the possibility of offsetting effects at different points. The significant question here is whether price discrimination ever tends to increase competition in the primary line or, stated conversely, whether the prevention of price discrimination ever tends to diminish such competition. It is widely believed that in certain oligopolistic industries, in which price competition is not keen and price movements are often sluggish, the tendency to maintain uniform and unvarying prices is reduced by discriminatory concessions. Some member of the industry seeks to get or hold business that he regards as attractive by quoting special prices, though he would be unwilling to make a general price reduction. His initial action is followed by defensive and retaliatory concessions by other members of the industry and by broader concessions to affected customers who were not beneficiaries of the original grant. In the struggle a new level of price may be established by sellers who were originally unwilling to contemplate it. Through discrimination they may find themselves backing into degrees of competition to which none of them would advance face forward. Where such a relationship prevails, the elimination of discriminatory pricing may be regarded by sellers as a contribution to the maintenance of a stable price level and should be regarded by the observer as a step toward the reduction of competition in the primary line. Patterns of this kind are unlikely except in industries in which price competition is initially weak.

However, in another way the vigorous application of the law against price discrimination may have broader effects in reducing competition in the primary line. A seller subject to a public policy that condemns injurious discrimination incurs legal risks when he establishes price differences. Although these differences are lawful when they are not injurious, when they are cost-justified, or when they are made in good faith to meet a competitor's prices, a seller cannot readily and infallibly know whether or not each given differential will work injury, whether or not it can be cost-justified, and whether or not the good faith of his action will be accepted by those who enforce the law. The fewer and narrower his price differences, the safer he is likely to be. Consequently, the law of price discrimination affords sellers an incentive to refrain from experiment with price differentials even when those differentials are not clearly unlawful or when they are probably lawful. All forms of competitive price adjustment other than uniform changes of price to all customers are thereby discouraged. The effect is likely to be some reduction of competitive incentive and of the intensity of competition on the seller's side of the market.

Where either or both of these influences are significant, it is quite possible that the effects of price discrimination will differ in the primary and secondary lines. Discriminations that contribute to competition in the primary line may injure it in the secondary line. In removing such injuries in the secondary line, the law-enforcement agency may also diminish the incentives to compete and the scope of competitive experiment in the primary lines. Certain critics of the law of price discrimination have described it as encouraging soft competition and have contrasted it with a policy of hard competition, which they assert would prevail if the standards of competitive injury were relaxed. These criticisms have seldom been clear; but, in general, the emphasis of the critics appears to have centered on effects in the primary line similar to those discussed above and to have given little or no attention to effects in the secondary line. If this interpretation of their views is correct, their contrast between soft and hard competition is neither accurate nor adequate. The significant point that underlies the criticism is the possibility that injuries to competition found to exist in the secondary line may coincide with benefits to competition in the primary line and that the correctives of the one may be detrimental to the other.

Under present legal standards, a discrimination that injures competition in either the broad or the narrow sense on either side of the market is unlawful regardless of its other effects. The law does not provide for an evaluation of the different effects the discrimination may produce at different points. Thus it is theoretically possible to condemn a discrimination that injures a limited class of disfavored buyers even though the removal of that discrimination would intensify the avoidance of price competition that characterizes an oligopolistic selling group. The law applies as fully in such cases as in other cases in which a discrimination injurious to competition among buyers has no effect on competition among sellers or has an adverse effect on that competition.

The importance of the law's failure to provide for an evaluation of the relative significance of the effects on competition at different levels is enhanced by the fact that the statute is not concerned only with broad types of injury. The extension of the concept of injury to cover effects on classes of sellers or buyers, even where these effects have no significant impact on market competition, gives the law a more pervasive significance. Where there are price differences to competing buyers, a statutory injury is likely to be found. Thus the possibility of conflicting effects in the primary and secondary lines is substantially enhanced.

It is noteworthy that, as a by-product of the controversy over the defense of meeting competition in good faith, legislative proposals have been made that might establish a sharp legal distinction between the narrow and the broad concepts of injury. Under the sponsorship of Congressman Patman and Senator Kefauver, bills, H. R. 11 and S. 11, have been offered for the purpose of modifying the Supreme Court's decision that good faith in meeting the equally low price of a competitor is a complete defense to any charge of price discrimination.[23] These bills provide that the defense shall not be adequate where the effect may be to substantially lessen competition or tend to create a monopoly. If such a bill were enacted, it might reasonably be interpreted to mean what it seems to say—that good faith in meeting a competitor's prices would continue to be a complete defense in cases involving only the narrow type of injury but not in cases involving the broad type of injury.[24] Such a distinction would emphasize the importance of findings in which one type of injury

[23] See below, pp. 571-73.

[24] In view of the long period during which the Commission and the courts have used the two concepts interchangeably, it is conceivable that if the bill becomes law it might be interpreted, in spite of its language, (1) to leave meeting competition still a complete defense against injuries of the broad type because the defense continued to be available for injuries of the narrow type; or conversely, (2) to make meeting competition less than a complete defense for the narrow type of injury because it was no longer a complete defense for the broad type of injury.

or the other was set forth and would evoke challenges if the Commission found the broad type of injury without showing the basis for the finding. The Commission would have an incentive to show injury to competition in the market sense where such a showing could be made. Respondents would have an incentive to challenge insufficiency of evidence or looseness of inference on the Commission's part if there was an effort to infer market consequences from evidence that pertained merely to injury to a competitive group. Thus it is reasonable to believe that, if a bill of this kind were to become law and were to be interpreted in this way, findings as to injury would soon become more explicit and distinctions between the broad and narrow concepts would be more carefully made. Whatever the appropriate policy toward the defense of meeting competition in good faith, this result would contribute to a desirable perspective in considering the injury resulting from discrimination. However, nothing in H. R. 11 or S. 11 would authorize the Commission and the courts to take offsetting effects into consideration where the results of a discrimination in the primary line differ from those in the secondary line.

17 / *Meeting Competition as a Defense*

AS ENACTED IN 1914, the price-discrimination section of the Clayton Act provided "that nothing herein contained shall prevent . . . discrimination in price in the same or different communities made in good faith to meet competition." Thus meeting competition was established as a complete defense to a charge of price discrimination regardless of the other circumstances of the case.

In the Robinson-Patman Act, reference to meeting competition in good faith was omitted from Section 2(a), in which the offense of discriminating in price is defined. In the procedural Section 2(b) appeared the provision "that nothing herein contained shall prevent a seller rebutting the prima-facie case thus made by showing that his lower price or the furnishing of services or facilities to any purchaser or purchasers was made in good faith to meet an equally low price of a competitor or the services or facilities furnished by a competitor." That the change in language was intended to reduce the significance of the defense of meeting competition has been shown in the discussion of the legislative history of the act in Chapter 2.

Under the language of the Robinson-Patman Act it is clear that the burden of introducing the question of meeting competition into a price-discrimination case and of submitting evidence pertaining thereto is placed on the respondent seller. In the light of the Supreme Court's decision in the Automatic Canteen case, it is possible, however, that when the Commission proceeds against a respondent buyer under Section 2(f), the Commission carries the burden of showing that the discriminatory advantage obtained by the buyer was not offered by the seller to meet competition in good faith.[1]

Apart from the questions as to the burden of proof, the amendment of

---

[1] See above, pp. 506-08; 511-15, especially footnote 33.

the statute raised major problems of interpretation concerning the legal
status of a discrimination if meeting competition in good faith is adequately shown. The controversy as to the meaning of the statute developed slowly because, prior to the case against Standard Oil Company
of Indiana, there was only one case in which the Federal Trade Commission dismissed a complaint because it found that the seller had met
competition in good faith, and in this case it found also that the discrimination was not injurious to competition. However, in the proceeding against Standard of Indiana, the Commission expressed the view
that, although the fact that competition has been met in good faith is
relevant where the probability of future injury to competition is at issue,
a showing that competition has already been damaged removes the need
to consider whether or not the seller met competition.[2] In argument before the Supreme Court, attorneys for the government expressed the
somewhat different view that the statute authorizes the Commission to
evaluate the impact of the discrimination in the light of facts as to meeting competition, and thus, in effect, to apply a rule of reason in distin-
guishing degrees of competitive injury. The Court, however, held 5 to 3
that meeting competition in good faith is a complete defense.[3] Though
this decision has produced efforts to establish a different principle by
amendment of the law, thus far they have been unsuccessful. A showing
that the seller met the equally low price of a competitor in good faith
terminates a case as conclusively as a successful cost defense.

Like the cost defense, the defense of meeting competition is relevant
to only part of the Robinson-Patman Act. Payment of unlawful brokerage contrary to the provisions of Section 2(c) is a violation of law whether
or not competition is met by the enterprise that engages in the practice.
The defense of meeting competition also appears to be irrelevant to disproportionate payment for sales service contrary to the provisions of
Section 2(d). Meeting competition is clearly relevant in cases involving
price discrimination under Sections 2(a) and 2(f) and presumably relevant in cases involving the provision of sales services under Section 2(e).[4]

[2] See above, pp. 319-20.
[3] See above, pp. 321-22.
[4] No proceeding has yet turned on such a defense by a seller charged with
violating Sec. 2(e); in the Arden case, however, the defense was offered and rejected as inconsistent with the facts. There appears to be little doubt that a showing that competition had been met in good faith would be a complete defense
under this section. The authorization for the presentation of the defense contained
in Sec. 2(b) applies to discrimination in price or services or facilities furnished

In practice, the defense of meeting competition has been offered in only one of the few proceedings in which the Commission has alleged a violation of Section 2(e); and in this case the claim that competition had been met in good faith was found to be untrue. The defense has not been offered in any of the cases concerned with alleged violations of Section 2(f). Except for the Arden case the relevance of meeting competition to the statute has been explored only in proceedings concerned with price discriminations by sellers.

A defense that competition had been met in good faith has been evaluated by the Commission in only twenty-one cases—twenty that resulted in orders to cease discriminating and one that was dismissed by the Commission.[5] In some cases, for example those against Standard Brands, Minneapolis-Honeywell and Champion, the defense was offered for only part of the discrimination. In such instances, even if the Commission accepted the sellers' contentions that some of the price conces-

---

and explicitly permits a showing that the furnishing of services or facilities to any purchaser was made in good faith to meet the services or facilities furnished by a competitor. The language of Sec. 2(e) makes it unlawful to discriminate in favor of a purchaser by furnishing services or facilities "upon terms not accorded to all purchasers on proportionately equal terms." Thus disproportionate provision of services or facilities is characterized in Sec. 2(e) as a discrimination, and the defense of meeting competition is explicitly made pertinent to such a discrimination in Sec. 2(b).

In this respect there is a sharp verbal distinction between the provision concerning the furnishing of sales services by the seller and that concerning the seller's payment for sales services provided by the buyer. Though disproportionate payments are forbidden in Sec. 2(d) in language loosely analogous to that of Sec. 2(e), Sec. 2(d) does not describe such payments as discriminations, and Sec. 2(b) does not explicitly authorize a showing of good faith in meeting competition to justify such payments. If the statute is interpreted literally, the defense of meeting competition is applicable to disproportionate services, not to disproportionate payments for services. However, in view of the parallel character of Secs. 2(d) and 2(e), it is possible that the courts, relying on the explicit language pertaining to Sec. 2(e), might interpret Sec. 2(d) as authorizing a similar showing that competition has been met in good faith.

[5] In 1957, Commissioner Gwynne summarized the Commission's experience with the defense of meeting competition: Since the Standard Oil Decision in 1951 the defense had been offered in 29 cases, of which 12 were still pending. Seven of the other 17 cases had been dismissed—6 because injury was not proved and 1 for failure of proof, on motion by the attorney for the Commission. The 10 remaining cases had resulted in orders to cease and desist, twice because respondents decided not to contest the case, and 8 times because the defense of meeting competition was rejected. See *To Amend Section 2 of the Clayton Act,* Hearings before the Senate Committee on the Judiciary, 85 Cong. 1 sess. (1957), Pt. 1, p. 636.

sions had been made to meet competitors' prices, it found lack of good faith as to a considerable portion of the concessions against which the proceeding was directed. Only in the Staley and Standard of Indiana cases was the rejection of the meeting competition defense given substantial consideration on appeal. In the Staley case the decisions on appeal turned on the question whether Staley's good faith could be established. In the case against Standard of Indiana, which reached the Supreme Court twice, the first decision was concerned with the legal adequacy of meeting competition as a defense, and the second with the merits of the effort of the company to show that it met competition in good faith. The defense was also considered on appeal in a compliance case against Standard Brands, and briefly considered on appeal in the Niehoff and Edelmann cases.[6] Meeting competition is now established as a complete defense, but the circumstances under which that defense is available to sellers can be ascertained only from 21 decisions by the Commission, 5 decisions by the courts in cases instituted by the Commission, and 1 or 2 court decisions in private proceedings.

Limitations Applicable to the Defense

The Commission's decisions in the cases involving Standard Brands and Minneapolis-Honeywell demonstrate that the defense of meeting competition is not adequate unless it is comprehensive. A seller cannot adequately show that he met competition in good faith by showing that in some instances his price concessions were made after and in response to concessions in equal or greater amounts by competitors. The Commission found that there had been concessions not responsive to the action of competitors and that the entire body of discriminatory prices could not be explained as mere defensive retaliation. In the Commission's view, a

[6] In the Edelmann case the Seventh Circuit merely remarked that Edelmann did not meet the different prices of its two principal competitors nor those of any other competitors and that Edelmann's discount system was not the same as that of the two principal competitors. Therefore, it held, Edelmann had not shown that competition had been met in good faith. In the Niehoff case the court summarized the Commission's relevant findings to the effect that Niehoff's prices reflected a nation-wide pricing system formulated to meet competition generally rather than to meet any particular competitor's prices and that Niehoff did not deviate from these prices. It then said that there was substantial evidence to support the Commission's denial that Niehoff had met the equally low prices of competitors in good faith.

discrimination can be justified as meeting competition only when the low prices of competitors are available to all who benefit from the discrimination.

Moreover, in the Commission's opinion, many circumstances are relevant to the good faith of the seller, and in consequence the presence or absence of good faith is far from self-evident. In the cases in which allegations of good faith have been examined, the Commission has denied the seller's good faith on a wide variety of grounds; and in the few cases in which the denial has been reviewed on appeal, only a few of these grounds have been considered. Thus the legal meaning of meeting competition in good faith remains only partially explored, and if meeting competition continues to be a valid defense, a considerable period of further litigation is to be expected before the limits of the defense become clear.[7]

In 1957, in testimony before a Senate committee, the chairman of the Federal Trade Commission said that the following propositions as to the defense of meeting competition had become "reasonably well-established."[8]

(1) The defense covers only situations where the prima facie proof of a discrimination as defined in 2(a) has already been met . . .

(2) The defense is an affirmative one and the burden of establishing it is upon the person claiming it . . .

(3) The defense is good only where the reduction in price is to meet the lower price of a competitor. It cannot be used to justify a price below that of a competitor. The defense does not permit predatory price reductions to destroy an individual competitor or the competition in a limited area . . .

(4) The defense is good only in meeting individual competitive situations. It cannot be used to justify discriminatory pricing systems based on some vague theory of meeting competition generally . . .

(5) The defense can be used only in defensive situations, that is, to retain a customer and not to gain a new one. While there is an

[7] The Attorney General's National Committee to Study the Antitrust Laws said in 1955: ". . . serious problems of statutory interpretation today confront tribunals —in government proceedings or private damage suits—adjudicating the legality of a seller's prices in the light of his 'meeting competition' defense. Difficulties cluster around the following complex issues: meeting a competitor's *unlawful* prices; *sporadic* or *regular* competitive differentials; exact *dollar-for-dollar meeting* or *undercutting* and *stopping short* of a rival's price; reductions to *retain old* or to *compete for new* business; the content of the *'good faith'* concept in the proviso." See *Report of the Attorney General's National Committee to Study the Antitrust Laws* (March 31, 1955), pp. 180-81.

[8] *To Amend Section 2 of the Clayton Act*, Hearings (1957), Pt. 1, pp. 631-34.

area of disagreement surrounding this premise, I believe that careful examination of the statutory intent plus adjudication will bear this out . . .

(6) The competitor's price which the respondent was meeting must be a lawful price—or at least the seller as a reasonable and prudent man must believe it to be lawful. Here there is a real area of disagreement, with cases pointing in two directions . . .

(7) The defense is good only when the lower price is given in good faith to attain the limited objective prescribed by law. The defense does not permit predatory price reductions to destroy an individual competitor or the competition in a limited area. . . .

Since this summary was limited to points that are regarded as reasonably well-established, it does not fully indicate the limitations and risks that bear on the defense of meeting competition. An effort is made below to analyze these. The complexity of the problem may be indicated by a summary of the various limitations inherent in the concept of good faith and of the various defects the Commission has perceived in the defenses thus far presented to it. Where court opinions have modified or extended the Commission's conclusions, their effect will also be summarized.

Good Faith and Purpose

Good faith is precluded in any case in which the seller's discriminations were incidental to an attempt to eliminate competition in violation of the antitrust laws. Thus the defense of meeting competition is unavailable for price discriminations that are part of a price-fixing conspiracy and for discriminations that are employed by sellers in an attempt to establish or maintain a monopoly. The Commission's findings of conspiracy in the cement case and its findings as to attempted monopolization in the chicory case led automatically to denial of the good faith of respondents. In the Staley case the dissenting opinion in the circuit court was based in part on the conclusion that Staley's purpose in discriminating in price was to avoid introducing competition into a noncompetitive price structure. The denial of Staley's good faith by the Supreme Court was couched in language suggesting that the court was impressed by a lack of competition between Staley and other producers, even though no conspiracy was formally alleged. Thus the court said that Staley had adopted the prices of its Chicago competitors, had maintained its prices at many delivery points at the level of competitor's high prices, and had never attempted to establish its own nondiscriminatory price system but had "slavishly followed in the first instance" the discriminatory prices of competitors. It concluded that Staley's purpose had been to establish outside Chicago the artificially high prices the discriminatory effect of which permeated Staley's entire pricing system.

That the seller's purpose must be defensive rather than aggressive is also necessary to proof of the seller's good faith. This limitation has been thought to be inherent in the language of the statute, which authorizes only a showing that the seller's lower price was made to meet an equally low price of a competitor. Initiative in reducing prices is thus expressly excluded from the scope of the defense. However, even when price reductions by competitors have preceded those by the respondent, the Commission may find in the respondent's conduct reason to attribute aggressive purposes to him and therefore to deny his good faith. In the Standard Motor Products case, the discriminations were held to be aggressive because, in giving them to buying groups some of whose members had been its customers, Standard obtained business not only from these customers but also from other members of the groups. The good faith of Anheuser-Busch in reducing the price of beer in St. Louis was denied, even though the company merely brought its price down to the level of other sellers, because its percentage of the St. Louis market had not been falling and because the purpose was to increase its local volume of business by selling without the customary premium. In the case against Standard of Indiana, in the modified findings of fact adopted by the majority of the Commission after the first Supreme Court decision (but subsequently set aside on appeal), the difference in prestige between Standard's gasoline and off-brand gasoline was mentioned as one of the reasons for denying Standard's good faith in meeting price offers by sellers of off-brand gasoline. The Commission said:

> In the Detroit metropolitan area, as elsewhere, off-brand or local-brand gasoline sells at lower prices than major brands, and distributors of off-brand gasoline find it necessary to undersell major brands in order to secure some share of the market. . . . Respondent has at all times been familiar with these competitive factors in the distribution of gasoline and could not have regarded the offer of Red Indian Oil Company to sell its Fleet Wing gasoline at 1½ cents per gallon lower price as a serious competitive threat.[9]

[9] 49 FTC 952. Since the circuit court thought that Standard had met competition in good faith, it must have rejected this reasoning, though its opinion was focused on other aspects of the issue of good faith.

Similarly, in the Standard Brands case, the Commission's findings recognized that in some instances Standard quoted off-scale prices "where there was keen competition and where prices lower than their scale were reported by customers to have been offered by competitors," but, nevertheless, denied the good faith of the price reductions. The denial was based in good part on the argument: "It was not shown that the price situations in which respondents found themselves were not of their own making. Respondents by reason of their service and goodwill were able to secure more for their yeast than could most of their competitors. . . ."[10] Subsequently, in the compliance proceeding against Standard Brands, the Commission's report on violations of its order gave weight to the fact that for several years Standard had consistently sold bakers' yeast at prices higher than most of its competitors and that, during a part of this period, its volume of sales had increased both absolutely and in percentage of total sales. The Commission found that in revising prices downward Standard had established new prices below its competitors in various instances, but the Commission's decision to reject the defense of meeting competition as to the entire structure of prices that followed the price reduction, rather than merely as to the portion of the structure that fell below competitors' prices, was apparently based on the finding as to Standard's customary prestige differential.[11]

In these cases the findings as to the significance of price differentials based on prestige were commingled with others pertinent to other circumstances. No case has yet been decided in which the problem of the prestige differential stands alone and is controlling.[12] Nevertheless, the

---

[10] 30 FTC 1136.

[11] See above, pp. 261-67.

[12] The Attorney General's National Committee to Study the Antitrust Laws favored the recognition of prestige differentials as consistent with meeting competition. "An inflexible cent-for-cent rule would enable a seller of the preferred commodity in fact to undercut the price for a less desirable product, or conversely, deprive the seller of a less popular product of the full benefit of the 'meeting competition' defense. We therefore urge a flexible rule which regards the nominal price of the rival product as only a presumptive boundary of a seller's permissible price reduction under the 'meeting competition' proviso, adjustable up or down upon satisfactory proof by the person questioning its reliability. In practical operation, such a test in some circumstances necessarily must permit a seller of a less accepted brand to cut substantially below the more popular product's price. Conversely, as the Commission has readily recognized, the seller of the premium commodity sometimes must not go down to the price level of the lesser product. In each case, the heart of the matter is whether actual competition, not merely a nominal price quotation, is equalized." See Report of the Attorney General's Committee, p. 184.

Commission's view appears to be that where a seller's product customarily commands a higher price, price reductions by the seller that diminish or destroy the customary differential are not in good faith, even though they merely meet a competitor's lower prices.

The good faith of a seller has also been denied on the ground that his purpose was not to meet a competitor's prices but rather to control a customer's resale-price policies. In the Minneapolis-Honeywell case the Commission rejected the claim that the price concessions of the company to two customers had been made in good faith to meet competition because the purpose in each instance was to eliminate a premium from the customer's resale price. Williams Oil-o-Matic and Cleveland Steel Products Company charged, respectively, $7.50 and $5 more for oil burners that they equipped with Honeywell controls than for burners equipped with controls furnished by other manufacturers. Minneapolis-Honeywell reduced its prices on the controls sold to these companies, the Commission found, in order to induce the companies to eliminate these surcharges. The Commission held that the reductions did not fall within the limits of good faith.[13]

In view of the fact that the decision of the Supreme Court as to the meaning of good faith in the Standard of Indiana case was rendered by a vote of five to four, the views of the minority of the court as to the significance of the purposes and attitudes of the respondents must be regarded as having potential importance. It is noteworthy that the minority of the court offered as a reason for its denial of Standard's good faith its belief that Standard had used an arbitrary and deceptive customer classification as a cloak for a price concession to large retailers. If in future cases this view should prevail, the candor of the seller's pricing practices would be significant in determining the legality of his discriminations.

Good Faith and the Scope of Discrimination

The good faith of a seller in meeting competition is appraised not only by considering his purposes and attitudes but also in the light of the scope of the discrimination adopted by him. In the Staley case, the

[13] Though the circuit court reversed the Commission's decision, it did so on the ground that the discriminations were not injurious to competition. It did not discuss the Commission's treatment of the defense of meeting competition. Certiorari was denied by the Supreme Court on procedural grounds.

Supreme Court focused its rejection of the defense of meeting competition on the finding that the discriminations of the company were incorporated in a general formula and did not constitute departures from a nondiscriminatory pricing system for the sake of meeting specific competitive situations. The court said:

> But Section 2(b) does not concern itself with pricing systems or even with all the seller's discriminatory prices to buyers. It speaks only of the seller's "lower" price. . . . The Act thus places emphasis on individual competitive situations rather than upon a general system of competition. . . . This test presupposes that the person charged with violating the Act would, by his normal, non-discriminatory pricing methods, have reached a price so high that he could reduce it in order to meet the competitor's equally low price.[14]

In the cement case the Supreme Court characterized the Staley case as holding "that a seller could not justify the adoption of a seller's basing-point pricing system under Section 2(b) as a good faith attempt to meet the latter's equally low price." It held that the proviso as to meeting competition in good faith does not permit a seller "to use a sales system which constantly results in his getting more money for like goods from some customers than he does from others." It concluded that the multiple basing-point system in cement was used by the respondents "as a practice rather than as a good-faith effort to meet 'individual competitive situations' " and, therefore, that the act was violated.[15]

This exclusion of pricing systems from the scope of the defense was reaffirmed in the case against Standard of Indiana. The Commission rejected the assertions of good faith by that company partly on the ground that the discriminations constituted a pricing system. The circuit court did not dispute the Commission's view that good faith could not cover an established method of pricing but held that the record affirmatively demonstrated that Standard of Indiana had made particular price concessions. In accepting this conclusion as to the facts, the Supreme Court explicitly noted that both parties before it acknowledged that discrimination pursuant to a pricing system would preclude a finding of good faith.[16]

[14] 68 S. Ct. 971, 975.
[15] 68 S. Ct. 793, 815.
[16] The Attorney General's Committee thought that, although the defense of meeting competition "should not permit collusive price-matching among sellers," the decision in the Staley case should not be interpreted as limiting good faith

Although it is clear that the law distinguishes between individual competitive situations and pricing systems, the scope of an individual competitive situation is far from clear. There was disagreement as to whether or not the concept of a pricing system fitted the facts of the Standard Oil case, with a majority of the Commission saying yes, the circuit court saying no, and a majority of the Supreme Court accepting the conclusion of the circuit court. In the Staley case the circuit court held that Staley could meet the price of Corn Products Refining Company in Chicago, where a majority of its business was done. In denying the legality of Staley's pricing practices, the Supreme Court qualified its condemnation by the statement: "It does not follow that respondent may never absorb freight when their factory price plus actual freight is higher than their competitor's price." In the light of the lower court opinion, this comment may plausibly be interpreted to mean that Staley might lawfully continue to absorb freight in its sales in Chicago for the purpose of meeting the competition of its Chicago competitor, even though freight absorption on such sales was continuous and a substantial share of Staley's business was involved.[17] Such an interpretation is supported by the decision of a federal court in the Balian case, a private triple-damage suit.[18] Arden Farms was accused of making discriminatory price reductions in Los Angeles. The court sustained the defense that Arden Farms had met competition in good faith and held that this defense was applicable not only to price reductions to individual customers but also to general price reductions in specified localities.

Between a price reduction to a customer in a single sale and the unvarying use of a market-wide pricing system lie many intermediate possibilities as to the duration of price reductions, the multiplicity of their

---

to sporadic price reductions. "A workable defense must authorize a seller to cope with competitive pressures so long as they exist, regardless of the frequency of the price reductions that competitive circumstances warrant." See *Report of the Attorney General's Committee,* p. 182.

[17] Since Staley's absorption of freight to meet the price of Corn Products Refining in Chicago would have given Staley a mill realization in Decatur lower than the mill realization of its Chicago competitor, the implication is that the Court did not think that the limitation to "the equally low price of a competitor" forbade this kind of price reduction. Concern has been expressed, however, lest such meeting of competition be prevented unless prices are conceived as delivered prices rather than mill prices. See *ibid.,* p. 183.

[18] *Balian Ice Cream Co.* v. *Arden Farms Co.,* 94 F. Supp. 796, 231 F. 2d 356. See above, pp. 459-61.

use, and the scope of each. Neither decisions of the Commission nor opinions of the court are available to trace the boundary line of good faith amid such situations. In answering questions from congressional committees, the Commission has indicated that it does not see inevitable illegality in a persistent concession that recognizes a persistently low competitive price or in the making of concessions in accord with a consistent principle.[19] Beyond the flickering light cast by this statement lies a shadow land of unexplored possibilities.

Question has also been raised as to whether the defense of meeting competition is valid where it might be reciprocally used by several competitors. In the case against Standard of Indiana the majority of the Commission thought it important that the respondent knew "that its standard for granting tank-car prices on its gasoline was in all substantial respects the same as the standards used by its major competitors." Since these standards antedated the Robinson-Patman Act, the Commission feared that the competitors might also defend their discriminations as justified by good faith in meeting those of Standard of Indiana. The Commission denied that the defense of meeting competition could be so used as "a means of effectively insulating any particular pricing pattern from attack." The court of appeals explicitly rejected this argument, seeing no reason why one seller should be deprived of the defense because some other might also invoke its protection. In reviewing the case, the Supreme Court held that the Commission had provided no adequate basis for its assertion that the various suppliers of gasoline were using a common pricing system and might reciprocally invoke the same defense, and therefore did not discuss the legal effect of such a showing.

Though the problem of reciprocal justification was not explicitly raised in the basing-point cases, the opinions of the Supreme Court in these cases justify doubt that the view of the circuit court in the case against Standard of Indiana may be regarded as a definitive statement of the law. The emphasis on individual competitive situations as distinguished from pricing practices in both the Staley case and the cement case implies that a defense of meeting competition would be greeted skeptically by the

---

[19] See, for example, an answer to question 34 submitted to Commissioner Ewin L. Davis by a subcommittee of the Senate Committee on Interstate and Foreign Commerce, in *Competitive Absorption of Transportation Costs,* Hearings before the Senate Committee on Interstate and Foreign Commerce, 81 Cong. 1 sess. (1949), p. 274.

Supreme Court in a situation in which competitive relationships were so orderly and price differences so sustained that reciprocal claims of meeting competition could be made. Indeed, the danger that such reciprocal claims might be used to cloak conspiracy appears to have been central in the thinking of the court about the matter.

Good Faith and Prior History

The prior history of a discriminatory price is also thought by the Federal Trade Commission to be relevant to the defense of meeting competition. The problem most frequently raised has to do with discriminations that were in effect at the time the Robinson-Patman Act became law and have not been subsequently changed. In the Champion Spark Plug Company case, one ground for the rejection of the defense was the finding that the company was using the same methods of sale and types of discount structure as before the passage of the Robinson-Patman Act. In the International Salt Company case, the Commission admitted that the company had altered the amounts of its discounts to conform to those of its competitors but, nevertheless, denied the good faith of the discounts because the practice of the company in granting volume discounts of a generally similar type antedated the Robinson-Patman Act. In the case against Standard of Indiana, the majority of the Commission held that the respondent had the duty of reviewing its pricing policy on the effective date of the Robinson-Patman Act in order to take such action as might be necessary to bring the policy into conformity with the new statute. The failure of the company to do this or attempt to do it was held to be inconsistent with good faith. On appeal, the circuit court decided that, since the Robinson-Patman Act preserved the defense of meeting competition, a concern whose discriminations could be justified on this ground had no duty to withdraw or revise them because of the act. The Supreme Court did not directly decide this controverted issue. The majority opinion declared that the crucial question was why the price reductions were continued after the effective date of the new law, and found a satisfactory answer in the price offers of competitors subsequent to that date. However, in the Staley case, the Supreme Court had found that the company's lack of good faith was evident in its adoption of the basing-point system employed by its competitors without any prior effort to devise an alternative system.

Though an automatic revision of prices on the effective date of the Robinson-Patman Act may not be mandatory, this decision indicates that the mere duration and general use of a pricing practice is insufficient to demonstrate the good faith of the user. Indeed, in the Moog Industries, Whitaker Cable, and Standard Motor Products cases, the fact that the discriminations were of long standing was cited as evidence that they were systematic and hence unlawful. Many questions remain to be answered as to the conditions under which time and changing circumstances may invalidate the good faith of price concessions that once were defensible.

In the proceeding against International Salt Company, the Commission adopted a test of good faith more severe than any of those yet discussed. It held that the good faith of the company was disproved by the fact that during the eight years following the Commission's complaint, the company had not attempted to eliminate or lessen the amount of discrimination, in spite of the fact that the complaint had brought to its attention "the illegal nature of this discount." Since the case was not appealed, this conclusion was not reviewed by the courts. Its necessary effect, if applied as a general standard, would be to deny good faith in all circumstances to which the defense of meeting competition is relevant; for the defense can be offered only after the Commission has complained that a discrimination is unlawful, and if the very fact of this complaint can be cited to show the bad faith of any respondent who does not change his practices, bad faith will be found in every case in which a respondent contests the proceeding by relying on the claim that he met competition in good faith.

Good Faith and the Level of the Price

Bad faith has also been perceived where the discriminatory low price was lower than the prices of competitors. In the Champion Spark Plug Company case, the Commission rejected the defense that competition had been met in a price concession to Atlas on the ground that, after the concession, the price of Champion Company was below that of A. C. Spark Plug, the only other supplier from which Atlas Supply Company had bought. This conclusion was inevitable in view of the fact that the statute explicitly limits the defense to cases in which the "equally low price" of a competitor is met. But to use the defense of meeting competition, a seller must not only avoid quoting a price lower than that of his competitor, but must also be careful not to apply the low price of the competitor to a range of transactions broader than those to which the competitor applies it. In the compliance case against Standard Brands, the circuit court rejected the argument of the company that it had merely met competition in good faith by saying:

> What Standard Brands did may be described in general terms as follows: A competitor of Standard Brands was selling to a customer a given quantity at a stated price, which was less than Standard Brands' price for that same quantity. In order to obtain some of this customer's business, Standard Brands would sell that customer a smaller quantity at a price below its competitor's price for that smaller quantity and also below its own scale price for that smaller quantity (but not below its competitor's or its own scale price for the larger quantity sold to that customer by the competitor). We think that the argument advanced to justify this practice answers itself. An "equally low price of a competitor" means an equally low price for a given quantity.[20]

The limitation as to the level of the competitor's price, coupled with the view of the Commission that good faith does not permit efforts to destroy a prestige differential, has curious results where competitors are selling at different prices. The concern with the higher prices cannot, in good faith, discriminate in a way that reduces the prestige price differential.[21] Nevertheless, if the price differential has been reduced, the con-

[20] 189 F. 2d 510, 513-15. The practice thus condemned by the court was apparently the same as that noted by the Commission in the findings that preceded the original order in the Standard Brands case. The Commission found that the volume discount of the company was determined by the customer's total monthly requirements, whether these requirements were bought entirely from Standard or from various suppliers. (30 FTC 1130.) Thus purchases from its competitors, as well as from Standard Brands, helped to make the customer eligible for a lower price. Since, in the original proceeding, the company's defense of meeting competition was limited to certain off-scale prices, the Commission had no occasion to evaluate the good faith of the volume-discount schedule in this respect.

The Attorney General's Committee recommended in 1955 that "an incidental undercutting of the prices quoted by others" should not invalidate a defense "when in the course of genuinely meeting one particular competitor's equally low price offer"; and that "a seller responding to a rival's price should not be confined to quotations for a pricisely equivalent quantity of goods." See *Report of the Attorney General's Committee*, p. 183.

[21] See above, pp. 553-54.

cern with the lower price cannot, in good faith, discriminate to restore it because the competitor's price is not equally low.[22]

In some instances good faith has been denied because a seller did not precisely and regularly meet the prices of his competitors. In the Fruit-vale case the hearing examiner rejected the defense of meeting competition because in some instances the price of the company to favored customers was higher than the prices of competitors. He drew the inference that "price was clearly not the deciding factor which gave respondent the business." The Commission's opinion in the case mentioned this finding with approval (though it added that in some instances the price reductions were below those of competitors). In the Edelmann case, deviation from the prices of competitors not only downward but also upward was mentioned among the grounds for denying good faith. In the Champion Spark Plug case, the failure of the company to meet certain verbal offers by competitors was similarly mentioned.

Good Faith and Information about Other Prices

Knowledge by the discriminating seller as to the prices quoted by his competitors has been regarded as indispensable to his good faith. In the Staley case the Commission rejected the attempt of the company to justify discriminatory delay in making a price increase applicable to certain favored customers on the ground that Staley had made no effort to find out in advance whether or not its competitors delayed price increases similarly to the same customers. In the Minneapolis-Honeywell case, the company asserted that it had met competition in good faith in reducing a price to one of its customers after learning that this customer had diverted a part of its purchases to another supplier. The Commission rejected the defense on the ground that the price concession had been made several months before Minneapolis-Honeywell knew what price the competing supplier had charged.

In some instances the good faith of the discriminating seller has been denied because of the timing of his price reductions. In the Minneapolis-

Honeywell case, the Commission rejected the good-faith defense as to various sales on the ground that Minneapolis-Honeywell had established the low prices in yearly contracts that were negotiated and made effective before the prices of its competitors had been finally established. In the Champion Spark Plug Company case the defect in timing consisted in being too late rather than too early. The company's price reduction to Socony Vacuum was held to be unjustified on the ground that it was made more than a year after the last competitive offer that might have justified it.

Good Faith and the Lawfulness of Competitors' Prices

The legal status of the competitor's price that is met is also regarded as relevant to the good faith of the concern that meets this price. The good faith of Standard Motor Products was denied by the Commission partly on the ground that, since the discounts the company met were granted on pooled purchases, the company must have known that they were unlawful. In the Staley case, the Supreme Court said:

> Thus, it is the contention that a seller may justify a basing-point delivered-price system, which is otherwise outlawed by Section 2, because other competitors are in part violating the law by maintaining a like system. If respondents' argument is sound, it would seem to follow that, even if the competitor's pricing system were wholly in violation of Section 2 of the Clayton Act, respondents could adopt and follow it with impunity. This startling conclusion is admissible only upon the assumption that the statute permits a seller to maintain an otherwise unlawful system of discriminatory prices, merely because he had adopted it in its entirety, as a means of securing the benefits of a like unlawful system maintained by his competitors. . . . We think the conclusion is inadmissible in view of the clear Congressional purpose not to sanction by Section 2(b) the excuse that the person charged with a violation of the law was merely adopting a similarly unlawful practice of another.[23]

In the case against Standard of Indiana the principle that a price discrimination is not in good faith if the price met is known to be unlawful was consistently recognized. The Commission's decision said:

[23] 68 S. Ct. 971, 974-75.

The provision for a showing of good faith to meet an equally low price of a competitor cannot be construed as a *carte blanche* exemption to a respondent to engage in discriminations in price which have the adverse effects upon competition proscribed under Section 2(a). Such a construction would constitute recognition of the soundness of the principle that one competitor's violation of law justifies its violation by another.[24]

The first opinion of the Supreme Court, which centered on the question whether meeting competition in good faith, if shown, was a complete defense, discussed this question on the assumption that a price differential had been made in good faith "to meet a lawful and equally low price of a competitor."[25] When the second opinion by the Supreme Court overturned the Commission's finding of lack of good faith, the four dissenting judges asserted and the majority of the court did not deny that only a lawful lower price may be met.[26] However, in *Standard Oil Company* v. *Brown*,[27] which was decided between the two Supreme Court decisions in the Federal Trade Commission's proceeding against Standard Oil, the Fifth Circuit held that the right to meet competition is not necessarily limited to meeting lawful prices. After a jury in this private suit had decided in favor of Standard Oil Company (the defendant accused of discriminating), a new trial had been granted because the jury had not been instructed that a seller may meet only a lawful price. With the jury thus instructed, the second verdict favored the plaintiff Brown. The Fifth Circuit restored the original verdict, holding that the instruction in the second trial was error. It interpreted the Supreme Court's decision in the first appeal of the Standard Oil case, not as limiting the kinds of prices that can be lawfully met, but only as a finding that, so far as the record went, the prices of the competitors of Standard Oil were lawful. The court said that the most that could be derived from the Supreme Court's treatment of the matter was that "if the seller discriminates in price to meet prices that he knows to be illegal or that are of such a nature as are inherently illegal . . . there is a failure to prove the 'good faith' requirement in Section 2(b)."[28]

[24] 41 FTC 283.
[25] 338 U.S. 865.
[26] 340 U.S. 231.
[27] 238 F. 2d 54.
[28] 238 F. 2d 54, 58. The Attorney General's National Committee to Study the Antitrust Laws recommended in 1955 that "a seller should be deemed to have met

Good Faith and Prospective Injury

There is some, though probably not sufficient, support for the view that the seller cannot operate in good faith if he knows that his discrimination probably will injure competition. In the Staley case, a dissenting opinion by Judge Evans in the circuit court set forth three grounds for rejecting the company's assertion of good faith, one of which was that Staley's pricing practice:

> . . . was not, and could not be, made "in good faith" when the result of it was to "substantially lessen competition and tend to create a monopoly" . . . we must hold that action which lessens competition or tends to create a monopoly is unfair within the meaning of the Federal Trade Commission Act . . . and good faith, as that term is used in the above-quoted exception found in the Robinson-Patman Act, cannot be ascribed to those who indulge in such practice.[29]

In the case against Standard of Indiana, the Commission cited the knowledge of the company that its discriminations were not justified by cost differences and its knowledge "that the manner in which it priced and sold its gasoline continually created the probability of injury to competition between retail dealers who bought such gasoline at different prices and resold it in competition with one another"[30] as a basis for the conclusion that Standard of Indiana had a duty to review and modify its pricing practices at the time the Robinson-Patman Act was passed. The circuit court, however, held explicitly that knowledge that the concessions were not cost justified and might injure competition was irrelevant to the question whether these concessions had been made in good faith to meet the price of a competitor. In sustaining the decision of the circuit court, the Supreme Court did not discuss the point. Acceptance of the interpretation of law set forth by Judge Evans or by the Commission in the Standard of Indiana case would drastically curtail the defense of meeting competition. According to the Commission's view, the defense would

---

a lawful price unless he knew or had reason to believe otherwise. The law must not be construed as forcing a seller to compete at his peril." But the committee agreed that "undiscerning application" of the proviso for meeting competition "could lead to serious abuse." See *Report of the Attorney General's Committee,* pp. 181-82.

[29] 144 F. 2d 221, 226-27.

[30] 49 FTC 953.

remain available only if the circumstances were such that the discriminating seller should not have known of the injury created by his discrimination or if, because of a valid cost difference or other adequate reason, his review of his pricing practices justified the continuance of the injurious price differentials. In the version of Judge Evans, the defense might also remain available where the injury to competition was too narrow to involve a substantial lessening of competition in the market sense or a tendency toward monopoly or where such results, though probable, were not yet realized. Otherwise, guilty knowledge would preclude good faith in spite of the fact that good faith precluded guilt.

Summary: The Meaning of Good Faith

In view of the fragmentary and partially contradictory nature of the decisions as to the nature of good faith in meeting competition, conclusions on the present state of law must necessarily be uncertain. In the C. E. Niehoff & Company case the hearing examiner said that the defense is inapplicable unless the discrimination is temporary, localized, individualized as to a particular competitor, not part of a pricing system, and defensive rather than aggressive; and unless the respondent knows or has reason to believe that the competitor's price is lawful. More fully, the decisions may be tentatively summarized as follows: The good faith of a seller cannot be established where his purpose is to eliminate competition by conspiracy or monopolization, to make an aggressive attack on the business of competitors who can maintain their position only through a price differential, or to modify the resale practices of the favored customer. Lack of candor in the form of the price reduction is also regarded as relevant to good faith by a substantial minority of the Supreme Court. The claim that competition was met can be used to justify price reductions in specific competitive situations, the breadth of which is uncertain, but not to justify broad pricing practices. Because of this limitation, the reciprocal use of the defense of meeting competition by competing sellers is necessarily curtailed, though it is questionable whether the courts will sustain the Commission in denying good faith on the basis of such reciprocal use alone.

The history of a price concession is relevant to the good faith of the concern that grants it. Adverse conclusions will be drawn from a failure to attempt to establish a nondiscriminatory price structure and, by the

Commission, also from a failure to abandon discriminatory price structures antedating the Robinson-Patman Act, although the latter basis for adverse inference has been rejected by the only circuit court that has considered it. The Commission has gone so far as to see lack of good faith in failure by a respondent to change his prices in response to the allegations of illegality set forth in the Commission's complaint, but this finding, which would destroy the good-faith defense, appears in a single case that was not appealed, and presumably does not express the Commission's considered views. Good faith is absent where price concessions are made without knowledge of the prices that are being met; where such concessions antedate the price offers of competitors or follow these offers after they have lapsed; where the concessions set prices lower than those of competitors; where, though not lower, such prices apply to smaller quantities or volumes than those covered by the competing price offers; and perhaps where the reduced prices remain higher than those that are being met. There can be no good faith in meeting the price of a competitor if that price is known to be clearly unlawful. Even knowledge that a discrimination injures competition may raise judicial question as to the good faith of the discriminating seller, though, where the question has been explicitly considered, the majority view has been that such knowledge does not preclude good faith.

From this summary it is obvious that there is no single simple test of the adequacy of a defense that competition was met in good faith; but instead, the good or bad faith of a seller can be established only after examination of a variety of circumstances as to the nature and history of his practice, the setting in which it occurs, and his purposes. Interpretations of the relevant law have been made by the Commission in only 21 cases, of which only 11 have been reviewed by the courts and only 5 have resulted in opinions that dealt with the matter. In some of these the handling of the problem was brief and unrevealing. Many of the relevant questions have not yet been adjudicated in cases that turned squarely on them. The only points that have been clearly established by the highest judicial authority are that meeting competition is a complete defense but that this defense is not available to justify general pricing practices or to justify concessions made to meet prices that are known to be unlawful. Presumably a long period of litigation lies ahead before the boundaries of the defense of meeting competition become clear. Meanwhile, price concessions that rest on this defense alone will necessarily be risky.

Problems for the Sales Manager

The present status of the defense of meeting competition is unsatisfactory both to businessmen interested in marketing their goods and to persons concerned with the maintenance of effective legal barriers against price discrimination.

To a sales manager who wishes to compete in good faith, the fact that good faith can be shown only in meeting a competitor's prices is a serious limit on price policy. If he encounters different demands and different degrees of competition in different markets, he wishes to adjust his prices to the varying market situations rather than to raise or lower prices uniformly everywhere. He wishes to be free to take the initiative in reducing prices, not to be limited to retaliatory action against competitors.[31] He also wishes to be free to experiment with new price policies in limited areas or to limited groups before he adopts them generally. If, however, his customers in different markets compete against one another, such flexible pricing probably will injure competition in the narrow sense. Moreover, it is improbable that all of the price differentials incident to such flexible pricing will reflect differences in cost or that the available cost information will be detailed enough to show whether or not they do so. In applying the concept of meeting competition to defensive measures only, the law exposes the sales manager to risks except where his flexible pricing is purely retaliatory. Since each competitor is thus exposed, the broad effect is to reduce the flexibility of prices downward by making reductions risky unless they are uniform in all markets.

The denial of good faith where the price that is met is not lawful is a further difficulty for the sales manager who is trying to compete. He is not, of course, required to become a detective or a judge. His good faith is denied only where he has clear reason to know the illegality of the competitor's offer.[32] However, the sales manager cannot be sure how

---

[31] In industries where competitors are numerous and prices are not orderly, the incentive to do more than retaliate instance by instance is peculiarly strong. See the discussion of the good faith of C. E. Niehoff & Co., above, pp. 249-50, 251.

[32] In two private suits, *Balian Ice Cream* v. *Arden Farms* (231 F. 2d 356) and

strong his suspicions must become before, in the eyes of those who enforce the law, they constitute knowledge that the prices of the competitor
are unlawful. When such knowledge is attributed to him, he is precluded
from meeting these prices and is thus left without defense against their
effects in the market during whatever period of time may elapse before
the legal remedies of the statute give him relief.

If he has been ordered by the Federal Trade Commission to cease a
discrimination, he is on notice that this discrimination is unlawful, and
thus is peculiarly helpless to protect himself by meeting competition if
his competitors continue to make similar discriminations and the Commission does not promptly issue similar orders against them.

Neither the uncertainty as to the limits of the seller's duty nor the inability to retaliate against a law-breaker is peculiar to the field of price
discrimination. Parallel problems arise with reference to other trade
practices. However, sellers are especially sensitive to the stresses created
by the differences between their prices and those of their competitors;
and the extension of the law of price discrimination, so that it applies
potentially to most differentials in price, has substantially enhanced the
possibility of such stresses.

Difficulties are also created for the sales manager who is trying to
compete by the fact that the defense of meeting competition in good
faith applies only to price concessions made to meet specific competitive
situations. In view of the uncertainty as to the legal boundary between
a specific competitive situation and a pricing practice, the magnitude of
these difficulties is likewise uncertain. The narrower the interpretation of
a specific competitive situation, the greater is the problem for the sales
manager. He often finds it simpler to anticipate a competitive offer that
he foresees instead of meeting it after his customer is tempted by it.
He commonly finds it appropriate to adjust prices in recognition of the
competitive offers that are typically to be expected, without detailed
inquiry as to whether these offers actually exist customer by customer
and moment by moment. If the concept of a specific competitive situation
is so narrow that he cannot act to anticipate competitive pressures or

---

Standard Oil Company v. *Brown* (238 F. 2d 54) federal courts have decided that
a seller charged with price discrimination is not required to show the lawfulness
of the competitor's price that he has met. In the Balian case the court indicated,
however, that the defense would not be available if the seller had reason to believe
that the price being met was unlawful.

adopt policies appropriate to what he regards as enduring competition, he feels himself handicapped in his capacity to do his job. So long as the legal limitations on him are uncertain, he feels handicapped by unpredictable risks.

Thus there is considerable gap between the legal conception of good faith and the meaning that a businessman is likely to give to that term in his marketing activities.[33] To the businessman meeting competition in good faith includes all adjustments to market forces that express merely an ordinary desire to improve profits by recognizing the impact of competition without attempts to monopolize the market, develop restrictive agreements, or destroy competitors. Apart from such predatory motives, he thinks that nearly all discrimination is in good faith, since there is seldom an incentive to make special price concessions to certain customers unless those customers have, or are likely to receive, attractive offers from competitors. But many of the activities that the businessman would consider to be thus justified lie beyond the legal boundaries of good faith because of their scope, their timing, their non-retaliatory character, their acceptance of uncertainty and approximation, their continuity, or their lack of concern about the legality of action by business competitors.

Problems for Supporters of the Law

For very different reasons, those who desire strong legal safeguards against price discrimination find the present status of the law of meeting competition unsatisfactory. They are concerned because the defense of meeting competition in good faith permits significant amounts of price discrimination injurious to competition where no considerations of efficiency can be offered to support the price differentials.

The defense of meeting competition may enhance the possibilities of discrimination in several ways. First, sellers may, if they choose, meet competitors' offers in selling to certain customers, yet refrain from meeting these same offers in selling to others; or may make a reduction to meet a large price difference by one competitor in selling to one customer

---

[33] In rejecting the defense of meeting competition in the Niehoff case, the hearing examiner said that he had no doubt "that what respondent has done, it has done in good faith, in an ordinary if not legal sense, but what it has done is not what the statute as interpreted requires it to do." 51 FTC 1132.

while meeting only the smaller price difference of another competitor in selling to another customer. Thus, by selecting the competitors whose prices will be met and the transactions in which this will be done, a seller may, up to the limits set by good faith, discriminate among the various recipients of price offers from competitors. Second, when sellers are exceptionally willing to make price concessions, enough of them may do so to produce recurrent situations in which it is impossible to determine which, among a considerable number of sellers that have offered concessions, took the lead in doing so. Third, a buyer may be able to buy a part of his needs from one or more sellers who can justify a price reduction by a showing of cost differences. Thereafter the buyer may be able to obtain additional supplies from sellers incapable of a cost defense but protected by the defense of meeting competition. Thus the existence of a cost justification in unusual circumstances may afford the buyer a larger supply at low prices than can be cost-justified. Fourth, the buyer may take the entire output of a small seller at a price that has no legal lower limit because the seller has only one customer and hence does not discriminate. Thereafter the buyer may obtain more of his requirements from other sellers who justify their price reductions as made to meet competition. In this case, as in the previous one, the defense of meeting competition may serve to convert a small supply of low-priced goods into a larger supply thereof. Fifth, the buyer may obtain some portion of his requirements abroad from sellers who are not under the jurisdiction of those who enforce the American law and may then obtain domestic supplies from sellers who meet the price quoted by the foreign seller. Here, too, the defense of meeting competition may operate to make available a larger quantity of low-priced goods than could be obtained without it.[34]

In general, the opportunity to take advantage of concessions based on the defense of meeting competition is more readily available to large and powerful buyers than to their smaller competitors. It is these large buyers who are most likely to receive offers of concessions from a considerable number of sources, to find some supplier who can provide a

---

[34] It is also conceivable, though perhaps not likely, that a buyer may be able to obtain a price offer from a seller from whom he does not buy and use it to obtain a price reduction from the seller who supplies him. If so, the initiator of the reduction has not violated the law because he made no sale, and the supplier who made the sale may be able to invoke the defense of meeting competition.

cost justification for unusually low prices, to buy the entire output of certain suppliers, and to buy goods abroad. Thus the general effect of the defense is to enhance the relative opportunities of the big buyer.

Efforts to Amend the Law

Dissatisfaction with the defense of meeting competition has evoked efforts, not to alter or sharpen the definition of good faith, but to change the legal effect of the defense. In the Eighty-Third Congress, 23 senators joined in sponsoring a bill, introduced by Senator Kefauver, designed to make the defense of meeting competition inapplicable to discriminations whose potential effect was substantially to lessen competition.[35] Congressman Patman introduced a bill providing for "a fair and intelligent balancing" of a seller's right to meet competition with the buyer's right to equal opportunity.[36] No action was taken on either bill. In the Eighty-Fourth Congress, the Kefauver bill was introduced again in the Senate with the sponsorship of 30 senators and in the House with the sponsorship of Congressman Patman and about 46 other congressmen.[37] The House passed the bill on June 11, 1956 by a vote of 394 to 3.[38] In the Senate, hearings were held and a similar bill was favorably reported by a subcommittee.[39] The Judiciary Committee, however, incorporated the

[35] S. 1357.

[36] H.R. 5848. See *Congressional Record,* Vol. 99, Pt. 5, 83 Cong. 1 sess., p. 6934.

[37] S. 11 and H.R. 11. The bill reported and passed in the House was H.R. 1840, identical with H.R. 11 except for omission of a declaration of policy, which, however, was added by the House. *Ibid.,* Vol. 102, Pt. 6, 84 Cong. 2 sess., p. 8204.

[38] As passed by the House, the bill contained a declaration that the purpose of the law prohibiting price discrimination was "to secure equality of opportunity of all persons to compete in trade or business and to preserve competition where it exists, to restore it where it is destroyed, and to permit it to spring up in new fields." The provision as to meeting competition in Sec. 2(b) was amended to read, "provided, however, that unless the effect of the discrimination may be substantially to lessen competition or tend to create a monopoly in any line of commerce it shall be a complete defense for a seller to show that his lower price or the furnishing of services or facilities to any purchaser or purchasers was made in good faith to meet an equally low price of a competitor, or the services or facilities furnished by a competitor." *Ibid.,* Pt. 7, p. 10051.

[39] As reported, the Senate version included a proviso "that nothing contained herein shall be construed to alter the law applicable to the absorption of freight or of shipping charges." (See *Corporate Mergers and Price Discrimination,* S. Rept. 2817, 84 Cong. 2 sess., p. 3.) The version passed by the House did not mention

bill with one to amend the merger provisions of the Clayton Act. Though this bill was reported favorably, it reached the Senate floor on the day of adjournment, and action on it was not taken. In the Eighty-Fifth Congress, the same bills were reintroduced.[40] The House bill was not reported or considered in hearings. The Senate version, as reported by a subcommittee, would have included a provisio that had been inserted in the Senate version in the previous Congress, that nothing in it should alter the law applicable to freight absorption. The full committee deleted this provision and rewrote the bill so that it would change the law of meeting competition only for food, drug, and cosmetic products for human consumption, and only where the reduction in competition appeared in the secondary line of commerce.[41] With these changes, the committee reported the bill favorably on July 28, 1958 by a vote of 12 to 2.[42] However, on three subsequent occasions when the bill was

---

freight absorption, but its sponsors said repeatedly that it was not intended to change the general status of that practice. (See *Congressional Record*, Vol. 102, Pt. 7, pp. 10024-25, 10034-52; also *To Amend Section 2 of the Clayton Act*, Hearings before the Senate Committee on the Judiciary, 84 Cong. 2 sess. (1956), pp. 192, 201, 221, 243, 260, 419.) However, in some of the statements an exception was made as to instances in which freight absorption was used to bring about a price discrimination. See *ibid.*, p. 243.

[40] S. 11 and H.R. 11.

[41] "Unless the evidence affirmatively shows that the effect of the discrimination may be substantially to lessen competition or tend to create a monopoly in any section of the country in any line of commerce in the sale of food, drug, or cosmetic products, it shall be a complete defense for a seller to show that his lower price or the furnishing of services or facilities to any purchaser or purchasers was made in good faith to meet an equally low price of a competitor or the services or facilities furnished by a competitor." That the bill was intended to cover only effects in the secondary line of commerce appears ambiguously in the bill but clearly in the report.

[42] *Strengthening Robinson-Patman Act and Amending Antitrust Law Prohibiting Price Discrimination*, S. Rept. 2010, 85 Cong. 2 sess., pp. 1-2. The report was accompanied by (1) a statement by Senators Kefauver, O'Mahoney, Carroll, and Wiley to the effect that the amended bill "repairs only negligibly" the damage done by existing law, that they had voted for the report only to get the bill before the Senate, and that the subcommittee's version should be restored; (2) a supplementary statement by Senator Wiley calling particular attention to the fact that gasoline dealers were not covered by the amended version and deploring that fact; and (3) a statement by Senators Dirksen, Jenner, Butler, and Hruska opposing the bill. The latter statement explained that opponents of the bill had voted to report it in modified form in order to clear the committee's calendar for other work. It advocated an alternative version by Senator Dirksen, which the committee had rejected by a vote of 9 to 6. In this version, meeting competition in good faith would have been a complete defense; but good faith would have been deemed not

called for consideration, it was passed over because of objection by a senator; and thus it died with the close of the Congress.

The proposal central to these bills might reasonably be interpreted to leave the defense of meeting competition fully applicable to the narrow type of competitive injury, but make that defense insufficient where the injury to competition is of the broad type. This was intended, as to the secondary line of commerce, in the latest Senate version. The committee report said that the purpose was to make

> . . . unavailable to such a supplier the so-called good-faith defense to a charge of price discrimination under Section 2(a) of that act where it is affirmatively shown that the effect of such discriminations may be (1) substantially to lessen competition or (2) tend to create a monopoly in the resale of such products. Where the adverse competitive effect in the resale of such products falls short of these 2 criteria of the original Clayton Act, but meets the third 1 [sic] of injury to competition, which was added by the Robinson-Patman amendment, good faith would continue to be a complete defense.[43]

Similarly, the strongest advocates of amendment said:

> Under S. 11, meeting competition would continue to be an absolute defense where the discrimination, while perhaps injuring competition with an individual competitor, was not of sufficient scope or dimension as to result in a probable lessening of competition or a tendency to create a monopoly. . . . It is only where the impact and effect of a discrimination extend beyond the injury to competition with a competitor to the substantial lessening of competition or tendency to create a monopoly that S. 11 would alter the present law.[44]

In the latest Senate version the defense would also remain open for all types of injury in the primary line.[45]

---

to include adopting the unlawful discriminatory pricing system of a competitor, acting pursuant to a conspiracy, attempting to monopolize, meeting a price known to be unlawful, or discriminating with an intent to eliminate competitors. Further, Senator Dirksen's version provided that it should not be deemed to prohibit "delivered pricing or freight absorption as such where independently pursued, regularly or otherwise, with the result of promoting competition." *Ibid.*, pp. 7, 60.

[43] *Ibid.*, p. 2.

[44] *Ibid.*, pp. 8-9.

[45] The Senate report declared that "Good faith would also continue as an absolute defense where the injury shown was only among sellers of such products." *Ibid.*, p. 2.

With such an interpretation, the effect would be that, where the broad type of injury was in question, at least in the secondary line, the good faith of the seller presumably would become merely one of the items of evidence pertinent to a conclusion as to whether or not such injury was probable. The possible significance of the bill in modifying the treatment of injury to competition under the law has been discussed above.

Opponents of the bill have challenged the effort to distinguish degrees of damage to competition. In the dissenting statement that accompanied the latest Senate report, four senators called the distinction "fine spun and technical" and "a vague and meaningless difference." They said that the courts and the Federal Trade Commission had used the terms *injury to competition* and *lessening of competition* interchangeably, and that in 21 years of enforcement only one district court had ever distinguished between the two types of competitive effect.[46] Moreover, they thought a seller could not, in practice, make the distinction.

> Whatever might be the ultimate Federal Trade Commission or judicial ruling . . . a businessman nevertheless would have to guess in advance which of the two kinds of competitive effect his prices would be found to have if he wished to avail himself of the right to meet competition under S. 11. Only by sheer word play can it be asserted that a business firm, forced to make such judgments in advance of quoting a competitive price, would enjoy any legal right to meet competition as a practical matter.[47]

In general, small business organizations and persons devoted to the policy of the Robinson-Patman Act have supported the bill, while bar associations, large business enterprises, organizations responsive to their views, and persons skeptical of the policy of the Robinson-Patman Act have opposed it.[48]

[46] *Ibid.*, pp. 31, 73-74.

[47] *Ibid.*, pp. 39-40.

[48] In 1957 the executive committee of the New York State Bar Association's section on antitrust law unanimously opposed S. 11 as inconsistent with competition. (*To Amend Section 2 of the Clayton Act*, Hearings, 1957, Pt. 1, pp. 498-502). Asserting that the right to meet competition is essential to a competitive economy and that S. 11 and H.R. 11 ran contrary to the basic objectives of the antitrust laws, the Illinois State Bar Association's section on antitrust laws also opposed the bills. (*Ibid.*, Pt. 2, pp. 1337-40.) The board of managers of the Chicago Bar Association expressed similar opposition because it regarded the defense of meeting competition as "of great importance to the maintenance of an effective antitrust policy based on free competition." *Ibid.*, pp. 1340-45.

The supporters of the bill regard it as a means of minimizing the use of the defense of meeting competition. Many of them have not concealed their wish that the use of this defense could be invalidated entirely. Assuming that this is impossible, they argue that at least the seller's right to meet competition in good faith should not be given such priority of importance as to permit serious impairment of market competition among buyers.

Opponents of the bill have argued against it on various grounds, not all of which are accepted by all of them. Apparently many of them regard the general policy of the Robinson-Patman Act as excessively severe and would like not only to preserve but to extend the defense of meeting competition. However, thinking such a program unrealistic, they limit themselves to an effort to preserve the defense in its present form. A characteristic argument is that of the National Association of Manufacturers.[49] NAM opposed the bill on the ground that it would deprive sellers of any lawful means of defending themselves against price raids by competitors and on the further ground that the proposed distinction between the broad and narrow concepts of injury involves standards so vague and indefinite that in practice the defense would cease to be available under any circumstances. NAM argued that the effect would be to induce competing sellers to charge all customers the same price, to create price rigidity, and thus to deprive sellers, buyers, and consumers of the fruits of competition.

Government agencies concerned with the question have not always agreed. The Antitrust Division of the Department of Justice and the Department of Commerce have consistently said that meeting competition should be a complete defense.[50] The Federal Trade Commission has repeatedly changed its mind.

[49] Memorandum by NAM Law Department, Jan. 8, 1957, entitled "Limitation of the Good Faith Defense—What It Means to Businessmen." This memorandum was duplicated and widely circulated.

[50] For recent statements, see, for example, the testimony of Victor Hansen, Assistant Attorney General, before a Senate Committee in 1957 (*To Amend Section 2 of the Clayton Act,* Hearings, 1957, Pt. 2, pp. 826-50); a letter from Warren Olney III, Acting Deputy Attorney General, to the Senate Committee on the Judiciary, June 27, 1956 (*To Amend Section 2 of the Clayton Act,* Hearings, 1956, pp. 688-89); a letter from Walter Williams, Acting Secretary of Commerce, on June 14, 1956 (*ibid.,* pp. 24-25); and a statement in 1956 by Frederick H. Mueller, Assistant Secretary of Commerce (*ibid.,* pp. 344-46). For an earlier statement, see *Study of Monopoly Power,* Hearings before the House Committee on the Judiciary, 82 Cong. 1 sess. (1951), Pt. 5, pp. 15-19.

On behalf of Commissioners Ayres and Ferguson as well as himself, Commissioner Davis, replying to inquiries by a congressional committee in 1949, said that "If good faith is present, injury to competition will be rare; and in general the policy of the law should not discourage active competition by preventing the meeting of competition in good faith." On February 17, 1949, speaking for the same three, he said, "I am in sympathy with the purpose of making the meeting of competitors' prices in good faith a complete defense against charges of price discrimination. However, I deplore any effort to circumscribe the concept of good faith itself."[51] On June 9, 1949, the Commission wrote to the House Judiciary Committee:

> . . . If good faith in meeting competition is not to be a complete defense, a seller who competes vigorously by reducing his prices where he encounters lower prices is exposed to the risk that he may thereby be violating the law, and he can avoid such risk only by caution and hesitancy in making price reductions. To refuse to make the good-faith meeting of competition a complete defense necessarily involves the risk of impairing the vigor of competition among sellers. . . . All of the Commissioners believe that on balance it would be preferable to make the good-faith meeting of competition a complete defense.[52]

Subsequently, with changes in the membership of the Commission, the belief that meeting competition should be only a partial defense was expressed by a new majority consisting of Commissioners Mead, Spingarn, and Carson. In April 1951, Commissioner Mead wrote to Senator McCarran, opposing the passage of a bill (S. 719) to assure that meeting competition in good faith was a complete defense.

> We do not believe . . . that discriminations which merely meet the price of a competitor are much less a force for destroying competition than are discriminations which undercut the price of a competitor. . . . We recognize that there is an area in which it may be desirable to permit justification on this basis. . . . We can see no particular objection to making the good faith defense available as to discriminations

---

[51] *Competitive Absorption of Transportation Costs,* Hearings, 81 Cong. 1 sess., pp. 275, 332.

[52] Quoted by Senator Capehart in a letter printed in, *To Amend Section 2 of the Clayton Act,* Hearings (1956), p. 638.

which injure, destroy, or prevent competition with a particular person, but which still fall short of substantially lessening competition or tending to create monopoly in a line of commerce.[53]

Commissioner Spingarn expressed the same point of view in July 1951 before committees of the Senate and the House of Representatives.[54] In March 1953, the same three Commissioners said that the defense of meeting competition in good faith was a fatal loophole in the statute. Their views were not shared by Commissioners Mason and Carretta. Indeed, on January 26, 1953, the latter wrote to Senator McCarran endorsing a bill that would have made meeting competition in good faith a complete defense but would have defined good faith to exclude instances in which the seller knew or should have known that the price he was meeting was unlawful.[55]

By June 1953, through the appointment of a new commissioner (Howrey), a majority had reversed the Commission's position. A letter by Commissioner Howrey, approved by Commissioners Mason and Carretta, said, "Our whole theory of trade regulation is based upon the existence of competition in every market. If such regulation is to remain effective, a seller must be permitted, when acting fairly and in good faith, to meet the equally low price of a competitor."[56] Dissent was expressed by Commissioners Mead and Spingarn.

Further changes in the membership of the Commission at first consolidated this position. In April 1956, the chairman testified before a subcommittee of the House Committee on the Judiciary.[57]

[53] *Price Discrimination, Defense under Robinson-Patman Act*, S. Rept. 293, 82 Cong. 1 sess. p. 10. Commissioner Ayres did not concur in these views, but expressed the opinion that the Standard Oil decision had made legislation unnecessary. Commissioner Mason dissented from the statement of the majority, and on April 23, 1951, wrote to Senator McCarran that he thought the bill would be useful.

[54] See statement by Stephen J. Spingarn, *Price Discrimination and the Basing Point System*, Hearings before the Senate Select Committee on Small Business, 82 Cong. 1 sess. (1951), pp. 236 ff. and *Study of Monopoly Power*, Hearings, 82 Cong. 1 sess., Pt. 5, pp. 20 ff.

[55] See *Congressional Record*, Vol. 99, Pt. 1, 83 Cong. 1 sess., p. 1046.

[56] Letter from Edward F. Howrey, Chairman, Federal Trade Commission, to Senator William Langer, June 16, 1953 (mimeo.). Quoted in *Congressional Record*, Vol. 101, Pt. 2, 84 Cong. 1 sess., p. 2412.

[57] Statement of John W. Gwynne, Chairman of the Federal Trade Commission, *To Amend Sections 2 and 3 of the Clayton Act*, Hearings before the House Committee on the Judiciary, 84 Cong. 2 sess. (1956), p. 202.

The Commission believes that freedom to compete, including competition in price, is so basic a concept of our economic system that a restriction upon the right of a seller to meet in good faith the equally low price of a competitor should not be enacted without a clear showing of the necessity therefor. . . . Since the Standard Oil decision by the Supreme Court, there has been no Federal Trade Commission case, decided either by the Commission or a court, in which a Section 2(b) good faith defense to a charge of price discrimination has been sustained. On the other hand, the Federal Trade Commission has issued cease and desist orders in a number of cases in which the good faith defense was involved. . . . Some of the cases decided by the Commission, including its modified order in the Standard Oil case, are now pending on appeal in the courts. It may be that the decisions in those cases or in cases now pending within the Commission, or the decisions in cases hereafter instituted, will furnish reason to believe that the "good faith" defense now afforded by Section 2(b) will hamper enforcement of the Clayton Act. There is no such indication now, however, and the Commission therefore opposes amendment of Section 2(b) at the present time as premature.

Commissioner Kern, who had already sent a personal dissent from this opinion to the Senate Judiciary Committee,[58] testified in dissent on April 19, 1956:

If price discrimination is to be allowed as a defensive tactic of large sellers in competing with themselves or in attempting to crush upstart wild-catters, irrespective of the injury thereby inflicted on those of their customers whom they do not favor, then I say the law in its present form is promotive of monopoly, for its natural result will be to squeeze small business to the wall . . . I would suppose . . . that practices which lessen competition or which tend to create monopoly, in any line of commerce, should be suppressed without regard to the motivation of the actors.[59]

In May 1956, a majority against the unlimited applicability of the defense of meeting competition developed within the Commission as a result of a change of attitude by two commissioners. With the concurrence of Commissioner Secrest, Commissioner Anderson sent letters

[58] See *Congressional Record*, Vol. 102, Pt. 4, 84 Cong. 2 sess., p. 5390, and *To Amend Section 2 of the Clayton Act*, Hearings (1956), p. 32.

[59] Statement of William C. Kern, member of the Federal Trade Commission, *To Amend Sections 2 and 3 of the Clayton Act*, Hearings (1956), p. 216.

to the judiciary committees of the two houses of Congress,[60] saying
that the decision of a circuit court as to the good faith of Standard Oil
Company of Indiana and the Supreme Court's refusal to review the decision of a circuit court in a private suit (*Balian Ice Cream Company* v.
Arden Farms Company)[61] had convinced him that amendment of the
law was desirable. In June, Commissioner Kern testified before a Senate
committee[62] on behalf of the new majority that these two decisions had
"emasculated" Section 2(a) and made it "pretty much of a dead letter."

> As we see it, large businesses will be free to "meet" one another's
> competition through discriminatory price concessions to select custom-
> ers, regardless of the competitive havoc thus inflicted on the small
> businesses required to pay higher prices while trying to compete with
> the favored accounts. And . . . the large companies utilizing price
> discrimination for the purpose of eliminating their smaller competitors
> will find it possible, because of their superior financial staying power,
> to subsidize less profitable or even unprofitable sales for long periods
> of time in order to achieve their ends.

Commissioner Gwynne now expressed dissent[63] on behalf of himself and
Commissioner Mason. He emphasized the point that the defense of meeting competition was narrowly circumscribed; challenged the majority's
view of the legal effect of the Standard Oil and Balian decisions; and
said that the right to meet competition was valuable to both large and
small business, "I do not think in an attempt to protect competition, we
should destroy it."[64]

This division of opinion continued in 1957. In March, the secretary
of the Commission wrote to the chairman of the House Committee on
the Judiciary:[65]

> . . . The current construction of that section [Section 2(b)] is incon-
> sistent with the basic principles of the Clayton Act, as amended, and
> the Sherman Act. . . . [It] places the interest of an individual seller of

[60] See *Congressional Record,* Vol. 102, Pt. 7, 84 Cong. 2 sess., p. 9048, and
To Amend Section 2 of the Clayton Act, Hearings (1956), p. 31.

[61] See above, pp. 459-61.

[62] See *To Amend Section 2 of the Clayton Act,* Hearings (1956), p. 225.

[63] *Ibid.,* p. 229.

[64] *Ibid.,* p. 235.

[65] *Price Discrimination in Dairy Products,* Hearings before the House Select
Committee on Small Business, 85 Cong. 2 sess. Pt. 3 (1958), p. 708.

meeting the price of a competitor by discriminating in price without
cost justification, over the obviously more important public interest
that such a discrimination which may have the effect of substantially
lessening competition or tending to create a monopoly should not be
allowed.

Commissioner Gwynne again filed a separate statement of his individual
views.[66] The same attitudes were expressed in hearings held by a Senate
committee.[67]

Bearing of Meeting Competition
on Public Policy

Thus the defense that competition has been met in good faith has been
criticized as too narrow and as too broad, as insufficient and excessive,
and as a curb on competition both in its narrowness and its breadth.
These apparently contradictory sets of appraisals are both substantially
correct. The present legal status of the defense arises from an inappropriate analysis of the place that the seller's good faith in meeting competition
should have in public policy toward price discrimination. This analysis
gives meeting competition a status in some respects excessive and in some
respects insufficient.

The policy of the law should be to reconcile so far as possible two
objectives: freedom for businessmen to price their goods flexibly in response to the varying pressures of the market, and curbs on exercise of
that freedom in ways that thwart the objectives of the statute as to competition and competitive opportunity. One may describe the reconciliation
in different ways by placing primary emphasis on the one objective or the
other. Thus, one may say that freedom of business price policy should
be limited only for clear reason, or that the law should protect the public
against the evils of price discrimination in a way that leaves as much
freedom as possible. Under either formulation, what must be sought is
a balance that reconciles the liberty of the enterprise with the continuance
of liberty in the relationships among their enterprises and among consumers.

[66] Commissioner Tait, appointed to replace Commissioner Mason, took no position because he had not been a member of the Commission for a long enough
time to have an informed opinion of the merits of the issue.
[67] *To Amend Section 2 of the Clayton Act,* Hearings (1957), Pt. 1, pp. 629-69.

The good faith of the seller in meeting competition is not a satisfactory basis for determining the relative importance of the values that are to be reconciled. Its great usefulness is as a standard for appraisal of the impact of a seller's price policies on other sellers—in other words, as a standard for determining injury in the primary line. Broadly speaking, the harm that one seller inevitably does to another in the course of competition can be distinguished from harm done to competition among sellers by considering the seller's purpose to compete or to reduce competition—a purpose readily summarized as the seller's good faith. If injury in the primary line were the only problem, the standard of good faith would be roughly appropriate in determining the amount of freedom of action that should be left for individual sellers.

However, the seller's good faith in meeting competition does not provide a satisfactory standard with which to appraise the scope and significance of injury to competition in the secondary line. Discriminations made in good faith might conceivably result in destroying such competition. Discriminations not made in good faith might conceivably have smaller anticompetitive effects. There is no reason to expect even a limited correlation between the scope and severity of anticompetitive effects in the secondary line and the presence or absence of good faith on the part of the discriminating seller.[68] In cases in which a discrimination produces significant anticompetitive effects in the secondary line, it is possible that denial of the right to meet competition in good faith will produce significant anticompetitive effects in the primary line. In these circumstances, the problem of public policy has to do with the relative weight to be given to the maintenance of competition in the two different lines of commerce. This problem cannot be satisfactorily answered on the basis of the seller's good faith alone. A decision to make good faith in meeting competition a complete defense is a decision to protect competition in the primary line in all circumstances, even when this means accepting great anti-

---

[68] At first glance, it appears that when a seller merely meets in good faith a low price already established by a competitor, he does not enhance the buying advantage of the favored customer and hence does not significantly increase the likelihood of anticompetitive effects from that buying advantage. As has already been shown, however, the standard of good faith does not apply adequately or solely to this type of relationship. On the one hand, the concept of good faith is so limited that the seller's good faith may be denied even in some circumstances in which there is no accretion of advantage to the buyer. On the other hand, the seller's good faith may be demonstrated in cases in which his discrimination substantially enhances the amount of low-priced goods the buyer can obtain.

competitive effects in the secondary line in order to avoid slight ones in the primary line. A decision to give no weight to the good faith of the seller is the obverse of this: acceptance of the effect in the secondary line as the controlling consideration even if that effect is slight and the effect in the primary line is severe. A decision, such as that foreshadowed by H.R. 11, to make good faith in meeting competition a complete defense where the injury is narrow but not where that injury is broad, has the merit of attempting to distinguish two classes of effects that differ in significance. However, it still fails to afford any basis for balancing the possible opposite effects that may appear among sellers and among buyers. The version of S. 11 reported in the Senate in 1958 reflected a partial recognition of this analysis: It sought to make meeting competition a complete defense as to all injuries in the primary line of commerce and as to narrow injuries in the secondary line, but not as to broad injuries or tendencies toward monopoly in the secondary line.

If this analysis is correct, the significant question that underlies the controversy over the defense of meeting competition has to do, not with the seller's good faith, but with the scope and character of injuries to competition. The good faith of the seller is a major (though not the sole) consideration in ascertaining the effects on competition that a seller's price policies may produce in the primary line and also in ascertaining the effects that legal curbs on those price policies may produce in that line. The seller's good faith has no significance in the appraisal of injuries in the secondary line. The problem of public policy is to determine the character of the injuries to competition that are to be prevented, the way in which those injuries are to be detected, and what is to be done about conflicting effects in the primary and secondary lines. If these problems are satisfactorily met, the good faith of the seller will fall into its appropriate place as a part, though a significant part, of the evidence relative to one type of injury. It is hopeless to try to correct defects in the handling of the problem of injury by offsetting defects in the treatment of good faith.

That men will differ in their beliefs as to the proper scope for a law of price discrimination is to be expected. The appropriate focus of such differences is on the extent and character of the damage to competition that such a law should try to prevent and the relative weight that should be given to the primary and secondary lines when the facts as to damage to competition in those two lines are conflicting. This has not been the focus of controversy in recent years in the United States. Instead, those who would ambitiously broaden the law of price discrimination have sought to do so by enlarging the concept of injury to competition, while those who would curtail the law have pursued their objective, not by attacking the enlargement of the concept of injury, but by strengthening the defense of meeting competition in good faith. Along these lines there can never be an intelligible clash between the protagonists of opposite policies or a coherent solution of the problems on which they differ.

18 / Cost Justification

DURING CONSIDERATION of the Robinson-Patman Act by the Congress, great weight was placed on the right to justify price differences by differences in cost. Both the House and Senate judiciary committees reported that the proviso as to cost was of great importance because it left trade and industry free from any impediment to the adoption and use of more economic processes. Relying on this provision, the House committee reported that there was nothing in the proposed law

> . . . to penalize, shackle, or discourage efficiency or to reward inefficiency. . . . Any physical economies that are to be found in mass buying and distribution, whether by corporate chain, voluntary chain, mail-order house, department store, or by the co-operative grouping of producers, wholesalers, retailers, or distributors—and whether those economies are from more orderly processes of manufacture, or from the elimination of unnecessary salesmen, unnecessary travel expense, unnecessary warehousing, unnecessary truck or other forms of delivery, or other such causes—none of them are in the remotest degree disturbed by this bill. Nor does it in any way infringe the seller's freedom to give a part or all of the benefit of the saving so effected to others with whom he deals.[1]

The Senate committee likewise regarded the cost proviso as "of greatest importance," because

> . . . it leaves trade and industry free from any restriction or impediment to the adoption and use of more economic processes, and to the translation of appropriate shares of any savings so effected up and down the stream of distribution to the original producers and to the ultimate consumer. . . .[2]

[1] *Prohibition of Price Discriminations*, H. Rept. 2287, 74 Cong. 2 sess., p. 17.
[2] *To Amend Antitrust Act Relative to Wholesale Prices*, S. Rept. 1502, 74 Cong. 2 sess., p. 5.

After the bill emerged from conference, Congressman Utterback assured the House of Representatives that through the cost provision:

> . . . The bill assures to the mass distributor, as to everyone else, full protection in the use and rewards of efficient methods in production and distribution. . . . There is no limit to the phases of production, sale, and distribution in which such improvements may be devised and the economies of superior efficiency achieved, nor from which those economies, when demonstrated, may be expressed in price differentials in favor of the particular customers whose distinctive methods of purchase and delivery make them possible.[3]

Although the passages quoted were applied to the entire bill, a showing of cost differences is not, in fact, relevant to all violations of the Robinson-Patman Act. Cost differences are pertinent only when the violation charged consists in the payment or receipt of discriminatory prices contrary to the provisions of Sections 2(a) and 2(f). Neither the payment nor the receipt of unlawful brokerage nor disproportionate payment to distributors for their selling efforts permits any cost defense. It is doubtful that a cost defense can be offered for disproportionate sales assistance to distributors.[4] So far as Sections 2(c), 2(d), and perhaps 2(e) of the statute may prohibit practices that tend to reduce costs, the law contains no proviso under which the cost advantages are relevant to a decision.

However, price discriminations that have the capacity to injure competition or that actually do so are lawful in spite of that injury if they make no more than due allowance for such differences in cost as are covered by the statute. Question arises, therefore, whether or not, as far as these parts of the law are concerned, the provision that discriminations can be justified by cost differences has accomplished its purpose by leaving scope for all price adjustments that permit efficiency. Though the evidence is fragmentary, it raises grave doubts whether efficiency has been adequately protected by the cost defense and whether it can be so protected. The grounds for these doubts will emerge in the ensuing discussion of experience with cost justification.

[3] *Congressional Record*, Vol. 80, Pt. 9, 74 Cong. 2 sess., p. 9417.
[4] In the Simplicity Patterns case, a circuit court decided in 1957 that cost justification is permissible under Sec. 2(e). The decision has been appealed. See above, p. 164.

The Burden of Proof

In a case in which a seller is charged with unlawful discrimination, cost differences are considered only on the initiative of the respondent. Having shown injurious discrimination, the Commission has established a prima facie case. The burden of proving that cost differences justify the discrimination rests on the respondent. If he offers no cost defense, the question of cost is not considered.

Conversely, in proceedings against buyers under Section 2(f), the Supreme Court decided in the Automatic Canteen case that the respondent buyer does not carry a corresponding burden. Instead, the Commission's duty to show that the discrimination the buyer induced or received was unlawful includes a duty to prove that this discrimination was not justified by cost differences. Accordingly, the facts about cost must be a part of every case brought against a buyer, but may be omitted entirely from a case brought against a seller unless the seller wishes to introduce them.

When costs are relevant, the language of the statute circumscribes the discretion of the Commission and the courts as to the types of cost that can be considered and as to the permissible methods of analysis. The law provides that "nothing herein contained shall prevent differentials which make only due allowance for differences in the cost of manufacture, sale, or delivery resulting from the differing methods or quantities in which such commodities are to such purchasers sold or delivered."[5] The purpose of this language was explained by the sponsors of the act in the debates in Congress. Concerned lest a respondent might take certain business at prices based on the out-of-pocket cost of an additional increment of activity, those who drafted the bill sought to preclude any defense of such a price concession on the basis of a comparison of this incremental cost with a cost for other business computed to include all the overhead charges. Overhead costs were regarded as properly allocable on an equal basis to all business done. The differences in costs that were to be used in justifying price differences were to include only those arising directly from the peculiarities of the transactions in which the different prices were charged.

The fact that the burden of proof as to cost rests on respondent sellers has brought forth an informal give-and-take as to accounting

[5] Sec. 2(a), 49 Stat. 1526.

questions. Sellers who wish to introduce costs into a price-discrimination case desire to make their arguments persuasive; consequently, they seek to employ cost concepts and methods of computation acceptable to the Federal Trade Commission. They usually consult the Commission in planning their analyses of cost data, and modify their plans in the light of suggestions by the Commission's staff. When the Commission investigates charges that a seller has discriminated unlawfully, the seller, if he believes that he has a valid cost defense, is likely to make it informally available to the investigators in the hope of forestalling the issuance of a formal complaint. Presentations of costs that are thus made informally are considered by the Commission in deciding whether or not to issue formal complaints. If the cost defense is thought to be adequate, no complaint is issued.

The Frequency of Cost Defenses

Since the Commission does not announce the results of investigations that terminate without complaint, no record is available to show the frequency with which costs have been successfully offered as defenses in this informal way. While the writer was director of the Commission's Bureau of Industrial Economics and thus in general charge of the accounting staff concerned with problems of price discrimination, a considerable number of investigations were terminated in this way.[6]

There can be little doubt that the desire to avoid legal proceedings has induced some business enterprises to analyze the relation between their prices and their costs and to change the prices that cost differences clearly would not justify. For a time after the passage of the Robinson-Patman Act, the Federal Trade Commission authorized its staff to hold informal conferences with business enterprises that wanted to find out how their pricing practices were affected by the new law. The writer, then an employee of the Commission, participated in many of the conferences. The possibility of cost justification was prominent in the discussions. There was indication that, in an effort to make the cost defense applicable, most of the conferees intended to make significant changes in their dis-

[6] John Parkany reports in "Federal Trade Commission Enforcement of the Robinson-Patman Act, 1946-52" (doctoral dissertation, Columbia University, 1956, p. 260), that in October 1953 he was told by Arthur Lundvall, the Commission's chief accountant, that more than half of the time of the Commission's accounting staff is spent on price differences that do not result in legal proceedings.

counts, particularly by reducing the quantity discounts granted for large purchases.[7] Presumably a similar informal review of discount structures has continued to take place in the business community. So far as this is true, the effect must be to reduce the occasions for investigation and the likelihood that investigation will result in complaint.

For these reasons the Commission's formal proceedings are necessarily misleading as a record of the substantive significance and practical effectiveness of the cost defense. The issuance of a complaint under Section 2(a) means either that no cost defense was submitted to the Commission during the preliminary investigation or that the Commission's accountants found what was placed before them less than convincing. It follows as a matter of course that the cases thus initiated were often decided without cost information having been submitted and that, where such information was submitted during trial, the Commission usually rejected it as inadequate.

Thus the cost defense has played a relatively small part in the Commission's price discrimination proceedings. Of the 311 orders issued by the Commission in Robinson-Patman cases, a majority were concerned with violations regarding which no cost defense was possible. There were 118 cases involving violations of Section 2(a), and only in these might the respondents have been acquitted if they had presented a satisfactory showing of cost differences.[8]

[7] In various conferences it appeared that the basis for cost justification was thought to be that, regardless of the size of a transaction, a lump-sum cost was incurred in making a sale and delivery. Where there was such a lump of expense, the fraction of it applicable to each unit sold grew smaller with each increase in the number of units included in the transaction. The whole lump of expense was applicable to a single unit if only one unit was sold; half of it to each unit in a transaction involving two units; a quarter of it to each unit in a transaction involving four units; and so on. Where this is the basis for cost justification, cost differences will justify substantial price differences at the lower end of a quantity-discount scale, but the possibilities of cost justification quickly become negligible as the number of units in the transaction increases. When a customer buys 500 units, each unit accounts for only one five-hundredth of the lump sum, and no further subdivision of that five-hundredth can afford much further reduction of unit cost or much further justification for a reduced price. Thus this type of cost justification may be used readily to defend substantial price differences among small customers who buy slightly different quantities, but cannot afford much protection for a substantial difference in discounts between buyers of moderate quantities and buyers of large quantities. This point was generally recognized in the informal conferences.

[8] Cost defenses were inapplicable to Secs. 2(c) and 2(d). Until 1957, they were thought to be inapplicable to Sec. 2(e) also; and a test case challenging this inter-

In the majority of these cases, however, the respondents chose not to contest the complaint. They filed admission answers, accepted consent orders, agreed that the decision should be rendered on stipulated facts, or otherwise agreed to waive some or all of their rights to a trial of the law and the facts. So general was this acquiescence to the Commission's orders that the respondents invoked their rights to a trial in only 32 of the cases in which orders were issued under Section 2(a); and in 7 of these they waived a part of their rights to submit evidence, briefs, or argument. The remaining 25 cases constitute the entire group in which a cost defense was relevant to the charges, and the respondents fully used their right to defend themselves.

Cost defenses were offered in 12 of these 25 cases, plus 1 case in which a study of costs was included in a stipulation of facts.[9] In some of the 13 cases, cost defenses were offered only for a part of the discriminations that had been challenged. Cost defenses were likewise offered in 5 of the 95 cases in which the Commission dismissed a complaint involving Section 2(a),[10] and in 1 case in which the Commission dismissed a price discrimination charge but issued an order to cease violating the Federal Trade Commission Act.[11] In April 1958, another case was dismissed because of a cost defense.[12] Thus, until the autumn of 1958, costs had been considered in deciding 20 cases under Section 2(a).

One reason that costs were not submitted more often appears to be that in other cases the price discrimination was such that cost justifica-

---

pretation has not yet been decided. Cases that involved no offenses other than these constituted 185 of the total of 311 in which orders were issued. Prior to the Automatic Canteen case, no cost defense was offered as to a charge under Sec. 2(f); and in that case the Supreme Court decided that the burden of showing cost in a Sec. 2(f) case rests on the government rather than the respondent. An additional 7 orders apply only to Sec. 2(f) and 1 to Secs. 2(f) and 2(c) only. A cost defense was relevant solely in cases involving Sec. 2(a). One hundred and one orders have involved this section alone, and 17 have involved it in addition to the other sections of the act.

[9] The cases are those involving Standard Brands, E. B. Muller and Co., Champion Spark Plug Co., International Salt Co., Morton Salt Co., Standard Oil Co., Curtiss Candy Co., Minneapolis-Honeywell Regulator Co., National Lead Co., C. E. Niehoff & Co., Doubleday & Co., Fruitvale Canning Co., and U.S. Rubber Co. (Docket 4972). The stipulation of facts was in the case last named.

[10] Docket 2935, *Kraft-Phenix Cheese Corp.;* Docket 2937, *Bird & Son, Inc.;* Docket 4636, *Bissell Carpet Sweeper Co.;* Docket 5677, *B. F. Goodrich Co.;* Docket 5728, *Sylvania Electric Products, Inc.*

[11] Docket 5701, *Horlicks Corp.,* 47 FTC 169.

[12] Docket 6721, *Hamburg Brothers, Inc.*

tion was considered impossible. This was true, for example, in cases in which the discrimination was incidental to the use of a basing-point or zone-pricing formula.[13] When prices differ in sales to customers who are differently located, the costs that are relevant to the price differences are those incurred in transporting the goods. Cost justification is possible only when prices vary with transportation costs. But such concomitant variation exists only if the seller prices his goods f.o.b. point of shipment or sells at delivered prices that consist of a uniform price at the point of shipment plus the actual transportation expenses. In a basing-point system some sales are made by some participants f.o.b. point of shipment, but other sales are made at prices that involve freight absorption or the addition of so-called phantom freight to the transportation charge. Neither the mill realizations nor the delivered prices in sales to different delivery points reflect the relative costs of shipment to those points. Similarly, in a zone-pricing system price differentials between zones may or may not be based on average costs of transportation to the customers in the respective zones; but even when they are computed in this way, they are almost certain to overstate the difference in transportation costs between points that are close to each other on opposite sides of a zone boundary and to understate the difference in transportation costs between points that lie at the extremities of the respective zones. Thus, in both basing-point systems and zone-pricing systems, the cost defense is automatically precluded by discrepancies between the price structure and the structure of transportation rates. It is not surprising that in such cases respondents have not sought to justify discriminations by cost differences.[14]

There were other discriminations, too, for which a cost defense was apparently impossible. In numerous cases some or all of the discriminations that were found to injure competition took the form of unsystematic price concessions made to individual customers. In these instances nothing short of a showing that costs differed concomitantly for each

[13] In the National Lead case, which was primarily concerned with zone pricing, the cost defense applied only to incidental quantity discounts.

[14] In one case of unsystematic territorial discrimination, that involving E. B. Muller, a cost defense was offered. However, the cost information pertained primarily to a charge of predatory sale below cost. Muller sought to justify price differences by cost only in the case of contracts with three quantity buyers. The other respondent, Franck, offered no specific cost defense for discriminatory prices. The cost aspects of the case are analyzed in Herbert F. Taggart, *Cost Justification* (1959), pp. 81-111.

customer could have laid the basis for a cost defense. There were also cases in which a respondent departed significantly from his own pricing schedule—for example, by allowing volume discounts to customers who did not buy the volume to which the discount applied. In these instances a showing that the discount schedule was justified by cost differences would not have justified the off-scale selling, and presumably a showing of cost differences appropriate to justify the off-scale selling would have implied a lack of cost justification where the scale was observed.[15] In some of the volume-discount schedules, purchases were pooled for purposes of computing discounts. The central office of a buying organization was given a discount on the aggregate volume of the purchases that had been separately made by and separately delivered to different branches of the buying organization; or a buyer was permitted to count as a part of his volume not only his own purchases but also purchases that had been made directly from the seller by the buyer's customers. Since costs arise from sales contacts, transactions, and deliveries, all of which were separate in such instances, the pooling of separate purchases in computing discounts would have been difficult to justify on a cost basis.

The Problem of Segregating Costs

There was a second reason for the infrequency with which cost defenses were offered and also for the fact that most of the cost defenses presented to the Commission in formal proceedings were rejected by it. The task was one of improvisation, for, in the words of a practicing lawyer who is also an accountant, "there is no well-established or accepted single set of principles in cost accounting which compare with those in financial accounting. . . . Further, accounting for cost differences is a completely new field, since accountants conventionally deal with *average* costs, rather than cost differences."[16] Moreover, the difficulty of the work

---

[15] Minneapolis-Honeywell undertook an elaborate reclassification of customers as a first step in its cost defense, in order to justify discounts on actual rather than imputed amounts bought. See above, p. 242.

[16] Mark S. Massel, "The Robinson-Patman Act: Cost Justification," in *Conference on the Antitrust Laws and the Attorney General's Committee Report, Symposium*, Trade Regulation Series, No. 2, James A. Rahl and Earle Warren Zaidens, eds., Federal Legal Publications (1955), p. 208. A similar point of view has been expressed by another practicing lawyer, Albert Sawyer, in a speech before the section on antitrust law of the Illinois State Bar Association ("Cost Justification of

was magnified by the complexity of many of the price structures for which cost justifications were needed. Many of the respondents in price discrimination cases were engaged in the sale of a considerable number of commodities, each bearing its own prices. When the price differences applicable to one of these commodities were challenged, a cost defense required a segregation of the cost pertaining to that particular commodity. This was difficult, for in the words of the Attorney General's National Committee to Study the Antitrust Laws, "a firm's expenditures comprising the differences in costs as between alternative methods of distribution are typically spread among numerous products in varying ways; the breakdown of these 'joint' costs among the several components involves largely subjective business judgments in choosing among several equally rational alternative methods of allocation."[17] According to one responsible estimate, about 85 per cent of all industrial companies did not allocate cost information on a product basis in 1946.[18]

Quantity Differentials," 1 *Antitrust Bulletin* 578-80). ". . . we are dealing not with the problem of record keeping on a day-to-day basis and provable as such, but with what are essentially numerous series of estimates, the validity of which rest, in large measure, upon the standard of care and good faith which brings them into being. . . . In all but the simplest cases the reliability of the evidence must be tested not against the accuracy and completeness of the data presented, but more largely upon the soundness of numerous subjective judgments of the witness as to the methods of allocation of various types of expenses common to several classes of products or classes of customers. . . . There is usually a choice of alternative methods. Objective tests, such as a time and motion study of representative samples, may fortify a particular selection. In many cases, however, such objective tests are impracticable or unavailable within the reasonable bounds of time and cost. . . . A cost difference will hardly ever be a precise amount. It is more in the nature of range of values."

[17] *Report of the Attorney General's National Committee to Study the Antitrust Laws* (March 31, 1955), p. 174.

[18] Paul M. Green, Deputy Administrator for Accounting of the Office of Price Administration, made this estimate on April 4, 1946. The Banking and Currency Committee of the House of Representatives was considering a proposal that prices fixed by OPA must provide for recovery of the total costs of each product plus a reasonable margin of profit. In discussing this proposal Mr. Green said, ". . . in some industries nearly all the companies have cost accounting records that will provide a breakdown of costs by products. In other industries none of the companies could produce cost information on a product basis. . . . Probably 85% of all industrial companies do not allocate cost information on a product basis and 15% are readily able to produce such information. Since there is some tendency for the cost accounting to be more complete in the larger companies (although not nearly to the extent usually supposed), the percentage of total over-all production that could be covered by total cost on a product basis is probably somewhat larger than the above percentage would indicate. I believe that I am very optimistic

In the Standard Brands case, for example, the costs of bakers yeast were appropriate to the cost defense. The company found it necessary to try to segregate these costs from the costs of a considerable number of other bakery products after segregating the costs of all bakery products from the costs of a considerable number of other commodities known as grocery products. The difficulty of such segregations becomes progressively greater with each increase in the number of commodities sold. It also becomes greater with each increase in the integration of the activities by which the seller produces and distributes his various products. Segregated costs for particular commodities can be ascertained easily only where the commodities sold are few, or each is produced and sold separately from the rest.

Moreover, in justifying price differences, the costs applicable to a single commodity must be segregated in such a way as to show the differences in cost appropriate to the transactions for which different prices are quoted. The more complex the price structure, the more elaborate this segregation must be. In a structure of quantity or volume discounts, the price difference between any two discount classes may be challenged and, if it is, must be justified by a cost difference applicable to sales to those particular classes. If there are seven discount classes, a full cost defense will be possible only if costs can be correspondingly segregated into seven groups. If quantity and volume discounts are both offered, segregations of cost appropriate to each must be supplied. If different discounts are available to different classes of customers, the costs of serving each class must be separately stated. If different discount

---

when I estimate that as much as 25% of total production could be so covered. The remaining 75% of production would be by companies which do not have total cost on a product basis." See Office of Price Administration, *A Report on Cost Accounting in Industry* (June 30, 1946), p. iii.

Mr. Green added in his comments to the committee, "In working out our cost studies, we have been forced to allocate costs that had not been allocated, and we have been forced to develop methods which were agreed upon with the company accountants. Many of our allocations have been somewhat arbitrary, but they were the best that we could do. . . . Naturally the problems are not so great with the single-line companies, but the multi-line companies have found many difficulties in producing product cost figures." From unpublished copy of original statement.

Mr. Green's estimate of the percentage of companies that had cost information by products was based on a survey then being conducted by OPA. When completed, the survey showed that unit costs on a product basis were believed to be available in 29,046 companies out of approximately 187,370 studied. See OPA, *A Report on Cost Accounting in Industry*, p. iv.

structures are available in different parts of the country, there must be a territorial segregation of costs followed by a further segregation appropriate to each discount structure. The demands of such an analysis are sometimes so great that even business enterprises that have sought to provide a cost defense based on a special cost study have developed cost classifications inadequate to the complexity of the price structures they were seeking to defend.

However, even a full segregation of expenses by commodities and discount classes would not assure the adequacy of the ensuing analysis of costs. Comparison of costs for different discount classes is possible only by comparing the average costs applicable to each class. But an average has significance only when the members of the class for which it is computed are similar and when all persons having these similarities are included in the class. If the class has been improperly defined, the cost justification based on that definition will be invalid.[19]

Yet there is usually more than one plausible way of classifying transactions or business enterprises for purposes of computing costs; and little guidance has been supplied, either by the statute or by the Federal Trade Commission, to the principles of classification that are acceptable. Indeed, discount structures and the circumstances underlying them are so various that it would be a formidable task to embody principles of classification intended to be generally applicable in language sufficiently specific to be useful.

Thus difficult problems regarding the coverage and homogeneity of discount classes are likely to arise in computing costs. Lack of homogeneity

---

[19] An assistant general counsel of the Commission wrote in 1953: "Practicality requires that, to the extent possible, each bracket be treated as a unit for cost and price comparisons. In turn, this requires that customers in each bracket be reasonably homogeneous in their buying practices. The legal theory for accepting such average costs is that no significant differences in costs exist as among customers within a given volume bracket. If this is not the case, the theory is inapplicable. If cost differences in serving customers in the same bracket are so great that averaging would create numerous inequities between them and customers in other discount brackets, the result would be to destroy any reason or legal basis for using average costs for the group as a unit. . . . Usually, the greater the width of a bracket in terms of quantity, the greater the number of substantial deviations from the average justification. . . . In turn, if the brackets are very wide in terms of price difference, this tends to accentuate the possibility of injury to competition. It is doubtful that a discount schedule having extremely wide steps either in discounts or in quantities, or in both, could successfully withstand attack." See Robert B. Dawkins, "Quantity and Cumulative Volume Discounts," in *Lectures on Federal Antitrust Laws* (1954), p. 113.

in a discount class may invalidate a cost computation. A large number of buyers may be grouped together for discount purposes in spite of the fact that the conditions under which they buy and the amounts of their purchases differ greatly in ways that appear to be likely to produce substantial differences in the costs of serving them. Where this is true, the computation of an average cost applicable to the group will be suspect on the ground that the group has no coherent identity and that the average is not fairly representative of any of the coherent subgroups. The discount class may be thought to be unduly broad.

Lack of proper coverage may also invalidate a cost computation. For example, a group of large customers who receive a substantial discount may include some but not all of those who buy in similar quantities with similar frequency and take delivery in similar ways. The exclusion from this class of buyers of some of the concerns that apparently belong in it may be sufficient to invalidate a cost justification even if the costs appropriate to the class can be segregated and can be shown to justify the discount. The discount class may be thought to be unduly narrow.

Where a cost computation is challenged on the ground that the group to which it applies is unduly narrow or unduly broad, this challenge can be met only by a further segregation of costs. Costs in serving the customers who have been excluded from the group must be compared with the costs attributed to the group; or costs in serving the various subgroups must be compared with average costs for the group as a whole. Thus, it may become necessary to show the propriety of a discount structure by segregations of cost even more elaborate than the structure itself demands.

Careful application of these principles of homogeneity and adequate coverage is essential to prevent discrimination by selective concessions based on nonexistent cost differences. For example, customers A, B, and C may be served at a cost of $1 and customers D and E at a cost of 80 cents. When A, B, C and D are grouped together, the average cost of serving them may appear to be 95 cents. If this inappropriate grouping is accepted, it will appear to justify a discount of 10 cents granted to E and withheld from D. The discrimination between D and E can be detected and evaluated only by grouping the customers appropriately.

Problems similar in difficulty may arise with reference to the location of the boundaries between classes of customers, particularly in discount schedules based on quantity or volume. Purchases by the largest buyer in any class of customers may be only slightly smaller than purchases by the smallest buyer in the next class. The difference in purchases between customers in different classes who are adjacent to each other at the class boundary may be less than the difference between customers who lie at the two boundaries of a single class. Moreover, there may be no clear reason why the boundary between classes should be located at one point rather than another. The fewer the classes and the larger the differential in price that separates them, the more important these boundary problems are likely to be. If class boundaries are to be justified on a cost basis, those who offer the cost defense must be prepared to present alternative segregations of costs capable of showing the significance of a relocation of the boundary or of a change in the number and breadth of the discount classes.[20]

The Problem of Allocation

Alongside these formidable difficulties in segregating costs, there are difficulties scarcely less great in determining the proper principles on which cost allocations should be based. Broadly stated, the theory of the allocation of costs is that each segment of business activity should be charged with the expenses that are incurred in the particular operations involved in it. Thus, the cost of a commodity properly includes the cost of the material incorporated therein, the cost of any material destroyed in making it, and the payments to labor for the particular operations by which the commodity was made and distributed. In practice, however, there is no exact correspondence between the flow of activities and the flow of goods, and therefore the attribution of activities to goods must be based on standards that commend themselves to the good sense of the observer. But unfortunately there are often several plausible ways in

[20] In an opinion in the Minneapolis-Honeywell case, Commissioner Ayres said, "It has been urged that there is necessarily a failure of cost justification where the quantities purchased by two competing customers at applicable price differentials are nearly the same, with one being just below and the other being at or slightly above the minimum quantity for a particular bracket. This argument may be persuasive in a case where such a situation is actually shown and where there is some indication that it is a matter of competitive importance. But there has been no such showing in this case. Any annual quantity system of pricing is vulnerable to this argument and may be controlling where it has practical aspects. Where it is purely theoretical, however, it does not constitute a satisfactory basis for disallowing the whole effort at cost justification." 44 FTC 394.

which that responsibility can be determined, each differing from the others in the resulting computation of costs.

The complexity of the problem appears clearly in the effort to ascertain the relative costs of making sales to different groups of customers. If salesmen call on these customers, the salaries, traveling expenses, and commissions of the salesmen are appropriate items of cost. It is reasonable to believe that such expenses are smaller per dollar of sales for the customers who place the larger orders. To give this belief a numerical value, however, one must determine the part of the expense attributable to the customers who buy different amounts.[21] When salesmen are compensated by salary plus a commission based on a percentage of their sales, one way of doing this is to determine the total number of calls made by the salesmen, to assign to each call an equal amount of the total expense, to compute the total number of calls on the larger and the smaller customers, and to attribute the segregated aggregates of expense thus obtained to the respective segregated totals of orders.[22] However, it may be objected that calls on small customers are shorter than calls on large ones, or that the salesmen who call on large customers have higher salaries and larger expense accounts; or, conversely, it may be objected that the larger customers have urban locations, so that calls on them require less travel time than calls on smaller rural customers. Such objections may suggest the propriety of a time study, followed by an allocation of expense at so much per hour rather than so much per call. Again, executives of the seller, as well as the seller's salesmen, may participate in the effort to make sales to large customers, and, if so, there may be need to allocate some part of the salary of these executives to the computation of sales expense, in spite of the fact that no records exist by which the appropriate fraction can be determined.

Problems similar to this abound when an attempt is made to allocate the cost of manufacture, sale, and delivery among the various groups of customers who pay different prices for the same goods. Unlike financial

[21] "Any allocation of costs based upon arbitrary assumptions, e.g., that each customer receives substantially the same number of salesmen's calls, or that all salesmen's calls last the same time or that costs necessarily vary with dollar sales, must not be attempted." See Jerrold G. Van Cise, "The Robinson-Patman Act and the Accountant," 3 *Antitrust Bulletin* 335.

[22] Acceptable methods of allocation will vary with the way in which salesmen are compensated. If, for example, there is a sliding scale of sales commissions based on the size of the customer's order, a division of total sales expense in proportion to the number of calls or the time spent would be inappropriate.

accounting, cost accounting has not developed generally accepted principles for allocation of expenses. Moreover, the objective of cost accounting has been to determine average costs for categories of activity, not to compute cost differentials.[23] Hence more than one method of allocation is typically possible. The propriety of the various methods is typically uncertain. Records sufficient to permit alternative methods to be readily used and compared are typically nonexistent.

The Federal Trade Commission has summarized the difficulties of accounting that underlie the justification of price differences as follows:

> If the effort or service for which there is a given expenditure were always wholly applied to the category of a given cost classification for which costs are desired, costing, whether for production or distribution, would be relatively simple. If, for example, where a firm is selling several commodities, the efforts of each salesman were wholly applied to the sale of a single commodity, no problem of allocation of direct selling cost would present itself in finding the distribution costs by commodities. A record of the expenses for salesmen, classified according to the commodities they sell, would suffice. Or where the firm is selling only one commodity but to customers classified according to volume of purchases, if each salesman sold to but one class of customers, the finding of the direct selling cost by such classes of customers would be comparatively simple. A record of the expenses for salesmen, grouped by the classes of customers to whom they sell, would be sufficient.
>
> It is where an expenditure is incurred for an effort or service, whether in production or distribution, which is applied to more than the one category for which costs are desired, that is, where the expenditure is of a joint nature, that an allocation must be made. This requires a basis of allocation which in turn calls for a reasonable standard or unit whereby the effort or service rendered by the function may be measured. When that unit is found, the costs for the function are allocated to the category in the proportion that the units of service rendered for that category bear to the total rendered for the function.
>
> Often it is difficult to find the unit of effort or service being costed which most uniformly represents the same amount of expenditure and for which statistical data are available. For example, if it is desired to ascertain the direct selling cost of a commodity by customer classes all of which are served by the same salesman, shall salesmen's selling

---

[23] That accounting for differential costs had not been seriously undertaken prior to the passage of the Robinson-Patman Act is surprising in view of the uses to which this kind of information could be put by management, and that little has been done to develop such accounting during a period of more than twenty years under the act is notable. Presumably, the meagerness of the development reflects the inherent difficulty and expense of such work.

effort be measured by the number of calls or by the number of minutes; that is, by the call unit or by the time unit? Or may there, under the given conditions, be some other measuring unit more satisfactory? For which unit is it most practicable to obtain the necessary information and will that unit represent a substantially uniform amount of expenditure? Regardless of the unit chosen, it frequently is necessary to make elaborate special studies to obtain this information.

While both types of accounting have this fundamental problem of cost allocation, distribution-cost accounting is different from production-cost accounting in these three important respects:

(1) It has to do with a process, that of distribution, not nearly so highly standardized, on the whole, as that of production, either as among industries or even within the same industry. Each of the operations of the distributing process, even for a given firm under given conditions, is open to wide variation of method, with varying costs. The entire distributing process often extends over a longer period than that of production and, unlike production, is for any one firm generally carried on at widely separate points under diverse conditions and, consequently, with greater uncertainty as to results. . . .

(2) Distribution costs are normally subject to more classifications or types of analysis than those of production, commodity being the principal basis for classification of production costs, whereas commodity, channel of distribution, territory, quantity-size of deliveries or volume of sales, and method of sale and delivery are all common bases for the classification or analysis of distribution costs. . . .

(3) Generally the proportion of the total number of items of distribution costs for a given concern, each of which can be charged wholly to any single category of a given cost classification, is small as compared to that of production costs. Consequently a larger number of allocations must be made, requiring for each such allocation the sound choice of a unit by which the functional effort or service may be measured. . . .[24]

Such is the problem facing the business enterprise that desires to keep its price differences within limits established by differences in cost. Informal conversations with business executives have convinced the writer that few, if any, enterprises believe they have solved this problem.[25] He

[24] See Federal Trade Commission, *Case Studies in Distribution Cost Accounting for Manufacturing and Wholesaling* (1941), pp. 28-30.

[25] However, William J. Warmack, formerly an accountant with the Commission and subsequently an adviser in various price discrimination proceedings, has expressed the opinion, in a letter to the author, that "by avoiding ever-present pitfalls involving expensive experiments," most interstate sellers can obtain "adequate Robinson-Patman costing at an annual expense that should seldom exceed the salary of a good clerk."

In an article elaborating this opinion, Mr. Warmack argues that the cost de-has found no instance in which segregated cost information sufficient to compute the cost differences relevant to the structure of discounts is regularly prepared and made available to those persons in the business enterprise who determine the discount structure.[26] In other words, he has found no case in which the routine of price adjustment is continuously subjected to a routine comparison of price differences with cost differences. The most that appears to be thought possible by business executives is a check on the relation of prices to costs at relatively infrequent intervals by a process involving studies that supplement the cost information that is regularly obtained from the books of account.[27]

Cost Defenses Offered

That these are the limits of possibility appears to be indicated by the nature of cost defenses that have been offered to the Federal Trade Commission in cases that went to trial. These defenses have one striking common characteristic: apparently, none of the respondents had devised methods of analyzing costs currently in such a way that management could base price differences on cost differences. Even the most careful of

fenses have often been expensive because they were hastily developed in support of prices not originally based on cost. The proper procedure, he thinks, is first, to examine a pricing plan to make sure that it is not inherently unlawful and might reasonably be capable of cost justification; second, to select representative territories and time periods for analysis; third, to analyze the principal items of cost (usually found in costs of distribution rather than of manufacture) in which differentials will appear. These, he thinks, invariably include selling, warehousing, picking, packing, shipping, and order handling. He recognizes that to allocate these costs, on the basis of time and effort expended, among product lines, customer groups, and quantity or volume brackets is not always practical, but argues that "needless and expensive experiment" can be avoided if each item of cost is considered in the light of previous legal rulings. He says that if a plan is formulated in this way "it is our experience that all necessary data for the territories and periods selected for study can be compiled currently by the seller's own personnel—and at but relatively little additional effort and expense." See William J. Warmack, "Robinson-Patman Costing Not Too Difficult or Expensive," in *1956 Trade Practice Annual.*

[26] The Attorney General's Committee commented in 1955, after noting the subjective elements of judgment in distribution cost accounting, "Such considerations are obviously not suitable for periodic entry in a seller's regular books of account." See *Report of the Attorney General's Committee,* p. 174.

[27] In private suits, resort to decision by juries tends to obscure these difficulties and to make it possible for dubious computations to be considered "for what they are worth." An example is *Reid* v. *Harper,* 235 F. 2d 420. In the lower court

the defenses were based on studies undertaken, after the price structure had been challenged, for the purpose of developing a defense in a pending lawsuit. The defenses were developed after the fact, in support of price differences that had not originated in a study of costs and had not previously been checked against costs.[28] It is not surprising, therefore, that the respondents encountered many difficulties in obtaining adequate cost information, in segregating costs, and in justifying the methods of allocation they used.

Harper had offered a cost defense for its discrimination against Reid and had won the case. Part of the cost difference consisted of differences shown in an accountant's analysis between billing, bookkeeping, and shipping costs in serving Reid and similar costs in serving three jobbers. The rest consisted of savings said to be due to the purchasing patterns of the jobbers and to the avoidance of certain collection expenses in serving them. The intangible items had been admitted for the jury to decide what they were worth. The accounting analysis covered the oldest available cost records, those for 1951, but had been applied to the period covered by the suit, 1941-50, by adjustments based on general salary rates as published by the Commerce and Industry Association of New York. The costs of serving the largest jobbers had been computed "by averaging total shipments on a cumulative basis for an entire year," which, the plaintiff contended, resulted in letting the savings of the large transactions justify the discrimination on the small ones.

The Second Circuit's opinion did not condemn either the accounting improvisations or the resort to annual averages. As to the former, it said, "Although such an accounting method obviously lacks the full measure of desired precision, it appears to have been undertaken in good faith and to accord with the minimal requirements of sound accounting principles. Indeed, under the circumstances, it appears to have been the best available procedure. Both the courts and the Federal Trade Commission have recognized the dilemma confronting defendants in suits such as these, and have liberally accepted data derived from litigation-inspired accounting methods." As to averaging, the court said, "To require a seller in these circumstances to justify the cost differential in each and every transaction with his buyers, rather than on the aggregate basis of their dealings, would prove unduly onerous. The impact of such a requirement might be to discourage *all* price differentials, even those actually justified by cost distinctions." (235 F. 2d 420, 425.)

Both as to the accounting procedures and as to the intangible costs, however, the court's final and conclusive ground for sustaining the verdict below was that the trial court had instructed the jury that it should determine the validity of the assumptions and methods used in the computations and of the conclusions reached from them. Thus the legal fiction of the competence of a lay jury to decide relevant technical questions provided a basis for acceptance of any decision for which a rationale could be subsequently evolved.

Cost aspects of this case are analyzed in Taggart, *Cost Justification,* pp. 494-510.

[28] In two private suits involving American Can Co., a cost defense was based on a study covering a test period at the time a volume-discount schedule was introduced. However, this study was neither continuously maintained nor repeated. See above, pp. 244-46.

In 7 cases the Commission has dismissed a charge of price discrimination after considering a cost defense. In only 2 of these cases, however, do the findings throw light on the Commission's handling of cost problems.[29] In the Kraft case,[30] in which most of the discriminations were found to lack competitive injury, one discount to buyers of more than 150 pounds of loaf cheese was found to be cost-justified. Such buyers received their cheese from the factory at a delivery cost of 7.5 cents per hundred pounds, while buyers of smaller amounts obtained them from Kraft's delivery truck, the average cost of whose deliveries of all products was $3.70 per hundred pounds. Although, in the absence of further information, the Commission thought the deliveries of loaf cheese by truck were probably not as expensive as the average for all products thus delivered, it drew a "reasonable inference" that they were more expensive than deliveries from the factory by a sufficient margin to justify a discount of 1 cent per pound to buyers of the larger quantity.

The Sylvania case concerned preferences to Philco on radio tubes for the replacement market. The differentials between the prices paid by Philco and those paid by Sylvania's dealers varied for different tube types. The aggregate price differences on the entire line of tubes were found to be approximately justified by the aggregate cost differences, whereas for

[29] In Docket 2937, *Bird & Son;* Docket 4636, *Bissell Carpet Sweeper Co.;* Docket 5677, *B. F. Goodrich;* Docket 5701, *Horlicks Corp.;* and Docket 6721, *Hamburg Brothers,* the Commission noted the existence of cost justification without indicating the nature of the analysis by which it was found. In the Bissell case the Commission apparently decided that there was no competitive injury, and in the Bird case sales to disfavored customers, which constituted about 1 per cent of Bird's total sales, were made only for three or four months, while Bird completed a change in selling methods that had been undertaken before passage of the Robinson-Patman Act.

In the Goodrich case, all discriminations were found to be cost-justified except a 13 per cent discount on waterproof footwear; and since less than .5 per cent of waterproof footwear sales were made at this discount, the discrepancy was regarded as unimportant.

The Bissell case was dismissed without public hearing. In the Horlicks case, the existence of cost justification was stipulated without public evidence relevant thereto. In the Bird case, evidence introduced by Bird was characterized as adequate to provide cost justification in testimony by an FTC accountant. In the Goodrich and Hamburg cases, evidence as to cost was received but was omitted from the public record at the respondents' request. Such information about cost as the records of these cases provide has been analyzed in Taggart, *Cost Justification,* pp. 461-62, 33-38, 340-64, 464-65.

[30] Docket 2935, *Kraft-Phenix Cheese Corp.* The cost aspect of the case is discussed in Taggart, *Cost Justification,* pp. 454-56.

certain particular tubes the price differences exceeded the cost differences. The case turned, therefore, on the question whether or not the comparison of aggregates was proper. The hearing examiner thought not. Sylvania appealed to the Commission, and the Commission's attorney did not oppose the appeal. The Commission found that the tubes for which price differences were not specifically justified were not sold in substantial volume, and that the largest price differences were on the tubes with the least demand. It saw no competitive significance in the variation in the price differentials, and therefore dismissed the complaint. In a concurring opinion, Commissioner Howrey elaborated the analysis by showing that a full line of replacement tubes must be carried in proportion to the relative demand for each, so that the average for the full line of tubes, rather than the price of a particular tube, determined market advantage.[31]

Among the 13 instances in which cease and desist orders have been issued after submission of cost defenses, 6 throw little light on the problems of cost justification, either because the respondent devoted little effort to this defense or because the Commission wholly or partly rejected the defense without stating its reasons.[32] The 7 remaining cases,

---

[31] He also noted that if all disputed questions as to accounting methods were decided against Sylvania, cost justification would fall, on the average basis, by 0.87 cents per tube. He regarded this as *de minimis*.

He used the case as an opportunity to comment that "the cost defense has proved largely illusory" and to urge that the Commission should abandon meticulous accounting detail, and instead attempt to assure merely that prices were reasonably related to cost differences.

The cost aspect of the Sylvania case is analyzed in Taggart, *Cost Justification*, pp. 365-98.

[32] In 3 of these cases the cost defenses have been analyzed in *ibid.*, the Muller case at pp. 81-111, the Morton Salt case at pp. 170-86, and the rubber footwear case at pp. 284-339. In the Muller case, cost justification was attempted by Muller only for certain contract sales, and Franck, the other respondent, did not explicitly offer a cost justification. The Commission's findings summarily said that price differences had not been cost-justified.

In the Morton case, the cost defense was rejected by the trial examiner as based on estimates and guesses without adequate factual foundation; and the Commission, silent as to the matter in its first findings, decided summarily in revised findings that price differences had not been cost-justified. On appeal, the Supreme Court sustained the Commission with a brief and unrevealing rejection of the cost defense, though Mr. Justice Jackson, dissenting, saw an obvious cost difference behind the carload discount.

The rubber footwear case was decided solely on the basis of stipulations of fact, most of which pertained to costs. After the stipulations had been twice amplified and refined to take account of the attitudes of FTC accountants, counsel for both sides agreed on the facts as to price and cost differences. Though the Commission

4 concerned with quantity or volume discounts and 3 with functional discounts, supply analyses sufficient to be useful.

In the cases involving quantity or volume discounts, the cost defenses offered by Standard Brands, International Salt, and Niehoff were rejected as inadequate on grounds that illustrate the problems discussed above. Standard Brands segregated the cost of bakers yeast by first using arbitrary percentages to segregate the costs of bakery products from those of grocery products and then using arbitrary percentages to segregate the costs of yeast from those of other bakery products.[33] The Commission rejected the use of these percentages, particularly in the segregation of bakery products from grocery products, as inconsistent with such evidence as was available to show the percentages that were appropriate. Although Standard Brands had several discount schedules applicable to different territories, it used computations based on nationwide aggregates of cost in an effort to justify the discount structure for one of its territories, and made no effort to provide a cost justification for the other territorial discount structures. The Commission did not directly challenge the sampling studies employed by Standard Brands to allocate cost to different volume brackets, but did challenge some of the principles of allocation that were used.

The scope of the customer classifications employed by International Salt Company was thought by the Commission to be inappropriate.[34] In justification of its volume discount, the company compared the costs of serving Atlantic & Pacific Tea Company with those of serving all other customers; but the Commission thought that in grouping together customers who bought in widely different amounts International Salt Company had computed averages that were not fairly representative of the smaller customers.[35] The Commission also objected to the use of the costs of serving

treated the agreement as conclusive in establishing the facts of the case, it did not explicitly adopt and may not have considered the thinking on which the determinations of fact were based. Though substantively interesting, the concepts formulated and the precedents established did not attain the stature of Commission decisions.

[33] For an analysis of the cost defense in this case see Taggart, *Cost Justification*, pp. 39-80.

[34] *Cf. ibid.*, pp. 140-69.

[35] Why the Commission emphasized the impropriety of treating this average as representative of the smaller customers is not clear. Presumably, the effect of including larger as well as smaller customers was to reduce the average cost for the group and thereby to reduce the cost differential between the group and A. & P. Thus if there was error, its tendency should have been to diminish rather than enhance the size of the price difference that International could justify.

A. & P. as representative of the costs of serving large-volume buyers, on the ground that the company had not shown that similar costs were incurred in dealings with other large companies. The Commission objected to the company's defense of its quantity discount, on the grounds (1) that the average sale to those who did not receive the discount could be shown to be substantially higher than the average assumed by the company, and (2) that, in any case, the company had failed to show the propriety of averaging the costs for all of the nondiscount customers in spite of variations in the amounts they bought. As in the case of Standard Brands, the Commission also challenged the propriety of some of the principles of cost allocation used by International Salt Company.

The precision demanded in an acceptable allocation of costs is illustrated by the Nichoff Company case.[36] Here a cost defense for volume discounts was rejected because (1) it rested on computations of the average size of orders in each volume class in disregard of the variation around the average; (2) it assumed, contrary to fact, that salesmen made the same number of calls on each jobber regardless of the volume he bought; (3) the expense for advertising and catalogues was allocated in equal portions to each customer rather than equally to each dollar of sales.

The Commission accepted the cost defense offered by Minneapolis-Honeywell.[37] However, no defense was submitted as to the discounts available to buyers in the three largest volume classes who took about 55 per cent of total sales of the company.[38] The Commission's order was based on the price differences that were not cost justified. In an opinion in the case, Commissioner Ayres expressed the attitude of the Commission toward efforts at cost justification:

> Cost studies of the sort presented in this matter ordinarily do not afford precise accuracy but must necessarily embrace a number of conjectural factors and allocations. There is inherent in them a reasonable margin of allowable error. Where they are made in good faith and in accordance with sound accounting principles, they should be given a very great weight. . . . Respondent's burden under the act is very great and it should have a liberal measure of consideration

[36] Cf. ibid., pp. 399-428.
[37] Cf. ibid., pp. 257-83.
[38] As to these classes, the Commission found the price differences were "greater than the amount of unallocated costs and it was deemed impractical to allocate additional items of cost which were excluded from the study." 44 FTC 381.

when it becomes apparent that it has made sincere and extensive efforts to discharge that burden.[39]

In two private cases, cost defenses for volume discounts offered by American Can Company have been reviewed by the courts, with conflicting results. In a case brought by Bruce's Juices, the lower court refused to accept a cost defense that grouped customers in broad classes instead of showing costs for individual customers, and the court of appeals affirmed the decision.[40] In a similar case brought by Russellville Canning Company, the lower court took the same position as to classification of customers and also criticized the cost study because it had not been continued beyond a trial period. The court of appeals, however, thought that a continuous check on the cost of serving each individual customer would be so burdensome as to preclude volume discounts; it reversed the decision and remanded the case for a new trial.[41] It should be noted that although the decision approved sample studies and the classification of customers for analysis of costs, it did not deny that the classification must be appropriate in the respects discussed above.

Cost defenses were analyzed and rejected in three of the functional discount cases. As in the volume-discount cases, the chief inadequacies consisted in improper segregation of costs and the use of unacceptable principles of allocation.

In the Champion Spark Plug Company case,[42] a cost defense was offered only for the company's special prices on spark plugs sold to Atlas and Socony-Vacuum. The Commission objected to the computation of an average cost for the other 485 customers of the company, especially because Cities Service Company, one of these customers, bought in volumes comparable to Atlas and Socony-Vacuum and might well have been served at costs as low or lower.

Curtiss Candy Company offered a cost defense only for its sales of candy to vending-machine operators.[43] The defense was based on a comparison of its costs in such sales with the average of its costs in all other sales. The Commission rejected the computation of this average on the

[39] 44 FTC 394.
[40] See above, pp. 244-46. Cf. Taggart, Cost Justification, pp. 467-72.
[41] See above, pp. 244-46. Cf. Taggart, Cost Justification, pp. 472-93.
[42] Cf. ibid., pp. 112-39.
[43] Cf. ibid., pp. 237-56.

ground that it lumped together transactions that took place at widely different prices and might have given rise to widely different costs. The Commission made specific objections to the computation of an average price for these sales by the company, derived from a division of dollar volume by physical volume and used instead of the varying prices paid by different groups of customers. Objection was also made because Curtiss Company, lacking a cost survey or adequate cost records, had allocated various costs on the basis of dollar sales.

The Standard of Indiana case illustrates the complexities of the problem of cost justification even where the discount structure is simple.[44] The discounts to be justified were only two—one and a half cents per gallon to three and later four customers over a given period of time, and one half cent per gallon to one of these customers during a part of the period. As to the former discount, Standard of Indiana compared the costs of serving the favored customers with costs of serving other customers in Detroit, where the favored four were located, and with costs shown by a survey in Kansas and Oklahoma. The Commission objected to the comparison with Kansas and Oklahoma because methods of distribution there were not comparable to those used in Detroit and because the figures used for Detroit consisted of computed averages that did not properly reflect the cost of serving the disfavored customers. It objected to the comparisons of costs within Detroit because the costs of serving disfavored dealers included costs incurred in suburban areas subject to higher costs than the metropolitan area. A similar objection was offered to the effort of the company to justify the half-cent differential by comparison of the cost of serving the favored customer with the cost of serving other resellers in Detroit. The Commission held that these other customers had been improperly lumped together and that Standard had incorrectly assumed that there was a consistent difference between methods of delivery to them and methods of delivery to the favored concern. In analyzing both sets of cost justifications, the Commission found reason to criticize allocations of cost, either because favored customers were improperly relieved of their share of certain costs or because disfavored customers were improperly charged with costs irrelevant to the problem, such as the landlord expenses of the company and its administrative and sales expenses outside of the Detroit area.

[44] *Cf. ibid.*, pp. 187-236.

The Advisory Committee

Considerable criticism has been directed at the Federal Trade Commission on the theory that the difficulties encountered by business enterprises in presenting satisfactory cost defenses were attributable to the use of perfectionist and doctrinaire standards of accounting by the Commission rather than to inherent difficulties.[45] Impressed by this criticism, in 1953 the chairman of the Federal Trade Commission appointed an advisory committee on cost justification, composed of outside experts.[46] This committee was asked to "ascertain whether it is feasible for the Federal Trade Commission to develop standards of proof and procedures for costing which can be adopted by the Commission as guides to business enterprises." It was hoped that if such standards and guides could be provided "sellers who wish to facilitate a determination of compliance with the Robinson-Patman Act would be able to organize their cost records accordingly."

The committee submitted a report made public by the Commission in February 1956. It said that the requirements of good management do not demand the extent of detail or continuity of records needed for an instantaneous solution of the problems presented by the Robinson-Patman Act and that business enterprises have not customarily kept such detailed records. It thought that the need for special studies of cost to meet an investigation or complaint by the Commission could not be eliminated, but that cost-accounting systems could be designed to provide suitable

[45] The Attorney General's National Committee to Study the Antitrust Laws, for example, said that "the Commission at times has wholly discarded and accorded no weight whatsoever to complex cost studies that merely fell short of accounting for the challenged differential by a fraction of a cent." *Report of the Attorney General's Committee*, p. 173. The statement is supported by footnote reference to the report of the trial examiner in the Standard Oil case and to the Commission's findings in 41 FTC 263, 276-81. To the present writer, the Commission's reasons for rejecting the cost defense of Standard of Indiana were clearly conceptual rather than mathematical. See above, pp. 314-16.

[46] The committee consisted of C. R. Fay, vice president and comptroller of Pittsburgh Plate Glass Co.; Alvin R. Jennings, partner in the accounting firm of Lybrand, Ross Bros. & Montgomery; E. W. Kelley, controller of Macy's in Kansas City (and assistant controller of Standard Brands during the Standard Brands case); H. T. McAnly, partner of the accounting firm Ernst & Ernst; Albert E. Sawyer, New York attorney; Herbert F. Taggart, professor of accounting at the University of Michigan; and Otto F. Taylor, New York certified public accountant. Professor Taggart was chairman.

raw material for special studies.[47] It opposed any effort by the Commission to adopt specific rules of accounting analysis on the ground that uniform methods and procedures in cost accounting were precluded by "the infinite variations of internal organization, methods of doing business, availability of accounting and statistical data, and other important factors." Stressing the elements of opinion and approximation in accounting, it urged a broad interpretation of the cost defense, with great weight given to cost studies made in good faith provided they relied on sound accounting principles, with leniency where realized costs had diverged from anticipated costs for reasons that could not be controlled or foreseen, with acceptance of sampling procedures, and with acceptance of approximate cost justifications that covered all but negligible fractions of the price differentials. However, the committee also emphasized the importance of classifying transactions and customers so as "to make sure that all members of the class are enough alike to make the averaging of their costs a sound procedure" and to make the class divisions "reflect actual differences in the manner or cost of dealing." The committee emphasized, too, the importance of the requirement that samples "be truly representative of the whole"; the impropriety of using incremental costs to justify price differences; and the need to justify the methods used in allocating costs.

The relation of the report to the previous practice of the Commission was seldom explicit; but, in general, the committee appeared to endorse the concepts and accounting procedures that the Commission had used in evaluating cost defenses, though with a warning against severity in their application.[48] This interpretation of the report is supported by the fact

[47] Professor Taggart, chairman of the committee, wrote in June 1956: "The committee has not come up with a magic formula which either eliminates the requirement for a painstaking and detailed cost study or materially decreases its scope or its cost. . . . The cost and complexity of a Robinson-Patman cost study does not decrease proportionately with the size of the respondent. . . .

"The report does not recommend continuous Robinson-Patman accounting. . . . Few laymen (in the accounting sense) are so unsophisticated as to believe that an economically feasible record-keeping system can be devised which would give an immediate answer to every Robinson-Patman problem. The experience of American Can Co., which actually carried out an ambitious project of this sort for nearly five years, does little to encourage emulation." From "Cost Justification under the Robinson-Patman Act," *Journal of Accountancy* (June 1956), pp. 52-56.

[48] Advisory Committee on Cost Justification, "Report to the Federal Trade Commission," February 1956 (mimeo.). Professor Taggart wrote subsequently that the report does what it can to encourage the "tendency to be reasonable" shown in a

that neither change in commission policy nor public controversy over the lack of change followed publication of the report.[49] The committee made several suggestions as to administrative matters—that the Commission's staff be more readily available for consultation while a cost study is being developed; that written drafts of expert testimony be exchanged in advance; that the Commission issue accounting opinions; and that an accounting adviser be appointed to serve the Commissioners and the hearing examiners in their judicial capacity.[50] Only as to written drafts of testimony does any serious criticism of Commission practice appear to have been intended. The recommendation in this respect expressed dissatisfaction with the prevailing practice of a purely oral presentation of the views of the Commission's accountants.

---

number of Commission decisions, among which he mentioned those involving Kraft-Phenix Cheese Corp., U. S. Rubber Co., Sylvania Electric Products, and B. F. Goodrich Co. He mentioned as other affirmative aspects of the committee's report (1) its advocacy of a broad interpretation of the phrase, "costs of manufacture, sale, and delivery," so that no costs are excluded as falling outside these categories; (2) its statement of the possibility of substantial cost differences in manufacturing; (3) a proposal as to a logical way to treat cash discounts; (4) a proposal as to a possible way of handling minor differences in the specifications of goods; (5) strong advocacy of the propriety of reasonable classification of customers, commodities, and transactions. As to the last, he specifically noted that the Commission has always accepted classifications of customers and transactions as proper, and in the Sylvania case accepted a grouping of commodities. The only instances in which he indicated that the committee's proposals imply criticism of previous Commission practice have to do with his second and third points, as to the scope of manufacturing-cost economies and as to cash discounts. With reference to the former, he noted a "visible reluctance" in the Commission's staff to concede that differences in manufacturing cost may play an effective part in cost justification. With reference to the latter, he noted that the cash-discount problem "occupied hundreds of the most unprofitable pages in the Sylvania case." ("Cost Justification under the Robinson-Patman Act," *op. cit.*, p. 55.) His views of the status of the cost defense have been subsequently elaborated in his book, *Cost Justification*, pp. 55, 527-49.

[49] Two careful analyses of the committee's report have appeared in legal publications: Harry L. Shniderman, "Cost Justification Under the Robinson-Patman Act—The FTC Advisory Committee's Report," 25 *University of Cincinnati Law Review*, Fall 1956, p. 389, and Albert E. Sawyer, "Cost Justification Report," *Proceedings at the Spring Meeting, 1956, of the American Bar Association Section of Antitrust Law*, p. 54.

[50] The Administrative Procedures Act, which sharply separates the judicial and prosecuting functions of regulatory commissions, prevents the judicial officers of the Commission from receiving advice from the accounting staff if that staff has participated in developing the case in support of the complaint.

Inherent Limitations of the Cost Defense

In the light of the committee's failure to find significant opportunities for improvement[51] as well as in the light of the analysis of the problems set forth above, it is reasonable to conclude that most of the difficulties of the cost defense are due to the provisions of the statute and the limitations of cost accounting, not the practices of the Federal Trade Commission.[52]

The inherent complexities and limitations of the cost defense raise a major problem as to the economic significance of the price discrimination law. The Congress undoubtedly thought that, in permitting business enterprises to differentiate their prices so far as they could show differences in their costs, the statute gave full scope to price policies designed to foster improvements in marketing methods and to reward customers for buying in ways that promote the efficiency of their suppliers. The cost defense, in other words, was regarded as the guarantee that economic efficiency would not be sacrificed in the effort to protect buyers from price discrimination. So far as price policies that promote efficiency give rise to ascertainable differences in cost, this presumption is reasonable. So far as cost savings cannot be identified and shown, the presumption has no basis.[53]

[51] The Attorney General's Committee also made recommendations about Commission policy toward cost defenses: that the Commission "adopt realistic standards acknowledging the inadequacies inherent in accounting measurements of price," and recognize that a cost-defense "is not susceptible to testing by precise or mechanical rules"; that justifications be accepted if they fall short by "a fractional amount," or if the unjustified portion could not reasonably cause injury; that "compulsory allocation" of joint distribution costs among *individual* transactions, or *individual* customers, or *individual* items in a seller's homogeneous product line be regarded as an "unwarranted burden"; and that a "reasonable approximation" of cost variances to price differentials "demonstrated in good faith through any authoritative and sound accounting principles" suffice to justify the differentials. (See *Report of the Attorney General's Committee,* pp. 174-75.) In effect, this seems to mean about what the Taggart Committee meant in recommending a broad interpretation of the cost defense, with weight given to studies made in good faith according to sound principles, and with acceptance of approximate justifications.

[52] The author does not assert, as to this or any other problem of public economic policy, that the possibilities for constructive work have been exhausted. But if there are unexplored opportunities here, they appear to demand more than the *expertise* of the accountants and government officials who have been enduringly concerned with the problem.

[53] Though it thought a change in the Commission's attitude could prevent the

In three respects the cost provision of the act is inadequate to perform the task of safeguarding efficiency in selling that has been entrusted to it. First, the inherent limitations on the segregation of cost data and the inherently controversial nature of many of the principles of allocating costs that must be used in providing a fine breakdown of cost information expose the concern that seeks to ascertain costs to exorbitant expense and considerable legal risk.[54] The burden of computing costs adequate to show the savings associated with flexible price structures is too great to be continuously borne even by a large enterprise.[55] With the standards of injury to competition so narrow that injury can be easily shown and with cost defenses so difficult as to be often unavailable, price variations are likely to be forbidden by law whether or not they contribute to the efficiency of the marketing process.

Second, the existing legal standard makes experiment perilous even if costs can be ascertained and proved. A seller who believes that a price reduction on a particular type of purchase—for example, purchase in excess of a given quantity—will be justified by the resultant savings is free to make the reduction provided he can show the savings. If, however, the savings do not develop, he has violated the law. Thus legal risks are inherent in any experiment with price differences the results of

---

cost requirement from impeding any price variation based on economies, the Attorney General's Committee described the situation in 1955 as follows: "Under such circumstances, only the most prosperous and patient business firm could afford pursuit of an often illusory defense. Pressure builds to gain legal safety by withholding price differentials from more efficient buyers, thus denying to the public the benefits of mass production and economical distribution processes which Congress intended to preserve. . . ." See *Report of the Attorney General's Committee*, p. 173.

[54] Although Warmack (see above, footnote 25, pp. 599-600) is undoubtedly right in saying that the risk has been enhanced by failure to consider cost-price relationships prior to challenge by the Commission, it is noteworthy that he thinks reasonable safety can be attained only by an enterprise that adheres closely to a pricing plan that avoids "expensive experiment."

[55] The cost study by the Sylvania Co. is estimated to have required 3,000 man-hours under supervision by corporate officers and independent accountants. See Sylvania's appeal brief before the Commission, pp. 22-24. Herbert Taggart estimates that the initial cost study by Goodrich had taken six men about five or six months, with part-time help from other persons, and that subsequent revisions required at least 495 man-days at a cost probably over $25,000. (See Taggart, *Cost Justification*, pp. 341, 361.) The cost defense of Minneapolis-Honeywell, according to an official of the board of directors, required nine months of work by from four to eight accountants and analysts. (See above, footnote 69, page 242.)

which are not certain. A concern desiring to avoid breaches of law must avoid such experiments.

Third, price concessions designed to promote efficiency are permissible only if the cost savings they produce are realized before the Commission challenges the concessions. It might be, for example, that if a considerable portion of a seller's customers were to buy in substantially larger quantities, the seller could make appreciable savings by using methods of sale appropriate to such large purchases, but that the savings could not be made until after the methods of sale were changed and the methods could not be changed until an adequate volume of large purchases was achieved. If price concessions on large purchases were to produce an immediate and substantial change in buying habits, followed by an immediate change in the seller's selling methods, cost savings would be available to justify the concessions. If, however, buyers' habits were to change slowly, there would be a considerable period without cost savings to justify the incentive prices. During this period the price concessions would be unlawful, and a seller who chose to make them would be accepting a calculated risk that the Commission would not promptly proceed against him. Since proceedings under the act are relatively few and slow, such a risk might be taken. Nevertheless, the law as written discourages experiment with price structures not only where the results are uncertain but also where they are slowly realized.

Apart from these difficulties, the principle of cost allocation which the Congress included in the statute appears to make it difficult to seize one possibility for enhancement of efficiency. Full and well-balanced use of plant is more efficient than partial idleness in some operations, accompanied, perhaps, by excessive activity in others. In a regulated industry such as those that sell electric power, public commissions have recognized, in certain circumstances, that discriminatory pricing makes it possible to promote efficiency by fuller off-peak use of existing facilities or by increasing demand to the point at which a larger and more economical productive unit can be employed. That such possibilities appear from time to time in competitive industries is probable. Cost accounting procedures, however, are not sufficient to identify them, and the right to a cost defense will not always be sufficient to enable a concern to seize them if they are perceived. Sales that permit efficient operation may require price differences that exceed cost differences, even when the price policies expressed in those sales are fully justified by their contributions to efficiency.

An example will make this clearer. It is possible that if the price is uniform for two methods of purchase the number of buyers using the X method will be so numerous, and those using the Y method so few, as to overtax the facilities of the concern for use of the X method and underemploy its facilities for use of the Y method. Let us suppose that under such pricing the sales cost per unit under the X method is 20 cents, as compared with 10 cents per unit under the Y method. Let us also suppose that the price difference that is necessary to induce a sufficient number of persons to change their method of buying from X to Y is 15 cents. Such a difference cannot be justified by existing cost differences. It may, nevertheless, promote efficiency. With a proper balance in the two methods of buying, the cost of sale by each method probably will be reduced. If the reduction establishes a cost difference of more than 15 cents between the two methods, the new price structure can be justified by the new costs, and the only problem springs from the possibility that uncertainty about the actual amount and speed of cost change may sometimes discourage desirable changes. But the reduction in costs, though enough to increase the aggregate spread between receipts and expenditures, may not be such as to establish a fifteen-cent cost differential between the two methods. For example, when operations are better balanced, the cost of selling by X method may fall to 10 cents and the cost of selling by Y method to 5 cents. It is quite possible that the aggregate saving will more than cover the reduction of gross revenue resulting from a price cut of 15 cents to customers who buy according to the Y method. But with a cost difference of only 5 cents between X and Y, there can be no cost justification for a difference in price of 15 cents.

The frequency with which this type of opportunity exists and can be realized only by incentive pricing that is not cost-justified is, of course, unknown. Since it requires a particular combination of cost structures and buyer reactions, it may be relatively uncommon. That it is not recognized at all in public policy toward discrimination results, to an unknown extent, in a discrepancy between that policy and the policy of encouraging efficiency.

The limitations summarized above make it probable that the price concessions that promote or reward better methods of purchase and sale will not be fully utilized and that experiment with the potentialities of price concessions to achieve better methods will be generally avoided. Since cost information is lacking not only for defense of marketing policies but also for purposes of appraisal of the marketing system, there is no way of determining the magnitude of the sacrifice of efficiency that is inherent in this tendency. It is clear that, in invoking a sweeping concept of injury to condemn differences in price that, by the cost standard, are undue while providing no adequate way of defending the differences that, by such a standard, would be appropriate, the law encourages businessmen to make their price structures unduly uniform rather than unduly diverse. However, it would not be desirable to correct this bias by applying the law to undue uniformity as well as undue diversity. In economic theory, both are wasteful. In public policy, however, to require that every cost difference be reflected in a price difference would be inappropriate. Although buyers should have an incentive to promote efficiency because they might receive lower prices by doing so, sellers, too, should have an incentive to adopt efficient methods because they might be able to retain the gains derived therefrom. The appropriate statutory standard as to the relation between price and cost is one in which cost advantages may be, but need not be, passed on to the buyer. Even if this were not true, the inadequacies of cost accounting would make it impossible to obtain a reliable and comprehensive analysis of cost differences for purposes of enforcing appropriate price variations; and the rigidity that such a requirement would impose on price structures would be intolerable.[56]

If the injuries to competition with which the law of price discrimination is concerned were limited to those that impair competitive protections in the market, this bias in the Robinson-Patman Act would be only a further example of a bias that is deliberately and consciously incorporated in antitrust policy. The antitrust laws generally contemplate that, in so far as any conflict appears between the maintenance of competition and the achievement of full economic efficiency, competition shall be preserved and efficiency sacrificed. The same principle appears in the quantity-limit proviso of the Robinson-Patman Act itself, though there it has been contaminated by its application to "unjust" as well as

---

[56] It is curious to note that under legislation controlling the sale of electric power in the United Kingdom, a private litigant (in *British Oxygen, Ltd.* v. *Scottish Electricity Board*) is asserting that a legal provision against price discrimination requires the seller of power to grant to his customer the full benefits of any savings in cost experienced in selling to him. In January 1959, the case had not yet been decided.

to monopolistic discriminations. In Section 2(a), however, the potential sacrifice of efficiency goes further than this. Price discrimination is unlawful, not only when it impairs the vigor of competition in the market, but also when it impairs the competitive opportunities of a particular class of sellers or customers. In the absence of the cost defense (and of the defense that competition was met in good faith), this narrow type of injury is sufficient to invalidate price differentials. Accordingly, the failure of the cost standard to protect efficient methods may result in the sacrifice of those methods not only for the purpose of protecting competition but also for the purpose of protecting classes of competitors.

In summary, insufficient provision is made to protect efficiency in the part of the law that applies to price discrimination, and no provision is made to do so in the parts of the law that apply to brokerage, advertising allowances, and perhaps also the provision of selling services. The objectives of the statute have not been reconciled with efficiency of distribution, but remain partially inconsistent therewith.

19 / *Appraisal of the Price Discrimination Law*

AN APPRAISAL of the effects of the Robinson-Patman Act must be tentative for several reasons:

First, broad changes in the environment in which business is done have obscured the effect of public policy toward price discrimination. Many of these changes were incident to the transition from depression to war and from war to postwar boom. Others involved such institutional trends as the growth of national-brand advertising, the development of supermarkets, the growth of the pre-packaging of foods, and the shift of demand from staples to specialties—trends which may have been affected by the law but certainly expressed many other influences also.

Second, the most significant consequences of the statute may have been indirect, and therefore practically untraceable. One effect that is to be expected from any public policy is an alteration of the relative advantages and disadvantages of different courses of private action and a consequent change in the direction in which private policies evolve; but since law is only one of the influences that establish the nature of risks and opportunities, its effect is to be observed clearly only if it is overwhelmingly predominant or if its impact is both immediate and uniform. A statute can have a significant influence if it brings about gradual changes in business conduct by slightly altering the balance of considerations that are almost equal in weight; but since such effects are deferred, and the decisions based on them follow no visibly consistent pattern, they can be traced only by inference. Even persons whose action is affected in this way may not be conscious of the statutory source of change.

Third, the fact that the law of price discrimination incorporates at least three legal principles makes it likely that the different parts of the law have varied in their impact on the business community. Yet, because businessmen have a considerable opportunity to change the form of their conduct so that it is subject to one part of the law rather than another, maneuvers to alter legal jurisdiction have modified to an uncertain extent the direct impact of each of the legal principles.

Fourth, there are serious gaps in the information both about what occurred before legal proceedings and about what occurred after. The record of the nature and effect of business practices that were subjected to complaint is defective because the complaints of the Federal Trade Commission were often couched in general terms; because most of the cases were not tried; and because it was not legally necessary in a trial for the Commission to bring out all the data relevant to an economic appraisal. Cases concerned with brokerage or disproportionality needed to contain nothing as to the economic setting or business impact of the practice, and cases concerned with price discrimination needed to make no distinction between the broad and the narrow concepts of injury. Gaps in the information about what happened afterward are traceable to such facts as the disappearance of the business enterprises directly concerned, the death of executives who had personal knowledge of the situation, the destruction of corporate records, the inability of private investigators lacking coercive powers to persuade the affected enterprises to take the time and trouble necessary to provide reliable and adequately specific information, and the reluctance of persons interviewed to speak candidly where they perceived legal risks.

What is available as a basis for appraisal is a series of scattered insights into particular situations. They differ widely in scope, degree of detail, and reliability. The conclusions that they severally suggest are sometimes inconsistent with one another, and in such cases information is generally lacking with which to evaluate their relative importance or to determine whether the apparent differences are characteristic of different industries or of different periods of time.

The best that can be done with such materials is to develop conclusions that appear to summarize a considerable number of instances, to be reasonable on logical grounds, and to be unrefuted by any of the facts that have become available. Some conclusions are more strongly supported than others, but none can be regarded as conclusively proved. The justification for tentatively offering them is the fact that the inquiry has been pushed as far as it can readily go. Some of the difficulties of appraisal are inherent in the nature of the subject matter. Others could be avoided only by a governmental investigation possessing mandatory powers. Other private students of the Robinson-Patman Act might differ from the author in their estimate of its effects, but they, too, would necessarily advance tentative hypotheses based on evidence obviously fragmentary.

Was There a Problem that Justified Action?

The cases that have arisen under the statute have confirmed the belief of Congress that there were problems of price discrimination significantly related to competition. These have appeared both in the competitive relationships among buyers and in those among sellers. Cases such as those against E. B. Muller and Maryland Baking Company involved deliberate efforts to destroy competitors, the success of which would necessarily have diminished market competition. Though the facts were such that proceedings under the Sherman Act might have been successful, it was appropriate and probably easier to invoke a law against price discrimination. On the buying side of the market, the associated buying power of large enterprises, such as was involved in the case against Atlas Supply Company, had obviously restrictive implications. To proceed against such groups under a law of price discrimination was easier and more appropriate than to attempt to treat their joint demand for discounts as a conspiracy to fix buying prices. In the spark plug cases, it was evident that the buying advantage given to automobile manufacturers in the purchase of replacement plugs enabled these powerful concerns to dominate the replacement market through their captive dealer organizations. Though the principle by which A. & P. was prevented from receiving allowances in lieu of brokerage may be questionable as a general rule of law, it is clear that the power of A. & P. was coming to have important anticompetitive implications.[1]

[1] Indeed, that power was so great that it led not only to the passage of the Robinson-Patman Act, directed largely at A. & P., but also to successful criminal prosecution under the Sherman Act and subsequently to a consent decree in a parallel civil case. In the criminal proceeding, a circuit court affirmed the judgment of the district court, and A. & P. did not choose to carry the case to the Supreme Court. The economic implications of this litigation have been matters of controversy (see Morris A. Adelman, "The A. & P. Case: A Study in Applied Economic Theory," 63 *Quarterly Journal of Economics* (May 1949) 238, and Joel B. Dirlam and Alfred E. Kahn, "Anti-Trust Law and the Big Buyer: Another Look at the A. & P. Case," 60 *Journal of Political Economy* 118). However, though the critics of the Government's position in the case have severely challenged parts of the economic analysis and legal theory on which the prosecution

Moreover, the cases under the Robinson-Patman Act have disclosed the prevalence of price structures that are of dubious economic usefulness and probable anticompetitive tendency. Big buyers have commonly been able to obtain volume discounts, special price concessions, and other types of advantage that recognize their bigness and that have little or no logical connection with functional efficiency as distinct from bargaining power. Examples are the volume-discount schedules of National Biscuit Company, Standard Brands, and Morton Salt Company. Under the schedule of the National Biscuit Company, only 213 customers received discounts in the first quarter of 1944. Under the Standard Brands schedule, the few buyers who could take 50,000 pounds or more of bakers yeast per month paid 44 per cent less than the smallest bakers. Under the Morton Salt Company schedule, the largest discounts required volumes of purchase so large that only four or five customers could attain them. It is reasonable to believe, with the Commission and the courts, that there was a tendency for such advantages to be received cumulatively by the big buyers on the various commodities they bought. That this type of advantage strengthened the position of the large buyer and tended to place a larger part of the total business in the hands of a big few can scarcely be doubted. That competition among the few tends to be weak competition is a reasonable hypothesis. To limit the buying power of big buyers was, therefore, an appropriate aspect of a competitive policy, even where such concerns had not yet attained dominance and anticompetitive effects had not yet appeared.

But the cases also supply persuasive evidence that the problem posed by discrimination was more complex than had been envisaged by the Congress. Discrimination was not solely a weapon of predatory sellers and a source of advantage for powerful buyers. Where there were price agreements, the effectiveness of these agreements was reduced, as in the corn products industry, through various forms of special and often secret concessions to particular purchasers. To attack this kind of discrimination was to curb a private means of enhancing competition and to place greater burdens on the parts of the law that forbid conspiracy.

In the case of the single large enterprise, too, discrimination had competitive as well as anticompetitive aspects. While a large seller may

---

was based, they have admitted the validity of other parts. There was in the case substantial evidence of A. & P.'s intention to dominate important retail markets and of anticompetitive effects in certain markets in which a few large chains as a group had acquired such dominance.

discriminate to destroy his competitors, he may also exercise his power by establishing rigidly inflexible prices not responsive to changes in the economic environment. Where such sticky prices appear, discrimination sometimes introduces an element of competitive flexibility. Moreover, the pressure of powerful buyers for discriminatory concessions may provide the principal leverage to overthrow the unduly rigid prices of powerful sellers.[2] Standard Brands dominated the market for bakers yeast. The tire industry was in the hands of a few very large enterprises. In seeking price concessions for themselves, the large bakers and the large oil companies, though they obtained advantages that increased their own power, also did something to diminish the power of the dominant sellers of yeast and tires.

The tendency to underestimate these difficulties was encouraged by the fact that the concepts of the law were developed both by the Congress and by the Federal Trade Commission with the food industries primarily in mind. Food manufacture is among the more competitive segments of American manufacturing. Food distribution is a field in which the mass distributor has become conspicuous. The dangers of conspiracy and of sticky prices and the possibility that each may be broken by powerful buyers are less obvious in this field than in certain other parts of the economy.

Although the Robinson-Patman Act contains no specific provisions

[2] In a study of discriminatory pricing practices in the grocery trade, Dr. L. A. Skeoch of the staff of the Director of Investigation and Research under the Canadian Combines Investigation Act noted the existence of substantial differentials in special discounts and allowances, with the less favored buyers enjoying "average rates of payment as low as one-third those of their favored rivals." He commented that differential treatment did not necessarily justify criticism since in some circumstances discriminatory terms might improve economic performance. However, he found in the data of the study no support for two possible justifications of discrimination: first, that the pressure of big buyers for favored treatment might foster price competition among oligopolistic sellers, and second, that such pressure might reduce promotional expenditures and thereby reduce marketing costs or might lead to more efficient expenditure for promotion. As to pressure on oligopolistic prices, he saw no support for the opinion that chains were particularly successful in obtaining special discounts and allowances from the largest sellers nor that they took their advantages in lower buying prices as distinguished from advertising allowances. As to marketing efficiency, he thought the tendency had been to increase total expenditure on promotion, sometimes with little or no evidence of results justifying the payments. See Restrictive Trade Practices Commission, *Report Transmitting a Study of Certain Discriminatory Pricing Practices in the Grocery Trade Made by the Director of Investigation & Research, Department of Justice, Ottawa* (1958), pp. 193-95.

designed to cope with such complexities, the principal provision set
forth in Section 2(a) and invoked by reference in Section 2(f) would
have been capable of interpretation in such a way as to deal with the
difficulties when they appeared. Discriminations were to be unlawful
only when they impaired competition in one of three stated ways. It
might have been possible to base a finding of injury to competition on
a broad analysis of the competitive environment, sufficient to show the
impact of a discrimination in its particular setting. Under such a standard, discriminations the chief effect of which was to strengthen powerful
buyers would have been regarded as injurious, while discriminations that
furnished the last remaining forms of competition or that resulted in ever-
widening concessions that broke down an over-rigid price structure would
have been held not to be injurious. But the Commission did not proceed in this way. Rather it saw injury in effects so narrow that the
broader implications of a discrimination were seldom examined. Moreover, the portions of the statute that were concerned with brokerage
services and allowances afforded no leeway for this kind of thinking.

Did the Act Meet the Problem Successfully?

There is strong reason to believe that the statute has afforded effective protection against the price-cutting activities of predatory would-be
monopolists and that it has substantially reduced the discriminatory advantages in price enjoyed by large buyers. Cases like those against E. B.
Muller and Maryland Baking Company illustrate the successful use of
the statute against selective price cutting with predatory effects. That
the previous advantages of large buyers have been curbed is apparent.
Brokerage payments to chain stores have become infrequent. Allowances and services are more broadly available than before. When payments are made for advertising, care is usually taken to see that the advertising is actually provided. Price differences in favor of the big buyer
have been eliminated in some cases and reduced in others. Under revised discount structures, more customers are usually eligible for discounts. The big buyer's pressure on sellers for price concessions has
diminished.

Though these sweeping conclusions are supported by fragmentary
evidence as to concerns involved in cases in which the FTC issued
orders, the available information all points in the same direction. In a

large number of interviews with sellers and with buyers who had formerly been both favored and disfavored, opinions consistent with what has
been said above were general, though there was a reiterated opinion
that effects of this kind have been reduced through covert violation of
the Commissioner's orders. What could be ascertained about the effects
of orders in particular cases tended to support the broad opinions.

A. & P. and Atlas Supply Company no longer receive their former
concessions in the form either of brokerage or of discounts, and those
who supply A. & P. and the oil companies served by Atlas Supply Company have experienced less buying pressure. The payment of overrides
by United States Rubber Company continues only to the oil companies
that are not customers of the company. The buying advantages of Aloe
Company on medical supplies have been substantially reduced. Volume
discounts have been dropped entirely by Sherwin-Williams Company,
Pittsburgh Plate Glass Company, Morton Salt Company, International
Salt Company, Simmons, American Optical Company, Master Lock
Company, Jacobs Manufacturing Company, and the producers of frit.
The spread between the highest and lowest prices has been substantially
reduced in the discount structures of National Biscuit Company, Standard Brands, and John B. Stetson. Off-scale selling for the benefit of large
buyers has been entirely abandoned in some cases and narrowly circumscribed in others. Even Minneapolis-Honeywell, which successfully
defended itself in the price discrimination proceeding, reduced the spread
in its discounts and abandoned off-scale selling.

Moreover, discount structures have been so modified that discounts
have become more widely available to relatively small enterprises. This
is conspicuously true for the packaged biscuits bought from National
Biscuit Company, for the bakers yeast bought from Standard Brands,
for the educational supplies bought from American Crayon Company
and Binney & Smith, and for the roofing bought from Ruberoid Company.

It is reasonable to suppose that the changes made in compliance with
the orders of the Commission and the courts in these particular cases
have been accompanied by voluntary changes of a similar character by
other enterprises desirous of avoiding legal proceedings. In the cases in
which effects can be traced, there have been substantial differences in
the amounts of price spread remaining after the proceedings. Doubtless there are similar differences elsewhere. There is no basis for an estimate of the extent to which the advantages of big buyers have been reduced. But that this has been the direction of movement is persuasively

indicated, and that the amount of the change has been substantial seems likely.

The trend of the economy has been such as to encourage this kind of development. The depression that produced the Robinson-Patman Act was followed by a war and then by a sustained period of business prosperity, which, to this day, has been broken only by recessions neither long nor severe. Sellers have been in a better position to maintain prices, and powerful buyers in a worse position to obtain concessions, than in the period before the act. Moreover, the rise of supermarkets has resulted in a variety of regional chains and substantial single retail enterprises through whose appearance the differential in power between the national corporate chains and the independent merchants has been reduced. The change in structure has been accompanied by an increased emphasis on national brands, broader promotional programs for those brands, and enhanced prestige for the successful national advertiser. The greater importance of national brands was repeatedly mentioned in interviews, particularly by persons interested in the voluntary chains. Such developments have tended, on the one hand, to diminish the seller's need to make concessions to powerful distributors and, on the other hand, to enhance his willingness to enlist the sales co-operation of a larger proportion of those who distribute his products. The law may have had some effect on the direction in which the business structure has evolved. If, however, one could assume that this evolution would have shown the same trend without the statute, one could say confidently that the circumstances of the late 1950's, in themselves, would have reduced the discrimination that was present in the mid-1930's.

But the law has only partly accomplished its purpose. It can be described as a partial failure as well as a partial success. Its failures have four aspects.

First, the statute itself has serious gaps. Sellers alone are liable for violation of the provisions about services and allowances, and partly for this reason there has been a tendency for powerful buyers to obtain immunity by seeking concessions in this form. Though buyers as well as sellers are liable where there are unlawful price concessions, the part of the statute that establishes the buyer's liability was badly conceived and has proved to be so burdensome that it cannot be expected to play a major part in future proceedings. Except in the case of brokerage, the recipient of discriminatory concessions is either hard to reach or unreachable.

Second, the fact that the law must be separately applied against each seller or buyer except where there is conspiracy has necessarily meant discrimination in enforcement. Particular enterprises have been subjected to orders while their competitors remained unattacked. If the statute were so written and so administered that the first proceeding was always directed at a powerful concern whose practices were conspicuously responsible for the discriminations in a particular market, selective enforcement would be no more than a minor problem. But when the Commission proceeds against one of a series of sellers who grant concessions to one or more powerful buyers not involved in the proceedings, the disadvantage of priority in the application of the law may be as great and as burdensome as market discrimination itself.

Third, the statute was designed to strike at manifestations of the power of the big buyer rather than at that power itself. This has meant that ways are available to obtain advantage for the powerful by means not within the scope of the statute. Goods that are not of like grade and quality are not subject to the law. Thus price concessions can be justified by the differentiation of products, and to a minor extent it appears that this has been done. More important, however, is the fact that selective buying and selective selling are weapons fully available to the powerful concern. A seller who may not discriminate against a class of buyers may cut them off. A buyer who may not obtain a discriminatory concession may purchase exclusively from concerns that sell only to him or only to customers who are also powerful buyers that obtain similar concessions. Moreover, even from a seller who does a general business, a powerful buyer may obtain advantages without limit in the form of preferential access to goods, quicker delivery, readier extension of credit, and the like. The weakness of the statute consists in the fact that it covers only price discriminations and closely related practices, whereas the manifestations of power and privilege can be infinitely varied. No law striking at the symptoms of power rather than power itself can be other than incomplete.[3]

[3] The ineffectiveness of the law in limiting the growth of the great corporate chains in the food industry is evident in the sales of the largest concerns. A. & P.'s sales, which were slightly more than $1 billion in 1927, were more than $4.3 billion for the year ended February 1956 ("Chain Store Sales," *Progressive Grocer*, March 1957, p. 49). Safeway, which sold about $76 million in 1927, sold $2.1 billion net in 1957 (*Moody's Industrial Manual*, 1958, p. 1503). American Stores, which sold about $121 million in 1927, sold $780 million in the 52 weeks ending March 31, 1957 (*ibid.*, p. 7).

Fourth, the law has curbed not only the practices of the powerful but also the practices of others designed to furnish protection against the powerful. Flexible adjustments designed to give independent small concerns some of the buying advantages of chain stores have been struck down where, as in the Southgate case, they gave brokers the status of buyers and where, as in the cases involving voluntary chains, they gave associations of independent mechants power comparable to that of the great buyers. The capacity of the independent to protect himself has been weakened, and thereby an increasing reliance has necessarily been placed on the enforcement of the statute.

The study affords no satisfactory basis for weighing the new legal protection of the small buyer against the damage done to his efforts at self-protection. In the nature of the case, however, the immediate effect of the former must substantially outweigh the immediate effect of the latter. What small distributors lost through the Southgate case and similar cases was the advantage of pool cars. What small buyers lost in the Biddle and Oliver cases was a cut rate on market information. The losses involved in the brokerage cases against co-operatives and voluntary chains had significance only for the actual and prospective participants in such organizations and only within the limits to which group buying could be carried without becoming vulnerable under the Sherman Act or the Federal Trade Commission Act. At most, the adverse impact of the law on small buyers pertained to limited savings and to bargaining advantages available to segments of the group, whereas the favorable impact of the law on such buyers applied generally wherever they were at a bargaining disadvantage. The ultimate importance that might have been attained by the voluntary groups is, of course, a matter of opinion. Nevertheless, it is probable that for the whole body of small buyers the gains were greater than the losses.

Information is not available for a broader comparison on which to base a judgment of the relative long-run importance of the successes and failures in accomplishing the purpose of the statute. It is noteworthy, however, that the failures fall into two classes. One class, including the incompletenesses in the law, the difficulties created by discriminatory enforcement, and various preferences that can be given and received without violation, may be regarded as merely limiting the success with which the statute curbs privilege. The fact that success has been incomplete does not destroy the value of what has been accomplished. The failures in the other class are more important. In checking the growth of voluntary groups and encouraging vertical integration, the law may have assisted the powerful in ways that will become more significant with time. Here the question is whether an immediate reduction of the advantages of the powerful has produced an institutional change that means even greater advantages for the powerful in the future. Though this question has no clear answer, its importance is obvious.

Did the Statute Reach Beyond
the Problem It Was Meant to Meet?

Many proceedings under the Robinson-Patman Act have involved neither predatory discrimination by sellers nor buying advantages for powerful purchasers. In each field of activity some of the cases have been irrelevant to the purposes of the law. Many of the brokerage cases have been concerned with relatively small transactions among relatively small enterprises; they have prevented petty chiseling or have merely enforced by Federal authority a rigidly orthodox theory of the brokerage function. The cases involving disproportionate services have included proceedings, such as that against Luxor, in which the Commission enforced the use of a channel of distribution that the seller had vainly sought to employ before the case, the use of which was found to be undesirable by the distributors themselves after the order. The cases against disproportionate advertising allowances made it difficult if not impossible to engage in selective advertising whether or not there was a harmful competitive effect. The cases concerned with price discrimination included some, like the automobile parts cases, in which the Commission perceived injury in the secondary line of commerce even though the disfavored customers were unanimous that they had not been injured; and some, like the rubber stamp cases, in which disorderly price competition among small sellers was held to be seriously damaging to competition among them. In policy toward discrimination, the comprehensive sweep that was given to the concept of injury determined the impact of the statute; for cost justification was so difficult that it could seldom be successfully invoked, and the statutory meaning of good faith in meeting competition was so far from ordinary business conceptions of such good faith that this type of defense held innumerable snares for the unwary. A considerable portion of the Commission's effort was spent in proceedings among small concerns directed against injuries to competition that had nothing to do with the big buyer or the predatory seller. Consequently, the statute has had an unnecessarily harassing effect on business conduct. Moreover, in applying the law in this way, the Commission was diverted from the substantial problems of power, which were the principal concern of the legislation.

Was Efficiency Affected?

In one respect, the pervasive application of the statute may have produced in some companies a variety of improvements in business practice. To minimize their legal vulnerability, enterprises have often found it advisable to analyze their price structures in considerable detail and, where possible, to compare price differences with cost differences. The close attention given to the minutiae of pricing appears to have led, in certain instances, to the discovery of various wasteful practices and to the adoption of new and sometimes useful devices.

Instances in which the application of the law by the Federal Trade Commission has increased efficiency do not appear clearly except in the case of educational supplies. Here various customers of American Crayon Company and Binney & Smith have indicated that, with confidence in their capacity to compete in the resale market, they have found it possible to buy in larger quantities and carry larger inventories. However, there are some indications that the impact of the act on quantity discounts and formulas for territorial price discrimination may have fostered efficiency. As to the former, the law has tended to deflate the belief of businessmen that substantial economies are achieved when sales are made in relatively large quantities and to make businessmen aware of the economies associated with relatively small increases in the size of small purchases. Thus, it has encouraged a revision of discount structures appropriate to provide incentives for more economical methods of buying. As to formulas for territorial price discrimination, changes in practice have been due more to the law of conspiracy than to the Robinson-Patman Act; but proceedings under both types of law have brought about the practical abandonment of prices that include phantom freight, have encouraged shipment by water and by truck as well as by rail, and have enabled buyers who wish to take delivery at the point of production to do so. These changes have facilitated the use of more economical methods of transportation and have probably diminished the amount of avoidable cross-hauling. Thus they probably have contributed something to the efficiency of physical distribution.

In important respects, however, the statute has created obstacles to the attainment of full operating efficiency. Under the standard of proportionality, concerns have had either to buy undesired advertising and provide services they regarded as valueless, on the one hand, or refrain from providing service or purchasing advertising they regarded as desirable, on the other. The tendency has been to undertake sales programs of dubious value at increased expense. Similarly, to avoid payments in lieu of brokerage, various sellers have found it expedient either to use brokers in transactions where they were not needed, or else to avoid using brokers in transactions where they were needed. Either choice tended to diminish efficiency. In view of the breadth of the concept of injury and the difficulty of the cost defense, sellers have found it dangerous to experiment with methods of sale and channels of distribution that might increase efficiency. They have been encouraged to make their prices insufficiently responsive to cost differences lest they be held to have provided differentials that were excessively responsive. Buyers, in turn, deprived of the opportunity to save money by economical methods of buying, have tended to buy more wastefully. The most conspicuous examples of the encouragement of wasteful practice are found in the application of the brokerage and proportionality provisions.

The records of the cases include various changes indicative of wasteful increases in the costs of distribution. Some of this decrease of efficiency appeared where buyers no longer had incentives to buy in the most economical way. Some of it appeared where sellers found it necessary to spend money for unwanted services in order to avoid legal risks.

Unable to get brokerage or allowances in lieu thereof, A. & P. adopted policies of hand-to-mouth buying and bought through brokers even when it was already in direct touch with the supplier. The oil companies that had bought through Atlas Supply Company set up duplicate buying organizations. Such canners as Columbia River Packers, Custom House Packing, and Ketchikan Packing set up expensive systems of consignment stocks and, instead of billing pool cars to the broker, billed every small customer directly. Garment manufacturers who were engaged in selective advertising found it necessary to choose between abandonment of publicity they found profitable and payment for publicity they did not think worth its cost. Similarly, cosmetic producers

that used demonstrators were able to retain this practice only by providing equivalent sales aids for small outlets, whether or not these additional expenditures justified themselves by increased volume.

Moreover, the excessive sweep of the law has tended to make business more expensive by requiring careful legal analysis as a part of substantially every decision concerned with prices, market channels, or
sales effort. The participation of legal counsel in marketing decisions is
both costly and time-consuming.

Was the Vigor of Competition Affected?

Excessive scope in the law has also tended to reduce the vigor of
competition. Even where there is no predatory purpose and no problem
of the power of the large enterprise, sellers and buyers tend to play safe
as a precautionary measure. Buyers tend to bargain less vigorously;
sellers tend to maintain prices that are less responsive to the varying
conditions of the market. Price structures that have proved to be legally
safe tend to be continued because change would involve new risk. Price
change tends to take place only where the pressures toward it are great
enough to justify an upward or downward movement of the entire price
structure.

These tendencies reach their maximum under the impetus of the
Commission's theory of injury to competition in the primary line of
commerce. It has come to be dangerous to compete by selective or localized price reductions, not only where the seller is large and the purpose
predatory, but also wherever a competitor is smaller and even (on the
authority of the rubber stamp cases) where there is no size differential.
When diverting business from competitors is legally hazardous, competition itself tends to become hazardous.

Did the Law Affect Price Movements?

The law has had various effects on prices and price movements. There
is a consensus of opinion among both buyers and sellers that the result
has been to diminish the flexibility of prices; indeed, many of the persons interviewed regard this as the chief virtue of the statute. It is probable that in oligopolistic industries the outlawry of discriminatory concessions has reduced the principal kind of price competition that still

existed under conditions of concentrated production and sale. It is probable that, in industries that have achieved conspiracy by direct agreement on price formulas based on reciprocal freight absorption, the elimination of unsystematic price cuts has removed the principal weakness of the conspiracy. Proof of neither of these propositions has been obtained during the study; but it was not to be expected that evidence pointing to possible violations of the Sherman Act would have been volunteered by participants in such arrangements. However, the interviews strongly support the inference that the reduced pressure of buyers for concessions and the enhanced risk of the seller who makes concessions have tended to make sticky prices stickier and thus to reduce the flexibility and responsiveness of the price system. The effect has been great enough to be prominent in the thinking of businessmen who like it as well as businessmen who do not like it.

We need not rely on such indirect inference in determining the immediate effect of the cases on the prices paid by buyers for the goods involved therein. It has been frequently asserted in political controversy about the Robinson-Patman Act that when concessions are forbidden, everybody pays the higher price, and, conversely, that general price reductions are made by sellers who can no longer make special price reductions. Since many influences underlie the long-run changes of prices, no one can prove that the orders in the price discrimination cases have or have not had a general upward or downward influence on price trends. However, it is clear from the cases that the price movements produced immediately by the price discrimination orders have not been uniformly upward or downward. In the volume-discount cases, discriminations were reduced by raising the lowest prices for salt, bedding, optical goods, and locks, but by lowering the highest prices for dental supplies, biscuits, and yeast. On industrial chucks, high and low prices both moved toward the middle, and the manufacturer obtained approximately the same revenue as before. In the basing-point cases delivered prices fell at points that had formerly been subject to phantom-freight charges. In the cement industry, delivered prices rose temporarily where shippers had absorbed freight, but freight absorption reappeared when the sellers' market weakened and the political controversy ended. Outside the fields of volume discounts and territorial price discrimination, such evidence as is available shows similar conflicting results. The effect of the Caradine Hat case and of the Southgate group of brokerage cases was to raise prices to the buyers who had formerly been favored. The effect of the school-supply cases and the roofing case against Ruberoid Company was to make the lower prices more generally available.

The mixed result is not surprising. Situations in which a few buyers get special concessions and situations in which a few buyers pay premium prices are equally subject to the law against price discrimination. The importance of retaining the business of the favored buyers and the difficulty of doing so can be expected to differ greatly in different situations. The proportion of the seller's total volume that formerly moved at the low prices can be expected to show a similar difference. There is no reason to expect sellers who are legally required to alter their price structures to disregard such varying characteristics of the markets they serve.

Thus theory and the scattered available evidence unite to support the view that when illegal price discrimination is ended there is no uniform effect of raising or lowering prices. Whatever general effect may be produced on the price level can be only the net residue of conflicting tendencies. Comparable information about prices is not available in a scale permitting inquiry as to whether there is such a residual effect; but if one could be computed, it probably would reflect nothing more significant than the accidental balance of the industries and markets in which price discrimination proceedings had been brought.

Do the Bad Effects Necessarily Accompany the Good Ones?

Some of the difficulties that have developed under the Robinson-Patman Act were obviously avoidable. There was no need to apply the proportionality sections against the seller alone, with exemption for the buyer. There was no need to make disproportionate payments and services or the payment of brokerage to a person on the other side of the transaction automatically illegal, regardless of competitive impacts. There was no need to deprive the offender under these sections of whatever benefit he might obtain from the defenses that are applicable to violations of the price discrimination section. Similarly, there was no need to make the treatment of buyers' conduct under Section 2(f) a mere corollary of the treatment of sellers' conduct under Section 2(a). It should have been possible to establish by statute or by interpretation a concept of injury to competition more closely related to the problems of predatory selling and of advantage enjoyed by the powerful. If the principles of Section 2(a) had governed the other sections concerned with sellers' conduct, if there had been a carefully drawn section of similar scope concerned with buyers' conduct, and if the concept of injury had not been exaggerated, a considerable number of the evils that have developed in the administration of the law would have been reduced or eliminated. What was important would have been more enforceable. There would have been less of what was unimportant or anti-competitive.

But other difficulties are more deeply imbedded in the plan of the statute. So long as the policy against price discrimination is enforced by law suits, legal counsel must be at the elbow of the sales manager or the purchasing agent in each enterprise, and selective legal proceedings must result in certain discriminations against the concerns that are first investigated and subjected to orders. The complexities and uncertainties that are inherent in the application of cost accounting to price differences are so great that cost justification will necessarily remain expensive and uncertain. In consequence the exemption of cost-justified discriminations cannot afford sufficient protection for efficiency where the statutory injuries are found. Moreover, there is an inescapable difficulty in the concept of injury itself. Since big business creates the dual hazard of predatory action and stand-pat inflexibility, and since aggressive bargaining by one powerful enterprise may reduce the stand-pat inflexibility of another, there will necessarily be circumstances in which discrimination has contradictory effects on competition. To disentangle these or to determine their balance of importance is a perplexing task. Thus far public policy has evoked a dual standard in such instances: it has been concerned about inflexibility in cases arising under the Sherman Act, but not in cases arising under the Robinson-Patman Act. It is not inevitable that policy under the latter statute should be indifferent to considerations of flexibility. It is inevitable, however, that difficulties should arise in appraising the relative importance of the two problems.

Could a Better Law Be Enacted?

What has just been said implies that the Robinson-Patman Act could be amended to accomplish its purposes more successfully. There is little doubt that a bill could be drafted that would be a great improvement on the present statute.

However, whether or not such a bill could be passed is problematical. In law-making, group interests and conflicting ideas come into conflict and result in modifications of legislative proposals in the search for a compromise that will win legislative and executive assent. This is always an uncertain process. The uncertainties are at their maximum when the subject matter is complex enough to be readily misunderstood, and when the groups whose interests are in conflict are numerous enough to provide opportunity for shifting alliances and for tactics based on concealment and sabotage.

Group conflict, obfuscation, and misunderstanding have been conspicuous in the efforts that have thus far been made to amend the law of price discrimination. The battle over the basing-point bill which is discussed at some length in Chapter XII furnishes a notable example of differences between actual and ostensible objectives, of efforts to accomplish purposes by round-about means, of confusion and uncertainty as to the actual effect of proposed statutory language, and of such change in the character of a bill during the legislative process that the original sponsors repudiated it. The later debates over the successive bills designed to change the status of the defense of meeting competition indicate diminishing confusion but rivalry of exaggeration in stating the effects of existing or proposed law. The latest versions of these bills are striking examples of the unexpected changes that can be introduced during the legislative process in a search for an acceptable compromise.

The central question for anyone who would amend the Robinson-Patman Act is whether the new statute would be nearer to or further from his objective. There would inevitably be political struggle between big and little business, between various classes of producers and distributors, and between spokesmen for different types of industry. Underlying the conflicts of interest would be unresolved issues as to the relative importance of different purposes: Is the vigor of competition among sellers or competitive opportunity among buyers more important to competitive vigor? What is the relative importance of fairness in competition and flexibility and vigor therein? What should be the relative emphasis on the immediate impact of a business practice and the less certain but possibly more significant future impact thereof? In approaching such problems under the pressure of warring groups, congressional action would be exceptionally unpredictable.

It is understandable, therefore, that people who do not like the Robinson-Patman Act may prefer it to the unknown statute that might emerge from a new legislative effort. Those who desire to strengthen the law may fear that it would be weakened; those who wish to weaken it may fear that it would be strengthened.

In a book such as this, however, neither the political feasibility of change nor the probable direction that would be taken by the unleashed forces of change should be considered. These matters may alter from year to year, and their appraisal at any one time calls for a political *expertise* to which the author makes no pretense. Today's impossibility often becomes tomorrow's program.

The proper question for a book such as this is what changes would be desirable and technically feasible if they were politically possible. There is a great advantage in having on hand legislative proposals unlimited by considerations of expediency. Public policy changes direction chiefly in time of crisis, when events move too rapidly for new programs to be formulated and evaluated. The crisis supplies the motivation, but the thinking of previous periods about what then seemed to be political impossibilities supplies the program.

Accordingly, the next and final chapter will attempt to state what the author believes would be worth doing and technically possible if people should ever be willing to do it.

20 / *Suggestions as to Policy*

A RECONSIDERATION of the Robinson-Patman Act should begin with an effort to determine the appropriate place of the law of price discrimination in the general body of antitrust laws and the scope and focus of a statute appropriate to that place. Do we need a law of price discrimination, and, if so, what is its proper function?

Objectives in the
Primary Line of Commerce

The need to prevent competition in the primary line from being reduced by the discriminatory practices of powerful competitors has been recognized since 1914. Though the cases concerned with this type of damage to competition have been few, they have been generally accepted as a useful supplement to Section 2 of the Sherman Act. Whatever doubts have been raised about them have been focused, not on the law of price discrimination, but on the broad question whether the growth of oligopoly has made it necessary to re-think our policy toward competition generally, in the Sherman Act as well as in the Clayton Act. This question is answered in the negative by most of those who consider it; in any event, it lies beyond the scope of the present study. The ground for a law against discrimination that is harmful, in this sense, to competition in the primary line remains what it was in 1914.

To prevent discrimination that works this type of injury was possible under the old law unless the discrimination took the form of quantity discounts. It is possible under the present law without this exception. The removal of the exception was appropriate. Appropriate, too, were the changes in the cost defense that were designed to make sure that differences in cost were related in kind and in amount to the discriminations for which they provided justification.

Other features of the Robinson-Patman Act, though largely unrelated to the problem of broad injury in the primary line, create no significant obstacle to effective action about this problem. The defense of meeting competition is seldom relevant; for a seller's price policies usually do not have broad anticompetitive effects in his own market unless he so intends; and if such effects are intended, the intention is inconsistent with good faith. The significance of the cost defense is less clear; but it too appears to be appropriate to the policy of the Sherman Act. Price discriminations are forbidden, not only when they produce monopoly or are part of a definite monopolistic plan, but also when they probably, but not certainly, will reduce competition and when their tendency is monopolistic. The law is concerned with risks, not certainties; with tendencies, not facts. It is proper in such circumstances, that a demonstrated increase in efficiency should be protected in spite of a still uncertain, though probable, anticompetitive effect. A successful cost defense is so difficult that no wholesale encouragement of monopolistic tendencies can spring from such a policy. If the risks of monopoly materialize, action under the Sherman Act remains available as a means to preserve competition even at some sacrifice of efficiency.

But efforts to prevent the narrow types of injury to competition in the primary line of commerce are not appropriate in a price discrimination law nor consistent with the policy of the antitrust laws. People will not compete without some hope of success; and successful competition necessarily diverts business from rivals. To make such diversion unlawful is tantamount to a complete prohibition of the tactics of making price reductions or price increases that result in nonuniform prices. It is to forbid limited experiment with new price policies, adjustment of prices to varying conditions of demand, and response to competitive pressures that are neither general nor strong enough to induce a general price change. It is to reduce competition, not to protect it. By invoking the narrow standard of injury and applying it to effects on sellers as well as buyers, the present statute has fostered such anticompetitive consequences.

Objectives in the
Secondary Line of Commerce

The more difficult and controversial problems in the policy of price discrimination concern discriminations that involve injury to competition in the secondary line. Do we need a law of price discrimination concerned not merely with the predatory discrimination by a seller but also with effects among buyers? If so, what are the effects that the law should seek to curb?

Two sharply different objectives have been incorporated in the present law, without recognition of their difference. One is to prevent discriminations injurious to market competition in the secondary line. This is the counterpart of the objective of the law in the primary line. It is incorporated in what has been called, in previous pages, the broad concept of injury. The second objective is to assure equality of opportunity for all competing enterprises that buy goods from the same seller. It has been expressed in the concept of injury previously described as the narrow concept.[1] Although inequalities of opportunity may be of a kind and scope

[1] Public policy toward price discrimination might conceivably serve a third objective, that of promoting the efficient production and consumption of goods and the efficient use of economic resources by assuring a correspondence between price differences and cost differences. The economic theory of competitive markets leads to the conclusion that an economic system is most efficient when prices accurately reflect the differences in costs of production. The economic concept of discrimination is the maintenance by a seller of price relationships that do not reflect relative costs. From this point of view prices may be discriminatory when, by the cost standard, they are either unduly different or unduly similar. A nondiscriminatory price structure would be one in which price differences exactly matched cost differences.

Whatever may be the merits of this conceptual scheme for economic analysis, it cannot be used as a basis for a law about price discrimination. To apply it by law would be to require not only that every price difference must exactly correspond to a cost difference but also that no prices be the same unless costs are the same. Thus the law of price discrimination would be converted into a program of complete price control based on detailed cost accounting. Freedom in pricing would disappear. Such a policy could be applied only if exact costs could be computed for each commodity, class of customer, and type of transaction. No one has ever seriously suggested that this type of policy could be or should be adopted.

Moreover, the incentives provided by a law designed to permit but not require price differences that reflect differences in cost are preferable to the incentives that would be implicit in a statute making such price differences mandatory. Where a change in methods of production or sale would promote efficiency, both buyers and sellers should be given incentives to facilitate the change. If a buyer can obtain a price reduction by adapting his purchasing methods to the change, he has such an incentive. If a seller can absorb the saving wholly or partly in increased profits, instead of passing it on in lower prices, he, too, has an incentive. In some instances the initiative in making the appropriate changes is likely to rest with sellers, in other instances with buyers. Hence it is desirable that both retain an opportunity to benefit. A law requiring that all cost savings attainable through

that have anticompetitive effects, there may also be inequalities that have no necessary relation to the maintenance of competition. Clarity in thought will be promoted by regarding equality as an end sought for its own sake and without reference to its bearing on the competitive pattern. In pursuit of this end, the law of price discrimination has been given a scope of application much broader than is necessary to protect market competition alone.

Problems of degree arise in the pursuit of both of these objectives. It would be possible to attempt to preserve competition from all risk, however remote, of any impairment, however small. The law does not attempt anything so comprehensive. Instead, it strikes at a reasonable probability of a substantial lessening of competition. Similarly, it is possible to invoke a rigorous standard of equality under which even the slightest inequalities are prohibited, or, alternatively, to attack inequality only where it is reasonably likely to be substantial. Under the Robinson-Patman Act, the narrow standard of injury has been applied rigorously in any situation involving a price difference large enough to have a perceptible effect on profits or market behavior. However, it would be possible to pursue equality in a different spirit and thus to develop a law different in the scope of its application.

It is unreasonable to use the law of price discrimination to attack minute inequalities among buyers. Where such inequalities are ephemeral or have no central pattern, they may well be offset at other times or on other commodities. Any one buyer may sometimes be favored and sometimes disfavored. Moreover, since the defense of cost justification is not readily available, insistence on equal treatment in all particulars except where cost differences can be shown tends to make price structures unduly inflexible.

The two central questions of policy that emerge are these: First, is there need for a law of price discrimination designed to prevent substantial impairment of market competition in the secondary line? Second, is there need for a law designed to prevent discriminations in the terms on which buyers acquire goods from bringing about substantial inequalities in the profits and competitive opportunities of those buyers?

---

methods of distribution be given entirely to buyers would unduly diminish the incentive for sellers to take their part in the improvement of the distributive process.

The principle is similar to that which it has already been suggested should govern policy toward the advantages of location. See above, pp. 534-37.

The first question cannot be disposed of by the simple comment that competition among distributors and industrial consumers is as important as it is among producers. Buyers are in competition as buyers, and in their resale markets are in competition as sellers, regardless of the scope of the law of price discrimination. Market competition in the secondary line may be affected by discrimination in one particular way, namely, that certain favored buyers convert their buying advantages into decisive selling advantages in resale markets. The question is whether this type of advantage is important enough to call for a precautionary law.

Experience under the antitrust laws suggests that the competitive problem created by discrimination in the secondary line is less serious than in the primary line. Both before and after the passage of the Clayton Act, Sherman Act cases have furnished impressive illustrations of the use of price discrimination as a monopolistic weapon against competitors and have thus attested to the significance of the injuries in the primary line to which the law of price discrimination is addressed. By contrast, there have been few cases against manufacturers and still fewer such cases against distributors in which discriminatory buying advantages have been found to contribute to violations of the Sherman Act. The function of the law of price discrimination in protecting competition is to stop injuries to competition in their incipiency, but these injuries appear from the record to be more common and more significant in the primary line than in the secondary line.

Nevertheless, competitive problems to which the law of price discrimination is appropriate have arisen in the secondary line. Their infrequency points to the limited function but not to the uselessness of this aspect of a price discrimination law. Moreover, there is a possibility that in some lines of distribution the quality of competition may be impaired by a progressive concentration of control in a few large distributive organizations. The Sherman Act has not been successfully used to prevent the rise of quasi-monopolistic oligopolies. The precautionary standards of a law of price discrimination may prove to be useful against such developments. It would be wise to continue to prevent discriminations that may injure market competition in the secondary line, but this part of the policy of competition is not so urgently needed as to justify the sacrifice of other important objectives of public policy.

The objective of preventing substantial inequalities of opportunity raises different issues. There can be little doubt that, if the law were to permit, inequalities in buying prices would be common among competing buyers. There can also be little doubt that in many cases the price differences would be important enough to affect the profits and opportunities of these competing concerns in their resale markets. The question is not whether substantial inequalities are common but whether their elimination by law is a proper public objective. It is apparent that the objective of establishing equality must stand or fall on its own merits, since it is not a necessary part of the objective of preserving competition.

There is little reason to try to assure by law an equality of prices so pervasive that it prevails generally in the relation among small and numerous buyers. Though price discrimination may create disparities of opportunity among such concerns, the likelihood of offsetting disparities on other goods or at other times is so great that little would be gained from an effort to curb such inequalities. Substantial, consistent, cumulative inequality is to be expected only where favored buyers are relatively large and strong. Only in such circumstances are we justified in considering an intervention that subjects the detail of price relationship to pervasive control.

To the present writer it appears that, even in the case of the powerful buyer, the objective of preserving equal opportunity is an inappropriate focus for a law of price discrimination. The pursuit of equality through the price discrimination law, even in this limited field, tends to give that law an unfortunately pervasive control over price relationships. Moreover, the definition of equality as the equivalent of equal buying prices distorts the conception of equal opportunity. A powerful buyer may obtain advantages not only by paying lower prices but also by receiving more generous credit, obtaining quicker deliveries, obtaining preferential access to scarce goods, and in many other ways. Piecemeal legislation addressed to particular types of advantage is not a satisfactory way of assuring equality, if, indeed, equality is to be assured by law. To keep public control over business activity within reasonable limits and at the same time to cope more effectively with the greatest disparities of bargaining power, the focus of public policy should be shifted from efforts to control market behavior to efforts to prevent undue concentrations of power. Section 2 of the Clayton Act cannot fill the need created by underuse of Section 7 of the Clayton Act and Section 2 of the Sherman Act.

This is admittedly a controversial position, and one that will be rejected by many of those concerned with the policy of price discrimination. In the suggestions that follow, an attempt will be made to distinguish clearly between those proposals for change in the law that presuppose the abandonment of the effort to secure equality, and those proposals that would be appropriate to a law that pursues the dual objective of preserving competition and establishing equality of opportunity.

But whichever scope is considered appropriate, the law governing effects in the secondary line should be focused on problems created by the powerful buyer. Only the inequalities surrounding the powerful buyer are important enough to justify legal action. Similarly, no substantial effect on market competition is likely to be produced by buying advantages except where the favored buyer is already a large and strong concern. Typically, there will be no such effect unless either the total number of buyers is few or the favored buyer is substantially larger than his competitors. Thus, whether the statute is concerned only with the broad type of injury or with the broad and narrow types alike, it should be conceived as one of the curbs placed on manifestations of concentrated economic power.

If discrimination that produces effects in the secondary line were covered by the law only where powerful buyers were involved, many small enterprises that do not sell to powerful buyers would be entirely exempt from the application of the statute. The number of cases would be significantly reduced. Cases that have no discernible relation to the policies of the antitrust laws would be fewer. Much would be done to restore the flexibility of market prices. Moreover, the Commission and the courts would be able to focus their attention more sharply and continuously on work that is important. By this change alone the economic impact of the law of price discrimination could be significantly altered.

To cope with the problem of the powerful buyer by imposing controls on the seller's conduct is inherently awkward, and so far as possible should be avoided. The present pattern, by which the law seeks to avert injuries in the secondary line by limiting the price differentials in the primary line, is anomalous. Unlike other parts of the antitrust laws, the law of price discrimination, when concerned with the secondary line, does not attack directly the power or the behavior of those who are its targets. Instead, it attacks sellers, who may be the victims of the powerful buyer. Whether or not curbs on the seller are comprehensive enough to reduce the strength of the buyer, they inevitably restrict the seller's freedom to experiment and the flexibility of his price policies.

An attempt should be made to define the types of buying conduct that express undue buying power and to prohibit such conduct directly through proceedings against the buyers who engage in it. This is an inherently difficult task, the possibilities of which have not been explored. The present writer does not profess to be able to provide a neat formula suitable to the purpose. Though a few suggestions are made in the more detailed discussion that appears later in this chapter, their purpose is illustrative, and none of them is advanced confidently. The formulation of satisfactory standards of buyer's conduct will be possible, if at all, only after extended discussion and controversy. It is possible, perhaps even probable, that a substantial part of the oppressive buying power of powerful buyers will prove to be incapable of legal definition.

In so far as direct attack on the conduct of the powerful buyer cannot be made, it will be necessary to continue the effort to cope with this problem through control of the price policies of sellers. So far as this is done, however, there will necessarily be a dual effect. The law will have consequences not only for the power of buyers but also for the incentives of sellers and the flexibility of their price structures. The problem of public policy will be to evaluate the effects in the primary and secondary lines in order to make sure that the accomplishments in the secondary line are not obtained at too great a cost of adverse effects in the primary line. To this end, the portion of the statute that has to do with injurious effects should be so worded that it permits the suggested kind of evaluation.

Objectives as to
Proportionality and Brokerage

The foregoing discussion of the broad objectives of the law of price discrimination has not dealt directly with problems of the disproportionality of payments and services or with the payment of brokerage to persons on the other side of the transaction.

The problems as to the provision of a payment for sales services that arise under Sections 2(d) and 2(e) of the Robinson-Patman Act are in part relevant to a price discrimination statute. In particular instances, such services and payments are indirect means by which powerful favored buyers obtain discriminatory advantages over others. However, the subjection of these payments and services to a special rule of law and their exemption from the general law of price discrimination deprives the statute of consistency and extends it in practice to cover situations where no injurious effect is perceptible. The part of the statute applicable to discriminations in price now covers and should continue to cover indirect as well as direct discriminations. Where the purpose and effect of sales aids or payments for selling service are to give the buyer a concealed discount, that discount could be treated as an indirect method of price discrimination. As such it would be neither more nor less unlawful than other discriminations, direct or indirect. To cope with this kind of problem, no special enactment is necessary.

To limit the selective purchase of advertising services or the selective provision of such services where sales effort rather than price reduction is in question is not an appropriate part of a price discrimination statute. It is true, of course, that selective advertising may be injurious to those not selected, just as it is true that a seller's selection of his customer or a buyer's selection of his sources of supply may be injurious to those who are rejected. Except for regulated public utilities, public authority has consistently refused to limit the right of private traders to choose those with whom they will trade so long as these traders make their decisions severally and without attempt to monopolize. There is no good reason for an exception to this policy in the case of the purchase of advertising.

The distinction between concealed price concessions and selective sales arrangements is undoubtedly difficult to make in certain cases. If the control over such matters depends on a finding that indirect price discrimination has taken place, the Commission and the courts will be forced to cope with the difficulties case by case in the light of each particular state of facts.[2]

Unlike the provisions regarding sales assistance, the brokerage provision has almost no relevance to a policy toward price discrimination. The only excuse for including it in the Robinson-Patman Act was the

---

[2] The Patman bill, as originally introduced, sought to leave room for selective advertising by permitting disproportionate advertising allowances, provided the participating distributors were not identified in the advertising. Mr. Teegarden, author of the bill, strongly opposed a substitute version that eliminated this provision, on the ground that the effect would be to make many advertising programs either unlawful or wastefully expensive. In practice the type of exemption contained in the original bill would have given little scope for selective co-operation in sales effort between manufacturers and distributors: Mention of the manufacturer's products in distributors' advertisements, special display of those products in distributors' establishments, and many similar customary methods could not have continued on a selective basis because the names of manufacturer and distributor were necessarily associated therein.

fact that the Congress desired to terminate the brokerage payments obtained by a few large food chains and was afraid that these payments could be cost-justified. The purpose itself was inconsistent with the reasoning that underlay the Robinson-Patman Act.[3] The inclusion of the brokerage provision in the act resulted in few proceedings involving powerful buyers and many proceedings unrelated to the problem of the powerful buyer. Indeed, some of the brokerage orders, such as that against Southgate Brokerage Company, tended to weaken rather than strengthen the small distributors and producers. So far as there is any special public problem associated with the payment of brokerage, this problem appears to center in sharp practice verging on fraud, the appropriate remedy for which would be disclosure of the ownership of dummy brokers. Whether or not such disclosure should be required by law, the question at issue has little to do with price discrimination. The brokerage provision has no proper place in the statute.

The Status of the Criminal Provisions

The criminal provisions of the Robinson-Patman Act constitute a special problem. Of the three offenses for which criminal penalties are provided, two involve predatory purposes in the primary line, which probably would be sufficient to justify a Sherman Act proceeding. The third consists in price discrimination among competing buyers on like quantities. Where this third offense appears, no proof of injury to competition is necessary, and no defense of cost justification or good faith can be offered. There is obviously no justification for a criminal provision which, on the one hand, applies penalties to offenses that the civil law does not recognize, and, on the other hand, exempts entirely discriminations among concerns that buy different amounts, in which the problem of the powerful buyer is most easily discerned. If this part of the criminal statute is to be retained, it should be harmonized with the rest of the law.

However, there is no good case for invoking criminal penalities in

[3] The Congress might reasonably have thought a cost justification insufficient in situations involving grave jeopardy to competition. Indeed, it took precautionary action on this ground to permit the Federal Trade Commission to establish quantity limits applicable to cost justifications generally. However, there was no basis for belief that brokerage payments are more dangerous to competition than other concessions to large buyers, and the statute forbade them without requiring any prior finding of jeopardy to competition such as is necessary before a quantity limit is fixed.

support of the law against price discrimination. When injuries in the primary line are involved, the function of the law is to cover practices that have not yet attained the scope and clarity of purpose justifying proceedings under the Sherman Act; and the grosser offenses for which criminal penalties may be appropriate can be subjected to them through a Sherman Act proceeding. When injuries in the secondary line are involved, the law must be used either to reach a powerful buyer over the seller's shoulder or to experiment with the formulation of concepts of unconscionable buying conduct. In the former type of proceeding, criminal penalties would be inappropriate; in the latter type, possibly appropriate but certainly premature. Moreover, whether the problems of discrimination are concerned with the primary line or the secondary line, violation is proved, not when damage has already occurred, but when there is a reasonable probability of future damage. Criminal penalties are inappropriate to reinforce the precautionary orders that are based on predictions about the future.

Outline of an Appropriate Law

A statute with the scope and focus of policy that have been suggested above would bear little resemblance to the Robinson-Patman Act. The brokerage section and the criminal provisions of Section 3 would be deleted entirely. Payments for selling service and provisions of selling help would no longer be dealt with by the requirement of proportionally equal terms now contained in Sections 2(d) and 2(e). Instead, the provisions of the general law of price discrimination would be applicable to such payments and services. This would have the effect of removing the special exemption of buyers that now prevails with reference to this part of the statute and of making legality depend on the same tests as to injury, cost, and good faith that apply to other forms of price discrimination.[4] The law

---

[4] It would be possible to alter the language of Secs. 2(d) and 2(e) so that disproportionate payments would become unlawful only when they had harmful effects and when the relevant justifications could not be shown. Though such changes could do much to harmonize these sections with Sec. 2(a), they would still leave the seller alone subject to the law. They would require that the effects in the secondary line be reached by proceedings against sellers rather than buyers. Thus, they would be inconsistent with many of the suggestions offered herein. Moreover, if the test of harmful effect were invoked, the test of proportionality would become irrelevant and might exempt some payments and services that were actually harmful.

of price discrimination itself would contain provisions covering the activities of sellers that injure competition in the primary line and the activities of buyers that injure competition in the secondary line. The breadth of the provisions about buying activities would depend on a basic decision whether the purpose of the law should be solely to protect competition or also to preserve equality of opportunity among buyers. Supplementary provisions concerned with discriminations by sellers who deal with powerful buyers would be included in the statute in so far as the provisions directly concerned with the activities of buyers were thought to be inadequate.

The Primary Line of Commerce

As to injuries in the primary line, the purpose of such a statute would be to authorize proceedings against discriminations that jeopardize market competition, but not to extend protection to sellers where no threat to market competition is involved. It would be unlawful for a seller to discriminate in price directly or indirectly where the effect may be substantially to lessen or to prevent competition or to tend to create a monopoly. The test of competition in the broad sense thus provided would be similar to that which has been applied in practice in cases such as those against Muller and Maryland Baking Company. In some respects, however, it would be broader than the law prior to 1936: Volume and quantity discounts would be fully subject to the law, and the cost defense would be more carefully limited. Moreover, discrimination would be unlawful when it prevented competition as well as when it lessened it. Thus, a powerful seller would be precluded from using discriminatory tactics that damage competition by preventing the entry of new competitors into his field.

Price differences based on differences in cost should be exempt from this prohibition. Although it is the policy of the Sherman Act to forbid monopolization whether or not it enhances efficiency, no such policy is appropriate in a precautionary statute that strikes at price discrimination wherever damage to competition is reasonably probable. Present efficiency should not be sacrificed because of future risks to the competitive structure against which, if they should materialize, other legal weapons are available.

But the cost defense, though narrower than in the old law, should be given a broader scope than in the existing law. An effort should be made to facilitate experiment with methods of cost reduction, even though the results are uncertain or may be delayed. Moreover, an effort should be made to diminish the burdens of cost analysis that must now be borne by those presenting cost defenses. The procedures that can best accomplish these purposes are not self-evident, and prolonged consideration by accountants and economists would be appropriate in devising them. It is tentatively suggested, however, that where forecasts of costs, if realized, would provide a cost justification within a reasonable period of time, those forecasts might be accepted as sufficient to establish the provisional legality of the price differences thus justified, subject to later review of cost experience.[5] It is also suggested that in so far as methods of allocation and analysis used in a cost defense are those generally employed by the seller in making decisions about other matters than price differences, this fact should go far to establish their validity. The accounting on which a seller relies for a whole range of managerial decisions cannot have been devised as a cloak for questionable pricing practices; and in view of the controversial nature of many aspects of cost allocation, a cost defense should be acceptable not because the accounting is good but because it is in good faith. Care should be taken, of course, to deny the good faith of bad accounting used primarily for purposes of cost justification, even if some other use is made of it in order to give it a protective coloration of general applicability.

When injury appears in the primary line, the question whether a seller should be allowed to justify a discrimination by showing that he merely met a competitor's price is relatively unimportant. Discriminations through which a seller damages market competition with his rivals can seldom be in good faith. Indeed, the seller's knowledge that the probable effect of a discrimination will be to reduce competition in the market the seller occupies may be sufficient in itself to preclude good faith. Thus, a successful showing of good faith where the requisite injury is shown will necessarily be rare. If the possibility of the good-faith defense is retained in the statute, the incentives for experimental price variation may be somewhat enhanced. On the other hand, there may be danger that such a principle will emphasize an undesirable distinction between initiatory and retaliatory price reduction and thus discourage sellers from taking

---

[5] Though delay in proceeding against discrimination now affords sellers an opportunity to realize prospective savings before they must show cost justification, this protection is not reliable; and the risk that it will fail is a deterrent to experiment.

the lead. Moreover, if market competition is actually endangered, the good faith of the seller should not be sufficient to justify the anticompetitive effect.

The most persuasive argument for retaining the defense of meeting competition is that a seller should be permitted to defend himself against a discriminatory attack by a rival. Unfortunately, the defense affords a weak protection for a seller who wishes to retaliate against such an attack. If the competitor's discrimination is cost-justified or if his low price is not discriminatory, price reductions to meet his prices cannot realistically be described as injurious to market competition—except perhaps in circumstances that would justify a proceeding under Section 2 of the Sherman Act. When a competitor's discrimination is not thus defensible, the defense of meeting competition tends to be less useful as the danger from that competitor becomes greater. It is a matter of grave doubt whether a discrimination that is illegal can be used—or should be capable of use—to justify another discrimination; and in practice the most dangerous competitive raids are those that are probably illegal or might reasonably be so. It is possible, of course, to give a seller the right to retaliate in good faith even though it is recognized that in many instances the good faith of the retaliation will be questionable. But if no such right is given, the standard of injury used in the primary line will probably afford equal or greater protection. A seller who merely retaliates against a competitor's price reductions will not readily be found to have damaged market competition by doing so. Indeed, in ordinary circumstances, a seller thus attacked might not only meet but also beat his rival's low price without hurting competition in the market. On balance, it appears preferable to assure freedom of action for sellers not through the defense of meeting competition, which unites uncertainty of application with rigidity as to the price reductions it permits, but through a realistic interpretation of the meaning of injury to competition in the primary line.

The Secondary Line of Commerce: Provisions About Buyers

The provisions concerned with discriminations that injure competition in the secondary line would depart sharply from the standards and procedures of existing law. They would seek to identify and forbid the exploitation of excessive buying power by powerful buyers. To focus their prohibitions on powerful buyers only, they would contain an exemption of small buyers, the concerns to be exempted being measured by asset size, percentage of the total product bought, or some similar convenient measure. So far as exploitative buying conduct could be defined and distinguished from the buyer's ordinary pursuit of economical sources of supply, it would be prohibited. In view of the exemptions, the practical impact of the prohibitions would be on the larger buyers only.

An initial decision would be necessary as to whether exploitative buying conduct should be conceived only as conduct that has the reasonable probability of reducing market competition either in the purchase of goods or in resale markets or whether, alternatively, this concept should be extended to include all buying activities that are reasonably likely to produce substantial inequalities in the buying prices of competing concerns. As has been indicated above, the present writer believes that the law should be concerned with market competition alone, and the ensuing discussion will proceed on this assumption. It would be possible, however, to include equality of opportunity among the purposes of the law, yet focus the statute on the definition and prohibition of the relevant activities of powerful buyers.

There are two ways, alternative or supplementary, to attack exploitative buying practices. The first is to declare broadly that buyers (other than those exempted because of their smallness) shall not engage in buying practices that probably will have the effect of substantially lessening or preventing competition or tending to create a monopoly either in the market in which the buyer buys or in his resale market. As in the case of other statutes that prohibit conduct having adverse effects in the market, the practical meaning of such a prohibition would necessarily be determined in case law as the courts considered the probability of injury to competition in various circumstances brought before them. The advantage of such a procedure is that it fosters flexibility and relevance in the development of legal standards. Its disadvantage is that uncertainty as to the meaning of the statute, though gradually diminishing, would limit the effectiveness of the prohibition and the guidance available to business enterprises that desire to minimize their legal risks. It would be possible, however, and probably desirable, to assist the courts and the business community in interpreting the concept of damage to competition by buyers by including in the statute a suitable definition of harm. This possibility will be discussed further below.

The other method would be to attempt to define the specific conduct that is thought to be harmful in its effect and to include in the statute prohibitions directed against that conduct. Such an attempt was made in Sections 2(c), 2(d), and 2(e) of the Robinson-Patman Act, though only Section 2(c) applied to buyers. Experience with these sections does not encourage further experiment along similar lines. The present writer does not recommend this type of statute; nor could he formulate a list of buying practices that might reasonably be regarded as sufficient for the purpose. Moreover, even if the law were framed in the form of specific prohibitions, it would need to be supplemented by a general provision along the lines suggested above.

Whichever method of attack is chosen, the prohibitions and permissible defenses applicable to buyers should be developed separately, not borrowed from the law that pertains to sellers. The defenses appropriate to discriminations by sellers are obviously not suited to a statute concerned with harmful conduct by buyers. In most instances the buyer cannot know whether or not the price concession by a seller is justified by a cost difference. He does not have access to the seller's cost records and should not be expected to accept unverified statements by the seller as to the nature of costs. Though he certainly knows whether he has received offers of low prices from other sellers, he cannot be expected to know whether the scope and motives of a price concession by the seller are such as to establish the seller's good faith in merely meeting competiton. Because of the limitations of the buyer's knowledge, the most that could be demanded of him with respect to the costs and good faith of the seller would be that he should not accept a concession damaging to the competition in which he is engaged when he knows that this concession was justified by neither cost nor good faith. An obligation thus limited would mean little. Moreover, it would be unwise to determine the lawfulness of the buyer's conduct by tests concerned not with that conduct itself but with the behavior of the seller.

To include in the statute a provision forbidding buyers to abet the unlawful conduct of sellers would be unobjectionable, but such a provision would serve a useful purpose only in those rare cases in which violation is candid and overt or in which there is an unusually full exchange of information.

A law concerned with the harmful conduct of buyers should attempt to leave buyers free to buy in the most economical way, to find those suppliers who quote the lowest prices, and to exert on sellers pressure for low prices sufficient to offset the pressure of sellers for high prices. It should encourage experiment with methods of distribution by leaving buyers free to take over distributive functions such as warehousing and transporting goods, which sellers may have previously performed, and to receive appropriate price concessions for doing so. To distinguish between such activities and the use of buying power in ways that hurt competition is difficult, and it may be desirable to include in the statute a definition of damage to competition or a declaration of policy designed to prevent such activities from being treated as harmful. The problem centers, however, on a suitable definition of the offense, not on a provision of exemptions.

Since such a definition or declaration of policy would determine the focus of the price discrimination law as applied to injuries in the secondary line, its language would need to be worked out with great care. The author is not equipped for this task and has not attempted it. However, the concept of injury to competition should be broad enough to cover:

(1) A reduction of the number of competitors so great that it unduly restricts the alternatives available to those who deal with these competitors;

(2) An increase in the power of particular enterprises so considerable that it substantially reduces the freedom of their competitors to make independent decisions;

(3) An increase in the proportion of total purchases or sales made by a particular enterprise so great that it substantially reduces the need for that enterprise to consider, in framing its own market policies, the possibility of diversion of business to its competitors.

(4) Exclusion of new competitors from a competitive field in which, by the above tests, existing enterprises are too few or too powerful.

The Commission and the courts would necessarily carry the burden of working out in case law the boundary between degrees of buying power that damage competition and the ordinary buying pressures that are a necessary offset to selling pressures and that are a necessary part of the process of keeping distribution efficient.

In the administration of such a statute, many difficult problems would be encountered. Nevertheless, it should be possible to use this kind of law successfully against practices such as those by which during the 1920's, the chain stores aroused the indignation that led to the Robinson-Patman Act. The aggrandizement of the chains to the point at which various groups of food producers were dependent on chain outlets; the use by the chains of regional price cutting to attain volume targets; the adoption of collusive price-raising tactics by the chains in certain urban markets in which they had become predominant; the use by the chains of manipulative controls designed to produce price fluctuations in wholesale markets—these and similar tactics were not only enough to show a probability of damage to competition but, in certain cases, enough to result in successful prosecution under the Sherman Act. The price concessions received by the larger chains were made in a setting in which there were wide differentials of size and power between those who obtained the concessions and those who did not and often between those who obtained them and those who granted them. In many instances, the concessions were made not in the form of price reductions available to all of those who performed certain marketing functions that had been undertaken by the chains, but as special concessions to particular concerns. Concessions such as these would not have been sanctioned by a statute that authorized the ordinary higgling of the market and the adaptation of prices to varying patterns of vertical integration. However, in correcting price structures that reflect such manifestations of power, a statute like the one proposed need not have provided chains with incentives to abandon practices that might be economical, such as the performance of wholesaling functions and the purchase of commodities in large quantities for storage and distribution to their outlets. Neither would it have entirely removed the influence of the chains in holding market prices down by seeking concessions appropriate to their way of doing business. In leaving such possibilities open, it might have done something to promote the efficiency of the distributive process. It probably would also have diminished the incentive provided by the present law for the chains to engage in manufacture, exclusive purchase, and the promotion of private brands in order to evade the statute.

The Secondary Line of Commerce:
Provisions About Sellers

So far as provisions directed against the conduct of powerful buyers may be insufficient to cope with the dangers to competition produced by that conduct, the statute might contain supplementary provisions which, like those of the present law, seek to curb buying power by preventing sellers from making concessions responsive to it. The writer has no enthusiasm for this suggestion. He doubts that the danger to competition apparent on the buying side of the market is so pressing and so pervasive as to justify it. Recognizing, however, that this attitude is not shared by many of those concerned with problems of price discrimination, he thinks it appropriate to discuss ways in which supplementary provisions against sellers might be fitted into a statute of the type proposed above.

Supplementary provisions of this kind should be set forth separately from those concerned with damage to competition in the primary line because their scope and focus are materially different. The purpose of the supplementary provisions should be solely to reinforce the protections against the powerful buyer. Accordingly, these provisions should be made applicable only to sellers who engage in transactions with powerful buyers. The exemption of other sellers would in itself prevent the use of the awkward proceeding that reaches the buyer over the seller's shoulder against the many concerns whose customers are not large and whose sales are unrelated to significant problems of injury to competition in the secondary line. It would eliminate the meaningless applications of a formal rule against discrimination that have appeared under the Robin-son-Patman Act.

Unfortunately, though powerful buyers are not numerous, there are many sellers who sell to them and who, therefore, would not be included in the exemption. For these concerns the law of price discrimination would retain unavoidably the awkwardness of the present statute in that the seller would be forbidden to discriminate where his action created probabilities of harm in markets in which he did not sell and could not readily estimate the damage. The only excuse for subjecting him to such a rule is the belief that the damage done is of great public importance and that the law concerned with buyers' conduct is insufficient to cope with it. Accordingly, the conception of damage in the secondary line that is used in this part of the statute should be the same as that used in the part concerned with buyers' conduct, and similar precaution should be taken to prevent damage to competition from being so broadly interpreted as to preclude ordinary higgling and the pursuit of efficiency.

In this part of the law the seller should enjoy protection for price concessions that reflect cost differences similar to the protection afforded for discriminations that affect the primary line. He should not, however, obtain a complete defense from a showing that his low price was made in good faith to meet the equally low price of a competitor. The nature of the other prices available and the good faith of his action should be regarded as parts of the evidence pertinent to a determination whether competition in the secondary line was likely to be injured; but where the probability of such injury was found, the good faith of the seller should not provide an automatic reason for sanctioning the injury.

However, the law should recognize that whenever sellers are forbidden to retaliate against their competitors, the prohibition may damage competition in the primary line. Appropriate consideration should be given to that damage. Accordingly, a showing of good faith in meeting competition should require the Commission and the courts to determine the impact of the discriminatory practice and of a judgment forbidding it in both the secondary line and the primary line and to issue an order against the discrimination only where, on balance, the order prevented more damage to competition than it caused.

The difficulties of this type of proceeding, both for the enforcement agency and for the business community, are so obvious as to provide compelling incentives to minimize its use. Accordingly, sellers who deal with powerful buyers might be required, when making price concessions, to give these concessions a form that would reduce the possibility of injury to competition in the secondary line. Thus they might be required, except when meeting competition in good faith, to adhere to published price schedules in which their low prices were announced to interested customers and were available to all buyers meeting objectively stated conditions as to the nature of the transaction or the function performed by the customer. The effect of such a requirement would be to preclude secret rebates and price reductions based on no intelligible criteria and to expose the seller to the criticism of customers who paid relatively high prices. That this would do something to diminish excessive concessions to powerful buyers is probable. Unfortunately, it would also do something to encourage concerted pressure among customers to prevent concessions that might be cost-justified or might have no harmful effect in the market. Moreover, such a rule would impose on the government a broad duty to enforce the publication of price lists by many enterprises of varying sizes and, among the many concerns that make sales to powerful buyers, to search out and proceed against price concessions that were secret, regardless of their scope and effect. A rule of this kind would be substantively dangerous and would involve the government in petty regulation of trade practices such as it should seek to avoid. The suggestion is offered for consideration only because of the embarrassments that are inescapable in proceedings that attack sellers for damage to competition in the secondary line.

Summary

The foregoing discussion may be summarized as follows. The brokerage provision has no appropriate place in a law of price discrimination and should be eliminated. Policy toward sales aids and toward payments for selling services should rest on the same principles as policy toward price discrimination, and such practices should be covered only in so far as they constitute indirect discriminations. Discrimination that is likely to affect competition in the primary line should be forbidden only when it reduces market competition; and the cost defense applicable thereto should turn on questions of good faith in accounting and in forecasting. Substantial revision is needed in the case of discriminations that are likely to hurt competition in the secondary line. Important features of that revision are: that the purpose to protect market competition should be clearly distinguished from the purpose to assure equality, and consideration should be given to the elimination of the latter purpose; that, whether or not both purposes are pursued, an appropriate exemption should be provided for small business, on the ground that jeopardy to market competition and significant jeopardy to equality arise only in the case of the large buyer; that the attack on the problem should be made, so far as possible, by rules governing buying conduct and proceedings directed against buyers; that in this sort of attack the traditional exemptions concerned with the seller's costs and good faith are irrelevant, and their place should be taken by a definition of the offense designed to assure action against real damage to competition among buyers, yet to prevent injury to competition from being so broadly interpreted that it precludes desirable buying practices; and finally that, if this attack on the problem of the powerful buyer is thought to be insufficient, supplementary rules governing sellers' conduct should be separately stated in order that they may cover only the sellers who deal with powerful buyers, and should include, instead of a blanket good-faith defense, a provision for the balancing of effects on competition on the two sides of the market. If such supplementary rules are invoked, consideration should be given to the idea of limiting their application by requirements that those selling to powerful buyers do so in published price schedules.

A political philosopher commented some years ago that if the temperature were to become a political issue the objectives of the rival factions would be, respectively, the boiling point and zero. He did not say, but it is nevertheless true, that the clash of zealots often produces a compromise at something like an acceptable temperature. In considering price discrimination, there are zealots who regard all price differences as major evils and are not concerned about the flexibility of prices; and there are zealots who favor complete freedom of action for powerful bargainers no matter what damage these may do. If—or when—we undertake the chancy and arduous task of revising our policy, the aim should be, not to substitute one extreme for the other, but to find a desirable intermediate temperature.

Appendixes

APPENDIX A / Tables

TABLE 1. Cases in Which Orders Were Issued Under the Robinson-Patman Act, 1936-57[a]

Docket Number	Name of Case	Date Decided by FTC	Circuit Court Date of Decision	Supreme Court Certiorari Denied or Date of Decision	Process of Decision				Offenses Found			References to FTC Decisions	Included in Sample of Cases Studied	Commodity	Remarks and Citations to Court Decisions
					Tried	Admission Answer	Stipulation of Facts	Consent Order	Robinson-Patman Act Subsection of Section 2	Other Sections of Clayton Act	Section of FTC Act				
2986	Standard Brands, Inc.	6-15-39	6-4-51		x				a			29-121; 30-1117; 46-1485; 47-1831	x	bakers yeast	189 F.2d 510
2987	Anheuser-Busch, Inc.	5-1-40				x			a		5	30-1209		foil yeast / bakers yeast	
3020	Hollywood Hat Co., Inc.	5-11-40	9-22-39	Certiorari denied	x	x			a			25-555		hats	106 F.2d 667
3031	The Great A. & F. Tea Co.	1-25-38		Certiorari denied					c			26-436; 29-1591	x	food products	
3032	Biddle Purchasing Co.	7-17-37	5-2-33; 1-18-41; 3-13-41		x				c			25-564; 26-1511; 32-1340; 32-1867; 33-1706	x	food products	96 F.2d 687; 3 S&D 354, 381; 117 F.2d 29; 305 U.S. 634
3050	Christmas Club	9-30-37						x	a			25-1116		savings systems	
3088	Oliver Brothers, Inc.	12-31-37	3-25-39	Certiorari denied			x		c	3		26-200; 28-1926	x	hardware & other mdse.	102 F.2d 763
3129	Reeves-Parvin & Co.	4-15-39	6-5-46	Certiorari denied	x				c			28-1429	x	groceries	156 F.2d 132
3153	Elizabeth Arden, Inc.	10-8-44			x				e			29-288; 42-916	x	cosmetics	
3154	Pittsburgh Plate Glass Co.	10-30-37	9-20-46		x				a, f		5	25-1228; 26-824	x	glass	147 F.2d 589; 157 F.2d 533; 333 U.S. 683; 334 U.S. 839; 4 S&D 765
3161	Golf Ball Mfrs. Assn.	2-25-38				x			a, d, f			37-87; 40-869; 43-1101	x	golf balls	
3167	The Cement Institute	7-17-43	7-27-48	4-26-48	x	x			a		5	44-1460; 45-1063	x	cement	
3214	The Webb-Crawford Co.	10-20-38	1-30-40	Certiorari denied	x				c			27-1099; 30-1630	x	groceries	109 F.2d 268; 310 U.S. 638

[a] Minus sign indicates that respondent did not fully invoke his rights to present evidence and argue the case.

661

TABLE 1. (Continued)

Docket Number	Name of Case	Date Decided by FTC	Circuit Court Date of Decision	Supreme Court Certiorari Denied or Date of Decision	Tried	Admission Answer	Stipulation of Facts	Consent Order	Robinson Patman Act	Other Sections of Section 2 Subsection of Clayton Act	Section of FTC Act	References to FTC Decisions	Included in Sample of Cases Studied	Commodity	Remarks and Citations to Court Decisions
3218	Quality Bakers of America	4-27-39	9- 6-40		x				c			28-1507; 29-1328; 31-1858	x	bakery products	114 F.2d 393
3221	United Buyers Corp.	11-15-39 11-18-41 6-17-47			x -				c			34-87; 43-619	x	groceries	Waived trial procedure. Complaint dismissed against several of the respondents. 142 F.2d 511 Also consented to order Also consented to order
3224	E. B. Muller & Co.	6-11-41	4-18-44		x						5	33-34; 38-868	x	chicory	
3232	American Optical Co.	1-21-39				x			a			28-169		optical goods	
3233	Bausch & Lomb Optical Co.	1-21-39					x		a			28-186		optical goods	
3263	Agricultural Laboratories, Inc.	1-12-38					x		a			26-296	x	commercial inoculants	
3264	Hansen Inoculator Co., Inc.	1-12-38				x			a			26-303		commercial inoculants	
3265	Urbana Laboratories	1-12-38				x			a			26-312		commercial inoculants	
3266	The Nitragin Co., Inc.	1-12-38					x		a			26-320		commercial inoculants	
3299	H. C. Brill Co., Inc.	2-10-38				x			a			26-666		preparation for home-made ice cream	
3305	United Fence Mfrs. Ass'n	7-13-38				x			a			27-377	x	snow fence	
3344	Atlantic Commission Co.	7-24-40				x			c			31-625	x	fruits & vegetables	
3377	Miami Wholesale Drug Co.	2- 9-39				x			f			28-485		drugs	
3381	Curtice Bros. Co.	4-15-40					x		ad			30-971	x	packed fruits & vegetables	
3386	Master Lock Co.	9-14-38				x			a			27-982	x	locks	
3511	Mississippi Sales Co., Inc.	5-15-40			x				c			30-1282	x	produce	
3633	Corn Products Refining Co.	3-16-42	7- 6-44	4-23-45	x				ae	3		34-350; 39-664; 40-892	x	corn products	144 F.2d 212; 324 U.S. 726
3646	The C. F. Sauer Co.	7-31-41					x		**ad**		5	33-812	x	mayonnaise & condiments	Testimony on first complaint; stipulation of facts on amended one
3685	The United States Rubber Co.	4-25-39			x				ad			28-1439	x	tires & tubes	
3736	Luxor, Ltd.	7-31-40				x			e			31-658		cosmetics	
3739	San Pedro Fish Exchange	7-18-40							c			31-536		fish	
3740	Metz Bros. Baking Co.	12-28-39							c			30-268		bread	
3749	Lambert Pharmical Co.	8-12-40			x				d			31-734		mouthwash	
3756	Nutrine Candy Co.	12-19-39				x			a			30-115	x	candy	
3765	Fruit & Produce Exchange et al.	12-22-39				x			c			30-224	x	fruits and vegetables	
3783	Modern Marketing Service, Inc.	9- 8-43	6-18-45		x				c		5	37-386; 40-988	x	groceries	149 F.2d 970

Table of Federal Trade Commission proceedings (docket numbers, respondents, dates, products, and citations):

No.	Respondent	Date(s)	Code	Product	Vol.–Page ref.	Citation / Remarks
3798	Anheuser-Busch, Inc.	9-25-40	a	corn products	31-986	Respondent submitted no evidence nor brief nor oral argument
3800	Clinton Co.	8-17-42	a	corn products	34-879	Respondent submitted no evidence nor brief; did not ask oral argument
3801	The Hubinger Co.	4-8-41	a	corn products	32-1116	Respondent submitted no evidence nor brief; did not ask oral argument
3802	Penick & Ford, Ltd.	11-29-40; 5-10-43	a	corn products	31-1494; 32-677; 40-906; 4 S&D 705 (revised findings)	135 F.2d 453; 144 F.2d 221; 324 U.S. 746
3803	A. E. Staley Mfg. Co.	6-10-42; 7-6-44	a	corn products	86-1126; 89-...	
3304	Union Starch and Refining Co.	12-11-40; 4-28-45	a	corn products	32-60	Respondent submitted no evidence nor brief; did not ask oral argument
3305	American Maize Products Co.	3-15-41	a	corn products	32-901	Respondent submitted no evidence nor brief; did not ask oral argument
3320	A. S. Aloe Co.	12-15-41	f	surgical products	34-363	
3834	C. R. Anthony Co.	9-12-39	c	women's and other apparel	29-922; 30-1103	
3840	The Simmons Co.	4-30-40	a	bedding	29-727	
3843	American Oil Co.	8-25-39	af	gasoline	29-857	
3844	The Williams & Wilkins Co.	9-9-39	a	scientific books	29-678	
3889	National Numbering Machine Co., Inc.	12-13-39	a	numbering machines	30-189	
3903	National Grain Yeast Corp.	7-13-41	ae	bakers yeast	33-684	
3916	Charles V. Herron	1-27-40	c	food products	30-445	
3926	Federal Yeast Corp.	9-23-41	a	bakers yeast	33-1372	
3955	Jasper W. Efird	4-14-45	a	wearing apparel	40-873	
3965	Champion Spark Plug Co.	1-8-43; 12-5-55; 10-8-56	a	spark plugs	36-25	
3977	The Sherwin-Williams Co.	7-10-53	ad	paint	50-30	
4142	The American Crayon Co.	12-31-40; 4-20-55; 2-6-57; 8-18-54	ad	school supplies	32-303; 49-1799	223 F.2d 264
4143	Binney & Smith Co.	12-31-40	ad	school supplies	32-315	4 S&D 729
4215	H. Stanley Jones et al.	11-30-40	c	canned food	31-1538	
4227	A. M. Florman & Bro.	8-19-45	c	millinery	40-207	
4229	Harry M. Bitterman, Inc.	7-8-42	c	fur garments	35-49	4 S&D 410, 583
4231	Isaac S. Dickler	7-8-42	a	fur garments	35-59	
4233	Parr Sales Co.	11-2-40	c	food products	31-1236	4 S&D 410, 583
4240	David M. Weiss	7-8-42; 7-28-45; 11-12-46; 7-16-45	c	fur garments	35-65, 41-437; 43-1176	4 S&D 410, 583
4249	Style & Merit Buying Services	8-17-42	c	women's ready-to-wear, fur garments	35-354	
4257	Jack Herzog & Co.	7-8-42; 11-12-46	c	fur garments	35-71; 41-426; 43-1175	150 F.2d 450; 4 S&D 582
4259	Central Buying Service, Inc.	7-8-42	c	millinery	35-77	
4275	A. Fletcher Sisk et al.	11-30-40	c	canned fruits & vegetables	31-1543	
4276	Giant Tiger Corp.	7-31-41	c	food products	33-880	
4277	Uco Food Corp.	8-7-41	c	food products	33-924	
4279	R. C. Williams & Co., Inc.	8-27-41	c	food products	33-1182	
4280	A. Krasne, Inc.	11-14-41	c	food products	34-121	
4281	General Grocer Co.	6-27-41	c	food products	33-977	

TABLE 1. *(Continued)*

Docket Number	Name of Case	Date Decided by FTC	Circuit Court Date of Decision	Supreme Court Certiorari Denied or Dates of Decision	Tried	Admission Answer	Stipulation of Facts	Consent Order	Robinson Patman Act Subsection of Section 2	Other Sections of Clayton Act	Section of FTC Act	References to FTC Decisions	Included in Sample of Cases Studied	Commodity	Remarks and Citations to Court Decisions
4282	Thomas Roberts & Co.	11-30-40				x			c			31-1551		canned fruits & vegetables	
4283	Chas. F. Unruh	11-30-40				x			c			31-1557		canned fruits & vegetables	
4284	Cecil G. Raeburn	11-30-40				x			c			31-1565		canned fruits & vegetables	
4285	Minetree Brokerage Co.	12-19-40				x			c			32-215		groceries	
4286	The Thos. Page Mill Co., Inc.	10- 1-41					x		c			33-1487	x	flour	
4290	Parker T. Frey Co.	10- 8-40				x			c			31-1084		canned food	
4292	H. Weldon Ruff et al.	11-30-40				x			c			31-1573		canned fruits & vegetables	
4294	W. E. Robinson & Co., Inc.	1-10-41				x			c			32-370		canned fruits & vegetables	
4298	American Brokerage Co., Inc.	11-30-40				x			c			31-1581		canned fruits & vegetables	
4299	Lawrence W. Powers	7- 8-42				x			c			35-83		women's ready-to-wear garments	
4303	George C. Bounds et al.	6-18-41				x			c			33-235		canned tomatoes & sweet potatoes	
4307	International Salt Co.	8-22-52	5-27-47	5- 8-48	x				ad			49-188; 39-35; 40-388; 43-1223	x	salt	
4319	Morton Salt Co.	7-28-44	5-20-49	2- 6-50	x				a			44-1499; 45-328	x	salt	162 F.2d 949; 334 U.S. 37
4340	William E. Silver & Co.	11-30-40				x			c			31-1589		canned fruits & vegetables	
4344	Vonnegut Hardware Co.	1-28-41				x			a			32-512		self-releasing fire exting. devices	
4355	Ramsdell Packing Co.	4-15-41				x			c			32-1187		sardines	
4356	Seaboard Packing Co.	4-15-41				x			c			32-1192		sardines	
4357	Machiasport Canning Co.	4-15-41				x			c			32-1192		sardines	
4358	Holmes Packing Corp.	4-15-41				x			c			32-1192		sardines	
4359	R. J. Peacock Canning Co.	4-15-41				x			c			32-1192		sardines	
4360	Jonesport Packing Co.	4-15-41				x			c			32-1193		sardines	
4361	Sunset Packing Co., Inc.	4-15-41				x			c			32-1193		sardines	
4362	Stinson Canning Co.	4-15-41				x			c			32-1193		sardines	
4367	Republic Yeast Corp.	7-18-41				x			a			33-701		yeast	
4389	Standard Oil Co.	10- 9-45; 8- 9-46; 1-16-53; 1- 7-55	8-11-49; 1-18-54; 5- 8-56	11- 7-49; 1- 8-51; 1-27-58	x				a			41-263; 43-56; 45-1091; 47-1766; 49-923	x	gasoline	173 F.2d 210; 338 U.S. 865; 233 F.2d 649; 340 U.S. 231

664

Docket	Name	Date filed	Date(s)	Product	Cease	F.T.C.		Type	Certiorari / Review	Remarks
4405	Samuel H. Moss, Inc.	5- 1-48; 10- 8-45; 6-19-46	3-29-45; 8- 8-46	rubber stamps	x	38-640; 40-885; 42-991	3	a		148 F.2d 873; 155 F.2d 1016
4410	Royal River Packing Corp.	4-15-41		sardines		32-1193		c	x	
4411	Belfast Packing Co.	4-15-41		sardines		32-1193		c	x	
4412	N. Labec Mfg. & Canning Co.	4-15-41		sardines		32-1193		c	x	
4413	Union Sardine Co.	4-15-41		sardines		32-1194		c	x	
4414	Booth Fisheries Co.	4-15-41		sardines		32-1193		c	x	
4436	Reed-Harlin Grocer Co.	8-21-41		food products		33-1114		c	x	
4519	Miles Brokerage Co., Inc.	10-22-41		food products		33-1380		c	x	
4547	J. T. Jarrell Co.	3-25-46		food products		42-198		c	x	
4548	E. J. Brach & Sons	12-21-44		candy	x	39-535		f	x -	Tried as to some allegations; admission answer on others. No oral argument. Two complaints were consolidated in one case
4556/4673	The Curtiss Candy Co.	11-12-47	Certiorari denied	candy	x	44-257; 48-161	3	ad / ef	x	150 F.2d 607. No oral argument
4571	Life Savers Corp.	12-23-41		candy	x	34-472		ad	x -	
4585	G. B. Shelton Brokerage Co.	3-25-41		crystal phosphate		42-114		c		
4589	C. H. Robinson Co.	1- 6-47		fruits & vegetables		43-297		c		
4677	Walter H. Johnson Candy Co.	6- 8-48		candy		44-1021		d	x	
4740	Benjamin L. Grebosky	4- 6-43		cigars		36-477		c	x	
4792	Britt McKinney Co.	4-19-45		food products		40-420		c	x	
4796	Maurice J. Keller	7- 8-43		food products		37-17		c	x	
4821	Southgate Brokerage Co., Inc.	6-12-44	7-19-45	food products		39-166; 41-430	3	c	x -	Certiorari denied
4323	Fraering Brokerage Co., Inc.	12- 5-44		food products		39-480		c	x	
4388	Stanley J. Remms & Co.	11-30-43		canned fish		37-587		c	x	
4835	Glover & Wilson	12- 5-44		food products		39-485		c	x	
4883	Booth Fisheries Corp.	8-29-45		frozen fish		40-690		d	x	
4915	Dentists Supply Co. of New York	8-17-43		dental supplies		37-345		d	x	
4920	Minneapolis-Honeywell Regulator Co.	1-14-48	7- 5-51; 2-22-52	automatic temperature controls	x	44-351; 48-1691; 49-1695	5	u	x -	191 F.2d 786; 344 U.S. 206
4928	W. M. Meador & Co., Inc.	19- 5-44		food products		39-489		l	x	
4933	Automatic Canteen Co. of America	3- 6-50; 1-12-55	1-18-52; 8- 8-52; 6- 8-53	candy & lease of automatic vending machines	x	46-861; 48-1788; 49-1768; 51-574	3	l	x -	194 F.2d 433; 346 U.S. 61. Respondent submitted no evidence, but argued case
4938	H. D. Childers Co.	12- 5-44		food products		39-492			x	
4939	Calif. Lima Bean Growers Ass'n.	5- 9-46		lima beans		42-292			x	
4957	Atlantic City Wholesale Drug Co.	6-14-44		drugs	x	38-631			x -	No briefs nor oral arguments
4972	United States Rubber Co.	6-30-50		rubber & canvas footwear		46-998			x	
5013	National Biscuit Co.	2-23-44; 4-26-54	5-26-52	bakery products	x	38-213; 50-932			x	189 F.2d 883; 191 F.2d 294; 343 U.S. 470
5017	The Ruberoid Co.	1-20-50		roofing materials		46-879; 47-1838; 48-1699; 48-1771			x	
5020	Holzbeierlein & Sons, Inc.	8-16-44		bread		39-82			x	
5027	Associated Merchandising Corp.	5- 8-45		department store merchandise		40-578			x	Waived trial procedure
5089	Columbia River Packers Ass'n., Inc.	8-25-47		canned seafood		44-118			x	

665

TABLE 1. (Continued)

Docket Number	Name of Case	Date Decided by FTC	Circuit Court Date of Decision	Supreme Court Certiorari Denied or Date of Decision	Tried	Admission Answer	Stipulation of Facts	Consent Order	Subsection of Section 2 Robinson Patman Act	Other Sections of Clayton Act	Section of FTC Act	References to FTC Decisions	Included in Sample of Cases Studied	Commodity	Remarks and Citations to Court Decisions
5048	Unity Stamp Co., Inc.	10-23-47					x		a			44-199		rubber stamps	
5049	American Art Clay Co.	5-12-44				x			ad			38-463		school supplies	
5059	Hutchings Brokerage Co.	12- 5-44				x			c			39-495		food products	
5087	Stacy Williams Co., Inc.	6-13-44				x			c			38-624		food containers & food products	
5115	General Baking Co.	4-25-44				x			d			38-307		bakery products	
5129	L. P. Maggioni & Co.	3-20-45				x			c			40-241	x	canned seafood	
5130	Austelle-Flintom Co.	8-12-44				x			c			39-46		food products	
5131	J. J. Finsten Co. et al.	2-12-45				x			c			40-126	x	canned seafood	
5137	Marine Products Co.	3-29-45				x			c			40-314	x	canned seafood	
5151	Caradine Hat Co.	8-16-44				x			a			39-86	x	men's harvest hats	
5155	Ferro Enamel Corp.	2-26-46									5	42-36		frit	
5164	Ketchikan Packing Co.	9- 3-47				x			a			44-158		canned salmon	
5172	John B. Stetson Co.	10- 8-45				x			ad			41-244		men's hats	
5189	E. H. Hamlin Co.	5-16-46				x			c			42-343		seafood	
5197	Coast Fishing Co.	3-26-45				x			c			40-286		canned seafood	
5217	B. F. Shriver Co.	10-23-44				x			c			39-397		packed fruits & vegetables	
5228	Washington Fish & Oyster Co., Inc.	3-25-46	12- 1-57			x			a			42-119	x	seafood	
5253	National Lead Co.	1-12-53	4-30-57 2-25-57		x				a		5	49-791		lead products	
5267	Halfhill Co.	5-12-45				x			c			40-610		canned seafood	
5270	C. C. Waddill Co., Inc.	3-25-46				x			c			42-125		food products	
5273	Phillips Sales Co., Inc.	3-25-46				x			c			42-192		food products	
5279	Carl Rubenstein (Whitney & Co. et al)	3-25-46	11- 1-51 4- 1-56			x			c			42-188; 48-1723		canned seafood	192 F 2d 746
5282	Paul Pankey & Co.	3-25-46				x			c			42-148		food products	
5284	Parrott & Co.	3-25-46				x			c			42-155		canned food	
5285	South Coast Fisheries, Inc.	3-25-46				x			c			42-165		canned seafood	
5295	William R. Hill & Co.,	3-25-46				x			c			42-173		canned food	
5296	Southern California Fish Corp.	3-25-46				x			c			42-180		canned seafood	
5297	Del Mar Canning Co.	3-25-46				x			c			42-188		canned seafood	
5303	Hoyden Food Products Corp.	3-25-46				x			c			42-196		canned seafood	
5333	J. V. Blevens Co.	9-17-45				x			c			41-160		food and misc. mdse.	

No.	Name	Date	Date 2	Code	No.	Citation	Product	Note
5388	National Modes, Inc., et al.	2- 3-50		c		46-404	women's dresses	Charge under 2(d) dismissed
5365	Sebastian-Stuart Fish Co.	3-25-46		c		42-202	canned fish	
5370	Robert Rosoff	10-30-46		c		43-232	furs & fur garments	
5383	Carroll E. Lindsey	4-15-46		c		42-256	fruit juices & fruit products	
5404	Custom House Packing Corp.	9-23-46		c		43-164	seafood fish & fish products	
5420	Union Fishermen's Cooperative Packing Co.	6-14-46		c		42-408		
5428	High Seas Tuna Packing Co., Inc.	10- 2-46		c		43-173	tuna & mackerel	
5432	West Coast Packing Corp.	9- 5-46		c		43-111	fish & seafood	
5433	Independent Grocers Alliance Distributing Co.	3- 7-52	4-20-53	c		48-594; 49-1751	food products	Some respondents filed admissions; others stipulated facts. 203 F.2d 941
5436	Draper Corp.	5- 5-47		a	3	43-480	loom parts, bobbins & shuttles	
5446	Jacques Kreisler Mfg. Corp.	8-11-48		a		45-136	jewelry	
5456	French Sardine Co. of Calif.	10- 7-46		c		43-190	canned seafood	
5460	The Cooter Co.	12-18-51		c		48-529	groceries	
5462	California Marine Curing & Packing Co.	2-18-47		c		43-304	seafood	
5469	Advance Realty Corp., et al.	8-11-48		c		45-145	canned seafood	
5471	New England Fish Co.	1-12-48		c		44-340	canned seafood	
5482	Carpel Frosted Foods, Inc.	2-18-48		cd		48-581	frozen foods	
5494	Jesse C. Stewart Co.	12-18-51		c		44-285	flour	
5501	Gevertz Buying Corp.	11-28-47		c		44-522	men's wearing apparel	
5502	Corn Products Refining Co.	2- 4-48		a	5	47-587	corn products	
5516	Krengel Mfg. Co., Inc.	11-20-50		a		46-75	rubber stamps	Respondents submitted no evidence or briefs; did not ask oral argument
5517	Adolph Gottscho, Inc.	8-16-49		a		46-100	rubber stamps	
5534	Bonner Packing Co.	11- 9-50		c		47-557	dried fruits	
5576	J. Richard Phillips Jr. & Sons, Inc.	2- 8-50		a		46-467	canned vegetables	
5579	F & V Mfg. Co., Inc.	3-14-50		a		46-632	jewelry	
5620	General Motors Corp.	7-10-53		a	3	50-54	spark plugs & auto parts	
5623	The Larsen Co.	2- 6-50		c		46-487	canned fruits & vegetables	
5624	The Electric Auto-Lite Co.	7-10-53		a		50-73	spark plugs	
5628	Alfred J. Harris & Co.	7- 1-49		c		46-10	canned food	
5640	Florida Citrus Canners Cooperative	7-14-52		a		49-37	canned citrus juice	
5643	Christian Brokerage Co.	9- 8-52		c		49-205	food products	
5646	Pacific Grape Products Co.	9-14-49		c		46-116	canned fruits & vegetables	
5648	National Tea Co.	5-15-50		f		46-829; 47-1314	groceries	
5651	Philip Barr & Co., Inc.	5- 8-51	6-22-50	c		46-967	canned food	
5658	Pan American Food Co., Inc.	12- 4-50		c	5	47-671	dried fruits & vegetables	

667

TABLE 1. (Continued)

Docket Number	Name of Case	Date Decided by FTC	Circuit Court Date of Decision	Supreme Court Certiorari Denied or Date of Decision	Tried	Admission Answer	Stipulation of Facts	Consent Order	Robinson Patman Act Subsection of Section 2	Other Sections of Clayton Act	Section of FTC Act	References to FTC Decisions	Included in Sample of Cases Studied	Commodity	Remarks and Citations to Court Decisions
5670	Ideal Cement Co.	9-28-50				x			a			47-221; 47-1080		cement	
5671	Monolith Portland Cement Co.	3- 8-51			x	x			a			47-1292		cement	
5696	Central Soya Co., Inc.	5- 4-51			x	x			a			47-839		animal feeds	
5721	Standard Motor Products, Inc.	1-11-51			x				a					automotive parts	
5722	Whitaker Cable Corp.	12-27-55	12-14-56	5-18-57	x				a			51-958		automotive parts	239 F.2d 253; 353 U.S. 938
5723	Moog Industries, Inc.	4-29-55	11- 5-56	1-27-58	x				a			51-981	x	automotive parts	238 F.2d 48; 355 U.S. 411
5735	Kay Windsor Frocks, Inc.	8-18-54							d			51-89		dresses	
5768	C. E. Niehoff & Co.	5-17-55	1- 9-57	1-27-58	x				a			51-1114		automotive parts	241 F.2d 37; 355 U.S. 411, 941
5770	E. Edelmann & Co.	4-29-55	12-14-56	2- 8-58	x				a			51-978		automotive parts	239 F.2d 152; 355 U.S. 941
5771	Namsco, Inc.	3-17-53		2- 8-58	x				a			49-1161	x	automotive parts	Respondent submitted no evidence
5773	Appleton-Century-Crofts, Inc.	6-13-51				x			e			47-1371	x	books	
5784	Lagomarcino Gruppe Co. of Iowa	9-15-53				x			e			50-248	x	food products	
5794	Atlas Supply Co. et al.	7-19-51						x	c, f		5	48-53		tires, batteries, automobile accessories	
5815	Hesmer, Inc.	3-22-51				x			c			47-1106		food products	
5819	Pacific Gamble Robinson Co.	4- 5-51					x		c			47-1202		groceries	
5828	Holite Mfg. Co.	10-22-53				x			a			50-379		rubber heels & soles & shoe findings	
5830	Bulova Watch Co., Inc.	3-17-52				x			d			48-971		watches	
5836	Gruen Watch Co.	3-17-52				x			d			48-979		watches	
5837	Elgin National Watch Co.	3-17-52				x			d			48-990		watches	
5865	Consolidated Cigar Corp.	7- 7-51				x			c			48-3		cigars	
5870	Consolidated Companies, Inc.	7- 1-51					x		c			48-254		food & other products	
5880	Dekle Brokerage Co., Inc.	8-16-51				x			c		5	48-192		fruits & vegetables	
5897	Doubleday & Co	8-31-55						x	a		5	—		books	
5898	Harper and Brothers	3-23-56						x	a			—		books	
5913	P & D Mfg. Co., Inc.	5- 9-56	4-30-57	11-25-57	x				c			—		automotive parts	245 F.2d 281
5921	Hastings Potato Growers Ass'n.	1-31-52			x				c			48-746		potatoes & other vegetables	

Docket	Respondent	Date	Date 2			Code	No.	Product
5960	Houghton Mifflin Co.	3- 6-52		x		a	48-861	books
5961	Little, Brown & Co., Inc.	3- 6-52		x		a	48-869	books
5962	Random House, Inc.	3- 6-52		x		a	48-878	books
5963	Simon & Schuster, Inc.	3- 6-52		x		a	48-886	books
5969	Benrus Watch Co., Inc.	11- 6-52		x		a	49-476	watches
5971	Kentucky Chemical Industries, Inc.	8- 6-52		x		a	49-87	animal feed
5972	Ubiko Milling Co.	8- 6-52		x		a	49-99	animal feed
5973	Early & Daniel Co.	8- 6-52		x		a	49-108	animal feed
5974	Page Dairy Co.	10-30-53			x-		50-895	milk
5982	American Greetings Corp.	10-28-52				de	49-440	greeting cards
5989	Fruitvale Canning Co.	6-15-56			x x	a	—	canned fruit
6018	General Foods Corp.	2-15-56				ae	—	food products
6039	Western Grain Co.	1-27-53		x		a	49-883	grain products
6042	American Biltrite Rubber Co., Inc.	7-29-53		x		a	50-133	rubber & composition heels & soles & other shoe products
6043	The B. F. Goodrich Co.	7-29-53		x		a	50-138	rubber & composition heels & soles & other shoe products
6044	The Goodyear Tire & Rubber Co., Inc.	7-29-53			x	a	50-143	rubber & composition heels & soles & other shoe products
6045	O'Sullivan Rubber Corp.	7-29-53		x	x	a	50-149	rubber & composition heels & soles & other shoe products
6052	P. Sorensen Mfg. Co., Inc.	6-29-56	5-28-57	x		a	49-1469	automotive parts
6061	Jacobs Mfg. Co.	6-24-53		x		a	49-1495	industrial chucks
6073	Jan. Warren Corp.	6-25-63				c	50-333	frozen foods
6103	S. S. Sawyer, Inc.	10- 1-53				c		potatoes
6104	Florida Planters, Inc.	10- 6-53			x	c	50-849	potatoes & other vegetables
6152	Aeration Processes, Inc.	1-10-54		x		a	50-994	aerated food products
6160	Topco Associates, Inc.	8-17-54		x		c	51-83	food products
6191	Sunshine Biscuits, Inc.	6-30-54		x		a	—	bakery products
6198	Frank F. Taylor Co.	7-29-54		x		a	51-51	baby walkers & velocipedes
6210	KC Snow Crop Distributors, Inc.	10-28-54		x		c	51-412	food products
6212	Henry Rosenfeld, Inc. et al.	6-21-56			x	d	—	women's suits & dresses

TABLE 1. (Continued)

Docket Number	Name of Case	Date Decided by FTC	Circuit Court Date of Decision	Supreme Court Certiorari Denied or Dates of Decision	Tried	Admission Answer	Stipulation of Facts	Consent Order	Robinson Patman Act Subsection of Section 2	Other Sections of Clayton Act	Section of FTC Act	References to FTC Decisions	Included in Sample of Cases Studied	Commodity	Remarks and Citations to Court Decisions
6215	Jonathan Logan, Inc.	5-29-55			x			x	d			51-1229		dresses	Section 5 charge dismissed. Respondents submitted no evidence. Remanded on appeal to hear cost justification
6216	Wooster Rubber Co.	10-31-54						x	e			51-430		rubber products	
6221	Simplicity Patterns	3-13-57	5-20-58						e		5	—		dress patterns	
6223	Lafayette Foods, Inc.	10-28-54						x	c			51-424		food products	
6230	Rocky Mountain Wholesale Co. et al.	6-7-56				x			c			—		candy, tobacco, sundries	Admission without acquiescence
6254	Spada Distributing Co., Inc.	3-11-55						x	c			51-789		food products	
6255	Florida Citrus Exchange	11-26-56			x				c			—		citrus fruit	
6259	F. C. Bloxom & Co.	9-8-55						x	c			—		fresh fruits & vegetables	
6263	Adams Bros. Produce Co. et al.	4-21-55						x	de			51-917		food products	
6264	Knomark Mfg. Co., Inc.	4-7-55						x	c			51-879		shoe polish	
6274	Northern Brokerage Co. et al.	3-10-55						x	a			51-784		food products	
6327	Maryland Baking Co.	6-29-56 / 5-31-57	4-8-57		x	x			a			—		ice cream cones	Respondent submitted no evidence, but argued case. 243 F.2d 716
6331	Anheuser-Busch, Inc.	9-10-57	4-13-59		x			x	a			—		beer	245 F.2d 60
6366	Union Malleable Mfg. Co.	9-23-55						x	c			—		plumbing products	
6370	Magnesium Co. of America, Inc.	1-6-56						x	a			—		dockboards	
6383	American Brake Shoe Co.	11-15-55						x	a			—		bearings	
6420	Druggists Supply Corp. et al.	1-17-56						x	c			—		drugs	
6440	Hudnut Sales Co., Inc.	4-4-56						x	d			—		cosmetics	
6441	Helena Rubinstein, Inc.	5-9-56						x	de			—		cosmetics	
6442	Yardley of London, Inc.	4-19-56						x	e			—		soaps & cosmetics	
6443	Elmo, Inc.	3-7-56						x	de			—		cosmetics	
6444	Clover Farms Stores Corp. et al.	4-24-56						x	c			—		food products	
6460	The Sweets Co. of America	11-12-57	5-27-57					x	d			—		candy	
6462	Tetley Tea Co., Inc.	4-26-56						x	d			—		tea	

670

No.	Name	Date						Products	Citation
6464	Atalanta Trading Corp.	12-20-56	x	x	d		—	meat products	258 F.2d 365
6465	Chestnut Farms Chevy Chase Dairy	5-21-57	x		d		—	dairy products	
6466	Minute Maid Corp.	7-27-56	7-23-58		d		—	frozen foods	
6467	J. H. Filbert, Inc.	9-19-37		x	d		—	salad dressing & oleomargarine	
6468	Pompeian Olive Oil Corp.	9-20-57		x	d		—	olive oil	242 F.2d 81
6469	Joseph Martinson & Co., Inc.	6-29-56	3- 7-57	x	d		—	coffee & tea	
6470	McCorrick & Co., Inc.	9-17-57	3- 7-57	x	d		—	spices, extracts, tea, coffee, condiments	242 F.2d 81; 353 U.S. 957
6480	Thomas Y. Crowell Co.	3- 6-56	Certiorari denied	x	a		—	books	
6434	Henry Froch & Co.	12-10-57			c		—	food products	
6519	Revlon Products Corp.	8-17-56		x	de		—	cosmetics	
6521	Bymart-Tintair, Inc.	9-25-56		x	d		—	hair coloring preparations	
6523	Johnson & Johnson	9-27-56	x	x	d		—	surgical supplies	
6524	Anahist Co., Inc.	12-20-56		x	d		—	medicinal preparations	
6552	O'Cedar Corp.	10-31-56		x	de		5	mops, waxes, polishes	
6580	Stephen F. Whitman & Son, Inc.	1-31-57		x	a		—	candy	
6569	Dolcin Corp.	8-31-56		x	d		—	pain reliever	
6606	E. A. Aaron & Bros., Inc.	12- 3-56		x	c		—	frozen fruits & vegetables	
6633	Daniel H. Sobo et al.	3-22-57		x	c		—	sugar	
6635	Bourgois, Inc.	3- 5-57		x	d		—	cosmetics	
6639	Arkansas City Cooperative Milk Ass'n, et al.	3- 4-57		x	a		—	milk	
6654	Sealed Power Corp.	5- 8-57		x	a		—	automobile parts	
6699	Pittsburgh Plate Glass Co.	4-19-57		x	a		—	auto. safety glass	
6700	Libbey-Owens-Ford Glass Co.	5-22-57		x	a		—	auto. safety glass	
6720	Haskins Canning Corp.	6-19-57		x	c		—	sardines	
6725	Colonial Mfg. Co., Inc.	6-18-57		x	c		—	food products	
6733	Institutional Foods Co.	6-21-57		x	c		—	food products	
6737	The Borden Co. et al.	11-13-57		x	a		—	milk	
6743	Grove Laboratories, Inc.	12- 2-57		x	a		5	drugs and hair preparations	
6747	Topps Chewing Gum, Inc.	10-25-57		x	ad		—	chewing gum	
6748	Philadelphia Chewing Gum Corp.	10-25-57		x	a		—	bubble gum	
6749	Leaf Brands, Inc.	9-18-57		x	d		—	candy and chewing gum	
6752	Riviera Packing Co. et al.	12-18-57		x	c		—	sardines	Charges under 2(a) & 2(c) dismissed.

671

TABLE 2. *Violations of Section 2(a) of the Robinson-Patman Act, 1936-57*

Docket Number	Name of Case	Nature of Discrimination[a]								Nature of Injury						Defenses Offered		Remarks
		Quantity	Volume	Functional	Territorial	Unsystematic	Selective	Off-scale	Other	Primary Line Narrow	Primary Line Broad	Primary Line Tend to Monopoly	Secondary Line Narrow	Secondary Line Broad	Secondary Line Tend to Monopoly	Cost Justification	Meeting Competition	
2986	Standard Brands, Inc.		x					x					x	x	x	x	x	Bakers yeast volume discounts based on total consumption from all sources. Foil yeast volume discounts available to chains regardless of volume. Meeting competition defense for off-scale sales only.
2987	Anheuser-Busch, Inc.		x					x					x					Volume discounts based on total consumption from all sources.
3020	Hollywood Hat Co., Inc.												x					Discount to largest customers.
3050	Christmas Club					x				x	x	x						
3154	Pittsburgh Plate Glass Co.				x					x	x	x	x	x	x			Two findings as to injury: one broad in primary line, narrow in secondary; the other limited to secondary line, with all three types.
3161	Golf Ball Mfrs. Ass'n.				x					x	x	x	x	x	x			Findings deny cost justification and good faith.
3167	The Cement Institute				x					x	x	x	x	x	x			Pooling volumes by multi-unit buyers.
3224	E. B. Muller & Co.	x		x						x	x	x						Findings deny cost justification.
3232	American Optical Co.			x				x		x	x	x						A private brand price to one dealer. Findings deny cost justification.
3233	Bausch & Lomb Optical Co.			x		x		x	x	x	x	x						Findings deny cost justification.
3263	Agricultural Laboratories, Inc.			x						x	x	x						
3264	Hansen Inoculator Co., Inc.			x						x	x	x						
3265	Urbana Laboratories			x						x	x	x						
3266	The Nitragin Co., Inc.		x							x	x	x						
3299	H. C. Brill Co., Inc.		x				x			x	x	x	x	x	x			Allowances to 3 chain stores only; findings have long disclaimer of cost justification. Finding on injury ambiguous.
3305	United Fence Mfrs. Ass'n.							x			x	x	x	x	x			Freight allowed to a few customers—one allowed to pool purchases of branches. Findings deny cost justification.
3381	Curtice Bros. Co.							x			x	x	x	x	x			
3386	Master Lock Co.					x		x	x	x	x	x	x	x	x			
3633	Corn Products Refining Co.		x		x			x	x	x			x	x			x x	Container differentials; different dates for price increase; special prices to 6 for gluten feed and to 2 on corn starch; exclusive dealing arrangement violated Section 3.
3646	The C. F. Sauer Co.			x			x		x	x		x	x	x	x			Private brand and commercial fleet sales. Findings deny cost justification. Different types of injury found for different discriminations.
3685	United States Rubber Co.							x		x	x	x	x	x	x			
3740	Metz Brothers Baking Co.				x			x	x	x	x	x	x	x	x			Different container surcharges. Container differentials and different dates for price increases. Container differentials. Special prices to Brach & Griffin. Differential dating of price increases. Selective volume discount on gluten feed only. Primary line injury only on discounts to Brach & Griffin.
3756	Nutrine Candy Co.				x				x	x	x	x	x	x	x			
3798	Anheuser-Busch, Inc.				x				x	x	x	x	x	x	x			
3800	Clinton Co.								x			x						
3801	The Hubinger Co.		x		x				x	x	x	x	x	x	x			

672

The following column of remarks appears for the listed companies:

- Different dates for price increases.
- Container differentials,
- Container differentials, different dates for price increases,
- Pooling store purchases and pooling through buying agent, cooperative or association. Findings deny cost justification.
- Probably volume discounts.
- Zone prices with difference based on freight not challenged. 10% to some chain lumberyards. Pooling for volume, accumulating orders for quantity discounts. Special price to a landlord,—split function not recognized.
- Cost defense for special prices to Atlas and Socony only. Exclusive dealing discounts.
- Pooling for volume. Special prices to a few. Latter only defended as meeting competition.
- Findings deny good faith and cost justification.
- 100 count to one customer, 60 count to some, special prices to some, special deals; some discounts conditioned on exclusive dealing and buying practices. Finding of injury in secondary line ambiguous.
- Pooling for chains. Bonus to jobbers on purchases by bonus dealers. Use of previous or estimated volume, with subsequent adjustment of price only downward. Off-scale to 76 customers. Inclusion of customers' direct purchases in volume. Meeting competition defense offered on off-scale sales only.
- Special prices to chains and mail order on unadvertised brands.
- Pooling for members of buying organizations only.
- Pooling for some stores.
- Cost justification offered on carload differential and on zone differential.
- Discount for exclusive dealing.

No.	Company
3802	Peniok & Ford Ltd.
3803	A. E. Staley Mfg. Co.
3804	Union Starch & Refining Co.
3805	American Maize Products Co.
3840	The Simmons Co.
3843	American Oil Co.
3844	The Williams & Wilkins Co.
3889	National Numbering Machine Co.
3903	National Grain Yeast Corp.
3926	Federal Yeast Corp.
3965	The Sherwin-Williams Co.
3977	Champion Spark Plug Co.
4142	The American Crayon Co.
4143	Binney & Smith Co.
4307	International Salt Co.
4319	Morton Salt Co.
4344	Vonnegut Hardware Co.
4367	Republic Yeast Corp.
4389	Standard Oil Co.
4405	Samuel H. Moss, Inc.
4556	The Curtiss Candy Co.
4571	Life Savers Corp.
4677	Walter H. Johnson Candy Co.
4883	Booth Fisheries Corp.
4915	Dentists Supply Co. of New York
4920	Minneapolis-Honeywell Regulator Co.
4972	United States Rubber Co.
5013	National Biscuit Co.
5017	The Ruberoid Co.
5048	Unity Stamp Co. Inc.
5049	American Art Clay Co.
5151	Caradine Hat Co.
5155	Ferro Enamel Corp.
5179	John B. Stetson Co.
5258	National Lead Co.
5436	Draper Corp.

[a] In this table, discrimination by quantity means that the price varies with the amount bought in a single transaction; discrimination by volume, that the price varies with the total amount bought during a period of time; functional discrimination, that the price varies according to the characteristics of the buyer; territorial discrimination, that the price varies with the location of the buyer; and unsystematic discrimination, that the price varies without ascertainable pattern. In selective discrimination, two or more patterns of pricing are used, each for a different group of buyers. In off-scale discrimination, one or more buyers pay prices that do not conform to systematic patterns of variation applicable to sales to others. Discriminations grouped under "other" involve variation for reasons not elsewhere specified, such as whether the goods carry private labels or whether there is an exclusive dealing arrangement. Peculiarities of pricing systems not readily accommodated in this classification are noted in the column for remarks.

TABLE 2. *Violations of Section 2(a) of the Robinson-Patman Act, 1936-57 (Continued)*

Docket Number	Name of Case	Quantity	Volume	Functional	Territorial	Unsystematic	Selective	Off-scale	Other	Primary Line — Narrow	Primary Line — Broad	Primary Line — Tend to Monopoly	Secondary Line — Narrow	Secondary Line — Broad	Secondary Line — Tend to Monopoly	Cost Justification	Meeting Competition	Remarks
5446	Jacques Kreisler Mfg. Corp.		X		X	X				X	X		X	X				Single and multiple and zone systems by agreement.
5502	Corn Products Refining Co.		X			X		X	X	X	X		X	X		X	X	Findings deny cost justification and meeting competition.
5516	Krengel Mfg. Co., Inc.			X			X			X	X		X	X				Jobber discounts to chains.
5517	Adolph Gottscho, Inc.			X		X	X			X	X		X	X				Discounts conditioned on exclusive dealing.
5579	F & V Mfg. Co., Inc.			X					X	X	X		X	X				
5620	General Motors Corp.								X	X	X		X	X				
5624	The Electric Auto-Lite Co.								X	X	X		X	X				Option to A. & P. to buy large volume exercised after price rose.
5640	Florida Citrus Canners Co.		X							X	X		X	X				Differential at plant between purchases for rail and truck delivery.
5670	Ideal Cement Co.		X						X	X		X	X	X				Differential at plant between purchases for rail and truck delivery.
5671	Monolith Portland Cement Co.		X						X	X		X	X	X				Franchise dealers credited with volume of associate dealers and paid after deducting payments due associates at their rates of discount.
5696	Central Soya Co., Inc.		X						X		X		X	X				Pooling volume.
5721	Standard Motor Products, Inc.			X			X	X		X			X	X			X	Private brand discounts.
5722	Whitaker Cable Corp.							X	X				X	X			X	Pooling volume. In P. & D. case commission opinion refers to finding here as broad injury, but language here indicates narrow.
5723	Moog Industries, Inc.			X			X	X					X	X			X	Pooling volume.
5768	C. E. Niehoff & Co.						X			X	X	X	X	X	X		X	Selective nature of discounts stressed, rather than discounts themselves.
5770	E. Edelmann & Co.						X	X		X	X	X	X	X	X	X	X	Pooling volume.
5771	Namsco, Inc.		X				X			X	X	X	X	X	X		X	Selective nature of discounts stressed, rather than discounts themselves.
5828	Holtite Mfg. Co.	X					X				X	X	X	X	X			Same.
5897	Doubleday & Co.			X							X	X	X	X	X			Same.
5898	Harper and Brothers	X	X								X	X	X	X	X			Same.
5913	P & D Mfg. Co., Inc.	X	X								X	X	X	X	X			
5960	Houghton Mifflin Co., Inc.	X	X								X	X	X	X	X			
5961	Little, Brown & Co., Inc.										X	X	X	X	X			
5962	Random House, Inc.										X	X	X	X	X			
5963	Simon & Schuster, Inc.										X	X	X	X	X			
5969	Benrus Watch Co., Inc.											X	X	X				
5971	Kentucky Chemical Industries		X							X	X		X	X				
5972	Ubiko Milling Co.		X							X	X		X	X				
5973	Early & Daniel Co.		X		X					X	X		X	X				
5974	Page Dairy Co.		X							X	X		X	X				
5989	Fruitvale Canning Co.			X	X					X			X	X				
6018	General Foods Corp.			X						X	X		X	X				
6089	Western Grain Co.				X	X				X	X	X	X	X	X	X	X	Special list price to one buyer.

674

No.	Company	Comments
6042	American Biltrite Rubber Co., Inc.	Multiple territorial price lists. Not clear whether at issue but order applicable to them.
6043	The B. F. Goodrich Co.	
6044	Goodyear Tire & Rubber Co., Inc.	
6045	O'Sullivan Rubber Corp.	
6052	P. Sorensen Mfg. Co., Inc.	
6061	Jacobs Mfg. Co.	
6152	Aeration Processes, Inc.	
6191	Sunshine Biscuits, Inc.	A few favored customers such as mail order and chain auto supply.
6198	Frank F. Taylor Co.	Only one competitor in territory where price was cut.
6327	Maryland Baking Co.	Price reductions limited to St. Louis.
6331	Anheuser-Busch, Inc.	Pooling purchases of branches. Payment of volume discounts though volume was not taken. Certain special discounts.
6370	Magnesium Co. of America, Inc.	A new competitor's territory—special price to one buyer.
6383	American Brake Shoe Co	Pooling volume by chains.
6480	Thomas Y. Crowell Co.	
6560	Stephen F. Whitman & Son, Inc.	
6639	Arkansas City Cooperative Milk Ass'n, et al.	
6654	Sealed Power Corp.	Pooling volume by jobber groups.
6699	Pittsburgh Plate Glass Co.	Special price to Ford Motor Co.
6700	Libbey-Owens-Ford Glass Co.	Special price to General Motors.
6737	The Borden Co.	Complaint included cash discounts; order broad enough to be applicable thereto.
6748	Grove Laboratories, Inc.	
6747	Topps Chewing Gum, Inc.	
6748	Philadelphia Chewing Gum Corp.	

TABLE 3. *Robinson-Patman Cases Closed Without Order, 1936–April 1958*[a]

Docket Number	Name of Case	Violation Charged under Sec. 2 Robinson-Patman Act; Sec. 3 Clayton Act; and Sec. 5 FTC Act	Date of Closing	Stage of Proceedings when Case was Closed			Reasons for Closing	Reference to FTC Reports and Decisions
				Before Trial	During Trial	After Trial		
2571	American Safety Razor Corp.	a	1/30/37			x	complaint issued before statute was passed; practice discontinued	24/1888
2935	Kraft-Phenix Cheese Corp.	a	7/17/37			x	no injury; met competition	25/537
2936	Shefford Cheese Co., Inc.	a	10/30/37	x			no injury; met competition	25/1209
2987	Bird & Son, Inc., et al.	a	7/17/37			x	cost justified; discount peripheral and discontinued	25/548
2951	U. S. Quarry Tile Co.	a, e, 5	5/28/41			x	no evidence	32/1652
2972	Bourjois, Inc. et al.	a, e, 5	12/27/40			x	cosmetic rules adopted	32/1636
2973	Richard Hudnut et al.	e, 5	1/9/53			x	cosmetic rules adopted	49/1562
2974	Elmo, Inc.	e, 5	1/9/53			x	cosmetic rules adopted	49/1563
2975	Coty, Inc. et al.	e, 5	12/27/40			x	no reason given	32/1637
3017	Charles of the Ritz, Inc., et al.	e, 5	1/9/53			x	cosmetic rules adopted	49/1564
3039	Primrose House, Inc.	e, 5	1/9/53			x	cosmetic rules adopted	49/1564
3076	Procon Grocery Service Co., Inc. et al.	c	5/19/37	x			dissolved	24/1402
3091	Cast Iron Soil Pipe Ass'n.	a, 5	7/30/48	x			Lapse of time (complaint March 1937). Many participants now out of business	45/670
3830	U. S. Hoffman Machinery Corp.	a	9/19/41			x	no reason given	33/1636
3873	Merck and Co., Inc.	a	7/9/41	x			no reason given	33/1633
3546	Superior Ceramic Corp.	a	5/28/41	x			no evidence	32/1653
3547	Trent Tile Co., Inc.	a	5/28/41	x			no evidence	32/1653
3548	Mosaic Tile Co.	a	5/28/41			x	bankruptcy	32/1653
3549	C. Pardee Works et al.	a	5/28/41			x	no evidence	32/1654
3550	Wenczel Tile Co.	a	5/28/41			x	no evidence	32/1654
3551	Wheeling Tile Co.	a	5/28/41			x	no evidence	32/1654
3552	Architectural Tiling Co., Inc.	a	5/28/41			x	no reason given	32/1655
3553	National Tile Co., Inc.	a	5/28/41			x	no evidence	32/1655
3669	General Baking Co.	a	12/13/40			x	no evidence	32/1635
3764	Chilean Nitrate Sales Corp. et al.	a, 5	4/1/46	x			Discontinuance of practices; delay in proceeding—result of court proceeding by Dept. of Justice and of War.	42/478
3799	Piel Brothers Starch Co.	a, d, 3, 5	12/15/39	x			liquidation	30/1384
3886	General Motors Corp. et al.	a, d, e	11/17/48	x			superseding complaint	45/723
3912	P. Lorillard Co.	a, d, e	3/17/48		rec.		no evidence	44/1180
3913	Brown and Williamson Tobacco Corp.	a, d, e	3/17/48		rec.		no evidence	44/1181
3914	R. J. Reynolds Tobacco Co.	a, d	3/17/48		rec.		no evidence	44/1182
3915	Larus and Brother Co., Inc.	a, d, e	3/17/48		rec.		no evidence	44/1182
3919	Philip Morris & Co., Ltd., Inc.	a, d, e	3/17/48		rec.		no evidence	44/1183
3921	Liggett and Myers Tobacco Co., Inc.	a, d, e	3/17/48		rec.		no evidence	44/1183
3922	Stephano Brothers	d	3/17/48		rec.		no evidence	44/1184
3927	The American Tobacco Co.	a	3/17/48		rec.		no evidence	44/1185
3962	Continental Baking Co.	a, d, e	5/31/40	x			no reason given	44/1185
4103	Globe-Union, Inc.	a	9/23/41			x	no reason given	30/1393
4149	Continental Baking Co.	a, 5	10/18/43		rec.		no evidence	33/1638
4834	Clover Farm Stores Corp. et a.	c	2/12/41	x			dissolution	32/1642
4835	Puritan Uniform Co.	d	12/4/41			x	no reason given	34/1550

No.	Respondent	Basis	Date				Disposition	Citation
4390	Gulf Refining Co.	a	4/3/57	x		x	delay waiting Standard Oil decision	49/1565
4391	The Texas Co.	a	4/3/57	x		x	delay waiting Standard Oil decision	49/1565
4392	Shell Oil Co., Inc.	a	1/9/53	x		x	delay waiting Standard Oil decision	37/669
4435	Coty, Inc.	e	1/9/53				cosmetic rules adopted	33/1639
4436	Bourjois, Inc., et al.	e	9/10/43				cosmetic rules adopted	40/738
4506	Callaway Mills	c	9/25/41	x			no reason given	38/725
4587	D. J. Easterlin	c	5/6/45	x	rec.		no competitive effect; cost justified	34/1537
4636	Bissell Carpet Sweeper Co.	d	2/1/44	x			no reason given	37/670
4637	Cranberry Canners, Inc.	a	3/12/42	x			no evidence	46/1087
4725	Kimble Glass Co.	a	9/10/43	x			no reason given	44/1015
4744	Tennessee Tufting Co.	a, e	11/15/49	x		x	discontinued (practice in 1939; complaint 1942)	44/1197
4841	Van Camp Sea Food Co., Inc.		7/8/49	x			dissolution	46/1170
4971	Hood Rubber Co., Inc.	c	3/25/48	x		x	isolated unauthorized instance of discrimination	46/1139
5152	H. A. Irving et al.	d, e	3/21/50	x		x	delay; practice discontinued 1941, complaint 1944. War intervened.	41/978
5243	Celanese Corp. of America, Inc.	d, e	3/13/50	x		x	practice discontinued in 1944; complaint 1944. Changed conditions.	51/733
5352	N. Erlanger, Blumgart & Co., Inc.		8/31/45		rec.		dissolution	47/1256
5421	Shirbee Hat Co., Inc.	f, 5	2/9/55	x			Canteen decision	46/1069
5483	Crown Zellerbach Corp.	a, 5	4/19/51	x			difference in actual price not shown	46/1061
5526	Clay Products Ass'n., Inc.	a	10/20/49	x			lack of injurious effect; discrimination discontinued	46/1062
5526	E. I. duPont de Nemours & Co., Inc.	a, c, d, e	9/23/49	x			surplusage of complaint	46/1062
5544	Wayne Candies, Inc.	a, c, d, e	9/23/49	x			surplusage of complaint	46/1062
5545	Melster Candies, Inc.	a, c, d, e	9/23/49	x			surplusage of complaint	46/1062
5547	Luden's Inc.	a, c, d, e	9/23/49	x			surplusage of complaint	46/1062
5543	D. L. Clark, Inc.	a, c, d, e	9/23/49	x			surplusage of complaint	46/1062
5549	The Williamson Candy Co.	a, c, d, e	9/23/49	x			surplusage of complaint	46/1062
5550	Bunte Brothers, Inc.	a, c, d, e	9/23/49	x			surplusage of complaint	46/1062
5551	The Sperry Candy Co.	a, d, e	9/23/49	x			surplusage of complaint	46/1062
5552	The Queen Anne Candy Co.	a, c, d, e	9/23/49	x			surplusage of complaint	46/1062
5553	The Switzer's Licorice Co.	a, d, e	9/23/49	x			surplusage of complaint	46/1062
5577	Wm. Wrigley, Jr., Co.	a, d, e	9/23/49	x			surplusage of complaint	46/1062
5578	Richmond-Chase Co.	c	1/11/52		x		one type of practice discontinued two years before complaint; no evidence on another.	48/1566
5585	Lever Brothers Co.	a, d	12/16/53		x		no injury in one practice; others not proved.	50/494
5586	Procter & Gamble Distributing Co. et al.	a, d	12/16/53		x		no injury in one practice; others not proved.	50/513
5587	Colgate-Palmolive-Peet Co.	a, c, d, e	12/16/53		x		no injury in one practice; others not proved.	50/525
5596	Minter Brothers	a, c, d, e	9/23/49	x			surplusage of complaint	46/1062
5587	Town Talk, Inc.	a, c, d, e	9/23/49	x			surplusage of complaint	46/1062
5558	D. Goldenberg, Inc.	a, c, d, e	9/23/49	x			surplusage of complaint	46/1064
5559	Cream-O-Specialty Sales Co., Inc.	a, c, d, e	9/23/49	x			surplusage of complaint	46/1062
5600	The Euclid Candy Co., Inc.	a, c, d, e	9/23/49	x			dissolution	46/1062
5601	Mason, Au & Magenheimer Confectionery Mfg. Co.	a, c, d, e	9/23/49	x			surplusage of complaint	46/1062
5602	Sweets Co. of America, Inc.	a, c, d, e	9/23/49	x			surplusage of complaint	46/1062
5603	Kerr's Butterscotch Inc.	a, c, d, e	9/23/49	x			surplusage of complaint	46/1062
5604	Delicia Chocolate & Candy Mfg. Co.	a, c, d, e	9/23/49	x			surplusage of complaint	46/1041
5605	New England Confectionery Co.	a, c, d, e	9/23/49	x			surplusage of complaint	46/1062
5606	Chas. N. Miller Co.	a, c, d, e	9/23/49	x			surplusage of complaint	46/1062

a List does not include cases in which a charge under the Robinson-Patman Act was dismissed while an order was issued under some other statute.

TABLE 3. *Robinson-Patman Cases Closed Without Order, 1936-April 1958 (Continued)*

Docket Number	Name of Case	Violation Charged under Sec. 2 Robinson-Patman Act; Sec. 3 Clayton Act; and Sec. 5 FTC Act	Date of Closing	Before Trial	During Trial	After Trial	Reasons for Closing	Reference to FTC Reports and Decisions
5607	F. B. Washburn Candy Corp.	a, c, d, e	9/23/49	x			surplusage of complaint	46/1062
5608	American Chicle Co.	a, d, e	9/23/49	x			surplusage of complaint	46/1062
5609	Planters Nut and Chocolate Co.	a, c, d, e	9/23/49	x			surplusage of complaint	46/1062
5610	George Ziegler Co.	a, c, d, e	9/23/49	x			surplusage of complaint	46/1062
5611	The Euclid Candy Co. of Illinois, Inc.	a, c, d, e	9/23/49	x			surplusage of complaint	46/1063
5612	Dante Candy Co.	a, c, d, e	9/23/49	x			surplusage of complaint	46/1063
5613	Fred W. Amend Co.	a, c, d, e	9/23/49	x			surplusage of complaint	46/1063
5614	Shotwell Mfg. Co.	a, c, d, e	9/23/49	x			surplusage of complaint	46/1063
5615	The Kimbell Candy Co.	a, c, d, e	9/23/49	x			surplusage of complaint	46/1063
5616	M. J. Holloway & Co.	a, d, e	9/23/49	x			surplusage of complaint	46/1063
5617	Universal Match Corp.	a, c, d, e	9/23/49	x			surplusage of complaint	46/1063
5618	Hollywood Brands, Inc.	a, d, e	9/23/49	x			surplusage of complaint	46/1063
5619	Paul F. Beich Co.	a, c, d, e	9/23/49	x			surplusage of complaint	46/1063
5675	General Foods Corp.	a	9/23/49	x			no competitive injury	46/1063
5677	The B. F. Goodrich Co.	a	4/13/54		x		cost justified; no competitive injury.	50/885
5720	Bohn Aluminum & Brass Corp. et al.	a	1/24/54		x		one respondent liquidated; other discontinued and sold relevant part of business.	50/692
5728	Sylvania Electric Products, Inc. et al.	a, f	5/22/55	x			(a) cost justified; (f) not proved.	51/1195
5928	Wildroot Co., Inc.	d	9/23/54			x	analogy to cosmetic cases, which were dismissed	
5990	Safeway Stores, Inc.	f	6/30/53	x			Canteen decision.	51/282
5991	The Kroger Co.	f	7/27/53	x			Canteen decision.	49/1578
6008	Purex Corp., Ltd.	a	9/ 8/53	x			no injury	50/125
6199	Argus Cameras, Inc.	a, d	8/24/54	x			discontinuance of practices	50/213
6227	Warren Petroleum Corp. et al.	a, 5	10/20/54			x	not proved	51/100
6232	The Yale & Towne Mfg. Co.	a	9/17/56		x		no injury	51/405
6329	The Elwell-Parker Electric Co.	a	6/28/56		x		no proof of injury	
6330	Hyster Co.	a	9/ 6/56	x			no proof of injury	
6340	Lewis-Shepard Co., et al.	a	9/ 6/56	x			no proof of injury	
6347	Clark Equipment Co.	a	9/ 7/56	x			no proof of injury	
6350	Otis Elevator Co. et al.	a	9/ 7/56	x			no proof of injury	
6386	Maine Fish Co.	c	9/ 7/56	x			allowance not in lieu of brokerage	
6522	Serutan Co.	c	7/30/56	x			wrong party respondent	
6593	Pepsi Cola Co.	d	8/ 1/56	x			wrong party; no commerce	
6594	Coca Cola Bottling Co. of N.Y., Inc.	d	2/26/58	x			no commerce	
6721	Hamburg Brothers, Inc.	a	4/30/58		x		cost justified	

TABLE 4. *Types of Violation Found Under the Robinson-Patman Act, 1937-57*

Year	Sec. 2a	Sec. 2c	Sec. 2d	Sec. 2e	Sec. 2f	Multiple Violations, Number and Section	Total
1937	2	2				1 (a, f)	5
1938	7	2				1 (a, d, f)	10
1939	8	4			1	1 (a, d) 1 (a, f)	15
1940	4	15	1	1		3 (a, d)	24
1941	6	24			1	1 (a, c) 2 (a, d)	34
1942	2	7				1 (a, e)	10
1943	4	3	1				8
1944	3	9	2	1	2	1 (a, d)	18
1945	2	9			1	1 (a, d)	13
1946	1	23					24
1947	2	5				1 (a, d, e, f)	8
1948	3	3					6
1949	2	2					4
1950	5	6			2		13
1951	2	5	1	1		1 (c, d) 1 (c, f)	11
1952	9	3	3			1 (a, d) 1 (d, e)	17
1953	12	4					16
1954	2	3	1			1 (d, e)	7
1955	8	5	1			1 (d, e)	15
1956	7	5	10	1		4 (d, e) 1 (a, c)	28
1957	10	6	7	1		1 (a, d)	25
Total	101	145	27	5	7	26	311

TABLE 5. *Complaints Dismissed, by Year of Dismissal*

Year	Number	Year	Number
1937	5	1948	12[b]
1938	0	1949	36[c]
1939	1	1950	2
1940	4	1951	3
1941	14[a]	1952	1
1942	1	1953	12[d]
1943	3	1954	5
1944	2	1955	2
1945	2	1956	9[e]
1946	1	1957	4[f]
1947	0	Total	119

[a] Includes 8 tile cases dismissed on the same day, mostly for lack of evidence.

[b] Includes 8 tobacco cases, dismissed on the same day for lack of evidence.

[c] Includes 32 cosmetic cases dismissed on the same day for the same defect in complaint.

[d] Includes 3 soap cases dismissed on the same day for lack of injury and lack of proof.

[e] Includes 5 similar equipment cases, dismissed on two successive days for lack of proof of injury.

[f] Includes 3 gasoline cases, dismissed on the same day because of delay while awaiting a final decision in the Standard Oil case.

TABLE 6. *Delivered-Price Conspiracy Cases Resulting in Orders, July 1, 1936–June 30, 1955*

Docket Number	Name of Case	Type of Delivered Pricing	Date Decided	Robinson-Patman Violation	FTC Reference	Appellate Reference
2565	National Electrical Manufacturers Association et al.	uniform delivered	12-20-36		24FTC306	U.S. v. American Steel & Wire Co. of New Jersey (civil penalty suit) April 30, 1947, 4 S & D 822. Penalties imposed.
2958	Water Works Valve and Hydrant Group of the Valve and Fittings Institute et al.	Zone	5-18-37		24FTC1253	
2650	Menasha Wooden Ware Corp. et al.	Zone	6- 8-37		25FTC57	
3092	Scientific Apparatus Makers of America et al.	Zone	8-25-41		33FTC1130; 40FTC169, 674	Eugene Dietzen Co. v. FTC, 142 F. 2d 321. Modified and enforced.
3107	Shelton Tubular Rivet Co. et al.	uniform delivered	6-14-38	territorial	27FTC225	
3167	The Cement Institute et al.	basing point	7-17-43	territorial	37FTC87	Aetna Portland Cement Co. v. FTC, 152 F. 2d 533. FTC v. Cement Institute, 331 U.S. 683. Affirmed.
3305	United Fence Manufacturers Ass'n. et al.	uniform delivered	7-13-38		27FTC377	
3317	Mathieson Alkali Works Inc. et al.	Zone	12-16-38		27FTC1413	
3393	Johnson & Johnson et al.	Zone	12-21-39		30FTC184	
3397	Food Dish Associates of America, et al.	Zone	12- 9-38		27FTC1267	
3418	The Hardwood Institute et al.	basing point	2-20-42		34FTC661	
3519	Columbia Alkali Corp. et al.	Zone	12-13-38		27FTC1354	
3544	Rowe Manufacturing Co. et al.	basing point	12-15-38		27FTC1376	
3555	United States Maltsters Ass'n. et al.	basing point	12-29-42		35FTC797; 37FTC342	U.S. Maltsers v. FTC, 152 F. 2d 161. Affirmed. Petition to review filed and withdrawn, 3 S & D 411.
3556	American Veneer Package Ass'n. Inc. et al.	Zone	3-15-40		30FTC665	
3591	Pine Hill Lime & Stone Co. et al.	Zone	6-30-41		33FTC427	
3670	Hardwood Charcoal Co. et al.	basing point	8- 9-40		31FTC706	
3760	Book Paper Manufacturers Ass'n. et al.	Zone	6-30-45		40FTC696	Allied Paper Mills v. FTC, 168 F. 2d 600. Affirmed.
3868	Southern Vitrified Pipe Ass'n. et al.	uniform delivered	5-31-40		30FTC1347	
4034	The Robinson Clay Product Co. et al.	uniform delivered	1-29-41		32FTC538	
4145	Agricultural Insecticide & Fungicide Ass'n. et al.	uniform delivered	7-24-42		35FTC201; 38FTC609; 39FTC518	Phelps Dodge Refining Corp. et al. v. FTC, 139 F. 2d 393. Modified and enforced.
4320	Salt Producers Ass'n. et al.	Zone	11-10-41		34FTC38; 37FTC339	Salt Producers Assoc. v. FTC, 134 F. 2d 354. Modified and affirmed.
4443	The Wire Rope and Strand Manufacturers Ass'n. Inc. et al.	Zone	12- 8-42		35FTC756; 36FTC790	American Chain & Cable Co., Inc. v. FTC, 139 F. 2d 622. Affirmed.
4452	Rigid Steel Conduit Ass'n. et al.	basing point	6- 6-44		38FTC534; 44FTC1532; 45FTC1103	Triangle Conduit & Cable Co. v. FTC, 168 F. 2d 175. Clayton Mark & Co. et al. v. FTC, 336 U.S. 956. Affirmed.
4551	The Milk & Ice Cream Can Institute et al.	frt. equalized	9-18-43		37FTC419	Milk & Ice Cream Can Institute v. FTC, 152 F. 2d 478. Modified and affirmed.
4602	Crown Manufacturers Ass'n. of America et al.	frt. equalized	8- 4-48		45FTC89	Bond Crown & Cork Co. v. FTC; Crown Manufacturers Ass'n. of America et al. v. FTC; Armstrong Cork Co. et al. v. FTC, 176 F. 2d 974. Modified and enforced.
4606	National Crepe Paper Ass'n. of America et al.	Zone	4-22-44		38FTC282	Fort Howard Paper Co. v. FTC, 156 F. 2d 899. Affirmed.
4613	Acme Asbestos Covering and Flooring Co. et al.	Zone; frt. equalized	4-27-44		38FTC342	Keasbey and Mattison Co. v. FTC 159 F. 2d 940. Modified and affirmed.
4675	Liquid Tight Paper Container Ass'n. et al.	Zone	5-29-45		40FTC630	
4878	Chain Institute Inc. et al.	basing point; zone; frt. equalized	2-16-53		49FTC1041	Chain Institute v. FTC, 246 F. 2d 231. Certiorari denied. Affirmed.
4900	American Refractories Inst. et al.	frt. equalized	4-13-48		44FTC773	
5155	Ferro Enamel Corp. et al.	frt. equalized	2-26-46	volume	42FTC36	

Docket		Type	Date		FTC Cite	Court Citation
6253	National Lead Co. et al.	Zone	1-12-53	territorial; quantity	49FTC791	National Lead Co. v. FTC, 227 F. 2d 825, FTC v. National Lead Co., 352 U.S. 419. Modified and affirmed.
5467	Structural Clay Products, Inc. et al.	Zone	5-28-48		44FTC892	
5463	Structural Clay Products, Inc. et al.	Zone	5-28-48		44FTC906	
5483	Clay Products Ass'n, Inc. et al.	Zone	4-19-51		47FTC1256	
5484	Clay Sewer Pipe Ass'n, Inc.	Zone	8-20-51		48FTC202	
5502	Corn Products Refining Co. et al.	basing points; zone	11-20-50	territorial; misc.	47FTC587	
5508	American Iron & Steel Inst.	basing point	8-10-51		48FTC123	
5528	Fir Door Institute	Zone	10-20-50		47FTC395	
5529	Douglas Fir Plywood Ass'n, et al.	basing point	10-20-50		47FTC416	Consolidated: Oregon-Washington Plywood Co. v. FTC, 194 F. 2d 48. Set aside. Consolidated: Oregon-Washington Plywood Co. v. FTC, 194 F. 2d 48. Set aside.
5657	Malleable Chain Manufacturers Institute et al.	Zone	4-10-52		48FTC1163	
5878	Sayles Finishing Plants, Inc. et al.	frt. allowed; basing point	6-10-53		49FTC1427	
6078	U.S. Steel Corp, et al.	basing point	4-28-55		51FTC921	
6107	The Blotting Paper Manufacturers Ass'n. et al.	Zone	10- 8-53		50FTC364	
6225	Barnes Metal Products Co. et al.	Zone	2- 8-55		51FTC706	

Department of Justice Activities under the Robinson-Patman Act

Prior to December 31, 1957, the Department of Justice had instituted eight proceedings under the Robinson-Patman Act.[1] Four of these were civil cases under the amended Clayton Act, and four criminal proceedings under the further provisions of Section 3 of the Robinson-Patman Act.

In each of the civil cases, violations of other laws were also charged—the Sherman Act in all four cases, Section 3 of the Clayton Act in three cases, and Section 7 of the Clayton Act in two cases. One of the criminal cases included a charge under the Sherman Act, and the other three were accompanied or followed by other proceedings in which there was such a charge. In no instance was legal action based exclusively on an offense under the Robinson-Patman Act. In most instances, and perhaps in all, the charges under the Robinson-Patman Act were made in a setting of alleged conspiracy, unlawful purpose, or dominant power. Had the charges resulted uniformly in corrective orders, they would have covered little or nothing that could not have been reached by other means.

The first of the proceedings was the so-called "Mother Hubbard" case instituted in the petroleum industry in September 1940.[2] Several hundred defendants were charged with violating each substantive section of the Sherman Act and Sections 2 and 3 of the Clayton Act. On four successive occasions charges against some of the defendants were dismissed. Finally, in June 1951, the case was dropped, because it was too cumbersome to try, with the intention of substituting a series of regional cases. The superseding litigation that has thus far been undertaken has been based on the Sherman Act. No charge under the Robinson-Patman Act has been made.

The second case, against General Motors, was also started in 1940.[3] The

---

[1] Nine proceedings were begun, but since one of them, against Safeway Stores, arose by dismissal of a case and prompt institution of another involving the same charges against the same defendant, the two proceedings have been counted as one. Another, against Fairmont Foods Company of Wisconsin, was begun on Nov. 7, 1958. It alleged violation of the criminal provisions contained in Sec. 3 of the statute.

[2] *U. S.* v. *American Petroleum Institute,* Complaint Sept. 30, 1940. See CCH, *The Federal Antitrust Laws With Summary of Cases Instituted by the U.S., 1890-1951,* Case No. 564, p. 236.

[3] *U.S.* v. *General Motors Corp. et al.,* Complaint Oct. 4, 1940, CCH, *Trade Cases 1952-53,* par. 67324.

complaint alleged that General Motors has attempted to coerce dealers to use a subsidiary finance corporation in financing installment sales of automobiles. Violations of the Sherman Act and of Sections 2, 3, and 7 of the Clayton Act were alleged. In a companion criminal case under the Sherman Act,[4] General Motors was convicted and fined. In the civil case, a consent decree under the Sherman Act was issued in July 1952; but the decree did not include any provisions addressed to the alleged violation of the Clayton Act.

The third case, begun in May 1945 and concerned with flat glass, involved charges that Libbey-Owens-Ford and others had participated in a conspiracy that violated the Sherman Act, Sections 2, 3, and 7 of the Clayton Act, and the Wilson Tariff Act. It ended in a consent judgment in October 1948.[5] Included in the decree was a broad prohibition of the sale of flat glass at any industry level at unreasonably low or discriminatory prices for the purpose of destroying a competitor or suppressing competition. Other provisions forbade refusal to sell or discrimination in filling carload orders for various specified reasons, such as pooling of purchases, resale in any territory, failure to buy chiefly from the seller, and failure to join a trade organization. Though these provisions are relevant to the alleged violation of the Robinson-Patman Act, their scope is such that they might readily have been included in an order pertaining to the Sherman Act alone.

The three civil cases that have been discussed were followed in 1948 by two parallel criminal cases, in each of which a dairy company was charged with violating Section 3 of the Robinson-Patman Act by granting rebates to A. & P. In the first case to be tried, against Bowman Dairy Company,[6] the court directed a verdict of acquittal in April 1951 because of insufficiency of evidence. In the following month the companion case against the Borden Company[7] was dismissed on the Government's motion.

These proceedings were then replaced, in June 1951, by a broader civil case, U.S. v. Borden Company et al., in which ten defendants were charged with violation of the Sherman Act and Section 2(a) of the Robinson-Patman Act. The latter charge was based on price cutting raids on the customers of independent dairies. Five of the respondent dairies accepted a consent order, which included a provision forbidding discrimination in price among customers.[8] The other five contested the case. At the close of the Government's presentation of evidence, the court dismissed the charges under the Sherman Act as not proved; disposed similarly of the price discrimination charge against one defendant; and held that, although price discrimination by the other defendants had been shown, the discrimination charge would be dismissed because an order covering it had already been issued on December 3, 1952, in a private suit, Dean Milk Co. v. American Processing & Sales Co.

[4] U.S. v. General Motors Corp. et al., 121 F. 2d 376, certiorari denied.
[5] U.S. v. Libbey-Owens-Ford Glass Co., CCH, Trade Cases 1948-49, par. 62323.
[6] U.S. v. Bowman Dairy Co., see CCH, The Federal Antitrust Laws, Case No. 935, p. 371.
[7] U.S. v. The Borden Co., ibid., Case No. 936, p. 371.
[8] U.S. v. The Borden Co. et al., CCH, Trade Cases 1952-53, par. 67441.

et al.[9] On appeal the Supreme Court sustained the decision as to the charges under the Sherman Act, but held that, since the Government had no right to seek enforcement of a decree that had been entered in a private suit, the Robinson-Patman charge should not have been dismissed. The case was remanded to the district court for further consideration.[10] There the record was opened for the introduction of further evidence. The case was still pending on November 14, 1958.

In July 1955, a criminal proceeding was undertaken against Safeway Stores, charging monopolization and conspiracy to monopolize under the Sherman Act and sale below cost to destroy competition under Section 3 of the Robinson-Patman Act. The case was dismissed in November 1955, and replaced by a criminal proceeding of similar scope and also by a companion civil case under the Sherman Act.[11] On June 18, 1957, the defendants in the case under the Robinson-Patman Act pleaded *nolo contendere* and were fined a total of $187,500. The civil case under the Sherman Act resulted in a consent order.[12]

The last of the criminal cases, begun in October 1955,[13] alleged that Maryland & Virginia Milk Producers Association had given Chestnut Farms Dairy a discount on milk to be supplied on Government contracts, and that Section 3 of the Robinson-Patman Act had been thereby violated. In a companion case, the association was indicted under the Sherman Act for price fixing. In the first case the defendants were acquitted in October 1956. In November the other case was dismissed at the Government's request.

In summary, the seven of these eight cases that have been concluded have resulted in fines in one case and in a consent order covering price discrimination in another case. In the case that is still pending an order including a provision against discrimination has been entered against certain defendants who chose not to contest the proceeding. In two of the remaining five cases the defendants were acquitted; in two, the proceeding was dismissed; and in one, the part of the case concerned with price discrimination was swallowed by the Sherman Act part, under which an order was issued.

[9] *U.S.* v. *Borden Co. et al.,* 111 F. Supp. 562.

[10] *U.S.* v. *Borden Co. et al.,* 347 U.S. 514.

[11] *U.S.* v. *Safeway Stores Inc. et al.,* CCH, *Federal Antitrust Laws, Supplement* (mimeo), Cases No. 1250, 1263, 1264.

[12] Information from the docket section of the Antitrust Division of the Department of Justice.

[13] *U.S.* v. *Maryland Cooperative Milk Producers, Inc. et al.,* CCH, *Trade Cases 1956,* par. 68517.

Index

Brokerage activity, 47–48, 71, 92–
103, 107–14, 151–52, 622, 623, 645;
buying power, legislative intent to
curb, 5–6, 9, 12, 63–65, 75, 102, 131,
158, 208, 237, 516, 619n, 647, 649–
53, 655, 656; buying practices and
advantages, 7, 10–11, 63, 71, 109–10,
112–13, 144, 152, 174, 205–06, 210,
522, 570–71, 579, 620–21, 622, 641–
43; ineffectiveness of law in controlling, 356, 625, 627; investigation
of, 7–10, 21; opposition to price
legislation, 23; private-label merchandise, 31, 109, 110–11, 115–30 passim,
173–74, 463–64; receipt of unlawful
concessions, 488, 495–511, 516
Champion Spark Plug Co. (3977), 292,
293, 297, 300–01, 311, 313, 314, 318,
319, 343, 462, 462n, 466, 467, 548,
558, 559, 561, 562, 589n, 606
Charles of the Ritz (3017), 200n
Chestnut Farms Dairy, 684
Chicago Seating Co. v. *Karpen,* 335n
Chicago Sugar Co. v. *American Sugar
Refining Co.,* 164n
Christian, G. A., Brokerage Co., 137
Christmas Club (3050), 462n, 468n,
524n
Cities Service Oil Co., 314, 606
Citrin-Kolb, 298, 305–06, 316n, 323
Clark, J. M., 358n, 361
Clark, Tom C., 371n
Clay Products Assn., Inc., et al. (5483),
365n, 433, 433n
Clay Sewer Pipe Assn. (5484), 433,
433n
Clayton Act (*1914*), 5–12, 64, 225, 421n,
571–80
Cleveland Steel Products Co., 554
Clinton Co. (3800), 372n, 373, 374n,
375, 376, 377, 466, 535
Clothing industry, enforcement activity
by FTC, 74, 75, 147–50, 181, 629
Colgate-Palmotive-Peet Co., 39
Colgate-Palmolive-Peet Co. (5587),
159n, 190n
Columbia River Packers Assn., Inc.
(5033), 142-45, 629
Competition (*see also* Injury to competi-
tion *and* Meeting competition): Ef-
fect of legislation, 630; test of effect
on, 31–32
Compliance. *See* Enforcement.
Conscious parallelism, 403, 404n, 414,
435
Conspiracy. *See* Price fixing.

Controlled markets, advertising allowances as payments for access to, 176–
80
Cooperative Food Distributors, 24, 47n
Cooperatives and voluntary groups:
Brands, trademarks, and private labels, use of, 115–30 passim, 172;
brokerage activity, 96–98, 99, 114–
30, 151, 172; buying advantages, 118;
impact of FTC's orders on, 122–23,
128–30, 151, 626; legislation, development, 41–42, 43–44; opposition to
price legislation, 22–23, 25n, 44n,
286, 439n; services available to, 118-
19
Cooter Co. et al. (5460), 121–22
Copeland, Royal S., 46n
Cordage Institute (5848), 435n
Corn Derivatives Institute, 413n
Corn Products Refining Co., 413n
Corn Products Refining Co. (3633), 168,
170, 193, 194–95, 373–80 passim,
383, 388, 389, 390–95, 405–06, 416,
462, 462n, 466, 556
Corn Products Refining Co. et al.
(5502), 364n, 372, 385–86, 390–95,
433n, 437, 524n
Cosmetic industry, 195–96, 198–200,
201, 629–30
Cost justification, 584–616; accounting
methods, 586–87, 591–99, 609, 612;
advisory committee of FTC on, 608–
11; basing-point and zone-pricing
systems, 590; brokerage savings as
cost defense, 92, 103, 645; burden of
proof, 58, 60n, 488, 504–08, 511–
16, 586–87; class boundaries, 595–96;
coverage and homogeneity of discount classes, 594–95; difficulties in
obtaining information, 570, 589–91;
functional discounts, 313–17, 606–07;
infrequency of proceedings, reasons
for, 82, 587–600; legislation on, development and analysis, 22, 25, 26,
33–36, 58–59, 60n, 81–82, 584–85,
586, 636, 637; legislation on, recommendations, 614–16, 647–48, 654,
656; limitations, 585, 611–14, 629,
633; miscellaneous price discrimination, 483; nature of defenses, 600–
08; proportionality, 164, 169, 170,
204, 204n; quantity and volume discounts, 59, 209n, 209–10, 237–46,
271, 365n, 588, 591, 604–06; text
(excerpts) of secs. 2(a) and 2(b) of
Robinson-Patman Act, 57n, 58n